GOVERNMENTAL AND MUNICIPAL
INFORMATION SYSTEMS

IFIP TC8 Conference on
Governmental and Municipal Information Systems
Budapest, Hungary, September 8–11, 1987

NORTH-HOLLAND
AMSTERDAM · NEW YORK · OXFORD · TOKYO

GOVERMENTAL AND MUNICIPAL INFORMATION SYSTEMS

Proceedings of the IFIP TC8 Conference on
Governmental and Municipal Information Systems
Budapest, Hungary, September 8–11, 1987

edited by

Péter KOVÁCS

and

Elek STRAUB

1988

NORTH-HOLLAND
AMSTERDAM · NEW YORK · OXFORD · TOKYO

ISBN: 0 444 70377 2

Published by:
ELSEVIER SCIENCE PUBLISHERS B.V.
P.O. Box 1991
1000 BZ Amsterdam
The Netherlands

Sole distributors for the U.S.A. and Canada:
ELSEVIER SCIENCE PUBLISHING COMPANY, INC.
52 Vanderbilt Avenue
New York, N.Y. 10017
U.S.A.

LIBRARY OF CONGRESS
Library of Congress Cataloging-in-Publication Data

IFIP TC8 Conference on Governmental and Municipal Information Systems
  (1987 : Budapest, Hungary)
    Governmental and municipal information systems : proceedings of
  the IFIP TC8 Conference on Governmental and Municipal Information
  Systems, Budapest, Hungary, September 8-11, 1987 / edited by Péter
  Kovács and Elek Straub.
        p.   cm.
    Bibliography: p.
    ISBN 0-444-70377-2 (U.S.)
    1. Public administration--Data processing--Congresses.
  2. Management information systems--Congresses.   I. Kovács, Péter
  1936-   . II. Straub, Elek, 1944-   . III. International
  Federation for Information Processing. Technical Committee for
  Information Systems.   IV. Title.
  JF1525.A8I448 1987
  350'.00028'5--dc19   87-34954
                                                          CIP

PRINTED IN THE NETHERLANDS

PREFACE

Dear Reader,

The booklet which you now hold in your hands is another major undertaking by the IFIP TC8 (Information systems). The professionals working in TC8 have been attempting for some time to deploy the results achieved in informatics research and practice to all walks of economic and social life. For this purpose we have decided to organize in 1986 an open conference where we could discuss and get an overview of the special aspects pertaining to public administration informatics and its various areas of employment.

The conference was held in Budapest primarily because we wanted to meet in a region where informatics-supported decision making in public administration is considered a primary goal.

The conference was a great success in all respects, with a large attendance, and an extensive number of high-standard lectures presented. We had some 200 participants and more than 70 papers were given. The large number of lectures set the program committee a difficult task. Under the direction of Gösta Guteland the program committee had set as its goal to present the scope of public administration informatics in various aspects.

Besides the papers presented at the plenary meeting the lecturers spoke about their work in 5 different sections. These were divided into 5 subject areas as follows:

- Governmental information systems
- Development of information systems
- Local information systems and land data bank systems
- Office automation and development of networks
- Security and database management.

The common platform for the sectional meetings was outlined by P.A. Tas's lecture on "Information System Policy in Government". Mr. Tas's introductory paper suggestively and convincingly confirmed the existence of public administration informatics.

The substantial lectures and the interesting comments made by the audience contributed to the valuable summaries given at the closing session by the rapporteurs (Brussard, King, Ohashi, Schultz and Sutherland) whose task was to point out the major ideas and suggestions presented by each section.

We consider a further significant result of the conference on public administration information systems that the audience agreed to establish a new working group under tha auspices of TC8 under the name of WG 8.5 Information Systems in Public Administration.

The scope and the aims of the new working group are as follows:

Scope

The working group focuses its activities on planning, realization and implications of information systems in public administration at all levels.

The working group will be a forum for the exchange of ideas and experience among academics and practitioners in the field of public administration. Its special focus will be on the relationship between central and local use of information systems and the provision of citizen services and the accomplishment of social goals.

Aims

The working group will

- evaluate and comment on information processing policies in public administration;
- discuss specific applications in government, and ways to improve them;
- promote analysis of the impacts of automated information systems inl public administration;
- work to deepen the level of international professional cooperation in the field.

We hope that we can present to you the newest research results in public administration informatics and their further practical application in our next publication.

P. Kovács and E. Straub

LIST OF CONTENTS

THEME "D": OFFICE AUTOMATION AND DEVELOPMENT OF NETWORKS

THEME "E": SECURITY AND DATABASE MANAGEMENT

CLOSING SPEECH

Governmental and Municipal Information Systems
P. Kovács and E. Straub (Editors)
Elsevier Science Publishers B.V. (North-Holland)
© IFIP, 1988

INFORMATION SYSTEMS POLICY IN GOVERNMENT

Prof. P.A. Tas / Nijenrode School of Business

1. INTRODUCTION

There are thirteen ministries in the Netherlands government. A
ministry has the following organisational structure.   The
minister and under-minister are formally responsible for the
policy and management of the ministry.   The secretary-general
(SG) is the head of the civil servants in the ministry and he is
responsible for its management, having a number of staff
departments to support him (finance, personnel, organisation and
information, legal, etc.).   He is also the top adviser to the
minister and the under-minister.

The position of the SG is rather ambiguous as there is a direct
line between the director-general and the minister or under-
minister where political issues are at stake.   The SG has a
strong position when these issues concern financial resources,
personnel, material, housing, information, etc. A policy
department is called a "directorate-general" and the head of such
a department is a director-general (DG).   A directorate-general
has its own directorates.

In 1979 the Netherlands parliament considered a policy paper
concerning information processing.   (Information processing is
used here in the sense of gathering, transporting, storage and
processing of data into information.)   In this a top-down policy
was laid out for information processing for the central
government, excluding the PTT (post and telecommunications) and
parts of the armed services. Ministries were obliged to have
information systems plans reviewed by the Minister of the
Interior.   The minister was assisted in this by an
interdepartmental committee consisting of secretaraties-general
and directors-general. Besides the review of these plans, it was
decided to consider systems with an interdepartmental or
intergovernmental aspect.

Interdepartmental systems are those which are used by all
ministries.   They concern personnel, finance and documentary
information systems.   Intergovernmental sector information
systems cross various levels of government and are concerned, for
example, with police matters, education and social security. As
a connecting factor between the levels of government and within
them, there are object systems which are concerned with
population, property, economic activities and ships and vehicles.
The population system, for example, has subsystems in each
municipality with a population data base with information on all
inhabitants in that municipality.   These municiple systems will
be connected to each other and to users of this population data
via a network.   Examples of users are the Taxation Service, the
General Pension Fund and Social Insurance Organisations.

During the past year, reports have appeared from the Government
Audit Office criticising the results of information processing
in the government.   Attention was drawn to failures and the high

cost of certain systems.   Planning the automation has not worked
well with the exception of a number of businesslike sections of
the government such as the Taxation Service and the Department
for the Maintenance of Dikes, Roads and Bridges.
As far as the interdepartmental systems are concerned, a central
payroll system is used by all ministries and slowly but surely
more and more ministries are making use of a central personnel
system which is connected to the payroll system.

In the financial sector a number of ministries are working
together on a logical design for a financial system which,
depending on the hardware and basic software in use in a
ministry, will be adapted to the appropriate technical design.

In the area of the sector systems, there has been some progress,
but mainly on paper.   The population system as one of the
objectsystems is in the design phase.   Furthermore, after years
of discussion, it looks as though integration will take place of
data files on vehicles in different ministries.   The remaining
systems are still being discussed in advisory committees.

The shortcomings of information systems have been analysed in a
number of ministries over the past two years and, based on this,
various recommendations have been made for improvement in this
area.   Attention is paid especially to the information systems
of the separate ministries and only where necessary is something
mentioned about interdepartmental and intergovernmental systems.

2.   GENERAL DEFINITION OF THE PROBLEM

For most organisations, the sixties and seventies are the years
of the computercentres which enthusiastically developed systems
which automated existing manual or mechanical applications.
Examples are well known from the banking and insurance world and
from businesses where bookkeeping, stock administration and
payroll are concerned.   But there are also many examples from
the government such as taxation, subsidy and personnel systems.
There were successes.   However, problems began to appear during
the seventies.   Systems became more expensive than foreseen and
were not completed at the promised date.   They did not conform
to the wishes of the user and a large part of the capacity of the
software development department was used for maintenance.   The
relationship between the automation department and the users
worsened.   The solution at that time was, among other things, to
call in the user and have more attention for his information
needs.

In the eighties, managers are becoming more and more involved in
affairs of information systems.   They are confronted by high
costs and obscure advantages and tensions appear in the
organisation.   Also the press, science and the literature are
all calling out that the "information society" is in sight.

The conclusion is that the automation which began from the
technical side and later under influence of the user, has now
become the field of interest of the manager.   Information
technology and everything connected to it appears to have a large
influence in business.   Management must bear in mind the
information systems.   It can no longer stand on the edge and

plead ignorance and just leave things to the technicians and the users. It must learn to handle information systems efficiently.

3. MANAGEMENT OF THE INFORMATION SYSTEMS (an overview)

3.1 Two main aspects in the management of the information systems.

A. How can automation be used to help the organisation fulfil its objectives. This concerns not only efficiency and effectiveness but also new possibilities of information systems for the strategies of the organisation.

B. The control of the process of designing and processing automated information systems. Good ideas must be turned into deeds effectively and efficiently and this is not easy.

For the management of the information systems, the following is necessary: a policy, a control of that policy and its execution. The boundary between policy and implementation is not always easy to define.

There follows an overview of the subjects which, based on experience gained in ministries of the Netherlands Government, played a role in nearly all of these ministries or certains parts of them. The subjects are aimed at management and concern policy as well as implementation.

3.2 Management and policy

- Organisation of information processing (who, what, where). The use of steering groups, committees and project groups. The setting up of the information systems organisation has much to do with (de)centralisation and (de)concentration. Specific attention must be paid to the position of the computer centre, the information centre, the data manager and "privatisation" of the data function.

- Planning of information systems at different levels of the organisation. Which systems must be developed with which priority?
Here the relationship between the objectives and the strategic possibilities of information processing to fulfil these objectives is of great importance. In choosing a system, the risks of failure must be considered.

- Hardware, software and communication policy. What do we choose now and in future? What are the expected developments in technology?

- Personnel aspects. General guidelines concerning work circumstances and opportunities. What is the relationship with the trade unions. General instruction and education in information systems.

- Auditing, security and back-up.

- Privacy guidelines.

- Definition of guidelines and standards for policy and implementation.

3.3 Management of the implementation

Management, directly responsible for the implementation, should pay special attention to the following subjects.

- Project approach to the development of systems.   Extra attention is necessary for large, complex systems.

- Relationship between organisation and information.

3.4 A policy on different levels.

An information systems policy must be implemented at different levels of the organisation.   The policy at one level will have to fit into that of a higher level in the hierarchy.   In the Netherlands Government, for example, there are four levels:

1. Ministry of the Interior for the total policy of the government.
2. The ministries which are responsible for the policy within a ministry.
3. The level of the Directorate-General.
4. The level of a Directorate.

A number of the most important subjects will now be further elaborated.

4.   THE ORGANISATION OF THE INFORMATION SYSTEMS

The most important criteria for a well-functioning information systems organisation must be considered here.   The organisation of information systems means: which people, groups of people and/or sectors of the organisation, at what level in the organisation and in what relation to one another, are responsible for the preparation of the policy and the decision making processes connected with it?
Important issues are: the role of top and middle management and the use of steering groups, policy groups and project groups.

It must be decided where and by whom the information systems policy must be implemented.   Who is responsible for, among other things, the following activities and where are these to be executed:
- Planning of information systems
- Information analyses
- Project management
- System design and implementation
- Operations (where are the computers situated)?
- (administrative) organisation

- Education and instruction
- Guidelines, procedures and standards.

Questions arise concerning centralisation and decentralisation, concentration and deconcentration.

At the centre of discussions at the moment within the Netherlands Government are, among other points, the following:

- Separation of policy and implementation.   Should these be two staff functions or should a information manager be made responsible for both?
Here should be taken into account the advancing specialisation of data management: definition of the essential data of the organisation, the possible relationships and the maintenance of the data model.   Who controls here the consistency of the data banks and their use?

- The place and role of the computer center. Splitting up of this service into an information centre and a production centre. Choices must be made concerning the place where, and by whom, the information analysis and the system analysis is carried out. The policy for subcontracting is important here.

- In the past, the organisation and the information functions have been merged in nearly all the ministries and also in the Ministry of the Interior.   These two functions are now under pressure in many ministries.   It appears to be especially difficult to integrate these two functions.   In some cases, the organisation function is scrapped and replaced by project managers for all sorts of projects including automation.

- An important subject at this moment is the privatisation of the information function.   Privatisation is one of the spearheads of the policy of the Cabinet.   It has much to do with the idea that a private organisation is more efficient.   Even in some private organisations, parts of the information function are subcontracted under the heading "externalisation".   Reasons for this are that the information function is seen as an alien activity and its management seems to be a problem.   The question arises whether privatisation is a good thing when it is known that the information systems forms the nerve centre of the organisation.   And that point is certainly valid for ministries which are an outstanding example of information-intensive organisations.

5. PLANNING OF INFORMATION SYSTEMS

Planning concerns the choice of systems, the relationship between them and the setting of priorities.   The planning within the ministries will have to be done at various levels.   The development of interdepartmental and intergovernmental systems will have to be taken into account here.   There are quite a few planning methods in practice.   Many of these are directed at the data in the organisation which are considered to be heart of the information systems. One of these methods is Information Systems Planning (ISP).   In this method all processes are placed in a row in a certain sequence along the y-axis of a matrix.   All data

bases are placed along the x-axis and in the matrix it is
indicated which processes create data and which use data from the
data bases.   Through the clustering of processes and data bases,
information systems can now be distinguished.

Use is made of critical success factors (CSF) for the setting of
priorities.   CSF's focus on areas of management which are
important for the fulfilment of the goals.

The method demands attention from management and monopolises the
organisation to an extent due to the fact that the construction
of the matrix and its completion must be done from many
interviews.

The experience with this method in one of the ministries is not
very favourable.   This is due to the fact that it appears to be
very difficult to define processes of similar order and detail in
a somewhat unstructured environment.   When the environment in
which this method is used becomes more structured, the better
applicable will be the results.
In practice it appears that few organisations have at their
disposal an adequate planning of the information systems.   The
most important cause of this is the fact that the information
processing is not an entity in itself but by its nature is
integrated with the policy and its implementation and therefore
with its planning.   Often it will be attempted to design a
global overview of the information processes and their
interdependence and thereafter a list of priorities will be made,
based on the most important bottlenecks in the organisation.   It
is largely a process of good sense and trial and error.

In the planning one encounters the policy of the organisation and
also the relationship with the strategy of the organisation.   It
becomes clear that the automated information processing can
greatly influence the manner in which the objectives of the
organisation are pursued.
Although there is some difference here compared to private
enterprise due to the fact that competition plays an essential
role, the relationship between information systems and objectives
is certainly present in government.   This concerns possibilities
such as:
- The fast and efficient implementation of a (complicated) law,
for example in social security.
- Fast and efficient exchange of information not only between
sectors of government, but also on behalf of external parties.
An example of this is the automation of the population
administration.
- Where the aim is to slim down government, a good personnel
system is essential.
- A better relationship with the services in the country, the
subsidised organisations and the municipalities.   - An improved
service to the citizen, for example through the automation of
theatre ticket offices of a large municipality.
- Decentralisation of responsibilities of central government
to province and municipality.
- Sale of data gathered by the government, such as, for example,
in the land registry.

When a choice of systems is made, the risks of failure must be
weighed carefully.   Factors playing a role in this are: the
number of manyears necessary for the system, the use of new

techniques, the management culture, is the organisation used to changes and how great are the organisational changes?

6. HARDWARE, SOFTWARE AND COMMUNICATION

The following factors play a role in the choice of hardware.
- One or more suppliers of mainframes, mini's and PC's?
- The continuity of the supplier.
- The operating system, especially the possibility of buying packages offered for sale.
- What is the strategy of the supplier?
- Network possibilities.
- The possibility of application of (defacto) standards.
- Does the supplier think in terms of solutions?

The choices can only be made when it has been determined where the various types of computers will be installed whereby the internal communication is of importance. This positioning of computers is of course dependent on the information systems in the organisation and also on the views concerning the implementation of the systems.
There are organisations which will install complete systems: hardware, software and application system with the accompanying instruction manuals. It has become a "black box" about which the user only has to know the directions for use.

However important the choice of hardware may be, it is the developments in software which determine the market. This applies to basic software, such as operation systems, data base systems, fourth generation languages, software support in systems design, retrieval languages, etc. This choice can be a major problem. Should the choice be for UNIX, can we choose more than one data base system? In one of the ministries, this problem had to be decided at the highest level due to the fact that it had an enormous impact on the cost of hardware and software.

Besides the basic software, more use will be made of standard packages for the solution to users' problems. These packages can be very general in nature such as for word processing, spreadsheets and data base programs, or more specific such as for bookkeeping and payroll packages, etc. The choice between making the software or buying it readymade affects the cost and the organisation

One of the hot issues in the future of this field is the application of networks. This means that choices must be made in relation to the hardware chosen. The following questions must be answered here..
- Should a hierarchical network be chosen, a partly hierarchical network with local area network or a mesh network?
- Are we going to use in this network a PABX?
- Should we choose a broad band or a base band local area network?
- What will be the role of an "integrated systems data network" (ISDN) in connection with integration of image, voice, data and text?
- What demands has office automation on the communication?

And in that whole area of hardware, software and communication
there are new developments such as the optical disc, the smart
card, etc.

It would appear that decisions concerning the subjects mentioned
can be made by technicians.   However, this concerns matters
which can have a great influence on the possibilities of the
information technology, the progress of the design of systems
and the cost of automation.   Furthermore management is being
confronted with the integration of office automation, EDP and
communication which are often developed by different
organisational units.
In one of the Government departments, automation has developed
partly centrally, but largely also decentrally with different
makes of hardware and networks.   The different parts of the
ministry have their own computer centres.   The policy, in the
hands of the deputy Secretary-general, is now aimed at unifying
the choice of hardware and software and it looks as though all
computer centres will be merged to form one large facility.

7.   PERSONNEL

Automation has consequences for existing functions.   These must
be adapted or scrapped.   This leads to surplus manpower or re-
education.   The work environment will change.

To prepare personnel for this, attention must be paid to general
instruction and education on information systems.   This applies
to the whole organisation including management.   In the Ministry
of Welfare, Health and Culture, all personnel is being educated
using the whole scale of education packages.
Besides general education, it is necessary to educate civil
servants to expert level due to the fact that automation
expertise is not available internally because of the high
salaries in private enterprise. Three ministries organise, for
example, a pilot course for the education of information experts,
who will function as a sort of link between management and the
rest of the organisation.

8.   SECURITY,CONTROL AND BACK UP

Security concerns the physical surroundings, such as the
arrangement of a computer centre in zones, to which entrance is
only possible by use of special passes to certain zones.   Some
centres even have a moat such as the computer centre of the city
of Amsterdam.

Security also concerns the prevention of system tapping or
destruction of data, or entry of "alien data".   Typical of this
is the break-in at the Institute of Health and Environment
concerning which there was even a parliament debate.   Much
attention is paid to the security of information transmission in
the automation of the population administration of
municipalities.

Accountants must take upon themselves the role of controllers.
This means supervising security measures but also taking part in
building the system and its processing procedures.

As the organisation becomes more dependent on automation, its
vulnerability increases.   Double computers, such as in the
cashpoint automation in the city of Amsterdam, and redundant
networks can be a solution.   Disaster back-up will also have to
be organised.   In the Netherlands, there are professional back-
up centres for such situation.   Management must realise that
these measures cost money.

9. PRIVACY

The guarding of privacy is especially important in government as
the authorities store a great deal of personal information and
there is now the possibility of linking this information by the
use of administration numbers.   In the Netherlands there is a
bill before parliament for the safeguard of privacy.   Privacy in
the population system is most often discussed.
Surprisingly there is little talk of privacy when it concerns the
systems of the taxation service or social security where files
are built up using information concerning the whole population of
the Netherlands with the appropriate administration numbers.
Although the safeguard of privacy is very important to national
government, just as much if not more attention must be paid to it
at local government level where there is more opportunity to link
privacy-sensitive data.

10. THE MANAGEMENT OF IMPLEMENTATION

10.1 Project Management

The management of projects is essential and project planning is
part of this.   It is a somewhat underestimated subject.
Activities which should be taken into account in project
management are, among others:
- How new is the technique to be used?   What knowledge exists in
the organisation about this technique?
- Is the application known?
- What is the time limit for the project?
- What is the size of the project?
- What is the knowledge and experience of the organisation in the
field of data processing?
- Is there a good project manager?

Before a project can be started, a risk analysis must be made.
Extra care is necessary with large, complex systems.   A number of
large projects in the Netherlands government have failed or have
exceeded the budget or have caused too much frustration due to
the fact that management has not paid enough attention to these
projects and has left their implementation to the data processing
departments and the suppliers of hardware and software.   A

painful example of this is the automation of the manpower offices
in the Netherlands - a project which cost more than a hundred
million guilders and is a total failure.   The most important
cause of this failure is the lack of management attention which
left the field open to the technicians.

10.2 The relationship organisation/information

Automation affects the organisation.   Procedures change, people
have to change their working habits and structures change.
Conversely information systems must change with organisational
changes.
Decentralisation is not well feasible without adequate
information systems.   Indeed the discussion immediately arises
what information is necessary at what level?   In the Netherlands
government, within the framework of the new management vision,
the subject of decentralisation of the personnel and financial
function is a hot-issue.   This is only possible if the
information systems are adapted to it, and that adaptation is
only possible where it is clear what information is desired at
different levels.

Automation often fails because the organisation is not first of
all adapted to the new situation.   Besides this, established
interests must be dismantled.   In one of the Directorates-
General, a large budget system is being developed which can only
function when the procedures and the working methods of the whole
organisation are adapted to it.
At the same time, the organisational structure is changed, the
organisation itself slimmed down, the administration improved and
the paymentfunction of the subsidy regulations decentralised.
It would seem almost impossible to implement such a large budget
system in an organisation which is in such a state of flux.
Experience shows that the changes in the organisation and the
education/reeducation of personnel can greatly influence the
planning of the project and that a large part of the resources of
the project must be directed to this.   We can talk here of 50%
of the budget.

11. SUMMARY

The following policy items have been discussed.
- The organisation of the information systems
- Planning of information systems
- Hardware, software and communication policy
- Personnel aspects
- Auditing, security and back-up
- Privacy
- Project management
- Relationship between organisation and information.

At each level of government organisation (interministerial,
ministerial, directorate-general, directorate) the question can
be asked: what can go wrong if no management action is taken on
the above subjects?   If the answer is "nothing", then there is
no policy needed.

In answering this question, a number of factors play a role:
- The structure of the organisation. Is the organisation more
like a holding company such as the Ministry of Transport and
Construction of Bridges and Roads or is there a strong connection
between the various services such as in the Directorate-General
of Works and Buildings.
- United leadership. The coordinating facilities of the Cabinet
for the whole government are much more limited than those of a
director of a directorate of a ministry.
- Is there a computer centre at the appropriate level with
capacity for system development. The availability of this
provides a certain power and grip on the situation. Examples of
two extremes are the Ministry of Transport which has no central
computer organisation, and the Ministry of Housing, Planning and
Environment which does have this facility.
- The previous experience of automation at the particular level.

When applying the question it appears that at interdepartmental
level (Ministry of the Interior) not much of a policy is
appropriate. Most ministries, on the other hand, have a central
information systems policy. For a few, such as Transport,
the main interest at top level is the connection between the
personnel and financial system and attention will be paid to a
documentary system. An information systems policy is essential
at the level of a directorate-general and a directorate.

Is information processing in government so different from that in
private enterprise?

To find this out, the American literature can be consulted in the
field of management and information processing. A typical
example is the EDP ANALYZER of January 1985. In this article, a
research project is mentioned in which the top 10 information
system issues, in order of priority, are identified. These are:
1. Improved information systems planning
2. Management and facilitation of end user computing
3. Integration of data processing, office automation, and
telecommunication
4. Improved software development and quality
5. Measuring and improving IS effectiveness and productivity
6. Facilitation and organisational learning and usage of
information systems technologies
7. Aligning the IS organisation with that of the enterprise
8. Specification, recruitment and development of IS human
resources
9. Effective use of the organisation's data resources
10. Development and implementation of decision support systems.

In a forward looking approach, the EDP ANALYZER thinks that the
six issues that will receive top attention of information systems
management during the next two years are the following:
- Strategic use of information systems
- Getting payoffs from IS investments
- Assessing organisational impacts of IS
- Managing end user computing
- Trimming the backlog
- Information security and privacy.

These general problem definitions are usually based on experience
gained in private enterprise. Comparison of the literature with
the experiences in the government indicates that the problems in

information systems in government do not seem to differ greatly
from those in private enterprise.   They are recognisable
problems.

There are, however, a few obvious points in which the government,
at least in the Netherlands, differ from a private organisation.

a) It is a very large, complicated organisation with very many
different areas of attention.   The top of the organisation does
not generally consist of managers.   A minister must take into
account his fellow ministers, the upper and lower houses of
parliament, his political party, public opinion and interest
groups.
b) It is not an organisation directed at a certain financial
result.
c) There is hardly any personnel policy.   Payment of groups of
civil servants is behind that of private enterprise.
d) There is hardly any management culture.   The manager in
government must constantly choose between policy on behalf of his
minister and the management of his organisation.
e) The openness of government is large.   A good example of this
are the Audit Office reports.

Obviously government automation is less efficient due to lack of
competition, but factors such as politics, personnel policy and
publicity make government automation more vulnerable and thereby
more difficult.

The conclusion is that there is a difference between government
and private enterprise, but that there is not to much difference
in designing and implementing information systems in government
compared to large companies in private enterprise.
In governent as in private enterprise management attention is
essential.

REFERENCES

- Brandt Allen.   An unmanaged computer system can stop you dead.
  Harvard Business Review, November-December 1982
- Henry C. Lucas, Jr.   Utilizing Information Technology:
  Guidelines for Managers. Sloan Management Review, 39 Fall 1986.
- Six Top Information Systems Issues. EDP ANALYZER, January 1985
  vol. 23, No. 1

Governmental and Municipal Information Systems
P. Kovács and E. Straub (Editors)
Elsevier Science Publishers B.V. (North-Holland)
IFIP, 1988

PLANNING OF INFORMATIONAL INFRASTRUCTURES FOR INTERGOVERNMENTAL USE

B.K. Brussaard
Ministry of the Interior/Delft University of Technology
P.O. Box 20011, The Hague
The Netherlands

The use of information systems in the public sector reflects the
distribution of authority and of activities between central, regional
and local governments. The application of modern information
technology tends to be influenced by it. It is argued that information
technology should be used to optimize the allocation of authority and
responsibility to governments and government agencies. For that
purpose an analytical tool with a corresponding planning methodology
has been developped. The resulting informational infrastructure is
described in terms of information systems and services for the public
sector. It also has implications for the informational relations with
the private sector. The organizational flexibility and the political
will, necessary to implement these structures predominate over their
rationality and efficiency. Therefore progress is slow.
Developments are illustrated by practical examples from the
Netherlands.

1. INTRODUCTION

The structure of a country's public administration is determined by a large
number of factors, among which information technology is only one. There is a
growing awareness, however, that in the long run its influence has been and is
growing to be more intrusive than was realized before.

When in the past new tasks were allocated to or taken up by government bodies it
was always taken for granted that the best (information) technology available
would be used to carry out these tasks and to provide for the information
required. The technologies available were well known and stable for a long
period of time. This changed rapidly after the fifties. This may be illustrated
by the organizational measures taken in the Netherlands to cope with these
developments. In the mid-fifties an interdepartemental committee was set up to
advise on computer procurement by central government agencies. The only reason
was that computers were expensive and expertise was scarce. The use of computers
was restricted entirely to the conversion of mass routine tasks up till then
carried out by manual or conventional punched card procedures. In the beginning
of the seventies, however, it appeared that the real subject was not computers
but information systems. Information systems do not consist of computers and
software only, but also of people, procedures accoording to which they are
supposed to do their work, and data collections which can be used for different
purposes . In the seventies a new committee was set up to advise on information
systems as a whole, but still for existing tasks within given organizational
boundaries. After seven years this approach was no longer considered
satisfactory too. In the beginning of the eighties for the first time in history

the council of ministers decided that the way in which information processing
was carried out within public agencies and ministries could no longer be the
sole responsibility of the hierarchical organizational units concerned. Again an
entirely new committee was set up and the directorate for government
organization and automation with the Minister of the interior should support
that committee to review multi-year information plans of agencies of all
ministries. The main purpose now was not to optimize information processing
within those organizational units. That was explicitly made the responsibility
of those units. The main purpose was to prevent similar information systems
being developed by several units and to promote the common use of data
collections where that seemed efficient. The subject changed from information
systems within organizational units to the whole of information systems and
services in the public sector, and concern of their interfaces and common
information resources. This situation did not last very long either. Within five
years and according to the advice of a heavy external commission the government
decided to reorganize the coordination of information systems and services for
the third time. Before going into the present situation which began last year
two points should be mentioned.
a. between 1975 and 1985 a parallel attempt was made to attain some form of
    coordination between central government departments, regional government
    (provincies) and local government (municipalities). Under chairmanship of
    the Minister of the interior himself it was tried to attune developments
    between the three government tiers, not only with a view to internal
    efficiency within the public sector but also with a view to the improvement
    of informational relations with the private sector.

b. The gradual introduction of more or less obliged multi-year information
    planning by central government institutions during the same period
    (1975-1985) did not mean centralization of decision making on information
    systems and services. The availability of cheap powerful equipment and the
    dispersion of expertise all over the administration made this impossible,
    even if it had been the objective. The true objective of the introduction of
    a planning methodology for organizational units was to make their management
    aware of their responsibility in the field of information systems. At the
    same time it gave some insight into the structure of information
    accumulation and information flows within the community as a whole. This
    could lead to improvements wherever required and feasible.

These two developments led to the present situation. Since 1986 a new committee
(the fourth in less than 20 years) has the mission to advise the government, not
to individual ministers or managers of administrative units in the first place.
It advises on long term measures to be taken and on the revision of
organizational and administrative boundaries; not only with a view to optimal
information processing, but with a view to the optimal operation of government
as such as far as this is dependent on the organization of information
processing. Taking into account the information intensity of the public sector
and the intrusion of new information technology for all types of information
(data, text, voice and images) this goes further into the structuring and
coordination of government activities than any other "resource", with the
possible exception of financial and personnel matters. On the basis of applied
research and practical experience in the field of information policy planning
the next paragraph gives a summing-up of earlier results and the third paragraph
gives an overview of present and expected developments.

2. ANALYTICAL TOOLS AND PLANNING METHODOLOGY

Information systems as the subject matter of applied informatics can be defined
both analytically and functionally. As indicated above information systems can
be described analytically as a whole of hardware, software, persons, procedures
and information; they process, store and transmit descriptions of other systems
(transformation in contents, time or space respectively).
These other systems called real systems in juxta position to information
systems, are those parts or aspects of reality (existing or imagined) we want to
know and perhaps control. The production of information systems may be called
record keeping, reporting, statistics, auditing etc. but also planning,
budgetting, designing and even (support of) decision-making. Information systems
in government may be categorized in a number of ways. In (1) it was proposed to
do so in three different types:

Type a. Information objects which describe society such as population,
        immovables (land, houses, other buildings, roads, public utility
        networks and so on), social-economic units according to legal,
        geographical or technical characteristics, road vehicles, shipping and
        so on. Usually they are recorded in public registers, both for use by
        the public and the private sector.
Type b. Information objects which describe activities in the public sector
        accoording to sectors of public endeavour e.g. in the fields of social
        security, public utilities, education, housing, taxation and so on.
Type c. Information objects which describe resources employed by the public
        sector in implementing the activities described as type b. as a result
        of which a new situation is reached as described under information
        objects of type a. Examples of type c. objects are personnel, materials,
        fixed assets, money flows, documents such as laws and regulations.
These three types of information objects occur at all government levels. It
applies to territorial decentralisation from city districts and municipalities
to provincies or states, and from national governments to international
organizations. Functionally it also applies to more or less government
controlled (financed) private organizations which take care of the productions
of goods or the rendering of services (e.g. in my country for social security,
housing and education).

This model in three dimensions (types of information objects) or four dimensions
(including government units) is the basis of the informational infrastructure
problem discussed in this paper.
In (2) a distinction was drawn between system management and information
¬anagement. System management (SM) consists of the determination of information
requirements, the design, development and maintenance of information systems and
indeed of all the system components (not only software but also hardware,
specialist staff, procedures and so on). Information management (IM) consists of
the utilization of information systems and the use of information both centrally
and distributed. It was also shown that it is necessary to distinguish sharply
between centralisation and concentration of systems management and information
management. Centralisation refers to the extent to which powers relating to
systems management or information management are taken together in a limited
number of decision making centres (government units, administrators, political

bodies or indivudual politicians). Concentration refers to the extent to which
activities relating to systems management and information management are pursued
at the limited number of geographical locations. Those locations may be
topografical points within a building or territorial areas.
This analytical tool for the description and the design of informational
infrastructures can be presented schematically as follows.

SM and IM	(de-)centralisation	
(de-)concentration	I	III
	II	IV

FIGURE 1. organizational and geographical distribution of system management
         and information management

Empirical research shows that each theoretical combination I-IV occurs in
practice. What is even more interesting is that it may be "right" from a number
of points a view and mutually independent for IM and SM. In other words it is
not always possible to determine beforehand what degree of centralisation and
concentration is the optimum for a particular type of information processing
activity.

The informatical*problem of informational infrastructures can now be described
as follows. Specific analytical components of information systems e.g. a
physical computer (or a databank) can be used by more than one functional
information system and this functional information system can be used by more
than one governmental unit. Not only at the same government level but also by
different government levels. The infrastructural problem is to allocate system
management and information management. It has to do with decision-making and
decision-execution (centralisation versus concentration) of governmental units
taking into account all kinds of relevant objectives and restrictions. Examples
of the latter are privacy of individual citizens, confidentiality of information
on commercial organizations, autonomy of governmental bodies and of course
efficiency and effectivity as defined in the usual cost benefits analysis of
information systems in the public sector and elsewhere.
For planning purposes it is necessary to have disposal of a methodology which
enables the administration to take all these considerations into account.

The conventional information planning theory shows three subsequent stages:
general policy planning, information requirements planning, and automation (or
information systems) planning. Schematically:

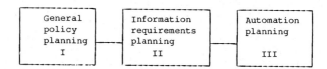

FIGURE 2.   Subsequent Planning Model

* The adjective "informational" is derivid from "informaticn" on the analogy of
relations/relational. The term informatical is reserved for the adjective of
"informatics" on the analogy of mathematics/mathematical.

The general idea is firstly that all strategic objectives of an organization are determined together with the most important constraints and a rough estimate of available resources (I). Secondly it is than supposed to be possible to derive deterministically from that the information requirements for a coming period and to determine detailed constraints and resources required (II). Lastly the actual automation planning for information systems may start. This hierarchical subsequent approach looks very logical but it does not work in reality. For one thing general policy plans seldom exist, and if they are available they are not suitable for information requirement analysis. Secondly information requirements can not be estamated without a thorough knowledge of existing information systems and experiences up till now. The logical order can not be the chronological order. On the contrary there are in each organization always more or less explicit planning activities going on at each of the three policy levels. These activities can be characterized as simultaneous, interdependent and dynamic. Information requirements are to a large extent determined by what is technically possible and organizationally feasible. Moreover the question is no longer, and in the past seldom was, automation or non-automation. It is and always was a question of using available resources such as computers for those parts of information systems and services for which it is profitable to do so. Not the smallest difficulty with the subsequent approach is that each stage may take so much time that it is outdated before the next one is ready.

For these reasons a so called simultaneous planning model has been developed. It consists of three parts as well. Schematically:

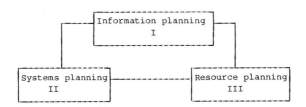

FIGURE 3. Simultaneous Planning Model

An information plan (I) consists of a structured description of all activities in the field of information systems and services which are planned to be carried out in a coming period e.g. three to five years. It includes all system management and all information management (see above) to be done by an organizational unit. Systems plans (II) do the same for each individual system. They include detailed information analysis, systems design, development and implementation for each individual system. Generally these systems may be used by more than one organizational unit. Resource plans (III) cover all informational resources of a specialized organizational unit which provide systems and services to one of more organizational units and for a number of information systems (e.g. a data processing centre).
The general idea is that no organizational unit is entirely independent. Each information plan should therefore correspond to information plans at higher and at lower hierarchical levels and with informations plans of organizational units at the same level. Secondly no organizational unit makes use of only one specialized organizational unit e.g. a computing centre or an information systems department for all phases for all information systems it needs. This

approach takes into account that most organizations already have more or less automated information systems already and that with each of the three parts of the planning model work is being carried out and plans are being reconsidered simultaneously. And lastly the three types or planning are intrinsically interdependent.

This planning method was developped by the ministry of the interior in the Netherlands for use with central government departments*. The only other known reference which goes somewhat in the same direction (with a different terminology) is (3). Our main objections to existing (subsequent) planning methodologies can be summarized as follows:

-    they consider organizations largerly as closed systems;
-    they suppose a one to one relation between the three parts of the simultaneous planning model in stead of a bi-directional n to m relation;
-    they do not take into account hierarchical and other formal and informal dependencies between organisational units.

This last point requires some further elaboration. The informational position of an organizational unit is dependent on the types of informational processes namely primary or secondary (both supporting and management) processes at different levels. If an information process is the main (primary) process of a organizational unit it still does not need to be independent, that is it may largely be determined by the environment (e.g. the financial information systems managed by an accounting department or a population register managed by a city administration). Secondly it may be dependent on the measure of influence the organizational unit has on contents and form of in- and outgoing information flows (by definition related to the measure of (in)dependency of main processes). And thirdly it is dependent on the measure of autonomy with regard to information policy at large e.g. computer system selection, information system priority setting, hardware and software standardization, methodology improvements, etc. The lower in the organization the more restrictions there are on the discretion with regard to information policy and planning of an organizational unit.

With help of the analytical tools shown in figure 1 and the planning model shown in figure 3 it is, under circumstances, possible to consider a change in the informational infrastructure between government agencies for the purpose of intergovernmental use.

3.   CAN INFORMATIONAL INFRASTRUCTURES BE CHANGED?

To answer this question it is first necessary to define more precisely what informational infrastructures are and secondly to explain what criteria will be used if a change is to occur at all. As information systems, informational infrastructures can be described both analytically and functionally. Analytically they comprise in principle the same components and these components are functionally serving different information systems as it was the case with information systems. The only difference appears to be that informational

* More detailed descriptions are at request available in Dutch only at request with the author.

infrastructures cover a wider area, both analytically and functionally. Their scope cannot be easily defined in terms of the real systems they describe. Also the distinction between information management and system management does not give much help here. Perhaps one could say that with informational infrastructures emphasis is on the system management side and less on the information management side. The difference between information systems and informational infrastructures becomes more clear when one realizes that we are talking about the fourth stage in the development of government interference with information processing in the public sector (par. 1). In this fourth phase the real discussion is about tasks and responsibilities of governmental units with a view to changes in their relations as a result of or accompagnying the introduction of modern information technology. If governmental bodies have relations they have information relations anyway, and in most cases they have informational relations only. Mutual supply of physical products or personal services is rather scarce. Also the relations of government with the private sector are highly information intensive, especially in the field of income redistributions (all kinds of tax-levy, personal allowances, and support to private organizations in one way or another). So if planning the informational infrastructure means anything, it means that we are talking about governmental and administrative changes in relation to the introduction of or a more intensive use of information technology. Recently at a conference in Speyer (Germany) the smouldering discussion came quite into the open. The main opponents were professor Kraemer from the United States and professor Reinermann from Germany (4), (5). The first one boldly claimed that information technology at least up till now and in North America, did not have any observable influence on public administrative organization and he did not expect it would get it either. The reason being that those changes occur only if there is a shift in power entirely independent of technological developments. On the other hand his opponent proposed that the use of modern technology does have and if it did not have it so much up till now should have, a far reaching influence on the structure of public administration. The main reason being that the requirements and expectations of the community and so of politicians with regard to the way in which government works are carried out, are changing in such a way that only with help of information technology they could be met. In the second place the use of information technology as such makes it a condition that in an increasing number of cases the division of tasks between government agencies and tiers of government are changed. Examples of these changes do occur in the continental north-westen part of Europe. The rather fundamental differences are not only of a methodological kind, as was suggested by some contributors. They argue that North American research in public administration is inclined to declare empirical facts to be normative standards for further action, whereas in Europe especially on the continent rational considerations do some times and after a time influence actual behaviour, that is to say they are considered as guidelines for action. Another explanation which could be heard is that the actual division of power did not change very much since the founding of the United States, whereas in Europe especially since the end of the eighteenth century in most countries several rather drastic changes in the structure of public administration have been made. In a way Europeans are accostumed to and therefore more inclined to consider possible improvements in government structures, also with help of modern information technology. Whatever may be the case or a correct explanation, it cannot be denied that infrastructures and therefore public administration are in discussion. Sometimes it seems that research is limited to changes in the organization of information processing as such. For instance Lenk came to the conclusion that quite apart of differencies between the individual states (Länder), there seems to be a new trend in the direction of some form of overall coordination between municipalities, regions and higher levels of government (6). An more theoretical approach is choosen by Ciborra, an Italian who is also discussing the reframing of the role of computers in organizations (7). He makes use of the so called transaction cost approach, the economic theory of Williamson which tries to explain the external organization in the private sector (sizes and forms of corperation and coordination between independent enterprises). Williamson is by the way not the first one who hints at the informational character of organizational structuring, especially Galbraith did the same and tested his theory also in the public sector (8). In stead of Galbraith well known strategies for improving organizational efficiency, Williamson distinguishes three organizational models which satisfy information requirements: the market model, the hierarchical or planning) model and the group model. The basic idea is that the cost of organizing is mainly the cost of coordination and control, i.e. of information processing. As markets function perfectly only if there are many independent suppliers and demand parties for standard products, and as in most cases information systems for the public sector are unique in any sence, some form of a planning model seems plausible quite apart from other reasons such as equality of rights and democratic control. This does, however, not necessarily lead to centralisation or big government. It is a pity that so little research is being carried out in this field. It is quite possible that the results of Attewell and Rule in their their examination of the literature on the effects of computing in organizations is restricted to American evidence only (9). It is quite possible that the contingency theory not only applies to the private sector but also to the public sector. On the other hand there are so many examples and serious deliberations going on that other conclusions are conceivable. Perhaps computers do not necessarily effect the distribution of authority and control but given the objectives of our governments under certain circumstances certain changes in the distribution of authority and control by way of information technology could be due.

A few examples from the author's environment are: reorganisation of national motor vehicle registration including drivers'licences, insurance records, motorcar taxes and technical inspections (formerly with at least four different agencies), reorganisation of population registration including informational relations to central government agencies but with decentralisation of information management to municipalities. Other examples are cooperation between organizations in the sectors of public health and education largely on a voluntary basis but both in the field of system management and information management with deconcentration of physical processing wherever that is more efficient. Especially these last two examples do come very near to the hard core of the question. Are we only talking about efficiency of information processing, or are we also and finally talking about redistribution of power which would not have occurred without modern information technology. This not so because somebody who has the power, now sees an opportunity to increase it, but because it is more efficient or more effective for the community as a whole.
After this support of intuitive formation of the notion (planning of) informational infrastructures we may try a more formal definition. An informational infrastructure can be defined as an administrative system which recognizes information as a resource by the provision of informational products and services to central, regional and municipal governments alike (and in some cases to the private sector as well). It may concern e.g. training of managers and users at different levels, the standardization of application independent

hardware and software, and the exploitation of datacommunication networks. It may also concern application development and maintenance, both to minimize cost of system management and as a prerequisite for the exchange of information and the joint use of databases.

The planning of the informational infrastructure can than be defined as the purposeful, if necessary new, arrangement of responsibilities and authorities for information management and systems management between central, regional and local governments (or even semi-public sectors). This rearrangement may be effected by voluntary and free cooperation (e.g. by mutual agreement) or by binding and regulatory coordination (e.g. by law) (2).

4. CONCLUDING REMARKS

The direction into which the development may go, can further be illustrated by two recent reports (available in Dutch only). These examples do not apply to particulair information systems or all information systems in a particular field of (semi-) public endeavour but seem to point at the organization of informational infrastructures as defined above. The first example is a recent advise to government by a working group charged to investigate whether and if so how, public agencies should be charged for the information they receive from other public agencies. To the surprise of many people, politicians and civil servants alike, and despite privatising and market thinking, it was advised not to do so on some restrictions. The restrictions are that all information exchanges should take place on a formal legal basis only, and apply to all public agencies in similar circumstances. This means if there is a right to ask for that information and a duty to deliver it. The reasons being not only that it saves a lot of expensive, difficult and often unreliable accounting work, but that under those restrictions charging back would undermine the responsibility of information providers to produce the information requested with minimum cost. In other words the market model would not work and other management tools such as planning should be applied.

The second example is the first interim report of the present government commission mentionend in par. 1 above. The highest priority should be given to the development of an interdepartemental and an intergovernmental telecommunication network. The preliminary conclusions of the commission after almost a year of intensive discussions supported by external technical research was that the only way to improve government by information technology is to promote free cooperation wherever possible (also by financial means), but to coordinate where necessary by regulatory measures e.g. with regard to the application of telecommunication standards.

These two examples may finally underline the necessity for scientists and managers of public administration to leave their sanctified legal and otherwise delimitated responsibilities in the public sector. At least they should entertain the idea that information technology could be an incentive for the consideration of administrative reform by way of planning the informational infrastructure.

References

1. Brussaard, B.K., Electronic Information Management for Administrative
    Government, Interdisciplinary Science Review, Vol. 8. No. 1, 1983. pp.
    56-64.

2. Bos, H and Brussaard, B.K., Intergovernmental relations in information
    Systems and Services in the Netherlands (a conceptual framework for
    comparative analysis), Proceedings of 1985 URISA conference, Ottowa, volume
    III, pp. 39-49.

3. Bowman, B., Davis, G., Wetherbe, J., Three Stage model of MIS Planning,
    Information and Management, no.6, (1983), pp. 11-25.

4 . Kraemer, K.L., Why technique-driven administrative reforms are not likely to
    happen, Proceedings of 55. Staatswissenschaftliche Fortbildungstagung, 10-13
    March 1987, Speyer.

5. Reinermann, H., Vor einer Verwaltungsreform? (Informationstechnisch
    motivierde Ziele und Systemkonzepte), Proceedings of 55.
    Staatswissenschaftliche Fortbildungstagung, 10-13 March 1987, Speyer.

6. Lenk, K., Einsetz der Informationstechnik: Die nenen Konzepte der
    Bundesländer, Offentliche verwaltung und Datenverarbeitung, Nr. 3, March
    1987, pp. 82-87.

7. Ciborra, C.U. Reframing the role of computers in organizations: the
    transaction cost approach, Proceedings of the 6th conference on Information
    Systems, December 16-18 1985, Indianapolis, pp. 57-69.

8. Galbraith, J.R., Organization Design, Addison-Wesley Publ.Co, 1977.

9. Attewell, P., Rule, J., Communications of the ACM, December 1984, Volume 27,
    No. 12, pp. 1184-1192.

Governmental and Municipal Information Systems
P. Kovács and E. Straub (Editors)
Elsevier Science Publishers B.V. (North-Holland)
© IFIP, 1988

CAD Thematic Mapping as Part of an Environmental
Information System

Dr.-Ing. Dieter Fischer
Umweltbundesamt, Bismarckplatz 1, D-1000 Berlin 33

1. INTRODUCTION

In the last twenty years, more and more data bases have been
established in many countries to perform a variety of functions. One of these functions is to provide backup for central
government activities, and it is in this respect that an environmental information system is being set up on behalf of the
government of the Federal Republic of Germany with the aim of
supplying up-to-date information for documenting environmental
research and describing the condition of and trends in the environment. This data can then be used as a basis for political
decision-making and to provide a public information service.

Environmental protection measures can only be successfully developed if the data on which they are based are reliable. In
reaching any decision in the environmental sphere, we must take
into account as many effects as possible on, for example, the
economy, town and country planning, transport policy, research
policy and a great many other aspects of social life. Only with
the aid of data base systems can the ever-increasing volume of
data relating to the environment be collected, edited and made
available. It is here that the environmental information system
(UMPLIS) of the Federal Environmental Protection Agency provides such an invaluable service.

The contents of the literature and research data bases are made
available in the form of lists, tables and reference works, for
example the Environment Research Catalog (UFOKAT), a comprehensive and periodical document of the research activities in the
environmental sector in the German-speaking area. Systematic presentation of the contents of the data bases for waste management (AWIDAT), emission source cadastre (EMUKAT), water pollution data base (HYDABA) and air immission data base (LIMBA) was
made possible with the introduction of a computer-aided interactive graphic system about six years ago. Up until then, the
measured values, system data and other statistical material
were printed out in the form of extensive lists.

The graphical representation of measured values, emissions and
pollution in the form of diagrams and maps was immediately
welcomed by the public, administrators and planners alike and
widely disseminated in newspapers and periodicals and by
television.

2. CONCEPT OF A SPATIAL INFORMATION SYSTEM

The term "spatial information system" often evokes the notion
of a supercompetent data network which produces graphics from
all the data of interest to the user, makes them available at
the touch of a button and perhaps even does all the reporting
automatically. It also conjures up perhaps the idea of a
spatial data base in which all the spatial data for a state,
for example, are stored in the optimum arrangement and are
readily accessible.

Even if these requirements have some justification as ideals
for designing such a system, they often have little in common
with actual fact. Environmentally relevant data are namely
sectoral in nature, coming from sectors such as meteorology,
hydroscience, economic statistics, population statistics,
agriculture and forestry, and in some of these cases the data have been available over a number of decades and in a
variety of forms, such as card files, data files and data bases in various public and private institutions. An integral
concept of a spatial information system builds on this situation, combines existing data sources with new collections of
data (data bases, for example) and makes use of the facilities
of interactive graphic systems. Fig. 1 shows the data flow
within such a system. The central graphic system takes data
from data bases, data files and lists, links these with threedimensional structures, allows the data to be weighted and
aggregated and provides the results in the form of diagrams
from the field of descriptive statistics, thematic maps,
tables, lists and text.

Combination and evaluation of geographical data and factual
data procudes information which expands the existing data
base. The two arrow directions in Fig. 1 illustrate this process of evaluation of existing data and the possible expansion
of the data base.

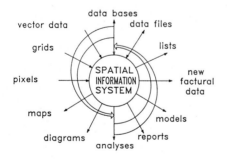

FIGURE 1
Data flow in a spatial information system

This concept is of particular significance as far as the functions of the Federal Environmental Protection Agency are concerned since the data situation in the environment sector,
particularly in West Germany, as a federal state, is anything
but homogenous. Systematic acquisition of data has only ever
been possible on a step-by-step, item-by-item and sector-by-
sector basis, and this is still true today. For this reason, a
great many data inventories are still in the course of preparation. This is true of environmentally relevant data at federal, 'Land' and local level and also applies to planning
institutions such as regional planning authorities, water authorities and research institutes. Some aspects of this system
have already been completed with the thematic maps produced;
these are:

- data base evaluation
- creation of new geographic structures
- preparation of reports
- numerical evaluation of geometric structures
- aggregation of primary data, and
- storage of aggregated data.

3. EXAMPLES

3.1 Results from the measurement network of the Federal Envi-
    ronmental Protection Agency

The diagram was prepared for the "1984 Data on the environment" report. It shows the trends in immissions at measuring
points over a period of time. The hourly values are stored in
the LIMBA data base and are aggregated in such a way that they
can be transferred to the graphic system for display.

The graphic method module consists of graphic structures (borders of the Federal Republic, measuring points in rural areas,
coordinate addresses for curves, text, connecting lines and
frames). These enable graphics to be produced for all the
substances stored and for various immission values. These parameters are interrogated in a dialog procedure system. Fig. 2
shows the trend in nitrogen oxide immissions in rural areas for
a number of statistical aspects.

0.2 man months were required to set up the methodic graphic
modules. It takes approximately one hour to produce a graphic
variant for other substances and/or immission values.

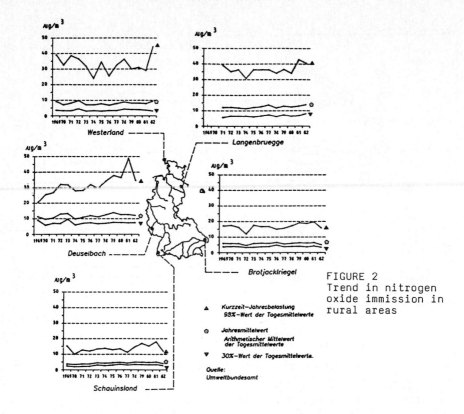

FIGURE 2
Trend in nitrogen
oxide immission in
rural areas

3.2 Charting the water quality from the Berlin environmental atlas

The current condition and the trends in the quality of the
flowing water in West Berlin are shown in Fig. 3 based on the
paramters of phosphate, amonium, oxygen saturation and minimum oxygen levels and also on the normality for escherichia
coli as an indicator of bacteriological pollution. Parallel
belts were set up for the selected measuring points alongside
the water. The measured values were evaluated and classified
according to a sevenstage quality scale.

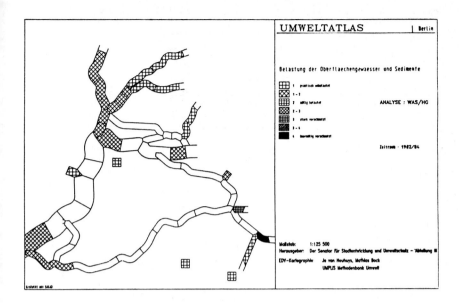

FIGURE 3
Quality of flowing water in Berlin

Measured values going back several decades are available for showing the quality of the Berlin surface water. It is therefore possible to produce time series for a large number of parameters. The graphic and methodic "Berlin water quality" module is a typical example of the extensive evaluation of measured values stored in a data base and of the versatility of this instrument in describing, for example, long-term trends and current situations. Approximately 2 man months were needed to develop the geographical basis for the belts and the dialog procedure system for data transfer and evaluation. It is possible to generate a new map within about 2 hours.

The "Berlin water quality" module is part of a spatial information system currently being set up for an urban region. The present geographical data base covers the Berlin transport network (roads, urban railroad and intercity railroad), flowing water, lakes, administrative boundaries, block structures and a 1 x 1 km grid pattern. On the basis of the network structure of the traffic routes, data are shown from the regular traffic censuses. This information then in turn forms the basis for

determining and thematically evaluating noise pollution in residential areas, taking into account the local conditions,
such as the type of road surface, width of road, density of
trees and hedges and the degree of development. Among other
things, the grid map shows nitrogen oxide and sulfur dioxide
emissions for the entire Berlin West area.

16 man months were needed to collect, check and correct the
graphic data. The resultant file occupies a storage space of
approximately 3.2 megabytes. The file is organized in such a
way that any rectangular section from the complete map can be
read, processed and plotted. In view of the large volume of
complex graphic data involved, this is absolutely essential.
Inquiries in a spatial information system which are carried
out by means of geometric structures are only possible if
logical connections are not split among a number of files (map
pages). In addition, the continuous organization of the data
base permits detailed organization of the data and detailed
analysis of any spatial entities (such as statistical areas,
traffic, cells, administrative areas, natural categories and
thematic categories).

3.3 Results from the EMUKAT data base

The EMUKAT data base contains data on emission sources broken
down into emitter groups and substances in addition to regular
rectangular grid patterns and network structures also at district level for the Federal Republic of Germany. For the purposes of evaluating these data and for portraying the economic
and demographic data collected at district level, a geographic
data base was created; this data base is known as the "Administrative boundaries of the Federal Republic of Germany" and
covers the state borders, 'Land' borders, the boundaries of
administrative areas and the boundaries of districts. Fig. 4
shows a graphic analysis from EMUKAT for sulfur dioxide emissions from the three emitter groups of traffic, private households and industry.

The thematic district maps have since become the standard output from the graphic systems and include data from a number of
different sources. Graphic data acquisition and correction and
development of the dialog procedure system required about 1.5
man months. The geographical data base consists of approximately 1000 connected lines and 315 area elements and requires
0.2 megabytes of storage.

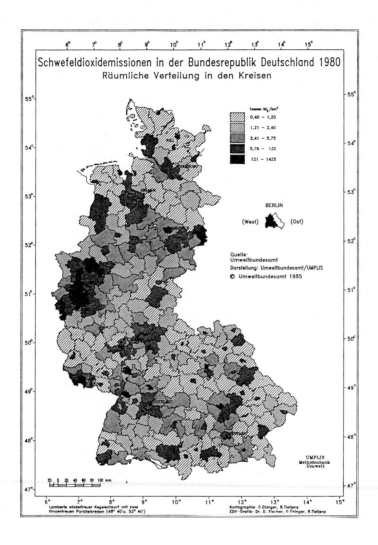

FIGURE 4
Sulfur oxide emissions in the districts of the Federal
Republic of Germany

3.4 Results from the 1983, 1984, 1985 and 1986 forest damage
    surveys

The analyses of forest damage carried out on behalf of the Federal Minister of Food, Agriculture and Forestry by the forest
administrations of the various Länder used a uniform random
sample method based on a 4 by 4 km grid network. The values
obtained were aggregated to provide representative statements
on the growth areas concerned. Growth areas are natural entities classified according to various criteria including the
composition of the soil, vegetation, altitude and climate. The
data supplied for the 58 growth areas were evaluated at the
forest area level cartographically on the basis of various
criteria such as year of survey, species of tree, degree of
damage and type of damage. The aggregated statistical values
were assigned to the forest regions in the growth areas in
order to reestablish the relationship to the forest areas. The
comparison of the results from the 1983 and 1984 surveys in
Fig. 5 and 6 shows the general escalation of damage in a very
short time and also shows regional peculiarities. Around 60
different thematic forest damage maps are produced in each
year of the survey. The reason so many are prepared is that a
wide variety of information is needed for scientific and publication purposes. The maps differ according to type of tree
(beech, spruce, oak, fir and pine), age either more than or
less than 60 years, degree of damage on a scale from 1 to 4
(slightly damaged, damaged, badly damaged and dead) and several classifications of percentage damage.

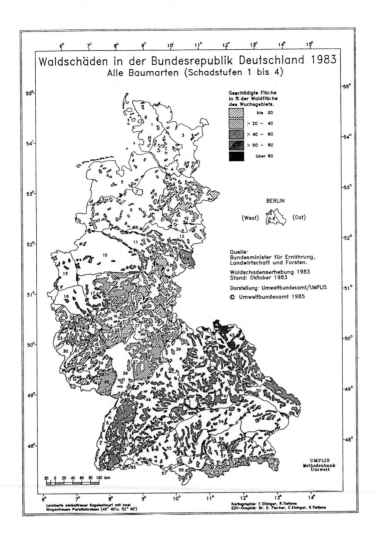

FIGURE 5
Forest damage map for 1983

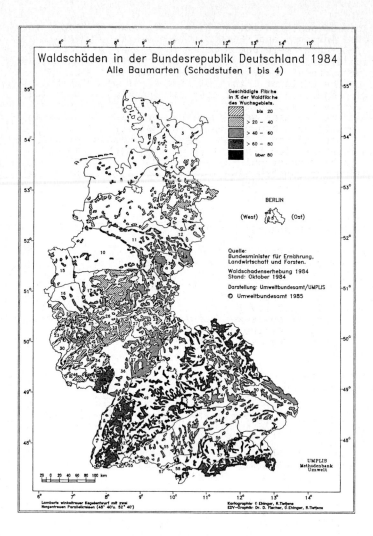

FIGURE 6
Forest damage map for 1984

The two cartographic entities of "Growth areas in the Federal Republic of Germany" and "Forest regions in the Federal Republic of Germany" were combined to form a new geographic data base which allows growth area data to be mapped on to forest regions or parts of these regions. The two basic maps generalized on the basis of 1 to 1 million scale maps (Lambert conformal projection with two standard parallels), digitized and provided with appropriate logical information (spatial references). The two maps were then automatically intersected so that the growth area boundaries thematically subdivide the forest regions. Around 3.5 man months were needed for the methodic module entitled "Evaluation of the forest damage surveys", including graphic data processing, data editing, intersecting and constructing a dialog procedure system. It takes about one hour to produce a new version of the map. The module requires 0.4 megabytes of storage space.

4. DESCRIPTION AND ANALYSIS OF THE ENVIRONMENTAL SITUATION

In comparison with other users of interactive graphic systems such as power supply utilities and land registries, environmental protection agencies have to maintain a large number of geographic data bases to be in a position to provide a cartographic illustration not only of individual items (for example emissions at district level and the sites of incinerating plants) but also of complex ecological relationships and also to perform analyses of the data obtained. A large number of different maps must be used to provide the cartographic basis. These include

- topographic maps,
- meteorological and climatic maps,
- geological maps, and so on.

The geographic data base comprises all the basic graphic structures, namely:

- areas (districts, nature reserves, biotopes)
- networks (water networks, roads, railroads)
- points (sites) and
- rasters.

The volume and complexity of the geographical information to be incorporated in a spatial information system imposes stringent requirements on the graphic system to be used as regards data management, data acquisition and the data structure, for example. Furthermore, as the scales and the projections used are not uniform throughout, valid transformation facilities have to be provided which guarantee correct conversion while retaining the logic of the geometry. The two main areas of application of graphic data processing are the description and analysis of the environmental situation. These two tasks it performs by linking the data evaluated in the factual data bases with a systematically produced geographic data base. I shall now deal with the two functions, starting with that of describing the environmental situation:

The purpose here is to produce high-quality up-to-date maps quickly and, as far as possible, without the need for an interactive dialog by specifying the desired graphic definition and allowing the system to link with the edited data. Experts in cartography who have no knowledge of graphic systems should also be able to produce such maps. In the decriptive dimension the geometric/geographic structures are support points for spatial statistical statements. Time series for measured values or distributions, for example, are shown with the aid of polygons, histograms, pie charts or symbols. The merit of the graphic system lies in the direct assignment of geometry and associated statistical data from external files and in freely selectable cartographic evaluation, for example by descriptive statistics, by symbols or the graphic development of areas and line elements by value-dependent hatching and/or the use of conventional signs. If the software itself only holds a basic stock of these, there must be facilities that the user can employ himself, without the need for programming, to extend the range of hatchings and symbols. This of course also applies to the classification of primary data, selection of the size of histograms and so on. This freedom of action at the user interface as regards value classification and cartographic detail is essential if environmental reporting is to be effective and up-to-date.

The second principal area of application for graphic data processing is the analysis of the environmental situation. In contrast the purely descriptive cartography, the geometric/geographic structures in analytical cartography are themselves the object of processing. By evaluation, assessment and modelling and by superimposition, intersection and computation new information is obtained, further thematic maps generated or the geographic data base extended. The geographic data base is also extended not by the digitization and/or incorporation of maps but by graphic methods such as intersection, generalization or imposing a raster.

Example of cartographic evaluation:

- intersection of areas, identification of areas of conflict (for example, biotopes versus amenity areas) with computation of the surface areas involved

- searches carried out for numerical and/or graphic information on the basis of distances or radii specified (for
example, all biotopes at a distance of 5 kilometers from
the freeway network or areas worthy of protection within a
radius of 10 kilometers from an emission source with a
source height of 300 meters)
- searches carried out for numerical and/or graphic information on the basis of paths specified (for example, temperature changes downstream of thermal inlets into rivers).

A further important analysis method is the assessment of spatial units by way of aggregating individual items of information. For spatial analysis of the environmental situation and
for preparing the way for planning decisions, information for
one particular spatial entity (the measurements taken at a
measuring point, for example) must be capable of being mapped
on to other spatial entities. The following are just some
examples:

- proportion of damaged forest area ('forest region' entity)
per district ('administrative boundaries' entity)
- proportion of intensively utilized agricultural area (the
'land utilization' entity) per water catchment area (the
'water catchmant areas' entity)
- balance of traffic on Federal freeways and Federal highways
(the 'road network' entity) for selected forest regions
('forest region' entity)
- balance of natural-area potential derived from indicator models per raster element ('natural area' entity mapped on a
grid system of, for example, 2 by 2 square kilometers in a
Universal Transversal Mercator (UTM) projection).

The Federal Environmental Protection Agency holds comprehensive
data inventories which describe the emission situation for
sulfur dioxide and the nitrogen oxides, for example, for the
entire Federal Republic of Germany. These data are available
for network structures (freeway sections), for administrative
boundaries (districts) and for raster areas in the Universal
Transversal Mercator projection (UTM grid). At the present
time, there are no measured immission values available for the
entire Federal Republic of Germany. Conclusions about immission
pollution are drawn from the emission situation by means of
modelling. These propagation models are fed from the existing
data files. The findings obtained with regard to local pollution and spatial distribution must be capable of being combined with other maps, such as those showing the extent of
forest damage.
Propagation models are based both on vector data (isolines)
and raster data. Appropriate graphic methods should be available for both types of model so that it is also possible to
map vector data on to grid data in numerical and graphic
analysis.

The new high quality of data evaluation is based on the ability of graphic data processing to process and present an extensive set of data, such as we have in the field of environmental protection, in terms of its physical effects and the interrelationships involved. In our experience, graphic data processing has proved to be an ideal communication interface for factual data:

- trends, patterns and critical conditions can be detected, noted, compared and evaluated, and
- the local and physical relationships of environmental events can be visualized.

In environmental reporting, there are two special data features which are of decisive importance as far as the application of graphic data processing for factual data is concerned:

- Social indicators require a spatial context. Social events take place in three dimensions. While for social data (economy, population etc.) the spatial link merely provides a frame of reference, this link is of material importance for environmental indicators and environmental data.
- The result of this is that in certain circumstances the various factors involved may have different spatial terms of reference, and aggregation within a single, threedimensional frame of reference may not be possible; instead these terms of reference will have to be superimposed and intersected.

It is therefore reasonable not to have the spatial relationship of the data added to the tables as additional verbal information but to use the threedimensional frame of reference as a basis and to link the statistical information logically as graphic highlights with geographical information, in other words to introduce thematic cartography for environmental reporting at national level.

As yet, however, there are no large-scale spatial information systems in use for national environmental reporting which combine data base systems with the available facilities for interactive graphic data processing.

At the regional level, we already have initial results from individual projects (water quality, condition of lakesides and river banks, and noise pollution) within the overall "Environmental atlas for Berlin" project. With the "Data on the environment" published in 1984 and 1987 and the thematic maps showing forest damage published in 1983, 1984, 1985, and 1986 the Federal Republic of Germany now has an instrument for environmental reporting at national level which evaluates factual data in graphic form both systematically and continuously. At European Community level, the intention is to draw up an ecological map of Europe by combining graphic data processing with hard data.

The application of graphic data processing as a communication
interface to the factual data bases is not restricted merely
to the preparation of reports and to spatial data analysis. In
its methodic role as an instrument of analysis it also feeds
new findings and new data back to the factual data bases.
Graphic data processing in the field of environmental protection can be developed as the central element of a spatial information system.

5. REQUIREMENTS ON THE GRAPHIC SYSTEM

Within the spatial information system, graphics provides the
geographic data base (digitized maps) and methods of spatial
data access and spatial data evaluation and data analysis.
This of necessity involves a series of methodic and specialist
requirements, and these are as follows:

- logical design of the basic graphic structures
- logical design of the spatial reference systems
- administration of the geographic references
- presentation techniques in thematic cartography
- spatial/geometric analysis techniques
- interfaces to statistical and alphanumerical data in data
  bases and files, and
- interfaces to other CAD systems for the purposes of data exchange.

As far as data acquisition, data processing, data management
and linkage to files and data bases are concerned, the following
minimum criteria have to be fulfilled:

a) Data acquisition
    - smooth and exact incorporation of the digitizing samples
      into a freely selectable frame of reference
    - operation possible with coordinate systems other than rec-
      tangular ones
    - acquisition of any map sheet sections
    - simultaneous acquisition of geometry and logic via pro-
      cedure handling and the menu principle
    - weighting of geometric information (origin points, fixed
      points)
    - automatic capture of points and lines by means of freely
      selectable tolerancing
    - reversible manipulation of geometric structures while re-
      taining the logical information
    - differentiated storage of geometric information according
      to content by means of menus and procedure handling (for
      example, the layer principle).

b) Data processing and data evaluation
   - linkage of the geometric data with statistical data and text information
   - logical selection of geometric data and/or factual data according to quantitative, qualitative and structural criteria
   - superimposition and intersection of geometric objects to form new geometric structures
   - computation of surface areas, lengths and distances, including storage of this information at the geometric objects or in files
   - optional graphic highlighting (inscription, hatching, symboles) of attributes or attribute words of the graphic elements
   automatic graphic highlighting of associated factual data in the form of histograms, polygons, pie charts or symbols
   - drawing up a balance of the geometric and logical information and associated factual data for any freely selectable region, and
   - superimposition of selected graphic information from various image files.

c) Thematic mapping
   - free definition of symbols
   - unrestricted design options for line modes, hatchings, conventional signs and parallel contours
   - separation of text
   - line-accompanying text, and
   - systematic presetting and revision facilities for color separations on the basis of the layer principle.

d) Data management
   - continuous organization of the maps in a variety of libraries based on thematic criteria
   - separate storage of images, symbols, procedures and menus
   - optimization of storage requirements, and
   - optimization of the plotting process

e) Interfaces
   - interfaces to data files, and
   - interfaces to data bases
   - interfaces to other graphic systems

The interactive graphic system used in the Federal Environmental Protection Agency, which is based essentially on SIEMENS SICAD program packages, already fulfils these requirements to a large extent.

6. THE FUTURE

The methods used successfully up to now for portraying individual aspects and situations relating to the environment are
to be supplemented by analytical instruments from the field of
graphic data processing, particularly in respect of the tem-
poral and spatial trends in a large number of parameters which
affect the ecological cycle. The aim will be to provide comprehensive reports on any area of interest by aggregating individual items of information and at the same time incorporating value judgments.
With the aid of this facility, it will be possible to perform
planning functions, such as finding suitable sites and areas
(what is known as site provision and regional planning) and
estimating environmental consequences, for the entire Federal
Republic of Germany. For this, it will be necessary to extend
the methodological scope of the SICAD program packages. The
transition from vector data to raster data and from raster
data to vector data, the intersection of spatial reference
systems of any size, the transformation of spatial references
into conventional cartographic projections, uniform storage
and the expansion of the generation and manipulation commands
for the cartographic expression of the spatial reference have
all to be accomodated in the new system of the future.

Governmental and Municipal Information Systems
P. Kovács and E. Straub (Editors)
Elsevier Science Publishers B.V. (North-Holland)
© IFIP, 1988

MANAGEMENT INFORMATION AND GOVERNMENT NEEDS:
THE UK EXPERIENCE

GRAHAM OATES*

1.   INTRODUCTION

Management information is crucial to the efficient and effective operation
of any large scale organisation. Despite this public sector bodies are
notoriously poor at developing and using management information systems.

The poor track record of the UK Government prior to 1979 in developing
well-targeted management information systems was primarily related to a
culture in which:

-     officials were seen either as policy makers, administrators or
      technical or professional specialists but not managers;

-     additional services were on the whole funded by additional resources
      not by improving the efficiency with which existing services were
      delivered.

The election of a new, Conservative, government in the UK in 1979, under the
Prime Ministership of Mrs. Margaret Thatcher, heralded the introduction of a
new managerial approach to the delivery of public services. The Prime
Minister appointed a personal adviser on efficiency - Derek (now Lord)
Rayner, the managing director of the well-known Marks and Spencer retail
chain - to assist her in the development and implementation of this new
managerial approach. Rayner quickly set in motion a programme of
"scrutinies" or reviews of selected governmental areas which soon
demonstrated that many departments and officials were peculiarly unaware of
the costs of their activities. Not only that but in many departments
responsibility and accountability was ill-defined, senior officials were
often badly informed on what was going on in their departments and junior
officials were given insufficient guidance on what they were meant to
achieve with the resources which were entrusted to them.

---

*   Graham Oates is a Senior Managing Consultant with Peat Marwick
      McLintock, London, England.

The mounting evidence concerning the lack of good financial management information in central government culminated in May 1982 with the launch by the Prime Minister of her Financial Management Initiative (FMI). "The time has come" said the Prime Minister "for a general and co-ordinated drive to improve financial management in government departments." [1]

The purpose of this paper is to review five years on the information systems implications of this drive to increase managerial awareness and activity in the UK public sector and identify some of the lessons which have been learnt from the process.

2.   THE NATURE OF THE FINANCIAL MANAGEMENT INITIATIVE (FMI)

The purpose of the FMI was to promote in each department an organisation and system in which managers at all levels would have:

"-   a clear view of their objectives and means to assess and, wherever possible, measure outputs or performance in relation to those objectives;

-      well defined responsibility for making the best use of their resources including a critical scrutiny of output and value for money, and

-      the information (particularly about costs), the training and the access to expert advice, that they need to exercise their responsibilities effectively." [1]

The thirty-two departments which make up the UK central government were asked to submit plans to the Treasury by the end of January 1983 indicating how they proposed to satisfy the FMI requirements. A prime requirement of the responses was that the departments should provide systems based solutions which were rooted in the departmental organisation structures. Failure to support previous management reforms with good quality information systems was seen as a prime reason for their failure.

In the event, departmental proposals encompassed three main types of system:

-      senior or top management systems;
-      financial and management accounting systems;
-      management information systems.

In addition, some departments also took the opportunity to review the adequacy of their operational systems and also included proposals for their improvement or replacement. The inter-relationship of the various types of systems is shown at Figure 1.

FIGURE 1: FMI SYSTEMS

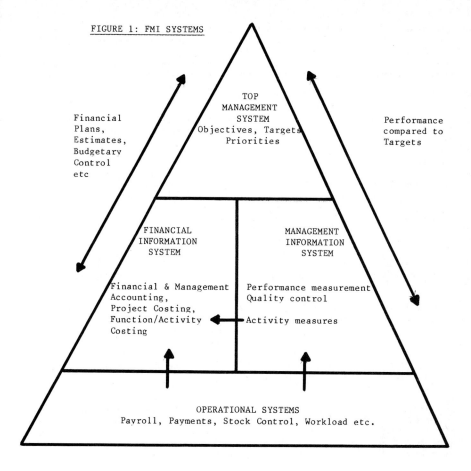

The first and most obvious lesson is that information systems are not an end
in their own right. They are, however, a necessary first step in most cases
to achieving improved management and decision making processes. Time,
however, is required to implement the new systems and, even once they are
operational, to build up a body of reliable information which can be used by
managers in making decisions about resource allocation and usage.

During this period managers are expected to service and support new systems
without receiving in return any significant tangible benefit. This is a
particular problem if, as in the UK public sector, many of the managers
regard this role as an unnecessary extension from their primary function of
caring for patients, assessing taxes, or carrying out academic research.
This has been one of the key problems in introducing new styles of
management into the National Health Service and more generally has involved
many public service bodies in becoming embroiled in a vicious circle whereby
it is difficult to introduce new management processes without major
improvements in management information and yet selling the necessary new
information systems to line managers is a problem when they only appear to
receive limited immediate benefits from the new system.

A second major lesson from the UK Government experience has been that
developing high quality management information systems in public sector
organisations involves major technical and conceptual issues. The sheer
size of the organisations, complexity of their operations and volumes of
transaction data mean that effective systems solutions rely heavily on
latest developments in computer software and hardware.

In addition, major problems are encountered in defining statements of
requirements and producing conceptual solutions to complex activities where
there are difficulties in defining and measuring outputs and levels of
performance. Initial attempts to develop all-embracing management
information systems using traditional step-by-step systems development
methodologies such as the one set out below:

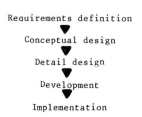

have on the whole failed. It is now recognised that a more flexible
development approach is needed which allows for requirements and the systems
supporting those requirements to evolve and grow as more is learnt about the
way the organisations work and the inter-relationships between resources,
activities and outputs. This revised approach has been reflected in the use
of flexible packaged software in the financial systems area and by the
increasing use of fourth generation languages, decision support systems and
prototyping techniques for some of the other applications.

Although most departments were clear at least, in theory, about the function and relationships of the various types of systems, there was less unanimity about the best overall systems development path. Some departments such as the Customs and Excise decided to concentrate their early efforts on getting the corporate planning process right before addressing the underlying management information issues; rather more departments, such as the Inland Revenue, the Department of Employment, and the Ministry of Agriculture, Fisheries and Food, believed that effective high level planning was impossible until they had built up a reliable database of good quality management information.

In systems terms, therefore, most departments responded by attacking the management information systems issues first. Moreover, since the FMI was primarily driven by the need to increase cost consciousness early developments concentrated on financial management systems.

3.   FINANCIAL MANAGEMENT SYSTEMS

The new financial information systems introduced the concept of management accounting into government departments and extended the range of cost analysis from the traditional concentration on cost types or cost elements (eg. salaries and wages, accommodation, etc.) to encompass cost centres or organisational units and, in a few cases, departmental functions and/or activities.

The design, development and implementation of new financial and management accounting systems was hampered in most departments by:

-    a shortage of accounting skills;

-    a shortage of data processing skills;

-    weak or inadequate operational or feeder systems;

-    the need to resolve a series of management issues relating to responsibility and accountability for budgets and costs.

The development of the new financial systems relied heavily on a series of key factors which included:

-    the availability of good quality and well proven general ledger software packages which enabled the systems to be developed in a shorter timescale and at a lower cost than if they had been designed and developed in-house;

-       the input of significant management consultancy resource in order to
        rectify accounting and data processing skill shortages.

4.   MANAGEMENT INFORMATION SYSTEMS

Developing and implementing non-financial management information systems has
proved a more difficult task both because the conceptual issues of defining
and measuring key output indicators and performance measures is more
problematic and ready made systems solutions are not available.   Such
systems, therefore, have in the main to be designed and developed in-house
and typically have a longer development timescale.

5.   TOP MANAGEMENT SYSTEMS

Developing good top management systems has proved even more elusive for many
departments.   The development of the underlying financial and management
information systems has ensured that top managers can receive large volumes
of information about costs, performance, workload and output.   In most
cases, however, there is far too much information, which needs to be
refined, restructured and presented selectively to senior managers in such a
way that it will support the decision making processes.   Providing senior
managers with accurate and comprehensive data about the activities of the
organisation in a way which can be easily digested and understood is a
problem in all large organisations, although some of these problems are
accentuated when dealing with government departments or other public sector
bodies.

In the UK central government the difficulties involved in developing top
management systems have included:

-       the need to wait for the development of the lower level management
        information systems.   Developing and implementing these systems has
        involved a significant amount of time and resource;

-       defining and agreeing upon the key pieces of information required by
        senior management to plan and control the department.   This is often
        difficult in relatively simple organisations which have a clearly
        defined objective such as to maximise profit or easily identifiable
        outputs such as cars, computers or packets of breakfast cereal.   The
        objectives and outputs of most government departments are much more
        difficult to identify and quantify;

- the existence and appreciation of the right technical solutions. It is only recently that decision support type software has appeared on the market. A logical technical solution for many government departments would be to use decision support software to support the Top Management System role based on data fed from the lower level management information systems. Decision support systems are, however, unlikely to provide a suitable answer to the top management system problem until the conceptual problems referred to above have been clarified. Even then their development is likely to be held back by the shortage of suitably qualified technical staff to program the systems;

- a lack of a proper appreciation by senior civil servants in many government departments of the top management role as a result of having been raised in a culture which gave priority to policy making and serving and supporting the relevant government minister over and above the managing of the department.

It seems likely that in some government departments, particularly the very large ones, that the concept of producing an all embracing top management system is too large and too difficult to cope with as a single project and that the way forward in this area will be by building decision support models covering discrete and well-defined activity areas. This approach allows experience to be gained in the techniques of model building whilst gradually improving the quality and relevance of the management information available to senior managers.

6.   KEY ISSUES IN THE SYSTEMS DEVELOPMENT PROCESS

An evaluation of the impact of the FMI five years on suggests that significant success has been achieved in the introduction of processes and systems which have increased the financial and management information available to government departments. The introduction of these systems and processes has been achieved despite acute shortages of accounting and data processing resource, the need to introduce new approaches to accounting and management alongside the information systems, and conceptual problems of defining, measuring and collecting data on outputs and performance.

The heavy dependence on external resources to achieve these changes and the sheer speed at which they have taken place has, however, raised major questions about the ability of some departments to effectively use and develop these systems now and in the future. As a corollary of this other observers are sceptical about the extent to which the new information systems will be accompanied by and reinforce a change in civil service culture. Solving the top management systems problem will be crucial in this respect for it is at this level that all the management information strands can be brought together to provide a complete picture of the efficiency and effectiveness of resource usage within a department.

The sheer scale of the information systems development problem has meant that in some departments designing, developing and implementing new management information systems has been seen as an end in its own right; rather than as a means to the ultimate end of changing the way in which government departments are managed.

7.   THE UK HEALTH SERVICE

The general principles of the FMI of:

-     bringing together within a single manager responsibility for using and controlling resources;

-     increasing the emphasis on what is achieved with resources, in terms of outputs and performance levels, rather than merely what volume of resources is consumed;

-     developing systems to provide management information to support the other objectives;

have been extended by the government beyond the 32 central government departments to other public sectors such as the National Health Service, Universities and other government sponsored bodies.

A series of "management budgeting" pilot schemes have been carried out in the National Health Service to widen the role of doctors and nurses from caring for patients to include an involvement in the control of the resources which are used to treat those patients. Once again the sheer lack of information about the use of resources in hospitals meant that much early effort was invested in the development of information systems merely to collect better data about how resources were used in hospitals and too little emphasis was placed on what analysis and information doctors and nurses really needed to carry out their managerial/patient care role more efficiently and effectively. The latest "Resource Management" pilot scheme is, significantly, concentrating on hospital sites which have relatively well-developed basic information systems, which means that development effort can be concentrated on clinical requirements rather than the implementation of lower level information systems which generate little immediate benefit to the ultimate end user.

8.   CONCLUSIONS

There are many lessons which can be learnt from the attempts of the UK Government during the last five years to improve the quality and quantity of management information available to administrative and policy officials and departmental managers. Two are particularly important.

This paper has concentrated on the difficulties and problems faced by UK public sector organisations in pursuing, over the last five years, an extensive programme of management information systems development. It would be a mistake, however, to assume, because of that, that no progress has been made.

There have been major changes in civil service culture during this period and the importance of positively managing government operations to increase outputs, reduce unit costs and generally improve both efficiency and effectiveness is now widely accepted.

Many government departments have powerful state of the art financial management systems; much effort has been invested in unravelling the complex interractions of government operations and in developing systems to monitor workload, performance levels and outputs; and there are an increasing number of examples of the use of decision support and prototyping approaches to cater for senior management needs.

The next five years will demonstrate whether what has already been achieved can be enhanced and expanded to fully realise the Prime Minister's original objectives.

[1] Efficiency and Effectiveness in the Civil Service: Government Observations on the Third Report of the Treasury and Civil Service Committee. HMSO. Cmnd 8616.

Governmental and Municipal Information Systems
P. Kovács and E. Straub (Editors)
Elsevier Science Publishers B.V. (North-Holland)
© IFIP, 1988

MANAGEMENT SUPPORT SYSTEMS IN FEDERAL GOVERNMENT

Klaus Lange

Institute for Applied Information Technology
Gesellschaft für Mathematik und Datenverarbeitung mbH
P.O.Box 1240
D-5205 Sankt Augustin 1

There is a great gap between the claim of Management Support Systems to support even top managers and the reality of their usage. Designers of MSS have misunderstood the nature of managerial work which is primarily communication of soft data and not isolated problem solving based on hard data. Indeed there is a growing use of PCs by the management of private companies but the tasks PCs are used for are rather ordinary. Examples of PC–use in the US federal government show that managers use computers primarily for communication purposes. In a pilot project the German PTT implements a MSS focussing on the communication habits and information needs of their managers. It is based on the interactive videotex system and a multifunctional telephone. Attracted by a high telephone comfort and the services of the public videotex system the managers learn to communicate electronically within their organization and to retrieve information out of internal databases. By using a basic system the managers also learn to articulate more precise requirements for a true MSS. These requirements will be surveyed by an evaluation team and will be fed back in the redesign of the basic system. This might be a way to lead managers to a creative and systematic use of modern information technology.

1. MANAGEMENT SUPPORT SYSTEMS: CLAIMS AND REALITY

The term *Management Support Systems* (MSS) is open to many interpretations. Scott Morton ([15], p. 326) defines it as "use of information technologies to support management". This very wide definition includes Management Information Systems (MIS), Management Decision Systems (MDS), Decision Support Systems (DSS) and Executive Support Systems (ESS); even End–User Computing (EUC) and the PC–use of managers could be submitted under the term [12]. With the terminological change from "information" or "decision" to "support" it is acknowledged that managers use computers for purposes other than information retrieval for decision making.

The classical decision theory's view [16] that information is gathered and used to make choices in decision situations is misleading. Organizations and individuals primarily gather information to scan the environment without any reference to actual decision situations. Information is gathered in surveillance mode rather than in decision mode [5]. There is no evidence that is not also true for managers.

Isolated data–based problem solving is rather the exception in the manager's activities than the rule. Most of the MSS designers have misunderstood management activities as rational, planned decision making based on hard data. This is an understanding which should be regarded with Mintzberg [10] rather as folklore than as fact:

- "managers work at unrelenting pace, ... their activities are characterized by brevity, variety and discontinuity and ... they are strongly orientated to action and dislike reflective activities"

- "managerial work involves performing a number of regular duties, including ritual and ceremony, negotiations and processing of soft information that links the organization with its environment"

- "managers strongly favor the verbal media – namely telephone calls and meetings".

The claim of MSS even to support chief executives (see [11] and [4]) is questioned . King [7] objects that the the real world of business is too complex to be captured in a computer model and that computers do little to support the vision and leadership that is critical to corporate success.

Concerning the activities of the top management Zmud ([25], p 91) has summarized the result of different field studies as follows:

- "Instead of managing people or resources, senior executives manage issues.

- Instead of reacting to decision situations, senior executives create decision situations.

- Instead of working through decision models, senior executives work through networks of people.

- Instead of making decisions, senior executives implement decisions.

- Instead of working with a well–defined, mostly quantitative and quite limited set of data, senior executives work with an ill–defined, mostly quantitative and wide–ranging set of data."

This disillusioning confrontation of design claims and management reality must not deny the fact that managers – up to the top – are slowly getting used to work with computers. However the increasing use should not deceive us with respect to the quality of the usage. 1984 DeLong and Rockart [2] have found out in a survey of the Fortune 500 companies, that in two thirds of the companies some executives have computers on their desks. The applications were rather ordinary: e.g. electronic mail, calendaring and word processing. An intensive PC–use comprising all executives with parallel integration into the company's data processing was the great exception. A survey among chief executives of the Fortune 500 companies in 1985 has shown that 12% of them use PCs in their work [6]. The most important applications were word processing and electronic mail apart from some information retrieval. An special advantage was seen in laptops allowing communication and word processing while at home or traveling. Traditional work styles of some executives seem to seduce them to work with PCs, such as the old habit to type texts and speeches himself. The executive's PC use has also symbolic qualities: He wants to demonstrate that he has realized the role of the new technology for the company and tries to motivate his staff to use this new technology too.

Moreover the above surveys allow to conclude that the great majority of executives has not yet got accustomed to use computers since top management works with or through secretaries and staffs. The better the support of the staff is, the less likely will the request be for a MSS. The potential competitive situation between staff and computer support has so far been neglected as an explanatory factor for the non–use of MSS. On the other hand, there may also be a positive reinforcing effect: If office automation is already implemented in the executive's office the executive could benefit directly from available data bases and applications and personal training and continuous assistance could be secured through the staff.

The very history of MSS shows that failures can mostly be explained by missing adaptation to users' interests and insufficient training and assistance. One generally failed to realize that system implementation is a continuous, lengthy and recursive process [9].

2. MANAGEMENT IN PUBLIC ADMINISTRATIONS

The above description of management activities by Mintzberg and Zmud hardly allows the inference of differences between the management in private companies and that in public administrations: The executives in public administrations work in the same manner as those in private companies: issue–centered, concerned rather with creating decision situations than with decision making, performing many regular ritual and symbolic duties. They favour verbal media and work with and through their staffs: *They manage by communication.*

But to some extent there are differences. Executives in private companies manage the production and selling of goods and services. The essential factors of this process are quantifiable, e.g. sales figures. Executives in public administrations – in our special case federal governments – formulate policies and supervise their execution. The main input and output factors in this process can hardly be quantified.

Managers in public administrations act less goal– and success–oriented as managers in private companies. To avoid internal conflicts they anticipate in time possible objections of other departments and therefore tend to withdraw initial goals or to reformulate them ("incremental muddling through"). Apart from the problem of the internal consensus public administrations are confronted with the problem of anticipating potential objections and resistance of external pressure groups or of public opinion. So their work is characterized rather by communication of soft data than by search for hard data in databases.

Another difference between private companies and public administrations is the degree of bureaucratization. The theory of bureaucracy is the theory of public administration. Characteristics of bureaucracy are strict hierarchies, clear distributions of responsibilities, strict rule–orientation and written documentations which secures the required precision, continuity, discipline, reliability and predictability of action. At first glance, public administrations thus appear as natural users of data processing since just data processing can secure these qualities. But administrative actions are seldom characterized by figures, but by texts of laws and regulations. Decisions are prepared in informal conversations and formal conferences. At present, modern information technology provides no sufficient support for these activities.

All in all, executives in public administrations are less inclined to use advanced information technology, if we disregard specific task groups dealing with budget and tax problems in classical departments and special service agencies.

3. MSS IN THE US FEDERAL GOVERNMENT

In no other country of the world modern information technology is such intensively used as in the US Federal Government which is the world's greatest buyer of information technology: In 1986, 15 billion \$ were spent on this purpose, in 1990, about 500.000 micros will be installed [8]. For this market, specific fairs are organized and specific periodicals ("Government Computer News") are published.

On the governmental side, several special agencies are involved in controlling this huge investment volume, namely:

- the Office of Management and Budget (OMB) with the basic guideline competence for the use of information technology, and

- the General Services Administration (GSA) as central service and procurement authority which has its own computer shops where PCs and software can be procured according to an approved list.

3.1 PC–Use of Managers

The Information Resources Management Service of the GSA conducted in 1985/86 a survey among microcomputer end users of the middle management in federal agencies [22]. The majority of the 208 interviewed managers regarded the microcomputer as an essential office tool. But they had great problems in describing the benefit of this tool: It was vaguely described with terms like "better timeliness, increased production, improved analysis and increased productivity". The most important applications for the PC were electronic spreadsheet, word processing, database management and statistical analysis. Only each 8th respondent said that used electronic mail. In future the respondents wanted to integrate their PCs into a local area network and to gain access to public networks. The respondents complained about the lack of adequate training and technical support, furthermore, they missed compatibility standards. The few senior level managers who already used a micro, fully understood neither microcomputer capabilities nor limitations. They expected from their word processing staff to act not only as trainers but also as operators and system administrators which meant to require too much from them. So it can be no surprise that almost every fourth micro installed in the Federal Government is used only seldom or not at all [18].

There are some rare examples of top officials using PCs for their work. The most prominent PC user in the Federal Government are (were) the Labor Secretary and the Secretary of the Interior [19]. Electronic mail and word processing were most intensively used by these top officials.

In the wide definition of MSS, the mere use of a PC is already management support. In the following, let us consider some prototype systems that were explicitly designed and implemented for the management in the Federal Government.

3.2 The White House Executive Office System

The Executive Office comprises i.a. the White House Office, the Office of Management and Budget, the Council of Economic Advisers and the National Security Council. For about 250 executives of these offices menu driven workstations were procured ([3], see also footnote). Standard software was flexibly integrated into one package. The PC menu include electronic mail and AP / UPI news services, word processing and spreadsheet. For the specific needs of the OMB handling budget and economic figures additional options were provided in connection with a mainframe; they are however not relevant in this context.

The training in one–to–one sessions and the permanent support by a specifically formed support team were essential to the acceptance of the system. The familiarization with the system was considerably facilitated by the menu concept; it was assumed that the executives were not willing to be confronted with the intricacies of an operating system [3]. Apart from training and guidance, much attention was attached to a short response time. Some resistance among the executives and their staffs had of course to be overcome. Some executives refused to put a keyboard device on their desks so that special desks were constructed for hiding the PC [3]. Since the system intervenes into the cooperation between the executive and his secretary, the secretaries showed some resistance against the system since some information ran past them through the system. In future, it is intended to integrate the whole word processing into the system and to replace the commercial electronic mail system by an inhouse electronic mail system which is required just for reasons of security. Furthermore, it is considered to use portable personal computers.

3.3 The System of the Department of Agriculture

The Department of Agriculture (DoA) uses an information system based on the Dialcom Electronic Mail System (see footnote). This is not only an electronic mail facility, but also provides other services:

- electronic bulletin board

- telex interface

- facilities for on-line discussions

- file transfer

- executive calendar and scheduling system

- electronic publishing for internal news

- electronic news services UPI and AP

- database management system

- forms processing.

The DoA, in particular its Office for Information, uses the system for the quick and effective exchange of information and documents with other federal departments and agencies, as well as with universities, state departments of agriculture and other cooperating institutions and organizations.

Currently, more than 400 users use the system on a regular basis; about 25% of the users are executives of the DoA, among them some senior executives. On average, electronic mail is used for 1–2 messages per day and per user. Unread messages are kept up to 30 days, the receipt of a message can be acknowledged. The daily news summary is of special interest for the users. It includes articles of the most important news services, newspapers and (technical) periodicals on agricultural policy and economy and the department in an abbreviated form. The editors of this service emphasize that they include "both favourable and unfavourable news". This news summary was of special interest for the executives when a former secretary of the DoA read it regularly.

For the issue–oriented analysis of public opinion Dialcom provides still another service: A 24 hour automatic clipping service selects articles with pre–selected characteristics out of the AP / UPI news services and sends them directly to an individual electronic mailbox. Via the Dialcom system, the Office of Information also distributes its own press releases to the interested public.

In other agencies of the Federal Government electronic mail systems and bulletin boards are mainly used by DP managers for communication going beyond organizational and local limits. These systems are gradually attracting managers of other areas, thus pervading slowly the whole organization. One example is an application in the General Services Administration, the central procurement and service agency of the Federal Government (see footnote). About 600 GSA managers – also of middle and upper levels – are currently using a network supplied by CompuServe, Inc. It is used primarily for the instantaneous transmission of electronic messages to GSA locations which are located in other areas of the US. Examples of the types of messages transmitted include: regional budget authorization, meeting notices, teleconference notices and authorization for travel. Moreover it allows communication with further nearly 200,000 other CompuServe users. The terminals on which electronic mail is handled are also used for word processing.

Apart from the comprehensive office automation [20], the PC–use of managers in US Federal Government is still underdeveloped and very heterogenous. An actual focus may perhaps only be seen in (mass) communication applications. Managers use the PC primarily to communicate within their department or agency and to monitor public opinion via electronic news services. The few systematic approaches are very pragmatic and not well planned or evaluated. The information needs of potential users and the actual use of the PC are not surveyed systematically. Qualitative training and assistance is often lacking. In the classical departments a real MSS is not in use; the additive comprising of standard software under one menu could not be regarded as a Management Information *System*. Not even in the computer wonderland US an information based government is in the offing.

4. ANOTHER APPROACH: CULI

At present a more systematic, user–oriented and well evaluated approach is pursued in the Federal Republic of Germany. In the FRG the use of modern information and communication technologies at governmental level is less spread than in the US. In some ministries first experiments with office automation or word processing are currently under way. A terminal on the desk of a manager is however still a great exception.

Against this background, the attempt to introduce a MSS into the Federal Ministry of Posts and Telecommunications is to be regarded almost as futuristic. The pioneering function of this ministry can be explained by the fact that it also manages all PTT services in the FRG. The communication with 26 mid–level agencies and the control of 451 post and telecommunications offices with about 500,000 employees require the use of modern information technologies [24].

The MSS is called CULI which stands for Computer Supported Management Information System. It is based on the public interactive videotex system (in German: Bildschirmtext, Btx) of the German PTT. The system with now about 70,000 primarily professional users has not been as successful as expected, especially if it is compared with the French system – Teletel – with more than 2,000,000 users. The success of the French system is however based on a fundamentally different strategy of introduction. Important services of the public Btx system are:

- electronic mailbox

- news services

- travel information

- home shopping

- home banking.

Each manager will be provided with a multifunctional telephone – MultiTel. This is a newly developed terminal which is currently marketed for professional Btx–users. It consists of a colour monitor and a small alphanumeric keyboard with additional function keys. MultiTel provides high telephone comfort: With replaced receiver, it allows open listening and loud speaking. 300 telephone numbers can be stored in a telephone register and called by abbreviated dialing; automatic redialing is provided. The MultiTel can also be used for calendaring and for storing notes and Btx pages. The user can program specific access procedure

macros to be triggered via function keys.

These facilities are described in such detail since quite a considerable part of the acceptance of CULI will depend on the MultiTel. Executives of the German PTT telephone rather frequently since this service is, so to speak, free of charge for them. With the attraction of the telephone comfort, it should be easy to make them use the public Btx–system and the electronic news services, in which the executives are particularly interested. So the managers will be stepwise trained to use the actual CULI–system.

The specific CULI–system comprises different components [1]:

- an electronic mail system for communication with other executives (individuals and groups),

- a retrieval system for information such as organization charts, schedules of responsibilities and internal telephone directories,

- a data manipulation system, which allows some calculating and graphic representation of inhouse statistics of the PTT.

The electronic mail system can also be used for simultaneous mailing of identical messages to different users. On request one can get get an acknowledgement upon message receipt. It is hoped that a part of the telephone communication will be shifted to this medium since usually every third call of an executive does not reach the requested person.

The information retrieval system currently provides organizational knowledge like organization charts and internal telephone directories. In future, it is planned to provide internal regulations, press releases of the ministry and a news review concerning the PTT. Furthermore, on request of the executives, the system shall allow inquiries about terminological regulations of the organization and the state of internal projects.

The so-called STATIS–system displays important statistical time series of the German PTT – e.g. number of received letters or number of telephone subscribers. Furthermore, simple mathematical operations can be performed on the time series, e.g. calculating the growth in terms of percentage, and the time series can be represented as bar charts. Thus, the executives obtain for the first time statistical information in condensed form, which is relevant for the controlling of the service corporation.

The system described above is tested in a pilot project with 300 (top) managers in the ministry, the mid-level agencies and the post and telecommunication offices. The project is evaluated by a team of the GMD, which understands itself as an advocate of the users. Several surveys investigated into the information needs and communication habits of the managers. Some results of these surveys have already been regarded in the design of the basic system [1]. Central aim of the evaluation is the adaption of the system to user requirements. By working with a simple basic system with an easy-to-handle interface, the executives shall learn to specify more precise requirements for a true MSS. During the course of the project, user criticism will be surveyed by questionnaires, personal interviews and group discussions for the redesign and further development of the basic system. The pilot-project thus tries to satisfy Lucas' demand "Let the user be the be the be the source of systems wherever possible" ([9], p 111).

Special emphasis is placed on training and guidance. Training is done in several phases, partly in one-to-one sessions or in small groups; special manuals have been produced for the training. The trainers will be the primary contact persons for the users during the whole project. In many organizational units, one trainer is responsible for only five users.

The organizational implementation of CULI met with some difficulties. One problem was the inclusion of the staff within the project. If the chiefs use CULI intensively, the cooperation between staffs – without a MultiTel – and chiefs will be disturbed. Furthermore, it was neglected to secure a high MultiTel density in order to stimulate an intensive use of the electronic mail system. Therefore, in a mid-level agency all executives and some support staffs will be provided with a MultiTel in a next step of the project.

Another problem is the fact that the requirements of differently interested and qualified users – soft and power users [16] – have to be met with a single system. A quite considerable minority of our pilot group preferred a powerful workstation while the majority was rather interested in an easy-to-handle information system. This target conflict will probably run through the whole project.

5. SOME LESSONS TO BE LEARNED

In spite of the fact that the above examples of implementing MSS in federal governments can hardly be compared, we will try to draw some conclusions from them.

- Managers in federal governments are less concerned with hard data. They primarily communicate soft data with their colleagues. Therefore a MSS should incorporate an electronic mail system for internal communication.

- The MSS should also function as an "interface" to the public. Therefore it should display the press releases of the ministry and allow to monitor the relevant news via electronic news services.

- Furthermore the MSS should display informations about the actual state of the organization (e.g. organizational charts, terminological regulations and internal projects.).

- Qualitative training and continuous assistance are essential to the success of MSS. User criticism should be surveyed for the redesign of the system. Participative system development and – probably – rapid prototyping is therefore indispensable.

- To guarantee the acceptance of MSS the manager's secretary and staff should be included in the system design and implementation process.   The MSS should be integrated into the general office automation.

- The Design of MSS should focus on the the soft user and offer him/her a transparent system with an easy–to–handle interface.

Organizational action – especially executive action – is done by verbal means and lengthy conversations. By designing MSS which can support these conversations one should consider user– oriented implementation strategies and – perhaps – the "new" design principles of Winograd and Flores [23].

FOOTNOTE

The informations in this and the following subsections, which are going beyond those in the references, have been collected during an informative trip of the author to Washington D.C. in December 1986. On this very point, I would like to express my thanks to my friendly interlocutors of the White House Executive Office, the General Services Administration and the Department of Agriculture.

REFERENCES

[1] Bornstaedt, F.v., CULI informiert Führungskräfte, net 40 (1986), pp 466 – 470.

[2] Delong, D.W. and Rockart, J.F., A Survey of Current Trends in the Use of Executive Support Systems, in [13], pp 190 – 205.

[3] Ditlea, St., Automation in the White House, Datamation, 15.8. 1986, pp 77 – 80.

[4] El Sawy, O.A., Personal Information Systems for Strategic Scanning in Turbulent Environments: Can The Ceo Go On– line?, MIS Quarterly 9 (1985), pp 53 – 60.

[5] Feldmann, M.S. and March, J.G., Information in Organization as Signal and Symbol, Administrative Science Quarterly 26 (1981), pp 171 – 186.

[6] Fersko–Weiss, H., Personal Computing at the Top, Personal Computing, March 1985, pp 68 – 73.

[7] King, W.R., Editor's Comment: CEOs and Their PCs, MIS Quarterly 9 (1985), pp xi – xii.

[8] Kirchner, J., Federal Computing: The Good and the Bad, Datamation, 15.8.86, pp 62 – 72.

[9] Lucas, H.C.jr, Why Information Systems Fail (Columbia University Press, New York and London, 1975).

[10] Mintzberg, H., The Manager's Job: Folklore and fact, Harvard Business Review, July–August 1975, pp 49 - 61.

[11] Rockart, J.F., Chief Executives Define Their Own Data Needs, in [13], pp 209 – 234.

[12] Rockart, J.F and Bullen, Ch.V., Introduction, in [13), pp vii – xxi.

[13] Rockart, J.F. and Bullen, Ch.V. (eds.), The Rise of Managerial Computing (Dow Jones–Irwin, Homewood (Ill.) 1986).

[14] Rockart, J.F. and Tracy, M.E., The CEO Goes On– line, in: [13], pp 135 – 147.

[15] Scott Morton, M.S., The State of the Art of Research in Management Support Systems, in [13], pp 325 – 253.

[16] Simon, H.A., Administrative Behaviour (Free Press, New York / London, 1976 3rd ed.).

[17] Stang, D.J., Supporting Micro Users Is a Many– Splendored Thing, in: Government Computer News, 29.8.1986, p 76.

[18] Stang, D.J., Govt. User Survey Reveals Many Micros Unused, Government Computer News, 24.10.1986, p 30.

[19] Sullivan, J.A., Top Officials Use PCs in Fed Offices, Government Computer News, 16.1.1986, pp 31 – 32.

[20] U.S.Congress, Office of Technology Assessment, Automation of America's Offices 1985–2000 (U.S. Government Printing Office, Washington, December 1985, Ota–Cit-287).

[21] U.S.Congress, Office of Technology Assessment, Federal Government Information Technology: Management, Security and Congressional Oversight (U.S. Government Printing Office, Washington, February 1986, Ota–Cit-297).

[22] U.S.General Services Administration, Information Resources Management Service, End User Microcomputing – A Federal Survey Report and Resources Guide [Washington, May 1986).

[23] Winograd, T. And Flores, F., Understanding Computers and Cognition: A new foundation for design (Ablex Publ. Corp., Norwood (N.J.) 1986).

[24] Zacher, F. and Dibbern, K., Bildschirmtext und die innerbetrieblichen Anwendungen der Deutschen Bundespost, in: Jahrbuch der Deutschen Bundespost 1986 (Verlag für Wissenschaft und Leben, Bad Windsheim 1986) pp 281 – 317.

[25] Zmud, R.W., Supporting Senior Executives Through Decision Support Technologies: A Review and Directions for Future Research, in: Mclean, E.R. and Sol, H.G. (eds.), Decision Support Systems: A Decade in Perspective (North–Holland, Amsterdam 1986) pp 87 – 101.

Governmental and Municipal Information Systems
P. Kovács and E. Straub (Editors)
Elsevier Science Publishers B.V. (North-Holland)
© IFIP, 1988

A GOVERNMENTAL INFORMATION PROJECT ALONG THE ADMINISTRATIVE REFORM
IN JAPAN

Tomohiro OHASHI

Administrative Management Bureau, Management and Coordination Agency
Prime Minister's Office, 4-33-11, Kasumigaseki, Chiyoda-ku
Tokyo, Japan

Since computer utilization in the government started in 1950s, it
has expanded its application area to various kinds of governmental
activities. At the moment, computer facilities installed in almost
all the ministries are playing quite important roles to improve and
upgrade public services as well as public administration.
In these years, as the financial situation is becoming severe, we
are forced to reduce governmental expenditures and the number of
public servants. From this point of view, computerization aiming at
improving efficiency of governmental activities is crucial for every
ministry, and the Management and Coordination Agency; MCA, is
carrying out some policies and activities to encourage each ministry
to promote its computerization.
Recently main concern of each ministry is to establish information
systems or data bases. A large amount of various kinds of data is
available in machine readable format through the computerization of
statistical and substantive applications. These data is stored in
data bases which provide government staff especially policy planners
or decision makers with adequate and timely information.
Nevertheless it takes much money and effort to establish information
systems or data bases. In addition various kinds of data which is
not necessarily available within each ministry, is required by
planners and decision makers.
It, therefore, would be a next important project to promote
information sharing among the ministries. There would be many
approaches for the project. Some measures already taken and future
approaches are described in this paper.

1. Introduction

When the utilization of computers began in the public sector, its main
purpose was simple technical calculation and statistical data processing.
Since then, the purposes of computer utilization have been upgraded and
diversified as can be seen in the fact that applications such as information
retrieval, and information analysis for forecasting have become common.
The computers used in the government sector are becoming indispensable
instruments for more efficient and effective public services. However, in
response to successive financial deficits in recent years, it has become
critically important to assure the efficient use of Government Information
Systems (GIS) resources such as hardware, software, computer readable data
and manpower.
Overview of the computerization in the government is as follows:

1.1. General Trends of Computer Utilization

Figure 1 shows the number of computers being used in the government from 1968
to 1986 by scale, and also indicates the computers set in on-line systems.
The recent increase ratio of the computers is rather low, because most of
major area has already been computerized. The ratio of large scale computers
is high in the national government compared with that in whole industries of
which large scale ratio is less than 10% as of 1985.
The number of computers used for on-line systems has been increasing as large
national-wide information systems have been built to connect regional or
district offices with central ones in Tokyo.

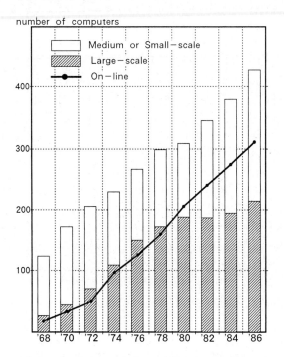

Figure 1. Trends of Computers Installed in the National Government

Large—scale Computer   : The price more than ¥250 million
Medium or Small—scale : The price more than ¥10 million
                          and less than ¥250 million
On—line   : The number of computers set in on—line
                          systems

Figure 2 shows the computer operating cost in all the ministries. The increase ratio is higher than that of the number of computers, and operating cost per computer unit is also increasing because the scale of computers is becoming larger, and the number of on-line terminals is increasing as the system are becoming nationwide. On the contrary, ratio of hardware cost to the total has rather been decreasing recently.

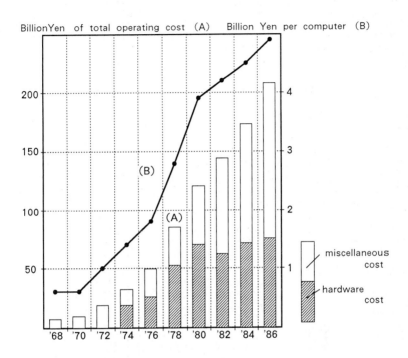

Figure 2. Trends of Computer Operating Cost

Operating Cost : includes experditures of hardware, software, telecommunicasion, and excluds cost of manpower, computer terminals.

Hardware Cost : includes rental fee and purchase cost payed in each year.

(Miscellaneous Cost) = (Total operating cost) − (Hardware cost)

Figure 3 and 4 shows the number of personnel engaged in computer divisions of all the ministries. The annual rate of computer staff increase is not high, because the number of key-punchers, in particular, has been declining recently due to introduction of input equipments such as OCR and OMR, and allocation of data preparation to private firms. In addition the number of system engineers and programmers temporarily hired from private firms are also increasing.

The number of computer staff in the national government (A)
The number of computer staff hired from outside (B)

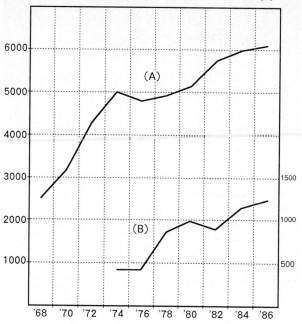

Figure 3. Trends of Computer Staff

Computer Staff : includes system analyst, system engineer,
computer programmer, operator, key puncher, and
general staff in computer section

The number of computer staff per computer section

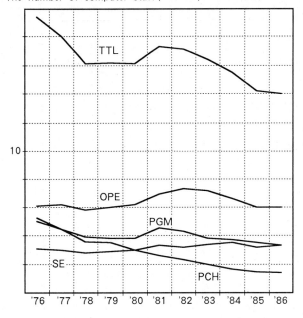

Figure 4. Trends of the Number of Computer Staff of Government per Computer Section

OPE : Operator
PGM : Computer Programmer
PCH : Key Puncher
S E : System Engineer
TTL : Total of above

1.2. Stages of Computerization in the Government

The computerization in the government has been progressed in accordance with development of computer technology, both hardware and software, and following four stages of the computerization could be identified:

i) 1st Stage (1950s);
In the first stage, major computerized applications were scientific and technological area, statistical activities and administrative work such as accounting and personnel management. For example the first computer in the government was installed in the Meteorological Agency for analysis of data and forecasting of weather; and the second one was installed in the National Statistical Bureau for compiling of the population census.
In this stage capability and capacity of hardware and technology of software were limited, and only specific staff made effort to promote the computerization under these restrictions. Although they covered limited area, the computerized applications in this stage have contributed to manpower saving and rapid data processing as well.

ii) 2nd Stage (1960s);
Thanks to development of technology and previous experience in the first stage, computerized area expanded to various kinds of major governmental activities such as drivers' licence control, migration records management, passport control, taxation, social insurance, motor vehicle registration, management of government-operated savings, job placement information service.
In these applications a great amount data was stored and was easily updated, retrieved and edited. As these substantive applications have close relation with the citizens, they have made remarkable contribution to not only effective and efficient public administration but also public services.
Especially in the latter half of 1960s, as most of them have been advanced to nationwide on-line systems, they have brought the people much benefit enjoying quick and high quality public services all through the country.

iii) 3rd Stage (1980s);
Through the computerization of statistical and substantive activities, a large amount of many kinds of data has been available in machine readable format, and planners or decision makers in the government have come to require data or information more and more. Therefore, main concern of computer divisions in the ministries is to establish information systems or data bases.
In this stage data or information has become to be managed as an important and valuable resource. It, however, is still very difficult for information systems to provide government staff with adequate and timely information, because most users of information systems are none-experts in terms of computer technology, and their requirement for information are vastly diversified.

iv) 4th Stage (1980s).
In parallel with mainframe computers, utilization of office automation (OA) equipments such as micro-computers, word processors and facsimiles has rapidly expanded in the offices of the government. Figure 5 shows the number of OA equipments being used in the upper level offices than provincial ones.
As indicated in the figures, increase ratio of the number of micro-computers, and Japanese word processors are quite high. It is more than 50% every year.
Reasons why these OA equipments have come to wide use in a few years are as follows:
a) The capability is high on the contrary prices are getting cheaper;
b) They have become so easier to use that general staff or none-experts can manage to use by themselves; and

c) They provide capability and functions in the field of document processing or paperwork which occupy most part of office work and were left behind the computerization by mainframe computers.

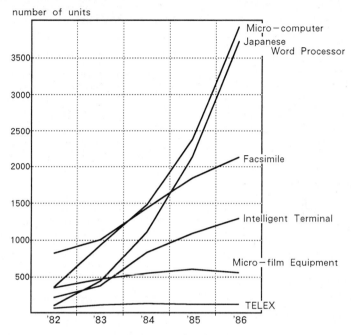

Figure 5. Trends of Office Automation Devices Installed in the National Government

Major computerized applications and information systems by ministry are listed in Appendix 1 and 2.

2. Major Policies and Activities for Coordination of the Computerization

The computerization in the government has fundamentally been promoted on a decentralized basis. It means that each ministry has responsibility on implementation, operation and maintenance of its system including hardware, software, data, manpower, and so forth. Major roles of the MCA, therefore, are to establish policies and to carry out activities common to all the ministries with respect to computerization.

As the computerized application area has expanded and the administrative reform has become important under the severe financial situation and social changes, issues to be resolved in consistent and uniformed way from a managerial and coordinative point of view are now increasing. Under this circumstance the MCA has been playing important roles identifying major issues through basic surveys on current status of computer utilization, data bases and OA; and discussing them in councils or working groups which consist of representatives or computer experts of all the ministries.

2.1. The Recent Administrative Reform

In 1980 the Provisional Commission for Administrative Reform was established. The Commission was composed of nine members who were executives of private firms and mass media, a professor, and representatives of labor unions. There were sub-committees and working groups to discuss specific area. Backgrounds that made the administrative reform crucial were as follows:

   i) There has been a slowdown of economic growth and an accumulation of budget deficits;
  ii) The nation's population structure has commenced a rapid aging process;
 iii) The interest, activities and life-styles of citizens have become diverse and multi-faceted; and
  iv) Japan's relations with the outside world have become more complex and multi-faceted.

In the final report of the commissions issued in 1983, following matters were recommended to promote with respect to computerization in the public sector:

   i) Enhancement of planning and coordinating function of computerization in the public sector;
      For this purpose the report proposed to establish a committee consists of representatives of ministries, and to establish master plan or basic policies regarding following matters through review of existing systems:
      a) Establishment of basic plans on data base systems and communication network;
      b) Training and recruitment of computer staff; and
      c) Measures for data privacy protection and freedom of information.

  ii) Strengthening of management of information as a resource;
      Stress should be put on management of information to promote effective and efficient utilization of information, privacy protection, and freedom of information.

 iii) Promotion of OA.
      It was recommendable to take following measures to promote OA in the government:
      a) To establish a meeting to discuss problems against promotion of OA;
      b) to build a specific section in each ministry, which be responsible for promotion of OA; and
      c) To promote training for enhancement of familiarization and basic understanding of top management and morale of general staff for OA.

2.2. Organizational Structure for Coordination of the Computerization

Several ministries have responsibilities on planning and coordinating computerization in various area including the private sector. Figure 6 shows the organizational structure for coordination by ministry.

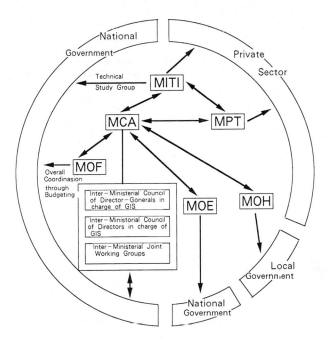

Figure 6. Organizational Structure for Coordination of Computerization

MOF : Ministry of Finance
MCA : Management and Coordination Agency
MITI : Ministry of International Trade and Industry
MPT : Ministry of Posts and Telecommunication
MOE : Ministry of Education
MOH : Ministry of Home Affairs
GIS : Governmental Information Systems

In this paper coordination functions of the MCA are mainly described herein-after.
In accordance with the recommendation of the Provisional Commission for Administrative Reform saying that a planning and coordination function of the computerization be strengthened, the Inter-Ministerial Council of director-generals in charge of governmental information systems of ministries was established in 1983 based on decision of the administrative vice-ministers meeting.
In the first meeting of this Council, following objectives were decided:
  i) To promote the efficient use of computers;
 ii) To promote the multi-purpose use of government data;
iii) To promote the effective use of government telecommunication networks;
 iv) To promote the mechanization of administrative work;
  v) To ensure data security and the protection of privacy; and
 vi) To ensure the safety of systems, establishment of computer staff policy, and others related to government information systems.

The Inter-Ministerial Council of Directors and six working groups were set up under the Council of Director-Generals to discuss and establish policies or measures for issues described above. In the organizational structure, each issue is discussed in each working group and report, guideline or recommendation compiled there, are to be approved in the Council of Directors or that of Director-Generals. A guideline for information sharing and a guideline for promotion of OA were approved and already issued, and basic approach to privacy protection was reported in the Council of Directors, so far.

2.3. Coordination of Budget, Organization and Staff needed for Computerization

In 1973 the MCA began to scrutinize and review budget requests submitted by ministries for computer installation and/or renewal, and major information systems development due to increase of the expenditure, relationship or interface among systems in the ministries, and necessity of technical and coordinative review. In this review, the proposals are examined with regard to justification, necessity, rationalization, feasibility, cost/benefit, and so forth. Results of the review are compiled as the opinion report which is submitted to the Budget Bureau of Ministry of Finance, and is referred to in giving final approvals. This review has been very effective to avoid redundant investments and to develop, in a well-coordinated fashion, information systems common or related to several ministries.
Since F.Y. 1970, "Budget for R & D on Administrative Information Systems" has been appropriated in block as a part of the budget of the MCA. This fund is to be used for R & D on information systems common or related to ministries, and also for basic R & D to improve information systems by transferring technologies researched or developed to other ministries concerned.
The MCA examines requests for the fund from ministries, and allocates it in view of necessity, importance, applicability, feasibility, and so on.
Regarding organization and personnel, it is the responsibility of the MCA to assess requests of ministries and agencies, to create or abolish organizations, and to increase or decrease the number of personnel. With a similar goal of budgetary review, the MCA judges those requests for organization and personnel related to computer utilization and information systems before a formal assessment is undertaken. The results of preliminary review based upon its expertise are then forwarded to the assessment division of the MCA in charge of the management of organizations and the number of personnel where a final assessment is conducted.

2.4. Promotion of Efficient Utilization of Computer Systems

As computer utilization within the government has expanded, the promotion of the efficient use of computers has become an important task with a view to curtail administrative cost as well as the expansion of administrative functions. For this reason, the MCA has been presiding over inter-ministerial joint study groups for the efficient use of computers since 1975 and based on the results of the study groups, the following guidelines have been published:
  i) Method of Cost/Benefit Evaluation for Computer Use (in F.Y. 1979);
 ii) Method of Measurement and Analysis for Computer Operations (in F.Y. 1979);
iii) Standard Documents for Development and Maintenance of Software (in F.Y. 1979);
 iv) Method of Computer System Selection (in F.Y. 1980);
  v) Method of Utilization of Software Development Technique (in F.Y. 1981);

   vi) Methods of Development and Management of Database (Method of Designing Database) (in F.Y. 1982);

  vii) Methods of Development and Management of Database (Method of Management of Database) (in F.Y. 1982);

 viii) Method of Implementation of Systems Control (in F.Y. 1982);

   ix) Method of Project Management for Software Development (in F.Y. 1983);

    x) Method of Quality Control of Software (in F.Y. 1984);

   xi) Method of Efficient Maintenance of Software (in F.Y. 1985); and

  xii) Method of Effective Application of System Development Technique (in F.Y. 1986).

In addition to the guidelines for efficient utilization of computer systems, the MCA is carrying out actual activities as follows to promote efficiency:

   i) Mutual use of application programmes which are developed in ministries and applicable or transferable to other ministries;
For the purpose, an inventory of application programmes was compiled and delivered to all the computer divisions of the ministries.

  ii) Mutual use of data/information;
This topic is to be described in detail in next section.

 iii) Administrative Telephone Network;
This Network was initially created in 1979 linking Tokyo to Osaka. Since then, the network service area has expanded to other major cities, 26 cities as of 1987. The Network works with a mechanism which enable to make calls directly from one extension to another between ministries, and has been contributing to efficient use of telephone line and cutdown on costs. Besides this Network is expected to expand OA systems such as facsimiles, on-line system using micro-computers as intelligent-terminals.

  iv) Data Communication Network.
Recently, various nationwide on-line networks for computer systems connecting different offices have been introduced, in accordance with the advancement of computer utilization. Therefore, since F.Y. 1981 the MCA has been conducting research on an exclusive Government network (Data telecommunication network) for data communications to facilitate data communications and cut down communication costs by sharing major dedicated data communication line between major cities, for example Tokyo and Osaka.

2.5. Operation of the Inter-Ministerial Computer Center

Joint utilization of computers and information systems is a subject frequently referred to in cabinet decisions, and in 1978, the Inter-Ministerial Computer Center was built in the MCA.

The Japanese Government did not adopt the system of centralized use of computers, and most ministries and agencies have their own computer facilities. However, it is not economical for a small agency to have its own computer facility. In addition, some information systems are common to most ministries and agencies. It is, thus, not economical to develop and manage such information systems in each ministry or agency. Therefore, the Inter-Ministerial Computer Center was built to serve small agencies with no computer facilities and to house information systems common to all the ministries. The Legal Text Retrieval System, Parliamentary Proceedings Retrieval System and Cabinet Decisions Information System are examples of systems now in operation.

In organizations like the Japanese government where lifetime employment is an established system, training is more important, because existing personnel cannot be easily replaced with persons external to the system who have sufficient expertise or techniques.

Thus, the training of computer personnel designed to enable them to acquire

computer literacy and sufficient technique, is considered to be very important by the government.
There are two types of training programs; government-wide training and training for personnel of each ministry or agency.
The Inter-Ministerial Computer Center has centralized training facility, where government staff from all the ministries, including director class participated to twelve training courses in 1986. Total number of graduates so far amounts more than four thousand five hundred.

3. A Governmental Information Project

Through the computerization of statistical and substantive applications, large volume of various kinds of data has been stored in each ministry, and the MCA has been trying to promote effective and efficient utilization of the data among the ministries as well as in each ministry. A project for it just started.

3.1. Data Stored in the Ministries

According to the MCA's survey on data file in machine readable format, total number of the files amounted to more than one thousand seven hundred, in all the ministries as of 1984, and most of them were produced and used for substantive and statistical activities (See Figure 7). It means that most of the activities which deal with large quantity of data have already been computerized. A quarter of data files are stored in data bases.

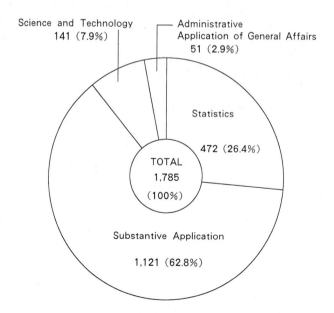

Figure 7. Number of Data File for Mutual Use among Ministries as of 1985

As for data bases, Figure 8 shows trend of the number. The increase ratio is high and in a few years more than three hundred data bases will be in operation.

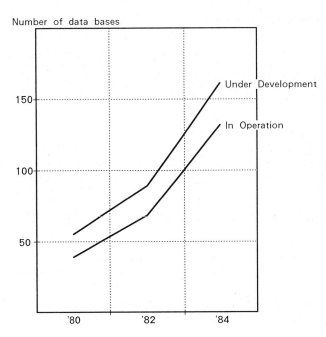

Figure 8. Trends of Data Bases in the Natinal Government

The number of data bases by area is shown in Figure 9.

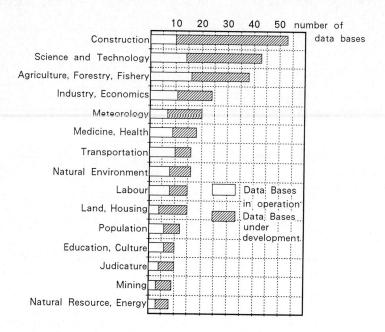

Figure 9. Number of Data Bases by Majour
15 Application Area

The number of data bases by main purpose is shown in Figure 10. Data bases of group I, II, III were established closely related to operational or substantive applications and most of data bases in operation belong to this category so far. However, the ratio of data of which main purpose is to provide planners or decision makers with information is increasing (Category II in Figure 10).

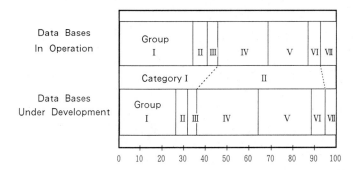

Figure 10. Data Bases by their Main Purposes of Establishment

Group I : Efficiency of governmental activities and public services ⎫
    II : Efficiency of programme maintenance and computer performance ⎬ Category I
   III : Efficiency of system development ⎭
   IV : Effective use of information
   V : Adequate management of information ⎫ Category II
   VI : Information Supply to other organization ⎭
   VII : Miscellaneous

Major data bases in each ministry are listed in Appendix 3.

3.2. Fundamental Approach for Information Policy

In Japan, there is an old proverb, saying 'He who knows ability of the opponent as well as himself would always win the game.', and today, it could be modified as follows; 'He who has enough information on the opponent as well as himself would always win the game.'
Needless to say, information is quite important and indispensable for government staff to carry out their activities or to make policies. There could be many cases that policies may fail due to lack of information or its inaccuracy. Under the situation that social and economic circumstances for policy makers are changing so rapidly, governmental activities and policies are becoming diversified and complicated, and decisions or policies of government have great influence on national economy or on life of the people, importance of adequate and timely policies based on adequate and timely information cannot be overemphasized.
However, gathering of information needs much effort and money. For example, direct expenditure per person of the population census in Japan is more than one US dollar, and it amounts three hundred million US dollars in total. If data or information is to be processed using computer facility, the data preparation costs very much additionally. Therefore, information which needs so much effort and money should be shared among ministries and agencies from effective and efficient point of view.
Information has unique characteristics, quite different from other resources, that is, once it is produced, it can be used many times without reducing its quantity, and even without additional cost. It means that the more it is used, the more the cost per information is reduced.
Another characteristic of information is that one information is more valuable or useful when other information are combines. It means one plus one could be more than two. That is one of the reasons that integrated information systems using data base technology are now being established to make full use of information available already.
Under these backgrounds, importance, cost and characteristics of information, various activities are being carried out and policies have been established in the Government of Japan, to promote efficient and effective utilization of information.
Information used for administrative and substantive activities, or for decision making in the government should be accurate, adequate, reliable, easy to use, timely, consistent, non-duplicated and transferable. Especially, the last three characteristics are crucial for information sharing among ministries and agencies. Ideally, some centralized body should carry out coordination and management functions to assure these characteristics of information. Relationship between characteristics required and activities to be done by the focal point is shown in Figure 11.

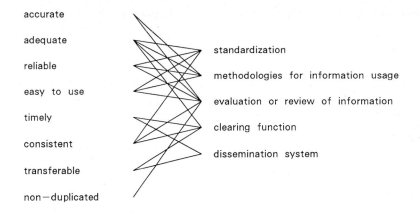

accurate

adequate

reliable

easy to use

timely

consistent

transferable

non–duplicated

standardization

methodologies for information usage

evaluation or review of information

clearing function

dissemination system

Figure 11. Characteristics of Information and
Managerial Activities for it

Major activities and policies which should be carried out are as follows:
   i) Standardization;
      Even after information needed for users are identified and are
      available, they are difficult or almost impossible to be shared or
      integrated together with other information, unless they are standardized
      in concepts, classifications, codes and so on.
      It certainly needs much effort to establish and maintain standards of
      information, and it would be impossible to establish standards of all
      the data and information in the government. Important and fundamental
      information to be shared, therefore, should be standardized. In Japan,
      standardization of data items of major statistics have been established
      and are being maintained by the Statistical Bureau of MCA.

  ii) Methodologies for information usage;
      Generally, decision makers or planners are not used to deal with data or
      information stored in computers, though computerized data or information
      has great potential capability to be put together, analyzed and provide
      various types of output. Recent data base systems provide these
      methodologies or technique how to extract, use, analyze data or informa-
      tion, and how to produce reports, using simple command or languages
      which are friendly for non-programmer users, planners or decision
      makers.
      It would be an important role for the focal point to provide information
      users with methodologies or techniques for information usage using
      computer facility. In addition, users' information requirements are
      not necessarily clear or concrete. Sometimes, the more, the better, and
      sometimes, on the contrary, too much information would confuse users.
      If an information system fails to meet users' requirements several
      times, users would lose interest or concern with the system. Thus, it
      is also an important function for the coordination body to identify
      users' requirement of information and to survey availability of
      information.

iii) Evaluation and review;
Information which is to be collected should be evaluated beforehand so that quality and consistency may be retained and so that duplication may be avoided.
In Japan, proposals of major statistics are issued to the MCA every time, and they are checked whether there is problem in quality, and are coordinated to retain consistency with other statistics concerned and to avoid duplication. Recently, privacy protection is becoming an important matter, and in this evaluation, those items that are sensitive in the light of privacy protection could be eliminated.

iv) Clearing function;
All the important information which could be used in other divisions or ministries, should be registered in the focal point so that every government staff can know where information exists, what kinds of items are available, and how they can be obtained.
Information registered in the focal point be compiled as an inventory of information and this inventory should be maintained periodically and be disseminated to every computer section and information users.

v) Dissemination system
Some dissemination system as well as clearing function is necessary in order to make information flow smooth and to promote sharing of information among ministries and agencies. In Japan, we have established the procedure for mutual utilization of information in the Government. It is described in detail in the next section.

3.3. Measures Taken for Information Sharing among Ministries

The MCA started a project which aimed to promote reciprocal use of information on magnetic media or data bases. Justifications of this project are as follows:
  i) In accordance with the social and economic changes, governmental activities and policies are becoming diversified and complicated in Japan recently. Therefore, timely and adequate information are required by planners or decision makers more and more;
 ii) It requires much effort and money to collect data and to establish data base systems, and it is recognized that a large amount of various kinds of data/information stored in each ministry in machine readable format should be made full use of; and
iii) Technological developments of computer hardware and data base systems have been enabling users to access data/information more easily, and each ministry is keen to establish data base system for effective and efficient utilization of data/information.
Term of "reciprocal use of data/information" hereinafter means restricted mutual use of data/information which is summarized so that each data cannot be identified in personal level considering privacy of individual data should be protected.

To promote mutual use of data/information among ministries, a guideline for mutual use of data on magnetic media among ministries have been established and issued to the ministries.

In completing the guideline, following approaches were taken:
  i) Making a cabinet decision beforehand on basic stance toward mutual use of data among ministries;
 ii) Conducting a survey on availability of data on magnetic media;
iii) Discussion on promotion of mutual use in the Working Group on Multi-Purpose Use of Government Data; and

iv) Compiling a draft report on mutual use of data among ministries.

The draft report was approved in the Council of Directors mentioned in 2.2. of this paper, and it was issued as a guideline to the Minister's Secretariat of each ministry by the name of Director-General of Administrative Management Bureau, the MCA in December 1985 (See Appendix 4).

In accordance with the Guideline following measures were taken:
  i) Compiling an Inventory;
     The MCA compiled the inventory of information on magnetic media which could be shared among ministries getting cataloging data from each ministry, and delivered it to all the divisions concerned. This inventory will be updated annually with cooperation of the ministries.
 ii) Identifying of Clearing Section.
     A clearing section which may be responsible for reference service and management of information within each ministry has been set up so that any government staff could easily reach the information available in other ministry. The list of these clearing sections of each ministry was compiled and delivered to all the divisions concerned.

Through these measures mention above, following effects could be expected:
  i) Strengthening management and coordination function of data/information in each ministry for effective and efficient use; and
 ii) Increase of reciprocal use of data/information among ministries from limited exchange on a give-and-take basis to one way or multi-lateral exchanges.

3.4. Future Approach of the Information Project

Although data/information in the government should fundamentally be collected, stored or built into data bases, maintained and utilized by each division in the ministries, and mutual use of data/information is still limited most of which is on magnetic media basis so far, it is sure that requirement of government staff for data/information in other ministries would increase more and more in easier way.
Therefore the governmental information project should be expanded, and major future approach would be as follows:

  i) Establishment of Basic Plan for Data Bases Development;
     A data base system is very helpful in terms of effective and efficient utilization of information. It enables non-programmers or information users such as planners and decision makers to access, analyze and produce reports.
     Under these circumstances, we are now establishing a systematic development plan for data base systems as a whole in the Government. The major contents would be as follows:
     a) Encouraging each ministry to establish an integrated data base or data bases for decision making;
        Major operational or substantive application data bases have already been built in each ministry. Therefore, much effort should be concentrated on establishing integrated data bases to provide planners or decision makers with adequate and timely data/ information. As this type of data base is built in each ministry, mutual use of data/information in data base could be expanded.
     b) Development of data bases common to ministries;
        At the moment several data bases common to ministries have been established in the Inter-Ministerial Computer Center of MCA, and they are provided to all the ministries through on-line terminals and butch mode as well. The number of this kind of data bases should be

increased from now on.
c) Establishing a central clearing function.
A central clearing function of computerized data/information available for government staff; catalogue data of books, papers and
reports issued by each ministries; data bases available in a commercial basis, and so forth should be established. This data would be
built in a clearing data base in the Inter-Ministerial Computer
Center and be available through on-line terminals installed in each
ministry.

ii) Development of an Inter-Ministerial Information Sharing System;
Mutual use of data/information stored in data bases should be expanded
through a computer-to-computer network system. There exists one example
of this system connecting non-compatible computers in the Economic Planning Agency and the Ministry of International Trade and Industry. The
former has a macro economic data base and the latter has a micro one,
and these data bases can be utilized in an integrated way in both
organizations.
This kind of computer network system should be expanded throughout
ministries using central switching function in the Inter-Ministerial
Computer Center. The concept of this system is shown in Figure 12.

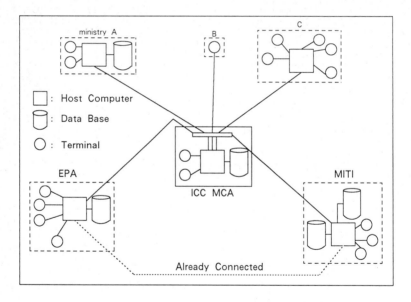

Figure 12. Concept of Information Sharing System

ICCMA : Inter—Ministerial Computer Center of MCA
EPA   : Economic Planning Agency
MITI   : Ministry of International Trade and Industry

iii) Promotion of data supply to the private sector.
As useful and valuable data/information has already been available, and it is almost impossible for private firms to collect the data by themselves, requirement for data/information stored in the ministries in machine readable format is becoming stronger, and each ministry has come to recognize the necessity and be rather willing to provide the private sector with data/information in machine readable format in a more convenient fashion.
The Statistical Council issued a guideline for promotion of computerized data supply to the private sector in May 1987. In this Guideline statistical data opened to the public by the ministries can be provided to data base distributers, which was prohibited before. By this provision it is expected that there would be firms which endeavor to build data bases adding value to data got from the government. From now on we will try to expand this system to governmental data which could be provided to the private sector.

3.5. Concluding Remarks

As described already the governmental information project is very important and crucial for Government of Japan at the moment, and there seems to be many approaches for it. In addition there might be a lot of problems or obstacles to be resolved prior to promotion of this project, such as technical feasibility, cost/benefit justification, getting consensus of the ministries, establishing measure for privacy protection (a privacy protection act is now under preparing), and so forth.
Although it would need much money and effort to promote the governmental information project, It is sure that the project could deserve of it, because data/information is an important and valuable asset for not only the public sector but also the private one and the people.

Appendix 1   Major Areas of Computer Utilization and Information Systems
sets: the number of mainframe computers

Ministry and Agency	Sets	Major Areas
Fair Trade Commission	1	Information Retrieval
Police Agency (National Public Safety Commission)	6	Reference of Identified Criminals, Reference of Motor-vehicles, Management of Motor-vehicle Drivers' Records, Statistics
Management and Coordination Agency	3	Legal Text Retrieval, Parliamentary Proceedings Retrieval, Payroll Management, Statistics
Hokkaido Development Agency	3	Technical Computation, Accounting of Public Works Cost, Payroll Management
Defense Agency	50	Procurement Management, Technical Computation, Meteorological Data Processing
Economic Planning Agency	1	Statistics, Economic Analysis
Science and Technology Agency	14	Technical Computation
Environment Agency	3	Information Retrieval, Technical Computation, Statistics, Payroll Management
Okinawa Development Agency	3	Payroll Management
National Land Agency	2	Payroll Management, Information Retrieval
Ministry of Justice	18	Management of Criminal Records, Management of Migration Records
Ministry of Foreign Affairs	7	Information Retrieval, Management of Passport Issuance, Exchange of Telegram Messages
Ministry of Finance	21	Statistics, Information Retrieval, Budgeting and Accounting, Capital Management, Taxation
Ministry of Education	9	Statistics, Information Retrieval, Analytical Calculation, Technical Computation
Ministry of Health and Welfare	19	Statistics, Information Retrieval, Management of Social Insurance Programs, Management of Pension Programs
Ministry of Agriculture, Forestry and Fishery	22	Statistics, Inventory Management, Technical Computation, Information Retrieval
Ministry of International Trade and Industry	22	Statistics, Analytical Calculation, Information Retrieval, Technical Computation, Patent Management, Management of Export Insurance Program, Management of JIS (Japanese Industrial Standard)
Ministry of Transport	79	Statistics, Analytical Calculation, Information Retrieval, Technical Computation, Motor-vehicle Registration, Meteorological Data Processing, Air Traffic Control, Management of Seamen's Records
Ministry of Posts and Telecommunications	87	Management of Savings, Management of Post Office Insurance Programs, Management of Radio Regulatory Programs
Ministry of Labor	12	Statistics, Management of Employment Insurance Program, Management of Employees' Accident Compensation Insurance Program, Collection of Labor Insurance Premium, Job Placement
Ministry of Construction	20	Statistics, Technical Computation, Accounting of Public Works Cost, Administration of Rivers and Roads, Digital Data on Land, Budgeting and Accounting
Ministry of Home Affairs	1	Statistics

Appendix 2 Examples of Major Information Systems

Police Information Management System (Police Agency): data on driver's license owners, cases of traffic offenses, cases of identified criminals, registered motor-vehicles, etc. are stored.

Migration Record Management System (Ministry of Justice): records of immigrants, immigrants and foreign residents are stored.

Taxpayer Record Management System (National Tax Administration of Finance Ministry): data on taxpayers (individuals and corporations) are stored for taxation.

Social Insurance Management System (Ministry of Health and Welfare): data on recipients of pension and insurance payment and records of applications and payments are stored for processing applications and calculating payment, etc.

Motor-vehicle Registration and Management System (Ministry of Transport): records of registered motor-vehicles and results of periodic inspection of them are stored.

Savings Management System (Ministry of Posts and Telecommunication): data on savings accounts and money orders are stored to provide on-line service at some 20,000 post offices.

Post Office Life Insurance and Annuity Programs Automation System (Ministry of Posts and Telecommunications): data on insurance and annuity policies of individual persons and records of transactions are stored; and on-line service is provided at some 1,100 post offices.

labor Information Management System (Ministry of Labor): data on employers and employees covered by employment insurance program are stored, and information on employment and job applications are also stored to provide job seekers and employers with suitable information.

Legal Text Retrieval System (Management and Coordination Agency): texts of laws and regulations, summaries of judicial precedents or leading cases of the supreme court and high courts are stored in the computer for quick reference.

Parliamentary Proceedings Retrieval System (Management and Coordination Agency): proceedings of parliamentary committee meetings are stored for quick reference by registered key words (subjects and items), names of speakers, data of meetings, etc.

Information Retrieval System of EPA (Economic Planning Agency): various kinds of economic data over a long period of time are stored for various kinds of economic analyses, planning and forecasting.

Land Information System (National Land Agency): digital data in square grids and aerial color photo-maps which show the state of land use are stored to be used for national and regional land use planning.

Appendix 3   Major Data Bases by Ministry

as of 1985

*: DBs under development

Ministry and Agency	The number of DB in operation	Major Areas
Fair Trade Commission	1	Marketing Structure DB, International Contract DB*
Management and Coordination Agency	5	Legal Text DB, Parliament Debate DB, Statistical Time Series DB, Population DB*, Cabinet Decision DB
Defense Agency	33	Logistic Management DB, Personnel Management DB, Meteorological DB, Procurement Management DB*
Economic Planning Agency	2	Macro Economic DB, International Economic DB, Economic Time Series DB*
Science and Technology Agency	2	Science and Technology Information DB*
Environment Agency	6	Public Pollution Information DB
National Land Agency	1	National Land Degital Information DB
Ministry of Justice	4	Foreign Citizen Registration DB, Immigrant Registration DB, Land Registration DB*, Judical Integrated DB*
Ministry of Foreign Affairs	6	Passport Control DB, Survey Report DB, Treaty DB*
Ministry of Finance	4	Trade Information DB, Integrated Taxation DB
Ministry of Education	3	Integrated Educational and Cultural Information DB, Clearing Information DB*
Ministry of Health and Welfare	5	Integrated Social Welfare Information DB, Social Insurance DB*
Ministry of Agriculture, Forestry and Fishery	15	Agricultural and Fishery Statistic DB, Bibliographic Information DB
Ministry of International Trade and Industry	13	Policy Planning Information DB, Research Report Information DB, Patent Information DB, Industrial Statistics DB
Ministry of Transport	9	Motor Vehicle Registration DB, Integrated DB, Marine Information DB, Meteorological Information DB*
Ministry of Posts and Telecommunications	3	Statistics DB, Medical History DB, Governmental Life Insurance Management Information DB*
Ministry of Labor	4	Labor Insurance DB, Employment Information DB, Labor Economic DB*
Ministry of Construction	16	Urban Development Planning DB, Road Management Information DB, Flood Control Information DB, Land Survey Information DB*, Water Quality Control DB*, Natural Disaster Prevention DB*

Appendix 4

12 Dec., 1985

To: Minister's Secretariat

From: Director General
        Administrative Management Bureau
        Management and Coordination Agency
        Prime Minister's Office

Guideline for Inter-ministerial Mutual Use of Information on Magnetic Media

I issue this Guideline approved in the Inter-ministerial Council of Directors in charge of Information Systems.

This guideline prescribes the procedures and documents necessary for promoting mutual use of information among ministries. I expect that you make effort to make this guideline well-known in your ministry and to positively provide other ministry with information on magnetic media along this guideline.

Guideline for Inter-Ministerial Mutual Use of Information on Magnetic Media

1. Purpose of the Guideline

This guideline prescribes fundamental matters necessary for mutual use of information, procedures for compiling an information inventory and identifying clearing function to promote effective and efficient utilization of computerized information.

2. Span of the Guideline

This guideline may be applied in the case of mutual use of computerized information among ministries.

3. Mutual utilization of information on magnetic media

3.1. Providing of information on magnetic media

3.1.1. A ministry which wants to use information on magnetic media stored in other ministry, request the ministry to provide the information.

3.1.2. The ministry which was request to provide information may accept the request form after negotiation was settled and the document (Form 1) must be exchanged.

3.1.3. The description 3.1.2. is applicable in the case of modifying content of the document exchanged.

3.1.4. In the case that information given to other ministry was publicly opened, there should not be any restrain in using the information.

3.1.5. In the case that information provided from other ministry includes items which should not be open to the public, the same procedure with that described in 3.1.2. should be taken after getting approval regarding how to deal with the information.

3.2. In the case that any thing which was not prescribed in the document exchanged took place, the ministry which received the information from other ministry must report to the supplier ministry and make arrangement necessary.
In the case that the ministry which supplied the information found the recipient used it against or beyond the prescription, can claim and request the recipient to make arrangement necessary including to stop the utilization of the information or to make it give back.

3.3. Confidence of information provided

3.3.1. The ministry which was provided with information from other ministry must not give it to other organization which is not referred to in the prescription of the document exchanged.

3.3.2. The ministry which was provided with information must keep confidence of the information provided.

4. Reference Section

4.1. Each ministry must set up or nominate unique reference section which is responsible for information providing. This section may have coordination function regarding information within its own ministry.

4.2. This reference section must compile an inventory of information on magnetic media which could be shared among ministries. Through this inventory the section carries out clearing function in response to queries from other ministries.

4.3. The Management and Coordination Agency, MCA, compiles the list of these reference sections of the ministries, and delivers it to the ministries.

5. Compilation of the Inventory (Form 2)

5.1. The MCA compiles an inventory of information on magnetic media which could be provided to other ministries.

5.2. The MCA delivers the inventory to the ministries.

5.3. The MCA updates the inventory periodically.

5.4. In the case that there happened any change, addition, delection in contents of the inventory or new data file which could be shared be created in each ministry, the ministry must report them to the MCA.

Form 1

Date:

Ministry A (Supplier)
Ministry B (Recipient)

Utilization of Information possessed by Ministry A

Ministry A and B have approved with utilization of information possessed by Ministry A under the conditions as follows:

  i) Names and contents of information _____

  ii) Measure to provide the information _____

 iii) Purpose of utilization of the information _____

  iv) Names of section(s) expected to use the information _____

   v) Measure of utilization of the information _____

  vi) Duration of the utilization _____

 vii) Management of the information

    a) Ministry B must not utilize the information provided by Ministry A beyond prescription above, nor give the information to other organization.

    b) Ministry B must deliverately keep the information and take actions necessary for confidence of the information.

viii) Miscellaneous _____

Form 2

Format of the Inventory

Name of file
Name of survey or resource of data
Classification of file
Name of reference section and TEL
Name of section which compiled data
Outline of content of data
Classification of field of data
Condition and procedure for data providing
Name of published report concerned Date of the latest issue Cycle of issue

Specification of record
  name of code
 	
  number of tracks of
  magnetic tape
 	
  density of magnetic
  tape data format
 	
  data format
 	
  label

Page number where detailed data items are described

Governmental and Municipal Information Systems
P. Kovács and E. Straub (Editors)
Elsevier Science Publishers B.V. (North-Holland)
© IFIP, 1988

COMPUTERIZATION OF WORK RELATED TO POLITICAL FUNDS

Masao Hanada

Secretary, Fukuoka Prefecture Election Administration Committee
4-19-10 Joseigaoka, Munakata City, Fukuoka Prefecture, JAPAN

1. THE BASIC CONCEPT OF THE POLITICAL FUND CONTROL LAW

The functions performed by political parties and political organizations under
the system of parliamentary democracy is extremely important. In order for a
parliamentary democracy to develop in a healthy fashion, political activities
of political parties and organizations must be carried out in a fair manner,
and must be conducted under constant supervision of the people. In response
to these requirements, the Political Fund Control Law establishes stipulations
and rules with regard to notifications of political parties and political
organizations, as well as public disclosure of the receipt and expenditure of
political fund and restrictions on the amounts that may be received properly,
etc.

The basic concept underlying the Political Fund Control Act consists of the
following two ideas:

[1] Political funds are donations put out by the people who would like to see
    a healthy development of democratic politics. Therefore, the [sources],
    receipt and expenditure of such funds must be publicly disclosed, and
    judgement related to these should be entrusted to the people, and nothing
    should be done to restrain the people's voluntary will with regard to the
    donation of political funds.
[2] Political parties and political organizations should be fully aware of
    their responsibilities, and in receiving political funds, they shall
    conduct themselves in a fair and correct way so that they will in no way
    create suspicion or distrust among the people.

2. SUMMARY OF WORK INVOLVED IN THE IMPLEMENTATION OF THE POLITICAL FUND
   CONTROL LAW

Under the Political fund Control Law, organizations that are mainly aimed at
carrying out political activity are required to submit notice of establishment
as a political organization to the Prefectural Election Administration
Committee (hereafter referred to as the Prefectural Election Committee), and
whenever there is any change in any of the item in the notification, or when
the organization is dissolved, they are also required to file notice. When
the Prefectural Election Committee receives such a notification, it will
announce that fact in the prefectural gazette; it is required by law to draw
up a registry of political organization(s).

All political organizations are required to submit a financial report covering
the receipt and expenditure of political funds from January 1 (or the date of
the establishment) to December 31 of each year to the Prefectural Election
Committee between January 1 (or the date of establishment) and March 31 of the
following year. The Prefectural Election Committee, in turn, is mandated to
publish the content of the financial report (report of receipt and

expenditure) in the prefectural gazette, and report the collated results from the financial reports to the Ministry of Home Affairs as "Survey Report on the Actual Situation Related to Political Funds."

Furthermore, through the revision of the Law in 1980, the system of "designated organizations" for candidates for specified public positions (that is, candidates for the National Diet, prefectural governors, prefectural assemblies, mayors and assembly of designated cities), and the system of reserve funds for them, were established. Along with this revision, the work related to notification of designated organizations, drawing up of candidate registry, receipt and publication of financial reports, has been added anew.

3. BACKGROUND OF SYSTEM DEVELOPMENT

In 1981, the number of organizations obligated to submit financial reports on political funds under the jurisdiction of the [Fukuoka] Prefectural Election Administration Committee (that is, the number of political organizations [in Fukuoka] as of December 31, 1980) came to 2,858, which was the fourth largest in all of Japan. These organizations submitted 4,452 financial reports and financial reports related to the dissolutions of political organizations, etc. (to be submitted before March 31 and June 30, 1980, respectively).

Formerly, the Prefectural Election Administration Committee had to handle all the work of publishing this huge volume of financial reports, and of drawing up the Report on the Actual Situation Related to Political Funds, manually.

It just so happened that in April of that same year (1981) there were special elections to fill the vacancies in the prefectural assembly, so the work of publishing the summaries of financial reports was delayed considerably, and the final deadline for publishing the summaries of financial reports was postponed from the latter part of September, the deadline period in normal years, to the latter part of November. And the work of printing and publishing the reports was shifted from the conventional letter-press printing to a quicker and simpler printing method based on electronic plate-making, which enabled publishing to be done immediately upon the completion of the draft.

This new method was effective in cutting down the time required for printing and proof-reading, as well as in reducing the printing costs. However, the tedious, time-consuming work required for drawing up the draft of the report to be published remained as before, and so various problems related to it remaind.

While the [Prefectural Election Committee] was somehow able to handle the publication of financial reports for 1981 before the final deadline was accomplished, a far greater degree of difficulty were expected for 1983. For, the nationwide unified local elections were scheduled to take place in April of that year, followed by the elections of the House of Councilors of the National Diet in June. The number of political organizations increased rapidly, and with the additional demands placed by the new establishment of the system of designated organizations and system of reserve funds, it was anticipated that it would be extremely difficult to complete the requisite work of publishing the summaries of the reports by the manual method that has been used up to that point.

Due to this situation, the Prefectural Election Administration Committee was compelled to seek substantial labor and time savings through the computerization of administrative and paper work related to the Political Fund Control Law.

In October 1981, as the Prefectural Election Committee moved into the new prefectural building, a mainframe general purpose computer was introduced, and the plan for computerizing the work related to the Political Fund Control Act became concretized in one sweep, leading to a decision to begin work on the basic design from November of that year.

In tackling with the work of developing this system, a number of problematic areas had to be faced:

[1] The forms for various types of notifications submitted by from political organizations and candidates for specified types of public offices had to be changed to new computer forms.
[2] If the various notification forms were changed to computer forms, then it would become necessary to inform and orient the staff members of political organizations in a thoroughgoing manner about the method of filling them out.
[3] With the shift to computerization, the contents of the existing registry of political organization (about 3,100 entries) and registry of candidates (about 350 persons) for specified posts must be registered with the master registry of political organizations, and input work must be carried out.

The staff members of the secretariat of the Prefectural Election Committee struggled hard for the goal of simplification and rationalization of the work related to Political Fund Control Law, and overcame these problems, which made it possible to start the computerization work from June 1982. It has now reached the point where this work can be handled by the staff members inbetween other types of work.

4.   SUMMARY OF THE SYSTEM

4.1. System Flow

The system flow is as shown in Table 1.

[Table 1.   The System Flow]

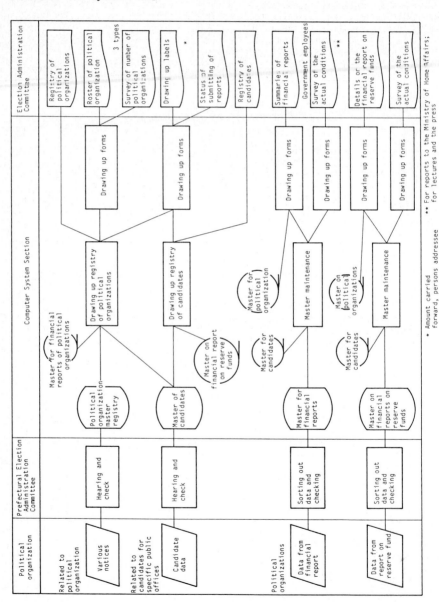

4.2. Summary of the System

When a political organization submits the notice of the establishment of a political organization, the Prefectural Election Committee enters the organization number to it (a serial number). And when the notice of establishment of a political organization is submitted by a political organization related to a candidate for a specific public office, the Election Committee registers the candidate for a specific public office through the candidate input form, and enter the organization's number of candidate number (also a serial number) to the notice of establishment of the political organization. Also, when a candidate for a specific public office submits a notice for the establishment of a designated political organization, the Election Committee will enter the organization number of the political organization and the candidate number of the candidate for a specified public office onto the notice, and by processing the respective input forms by computer, it has become possible to have a good grasp of the relationship between the candidate for a specified public office, and the political organizations and designated organizations related to that condidate, in a clearer manner.

The master for the political organizations and the master for candidates are used in this way. When various types of notices are submitted by the political organizations and/or candidates for a specificed public office, computer processing is carried out once a month, and each master is updated with the additional input. These masters are processed for permanent use, which means that the data on the amounts carried over in the financial reports of political organizations can be recorded for 15 years.

Note: The input forms for candidates has been developed by this prefecture on its own because of the need in computer processing. The secretariat of the Election Committee draws up the candidate input form from the bylaws of political organizations linked to the candidate for a public office or from recommendations written on the candidate's behalf.

From the master for political organizations and master of candidates, important items are produced as outputs such as: the registry of political organizations, registry of candidates, the roster of political organizations (three types), and address labels for various types of notices.

On the other hand, when financial reports are submitted by political organizations and candidates for specified public offices, then the appropriate accounting year, date of submission, and organization number or candidate number, are affixed onto it, and the reports are put through computer processing. From this data, the master on receipts and expenditure and master on reserve funds are drawn up. Both these masters are masters for single-year processing, but in order to make the Report on the Actual Situation Related to Political Funds, it needs to be computer processed in the following year as well, so the master tape is kept for at least one year.

From the master on receipt and expenditure and master on reserve funds, the master for political organizations and master for candidates can be processed simultaneously, and through this processing, the following items are outputted: publication draft of the summary of the financial reports, Report on the Actual Situation Related to Political Funds, the comprehensive list of organizations that have not yet submitted the financial report as well as address labels for prompting them to do so, comprehensive list of organizations that are assumed to have dissolved, and comprehensive list of amounts carried forward in the financial reports and labels for amounts carried forward.

5. VARIOUS TYPES OF INPUT AND OUTPUT FORMS

The input and output forms related to the computer system for the
implementation of the Political Fund Control Law and the processing cycle are
as shown in Table 2 and Table 3 below.

[Table 2. Input Forms, Processing Cycle]

Name of form	Submitted by	Processing cycle
Notice of the establishment of the political organization	Political organization	Every month
Notice of change in political organization	Political organization	Every month
Notice of dissolution of political organization	Political organization	Every month
Notice of designation organization	Candidates for specified public offices	Every month
Financial report of political organization	Political organization	Every year (January - June)
Report of receipt and expenditure on reserve fund	Candidates for specified public offices	Every year (January - June)
Input form for candidates	Election Committee Secretariat	Every Month
Input form for amounts carried forward	Election Committee Secretariat	Periodically
Input form for change in amounts carried forward	Election Committee Secretariat	Periodically

[Table 3. Output Forms, Processing Cycle]

Name of form	Processing cycle	Kanji processing (Kanji character processing)	Distributed to
Registry of political organization	Every month	Yes	Kept by Election Committee
Roster of political organizations	January of each year	Yes	Ministry of Home Affairs, municipalities
List of political organizations and address labels	November of each year	Yes	Only labels to political organizations

- to be continued -

List of organizations submitting financial report and address labels for prompting for report	February, April and November of each year	Yes	Only labels to political organizations
List of organizations assumed to have dessolved and address label for guidance related to dissolution	April of each year	Yes	Only labels to political organizations
Publication draft of summary of financial reports	August of each year	Yes	Public document
Survey Report on the Actual Situation Related to Political Organizations	August of each year	Yes	Ministry of Home Affairs
List of amounts carried forward and labels for amounts carried forward	August of each year	Yes	Kept by the Election Committee
Registry of candidates	August of each year	Yes	Kept by the Election Committee
List of candidates and address labels	November of each year	Yes	Only labels to candidates for specified office
Publication draft of summary of reports on receipts and expenditure of reserve funds	August of each year	Yes	Public document

6. IMPACT OF INTRODUCING THE SYSTEM

We can mention the following types of work as areas in which there have been significant amount of labor saving effect through the computerization of work related to the Political Fund Control Law.

6.1 Publication of Summary of Financial Reports

In the work related to publication of summary of financial reports, the summary is printed in the prefectural gazette only after checking of many items contained in a huge number of reports, and formerly, a considerable number of days of largely tedious work was required to do the various types of work involving everything from writing the draft to proof reading. However, by computerizing, all we now have to do is do the necessary work on the financial reports that we receive, do data punching, and verify the check list after processing. The publication draft can be outputted in Japanese-language line printer (i.e., put through kanji processing), so it is much easier to carry out light printing based on electronic plate-making; and the time needed for proof-reading and making of corrections has been eliminated. Thus, it has been greatly effective in cutting down on the necessary work time. Also, it has been instrumental in sharply reducing the amount of overtime, as well as in reducing the printing cost.

6.2 Work related to Survey Report on the Actual Situation Related to
     Political Funds

The work of drawing up the Report on the Actual Situation Related to Political
Funds involved a huge volume of simple calculation and collation work, and
formerly it took two staff members to work on the computation and drawing up
of the report for a period of one month. Through computerization of this
work, however, as soon as the publication draft of the financial reports (the
master on receipt and expenditure) is drawn up, it has become possible to
output the Survey Table on the Actual Situation at any time.

6.3 Work of writing address labels on notices to prompt for the financial
     report, to be sent to political organizations that have not submitted
     financial report.

6.4 Work of writing address labels on notice on guidance on dissolution, to
     be sent to organizations that are assumed to have dissolved.

6.5 Work of writing address labels for notice on the holding of explanation
     meetings on political activities directed toward political organizations
     as well as candidates for specified public offices.

In the past, staff wrote address labels for envelopes for items in 6.3 through
6.5, directed toward political organizations and candidates for specified
political offices, but with the computerized system, it is now possible to
output the necessary address labels at any time.

6.6 Drawing Up Roster of Political Organizations

With regard to the work of drawing up the roster of political organizations,
it is possible now to draw up a list of political parties and of other types
of political organizations (separately) in an alphabetical order, that is,
their names, addresses of their offices, names of their representatives, names
of the persons in charge of accounting, and whether or not there are any
preferential treatment given, etc., and submit this roster of political
organizations to the Ministry of Home Affairs readily by December 31 of each
year, and at any time necessary through the process of computerization.

Also, in Prefecture of Fukuoka, due to the necessity generated in this work,
the data is outputted in an alphabetical order according to type of public
office for political organizations linked to members of the National Diet,
Governor, members of the prefectural assembly, and mayors and members of city
council of the designated cities. With regard to the political organizations
linked to the heads of other municipalities (that is, cities, towns, and
villages), rosters of political organizations are outputted in accordance with
the type of public office as well as by municipality in an alphabetical order.
Brochures are produced by light printing based through electronic
plate-making, and distributed each year to the municipalities within Fukuoka
Prefecture.

6.7 Work of Preparing Various Types of Registries

With regard to the registry of political organizations, formerly the notice on
the establishment of political organization was first submitted, and after
this was published in the prefectural registry, the registry was prepared by
hand. However, with computerization, as soon as the master for political
organizations is made, it can be outputted at any time.

6.8 Work of Transcribing the Amounts Carried Forward to the Registry of
     Political Organizations

The work of transcribing the data on amounts carried forward to the registry
was formerly done by transcribing the amounts carried forward from the
financial reports to the reverse side of the registry of political
organizations. With computerization of our work, as soon as the master on
receipt and expenditure is completed, the labels on the amounts carried
forward can be outputted any time, and these, in turn, are placed on the
reverse side of the registry.

The types of work outline above can now be done quickly as well as accurately.

After the development of this system, the administrative and paper work has
been speeded up and rationalized to a significant degree so that the work
which was handled by 8 employees has been reduced, and the remaining work can
be handled adequatly by two staff members assigned to this area of work. This
elimination of repetitive and tedious work has contributed greatly to the
uplifting of the morale of our staff members, and today, the motivation and
energy of our staff members can be allocated more to the work of administering
elections and carrying out public education programs related to elections.

7. IN CLOSING

In recent years, the system of disclosing government information by local
governments to the general public is beginning to be introduced in Japan.
Now, under the operation of the Political Fund Control Act, information
related to the registeration of political organizations, etc., is published in
the prefectural gazette, and financial reports of political organizations are
published in a summary form, and the financial reports themselves are made
accessible for public perusal. In this sense, it can be said that this system
on political funds is in the forefront of the trend for public disclosure of
government information.

Now, with regard to the perusal of financial reports, it is legally
established that the financial reports are to be made available for public
perusal after the publication of their summaries, so the time for perusal used
to be delayed somewhat, depending upon when the summaries are published.
However, with the introduction of computer processing of work related to
political funds, the time required for publication of the summaries of the
financial reports and public perusasl of the reports themselves has been cut
down considerably, which is a major contribution in improving the government
information service in this sphere.

Governmental and Municipal Information Systems
P. Kovács and E. Straub (Editors)
Elsevier Science Publishers B.V. (North-Holland)
© IFIP, 1988

POPULATION REGISTER IN HUNGARY

A. KÉRY and A. KOVÁCS
State Office for Population Registration

Information is of similar value both at the macro- and micro level but only if it is available at a given point of time, at a given place, corresponding to the demands and by eliminating parallel processings it saves time on the part of the data supplier and of the user, as well.

The information demand in performing administrative and managing functions is well known.

One of the most important elements of the "macro and micro" systems is the information system of population register satisfying both social and individual demands.

The system of population register - considering its function and its characteristics based on the individual - has to satisfy several demands that relate to the individuals and to their position held and role played within the society.

/The citizen is the most important element of the society - elector, labour force, utilizer of health care and other services; law-abiding and occasionally law-breaker individual; a solder safeguarding our social order, our peaceful life, and so on./

The significance of population register has considerably increased simultaneously with the development of economic mechanism; the close interest-relation between the individual and the economy became more powerful.

Information relating to individuals is demanded at several places, thus such a method was to be developed, which eliminates parallellisms and where the stored information can be exchanged among the different users' fields and where these information form a unified system, resp.

The establishment of a computerized register based on personal indentifiers was demanded also by the tendency aiming at cost- and labour-efficiency.

The identifier satisfies several collection-, classification- and processing demands by the means of completing it by several other code-numbers. The cost-factor of the manual register of the preceding years is nearly inestimable.

Today there is a multi-level computerized population register available; that satisfying several "different" demands; this
register was developed on basis of the personal data collected on
the occasion of the 1975 population survey. It comprises the following: family- and given name; sex; maiden name; mother's name;
day, month, year and place of birth; marital status; Hungarian or
other citizenship; address of permanent residence; address of
temporary residence; personal identification number: a data derived from the basic ones; validity of the personal identification
card. The survey and recording of educational attainment and
qualification obtained within the frame of the school-system education will take place on the occasion of widening the scope of
data, while the linking of the father's, mother's, child's- and
spouse's personal identification number within the frame of developing the scope of data relating to family relations.

Development principles
Interestedness

The user's interest in establishing and operating the state
population register should be the fact that through the services
offered concrete results can be obtained. Such result might be
the obtaining of new information, filling-in a gap and also in
the form of simplifying a working-phase. Creation of the interestedness of data suppliers /citizens, institutions, councils
etc./ forms the basis for operating and improving the system. The
living guide of our activities is the harmonization of interests
of the departments and institutions and of the individuals concerned by the population register.

Cooperation

The population register is based on a wide-scale cooperation
with electronic data processing. The main factor of all the social and economic processes is the human being and its personal
criteria, resp., the recording of which is the task of the population register. The cooperation between the computerized population register and the citizens, councils and other organizations is inevitable both at the national and international level.
Basic registers play a cooperating and linking role.

Rentability

The population register demands for not negligible inputs. Its benefits are represented primarily in the social and economic development. It may have considerable cost-saving effect in administrative- and managing processes. In the whole process of population registration the individual products must be followed by prime cost calculation. The population register can be enlarged to such a state venture which will become more and more self-supporting and will solve the problems of employment as well as the renewal of devices utilized from its own resources to an ever increasing extent. This is the basis of the interestedness of both the individuals and the semi-independent groups working within the system.

Deliberateness

Computer-science, the electronized population register is the science and the practice of our days but also of our future. The greatest effort is demanded by the creating of mental capabilities.

The nation-wide electronization of the population register can be realized only in harmony with and integrated in the modernization of the state administration. And such objectives demand for administrative and data processing organizers who can apply computer techniques in each community and town. Moreover, several specialized organs, computer centers must be established, too.

Openness

Data of the register are accessible for all the data suppliers /i.e. first of the for the citizens/ and for those who make use of them in their work. At the same time, the confidentiality of data relating to individuals must be provided.

Development objectives
Integration, service abilities

When determining the directions of further-development, the conclusion of experience obtained in the introductory phase, the evaluation of international experience and the revision of faulty methods applied in the course of constructing the system are inevitable tasks.

In the development phase - with realistic consideration to
the mental and material capabilities available - such objectives
were set that could be realized, that were in harmony with the
original objectives and satisfy at the same time new demands
arisen in the meantime.

The population register is expected to offer rapid, correct
and reliable services. The exactness of the system must be approached - by the means of permanent improvement of the checking
system - to loo per cent and the rapid correction of errors must
be emphasized. The objective of the reliability of our services is
to provide for documentary evidence. To this end a comprehensive
quality-developing programme is already in progress, similary to
the provision of preconditions needed for the execution.

Maximum possible use should be made of the wide-scale application possibilities of the information carried by the population
register system of enlarged data content. Services of venture
character should be spread in the work of social, economic and
scientific organs.

Accordingly, the objective of the development is not only
the further improvement of the operational capabilities of the
already existing system, but also the outlining of such a new
information system which - taking into account also the poten-
tialities of the system - performs its tasks in a service-orient-
ed way, with enlarged data content and with consideration to the
users, satisfying efficiently both the individual and agregated
data demands.

The services of the state population register must be approached to the state administration. Development of the information system must be adjusted to this objective, which a three-
level, hierarchic, divided structure corresponds to. This facilitates that regional systems developing within the frame of the
population register should be integrated in the two-level deci-
sion-preparatory system of the council management as a part of
the unified information system of this latter. Thus the tasks of
local manual data bases will be solved also electronically.

The establishment of this divided system can be realized but
gradually, by proceeding from the present centralized system
towards decentralization. The rate of development is determined
by the available financial, organizational and personal condi-

tions. Standardization of basic personal data of material expenditures of individual respect and of the personal data of the individual sectors belong to the basic development objectives. With due consideration to sectoral peculiarities, the establishment of relations must be rendered possible at each level of the administration, by means of the wide-spread dissemination of personal data. The objective is to realize the exclusive use of personal numbers as personal identification. The standardization of registers should be organized in close interrelation with the development of a divided system, creating this way the preconditions for linking to the needed extent and for the exchange of data, reducing unnecessary parallellisms experienced in different, already existing registers and simplyfying data supply.

The increase of service capabilities

Aiming at a more wide-scale utilization of the state population register, the central data base must be transformed to a service system. By the help of computer services of the population register the immediate satisfaction of a significant part of personal information demands must be facilitated in the transactions of authorities' affairs. The satisfaction of individual data demands of the population should be started with by the help of the computerized information system of the population register.

By increasing the coordinating role of the State Population Register /SPR/, the harmony between register developments of personal character and the SPR must be further improved, for the sake of enlarging computerized services.

The most important objectives to be realized for increasing the service capabilities are the following:

- Harmonization between the SPR central system and the development of sectoral registers of personal character, first of all in the field of health care, of landed property register, of social security, of dwelling economy, of financial administration and of education.
- Modernization of the forthcoming population and housing census by making use of the population register, enlarging the scope of data of the SPR in the course of the census.
- Experiments aiming at the establishment of a computerized relation between the systems of social security and

population register.

Regional sub-centers

On basis of the regional sub-center experiments - as an element in the development of councils in the field of informatics and electronic data processing - local computerized data bases of the SPR should expediently be established gradully in the capital and in the counties; such local data bases would serve directly transactions of the population by administrative and provision districts /health care, education, election-districts etc./. The furnishing of local councils with computers - simultaneously with the establishment of county/capital systems - should be begun expediently first of all in the districts of the capital and in towns.

Sub-center of the capital

Within the population register, the tasks connected to the capital have been playing by now and will play also in the future development plans and outstanding role. This objective is justified by several factors, such as the specific council-administration pattern of the capital, the number of inhabitants, the number of events in the field of vital statistics exceeding the rate of the population, the mass of individual and agregated information demand, the problems arising from the life of a large town.

Decentralization of the common, computerized vital statistical-population register data collection is already realized up to the level of district councils, and local data capture of changes in the residential addresses will be started in the near future.

The sub-center of the capital is built up on basis of the principles set forth in the approved national decentralization programme.

Its tasks are:

1/ To furnish the council management of the capital and of the districts, further the social, state and economic organs contacting the capital with the needed, actual information /list of names, notice cards etc./.

2/ To furnish council employees and the citizens with timely individual data.

3/ To furnish the council- and other information systems
at the level of the capital with timely data in the form
of magnetic tapes or records.

The use of data supplies is multiplied by the fact that the
sub-center can handle and supply both agregated and individual
data in different breakdowns by districts /such as e.g. by district doctors, by district pediatrics, by screening stations, by
election-districts, by city-planning and school-districts/.

Ventures

Ventures can be further developed on basis of the existing
and not yet outdated population register system. We possess an
information-base of national economy level, which - due to its
nature - satisfies socio-economic demands and which is of significant value.

Issues relating to the use of the data base of the SPR

As proved by the Hungarian reality, the development of a new
system is based only in part on already existing ones - rather
entirely new, modern systems are established.

The question of utilization is connected also with the
circumstance that in several cases even those who know the system,
cannot use it in a purpose-oriented way.

Within the scope of users there are several who stick themselves to the old systems and refuse therefore the new ones, that
is they do not undertake the difficulties involved with getting
acquainted with a new system.

Some problems of the operation and development of the system

It is a multi-level, sophisticated, large system based on
the cooperation of several organizational units and the machine-
park.

The most important prop of the system's operation and utilization is the exactness of data and the timeliness of data
supply.

Beyond and over the demand for technical devices of data
collection, data transfer, data processing, one of the most
important questions is the problem of data base management.

Governmental and Municipal Information Systems
P. Kovács and E. Straub (Editors)
Elsevier Science Publishers B.V. (North-Holland)
© IFIP, 1988

The Technical Research Council on Computer Utilization
and its work in Japanese Government Agencies

Nobuhiro ISHIBASHI, Yasuo SUGIHARAI*

Computer Utilization Technology Office
General Coordination Division
Agency of Industrial Science and Technology, MITI
1-3-1 Kasumigaseki Chiyoda-ku TOKYO 100, JAPAN

This paper describes the establishment, history,
organization, main research topics and activities of
Technical Research Council on Computer Utilization.
Its object is to make clear the importance of cooperative
on computer utilization technology in government
agencies.

1. Introduction.

In Japan, circumstances affecting government administration are
becoming increasingly complicated as a result of such influences
as internationalization, the coming of the "information age", and
the maturing of society. From a long-term point of view, the
present time may be regarded as a transition period toward the
"Highly Information-oriented Society" envisioned for the 21st
century.

Expectation for administrative service are changing rapidly.
Government agencies plan policies based on relevant information,
and enforce them after consensus has been confirmed in the
community. Government agencies, then, are heavily dependent on
information, and as information services assume an increasingly
important role in society, it will become vital for government
itself to use them more efficiently and on a wider scale.

2. Establishment and activities

2.1 Establishment

The Japanese government has already installed computer systems to
increase efficiency in office work. In the 1960's, when the
first computer systems were introduced in government offices,
attempts were also made to find ways to use this new technology
to best advantage in the administrative field. After a period of
trial and error, the ministries and other agencies recognized
several common problems they had to solve, such as the varying
levels of skill of technicians, ambiguous methods of evaluating
cost performance, the lack of inter-operability for programs and
data, and so on.

---

* Policy Planning Information Office, MITI
  (The former secretariat of the council)

In 1968, to promote joint research on computer utilization by
government agencies, the Technical Research Council on Computer
Utilization was established in the Agency of Industrial Science
and Technology(AIST) which is in charge of scientific and
technological research for industry. The Computer Utilization
Technology Office(CUTO) was set up as its secretariat.
Specifically the tasks of the council were as follows:

(1) To increase the exchange of computer utilization
techniques among various governmental organizations and to
improve their standard.

(2) To establish a system which copes with new technical
developments.

(3) To effectively eliminate overlapping developments in
techniques.

(4) To insure the compatibility of data and programs
through standardization.

(5) To develop sophisticated computer utilization
techniques which can be shared by various government
organizations.

From that time down to this day, several times, the council had
changed its organization to keep up with progress of utilizing
technique. The change of the organization is shown in Figure 1.
Now, almost 20 years since its establishment, 420 experienced
professionals from leading 27 government agencies participate in
the council, and nine research groups work on various themes.
Participating government agencies are shown in Table 1.

Table 1. Participating government agencies (as of 1987)

Board of Audit
National Personal Authority
National Police Agency
Management and Coordination Agency
Defence Agency
Economic Planning Agency
Science and Technology Agency
National Land Agency
Ministry of Justice
Ministry of Foreign Affairs
Ministry of Finance
National Tax Administration Agency
Ministry of Education
Ministry of Health and Welfare
Social Insurance Agency
Ministry of Agriculture, Forestry and Fisheries
Food Agency
Ministry of International Trade and Industry
Agency of Industrial Science and Technology
Patent office

Ministry of Transport
Maritime Safety Agency
Meteorological Agency
Ministry of Posts and Telecommunications
Ministry of Labour
Ministry of Construction
Ministry of Home Affairs

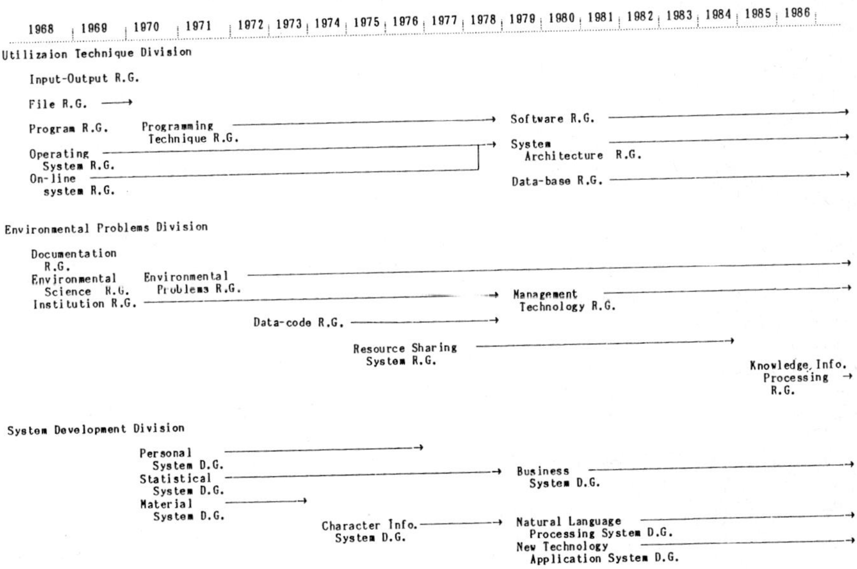

| 1968 | 1969 | 1970 | 1971 | 1972 | 1973 | 1974 | 1975 | 1976 | 1977 | 1978 | 1979 | 1980 | 1981 | 1982 | 1983 | 1984 | 1985 | 1986 |

Utilizaion Technique Division

Input-Output R.G.

File R.G. $\longrightarrow$

Program R.G. Programming ────────────────→ Software R.G. ─────────────→
            Technique R.G.
Operating ─────────────────────────────→ System ─────────────→
  System R.G.   Architecture R.G.
On-line ───────────────────────────────→
  system R.G.   Data-base R.G. ─────────────→

Environmental Problems Division

Documentation
  R.G.
Environmental   Environmental ──────────────────────────────→
  Science R.G.   Problems R.G.
Institution R.G. ───────────────────────────→ Management ─────────────→
                                               Technology R.G.
            Data-code R.G. ─────────────→

              Resource Sharing ─────────────→
                System R.G.
                                                    Knowledge, Info.
                                                      Processing →
                                                      R.G.

System Development Division

Personal ───────────────────→
  System D.G.
Statistical ─────────────────────→ Business ─────────────→
  System D.G.   System D.G.
Material ───────────→
  System D.G.
            Character Info. ───────────→ Natural Language ─────────────→
              System D.G.   Processing System D.G.
                                         New Technology ─────────────→
                                           Application System D.G.

Figure 1. The change of the organization

2.2 activities

The current organization of the council is shown in Figure 2. The research activities of each research group are briefly introduced below.

Utilization Technique Division

The division conducts studies on utilization techniques of computer systems.

Software Research Group

The group conducts studies on method of software design, development, maintenance and evaluation, programming languages and circulation of the existing software.

System Architecture Research Group

The group conducts studies on system architecture, especially on communication technology which combine various processing units and local/terminal station and operating system.

Data-base Research Group

The group conducts studies regarding advancement of data-base utilization techniques and promotion of data utilization/circulation.

Environmental Problems Division

The division conducts discussion on various problems surrounding computer systems.

Environmental Problems Research Group

The group conducts studies on general sciences which delineate and determine structure to utilize computer and other related problems such as relations between information processing organs and general administrative organs.

Management Technology Research Group

The group conducts studies on operation and management of computer such as improvement of system-efficiency, data-protection, system-security and data-compatibility.

Knowledge Information Processing Research Group

The group conducts total studies to apply the problem solving techniques of knowledge such as decision making, reasoning, natural language and recognition on administrative information processing system.

System Development Division

The division conducts deliberations on the system development which performs common business to various governmental organizations and the technical problems created along with various system development.

Business System Development Group

The group conducts studies on the development of administrative data processing systems and on the problems encountered in the development.

Natural Language Processing System Development Group

The group conducts studies on the development of Japanese language processing system and on the problems encountered in the development.

New Technology Application System Development Group

The group conducts studies regarding new technology and applicable areas of those development of application systems and the problems encountered in the development.

Figure 2. Organization of the Technical Research Council on Computer Utilization (as of 1987)

2.3 Recent research

The history of research and development is shown in Table 2,
Table 3 and Table 4.   At first, many of research themes were
basic utilization techniques of computer, problems of
computerization and developments of statistical system. The
Council's recent research has ranged from technical themes such
as video-tex utility at government offices, a micro-computer
data-base with user-friendly interface, an expert system and
natural language processing, to broader aspects of computer
systems such as the types of administrative information systems
which will be needed in the future, computer security and system
auditing.

Table 2. History of Research and Development Activities
(Utilization Technique Division)

<u>File Research Group ('68-'69)</u>

Trend in file program systems in government agencies	'68-'69

<u>Programing Technique Research Group ('69-'79)</u>
(including Program Research Group)

A list of programs in government agencies	'68
Compiler techniques	'69-'70
Information Retrieval Systems	'69-'71
General-purpose data processing programs	'70-'72
Point of system development	'72
Information retrieval on statistical data	'72
Programing language used in government agencies	'73
Programing language for on-line system	'74
Structured programing	'75
New programing technique	'76
Points of program making	'77
Software development support system	'78
Documentation support tool	'79

Software Research Group ('79-   )

Software productivity promotion technique	'79
Software design	'80
Requirement definition and specification	'81
Testing and quality evaluation	'82
Software maintenance	'83
Programing language	'84
4th generation language	'85
Software life cycle	'86

<u>Operating System Research Group ('68-'78)</u>

Establishment of OS concept	'68-'69
Possibilities of OS standardization	'69-'70
OS evaluation	'70-'73
OS in general and specialized uses	'71-'73
Other problems of OS	'69-'73
OS generation language	'74-'78
Future trends of OS	'77-'78

<u>On-line System Research Group ('68-'78)</u>

Trends in utilization of on-line systems	'68-'71
On-line network systems	'71-'77
Network Architecture	'77-'78

System Architecture Research Group ('79-   )

Architecture of computer systems	'79
High-level mini-computer	'80

Technical trend of Local Area Network	'81
Distributed processing system	'81-'85
New architecture computer	'86

Data-base Research Group ('79-   )

Survey on DBMS	'79
Utilizing DBMS in government agencies	'80
Problem of utilizing DBMS in government agencies	'81
Data dictionary/directory	'82
Distributed data-base system	'83
Multi-media data-base system	'84-'86
Data-base system for small computer	'85

Table 3. History of Research and Development Activities (Environmental Problems Division)

Environmental Problems Research Group ('68-   )
(including Environmental Science Research Group)

NIS	'68-'69
IR's and OR's	'69-'71
Networks and data banks	'70-'72
Systems engineering	'70-'72
Organization problems	'70-'72
View of information processing technique	'73-'74
Information processing in the administration	'73-'74
Environmental problems on resource sharing system	'75-'76
Relations between information processing organs and general administrative organs	'77-'78
Desired image of information systems in government agencies	'79
Problems of office automation in government	'80
Office work analysis	'81
Techniques of office work analysis	'82
Progress of OA and its effects and problems	'83
Information system in government agencies	'84-'86

Institutional Research Group ('69-'78)

Rental arrangements	'69
Personal, organization, and other aspects of computer room management	'70-'72
Validity of recording media as evidence of proof	'70-'72
Difference of computer utilization between Japan and other foreign countries	'73-'74
Facility management service	'74-'75
Clearing information systems	'76-'78

Management Technology research Group ('78-   )

Computer management control technique in government agencies	'78-
System audit in government and trend of operation support technique	'80
Trend of system audit	'81
Data management and automatic operation	'82
Automatic operation of computer system	'83-'84
Computer security	'85-

Data Code Research Group ('72-'78)

Date code hand-book in government agencies	'72-'75
Compatibility and standardization of data code	'75-'78

Resource Sharing System Research Group ('74-'84)

Preliminary research for developing a resource sharing system	'74-'85
Development of basic protocols	'76-'77
Development of high level protocols	'78-'79
Development of data sharing system	'80-'83
Summary of resource sharing system	'84

Knowledge Information Processing Research Group ('85-   )

Abstract of knowledge information processing	'85-'86

Table 4.   History of research and Development Activities
(System Development Division)

<u>Statistical System Development Group ('69-'78)</u>

Statistical language	'69-'72
Statistical data file subsystems	'73-'74
Statistical survey retrieval subsystem	'75
Statistical information using subsystem	'76-'77
Research for input/output device	'78

Business System Development Group   ('79-   )

Preliminary research for developing business systems	'79
Chinese character and graph processing	'80
Abstract design of graph processing and small computer	'81
Abstract design of graph administrative information filing system	'82
Promotion and application of OA	'83
Total office automation system	'84
Systematization bend on business analysis	'85

<u>Character Information System Development Group ('73-'78)</u>

Document management data generating subsystem	'73-74
Document retrieval subsystem	'75
Research for Japanese language processing	'76-'78
Design of automatic word extract system	'78

Natural Language Processing System Development Group ('79-   )

Japanese language processing system in government agencies	'79
Information reference with natural language	'80
Text data-base	'81
Retrieval system of text information	'82
Question-answer system by natural language	'83
Data-base retrieval system in Japanese	'84
Data-base query system in Japanese	'85

New Technology Application System Development Group ('79-   )

Patten information processing technique	'79-80
Feasibility of speech recognition	'81
Image mixed text prcessing system	'82-83
Examination of New-media's feasibility in administrative service field	'84
Video-tex utility at government office	'85
Machine translation	'86

Personnel System Development Group ('69-'76)

    Personnel systems   '69-'76

Material System Development Group ('70-'73)

    Material systems   '70-'73

2.4 Diffusion and Reinforcement of the Outcome of Research

With respect to diffusion of the results of research achieved by the Council, we are trying to promote the application of the results of research by reporting at the plenary session and the subcommittee of the Council and holding an annual meeting for the presentation of research.

The participants were only those from ministries and agencies. However, in accordance with the request from prefectural governments for utilization of the results of the Council, the participation to the above annual meeting is recommended to prefectural governments.

2.5 Dispatch of Overseas Trainees

The Research Council dispatches trainees overseas every year. One purpose of this program is to do diversified research and studies of advanced data processing technologies of other countries. Other purposes are to acquire such technology, thereby contributing to the improvement of computer utilization technology of the government agencies, and also to keep up-to-date with new technologies.

3. Conclusion

New technology is developing faster than our understanding of how to use it effectively, yet government agencies must apply this technology if they are to effectively computerize their operation. Thus the work of the Council will take on even greater importance in the years to come.

Governmental and Municipal Information Systems
P. Kovács and E. Straub (Editors)
Elsevier Science Publishers B.V. (North-Holland)
© IFIP, 1988

THE INFORMATION SYSTEM IN THE MINISTRY OF INDUSTRY /HUNGARY/ BASED
ON MAIN-FRAME AND PC NETWORK

Janos Lendvai

Ministry of Industry Hungary
P.O.Box 96
1525 Budapest, Hungary

1. INTRODUCTION

The authority of the Ministry of Industry covers seven braches of the Hungarian
industry and more than thousand state-owned enterprises and cooperatives belong
to these branches which are mining, production of energy, metallurgy, engineering, chemical industry, light industry and miscellaneous. The main duty of the
Ministry is to manage the short and long term activities of the industry in the
field of production, sales, R&D. For this purpose it is necessary to track and
controll the realisation of the planned economic development. The information
system should support this activity.

The information system has three main parts:
- the collection and selection of the data,
- reporting system for the staff and the top management in the Ministry,
- mathematical-statistical methods to analyse the industrial development.

2. GENERAL ASPECTS OF THE INFORMATION SYSTEM

2.1. The collection of the data

The ministries and agencies in the Hungarian administration have the right to
collect information from the firms. They process the gathered data and there
is a permanent exchange of the information among the authorities to avoid the
collateral data processing. This exchange in the information is carried out on
magnetic tapes.

The industrial information system takes part in this exchange and has four
different main data sources:
- data collection system of the Central Statistical Office,
- data collection from the accounting and balance system managed by the
  Ministry of Finance,
- statistical system of the foreign trade,
- Ministry of Industry's own data collection.

These sources include a lot of important information by firms, i.e.
- value of production, number of employees, wages, worked hours, sales by
  region, etc.,
- balance sheet, distribution of costs and revenues, etc.,
- turnover of foreign trade by products and countries,
- information about the R&D, the technical development, utilization of capacity,
  etc.

The information arrive to the computer center working for the Ministry on
different media but finally they are stored on magnetic devices. /The main-
frame computer is an R-55 one/. A data-base was selected from these primary
mass of information which includes about 400 data by firms and a special

handling-system would be developed /it is called VIR/ on the main-frame
computer.

Some characteristics of VIR are as it follows:
- it is able to work with four different sources /files/, a maximum of 16 data
  by sources,
- it can select by ten different codes and by six of them summarize,
- we can make calculations with the data in a rational fraction form where the
  numerator and the denominator consists of maximum six parts,
- the program tabulates the data and the results of the calculations.

The functions of the VIR are commanded by parameters and these are the main
means to process the data for the regular and occasional reports.

2.2. The reportinq system

The reporting system in the Ministry has monthly, quarterly and yearly reports.

The main ideas in the reporting system are that
- every department has got the information about the topics which it is in
  charge in,
- on the higher level of the hierarchy we provide less but more general information than on the lower level,
- we use the practice of the "management by exception" which means that we
  select with different methods the exceptional information and report only
  them instead of the detailed ones.,
- everybody has the possibility to get occasional reports for his request
  based on the database,
- the quarterly reports have more information than the monthly ones and the
  yearly have more than the quarterly ones.

In order to illustrate the system i.e. we have a monthly report about the
value of production, the number of employees, the export and import by sub-
braches, etc. and a comparison with the previous year. But we report the list
of the enterprises too, which have declined in the mentioned fields compared
with the previous year.

In the quarterly reports we give information on the balance and accounting
system i.e. net revenue, production costs, profit and profit-rate, fixed
assets, etc.

The regular reporting system has a standard form of tables and charts and a
strict timing of publication.

2.3. The analysing methods

The analysing methods cover the application of the mathematical-statistical
and econometrical means, partly to analyse the economic behaviour of the
industry partly to modell it for the purpose of forecasting.

We use in this frame the calculation of trends, correlation and regression,
standardization, statistical distributions.

But we apply the input-output tables of the Hungarian economy and the Hungarian
industry and make calculations with Cobb-Douglas production functions, too.

The calculations and estimations are based on the information collected and
stored on the main-frame and we use different program packages for the purpose.

3. THE PC SYSTEM

The information system described shortly was built up in the first half of the 80's but in the middle of the decade we had to realize that with the spreading of the PC-s we arrive to a new phase in the development.

It became clear that the growing number of PC-s in the Ministry should change the functions of the main-frame, some of the functions would be worth transferring to the PC.

Another important point was that the development of the local aerial network /LAN/ began began in the Ministry which should mean a qualitative change of the information system.

3.1. Hardware

For the time being the LAN consists of 10 IBM PC XT-s or compatible computers and two of them fulfill the server function.

The connection between the main-frame and the PC-s was established in two ways, partly via file transfer and partly via floppy disc which is produced as an output by the main-frame.

The file transfer works only from the main-frame to one of the server computers and the speed of the data transfer is low. Therefore, the greater part of the communication goes on with floppy disc.

In the hardware-field we had to introduce some standards to secure the exchange of the software products and the data among the computers in the network.

In this way the configuration of the PC work-place consists of

> 640 Kbyte RAM
> 10 Mbyte Winchester /minimum/
> 360 Kbyte floppy drive
> printer /Epson FX type of similar/
> DOS 3.1 version

The other very important part of the standard is the unified Hungarian character and code set. In order to overcome this special problem we had to analyse a lot of possible solutions because each had some disadvantages beside the advantages, as well.

/There are ten additional PC in the Ministry which have not been yet connected in the network./

3.2. Software and information

In the development of the software we followed two directions. The first one assumes that the users have some knowledge about the computers so they can solve the problems using software packages.

The second type of software - worked out by the specialists - does not need any knowledge of PC, it leads the user step-by-step in the processing.

The frame of the software is a master menu system which was installed on each PC.

The master menu has three levels, the first one works in the network, the second one goes out of the LAN but still remains in the menu and the third level goes back to the DOS.

The master menu contains:
- a word-processing package /Personal Editor/,
- a spread-sheet handling program /Symphonie/,
- a database handling package /Dbase III+/.

There was a special directory built up on the server computers for the regular reports, in this way each user can acces to the new information not only on hard copy but on his display too, and he is able to do further processing with them.

On the other hand we built up a restricted data-base by enterprises which consist of 34 monthly and 40 quarterly data and the users can select them for further analysing, processing.

These mentioned information are handled by the program packeges but a special user-friendly system was developed too.

It handles several ten thousand basic data from which the user can select the level of aggregation, the indicators calculated from the data, etc. The program is able to line up the firms by given indicator, calculates elasticities between different economic terms and all these facilities are directed with Hungarian commands.

Last but not least there is a very important possibility to get some information on floppy disc from the main-frame database.

Another feature of the system we installed a special program which allows to simulate the economic processes.

The algorithm of the dynamic simulation program is based upon the combination of the step-by-step method with the solution of the simultaneous equation systems. /The computer program was written in BASIC./ The basic idea of the system is that there are 200 elements which can be assigned different functions or meaning and that the meaning determines the connections among the elements. The meaning of the elements could be economic or physical. The contents of the element depends on the type. Currently there are five different types of elements in the program with economic meanings. These are the following:

> Integrator
> Summarizer
> Multiplier/divider
> Fractional function
> Cobb-Douglas function

There are two further possibilities in the program. We can use constant values in the inputs and order initial values to the integrator's element. During the run all parameters could be changed after every time step. The initial parameters and the results could be written on a diskette for repeated of further application.

Besides the master menu in the DOA every "professional" member of the Ministry's staff has the opportunity to work with the compilers for example BASIC, FORTRAN, PASCAL, etc.

4. CONCLUSIONS

We started with the PC system in the last quarter of 1986 and we have two important experiences. The first is that it is necessary to form the special distribution of tasks in the information processing between the main-frame and the PC using the flexibility of the latter.

Our second experience is that it is very substantial to demonstrate the advantages and the easy handling of the PC-s because without this conviction of the staff we cannot go further in this direction.

Governmental and Municipal Information Systems
P. Kovács and E. Straub (Editors)
Elsevier Science Publishers B.V. (North-Holland)
  IFIP, 1988

POLICIES FOR EDP IN PUBLIC ADMINISTRATION IN NORWAY

Arild Jansen
Ministry of Consumers Affairs and Government
Administration, Oslo, Norway

IFIP TC 8 Conference on
Governmental and Municipal Information Systems
Budapest, Hungary, September 8-11, 1987.

Abstract:
This presentation will discuss general strategies for managing the
information technology in public administration in Norway. One key
issue in these discussions is how to develop and maintain a
decentralized administration, while at the same time take care of
the co-ordination that is required. Two different approached are
being discussed, either to manage the "hard way" through central
regulations and guidelines, or the "soft way" by providing
attractive services that intentionally may have a conforming impact
on how institutional solutions are designed.

As one example of the latter strategy, the paper outlines a plan
for developing a common data communication system in the central
government in Norway. The long term goal is to develop a technical
infrastructure for the public administration based on the
principles in the Open Systems Interconnection (OSI) reference
model. This model shall allow for decentralisation and
institutional autonomy, while at the same time act as a coordinating and unifying structure.

Other elements of this strategy are to emphasize the importance of
focus on organisational and administrative aspect, to promote
user participation, and to stimulate the awareness on management
level of these matters.

1. INTRODUCTION

EDP in governmental administration in the nineties must be managed in
quite different ways than in the past. This is due to at one hand new
technical potentials and the increased use of edp to a wider range of
tasks, which is the result of the distribution of computing power and
the development of enhanced office automation tools. The significant
growth in the use of EDP in the public administration have created
substantial potentials for improving efficiency and effectiviness,
and constitutes important elements in the modernisation of the public
sector in general.

At the other hand, as EDP is integrated in daily worklife, there is
an increasing understanding of the importance of the relationship
between technology, organisation and human factors. Widespread
demand for equipment and personnel combined with budget constraints
and institutional sovereignity have resulted in piecemal and uncoordinated development, and consequently imposing management problems.
This paper discusses the growing demand for better co-ordination and
central initiatives and outlines elements of revised strategies that
we are considering.

2. GENERAL PRINCIPLES AND POLICIES

2.1 Overall political framework

It is essential to emphasize that using information technology in
public administration is _not_ a goal on itself, but merely tools for
improving the effectiveness of the information handling. Accordingly,
before designing and implementing new technological solutions, it is
necessary to identify the overall conditions and constraints, or the
political context. In Norway, this context have been expressed in a
program for modernising the government administration. The superior
goals are briefly expressed as:

* To provide better services.
* To utilize the resources more efficient
* To improve information handling.

In order to achieve those goals, various types of measures have been
selected:

1. Goal orientation and focus on political priorities, which implies
   that each organisational unit shall define its goals explicitly,
   develop plans and report the achievement regularly, in order to
   improve the basis for decision making and overall management.

2. Budget reforms have been implemented and other economic
   constraints are being reviewed, in order to provide each
   organisational unit with greater autonomy.

3. Improved economic planning and management has been initiated,
   including cost-benefit analysis, internal pricing, advisory
   assistance in planning, in service provision and in the
   implementation of the budget reform.

4. Education, training and recruitment of leaders and key personnel
   are in focus, and a program for implementing the equality
   act in the government administration has been initiated,
   aiming at increased utilisation of the personnel.

Concerning the use of IT in particular, we should mention important
considerations:

* Make sure that technology as such does not restructure the
  existing organisational and decision making structures.

* Promote user participation and local unions involvement along
  with focus on environmental matters.

* Maintain the correctness and openness in the information
  handling, and at the same time focus on security and make sure
  that vulnerability is not increased.

2.2 EDP in the Norwegian government administration

The Norwegian state sector comprices about about 500 institutions
with 175 000 employees. The decision and management structure related
to EDP is highly decentralized. Each institution is responsible for

the planning and implemention of its EDP-solutions as an integred
part of its internal organisation.

A recent survey that we have conducted indicates that there are today
about 30 000 terminals or work stations in these institutions. This
implies a coverage of almost 20 %. The annual investment is about
$100 mill. We have one state Computer Centre, with an annual gross
revenue of $20 mill. This figures tells that more than 80 % of the
government computing is managed by the institutions themselves.
Furthermore, there are 7 municipal computer centres, but their share
of service provisions to the state institutions is rather modest.
There exist no general central funding body or controlling agency.

2.3 Problem and bottlenecks in public computing

In general, many will claim that overall emphasis on public
expenditure restraint has promoted a bias towards efficiency which
influenced the way other qualities is perceived, and flexibility is
seen more a way to reduce cost than adjusting to the need.
Subsequently, we have experienced various problems with the current
situation, which may be illustrated by:

- There is an uneven distribution of IT resources between
  sectors, and many institutions do not have sufficient competent
  and trained personnel to succesfully manage such tasks.

- There is a lack of a general available, adequate technical
  infrastructure and data communication facilities between
  different computer systems, which should provide efficient
  access to central services and main national registers and
  systems.

- There is a general lack of adequate methods and systems to be
  implemented and used in environments of great diversity, e.g.
  poor system quality, significant maintenance burden, no
  portability or incompatibility between systems.

- There is a lack of standards for data administration and common
  procedures for exchange of information between institutions and
  sectors.

- There is little emphasis and knowledge about organisational
  aspects related to introduction of new technology, and in
  particular, a lack of awareness of such issues on management
  level.

2.4 The emerging of new EDP-strategies in public administration.

In Norway, as in many other countries, I think it is fair to say that
existing government EDP-strategy is the collection of non-integrated
individual agency plans. At the same time, there is a need to
incorporate edp into the daily work and making the institutional edp-
solutions more unified and compatible, at least on a functional level.
We are experiencing the increasing demand for more integrated
services, both within and between institutions, and even across sector
The technical development offers potencials to do so.

This leads to the question whether or not a more coherent,

governmentwide EDP-strategy should be defined, in order to address the
problems more adequately. Some hold the position that an EDP-strategy
should only be seen as an integral part of the general strategy of any
business, and that this should apply to the government as to national
policies in general. A separate EDP-strategy may isolate the various
responsibilities and make the overall goals less visible.

Others, however, claim that the public sector with its range of
institutions, competence and responsibility related to EDP require
common guidelines and rules of the game. They have several task and
problems in common, and the need for effective exchange of information
is increasing. Accordingly, one clearly observes the necessity for
co-ordination, as well as a need to stimulate further innovation
on the local level.

Our view is now that an EDP-strategy should be defined, but as <u>an
integrated part</u> of broader strategy, aiming at achieving the superior
goals. It should serve as basis for developing <u>long term</u> EDP-plans, fo
making <u>tactical</u> decisions, and determine the <u>operational</u> procedures fo
the executive bodies. Thus, such a strategy can be thought of having
three levels:

1.   A highest level, to determine the general <u>principles</u> and <u>goals</u>
     that determine the use of EDP. This will include decentralisation
     and greater managerial responsibility, competition, overall
     effectiveness and furthermore, information accessability,
     integrity and quality.

2.   A middle level of <u>governmentwide policies</u> and <u>procedures</u> and the
     organisational structure for implementing them. Examples are the
     separation of tasks and responsibility between central and local
     institutions, general principles for system design, development
     and acceptanse, standards for communication and exchange of data,
     etc.

3.   A lowest level, comprising <u>institutional operations</u> with specific
     plans and means that an individual agency uses to design,
     implement and operate systems for a specific tasks or
     administrative function.

It should be clearly observed that these guidelines and principles
may partly be conflicting.

3. ELEMENTS OF NEW POLICIES.

The spesific goals for the use of EDP in the individual institutions
will be to provide cost/effective solution to dedicated taks, while
the overall goals related to EDP in government at large will have a
broader scope, e.g. aiming at:

<u>To improve public services</u>: improve the quality and accessability of
    information and the way they are provided to the public.

<u>To increase utilisation of information and data:</u> simplify the
    exchange of information within and between institutions.

<u>To</u> <u>support the administrative tasks and problem solving</u>, by providing
    better tools for automating routine tasks, and helping in making
    laws, regulations and guidelines more accessible and easier to use.

Focus on such goals is essential, when designing an EDP-strategy and defining operative measures:

THE STICK OR THE CARROT?

The means or initiatives to be used may be of two different types:

The stick, by defining policies, general principles and
  guidelines that are enforced upon the individual institution
and
  the carrot, by providing a variety of services that are sufficient
  attractive, and when used properly, will have a unifying effect on
  the various solutions.

Clearly, we will need both approaches. But it is also necessary to take account of the successful applications that has been developed, as well as carefully notice the problems and, not to forget, the painful experiences that has been made. Such experiences tells us that we should relief the pain of the stick as much as possible, and rather focus on the benefits from finding the carrots. The requires new ways of management. Examples of such stimulating initiatives are:

Administrative and economic means:

- Through the budget reform, provide for long range planning and encourage more economical profitable investments and the means to implement them.

- Increase the independence of certain government institutions in order to make funding possible from the private sector.

- Wherever possible, implement a system of internal pricing on services that have so far been free.

Infrastructure and common support functions:

- Enforce the efforts to improve the nationwide technical infra-structure in the public sector, by specifying and implementing standardized communication procedures, increase the utilisation of telecommunication services.

- Improve means for information exchange between sectors and institutions, by defining common procedures for data exchange on various levels, as between general software products, between application programs and between institutions.

- Stimulate the design and implementation of modern, high quality systems, dedicated to solve important tasks within the administration. Important elements are to develop standard system-independent (portable) specifications, e.g. for accounting, budget and archive routines, and to implement experimental prototypes for evaluation of their usefullness.

- Focus on data administration in order to provide correct, relevant and sufficient information easy accessible. Essential is the mapping of data flow between major institutions and between major databases, and the standardisation of data elements.

Management and organisational aspects:

- Promote awareness and understanding among senior public
  administrators on EDP-matters, and emphasize the importance of
  strategic planning and well-developed implementation schemes.

- Make available general advisory guidelines for procurement and
  contracting work, and prepare "cookbooks" for planning,
  implementation and maintenance of various EDP- systems.

- Survey existing central and local advisory and support agencies,
  in order to strengthen and co-ordinate their activities and make
  them easier to access.

- Increase the focus on organisational and environmental aspects
  related to the increased use of IT, by initiating studies and
  pilot projects, distribute reports, exchange of experience, etc.
  Stimulate involvement from all levels of employees in design,
  implementation and operation of application systems through
  education opportunities, training packages, etc..

- Carefully consider vulnerability and security aspects, on
  technical, funstional as well as management levels.

The relation to the Norwegian computer industry has been much
discussed and created some emotions, too. In some cases, selected
development projects and other co-operative efforts has been
conducted to support local computer vendors, and similar
discriminating measures has been applied for same reasons. Some of
these intiatives has been rather successful, the result of others has
been of more partial success. Today, the Norwegian hardware and
software supply marked is more diversed and desentralised, and
accordingly, the such policies are adjusted to the changed
conditions.

4. GOVERNMENTAL INFORMATION MANAGEMENT AS OPEN SYSTEMS

4.1 Data communication as strategic instrument.

The great challenge we are facing now, is to implement these new
policies successfully. In the hierchical decision structure in the
government, the communication lines and the separation of task
follows traditional, well-defined procedures. Each institution of
organisation unit appears rather "closed" and has limited
communication with its environment. To a certain extent, these rules
of the game must be maintained. However, our modernisation efforts do
include the review of administrative procedures. The merging of tele-
and datacommunication technology, in fact the integration of text,
data, and pictures (grahpical information) will provide radical new
ways of information retrieving and distribution in general. These
possibilities can be exploited without changing the decision
structure, and will offers opportunities for increased co-operation
in the government.

One well-known approach when designing data network is the Open
Systems Interconnection, (OSI)- Reference model), which defines a
common framework for allowing systems to cooperate according to
established standards. The basic principle and rules is that each
system has to obey a common set of standard procedures and service

interfaces, and that the systems can be divided into corresponding
sets of functional equivalent peer layers.

A simple illustration of an open communication model:

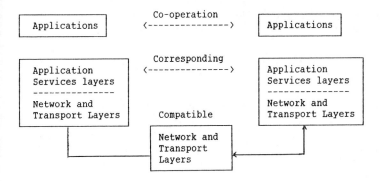

Figur I: A simplified OSI communication model

4.2 COOPERATION BETWEEN OPEN GOVERNMENT SYSTEMS.

These general principles are not restricted to networking, and its
applications may be extended beyond that of data communication. The
government should be viewed as a collection open, interconnecting by
autonomous systems and the communication services as an integrated
part of the general infrastructure that should serve the public
sector in general. What is then requires is a sets of advisory
standards for governmental computing which should not only include
data communication procedures and interfaces, but also standards for
data elements, archiving and database functions, data modelling
rutines, etc. This involves focus on different managements levels,
and includs various aspects, as e.g:

A. The organisational perspective, concerning management issues
    and cooperation between institutions, including the planning,
    development and operation of the common infrastructure and
    support bodies.

B. The functional aspect, focusing on the accessability, relevance,
    and quality of information, including system integrity and
    security.

C. The technical and operational matters, which includes
    connectivity and compatibility problems, how to provide
    interconnection of the computer systems throughout the
    administration, and how to ensure that exchange of data and
    information between relevant systems is offered in adequate ways.

The design of a governmental "open systems model" is, however, a very
ambitious task and requires a new way of structuring and managing the
data processing in the government. It is obvious that a lot of
functions should not be included. The use of such "standards" should
be voluntary, and their use should be made attractive by implying

less cost or increased benefit when adapted to. The number of
standards or guidelines should be kept as low as possible, and each
standard should serve a well-defined purpose.

Criterias for defining a standard may among others be:
- It exists an national or international accepted standard
- A common standard is necessary in order to accomplish tasks that
  involves several individual systems
- The use of standards or common procedures is clearly justified by
  cost/benefit or other high priority arguments

5. A CASE STUDY - A DATA NETWORK FOR THE CENTRAL GOVERNMENT

To illustrate some of the implications of the general principles
stated above, I will briefly outline the plans for a general data
communication network for central government administration in
Norway. The first step in designing a data communication system will
be to determine the desired objectives or functional requrements of
the network, and furthermore, the organisational structure it should
operate within. This implies that it is crucial to understand the
information and data flow within the various parts of the
administration which may be illustrated in this simplified manner:

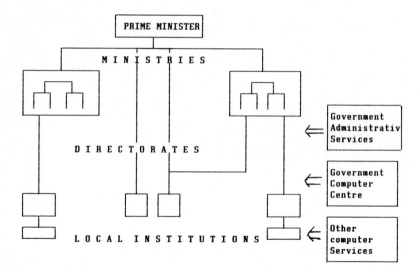

Figur II: <u>Organisational structure and information flow
              in government</u>

We may define the following categories of communication:

-   <u>Intra</u>-agency communication, e.g. between departments and offices
    within a ministry. This usually covers short distances (in-house,
    or on same floor), and will constitute a considerable amount of
    information, which should <u>not</u> be public accessible.

-   Data flow <u>between the ministries</u>, which may extend across building. This type of communication is more formal and comprises less amount.

- **Data flow** related to the use of <u>central computer services</u>, comprising considerable amount of data (budget, accounting, payroll statistics) and larger documents for duplication, printing and publishing.

- Communication <u>between</u> the <u>ministries</u> and other <u>governmental agencies</u>.

- <u>External use of public information services</u>. It is believed that use of public accessible information services will increase ssubstantially when they become electronic available through data network.

Today, the status on existing computer and communication facilities characterizes as follows:

- A diversity of equipment in the government, with separate and incompatible networks between these systems.
- Inefficient and costly use of public PTT services.
- Poor data communication facilities between ministries or even between departments within each ministry.

Evidently, there is a need to improve existing datacommunication facilities and to develop new services. We have estimated that there are more than 700 terminals within the ministries today (30 % coverage), and we do believe that within 3-4 years, most offices will be equipped with an intelligent terminal or work stations. This implies that a majority of more than the 3000 civil servants in the central administration will need appropriate computer networking facilities. The future data network that can meet the needs and manage the load generated by these people. Services that should be provided through the network are general interactive access to a variety of systems, electronic mail, file transfer, document handling, mass storage and publishing services.

5.2 AN OVERALL MODEL AND IMPLEMENTATION STRATEGY

The technical and organisational solutions, and the implementation strategy have to meet both short-term and long-term goals. Subsequently, we have defined a strategy as a step-by-step realisation of HYBRID network structure. It should allow the integration of various techniques, and provide flexibility that ofers potential for adjusting solutions to future needs and changed conditions. Important elements in this solution are:

A. Establish a high capasity (broadband) backbone network that covers the central government building square, with extention to remote computer centers. Emphasize will be placed on general and flexible cabling structures, with outlets in each office.

B. Allow for installation of local network and terminal connections to be based on either twisted pair circuits, PC-LANs or general LAN segments.

C. Develop guidelines for implementation of local computer systems including recommendations for services, protocols and important

application development tools to be used. Furthermore, one should
aim at providing standard interfaces, both when connecting,
terminal works stations, host computers and local LANs.

D. Specify and implement higher level services and provide a set of
common network services, as MAIL, message handling, file
transfer, etc. Common protocols for such functions must
be a long term goal, but interim solutions should be allowed when
gateways between these can be provided. A future network
architecture will be based on ISO and CCITT standards (X.25,
TELETEX, MHS, etc.)

E. Co-ordinate the use of PTT services through providing common
gateways and access ports to public network. Simplify access from
outside world to public available data bases in the
administration, while appropriate security messures are taken.

6. CONCLUSIONS

The lesson to be learned from the present situation with uncoordinated approaches is that new technology should not be introduced
partially or unplanned into a functional unit. Even from a
governmentwide perspective it seems to be a demand for better
coordination, or allow for viewing the government as one company.

The intention of this presentation has also been to illustrate how a
well-developed data communication system may serve as a key element
in co-ordinating the use of information technology in the government.
The ultimate goal should be to have individually developed and
operated systems interconnected and voluntarily co-operating by
providing attractive services. Thus, it is widely accepted that
common traffic regulations and rules of the game is required, in
particular when everybody drives his own car.

There will always be a dialectic conflict between standardisation and
individual freedom. The former which requies a central agency or body
with the authority to implement and maintain this structure and may
also prevent innovation and required changes. The decentralized
approach, emphasizes on local autonomy, innovation and
experimentation. It is therefore necessary to evaluate and review the
standards and guidelines that are determined continuously, in order
to avoid a rigid and resource-demanding bureaucracy which maintains
it own existence.

The pendulum will evitably swing in both directions, but not at the
same time.

Governmental and Municipal Information Systems
P. Kovács and E. Straub (Editors)
Elsevier Science Publishers B.V. (North-Holland)
© IFIP, 1988

A COOPERATIVE COMPUTER CENTER OF STATE ADMINISTRATION

by Dr.G.Nyíry - Dr.G.Széphalmi - Dr.J.Tankó

1. INTRODUCTION

The Computer Center of State Administration (CSSA) is unique in Hungary because it is the common computer center of several ministries and state institutions. Other computer centers of the state administration serve only one ministry or institution and they may sell only their excessive capacity to outside users.

CSSA was founded in consequence of a governmental decicion by the Central Statistical Office in Budapest in 1975. It is, however, an independent organization of income interest. Its computer equipments and other means of production are provided by the state budget, but the functional expenses must be covered by fees of services offered. The major task of Center is to satisfy computer demands of institutions financed by state budget, first of all demands of certain fields of state administration assigned to CSSA. CSSA really povides means for and develops several important national basic information systems.

At the time of foundation CSSA was intended only to operate a large common computer system (central computers and network) and to support users. In this early period of planning users were supposed to solve the development of their data bases and systems by themselves and pass them to CSSA for running. It was, however, obvious after a short time, that most of the users were not fully prepared for this task and needed CSSA also to design and develop systems for them. Since 1978 CSSA provides complete computer service for its users on a contractual basis. To meet these demands CSSA has grown up to 350 employees and has been organized accordingly. Through the user institutions the state budget provided more than one billion Ft to develop information systems of state administration based on the computers of CSSA. The realized data bases and application systems altogether are worth of billions of Ft.

2. USERS AND THE MEANS OF CSSA

We give a list of most important users here as follows:
    State Office for Population Registration
    Ministry of Food and Agriculture
    Hungarian Academy of Sciences
    Ministry of Justice
    State Office of Payment and Labour
    General Directorate of Social Insurance
    National Office of Environment and Nature Protection
    National Committee of Technical Development

CSSA is in possession of five Honeywell-Bull computers, some mini- and a lot of microcomputers and a significant number of terminals attached to them. CSSA uses the public information transmission networks of the Hungarian Post, can reach international data bases abroad as well, and will soon join the national packet switching computer network and will take part of different services of these networks.

User institutions of several dozens use our computers via one or more terminal connections. In addition to the interactive program development, the interactive data base retrieval and information flow combined with batch processing represents a greater and greater proportion. This latter activity is growing rapidly and this process will be improved by a planned innovation of the computer basis of CSSA and its connection to the network services in the near future.

3. INFORMATION SYSTEMS ON THE COMPUTERS

Several information systems of national importance operate on the CSSA's computer system. The undisturbed functioning of them is indispensable for the management of certain tasks of the state administration. The simultaneous processing, the management of the shared resources, the scheduling of user activities and processes to coordinate their peak periods require a high degree of organization of CSSA and a lot of management works.

To ensure all these CSSA continuously improves its own capabilities using reasonable computer resources - mainly out of intensive time. The resources used by CSSA to develop application systems for its users are also remarkable. These parts of usage of the resources and services gradually loose their weight. The more and more extending services provided by the information systems and the maintenance of the data bases for these services dominate in the usage. We can demostrate this by a list of the most important information systems in operation on CSSA's computers.

1. Undoubtedly, the biggest state administrative system on CSSA's computers is the Population Registration (PR) System. It contains the most important personal and address data of more than 10 million inhabitants of Hungary together with the personal identification number. The system has been operating continuously since 1980 and it can follow changes in data with a two weeks delay. The system will be developed in two directions in the near future. On the one hand decentralized regional and local data bases will be established beside or instead of the central data base. On the other hand the contents of personal records will be extended by some important additional data like qualification, employment and family relations.

Naturally also the range and content of the system services will be upgraded. Besides, an automatic information service will be set up for other data bases and information systems of state administration which contain data related to persons (social insurance, registration of real estates, financial, cultural and labour systems, etc.). The PR System is getting to be a basis of these systems and a possible connection between them.

2. The second greatest system operating on CSSA's computers and network is undoubtedly the Agrochemical Information and Management System (AIMS). The great quantity of soil test data referring to units of cultivation, collected in laboratories of regional agrochemical centers, as well as data on arable land, crops, soil cultivation and amelioration are stored in AIMS. Its services extends from statistics on soil conditions, production and others to an advisory service and all these are produced in forms of tables, coloured maps and in dialogs. The circle of data and the scale of services of this system are constantly widened and improved.

3. System of Real Estate Registration on CSSA's computers is also an important one. It contains the most important (e.g. geometrical, contextual, functional, legal and application) data of about seven million real estates being revised monthly. Its services carry out not only traditional office functions but orders of different interested institutions as well.

4. Data Base of Land Survey and Cartography is being loaded for some years. This will digitally store mapping data of the territory of the whole country, when it is finished. Data describing geometrical and regional characteristics, the surface, the natural and artificial landmarks, geographical objects, waters, pipes and power lines etc. will be stored so that maps of different functions and of details could be produced from them.

Till now the data for town Szeged and several districts of Budapest have been stored. We continuously actualize stored data. After loading the data an extensive service starts immediately about a given region. A faster loading of data base is not possible now because of shortage of technical means, manpower and financial resources. Our experiences, however, are utilized in the improvement and further development of the system.

This system is of course in close connection with the previous Real Estate Registration System and the range of its utilization and services is almost unlimited.

5. The Information and Management System of Forestry and Wood Industry contais important data on Hungary's forest stand, forest territories and growing stock and it facilitates planning and optimization of stocking, rehabilitation and lumbering.

6. Environment Protection Information System is not yet completed, it is under development. This system will contain a central data base, data bases of different special fields of environment protection and a system integrating these data. Contents and services of the system widen permanently and its importance and volume will significantly increase in the coming years.

7. Legal Information System is storing the text and contextual data of acts and orders of different levels, directions given by the Supreme Court as well as contextual data of jurisprudence. The textual data base is accessigble on-line. The loading of the data base is almost finished, maintenance and service programs are ready, actualization of the text is continuous.

8. The data of different health surveys stored on CSSA's computers are also of great value because they can help the development of health service, the prevention and partly the management works in public health. There are also some operative information systems of smaller significance, e.g. Network of Onkological Radiation Planning, Information System of Hospital.

9. Data bases and functional systems on CSSA's computers in connection with social insurance and social politics realized an important function during many years but these systems where decentralized and transferred to microcomputers after the propagation of PC-s in Hungary.

10. The Hungarian Academy of Sciences also established some data bases on CSSA's hardware providing information for its research and development activities. The National Instrument Registry, the Isotope Registry and the Nuclear Materials Registry are worth to mention here.

4. PROSPECTS

In the second part of the 1980-s it became clear that in order to satisfy the demand of the different management levels for more precise and reliable information, there is a need for organised cooperation between the different information systems of the state administration.

The development of the microelectronics in the previous years has resulted in flexible microprocessor based computers and their usage improves the availability of these information systems. This trend is also strenghtened by the aspiration to further democratize the public life. The informatics of the state administration would promote the service functions against the authoritative aspects. The mentioned principles create new situation also for the base registers of the state administration realized on the CSSA's computers.

The base registers of the main data for natural and artificial persons of the country, for elements of national wealth and for intellectual goods and procedures have to be more reliable because they serve as a base for the whole state administration. Though the registration as a function is independent of the other functions, its preparation, update and usage are parts of the information flows of the state administration.

After the setting up of the base registers in the previous years, their decentralization comes to the front today. The first level of the decentralization is that of the county, which is followed by the local (city, district) level. The definition and establishment of the connection between the information systems of the local authorities and the base registers is a very important and difficult job. Other functional administration systems containing indispensable information to the management on the national economy also belong to the central information systems of the state administration. These are the planing, finance, statistics, labor, foreign trade, priceing and market control systems, etc. Though their development is not a CSSA's mission, the connection of these is a real job for CSSA because of the interdependent nature of the organizations and levels of the state administration.

The development of these multidirectional connections has a great importance in the utilization of the base registers. To reach this aim, we should consider not only hardware and software requirements, but also other aspects, such as appropriate legal environment, proper organizational structures, the necessary resources and the whole complex informatic tools system.

In the establishment and operating of the base registers, the organisation of the state administration as a whole and the legal environment have a particular role. Depending on the actual conditions of informatics and on the organization and democratization of the management, the type of registers and their content and functioning vary.

The CSSA's mission is to support and enforce the general progress of our society on the field of informatics.

Governmental and Municipal Information Systems
P. Kovács and E. Straub (Editors)
Elsevier Science Publishers B.V. (North-Holland)
© IFIP, 1988

REVIEW AND UTILIZATION OF THE STANDARD NATIONAL COMPUTER
LEGAL INFORMATION SYSTEM (LIS)

by Benedek Srajber, Computer Service for State Administration,
H-1119 Budapest, XI. Andor u. 47-49

László Seprődi, Ministry of Justice
H-1055 Budapest, V. Szalay u. 16.

The authors summarize the sub-systems of LIS, created as a result of
several years' development, their substantial and functional characteristics. They outline the technical possibilities of accessing the LIS
and the expectable development, extensions of the application environment.

1. ANTECEDENTS

The starting point for the development of the Standard National Computer Legal
Information System (LIS) is resolution No. 2022/1980 (IX.9.) of the Council of
Ministers, which specifies for the Minister of Justice to organize the Standard
National Computer Legal Information System as a basic state record system of top
significance.

The purpose of this Resolution is "to simplify and speed up for legistlators
and applicators of law the provision of data on laws and legal directives".

The Resolution assigned the function of legal organizational base of LIS to the
Ministry of Justice, and the functions of computer engineereing/organization/op-
erational base to the Central Bureau of Statistics.

The two authorities commissioned the Computational Engineering Applications
Centre of the Ministry of Justice (IM SZAK) and the Computer Service for State
Administration of KSH (ÁSZSZ) with the execution of the above functions.

According to an agreement concluded between the two institutions, the implementation of the information system began in 1982.

The individual stages of implementation are:

1983 - Detailed system plan;
1984 - Data acquisition and maintenance sub-system;
1985 - Interactive and batch output sut-system;
1986 - Integrated testing of sub-system, start of "real" data acquisitions;
1987 - Trial operation, demonstration of the functioning system.

2. DATA CONTENTS OF LIS

Put briefly, the LIS has been created to keep record of laws legal regulations.
When the loading is completed, its data contents will cover about 4 to 5000
laws and legal regulations - those in force from the pre-1982 years and all
laws and regulations published in Magyar Közlöny after 1982.

The levels of regulations contained in the system range from laws enacted by
Parliament to decrees issued by the heads of agencies of national authority

(Ministers, Secretaries of State). Furthermore, the system contains directives issued by the same agencies and "court diretives" issued by the Supreme Court. In addition, the system will include a limited number of legal literature re-ports review of books, articles.

3. SUB-SYSTEMS OF LIS

3.1. Data Acquisition and Maintenance Sub-System

The data acquisition and maintenance sub-system of LIS has the function of gath-ering the data of laws, directives and legal literature reports, to make them suitable for computer processing, to check and continuously up-date them.

The data contents of LIS are classified in the following categories:

- normative laws and regulations
- non-normative laws and regulations
- international treaties
- pre-1945 regulations
- directives issued by ministries and agencies of national scope of authority
- court directives
- legal literature.

Since the acquisitioning and recording of the data are tasks calling for legal qualifications in the legal area concerned and the knowledge of the rules of data acquisitions, these tasks are carried out by staffs of specialists employed in different fields of law and trained in special fields of knowledge, under the supervision and coordination of IM SZAK.

The data acquisitions consist in a thorough perusal of the material to be record-ed, and filling special data forms. The essential feature of this filling pro-cedure is to use only the information in the text of a law, regulation, direc-tive or piece of literature to be recorded, i.e. the data in the text of a law are picked in the order of perusal and entered in the data form.

If, for example, the text of regulation $\underline{A}$ makes reference to the modification of a regulation $\underline{B}$, this piece of information is extracted as MDT=B where MDT (modified) is the name of extraction, $\underline{B}$ being the identifier of the modified law or regulation. If a regulation covers marriage, the words "marriage" is entered in the data form. Such and similar word making reference to the contents are called "descriptors".

As a result of data acquisitions and entries, the laws, regulations and direc-tives as well as the paragraphs thereof are converted into <u>documents</u> and the extracts are converted into fields in the computer system. These terms referred to notions of computational technology alone. The document, the basic unit of records, has an unequivocal identifier and consists of definite fields. The identifier is given an the outset for a regulation; only a few simple rules had to be introduced to establish standard notations. (Act I of 1974 is e.g. denoted as 1/1974. TV:.)

In this case, the fields of the document are the data to be recorded from the regulation or directive - e.g. name of issuing agency, date of entering into force, journal of promulgation etc.

Within a given type of document, each document in the computer system contains the same fields; of course, one or several of them may be blank as well.

As has been mentioned above, it is not necessary at the time of filling the data form to fill all fields of a regulation completely with data. Some of the fields will be filled by programs.

The process of creating the documents and then fields is referred to as "generation". The name of the issuing agency is e.g. an important data of a legal regulation.

In the above example, in recording 1/1974. TV, no reference is made to the
Parliament being the issuing agency; the program can infer this from the identifier. A similar procedure is adopted with legal literature where a simpler
process is involved because the fields are present at the outset.

Legal regulationscontain a number of important data that are not included in the
journal of promulgation. If, for instance, a regulation is repealed, this fact
is never encountered in the text of the journal promulgating that regulation,
but always in the text of another regulation repealing the former one. Accordingly, the date of repealing and the field contents of the repealing regulation
can only be entered in the system at the time of recording another regulation,
as the data of this latter one.

The term "correction" refers to the process of entering a subsequent data in a
field of a law or legal regulation, as a consequence of recording another regulation. The automatic correction by the program is the basic principle of
up-dating the data sets in the LIS, by combining the processes of data acquisition and data maintenance in a common human activity.

The LIS reflects the hierarchic structure of legal regulations.

The top level is the entity of the law or regulation proper. It consists of
paragraphs. Structural parts of the law or legal regulation on the same level
as the paragraph are the clauses, articles, enclosures and appendices. (They
may be referred to as "clauses", but when the term "paragraph" alone is applied,
this refers usually to structural parts being at the same level. A paragraph
may consist of indents, and the latter may consist of sub-sections.)

The LIS contains a stock document of each legal regulation. This is the law or
regulation proper. The values of its field are equally applicable to each part
of the regulation. A document is made of each paragraph (clause, article,
enclosure, appendix), the data of which are applicable to the given paragraph
only.

Against the stock data of the regulation proper, these are referred to as
"partial data". For reasons of economy, the stock data of the regulations are,
as a rule, not stored in the partial data as well; the only exceptions are a
few brief data (e.g. date, name of issuing agency); to facilitate the retrieval,
they are stored in the partial data even when they coincide with the stock data.
In printing the paragraph fields, the program reads the title of the law or regu-
tion , or the regulations on applications, from the stock part of the regulation, when the relevant fields of the paragraph are empty.

3.2. Interactive Sub-System

The functions of the LIS's interactive sub-system are to construct structured
textual data bases and to provide the means of interactive retrieval. These
functions are performed by a software developed on the basis of an Interted File
Processor (IFP) developed earlier at ÁSZSZ.

In the following, the term "data base" refers, in a broad sense, to the storage
in computers of the documents of law/regulation, directive and legal literature
report in a way optimum for retrieval.

Within this complex of data storage, the data base in the strict sense is
differentiated from the thesaurus storing the descriptors in a hierarchic order.

The basic storage unit of the textual data base is the document made up of
fields. As for storage, the fields of a document are classified into four
categories. They are:

- primary,
- secondary,
- ternary fields,
- external identifiers (special fields).

The external identifier (briefly "identifier") is an alphanumeric mark for the
differentiation of the documents of laws/regulations, directives, legal literature reports.

In the structure of the data base, an internal identifier is assigned to each
document in addition to the external identifier.

The internal identifier or serial number of document expresses the number at
which the document has been filled in the data base.

The primary field is a field, the value of which is stored in an inverted file.
A separate inverted file is made for each primary field. The inverted file contains once each value encountered in the field, linking a list of occurrences
to each value; the list includes the internal identifiers of the documents that
contain the given value in the particular field concerned.

The "primary retrieval" is made with reference to the primary fields. It has
the function of retrieving the set of documents containing a value of a field.
The primary retrieval is particularly useful for searches by complex conditions.
A retrieval question formulated in accordance with a complex logic condition
corresponds to logic operations performed in the computer between sets of occurrences.

The secondary fields are the fields, the values of which are stored in documents
(and in fields within a document), and for which secondary retrievals can be performed. The secondary retrieval question may contain various relations for the
values of the individual fields (smaller or greater than, equal to etc.), contained in a complex logic condition. The software system will perform the
secondary retrieval on the documents of a result file containing the result of
the previous retrieval, by checking each field of the document included in the
search question, evaluating the specified relations (true - false) and, on the
basis thereof, the complex logic condition.

The ternary fields are stored in groups in a document, which cannot be the basis
of a retrieval. A ternary field can be displayed only.

The data base in complete with a tesaurus containing the descriptors in a hierarchic order. The tesaurus file implements the relationship between the descriptors with a set of pointers. The following relationships are possible:

- subordinate - superordinate
- synonim
- related
- associated.

An IFP data base can include max. 262143 documents.

About 100000 documents are expected to be contained in the LIS.

Each document may have 63 fields.

The LIS will utilize 62 fields.

Each value in a primary or secondary field may be 60 characters long.

This limit is utilized to full extent by the primary fields; a value in a secondary field is not longer than 10 to 12 characters.

A ternary field may have max. 4095 characters. This limit is by far not utilized in most documents, and will be approximated in a few exceptional instances (e.g. full text of an Appendix).

A document may be about 8000 characters in length.

This is not utilized in most cases.

The tesaurus can manage an 18-level hierarchy.
The LIS utilizes 7 levels.

Each notion may have 20 synonims and 10 relatives at most.

Each notion may have max. 63 subordinates.
Of them, about 10 are utilized in the LIS.

The number of notions in a tesaurus is practically in the tesaurus of LIS.

Two data bases are planned to be used in the LIS. The larger one includes the legal regulations and directives; within this category, the documents are classified in different data spheres (section codes are applied). The smaller one contains the material of legal literature. It consists of a single data here (no section codes are applied).

3.3. Batch Output Sub-System

The batch output sub-system of LIS has the basic function of providing pieces of information suited to the actual purpose, from the stored and systematically arranged data - by batch processing operations.

The functions of the batch output sub-system include

- making output information feasible with a table generator and
- making statistical reports.

3.4. Text Filing Sub-System

This sub-system was elaborated in 1986. Its purposes are handling the entire text of the legal material (input, text change, correction, establishing archive stock, its up-dating and retrieval), separation of legal materials in force from the repealed ones, and making them accessible. The complete text stock is divided into two parts.

a.) The active stock

   includes the complete text of the legal material in force (and the material
   not yet in force but already promulgated). It is up-dated continuously by
   the entry of new text, text changes and corrections (repealing, re-number-
ing).

b.) The archive stock

   is made up of the pre-change state of documents changed in the course of
   up-dating the active full-text legal material and of the repealed documents.

The documents of the active full text can be retrieved by the commands of the interactive sub-system just as the data of the reference data base.

4. TECHNICAL CONDITIONS AND METHODS OF EXTENDING THE LIS

The hardware device base of LIS in constituted by a network system (TPA 1148, terminals) connected to an Honeywell Bull 66/20 D system through a network control unit (FNP) and a background configuration warranting the safety of operation (HwB 66/60). The conditions are provided for the addition of other concentrators and terminals. Developed for the IBM AT, the Micro-JIR software renders assistance in utilizing the actual data base of LIS, above all the sub-set selected to meet the user's demand; it is advisable to use this software primarily in narrow professional applications of law.

5. USER ENVIRONMENT OF LIS

The Ministry of Justice is the primary user of LIS. The supreme authorities utilizing the data base (government agencies, Ministry of Home Trade, Ministry of Internal Affairs, Ministry of Health etc.) are connected to the system through the concentrator installed at the Ministry of Justice.

In the first stage, about 15 to 20 new users are to be added to the system; in the second stage, further jurisdictional and state administration agencies (about 150 in number) are expected to be attached.

The universal demand encountered in council administration work requires a special attention to be focused on the applications of LIS in this environment and to supplementing the system with specific regulations and rules of council work.

BIBLIOGRAPHY

1. Országos Jogi Információs Rendszer (JIR) részletes rendszerterve (Detailed System Plan of LIS)
    ÁSZSZ, 1983.

2. Kovács, A. - Sugár, P. - Vig, E. - Kormos, K. - Apor, Gy.: Az IFP Szöveges Információkezelő Rendszer és alkalmazásai (The Text Information Management System IFP and its Applications)
    2nd Neumann Conference, Székesfehérvár (Hungary), November 14 to 17, 1983.

3. Dr. Seprődi, L.: A szoftverfüggetlen adatlap jelentősége az országos Jogi Információs Rendszerbbben (Significance of Software-Independent Data Form in the LIS)
    2nd Neumann Conference, Székesfehérvár (Hungary), November 14 to 17, 1983.

4. Kovács, A.: A Jogi Információs Rendszer programrendszerének megépitése (Construction of the Software System of the LIS)
    Információ Elektronika 85/4

5. Sajtós, I. - Kovács, A.: Az egységes országos számitógépes jogi információrendszer programrendszere és müködése
    3rd Neumann Conference, Szolnok, 1986.

Governmental and Municipal Information Systems
P. Kovács and E. Straub (Editors)
Elsevier Science Publishers B.V. (North-Holland)
© IFIP, 1988

AN OLD LESSON FROM A RECENT PROJECT

Mihály CSÁKÓ

Sociologist, Dohány u. 16—18, Budapest, Hungary 1077[*]

In the early eighties several office development projects failed because of the employees' reluctance or resistance to use new systems deteriorating their working conditions. Application software tends to be considered complete by experts only when accepted and used by the end-user. An office project aimed at creating a DBMS for the local offices of the house maintenance and management companies in Budapest, Hungary, nearly failed in facing the defaults of the hardware, insufficient memory capacity, a conflict between the needs of everyday functioning and those of innovation in user organization, conflicts between local offices and central management as well as between the user and the computer people, a shortage in space, time, and manpower, employees' insufficient computer culture, etc. It is stressed that even highly qualified analysts, programmers and users with positive attitude to computerization cannot bring success to projects without fulfilling organizational conditions.

1. INTRODUCTION

1.1. General background

A rapidly growing use of personal computers and workstations placed the attitudes to computing in the focus of managers' and consultants' interest. In the eighties a new branch of literature was born to analyze the factors of people's resistance in user organizations and to find methods of eliminating or decreasing it. Even a new interpretation of the concept of a "complete" system is emerging from these publications, withdrawing this qualification from the systems that people refuse to use in practice. Collins [1], Kaye and Sutton [2], Meyer [3], Strassmann [4], and others stressed that employees or at least their representatives have to be involved into the innovation process from its very beginning and that managers' role is critical in this aspect.

When I began to follow an office development project, as a sociologist, I was happy to read these views and shared them. My first hypotheses formulated in a paper at the INTERACT '84 conference of IFIP Working Group 6.3. on human-computer interaction [5] underlined the role of the human factor in the predicted failure or at least difficulties of the project.

Although predictions turned into reality, the hypotheses concerning the predominant role of the human factor could not be proved. [6] There were stronger factors operating to hinder the project studied.

1.2. Basic information on the project

Data of flats and houses are even today gathered manually and stored on paper in the local offices of the companies for the maintenance and management of state-owned properties in Budapest and processed for higher authorities (e.g. for the city council) by a computing centre. (See Figure 1.) Local offices are given a hardcopy of the processed data, but they usually do not use it because it is outdated after an off-line batch processing.

General conditions seemed to be given for a development project in 1983. Number of microcomputers rose sharply in Hungary, the autonomy of public enterprises was growing and the central data base

[*] The study was carried out with the research grant no.395/85-296 of the Soros Foundation and co-sponsored by the Research Institute for Culture, Budapest.

of state-owned flats in Budapest was recently updated and could serve as a starting point to the further development at the same time. In these circumstances decision-makers became convinced that it was high time to start a computerization project at the level of the local maintenance offices.

Following the instructions of the city council and proposals of its computing centre, some of the fifteen companies decided to equip their local units with personal computers to modernize the collecting and preprocessing of data by a DBMS for state-owned flats generating all reports needed at higher organizational levels. The offices to be equipped first with the new system were selected regarding their willingness to participate in the project.

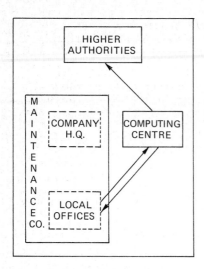

FIGURE 1
Information flow between the
organizations

FIGURE 2
Hierarchy of organizations
participating in the project

Hardware was to be installed and software developed by a subsidiary of the computing centre founded directly for this purpose. (See Figure 2.) The subsidiary engaged analysts and programmers with high qualifications and professional experience. They were motivated by greater autonomy and rewards expected from the new firm as well as by a professional ambition they could not satisfy at their previous jobs. An atmosphere of enthusiasm prevailed: "At last we can show what we are able to do!"

2. FACTORS HINDERING DEVELOPMENT

2.1. Hardware problems

Advantageous signs turned soon into their opposite. A unique situation arose: Hungarian decision-makers reacted too quickly to new technology! Although 1983 seemed to be an ideal moment to start a microcomputerization project since micros entered Hungary in a rapidly growing number, only models with low performance were available.

At the same time, analysts realized that the great quantity of data on state-owned flats cannot be stored and managed with reasonable response time without using Winchester-discs. But this type of device became available in Hungary only two years later.

Why did they not postpone the project until efficient hardware would be available? There were several reasons for it:

(1) No one could actually tell how long they should wait.
(2) Development decision was made by higher officials thinking in political and economic terms rather than technological ones.
(3) Once the new subsidiary of the computing centre was founded and the development perspectives for the house maintenance offices were defined it would not have been possible any more to stop the project and wait for PPCs with Winchester-discs several years.

Thus new system had to be developed with the means available at that moment, i.e. low-scale micros.

Even the software staff's enthusiasm turned into a negative factor facilitating to overlook hardware problems. Analysts and programmers did all they could to match system needs and hardware possibilities. From 1983 to 1986 they developed the DBMS for state-owned flats on four different hardware appearing successively on the hardware market in Hungary: Robotron 5420, TAP 34, Proper 8, and IBM PC. Programmers worked hard all the time to keep pace with the evolution of the market and they succeeded. They were satisfied: their systems run and if they were not used that must be the users' fault.

2.2 Organizational problems

Why did local offices not used the sytems? The main reasons are the following:

(1) The 17 sec minimum response time was found too long by the end-users and considered true only under laboratory conditions. In practice data retrieval in the new computerized data base demanded much more time than in the old paper-based one because of spatial and organizational conditions.
(2) The new data base system did not fit into the work organization scheme of most local offices.
(3) Changing of data base system raised significantly employees' workload in local offices.
(4) Local offices do not really need the new system, while their positive needs remained unsatisfied.

Organizational problems arose because microcomputers were installed in the offices following a "one machine/one office" scheme. So data can be accessed via only one keyboard and one display in each office in spite of the fact that should be used by several employees at the same time. This problem can be solved only by a multiuser system. It is true that using the old manual system employees could have access all at once to the filing shelves.

The newly developed system met the demand of the higher authorities for global information once a month, but it could not support the everyday activities of local offices. In consequence, employees have to continue using paper-based filing system in their everyday work and, in addition, update computerized data base to generate reports to higher authorities once a month. (See Figure 3.)

BEFORE				
Non-computerized activities	Paper-based filing	Generating reports to higher level		
AFTER				
Non-computerized activities	Paper-based filing	Updating computerized data base	Generating reports	Train-ing

FIGURE 3
Activities of local offices before and after the installation of computerized data base

Besides their growing workload, office workers were obliged to take part in training courses, too. It is a poor consolation for them that generating report with micros needs only a couple of hours instead of a couple of days like before: these days are now spent to update the new data base.

So neither time, nor space, nor work could be saved by the new system in the end-user offices. Why should office workers be ready to use it under these conditions?

2.3. Local managers' role

If the employees of local house maintenance offices did not go on strike nor listed their demands in petitions nor began to negotiate through unions like their colleagues in Western countries do in similar cases, it is because they were saved from the disadvantages of the PC project by their office heads. The latter are forced to defend the staff's interests by a grave shortage in manpower and a high turnover rate in the state-owned property maintenance offices. Offices work constantly with minimal personnel and follow a scheme of work organization that cannot bear one person missing without troubles in functioning.

This fact was overlooked in feasibility studies, and managerial promises to solve problems were accepted. In practice, it is staff rather than new technology that managers need: the activities for everyday functioning are of higher priority than those for innovation under the conditions of scarce resources.

Higher management did not offer supplementary resources to support the project at local level, considering microcomputerization as a resource-saving innovation. Thus the needs of higher authorities were to be satisfied through a growing workload at the office level.

This inner problem of the house maintenance companies manifested in an overt conflict between the computing service company striving to install the new system and local office heads resisting this effort in defence of normal functioning of the offices. (See Figure 4.)

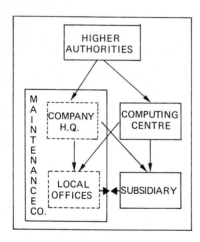

FIGURE 4
The point of conflict:
resistance to development

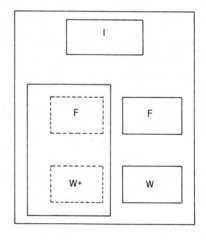

FIGURE 5
Distribution of advantages
and disadvantages

Most innovative office heads had another reason to resist the development of a computerized data base system. They realized that they rather needed financial and storage management programmes to support their own managerial work. As they had to accept the higher decision giving priority to the data base of flats and postpone their local needs, they felt frustration and lost enthusiasm toward the project.

When surveying office heads I found that those participating in the project felt having less autonomy in their work than others did, contradicting the reality. As a consequence of their situation they began to consider computer people as the representatives of higher authorities.

2.4. Structural problems

The organizational structure of decision-making and execution of the studied project offered only one point where problems, tensions, conflicts could explose: between the local offices and the service subsidiary. This statement can be supported by answering the following questions:

(1) Where is the output information of the new system needed? (The answer is marked with "I" on Figure 5.)
(2) Where should the financing of the project come from? (These places are indicated with "F".)
(3) Where should people work for the project? (In this case "W" indicates fully paid work, "W+" marks supplementary work without supplementary payment.)

Answers marked on Figure 5 show that the advantages of the project do not appear at the same organizations where the disadvantages occur. Such a distribution could cause conflicts, but it was experienced only between the organizations at the lowest level: local offices on one side and computing service subsidiary on the other.

A trivial question arises: Why did house maintenance companies start a development project under these conditions? Why did local offices want to participate in the project?

First, general directors felt a pressure of higher authorities (e.g. city council) and hoped — at the same time — that a project supported by these authorities should be successful at least in the long run. Regarding the office heads, after the decision made at company level they had no other choice left that "take it or leave it". As Mayo's old experience on "Hawthorn effect" proved: a guinea pig's position is always a desirable one, and particularly desirable in a socialist economy.

To be selected for an experiment offers practical advantages and privileges that every ambitious manager should grasp. It is true that the studied project has not yet offered such rewards at local level, but it can be expected to do so in the future because this belongs to the very essence of the socio-economic system. Office heads can even hope that local needs will be met in further steps of the development.

3. CONCLUSIONS

The authors I have referred to at the beginning of this paper would say the project failed, since it has not achieved any of the goals defined and put on paper at the starting point. After three years only a couple of the offices involved try to use the new system.

But success and failure are relative terms depending on the criteria used. The fact that some kind of hardware and software is installed and can be used in these offices, some employees and office heads have had their first experience with them, are considered by the decision-makers and project managers as the first step on a long way towards computerized offices. In this sense, changing criteria defined earlier, they do not tend to qualify the project failed.

Willing to express this attitude, I published the case study on the project with the title "Micro-success" indicating the subject, the result, and its measure at the same time. [7]

Most of the lessons offered by the project could be drawn before starting it. The moment the project started in 1983, an explicit warning could be read: "Commitment by the organization does not necesserily show commitment by people." (Conner [8]) As we have seen this does not apply only to organization/people dichotomy but to the relationship between grades of an organizational hierarchy.

The author quoted distinguishes more than 25 reasons for people's resistance. In the project studied these motives were taken into account by local managers without knowing the list. Employees were not directly involved — usually they are not in other countries either, except perhaps Sweden — but their interests were defended by office heads. Thus the managers' role proved to be even more important than several authors underlined it (e.g. Gibson et al. [8] and EDP Analyzer [9], [10]).

Organizational conditions of development projects tend to be more complex in Hungary than in Western economies, since development decisions are often made at a level higher than that of the target organization. So development planning should tackle not only the inner problems of one organization as it is usually done in Western countries, but also the problems of relationship between organizations (central and municipal administration, industrial and service companies, even political organizations). If such a wider approach to organizational problems is neglected in decision-making and planning process, projects can achieve only "micro-success" under the conditions of the institutional and economic systems of Hungary.

REFERENCES

[1]   Collins, Frank and Mooroe, Tom, Microprocessors in the Office: a Study of Resistance to Change, Journal of Systems Management, November 1983.
[2]   Kaye, A.R. and Sutton, M.J.D., Productivity and Quality of Working Life for Office Principals and the Implications for Office Automation, Office: Technology & People, Vol.2, No.4 (December 1985).
[3]   Meyer, N. Dean, Power and Credibility in Office Automation, Datamation, Vol.31, No.15 (August 1, 1985).
[4]   Strassmann, P.A., Information Payoff: the Transformation of Work in the Electronic Age, The Free Press, New York, 1985.
[5]   Csákó, Mihály and Tolnai, László, Microcomputer Installations in "Computer-untouched" Environments. Paper presented at INTERACT '84 the 1st IFIP Conference on Human-Computer Interaction, London, 4—7 September 1984.
[6]   Csákó, Mihály, The Quasi-zero Degree of Microcomputerization: Its Social and Human Background and Impact in Hungary. Paper presented at the 4th Workshop on Capitalist and Socialist Organizations, Budapest, 3—6 June 1986.
[7]   Csákó, Mihály, Mikrosiker, Művelődéskutató Intézet, Budapest, 1987. (Micro-success)
[8]   Conner, Daryl R., Building Commitment to Technological Change, O.D. Resources, Atlanta, 1983.
[9]   Gibson, Cyrus F., Davenport, T., and Schnidman, A., Strategies for Making an Information System Fit to Your Organization, Management Review, January 1984.
[10]   Human Side of Office Automation, EDP Analyzer, Vol.20, No.5 (May 1982).
[11]   Manage the Impact of Systems on People, EDP Analyzer, Vol.23, No.5 (May 1985).

Governmental and Municipal Information Systems
P. Kovács and E. Straub (Editors)
Elsevier Science Publishers B.V. (North-Holland)
© IFIP, 1988

EVALUATION OF ASPECTS OF COMPOSITION AND DECOMPOSITION IN THE
DEVELOPMENT OF INFORMATION SYSTEMS

Cees SCHRAMA

European Institute of Public Administration
O.L. Vrouweplein 22
6211 HE Maastricht, The Netherlands

Abstract

The development of information systems (IS) has often been treated
too simply. The steps taken were: analysis, design, implementation,
verification and production.
The very large load on maintenance (including migration,
adaptations and corrections) has almost become a burden and many
attempts are being undertaken to improve the development process in
order to avoid, or rather anticipate, changes at a later stage.
The steps to be taken in these architectural layers will be
illustrated and the individual contents discussed. These steps are:
enterprise analysis, business analysis, information systems
analysis, project study, implementation plan, composition of
functions and data, system analysis, data analysis, network
analysis, application analysis, design, implementation and
verification.
When each step is considered in detail it becomes apparent that
while one step is more decomposition-oriented, another is more
composition-oriented. The method of development should not focus on
composition or decomposition individually but should, where
applicable, use both concepts.

1. INTRODUCTION

The area of automation is increasing dramatically. Where only a few years ago
a select group of specialists created and used sophisticated machinery in a
complex way, nowadays more and more computers are being used by more and more
people reaching more and more areas of our society.
This will inevitably lead to enormous problems. Computers and their software
will increase in capacity and internal complexity, while the increase in the
number of users will require easily accessible programs.
The specialists in the automation profession will have to proceed according
to certain criteria. However, the experts have not yet come to a general
agreement on the methodologies to be used in the system/application
development.

In general, two streams can be distinguished in system development: top-down
(decomposition) and bottom-up (composition) development. Both methodologies
have been used with varying results and no agreement has been reached on the
best way to develop systems. As the need for automation experts is increasing
sharply, nearly every form of implementation has been accepted by the user,
as long as solutions to the urgent problems are found.

It is time that the experts reach agreement on the methodologies to be used
in what phase of a development process, which will lead to an acceptable

standard way of working. This paper intends to start combining various aspects and to indicate how the development process can be performed on a coherent basis.
It will not only reflect the implementation aspects but also address the (often overlooked) point of serving the changing world which implies the evolution of the systems to handle changing processes, data and organizations. When large systems have to be implemented, an overall architecture needs to be provided to keep control. Aspects reflecting business or public domain, the necessary information, the required network, all have to be architecturally described so that a coherent system can be provided.

2. OVERVIEW OF SOME OF THE IMPORTANT ASPECTS IN THE SOFTWARE DEVELOPMENT PROCESS

The software development process is evolving in a strange way. On the one hand the implemented systems and the total environment which has to be served are becoming more and more complex. Knowledge as to what is contained in certain procedures and how business processes are being performed is often no longer obvious as it is 'hidden' in some complex application.

On the other hand the availability of personal computers makes a set of small applications accessible to the end user. In this overview only some of the many aspects will be addressed briefly: information systems, the increasing demand on human resources, maintenance, composition, decomposition.

2.1 Information Systems

To support an organization in its information needs, information systems (IS) have been developed: often large to very large systems covering most of the information needed in an organization. In the past IS were developed as large systems, providing services, with static orientation. The users had to follow the structures and the way of working which were established by the IS. The developers of the system were seen more or less as magicians; they decided if and how certain functions could be performed. The users were mostly incapable of acting as a reasonable discussion partner for the automation expert and vice versa. The systems developed were often very unfriendly and access often encountered considerable resistance. Organizational aspects were not considered in the design of an IS at all. This led to dissatisfaction and resistance by the users and to the statement often heard: 'The computer is not doing what we want' or 'it makes nearly all human labour superfluous'. Of course many activities, especially the routine labour can to a large extent be performed by a computer, but more than being used instead of human labour, computers should be used as addition to human activities; computers can assist users by providing information, performing calculations and permit large filing possibilities in addition to opening up nearly unlimited communication capacities. The large penetration of personal computers and home computers made the user more aware of its possibilities and its (few) impossibilities. The market is providing many computer languages claiming to be easy to use and have many capabilities. They are making the user more aware of how to use a computer in order to support his activities. This will lead to new or changing requirements and subsequently to the development of application software leading to new or adapted information systems. An increasingly important factor in the development of an IS is the organization: how is it working today and how will it work tomorrow.

The systems developed will have to be flexible in order to anticipate changes in the near future. In addition it is recommended that they be integrated into the total organization, linked to other systems and fitted into the infrastructure of the organization. This tailoring to the specific needs of the users shows a shift from centralization towards decentralization. This has an organizational consequence as well: decentralization of functions will be accompanied by decentralization of power.

The information system should contain all the ingredients of the organization, its processes and its information. To be able to describe them with all the consequences, the need for architecture becomes apparent. Of course, in theory, architecture should always have been made first, but in the development of information systems in the past the development process often started by designing parts bit by bit and later gluing them together. Development without architecture will generally fail when a complex system has to be developed.

2.2 The Increasing Demand on Human Resources

Software is developed and used by people. In the near future there will be an increasing number of requests for specialists in the software and hardware professions to not only keep the existent systems going (and possibly reduce maintenance effort) but to assist in the development process. Great efforts have to be made to improve the knowledge in this relatively new software development profession.
There will be a large demand for specialists:
- to create increasingly complex computers able to handle specific requests for new functions (e.g. voice recognition, high density megachips, associative memory);
- to create systems capable of accessing newly developed computers (expert systems, applicable operating systems, CAD/CAM and CIM systems);
- to create user-friendly programs to improve communication between the complex systems and the user;
- to create networks for implementing infrastructures and allow easy access to different computers, systems, applications and users.

At the moment there is already a shortage of these specialists and in the near future this shortage will increase. At the IFIP conference in Dublin (1986) it was stated that in Japan a shortage of 900 000 software specialists is expected by 1990.
That is not all. More and more areas of our society have plans for automation. This will lead to a large demand for system analysts needing to know the specific area for which a system has to be developed as well as the possibilities of the computer.
These analysts have to be recruited from the user community which, in the years to come, will need many educational programmes mainly on how the specific specializations can be assisted by automation, which parts can be automated and what role the computer can play. But the computer expert also needs education to be able to acquire more and more knowledge of the society and organizational aspects which will be required. The user analyst and the computer expert need a basic understanding of each other profession to be able to communicate. It is necessary to take a look at how application systems have been developed, what the problems which have been encountered are and in what way solutions can be identified. It is of great importance to agree on a standardized way of developing systems and applications to be able to provide the necessary integration. An agreement is needed about the methods to be used in the software development process.

2.3 Software Development Process - Maintenance Aspects

It is surprising that program development, which is basically very mathematically-oriented, was performed in a trial-and-error manner for many years. Of course there were both exceptions and excuses. It was possible for very small programs to be developed without error and some experts stated that this could be extrapolated to large programs and complex systems as well

(Dijkstra). However, in reality it was not that simple: customers were not willing to pay a very high price for the products and preferred a lower price with some risk of small problems. Repair workshops earned their living because of the imperfections of various products ranging from cars and houses to computers. The request was increasingly heard that these repairs had to be reduced because labour costs for repairs were going up. So industries looked for better materials for their products, needing less repair and with all kinds of detecting mechanisms for preventing problems from occurring and indicating as far as possible the cause of a problem when it occurred. For quite a time in software development structured concepts were followed (1).

Development was performed in the following steps:
- gathering of requirements
- make a design
- implement design by coding
- testing
- maintenance.

The opinion was that whenever the design and coding were done correctly (structured) and adequate testing carried out the final product should work fine and maintenance should be minimal. However, this was proved to be wrong; maintenance has absorbed 70-80% of the total software budget. Not only due to real errors, but mainly to:
- improvements - due to the dissatisfaction on the users' side (e.g. performance);
- adaptations - due to changes in the users' environment;
- migration - due to the capabilities of new technology (e.g. use new equipment);
- linkage to other systems - due to infrastructure requirements;
- restriction removal - some limitations are no longer needed.

M.M. Lehman proposed that maintenance not be seen as the final step, but to integrate maintenance in the total life-cycle from the start. His papers were generally accepted with enthusiasm by the experts (2).
They gave an explanation of the inevitable existence of maintenance due to the evolutionary process of the information systems in support of an evolving society.
The evolving principles will apply fully to the Information Systems development.

2.4 Decomposition Aspects

Decomposition has often been carried out in order to refine broad functions resulting in a set of tasks. This process is called 'Functional Decomposition'.
But that is not all. Whenever a task is to be implemented, the necessary steps to be taken are design and code. In this process a decomposition process is often followed to be able to provide a high level as well as a detailed design. These two decomposition processes are known and often extensively used.
For all but the most trivial of application concepts, transformation has to be carried in order to achieve a piece which is sufficiently small to be viewed as a single act.
This sufficiently small piece can also be called an 'independent procedure'.

The development process can be seen as being two large steps:
(a) Abstraction process to be able to provide a formal specification from an application concept.
(b) Reification process to decompose a formal specification into an operational system.
The first step, abstraction towards a model, has some composition aspects.

Going from a real world, which is not mathematically described, towards a model, is never possible to prove to be totally correct.
The second step, decomposition into smaller (sub)processes can be proved as to correctness.

Quality has become one of the most important aspects of software. Aiming at error-free code and reduction in development costs necessitates regular reconsideration of the working methods and tools used. Improvement in the implementation aspect by performing inspections and testing has been a step forward towards quality achievement. Software engineering principles, as indicated by Mills (3), provide a way to rigid design and implementation and the number of errors is decreasing; it seems to be the right way.

2.5 Changing User Requirements

Information systems have to serve a changing world and to be effective the systems have to be flexible. Because it is a costly affair to regularly create new systems, the following possibilities have to be investigated:
(a) Creation of flexible, modifiable software by modular design.
(b) Change static life cycle into evolving development process.
(c) More independence of hardware.
(d) More involvement of end-users in increasing the reality of the model (e.g. prototyping).
(e) Shorter planning cycle.

How does a system act? How is it viewed? The fact that there is more than one view of a system is often overlooked. Various (types of) users have different perspectives. It is important to collect these views and represent them in a model. New requirements have to be analyzed with regard to that model. These views can be collected via interviews, surveys, studies of the existing systems and studies of the procedures which have to be followed.
In principle the requirements expressed by multiple users in their (multiple native) languages are not exact, often ambiguous and sometimes contradicting.
In addition, it is not possible to prove if a model, made as an abstraction of the real world, is correct.
The goal should be to optimalize the requirement analysis process and to achieve optimalization the following principles are recommended:
(a) uniform expression
(b) exact expression
(c) user-friendliness

Many attempts have been made to develop methods to be used. However so far no agreement has been reached on a standard.

It is necessary to be able to compose the various requirements in a comprehensive model. However this is still an area where no rigid methods are available and where much time (and money) is spent with little guarantee of success as to quality improvement and cost savings.

How are requirements collected, analyzed, turned into specifications and design? What is the linkage between the requirements and the existing systems? How can the final design be realized with minimum cost and maximum quality? At the 2nd Conference for Software Maintenance in Washington in 1985, 'Les' Belady, director of MCC, stated that in large systems the cost of software is only for 50% related to 'downstream' activities: specifications, languages, compiling, testing. The other half is spent on 'upstream' activities: to explore different design alternatives, (fuzzy) requirements collection and analyzing. In these areas so much time is lost because of the lack of computer aids and 'try and redo' because of lack of knowledge.
Limiting improvements to these 'downstream' activities can only provide a theoretical productivity improvement of at most 50%.

2.6 Implementation Composition Aspects

As an entire application is often very difficult to survey, M. Jackson (4)
encourages composition methodology. Take small pieces of the real world which
are surveyable and develop an application to support their pieces. Later,
combine many of these smaller units into a larger system. Jackson's design
methodology is based upon a formal description of a program's input and
output data structures. An feasible program is constructed through a series
of small sequential steps.
The design steps to be taken are:
(a) The real world is described in terms of events and their sequence.
(b) A working model of the real world is specified in terms of sequential
    processes.
(c) The functions of the system are specified by adding operations and
    processes to the specification.
(d) The resulting specification is implemented on one or more processors.

The main difference from the decomposition view is that at the start of the
composition real events are selected ('data'), around which processes emerge
at at later stage. It is often easier to start discussing real events than
some abstract data type.
We have to look at the development process at a whole to indicate the value
of the composition and decomposition.

3. SOFTWARE DEVELOPMENT ARCHITECTURE

An application development life cycle which reflects the changing nature of
requirements is proposed as one solution to these problems. The needs
expressed above should be handled in this life cycle. The evolving aspect
should lead to small applications being developed which can be produced in a
short time, changed quickly, installed easily, and made portable.

When developing a large system it is necessary to define a system, network
and data architecture to control the interfaces between the applications.
When a large application is split into a set of small applications it is
necessary to have a system architecture overview to be able to indicate the
links between sub-applications and with the external systems. Many
applications need a life cycle which does not assume fixed requirements. This
life cycle has to focus on a staged and modular approach where stress is on
fast delivery and easy change rather than total completeness. This life cycle
creates a natural link between IS development and end-user programming. It
will increase IS and user productivity by allowing IS to focus on tasks that
require systems skills and users to focus on tasks that demand detailed
knowledge of functional requirements.

This life cycle also promotes a stronger relationship between IS and users.
IS will have to become more aware of business changes, and users will have to
understand how business changes make an impact on their systems. For the
development of a large application, a breakdown into smaller applications is
necessary. This type of application development must be preceded by a
business architecture layer and an information processing architectural
layer, which includes system and data architecture.

3.1 Architectural Strategy

In the evolving development life cycle three layers are recommended:
(a) Business architecture, which sets the strategic direction and defines the
    processes and data at high level.
(b) Information processing architecture, which defines the set of
    applications needed to carry out the processes defined in the business

architecture. It will identify detailed processes, leading to functions, define the data needed, define interfaces with other applications and systems in line with a network architecture and, finally, define the support needed to run the applications.

(c) Implementation architecture, which defines the implementation steps of a (sub)application. Here well-known phrases like design, implementation and testing are used.

Business (/Administration) Architecture

Business architecture is required to provide a solid base for the total development process. It contains the fundamentals for the information processing architecture, where process data, support systems and network architecture are performed. In business architecture the following can 'be identified:

- enterprise analysis: to indicate the business domain
- business analysis
- information systems planning.

There are some basic elements in business architecture: management, organization, processes to be performed and data to be made available/delivered. In the past, when mainly operational systems were developed, the processes received considerable attention. Information was seen as being needed to perform processes. This is changing. It is becoming important to have data available to serve information retrieval needs as well. Information centres and personal computers have had great impact on the information world. If we want to anticipate this with the business architecture for the near future as well as for the current situation, it will be clear that the data definitions have to receive a high level of attention. The responsibility for defining the business data is with data administration.

Information Processing Architecture

The information processing architecture will contain various aspects. The user will express his needs at a high level. An investigation will be performed as to the way in which this need can be fulfilled by transforming these basic needs into high-level requirements. Data needed to serve the functions needed will be expressed. Refinement of processes can be performed. In this phase the following can be distinguished:

- process decomposition: leading to implementable functions;
- data architecture: leading to data base design;
- network architecture: define both inter- and intra-system connections;
- support architecture: define the way the applications will be run.

When we are defining our functions and data a fundamental problem arises: while it is possible to refine processes to a large extent, data is described by:

- entity
- relationship
- attribute

It is important to relate these entities to each other: identify relationships.

It is apparent that the nature of data easily leads to composition.

Implementation Layer

Application development should reflect the evolving nature of requirements. It should be quite easy to make changes. Each application will be developed as follows:

- delivery in stages with a short life cycle
  Stages are characterized by:

  * fast delivery
  * limited number of functions.

Each stage will be run in production. At each stage an investigation will
be carried out to find out if new requirements will fit the existing
application. If not a new application will be defined and developed.
Emphasis will be put on developing a set of small applications rather
than a very large one.
- Phased development of stages.
  In this stage the 'known' steps are:
  * model application with a subset of the high-level requirements
  * design: use prototype
  * implementation: conversion of design into coding
  * verification test
  * finally: production.

This phase concept is very similar to the existing life cycle but the
fundamental difference is that the implementation layer is preceded by the
business and information processing layer.

4.   SEQUENCE OF STEPS IN THE DEVELOPMENT PROCESS

4.1 Enterprise Analysis

Before anything else can be done an enterprise should first perform an
analysis of its current and future directions. Studies of the general market
and a financial analysis should lead the enterprise to strategic planning of
its business. In the past this was practically neglected due mainly to the
stability of the market. Take as an example stores where people can buy their
goods: one store sold books, another records, another meat, another cheese
and milk, another flowers, etc. Every shop has its own speciality and knows
the market, the competitors and the wishes of the clients. Nowadays an
enterprise has to be much more flexible and frequently consider whether the
range of products to be sold (or manufactured) should be increased to reach a
wider set of customers or simply decreased to shed products which do not sell
well. A company can consider entering the computer business, but then which
sector: hardware (PCs, large computers, printers, screens), software
(operating systems, applications, expert systems), network (OSI), etc.
For a public organization the driving forces are often political and
budgetary driven, leading to an increase or simply to a decrease in services
(privatization). The output of the enterprise analysis is to identify the
businesses (or services) which should be performed.

4.2 Business Analysis

For each business an extensive analysis should be performed. The critical
success factors for the business and the business processes needed to achieve
this have to be defined. Organizational and management structures necessary
to obtain the CSF have to be analyzed. van Schaik (5) identified as
management aspects:
(a) Setup of management system
(b) Growth of management system
(c) Control technology aspect in relation to management system
(d) Planning of development, resources and services
(e) Strategy planning

The output of the business analysis is the identification of information
systems.

4.3 Information Systems Planning

Part of the business architecture is an information systems planning. To do
this a method has to be followed to achieve optimal results. A possible

method is Business Systems Planning (BSP), currently being supported by a tool: ISMOD (see Blokdijk (6)). It provides an excellent overview of the organizational process and data aspect and can be used to provide a cost-benefit analysis.

It is important to perform studies in a uniform way to be able to merge studies from various functions to acquire an overall view of the enterprise. The basic elements in the business architecture are: management, organization, processes to be performed and data to be available/delivered. The output of information systems planning are projects possible to be implemented.

4.4 Project Study

For each project identified a cost-benefit analysis has to be performed to justify possible automation.
Existing (information) systems have to be studied to find out whether adaptation can fulfil requirements.
A system has to be created and resources have to be allocated. The output of the project study is an identification of an implementation system.

4.5 Implementation Plan

An implementation plan has to be made, needs have to be described and a conversion of the needs into functions has to be performed. High-level requirements have to be defined. User interfaces have to be defined; a first prototype may be used to illustrate the user interfaces. The output is a set of implementable functions.

4.6 Composition of Functions and Data

So far the steps are in general top-down oriented. To continue however it is necessary to perform a **composition**. Data has to be defined and as it is often already available in existing data bases studies have to be made into how far a composition of data can be performed.
Functions may be available already in implemented form and can then be re-used. These existing 'building blocks' can be composed from a framework of the implemented system. Currently the re-use of functions (or code) is not often performed, mainly due to a lack of information about where those functions can be found. Finally the interfaces with existing systems has to be analyzed, which lead to another composition: integration of a new system into the existing systems. This process leads to a system analysis, data analysis and network analysis.

4.7 System Analysis

Once a system is composed, a decomposition into smaller units, sub-systems, is performed. Note that these sub-systems are not equal to the implementable functions defined in 4.5. They may contain one or more of these functions, contain links to existing systems, in short be a composite set of functions and data.
Investigation of hardware and software criteria should be performed. Performance and security criteria should be defined.

4.8 Data Analysis

With regard to data analysis the following areas can be distinguished:
(a) entity - relationship definition
(b) identification of attributes
(c) logical data design
(d) performance analysis

(e) investigation of connection to existing data bases
(f) physical data base design
(g) tuning performance of operational system

These steps illustrate the composition process which occurs between the
logical and physical design.
It is the job of the data analyst to discuss with the client the elements of
the final system and derive the entity/relationship model from these.

4.9 Network Analysis

The infrastructure of the organization can necessitate the analysis of the
network in which the new information system will have to be located.
Decentralization requirements and the availability of various equipment
(personal computers) will make analysis of the network necessary.

4.10   Application Analysis

The system, data and network analysis has led to the definition of set of
applications to be developed. To be able to implement these applications an
analysis is needed to refine its contents: refinement of requirements,
refinement of data and a definition of implementable stages. Note that there
is no definite separation between this step and the previous three steps. For
not too large applications the application analysis is not considered a
separate step.

4.11   Design

Decomposition of the stage to be developed will be performed. Design
statements will be provided ('pseudo-code').
A prototype will illustrate the interfaces with the user and with other
applications and systems in detail and provide a window to the underlying
design.

4.12   Implementation

The 'pseudo-code' will be converted into real code. Environmental aspects
will be implemented. Note that code generation will eventually automate this
step but not all the previous steps. Of course, as the conversion process is
very time-consuming, significant reductions in time will occur, but not as
much as the sellers of code generators want the user community to believe.

4.13   Verification

Whenever the code is written it has to be tested against the stated
functions. Performance and security constraints as defined have to be
evaluated. The application has to be adapted to the overall system to which
it belongs; this requires an extensive test to guarantee that the original
functions are still being performed.
Performance and tuning aspect when running the application in reality has to
be evaluated.
To foresee problems at an earlier stage with regard to the performance and
tuning for complex application, a simulation model is often made early in the
process.

5.   CONCLUSION

The evolution in information systems, in addition to an increase in user
participation, necessitates a clearer view of the development process than is
mostly obtained. A coherent architecture has to be defined to be able to have

a framework for discussion between the information technology expert and the user.

Elements which are composing as well as those which are decomposing in nature have to be taken into consideration. This report is intended to give some indication of what the linkage is between the various elements of the development process.

A detailed breakdown of the total information system development process has been discussed; these steps fit into an overall architectural framework and might be the start towards an eventual general agreement on what a standardized development process should contain.

NOTES

(1) Stevens, W., Meyers, G., and Constantine, L., in their work: 'Structured Design', 1972.
(2) Lehman, M.M., 'Programs, Life Cycles and Laws of Software Evolution', IEEE proceedings, Vol. 68, No. 9, September 1980; and 'Program Evolution', presentation at the IFIP Working Conference on System Description Methodologies, 1983.
(3) Linger, Mills and Witt, 'Structured Programming', Addison-Wesley, ISBN 0-201-14461-1.
(4) Jackson, M.A., 'Principles of Program Design', Academic Press, 1975.
(5) van Schaik, E., 'A Management System for the Information Business: Organizational Analysis' by Prentice Hall, Inc., ISBN 0-13-5499665-8). The output of the business analysis is the identification of information systems.
(6) Blokdijk, A. and P., 'Planning and Design of Information Systems', Academic Press, 1987.

Governmental and Municipal Information Systems
P. Kovács and E. Straub (Editors)
Elsevier Science Publishers B.V. (North-Holland)
© IFIP, 1988

INSTRUMENTAL SYSTEM FOR COMPUTER — AIDED MANAGERIAL SYSTEMS DESIGN

Dr. Yu.M. Cherkasov, Dr. V.I. Yalovetsky

NPO ASU "MOSKVA", Moscow, USSR *

The dialogue system considered in this paper is an instrumental facility for   designing and realization of application dialogue systems in a complex   computer-aided management system called "Moscow" (CAMS "Moscow").

The "Moscow" computer-aided management system consists of hierarchical assembly of the interactive control systems of different levels and represents a facility of perfecting the municipal management by applying econometrical methods and new information processing approaches. The CAMS "Moscow"   provides automatic data acquisition and processing of information on economic, social, political and ecological processes taking place in a sity to make scientifically based, planned and effective decisions on purposeful, proportional municipal development [1].

Within the framework of general conception of typical   program facilities of developing the CAMS "Moscow", software complex, an instrumental dialogue system (IDS) is designed [2].

The most important requerement of a dialogue system is invariability in relation to a concrete task and subject. The process of man's decision in his subject area happens to have no formal analogue yet, as it represents the intellectual activity due to the knowledge of problem   conditions. The outer manifestation of this activity is the natural language.

The dialogue system is oriented on realization of man-computer procedures for taking decisions and developing information systems.

The descriptive means of the dialogue language are oriented on the problem user. The instrumental dialogue language is a tool for constructing an information-computer model of the dialogue process i.e. a script of the decision-making process. When describing the script the user introduces the terms of the subject field in which the task is solved. As the result of the learning stage the script obtained is the model of the problem task.

Realization of the decision-making procedure consists in the dialogue interpretation of the model in the terms of the problem area. As far as the instrumental dialogue language doesn't possess the progmatic power of the natural language, the lexics of it developped in such a way, that the problem user should be the intellectual link in the man-computer procedure. Then interaction of the non-formulized problem knowledge and the information-computer model will allow to realize complex decision-making tasks.

In the instrumental dialogue system the following main principles are realized:

1. The IDS represents an integrated system the function of which is realized by a data set with a unified interface between the program components.

2. The IDS is realized according to the module principle.

3. The interface between the user and the applied programs in based on the conception of "window", "menu" and functional commands (orders).

4. The bases of the dialogue model is the algorithm specification of the problem task (screen formatting, construction of the information-logic structure etc.).

5. The script of the man-computer procedure is interpreted by the dialogue processor.

In the architecture of the instrumental dialogue system we may allocate the following components: specification of the dialogue processes language and their implementation; syntactic analizer; semantic processor of the information model realization DP; the driver maintaining the videoterminals; the interface facilities to switch on the application programs; the information entry and data communication in the dialogue processes.

---

* 113054, Bahrushina st., 18, NPO ASU "MOSKVA", USSR.

The information model of the dialogue process (DP) is mastered in the form of a graph of the dialogue process, the verteces of which define actions and the arcs : the order of these actions. In the process of the information model construction control of logic structure update is executed.

The IDS possesses 9 types of verteces, which in the respect of informational content and the operations assigned.The verteces and their functions are as follows:

1. Initial vertex (type 01). It contains a unique name and a dialogue script (DS) identificator, which is a key to a look-up of a script, pointed out by a user from the directory. An Initial Vertex contains also an information about the purpose of a dialogue process (DP) of the problem solving. This vertex should be the first and unique in a script.

2. Information vertex (type 02). It may contain any information: reference information, explanatory or prompting. The number of informational vertex is arbitrary as well as their place in a graph.

3. Receiving vertex (type 03) is aimed to receive the values of parameteres, which the user is suggested to type at the display during the interface session with a system. The values of parametres are used in the user's application programs, which should be executed during the DP. At the stage of a DP script design, while writing the application program, a user defines the changable parametres, writes down their identificators and length at the receiving vertex. At the stage of a dialogue regime, when the receiving vertex is processed, the user input values of patametres into the indicated fields.

From the receiving verteces the information passes to the permanent file of the direct access. This file may be updated or left the same according to user's request in the following way: while processing the first receiving vertex, the system asks the user whether he wants to save the file, or to creat a new one.

The file consists of a directory record and data records with the information, which was input by the processing of each receiving vertex during the DP. The directory record consists of a sequence of number of receiving verteces and relative number of records in this file. A record is an information, read up from one of the receiving verteces. The record consists of fields, marked by a sign ''&'' during the DP design. This field is for the numerical values of parametres, to be used later in the application programs during the processing of the consecutive verteces (types 07, 08). Application program must read the record from the file of the receiving verteces according to the formats, denoted by the fields in the receiving vertex.

4. There are 4 types of the alternative verteces:

4.1. The ''menu''-type vertex (type 04) is labels by the choice condition of the parth in the problems solutions space. While working with this vertex, the user should make a decision about the alternative path of problem solving, pointing the number of the chosen vertex by the cursor. There are several alternative paths at the ''menu'' vertex, i.e. numbers of reference verteces (their total quartity is no less then 2 and no more than 5).

4.2. Alternative arithmetic vertex (type 05). This king of vertex also suggests parh choosing, but in this case, the system makes a decision based on the analysis of the results of arithmetic calculation. An arithmetic expression, the identifier and values of variables, which it possesses, can be written in the vertex at the stage of the DP design, or put by the user in the display while solving the problem during the dialogue session. An alternative arithmetic vertex provides 3 outputs. While developping the DP script, the user should make a graph of the problem solving in such a way, that the arithmetic vertex gets 3 reference numbers of verteces, one of them be the vertex, to which a control of the process is delivered, when the system finishes processing the arithmetic vertex. This processing is done in the following way: the system makes a syntactic and semantic analysis of the input arithmetic expression, analysis the presence and correctness of names and values of variables and displays diagnostic message about the mistakes with the request to correct them right at the display. After the user edits his mistakes, the system again tries the syntactic analysis of expression, and, when it is correct at last, calculates the atirhmetic expression (AE) according to the user's given variables values. Then the system gives out the result of calculation at the display and passes over to the first pointed reference vertex, if the meaning of AE is positive, to the second vertex — if it's equal to zero, and to the third — if it is negative.

4.3. Alternative logical-arithmetic vertex (type 06) is similar to the arithmetic one, described at paragraph 4.2. The vertex should posses two reference verteces for the subsequent control after its processing finishes. The processing of that vertex is as follows:
— readout of the vertex at the display;
— input of a logical-arithmetic expression (LAE) and the identifiers of variables and values of variables to the given fields of a display;
— syntactic and semantic analysis and the diagnostics of user's mistakes;
— editing of input;
— calculating of LAE by the system;
— readout of the expression meaning and choosing of subsequent vertex of the graph.
The transference of control to one of the reference verteces is made according to the results of the calculation: the first vertex becomes activated, when the meaning is "true", the second one — when it is "false".

4.4. Alternative-consequtive vertex (type 07). This vertex also demands the sustem's choice of an alternative way of the sequence of steps from one vertex to another. This vertex is intended to execute application programs, which must be compatible with the Operational System of the Unified System (OSUS), adopted for the Instrumental Dialogue System (IDS). Application programs (AP) use the parametres vector, processing (type 03). The alternative-consequtive vertex should contain numbers of the receiving verteces, where the data, necessary for the given AP is stored. The result of the AP's execution can be placed by the user in the data set, which the system readouts on the screen of the monitor just after this program run.
The AP may have alternatives in its finishing. The user (while writing the program) may form several corresponding complete flags and gives them the values from 1 to 5. The vertex should provide as many outputs (from 1 to 5), as the complete flags are formed in the AP. When the AP is executed, the system analyses the flag value and passes the processing to the corresconding reference vertex.

5. Consequtive vertex is interpreted by running the AP with the name, contained in this vertex. It differs from the previous vertex in one respect: in AP, attached to it there's no complete flag, And the control transferes to the only possible reference vertex, stated by its number.

6. The transference vertex is provided for the transference from one DP script to another, when there's necessary to use the previously gained results of other AP processings and in some other cases.
The above discussed types of verteces provide the process of algorithms description for considerably wide class of problems, irrespective of their problem are.
The language syntax is constructed on the basis of the verteces type classification. The particularity of the dialogue language seems to be the fact that the user has the possibility to input the computing procedures in the form of the arbitrary logico-arithmetical expressions with source fata for online appraisal and strategy selection from the terminal in the dialogue regime. An important feature of the instrumental language is the possihility of creating a "friendly" interface for the user, at the basisis of which lies the principle of entity-orientation approach — "What you see is what you get" [3].
The object-oriented programming, realized here, allows the possibility of the direct contact of user with the model of his application problem. This approach widely uses the concepts of "windows", "assisted panels", "menu", "pictograms", etc. The display is divided into windows, each for a certain process readout. Besides, the menu of possible alternative steps is also readouts to a display. Using a quided cursor, it is possible to invoke necessary windows, menu elements etc., without any language means. This system is an instrument to be used for problem solving.

The user's specific problem can be regarded as a microworld model, consisting of interactive elementary objects, forming up the superobjects. In a real problem area several problems can be interacting in the frame of the whole management system, i.e. several superobjects.

In a new version of the Instrumental Dialogue System (IDS) the interactive moled of the superobject is represented by means of a spreadsheet. A spreadsheet bears all main qualuties of a "friendly interface" and, at the same time, is an active dinamic tool for problem solving. A spreadsheet is a 3-dimensional model, in which two dimensions corresponds to the rectangle table of elements (elementary objects), which the user has a direct access too. The third dimension is constituted by functions, elements' semantics, logics and the interface functional of the elements of a spreadshat.

The approach of an instrumental dialogue system of a new generation implies the maximum adaptation of software to the user. That's why, the most useful way is to integrate all the subsystems into one complex software tool — a Technological Complex of Data Processing, considering the whole technological sycle of user's interaction with application programs.

The main purpose of integration is the ability of a system to adjust to different programming techniques, different kinds of processing, data structures the user's level of training.

An integration of software tools and information resources makes it possible for a final user to develop application dialogue systems of different purposes: from information analysis to predictions, planning, etc.

The integration extends also to interface software tools, dynamic table methods of problem solving, DBMS graphic representation means and, consequently, developped languages of speciaficatior, control and man-machine dialogue. User's interaction with the application software is done through the unificated user's interface, using spreadshects. The most isportant here is the specification of a display, windows, spreadsheets and fields of spreadsheets. The topologic specification of a display and windows, as well as the algorithmic specification of spreadsheets and their interfaces are executed.

The specification is translated into a 3-dimentional actual model of Multi-windows Application Dialogue System.

Such a System must posses the following necessary characteristics:

robustness to user's errors, availability of input—output format's control means, the possibility of virtual console, the adjustment of unterface to different user's levels, quick and easy modification and extension means, the display of gystogramms, and diagramms at the research of DBS and the results of calculations, means of interface with the distributed DBS.

The IDS includes:

— the multi-windows interface control system, which provides the object — oriented "user-application software" dialogue;

— the subsystem of spreadsheets control, which realezes an application problem in the form of a 3-dimensional table, giving the problem more convinient and simpler form;

— relational vocabulary subsustem, which executes the information control functions for IDS.

The multi-windows control sybsystem plays the role of a mediator between a user and application software, and provides the following functions:

— the screen formatting, i.e. deviding of a screen into windows with their possible over lapping;

— multi-windows driver for several processes display at a time;

— operational window with a menu of instructions;

— the cursor control for the windows managing;

— window moving through the text;

— dinamic change of windows place and parametres;

— input—output formats control;

— hard copy printing of the content of windows.

The subsustem of the spreadsheet control provides the realization of arbitrary application program and arbitrary screen functioning. The main point with a spreadsheet is as follows: the graphic means of a dialogue problem solving is an arbitrary table, the elements of which are the objects of the given problem. For a given problem the topologic specification of a table is done, that is the breadboard and the parametres of its fields are given, among them: brightness control, fields' protection, etc.

The topologic specification concerns the 2-dimensional surface of a spreadsheet. After that there follows the algorithmic specification, which gives the third dimension of a spreadsheet. The algorithmic specification means the rules of fields identification, which comprise: field name, data output format the constant value, variable field for data input in a dialogue regime, data retrieval criterion (in a Data Base), subrutine identifier, logical-arithmetic conditions of fields' interaction, etc.

The topologic and algorithmic specifications of a spreadsheet provides the dinamics of a dialogue process (DP). The DP is realized by a DP-processor of 3-dem. spreadsheets. The subsystem of the spreadsheets control executes the following functions:

— display breadboarding;

— topologic and algorithmic specifications;

— the control over the fields pointly for their reprocessing initiating;

— the spreadsheet initiating (problem solving);

— the user-problem interface, based on multi-windows tool;

— information control support of spreadsheets, based of relational vocabulary system;

— special system functions.

There are two kinds of spreadsheets:

a) system ones, fulfilling common purposes. They are as follows: operational spreadsheets, containing the menu; speeded up DB look in local and network regime; speeded up DB updating; dinamic construction of column gistogrammes; the calculator with the extendable library of routine functions; the calendar; the pad; the relational vocabulary system administrator; the design of spreadsheets;

b) application spreadsheet, which realise the dialogue model of application problem.

The relational vocabulary system (RVS) is aimed to logical centralizing of information (metadata) about the informational-algorithmic resources of the IDS. The concept of RVS is innovative in the way, that the user's problem media is displayed in the terms of the relational model in a form of an integrated conceptual scheme. DB is considered as an object from the problem media and, thus, can be viewed as a logical object of RVS, contained in a conceptual scheme of a metabase.

RVS stores the data, meta-data, topologic and algorithmic specifications of a display, windows, spreadsheets and their fields.

Metadata serve for identification and description of characteristics of user's objects (data, algorithms, specifications etc.). The main function of RVS is the control over functional resources of IDS. RVS is the only block, which may activate the objects during the user's dialogue model functioning. There are general formal rules and control procedures of the RVS metabase, such as metabase description, access control, provision of integrity, security means, metabase updating, DB maintenance.

The IDC is a functional part of the Technological Complex of Data Processing (TCDP) [4]. The system is oriented on virtual terminal US (united system) computer. TCDP serves as the basis of the typical technology to elaborate the application software.

REFERENCES

1. Yu.M. Cherkasov. The main principles and theses of developing a complex of automated systems if municipal management. Moscow, (SEV). The Committee for science and technology cooperation science — industry Complex, ASU "Moskva", Moscow City Soviet. Report of the seminar on management automation of territorial renits. Issue 7, 1983.

2. Yu.M. Cherkasov, V.A. Grynshtein, V.I. Yalovetsky. Instrumental Dialogue facilities in the organization management systems. Kiev, V.M. Glushkov Cyberneties Institute A.S. UcSSR, The papers of the All — Union conference "Dialogic man-comuter", 1985.

3. Allen Key. Sofrware Computer. In the world of science, translated from English. Moscow : Mir, November, No 11, 1984.

4. V.A. Grynshtein, Yu.M. Cherkasov, V.I. Yalovetsky. Interpriting program facilities of information processing. Moscow. Radio and Communication, 1984.

Governmental and Municipal Information Systems
P. Kovács and E. Straub (Editors)
Elsevier Science Publishers B.V. (North-Holland)
© IFIP, 1988

THE USE OF AUTOMATED TOOLS DURING INFORMATION SYSTEMS
DEVELOPMENT

Kathleen SPURR

Department of Computing, Mathematics and Statistics,
Polytechnic of North London,
Holloway Road,
London N7 8DB

Since the early 1960s it has been recognised that automated
tools would benefit the development of information systems.
The first automated products concentrated on the later stages
of the life-cycle, i.e. maintenance and implementation of
systems. These products were generally known as data
dictionaries. As the techniques became more widely used and
the concept of systematic development of software systems more
widely understood, it was recognised that these concepts and
techniques could be applied at earlier stages of the life-
cycle, in particular during analysis and design.

This paper explores the development of such data dictionaries
and automated tools. It provides a critical exposition of the
current state of the art, particularly with reference to the
existing formal methods for analysis and design, and the
associated software tools.

1. INTRODUCTION

The Data Dictionary has been considered for some time to be a useful
tool when implementing an information system. It has also been regarded
as being potentially beneficial during Analysis and Design. Such
potential benefits are now being realised with the production of
automated tools to assist the development of information systems. This
has been caused by the general acceptance (even if somewhat reluctant)
of a methodology-based approach to Information Systems Development.

This paper describes the development of the data dictionary concept to a
point where it may be considered useful for information systems
development. It outlines essential features of several methodologies
which may be included in an automated tool to be used for the
development of information systems.

Maddison [21] and Olle et al [22] describe various methodologies for information systems development. With the advent of associated supporting automated tools, an obvious sequel to those publications is a Directory of these software tools. We are currently in the first investigative stages of producing such a Directory. Our preliminary findings are reported in this paper.

2. THE DEVELOPMENT OF DATA DICTIONARY SYSTEMS

2.1 Early Developments

The late 1950s and early 1960s saw the emergence of large data processing systems providing systematic solutions to the handling of large quantities of data. Unfortunately, many of those data processing systems were not themselves always managed in a systematic way. During this period, the importance of rigorous analysis techniques was established and the need for effective system management and system documentation became apparent.

The data dictionary concept arose out of the idea that a data processing system should itself be documented by means of a data processing system. The term "data dictionary" is said to have originated in King's 1967 paper on "Systematics" [14]:

> "a data dictionary...should aim...at being a list of items which must occur in the course of processing"

King had developed ideas that appeared in an earlier paper by Fisher in 1966 [7]. As Fisher says, the problems of inadequate documentation were apparent:

> When systems analysts and programmers find it impossible to analyse and modify programs within reasonable time limits, the difficulty may be in the way the system is documented. Indeed, inadequate documentation may be regarded as one of the most serious problems confronting computer users."

Fisher recognised the need to document not only the data, but also the processes and the data-process interactions. His solution was to propose a system based on tables consisting of:

> (i) descriptive tables, one for each class of entry (data elements, programs and files)

> (ii) Cross-reference tables using the decision table approach indicating interactions between the entries.

2.2 The Data Dictionary Tool as a Tool for Systems Analysis and Design

As time went on, commercial data dictionaries were produced as a tool to
manage the information resource. They were very much aimed at databases,
and as such were repositories of data about data. But the notion
persisted that they should be of use during Systems Analysis and Design.
In 1969, King [15] proposed that "the work of a data dictionary aids
analysis by documenting and clarifying work as it proceeds." The Data
Dictionary Systems Working Party of the British Computer Society
endorsed this in their 1977 report [4].

In 1978, Gradwell, speaking as chairman of the British Computer Society
Data Dictionary Systems Working Party at a conference on Data Dictionary
Systems again proposed the use of data dictionary techniques during
Systems Analysis and Design [10].

> "The DDSWP sees a data dictionary as a tool with several major
> objectives. These are
>
> a) to provide facilities for documenting the information
> collected and created during all stages of a computer project;
> analysis, design and implementation
>
> b) to provide facilities that will continue to be used in the
> re-analysis, redesign and re-implementation that will occur
> after the first phase of the first project. Thus facilities to
> update the information are as important as facilities to
> create it (an unchangeable system specification is worse than
> none)
>
> c) to ensure that the documentation is structured, selectable
> subsets are easily available, and that all is properly indexed
> and cross-referenced
>
> d) the system should help analysts and designers follow well-
> structured methodologies.
>
> e) because no system available in the next few years will
> cover all these requirements, systems should be readily
> extensible."

The suggestion was made that the term "data dictionary" was no longer
appropriate in this context [4].

> 'The DDSWP has studied many commercially available and in-
> house data dictionary systems ... from simple data directories
> describing existing files to full-blown systems analysis,
> design, implementation and operational tools which could only
> be termed "systems encyclopoedias" '.

Other terms have been suggested (eg 'analysts workbench', 'analysts toolkit'), but there does not exist Universal agreement on the appropriate terminology or the definitions of the terms used.

2.3 Extensibility

In the late 1970s and early 1980s, commercial data dictionary products (eg ICL's Data Dictionary System, IBM/DC Data Dictionary, DataManager) were being used with great effect. Generally, these products were expensive, and were geared to run on large mainframe computers which catered for large data processing systems. These products had been developed in close co-operation with the users. Hence they proved to be effective databases for storing data about data processing systems, and had a comparatively high degree of user-friendliness. The development of such products was very much 'user-driven' and at about this time the users began to request that the products be used for applications other than data processing. Users required the capability to define their own dictionary entities. Files, Records, Schemas were not enough - the users wanted to store and to cross-reference details related to systems analysis and design, or even their own applications (accountancy, library records etc.). Many of these requirements could easily be handled by any commercial database, but the user-friendliness of the data dictionary and the user's familiarity with it made further extension of the data dictionary particularly attractive.

The key word in the early 1980s was "extensibility". In 1983, a 'state of the art' conference on Data Dictionaries was organised by the BCS Database Specialist Group [1]. Both IBM and ICL's data dictionary systems were portrayed as including the "extensibility" feature [17] [11].

There are two senses in which extensibility may be used:

> (i) As a tool for recording facts about the earlier stages of the information systems development life-cycle (e.g. Analysis and Design). There may be some merit in this if it facilitates automatic progression from one life-cycle stage to the next. For example, an entity at the Analysis stage may be associated with the corresponding record at the design stage.

> (ii) As a tool for recording information not directly related to data processing. This type of activity should not be seen as a necessary function of a data dictionary system, since any database could provide the same mechanisms, with an appropriate query facility. In a sense, it is misleading to adopt this approach.

Gradwell [11] summarised the situation well.

> "Architecture in 1982: By this point the Data Dictionary
> System is beginning to collect quite a number of different
> processes around it. It is becoming a typical database used by
> many applications. The only difference is that these are data
> processing applications"

It should be noted that, although extensibility enables users to include
analyis and design information in the data dictionary, it does not mean
that the data dictionary can be used as a tool to drive the analysis and
design process. There is no implication that, for example, a data entity
identified during analysis is automatically converted to a data record
during implementation.

2.4 The Information Resource Dictionary System

Currently, there is considerable activity directed towards producing an
International Standard for the Information Resource Dictionary System
(IRDS), based on the concept of a data dictionary system. The group
working in this area come under the umbrella of ISO/TC97/SC21/WG3 and
are known as the IRDS Rapporteur Group. Work is still in progress, but
agreement on an overall framework for the IRDS is near at hand. At the
heart of the framework is the IRDS Services Interface, which contains
the essential data elements and functional facilities for the Dictionary
System. The Standard for the Services Interface is progressing well and
one would expect an International Draft Proposal to be ready in a year
or two.

The Intention is that the IRDS will provide essential support in many
areas and that one of these areas would be related to Analysis and
Design of Information Systems. One way of providing this facility is
through Extensibility; another is to include appropriate components in
the IRDS. The best way of using the IRDS to support Analysis and Design
has yet to be addressed.

3. FORMAL METHODOLOGIES FOR THE DEVELOPMENT OF INFORMATION SYSTEMS

3.1 Description of Terms

The general development of computing systems stems from a desire to
discipline and systematize many different sorts of procedure. It was
inevitable that this desire be extended to the procedures for developing
computerised systems themselves. In recent years, many attempts have
been made to formalise the development of Information Systems. Three
IFIP conferences have been held on this subject [22,23,24] and the
Information Systems Analysis and Design Working Party of the British
Computer Society have produced a summary report [21].

Such techniques are generally known as "Methodologies for the
Development of Information Systems", but the three concepts involved,
namely

> (i) The methodology

> (ii) The Information System

> (iii) The Development of the Information System

are not well-defined.

Langefors [16] did much of the early work on formal techniques for the
development of information systems. He defines an Information System as:

> "A system of information sets needed for decision and
> signalling in a larger system (of which it is a
> subsytem) containing subsystems for
> > collecting
> > storing
> > processing
> > distributing
> information sets"

In order to understand the definition, one needs to understand the
particular frame of reference to which Langefors was working.

Maddison [21] defines an information system as a

> "means of catering for flows and storage of all
> relevant information for all end users; includes
> conceptual schema, information base, information
> processor"

Neither of these definitions give a clear understanding of the term
"information system". For our purposes, there is little to be gained
from attempting to define the term precisely. It is sufficient that one
is able to recognise an information system when we see one.

Jackson [13] criticises the use of the term "methodology":

> "The subject of computer system development is
> excessively disadvantaged by infatuation with
> destructively polysyllabic terminology. One of the most
> notable examples is the almost universal substitution
> of the word 'methodology' for the word 'method'. A
> method is a way of doing something; methodology is, or
> should be, the study and science of method. The penalty
> paid for the substitution is arguably that we discuss
> methodology less than we should because its name has
> been stolen".

Jackson is only partly correct in his criticism. Collins English
Dictionary [12] verifies Jackson's interpretation of 'methodology', but
also gives an alternative definition as

> "the system of methods and principles used in a
> particular discipline"

It is this definition that is more appropriate to our work.

As regards the development of information systems, there are many
theories as to the best way to proceed. Each methodology has its own
view of the life-cycle and although there exists some measure of
agreement between the methodologies, not all techniques conform to the
general pattern. Maddison [21] and Fitzgerald et al [8] give a general,
all-embracing definition for the life cycle as consisting of

> a general planning or strategy stage
> a feasability or evaluation phase
> an analysis phase
> a design phase
> an implementation phase
> an overall review and maintenance phase

It is intended that all methodologies should be able to fit into this
life-cycle definition, even if only into part of it. However, one only
needs a single counter-example to disprove a theorem. One example of a
development technique which does not conform to the general definition
may be found in [5]

Nevertheless, there are several methodologies for developing information
systems. Some of these are described in [21]. Most of the methodologies
involve a measure of activity analysis (sometimes known as function
analysis or process analysis) and some measure of data analysis. In our
study of methodologies, we have concentrated mainly on D2S2 [19],
SASD[6,25,29] and JSD[13] as being representatives of particular classes
of methodology. Other methodologies have been considered when
appropriate.

Any methodology may include models which relate to

>   data
>
>   activities
>
>   interactions between data components
>   (termed data interactions in this paper)
>
>   interactions between activity components
>   (termed activity interactions in this paper)
>
>   interactions between data and activity components
>   (termed data-activity interactions in this paper)

3.2 Data Modelling

Where methodologies pay any attention to data analysis, the modelling approach used is generally some form of entity-relationship model. The standard reference to quote with respect to the Entity-Relationship model is [3], but many other people have done work on the approach. Chen's model included a mechanism for dealing with certain sorts of constraint (existence dependency, ID dependency, and constraints which may be expressed using set-theoretic notation), a mechanism for representing n-ary relationships and a mechanism for representing recursive relationships.

Within the methodologies that pay attention to data modelling, the approach used will usually represent binary and recursive relationships, but relationships of order greater than two are not always catered for. Constraints are usually dealt with in a limited fashion. Relationships of degree 1:1, 1:m and m:n are almost always considered, but existence and ID dependencies are not usually included. Some methodologies include a mechanism for representing optional participation by an entity in a relationship [19,20]

Another aspect of data analysis that is important to the information systems developer is that of sub-typing or Generalisation. Smith and Smith's two papers are the classic references usually quoted in this context [26,27]. Some methodologies do include a subtyping mechanism [19,20] but this may be treated in an ad hoc manner, with no formal rules for the manipulation of sub-types.

3.3 Activity Modelling

"Activity" is taken to be the generic term to cover functions, processes, procedures or actions. As such, we follow the interpretation given in Collins English Dictionary [12]

"Activity: Any specific deed, action, pursuit"

Activity modelling features in all methodologies to varying extents. In terms of the relationships between the activities there are three considerations:

(i) Decomposition of activities

This features in most methodologies. References [19] and [13] give examples of decomposition of activities. Different terminology is used depending on the methodology. JSD, for example, calls such activity decomposition diagrams "structure diagrams" whereas the term used in D2S2 is "function hierarchy". SASD [6] uses the concept of "leveled data flow diagrams" during Analysis to model activity decomposition, whereas the mechanism used in SASD for design is the "structure chart"

(ii) Dependency of activities

This is where the occurrence of one activity depends on the occurrence of another in time, or because the output of the first activity must be used as the input to the second. The classic example of such dependency modelling is the dataflow diagram of SASD [6]. The data flow diagram shows how data flows from one activity to the next. D2S2 [19] uses a function dependency diagram for similar purposes and Information Engineering [20] uses the process dependency diagram. The System Specification Diagram of JSD [13] also comes into this category.

(iii) Type of activity being modelled

SASD [6] recommends that four different types of data flow diagram be drawn:

> A Physical model of the current system
>
> A Logical model of the current system
>
> A Logical model of the proposed system
>
> A Physical model of the proposed system

Here, 'logical' refers to 'what is being done' and 'physical' refers to 'how it is done'.

D2S2 [19] uses the notion that one should initially model the 'business functions' and that the modelling should be continued and refined until the level of 'elementary function' is reached. This elementary function may then be implemented as a computer transaction.

JSD [13] concentrates on constructing activity models based on the concept of communicating sequential processes. The JSD activity model attempts to be a logical model (in the SASD sense) rather than a physical model. JSD models the 'real world' in the computer system but it is not clear whether one should model the current real-world, the proposed real-world or some ideal real-world. The JSD model employs the concept of an 'action' which must occur at a point in time and may not be further decomposd. One is not therefore able to model broad business activities using JSD.

Thus the type of activity being modelled may refer to:

> (a) whether the activity is part of a logical or a physical model
>
> (b) a business activity or an elementary activity which may be represented as a computer transaction
>
> (c) a current activity or a proposed activity

These categories need not be mutually exclusive

3.4 Interaction Models

Data interactions and Activity interactions are included in the
discussions of §3.2 and §3.3. Some of the models discussed in these
sections also show data-activity interactions. For example, the SASD
data flow diagram, although primarily intended as a representation of
dependency between activities, also shows the interaction between the
input/output data and the activity. Another example is the SASD
Structure Chart which is primarily a representation of activity
decomposition, but also shows data being passed from one level to the
next [6].

D2S2 [19] includes other data/activity interaction models such as the
entity/function matrix, the entity life-cycle diagram and the function
logic model. LSDM [18] uses Entity Life Histories. In our preliminary
investigative work, we decided to concentrate on data models and
activity models and more work needs to be done on interaction modelling.

3.5 Components and Models

We have identified two essential elements in the methodologies. We will
use the terms **component** and **model** to name the elements.

Being aware of the problems associated with definitions of terms, we
prefer not to define the terms but instead to give examples, and hope
that the reader could identify a component or a model on seeing one.
Some examples of components are entities, functions and activities. Some
examples of models are entity-relationship models, data flow diagrams
and function decomposition diagrams. Each model will be associated with
a particular structural form (defined in § 3.6) and each model will
include components.

3.6 Categorisation of Models

We have examined approaches adopted by various methodologies to data and
activity modelling and our preliminary findings are shown in Fig 1

Structure of Model	Data Model	Activity Model
Heterarchy	Entity Relationship [19,20,18]	Data Flow[6] Process Dependency [20] Function Dependency [19]
Hierarchy	Sub-Typing Generalisation [19,26,27]	Activity Decomposition Function Decomposition[19], Structure Charts[6], Levelled Data Flow Diagrams[6] Structure Diagrams[13]

Figure 1   Categorisation of Models

We have categorised the structures of the models in two ways,
corresponding to the following forms:

(i) Heterarchy: where the components operate on a single level and each
component has the same value as any other. Such models include the
Entity Relationship model (where all entities appear to have the same
value) and the data flow diagram (where all transforms appear to have
the same value). This categorisation agrees with the definition given in
[12]

> "Heterarchy: A formal organisation of connected nodes,
> without any single permanent uppermost node"

(ii) Hierarchy: where one component may be considered to have a
different value to another, because of that component's place in the
structure. Examples include Generalisation hierarchies, as originally
defined in [26,27], activity decomposition as in D2S2 [19] and levelled
data flow diagrams [6]. Note that such diagrams need not corresepond to
a strict hierarchical form where one 'child' may have only one 'parent'.
Our interpretation corresponds to the definition given in [12]:

> "Hierarchy: A formal structure, usually represented by
> a diagram of connected nodes, with a single uppermost
> element"

For each occurrence of a model, relevant information would include:

> - the type of model (eg Entity Relationship, Activity
> Decomposition, Data Flow diagram of the current
> system).
> The structural form (hierarchy/heterarchy) is dependant
> on the type of model, as is its data/activity
> categorisation
>
> - the life cycle stage to which the model relates (eg
> Analysis, Design etc)

3.7 Categorisation of Components

Our preliminary conclusions are that for any occurrence of a data or
activity component there are three considerations:

(i) The type of component (eg entity, function, relationship)

(ii)The models in which the component participates (eg occurrences of
Entity Relationship models, logical data flow diagrams etc)

(iii) For each occurrence of a hierarchy in which the component
participates, the position of that component in the hierarchy

A component may participate in several models

3.8 Methodologies: the Current State of the Art

It is recognised that methodologies do not provide the complete solution
to information systems development. Bubenko [2] states that

> "as the situation is today, the total methodologies
> are too superficial and they have too many 'gray' and
> unexplored areas and problems"

Floyd [9] advises that

> "one should not expect that introducing a method will
> solve all problems, neither can the shortcomings
> discovered in the methods be eliminated by computer
> support of the methods"

In our analysis of 'methodology' we have attempted to focus on the
essentials that will provide coherent and comprehensive coverage of the
development process. We are looking at the methodologies with a view to
selecting those aspects that may be automated, and thus we have
concentrated on aspects related to data modelling and activity
modelling. We recognise that the methodologies have failings, and that
the methodologies cannot provide the complete solution. Hence,
automation of the methods cannot solve all our problems. Nevertheless,
we feel that there are some benefits to be gained from automation.

4. AUTOMATED TOOLS

4.1 Ground Rules for the Investigation

We are currently in the early stages of a project to evaluate and
compare automated tools for the development of information systems. The
existence and production of such tools is an obvious consequence of the
work that has been done in the two areas of data dictionaries and
methodologies for the development of information systems. Our results
will be published towards the end of next year. We hope that our
findings may be relevant to International Standards work on the Role of
the Information Resource Dictionary System in the development of
Information Systems.

Currently, we have carried out preliminary investigations into some 14
such automated tools. The purpose of the preliminary investigation was
to lay the ground rules for further investigation. It is our conclusion
that the tools investigated fall into two main categories:

(i) Diagram tools, for the purpose of constructing models such as data flow diagrams, entity relationship diagrams and entity life cycle diagrams. Such tools have obvious and immediate uses, but do not enforce consistency between the various models used. They can be used by analysts who are not harnessed to a particular methodology but do not ensure that a well-ordered, coherent approach to systems analysis is applied.

(ii) Data dictionary (or Encyclopoedia) based tools which have a central resource for the systems analyst. These tools will generally support the use of a specific methodology and will produce diagrams, pseudocode etc which is consistent with the techniques in the methodology. If such tools are to be effective they must have a central information resource which is based on the data dictionary concept.

Most of the tools investigated provided support for both activity modelling and data modelling.

4.2 Development of data dictionary based products

In order to obtain comprehensive support for the development of information systems throughout the life cycle and over the spectrum of development, tools in category (ii) are the ideal. But the development of such tools is still in the early stages. There appear to, be two approaches to the development of these data dictionary based tools:

(i) The 'bottom-up approach' whereby several existing diagram type tools are incorporated in order to give a more integrated coverage. Thus the resulting products may be said to be integrated and complete according to the stated result, but may not necessarily provide coherent coverage of the development process.

(ii) The top down approach whereby the global requirements are initially stated and then implemented by degrees until the final product is produced. Such products will aim to provide coherent coverage of the development process. But as they are implemented by stages, they may not provide complete coverage until the final stage of their implementation.

There appears to be no product at present which provides complete coherent comprehensive coverage of the whole spectrum of the development throughout its life cycle.

4.3 Essential Requirements

Following Fisher's early solution [7], an automated product intended to provide comprehensive coverage of the information systems life-cycle should support both data modelling and activity modelling, as well as interaction modelling.

The product should facilitate the heterarchic and hierarchic interactions shown in Figure 1. In addition, the product should enable progression through the information systems life cycle. Of the products investigated so far in the study, it is not clear that any product satisfies all of these requirements, but most products attempt to satisfy some.

The product should enable relevant diagramming techniques to be used and should enable consistency of definition throughout. Most of the products investigated appear to satisfy this, within their stated capabilities

4.4 Other requirements which may be included

Some products will generate code (eg Cobol data definitions, Cobol procedure code) or database definitions. These are not seen as essential requirements since they would be easily produced enhancements, provided the product has been modelled on sound basic principles.

Some products also provide a facility for designing screens and controlling progression through menus. The study has considered this to be a useful feature but not an essential one.

4.5 Features not Included

Partitioning systems into subsystems is a principle fundamental to the development of information systems. In terms of partitioning data and activity components, it includes the hierarchic approach mentioned in Figure 1. But, of the methodologies and automated tools investigated so far, there does not appear to be an effective mechanism to partition information systems into coherent whole subsystems with definable interfaces between them.

It could be argued that automated tools for the development of information systems should provide 'expert system' features to aid the developer with regard to the design of the system. For example, one obvious feature is to ensure that the data is in third normal form. Only one of the automated products investigated during the preliminary study claimed to support this. At this stage, such features are considered to be useful but not essential

4.6 User Interface

Most of the products investigated provided a graphical screen interface which could be manoevered using cursor control keys or a mouse. Sections of Diagram could be enlarged or reduced as necessary, but it must be said that the quality of the graphics produced deteriorated to illegibility in some circumstances.

5. CONCLUSION

This paper has described the first stage of a project to evaluate comprehensive automated tools for the development of information systems. Such tools are seen as employing two concepts:

(i) The data dictionary concept - ie that a data dictionary should support the development of information systems

(ii) The methodology concept - ie that the development of information systems should be based on sound, recognised, coherent techniques and procedures. Similar procedures are already employed by Architects and Engineers [28] when designing Buildings or Engineering structures such as bridges.

It is recognised that most of the automated tools available so far are diagram tools or provide only partial coverage of the information system development process. More integrated and coherent tools are appearing on the market.

The project is continuing and the next stage will involve more detailed analysis, with a view to publication of the results at the end of the next year. The aim of producing and evaluating such automated tools is that when developing information systems we may be able to concentrate more on the quality and aesthetics of the final product, and less on the techniques and tools required for the job.

ACKNOWLEDGEMENTS

My thanks to all the manufacturers who have provided information about their products and to their representatives who have given their time in discussions. In particular, may I express thanks to Ian MacDonald of James Martin Associates, David Last of ICL, Alan Davis of Entel, Richard Waltham of BIS, Ary Velstra of Interprogram B.V. and Tony Webb of LBMS. The opinions expressed in this paper are my own and any errors or ommissions are mine and not attributable to any manufacturer.

REFERENCES

[1] Baker, G.J. (ed), Data Dictionary Update published by the British Computer Society Database Specialist Group 1983

[2] Bubenko, J.A, Information Systems Methodologies - A Research View in Information Systems Design Methodologies: Improving the practice (North Holland) 1986

[3] Chen P,P,S, The Entity Relationship Model - Toward a Unified View of Data in ACM TODS vol. 1 no. 1 pp 9-36 March 1976

[4] Data Dictionary Systems Working Party Report (Wiley Heyden) 1977 also published in the USA as a joint special issue of DATABASE (Journal of ACM SIGBDP) vol 9 no 2 Fall 1977, and SIGMOD Record (Journal of ACM SIGMOD) vol 6 no 4 Dec 1977

[5] Dearnley P.A, and Mayhew P.J, In favour of system prototypes and their integration into the systems development cycle, The Computer Journal vol 26 no 1 February 1983 pp 36-42

[6] De Marco, t, Structured Analysis and System Specification (Yourdon) 1978

[7] Fisher, D.L. Data, Documentation and Decision Tables, CACM vol 9 pp 26 - 31 1966

[8] Fitzgerald g, Stokes N and Wood J R G, Feature Analysis of Contemporary Information System Methodologies. The Computer Journal vol 28 no 3 1985

[9] Floyd, C, A Comparative Evaluation of System Development Methods in Olle T.W, Sol H.G, Verrijn-Stuart A, Information Systems Design Methodologies: Improving the practice North-Holland 1986

[10] Gradwell, D, Objectives and Scope of a Data Dictionary System, The Computer Bulletin, December 1978

[11] Gradwell D, ICL's Data Dictionary System in Baker G,J (ed) Data Dictionary Update published by the British Computer Society Database Specialist Group 1983

[12] Hanks P. (ed) Collins Dictionary of the English Language 2nd edition (Collins) 1986

[13] Jackson M A, System Development (Prentice Hall) 1983

[14] King P J H, Some Comments on Systematics, The Computer Journal vol 10,pp116-118 1967

[15] King P J H, Systems Analysis Documantation: Computer-Aided Dictionary Definition, The Computer Journal vol 12 (1) 1969

[16] Langefors, B, Theoretical Analysis of Information Systems, 4th Edition (Auerbach) 1973

[17] Lankester, A. Aspects of the IBM DB/DC Data Dictionary in Baker G,J (ed) Data Dictionary Update published by the British Computer Society Database Specialist Group 1983

[18] Learmonth Burchett Management Systems, Introduction to LSDM, published by LBMS, Evelyn House, 62 Oxford Street, London W1N 9LF 1986

[19] Macdonald I.G. and Palmer I.R. System Development in a Shared Data Environment - The D2S2 methodology in Olle T W, Sol H G, Verrijn-Stuart A (eds) Information System Design Methodologies: a Comaprative Review (North- Holland) 1982

[20] Macdonald I.G. Information Enginering - an Improved Automable Methodology for the Design of Data Sharing Systems in Olle T.W, Sol H.G, Verrijn-Stuart A, Information Systems Design Methodologies: Improving the practice North-Holland 1986

[21] Maddison R N (ed) Information System Methodologies (Wiley Heyden) 1983

[22] Olle T W, Sol H G, Verrijn-Stuart A (eds) Information System Design Methodologies: a Comaprative Review (North- Holland) 1982

[23] Olle T W, Sol H G, Tully C J (eds), Information System Design Methodologies: a Feature Analysis (North Holland) 1983

[24] Olle T.W, Sol H.G, Verrijn-Stuart A, Information Systems Design Methodologies: Improving the practice North-Holland 1986

[25] Page-Jones M, The Practical Guide to Structured System Design (Yourdon) 1980

[26] Smith J M, Smith D C P, Database bstractions: Aggregation and Genaeralisation, ACM TODS 2,2 June 1977 pp105-133

[27] Smith J M, Smith D C P, Database Abstractions: Aggregation, CACM June 1977, vol 20 no 6

[28] Building Beauty at the Hard Face of Information, Times Higher Educational Supplement, 16th January 1987

[29] Yourdon E, Constantine L, Structured Design (Yourdon) 1978

Governmental and Municipal Information Systems
P. Kovács and E. Straub (Editors)
Elsevier Science Publishers B.V. (North-Holland)
© IFIP, 1988

CULTURE OF DECISION-MAKING AND THE USE OF DSS IN MUNICIPAL ORGANIZA-
TIONS

By Péter GELLÉRI - Ferenc MARTINEZ
                    Hungary

Culture of decision-making is determined by the broader culture and
by the culture of the given type of organization. Its state is a key
factor of DSS application. Models are proposed to represent the externally determining and the internally characteristic factors of decision culture. The logic of decision motivation is of particular sociological importance. In the conclusion, a set of the necessary functional DSS criteria is presented on basis of elicited user needs and
specific attributes of municipal organizations.

1. STARTING POINTS

1.1. On the cultural determination of decisions and on decision culture

People or groups of people have always made decisions and are often concerned
as much about the manner of making it as about the contents. Historically, however, the issue of decision-making as such entered into the scene and has received ever increasing emphasis only in the last era, as from early capitalism.
In terms of sociology the process can be reasonably considered a distinct symp-
tom and attribute of modernization. [1]

It is assumed that the simultaneous presence of several conditions, as a combined environment, is necessary to identify a decision problem as we mean it today. The necessary conditions are the following:

- a substantial stake,
- time pressure,
- decision should typically imply a situation of choosing between
  available alternatives or ones to be generated or expanded in the
  course of the process,
- a sufficiently "thick" information medium to provide matter for consideration,
- a social environment to be reckoned with and being equally responsive to decision content and eventually decision manner and to the
  outcome,
- frequent need of decision.

Remarkably, the manner of decision depends not only on the type of task or the
type of organization, but also on other qualities of cultural traditions. This
accounts for the difference between decision processes e.g. in the English-
speaking world, Japan or Hungary. Just for a hint:

- English:
the election of the decision method to be applied is up to the leaders of autonomous organizational units, however, decisions are actually taken by individuals and they are not obliged to give reasons.
(Value preference: quick decision rate.)
- Japanese:
broad circles of subordinates, managers and eventually experts are involved in
decision-making (in organizations of hierarchic structures!). Discussions are

typically held until consensus is reached.
(Value preference: unity of interpretation and commitment.)
– Hungarian:
managerial autonomy is in many respects and often restricted; coalition type
tradeoff and reconciliation are postulated but unestablished in the decision
process; there is no set routine for cooperation between leaders and experts. [2]

The above is an outline of a few features of three kinds of decision cultures.

By definition, decision culture is understood to mean a coherent combination of
the following factors existing at a given place and time:

  – the usual decision routine (e.g. how problems are formulated consid-
    erations and outcomes weighted, third parties involved in the pro-
    cess),
  – the actual "physical" conditions of decisions (e.g. availability and
    filing of data; decision aids),
  – knowledge and assumptions concerning the decision (e.g. which attri-
    butes are considerent to be salient; the tradeoff between alterna-
    tives; who should reasonably participate and how).

Beside cultures, also the types of organizations represent different conditions
from the decision point of view. For example the decision cultures of the mili-
tary, economic or administrative bodies of one given culture usually show marked
differences.

It is proposed to discuss the specific attributes of administration, as factors
determining a decision culture, in the context of various types and levels of
institutions. Administrative decisions are made in governmental, regional, rural and local units (councils and other authorities) by different types of organizations discharging contentually different functions.

The following statements are made about the decision culture of Hungarian municipal authorities (councils). In their content the statements may be valid for
some broader range as well, such as another council level, another type of administrative organization or, in some of its elements, concerning a given foreign process. As regards the structure of correlationships, however, we should
like to outline a comprehensive framework of reference i.e., a model approach.

The specific municipal attributes comprise, from the decision-making point of
view, the types of task content on the one hand and the conditions of the organization as well as the actual decision situations on the other hand. [3]

Referred to decision type, tasks may be classed by content as follows:

– Decisions where the task is to correlate two sets consisting of discrete elements, as, for example, the distribution of housing, property management, or
  assignments.
– Allocation type decisions, continuous in their quality of being variable, where
  the task is to apportion resources between an optional number of beneficiaries.
  Typical examples are: distribution of benefits and allowances, distribution of
  development funds.
– Strategic type decisions where the task is to choose the right or the best one
  of actual or generated alternatives. Such decisions are the stating of development objectives, aversion of sudden conflicts, or forecasting the limits of
  planned measures.

In the municipal sphere it is an essential feature of decision situations that
resources and demands are to be concerted in a way to meet certain objectives
and to bear in mind certain (statutory, financial, etc.) restrictions on use.
The already difficult situation is further aggravated by a number of organizational conditions, such as:

– The need of coordination with several organizations, typically one by one. [4]
– Coordination is not initiated by the council alone but it may appear as as un-
  expected requirement in any phase of the decision-making.

- The cooperating actors of decisions may pursue different objectives or may be in conflict.
- Coordinations may be of codified or traditional nature.
- Decisions are typically reached in several rounds in resumed processes.
- The "audience" of decisions is typically big.

It is obvious from the comparison between the attributes of the administrative type organization and profit oriented organizations that their respective staffs differ also in role-identification and value structure. [5] In the sphere of bureaucracy the goodness of a decision cannot be measured as finely as the profit of a business organization, and, typically, there is no indicator for its measurement. Consequently the problem of decision-maker's responsibility is formulated in different ways. In business organizations a decision is judged after the adequacy of its content which might even justify a conflict. In the case of municipal organizations, acceptance by the relevant environment may become more important and decision-makers are more vulnerable to any resulting conflict. Deliberate procrastination of decision and trying to withdraw from decision-making are not rare in this sphere.

1.2. Decision Support Systems (DSS): A new opportunity

The modernization process outlined in the introduction is accompanied, also because of the quality of tasks, by the ever growing demand for decision aids. Decision-makers typically find that decision situations are more and more cumbersome and troublesome and so they seek the ways of disburdening themselves.

The effects of the use of data bases are inconsistent in this respect. The availability of data offers the opportunity to tradeoff and so it is reassuring. At the same time their amenable use can be a real problem, meaning the comparison and evaluation of data and the finding of correlations. Similarly frustrating is the lack of relevant information of obvious importance just because the "hard" data are missing. [6]

The so-called multiattribute analysis systems have not come on stream here. One of their advantages is that they offer a means of tradeoff between alternatives by factors. [7, 8] Their shortcomings are that, partly, they only support certain phases of the decision process and, partly, they are applicable only in special cases. Problems do not always keep within such scopes. [9]

In principle, the expert systems are capable of overcoming the limits of the use of data bases and multiattribute analysis systems. The problem is about their extraordinarily high input costs and the narrow scope each system can cover. Such systems do not support reconciliation between actors although this is often a crucial point in decision making. Nor are these systems really convenient in tackling the salient problem of subjective preferences. [10]

The so-called decision support systems function and apply in a perfectly different way. DSS may be considered to be a process system including various means, decision techniques and methods with definite data connections, which methods support the clarification of goals, the generating of decision alternatives, the establishment of the set of assessment attributes, the different kinds of evaluations, the stating of correlationships and, finally, the comprehensive evaluation of decision alternatives (proposed decision).

Lately DSS has been utilized also in the process of reconciliation between several actors. [11] The future is obviously the integrated system of DSS-s, data bases and expert systems functioning in an environment of office-automation.

To put it in another way: DSS is supposed to assist in the process of thinking and discussion. It follows that it would be perhaps justified to use, instead of DSS, the more general term of DMMSS (Decision Maker's Mind Support System). For similar reasons a DSS product of ours is named "BÁBA" ("MIDWIFE"), expressing the relationship between the coming (newborn) decision of the bearer pregnant with the problem on the one hand and the assistant helping the latter on the other hand.

It can be easily appreciated that DSS could be successfully used for the purpose of a broad range of decisions made in administration. The interfaces, however, are of decisive importance. The election of the appropriate DSS is reasonably done by considering the task types (e.g. allocation type, strategic type) on the one hand and the correlationships that can be described in the following model on the other hand. (Fig. 1)

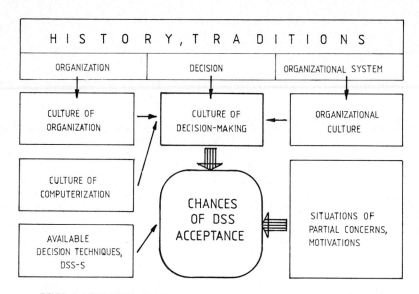

FIGURE 1 : THE MODEL OF THE CORRELATIONSHIPS OF DSS ACCEPTANCE

The elements shown in the above model need some complementary remarks.

- The term partial concerns and motivations is used for the personal interests of the decision maker, unrelated to the goodness of the decision (this will be covered more detail hereunder).
- Culture of computerization means the combination of knowledge about computing, attitudes toward computing, existing assets and the way of their actual use. Note that data processing culture is not particularly important from the point of view of DSS application because such aids are extremely user-friendly.
- Culture of organization defines the knowhow of structuring, the existing instruments of organization, the intelligent use thereof, as well as the actual structuring routine and the required degree of organization.
- Organizational culture includes the way of task and responsibility distribution between organizational units and individuals, the way of tackling individual and organizational problems and/or conflicts, the attributes of the communication process and the system of principles and processes of the regulation of behaviour. (As it is suggested by the definition, the state of democratic culture in the given organization and in its environment is an essential factor of organizational culture.)

The model indicates the correlationships considered to be salient.

In the following the determination between culture of decision-making and DSS acceptance will be discussed on basis of the correlationships elicited in the model. Ultimately we should like to make inferences about another dimension of correlationships, namely, the relation between the available DSS and the chances of DSS acceptance. The concluding question will interrogate the characteristic criteria of decision support systems with the best chance of application, in the light of the attributes of the given decision culture.

2. SOCIOLOGICAL CONDITIONS OF DSS ACCEPTANCE

2.1. The feasible ways of analysis

It would seem to be convenient to review and evaluate the experience of DSS application in municipal administration. However this cannot yet furnish sufficient data for analysis. [12, 13] The other approach, the one we, too, pursue, follows the usual logic of prognostication. In this approach the generic attributes of administrative decisions are explored first and then follows the study of what is required, what are the required types of decision aids, which are the typical characteristics of DSS-s with a "Nische" (void).

For this purpose a review is made of some major contentual attributes of decision-making and in this course the decision maker's motivation and the correlationships between the value structure imparted by the human–societal environment of decision-making and decision behaviour are analysed.

2.2. On the motivational logic of decision-making

The personal aspirations and motivations of the decision maker, of whatever content, can be enforced through the entire decision process, across the various consecutive phases. Concerning each decision phase the decisions taken in the organization are surrounded by a judging environment, a public opinion, which is strongly articulated in terms of representatives and which powerfully asserts itself. Beside considering the physical attributes of the given problem (for instance the use of an available resource in case of allocation type decisions), the decision maker has to reckon with this environmental condition as well and he has to enforce his ideas about the decision process through it. The way he chooses for this purpose is named the decision tactics of the leader. The correlationships are depicted in the following model. (Fig. 2)

The model apparently concentrates on the circumstance of reconciliation, an issue usually regarded to be a problem arising merely between the direct actors of the decision process. [14] From this point of view more can be expressed by the model than the obvious content. It is also possible to represent the contentually different judgments by different groups conveying the public opinion or the participation of more than one competent decision maker (leader) vested with the same influence.

From the elements of leader's motivation mentioned above, the category and subject of organizational partial interests should be discussed first. The range of such interests is extremely broad and they are always valid in a given actual constellation (that is, the decision maker may have several types of interests which may be partly conflicting as well). The major categories are the following:

- aversion of being called to account about a good decision,
- avoiding of internal and/or external tensions accompanying the decision process,
- devotion to the goal concerning the organizational conditions (development of communication between and/or democratism of organizational units, establishing or transforming the system of organizational standards),
- assertion of interests concerning inputs (time, cost, energy, knowledge),
- enhancing the role of professional knowledge in decision processes,
- increasing of unambiguous leader's competence and responsibility.

Decision strategies actually mean procedural preferences and the technique of having them accepted. [15] The choosing and enforcing of such procedures are

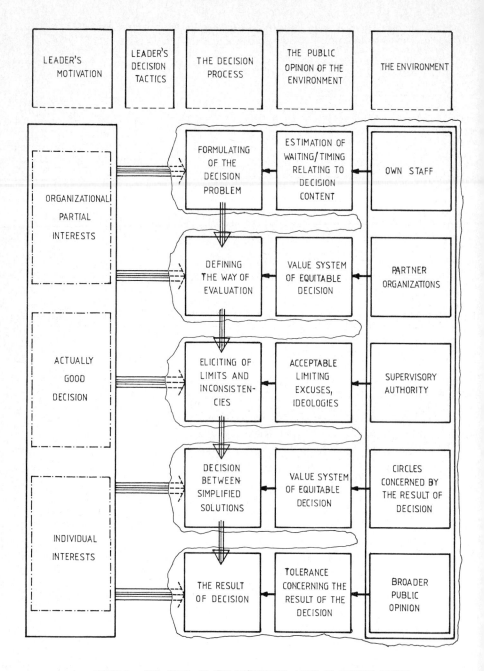

FIGURE 2 : THE MODEL OF THE MOTIVATIONAL LOGIC OF DECISION-MAKING

subsequent upon the tradeoff of acceptance, that is, the collecting of reasons that may be quoted in support of the leader's aspirations. The most frequent justifications are the following:

- the necessary resources are missing (time, information money, knowledge, energy, etc.),
- there is no universally equitable decision procedure,
- no adequate and dependable methods are available,
- the leader is responsible anyway.

Such arguments are usually accepted by the public opinion and are suitable for the selection and justification of the procedural methods in accordance with the objectives of the decision maker.

Let us illustrate the correlationships through a case where the leader's motivation is directed to <u>responsibility aversion</u>.

The following solutions offer themselves:

. the problem is not scheduled, it is not made an issue of decision,
. the decision problem is qualified as immature because of the lack of resources, and the process is stalled in some phase,
. no personal participation in decision-making,
. involving of numerous and respectable actors in the decision,
. the decision is removed from the organization, referred to another organization or transformed into an interorganizational one,
. decision is passed on to "science".

The above list illustrates the contentual relationship between these solutions and the above-mentioned arguments. In our example, assuming that the lack of time is an acceptable justification, the leader can postpone the decision and so this can be his chosen decision strategy.

Public opinion is the second model factor of sociological bearing.

Here we will only present a few stereotypes we have observed and which pertain to the equitability of the decision process. It can be seen from the model that these stereotypes can be readily associated with phases of the decision process. Naturally they represent various contents, not specified here, in the case of the different groups and subgroups in the environment.

Stereotypical arguments

Decision attribute related stereotypes:
. The attributes are not equally important
. Only the salient attributes matter
. Each attribute must be taken into account
. We decide on basis of objective attribute and data alone
. Subjective judgments matter as well
. The set of evaluation attributes must be constant.

Decision manner related arguments:
. In identical situations the manner of decision must be identical
. The outcome needs to be convincingly justified
. Prohibitive conditions may be given
. There is no inherently prohibitive condition
. The best solution is always offered by the "golden mean", i.e., by compromise
. Compromise solutions are always inferior

Actor contribution related arguments:
. Each contribution is equally important
. Not everybody's views deserve equal consideration
. Expert opinion ought to be considered
. Those concerned by the outcome of the decision ought to participate
. Nothing is worth a quarrel.

The stereotypes concerning equitable decision naturally show the same marked differences by cultures and are, as modernization attributes, variable. Sociologi-
cally, the related ideas are considered to be value system factors.

2.3. Circumstances of sociological relevance

A simplification was used for the model presenting the logic of decision motivation: we ignored numerous circumstances of decision-making that would produce
different conditions even for the same organization, decision maker and type of
affair. For example no mention was made of the degree of time pressure, the historical antecedents of the case if any, the content of actually available information, and number of other circumstances. [16] These circumstances clearly do
not work in isolation but through their actual constellation. The model is nevertheless considered suitable for describing symptoms causated by the thus determined circumstances.

3. DSS AS THE "WOODEN HORSE OF TROY"

The symbol used in the title above raises several reflections. It offers, we hope,
a relevant analogy for our inferences.

3.1. Developer and user motivation

The "wooden horse" or the DSS, can be put in the fortress provided that the inhabitants find it attractive and useful. So there are two different conditions
and each condition is further articulated in the judgments made by more than one
group (e.g. decision-makers, closer and broader public opinion). As far as its
attractivity is concerned, DSS usually has an appeal, it is welcome and it lends
itself to further adorning. Use value is judged partly according to the help it
is actually expected to give in problem solving. This judgment is predictably
positive as DSS is a help in several problem cases. [17] On the other hand, decision-makers judge it according to their own interests and motivations, in view
of its subservience to the assertion of their respective decision strategies.
The question of acceptance by public opinion is naturally implied in this latter
judgment. This is the very attribute that cannot be seen from a distance, from
the wooden horse, unless it is deliberately built so, with strong concentration
on that attribute. The wooden horse (DSS) must be apparently suitable for several uses ranging from worshipping to playing games. [18] At any rate, compact size
is certainly an advantage. If it is not oversize, its input will not require destruction, restructuring or knocking down on walls.

There are always two goals on the mind of the builder of the "wooden horse".
First of all he wants to put his product inside the walls and then he wants to
expose the inhabitants to delayed effect, mainly by means of the things conceal-
ed inside of the wooden horse.

Succesful use of the aid is only one of the ambitions of those engaged with DSS.
From their point of view, the influence achieved through being inside, through
being used – as a wooden horse – is far more important. This influence comprises
the transformation and updating of intra-organizational communication, decision
mechanism, organizational structure and decision culture in general. [19, 20]
This manifests the personal interest of the decision expert as well. With the advancement of decision culture, there is growing and increasingly qualified demand
for the wider use of DSS-s and their combination with other information systems.

So if the problem is considered from the aspect of requirements, the specification of the wooden horse must be set out of two points beside the aspect of functional competence. Specification must be based partly on the ideas of the build-
ers about the future effect and partly on the receiver's decision maker's assessment of the scope of decision manoeuvring.

The input of the horse, as an act of a "coup", naturally has a technique of its own. The theories of innovation cover such problems among others. [21, 22] As the problems to be discussed in this context are much more specific of organization then on subject-matter, in this respect we do not have much new to say about the case of DSS.

3.2. Some additions to the specification of DSS

From the above review of decision culture and from the summary of the sociological conditions affecting the use of DSS, the following criteria are concluded about decision support systems of municipal applicability:

- The DSS should cover an optional sphere of the decision process existing in the organization (eventually the whole of it, starting from the stating of objectives through generating of alternatives and eliciting and specifying the set of attributes to outcome justification).
- Capacity for problem solving on various levels of intricacy (omission of some phases when requirements are simpler).
- Furnishing each phase of work with optional means of tradeoff support.
- Permitting individual way of work (independent choice of the sequencies of decision steps, requests for explanations, etc.).
- Several types of decision algorythms should be provided or available for comparison.
- Supporting multiactor decision processes so as to permit, beside phase by phase evaluations from vote-like averages, the treatment of each opinion in isolation.
- Capacity for taking into account the different "weight classes" of the actors of decision-making by professional competence etc.
- Permitting the choice between the options of teamwork or individual (though simultaneous) work of the actors of decision, with or without supporting interactions between team members.

It must be admitted that the routine use of DSS might do some harm to decision culture on the long run. However, we expect that its advantages are more than preponderate and we have time to get ready for prevention before the adverse effects could manifest themselves.

References:

[1] Eisenstadt, S. N. (1966), Modernization: protest and change, Prentice-Hall, New York.

[2] Vári, A. and Vecsenyi, J. (1983), Decision analysis of industrial R and D problems : pitfalls and lessons, in: Humphreys, P., Svenson, O. and Vári, A. (eds.), Analysing and aiding decision processes, Akadémiai Kiadó, Budapest, pp. 183–189.

[3] Hawgood, J. (1985), Information morphology in bureaucratic subsystems, in: Methlie, L. and Sprague, R. (eds.), Knowledge representation for decision support systems, North-Holland, Amsterdam, pp. 237–244.

[4] Kunreuther, H. (1983), A multi-attribute multi-party model of choice: descriptive and prescriptive considerations, in: Humphreys, P., Svenson, O. and Vári, A. (eds.), Analysing and aiding decision processes, Akadémiai Kiadó, Budapest, pp. 69–89.

[5] Thompson, V. A. (1969), Bureaucracy and innovation, University of Alabama Press, Alabama.

[6] Naylor, T. H. (1982), Decision support systems or whatever happened to MIS?, Interface, Vol. 12, Aug.

[7] Eyraud, F. (1982), Aspects théoretiques et méthodologiques de la comparaison international dans l'optique d'une analyse societal. La cas des nouvelles technologie, L.E.S.T. – C.N.R.S., Aix-en-Provence, Third international training seminar on cross-national comparative research.

[8]   Inston and Llewelyn (1974), A discussion of some methods for the compara-
      tive evaluation a set of projects, Progr. Anal. Unit, Chilton, Didcot,
      Oxon.

[9]   Dawes, R. (1982), The robust beauty of improper linear models in decision
      making, in: Kahneman et al. (eds.), Judgement under uncertain heuris-
      tics and biases, Cambridge Univ. Press.

[10] Stamper, R. (1985), Knowledge as action : A logic of social norms and in-
      dividual affordances, in: Gilbert, N. (ed.), Language and knowledge,
      AI and sociological approaches.

[11] Wagner, G. R. (1982), Groups DSS experiences and implications. Proceedings
      of IFIP conference on processes and tools for decision support. Laxen-
      burg, Austria.

[12] Larichev, O. (1985), Problem of man-machine interaction in decision sup-
      port systems, in: Methlie, L. and Sprague, R. (eds.), Knowledge repre-
      sentation for decision support systems, North-Holland, Amsterdam, pp.
      27-39.

[13] Winterfeldt, D. von (1983), Pitfalls of decision analysis, in: Humphreys,
      P., Svenson, O. and Vári, A. (eds.), Analysing and aiding decision
      processes, Akadémiai Kiadó, Budapest, pp. 167-181.

[14] Phillips, L. (1984), A theory of requisite of decision models, Acta Psych.
      Vol. 56, I-III, pp. 29-48.

[15] Montgomery, H. (1983), Decision rules and the search for a dominance
      structure: towards a process model of decision making, in: Humphreys,
      P., Svenson, O. and Vári, A. (eds.), Analysing and aiding decision
      processes, Akadémiai Kiadó, Budapest, pp. 344-369.

[16] Humphreys, P. and Berkeley, D. (1984), Handling uncertainty: levels of
      analysis of decision problems, in: Wright, G. (ed.), Behavioral deci-
      sion making : Theory and analysis, Plenum, New York.

[17] Landry, M., Pascot, D. and Briolat, D. (1985), Can DSS evolve without
      changing our view of the concept of "problem"?, Decision Support Sys-
      tems, Vol. I, No. 1, pp. 25-36.

[18] Gelléri, P. (1986), Smaller sizes-changing roles: new dimensions of the
      man-computer interactions, in: Klix, F. and Wandke, H. (eds.), Man-
      computer interaction research, MACINTER-I, North-Holland, Amsterdam,
      pp. 71-75.

[19] Pulkkinen, K. (1985), The phases of development of an organization and
      knowledge representation within DSS, in: Methlie, L. and Sprague, R.
      (eds.), Knowledge representation for decision support systems, North-
      Holland, Amsterdam, pp. 41-54.

[20] Migliarese, P. (1985), Knowledge representation and organizational noise:
      an organizational framework about decision support systems, in: Methlie,
      L. and Sprague, R. (eds.) Knowledge representation for decision support
      systems, North-Holland, Amsterdam, pp. 237-244.

[21] Dennis, G. (1970), Innovations: scientific, technological and social, Ox-
      ford University Press.

[22] Himmelstrand.(1982), Innovative processes in social change: theory, meth-
      od and social practice, in: Sociology the state of the art, Sage, Lon-
      don.

Governmental and Municipal Information Systems
P. Kovács and E. Straub (Editors)
Elsevier Science Publishers B.V. (North-Holland)
© IFIP, 1988

F A R - S I G H T E D   P L A N N I N G
==

SICAD - SIEMENS INTERACTIVE GRAPHICS SYSTEM

S I E M E N S AG
D V 581
Guido Dirnberger
Otto-Hahn-Ring 6

D-8000 München 83

1. Introduction

This article deals with the objectives and scope of interactive graphic data processing in cartographic applications, with emphasis on
rural development and town planning. The characteristics and advantages of the SIEMENS software product SICAD (SIEMENS Computer-Aided-
Design) will be presented and illustrated by examples from actual
practice.

2. Particular demands on an interactive graphic informations system

Modern administration is practically unthinkable without the use of
data processing technology. For administrative tasks of an executive
nature, where data volumes and handling guidelines are normally
clear, data processing helps authorities to cope with large amounts
of information and routine tasks. Where planning tasks are concerned, the situation is different. In many cases, the volumes of data
in- volved are very difficult to predict and criteria may often have
to be modified, or even changed completely. Each criterion and each
object enter scruting must therefore be treated individually. Fully
automated procedures cannot be used. A flexible instrument that can
be controlled as desired in a man-machine dialogue is required.

- **Better quality of information and presentation**

The volume of information required in the course of planning and decision making processes is constantly increasing. An interactive graphics information system offers a
wide variety of options with regard to data intersection,
data overlays and representation of thematic information
in tabular, cartographic or any other graphical format.
These features mean that complex interrelationships can be
shown in a clear and easily understandable manner.

The various possible ways of dealing with problems can be
quickly visualized and evaluated, the interconnections between different planning, executive and decision making
bodies can be shown; carrying out tasks of this kind manually is nonsensical.

This is all the more true in cases where a very high quality of representation is demanded; in maps for political
and public bodies, for example. Rapid and accurate revisions need to be made to take suggestions and objections
into account, and these revisions can hardly be carried
out manually.

- **More efficient and economic carthography**

The revision of existing maps ties up a large amount of
time and money, and a large number of staff. Revisions are
frequently necessary as a result of surveys, additions and
local government decisions. But many of these revisions
only require modification of a single map section, maybe
only of minor details. The outlay required for manual execution of such relatively small changes is inordinately
high. An interactive graphics information system saves
both time and your money.

Better coordination between the various planning bodies

Most planning, decision-making and executive authorities maintain extensive links with each other. These links are used for a wide variety of coordinatory functions, from acquiring data and information on which plans and decisions are to be based, to passing on suggestions and opinions for approval.

With an interactive graphics information system, all users always have access to the same information and basic cartographic criteria, in a uniform format. This means that the outlay for entry, editing and transfer of data is considerably reduced.

Appropriate methods of representation can be selected to suit the various target groups. These can involve desired levels of aggregation and complexity in any scale. It is possible to produce a large variety of overall, section, and detail maps with a relatively small amount of time and effort.

SICAD provides the planner with an interactive graphics system comprimised of finely-tuned hardware and software components, with all the state-of-the-art features such as menus, symbols and procedures. An interactive system responds to every command entered by the user whereby:

* graphics can be created and manipulated

* calulation can be carried out

* technical and geometric data can be
  linked and analysed

* results can be visually represented

Interactive graphics with SICAD provides an efficient instrument for the processing, representation and annalysis of
technical and geometric information. It opens up new perspectives for the portrayal of information, data validation and
decision-making.

Thematic maps are extremely useful for representing complicated spatial factors in a clear and easily recognisable fashion. Maps of this kind are used especially by planning
authorities for inventories, analysis and the preparation of
documents for decision-making:

        * regional development

        * district planning

        * town planning

Compression of information and a wide overall view are of the
utmost importance here. Only after data has been pictorially
represented is it possible to draw all the potential conclusions and decide on subsequent actions . An interactive graphics information system enables it to use the form of picto-
rial representation - in a short space of time and in any
degree of detail- as the basis for planning decisions.

SICAD provides the planner with a powerful tool for the compression of large volumes of geographic data into clear and
concise planning documents. Thematic maps show relevant planning information far more effectively than printed lists.

Obvious areas of application include:

  * regional development and area planning

  * urban planning and development

  * local and district planning

  * environmental protection

  * village modernisation

Functions of the SICAD-THEA module

SICAD contains functions for the analysis and representation
of spatially related data as well as functions for collection
and evaluation of other information.

These functions include:

  * area hatching corresponding to assigned
    characteristics

  * representing results of a conflict
    analysis of areas

  * bar-charts, pie-charts, curves

  * filling of areas with symbols

  * interface facilities for the use of data
    from external files and data bases

3. Conclusion

Continual improvements in the performance of memory and processors, coupled with the anticipated fall in the price of
electronic components, are making interacitve computer systems more cost-effective and efficient. It is further expected that intensive current development of specialised application functions, plus greater efforts in standardisation,
will result in a considerable reduction in the compatibility
problems currently being experienced between hardware and
software of different manufacturers. At present therefore, it
is difficult to estimate accurately the time required for interactive graphics systems to become a standard tool of the
cartographer. An important influencing factor in this process
will not only be the availability of powerful hardware and
software, but also the willingness of the departments and offices responsible for providing carthographic services, to
invest.

Governmental and Municipal Information Systems
P. Kovács and E. Straub (Editors)
Elsevier Science Publishers B.V. (North-Holland)
© IFIP, 1988

SOCIAL INSURANCE ON-LINE SYSTEM TO SERVE NATIONAL WELFARE

TAKAAKI YAMANAKA

Data Communication Bureau,
Nippon Telegraph and Telephone Corporation (NTT)
5-7-1 Shimorenjaku, Mitaka City, Tokyo, JAPAN

The Social Insurance Data Communication System is a very large
on-line system with capabilities of processing, in real time, an
enormous volume of data from all over the country.
This is an administrative system developed by NTT at the request of
the Social Insurance Agency.
This paper outlines and evaluates the design and development of this
system.

1. INTRODUCTION

NTT currently provides services with 92 data communication systems and each
system shows a tendency to become increasingly larger in scale year after
year. This is particularly true of those systems set up as national projects
on a nationwide scale, the volumes of data and processing handled by both
these systems having been expanded in general. One of the largest of these
national projects is the Social Insurance Data Communication System.

This system includes 4 individual programs under the jurisdiction of the
Social Insurance Agency in the Ministry of Health and Welfare: health
insurance, national pension, welfare pension insurance and seamen's
insurance. The system was designed to improve and expand social insurance
services by upgrading the level of administrative services and by enhancing
the efficiency and speed by which operations are carried out.

Under the social insurance service approximately 70 million people are covered
by the above-mentioned programs. In addition, approximately 17 million people
are entitled to receive pension benefits. This includes wide-range and
long-term services such as various kinds of processing (which occur from the
time a person enters one or more of the systems until he begins to receive old
age benefits), collecting insurance premiums and paying pension benefits.
Thus, the service provided by this system is extremely complex in structure
and massive in volume.

The main features of this system are as follows.

[a] It has taken more than ten years to complete the entire system, beginning
    from the planning stage in 1975.
[b] The software to be developed is approximately 9 megasteps in total,
    utilizing as many as 10 large mainframe computers.
[c] Approximately 1,000 staff members are regularly engaged in development of
    this system.
[d] The current amount of databases has reached approximately 200 gigabytes,
    and is expected to total an approximate 260 gigabytes in 1988 to form an
    extremely large database system.

2. OBJECTIVES AND DEVELOPMENT PLAN OF THE SYSTEM

The objective of the system is to improve administrative services. As for the development plan, special consideration has been given to the smooth process of development at each stage, due to the large scale of system development.

2.1. Objectives of the System

Fundamental objectives of system development have been to provide the general public with correct, speedy and carefully thought out services, while relieving public service officials in social insurance offices from such monotonous jobs as manually posting records. As a result, these officials are able to devote their time to more important tasks such as examination, counseling and guidance which have been increasing every year. The details of these objectives are as follows.

[1]   Improvement of Administrative Services
    [a]   Correct and speedy office work
    [b]   Offering of uniform services throughout Japan
    [c]   Improvement of service at the social insurance office and
         introduction of new services

[2]   Enhancement and Advancement of Management Efficiency
    [a]   Enhancement of operational efficiency by streamlining office work,
         and keeping work time in reserve
    [b]   Providing the necessary speedy information

2.2 Development Plan of the System

The development plan of the system is divided into two plans. The first plan, counseling/inquiry for pensions and collection for health insurance/welfare pension insurance premiums, began in January 1980.

In succession, the second plan is now under way, greatly enhancing the capacity of the system configuration, while aiming at expanding system capabilities into those of a total system which can handle all tasks, from applications for people insured up to payments for people entitled to receive pension benefits.

Due to the size of the project, the second plan of system development consists of four phases, with new services/programs having been added step by step. The services in the first phase, which includes a newly added national pension service, started in September 1984 with the utilization of the new system with such new control programs as a service management program. The fourth and final phase is expected to be completed in 1988 about eight years after the beginning of the second plan.

Table 1 shows the tasks for services (including current services offered and future services under development) by program.

Table 1   Tasks for Services by Program

Task		Application Program			
		National Pension	Health Insurance	Welfare Pension Insurance	Seamen's Insurance
Short-term Task	Insurance Application	CS	CS	CS	FS
	Premium Collection	CS	CS	CS	FS
	Benefit Payment	FS	CS	--	--
Long-term Task	Benefit Payment	CS	--	FS	FS
Counseling and inquiry		CS	--	CS	CS

[NOTE]   CS: Current Services offered by this system
         FS: Future Services under development
         --:   None

3. SYSTEM CONFIGURATION

This system has a functionally distributed configuration with BEPs (Back-End Processor) which are exclusively used for database management and an on-line/off-line HOST which performs the processing operations because of the massive scale of record management of the insured persons. The database utilizes a 400-megabyte magnetic disk as a storage medium, and it is expected that eventually there will be an approximate 1,000 spindles. As for the links between the host processor and BEP, CPU multiconnectors are used in the centers, with high-speed lines being utilized between the computer centers.

Each center and social insurance office is linked by a 4,800 b/s line through TDM on a high-speed line.

Each of the terminals, installed in some 280 social insurance offices throughout Japan, has a TC (Terminal Controller) for a work station, with KWM (Kanji Window Machine), KLP (Kanji Line Printer), MIU (Magnetic Tape Unit) used for data interchange with municipalities, and OCR (Optical Character Reader) for reading notices for insurance premium collection, etc. The total system configuration is given in Figure 1.

4. SYSTEM DESIGN AND DEVELOPMENT

In accordance with the objectives of the system mentioned above, high efficiency and easy operability are required, incorporating new technologies.

The following sections explain the design policy and development methods.

4.1. Design Policy and Noted Points

[1] Management System for Recording
A BEP is employed in order to manage massive records, while a distributed
database system (DBMS) is adopted with a view to allowing access to
divided and allocated databases among multiple BEPs.
Not only can this method cope with the system construction flexibly in
proportion to the processing amount, but it can also cope with the
exclusive control of a concurrent processing system for batch and on-line
processing.

[2] On-line Tightly-Coupled Batch Processing and Its Automatization
Most of the batch processing is conducted according to the job schedule
at each social insurance office, with the processed amount totaling some
10,000 jobs a day at a center.
As for the batch processing schedules, they can be registered, changed or
inquired about from each social insurance office.
At the centers, scheduled batch processing is automatically implemented
according to such job net information as orders or priorities for every
social insurance office or jurisdiction.
Batch processing is conducted when data is transferred from a database or
an online transaction, and when it is completed, a message of process
completion is automatically given to the social insurance office
concerned. The processing result is distributed in response to the
requests from each social insurance office. In other words, batch
processing is performed in a similar way as on-line.

[3] Remote Maintenance of Terminals
Any change or addition of terminal program or table, due to revision of
laws or addition of programs, can be performed from a center to each
terminal at the various social insurance offices.
For trouble at terminals, automatic transmission of trouble messages to a
center or remote diagnosis is executed in the troubled division at the
center concerned.

[4] Backup of Massive Database
Since it is all but impossible to backup such a massive amount of data on
a daily basis, such measures as picking up only the changed data and
accumulating them during the day have been devised.

[5] Improvement in the Center Operation
  [a] Because of the great number of CPU sets installed, the BEP system is
       not only operated unattended with a DASD (Direct Access Storage
       Device) journal, but it is also operated at one location by
       utilizing a centralized supervisor system.
  [b] Data transfer between the online and batch can be performed
       automatically by means of the original file access method that uses
       the magnetic disk units shared by the host computers.
  [c] Malfunctions are prevented on tens of thousand of magnetic tapes by
       means of an automatic management program for every function of the
       system.

4.2. Software Development

In the second plan of this large-scale project, there have been about 9
megasteps for software development, handled by an approximate 30 development
groups. These groups, which are constantly engaged in developlment
activities, include some 1,000 staff members. This software development is
explained in the following sections.

4.2.1. Development and Plan of Introduction

As the amount to be developed is so huge, processing tasks are classified into sevelal categories, each being developed in separate stages. The development phases of every task overlap each other, taking two to three years respectively. A total of 280 social insurance offices are partitioned into a few groups, with service operations separated into on-line works introduced one after another to each group, and eventually expanding throughout all of the offices. Such a process takes between one month and three years to be completed. The process of introduction is shown in Figure 2.

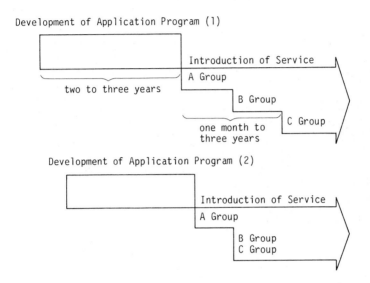

Figure 2. Development of Application Program and Introduction of Service

4.2.2. System Design and Development

[1] Development Organization

The massive scale of this project requires a large number of people in development, maintenance and management, totaling 1,000 regular staff members. There are presently 28 development groups, each developing a total of about 100 detailed events.

Generally speaking, it is now said that there is a deficiency in the number of people involved in development. However, since we have a sufficient number of such staff members for new task development, we can successfully ensure a high-level of know-how in this system over a long period of time.

The development organization, given in Figure 3 below, comprises the Social Insurance Agency, which presents development plans and operates the system, with NTT and the various manufacturers engaged in the design and development of the system.

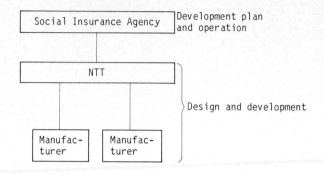

Figure 3. Development Organization

The greater the number of groups, the greater the adjustment between each group becomes indispensable. It is also important to find underlying problems, and to take the appropriate actions to solve those problems. Accordingly, arranging a structured conference system to which the respective working groups belong, and creating a system organization which has intersectional adjustment functions between groups are considered to be of great importance.
The more trouble the system confronts, the more important this becomes. However, reality does not always comply with theory.

[2] Standardization of Design and Design Method
   [a] With a large number of people involved in system development, standardization is indispensable. From this viewpoint, a standard design rule for documentation was established, while introducing such structure design as HIPO as well as a common module program, etc. When writing programs, high-level programming languages such as COBOL and a HDML (High-Level Database Manipulation Language) for database access are being used.
   [b] In the social insurance business, it is necessary to record and keep individual records accurately over a long period of time. In addition, individual records themselves are often complicated, and often vary, due to diverse factors such as law amendments. On the other hand, practical alteration in developing a system is of vital importance in order to smoothly convert manual work to online work. Consequently, system development which deals with various kinds of variations is so complicated that detailed design and review are required. At the same time it is necessary to take into account task analysis, historical task process, and expansion potentiality for the future in the process of development.

[3] Test Method
   Because of the system configuration with two or more distributed computers, a VM (Virtual Machine) system, in which plural computers are simulated on a single computer, is employed. Both remote and local common debug systems are also introduced to operate the computer efficiently, with the proper system being utilized depending on the development processes.
   Tools for large-scale confirmation tests on the bare machine prior to the service operation, or those for performance tests by high-load transaction, are also equipped.

[4] Quality Requirements
In the social insurance business, long-term records must be kept exactly
and efficiently, and many money-related transactions, such as insurance
premium collection, can be expected. What is more, the various
transactions are so closely related that, with for example, insurance
premiums being transferred into the form of pensions in the future, high
quality processing becomes necessary.
Accordingly, not only individual functional tests and overall operation
confirmation tests, but also quality improvement tests, taking aim at
some specified viewpoints, have been conducted repeatedly to confirm
quality.

4.2.3. Notes on Large-Scale System Construction

According to our experience, matters to be attended to for a large-scale
system are as follows.

[1] The greater the number of people involved in development, the stronger
the leaders are required.

[2] When a large-scale system is being developed, the minimum amount of
people necessary for development and the minimum number of tasks to be
perfomed by the software must be estimated in advance. At the same time,
it is risky to introduce too much new technology at one time.
These points, however, are apt to be underestimated at the initial stage.

[3] For system development, it could be a bitter blow to the task processing
development if a control program, which provides a fundamental base, is
not created beforehand.

[4] It might be better to conduct system development in two different steps:
the first dealing cautiously with inexperienced fields, and the second
gradually introducing labor-saving processes.

[5] When there are many groups, such required media as machine time and
magnetic tapes for program tests are apt to be underestimated, resulting
in a shortage of such media.

[6] Since system generation or performance evaluation requires highly
advanced technology, it is essential to have experts on hand who
thoroughly understand the situation, even more so than deemed necessary.

5. EVALUATION AFTER IMPLEMENTATION

Evaluation of development and operation is as follows.

5.1. Evaluation as a System and Points to be Noticed

[1] Super Large-Scale Software Development and Creation of Databases
Since this large-scale system is unprecedented in size, many cases
occurred in which the normal rules did not apply.
Consequently, various kinds of actions have been taken in an attempt to
improve the project management, such as early abstraction of problems,
intersectional adjustment and team coordination. As a result, we
believe, a super large-scale system developed by 1,000 people can be
operated properly under the proper setup. Creation of a massive database
based on manually-filed ledgers was completed during a short period of
time. Accordingly, this task proved to be very intensive both physically
and timewise, hindering the main development of the computer system.

[2] Traffic Concentration
     While a task can be rapidly processed after being computerized, that same
     processing is apt to be concentrated into a certain time period. Without
     the sufficient verification of such evaluation of operation, the
     performance of the system frequently drops down sharply.
     In reality, it is indispensable to keep up with the various modifications
     as they occur, supervising the situation and the resulting tendencies.

5.2. Evaluation of Operation

[1] Attainment of the Initial Objectives
     It is estimated that the initial objectives of improvement of national
     service and task operation, such as correctness, speed and national
     uniformity, have been attained when evaluated by the current service,
     although some of the tasks are still under development. Particularly,
     real-time response has become available with regard to individual
     counseling on pensions, something which is attracting more and more
     interest, at the various social insurance offices.
     The task of collecting insurance premiums has been recorded accurately
     and speedily through financial institutions. As a result, decision of
     insurance premiums can now be conducted precisely, based on previously
     recorded data.
     It will be possible to decide pension settlements within a week at most,
     although this job used to take over several months to complete. In a
     word, the system has provided with ever-increasing services in a wide
     range of tasks, with application areas being expanded to a wider range of
     new services.
     Being confronted with an ever-increasing number of insurers, efficient,
     correct, speedy and detailed service is by no means a negligible
     requirement.
     In conclusion, it is indispensable to introduce an advanced computer
     system.

ACKNOWLEDGEMENT

The author would like to thank the Social Insurance Agency in the Ministry of
Health and Welfare for giving the author the opportunity to participate in the
development of this system.

Social Insurance On-line Center

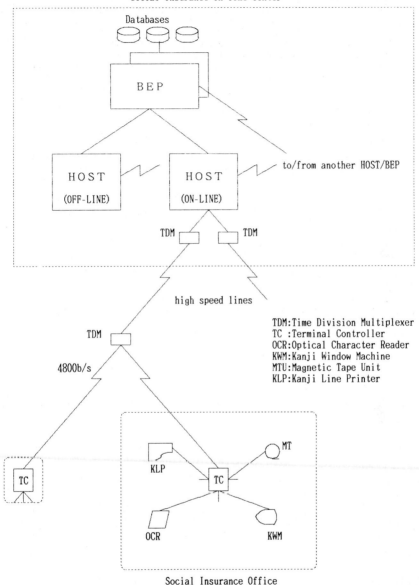

Figure 1.   Social Insurance System Configuration

Governmental and Municipal Information Systems
P. Kovács and E. Straub (Editors)
Elsevier Science Publishers B.V. (North-Holland)
© IFIP, 1988

Designing Forces in the Informatisation of Public
Administrations

Problems and Chances of Future-Orientated Application
Research

Prof. Dr. Klaus Grimmer

Forschungsgruppe Verwaltungsautomation,
Gesamthochschule Kassel - University -
Federal Republic of Germany

The use of information technology in public administrations seemingly advances without interruption. In connection thereto a great number of targets is envisaged: increase of service offers, improvement of service quality,
better compliance with the needs of the clients, more
efficiency, and humanisation of the working conditions.
The expectations of administrations towards the new
communication technologies, however, remain vague.

Electronical data processing and communication technology
unite. As far as the offerers' side is concerned individual technical systems such as personal computers, interconnected to working stations, integrated office commmu-
nication systems for the processing of texts, data, graphics, and documents, local networks, data bank-, and expert systems, public networks like ISDN determine the development. It seems at the moment as if the technical-
industrial capability to deliver new potentials of information and communication technology increasingly deviates
from the technical requirements in the administration
practice (not only in the public service) and its possibilities for application.

A stronger scientific engagement in the sense of a
future-orientated application research is required. Up to
now this is scarcely represented at universities and
large research institutions. Application research cannot
merely be considered as an instrument of industrial marketing but demands public promotion in order to deliver a
secured and politically justified basis for the development and application of new information and communication
potentials independent from commercial interests and
general routine requirements of administrations.

Subsequently the design targets and designing forces of
foregone computer-installations in public administrations
will be followed up. Afterwards the tasks and possibilities of application research in view to the development
and application of new information and communication
technology (IT and CT) will be discussed.

1. Modification of Design Targets and Designing Forces

In order to be able to estimate prospective demands for IT and CT and to consider their chance to be applied in practice it is advisable to have a look at the conditions, influencing factors and designing capacities which determined the application of IT in public administrations in the FRG in the past and at present.

The historical review of more than 25 years of technology use shows that first resource bottlenecks, above all a lack of personnel, stimulated the use of technology in mass administrations. Nowadays mainly economic problems and rationalisation requirements support further technology use. Convincing cost-profit-calculations, however, have not been realised yet.

Whereas in former times vague ideas of progressiveness were linked to the installation of technical equipment without any precise productivity expectations, today the importance of efficiency and effectiveness grew.

Whereas formerly the use of IT in public administrations was strongly determined by technical standards, and consequently by "technicians", nowadays technology offers a great range of application possibilities, and the "technicians" have to cope with precise ideas and expectations of the applying administration. This also resulted from technical deficiencies of both hardware and software becoming obvious in practical use only and thus demanding manifold adaptations.

Hence the choice of technology and its application, as well as the provisions required for the mastering of technically supported duties, was mostly done by EDP-centers, data administrations, and its coordination committees. Today, however, we can find in administration departments a - limited - understanding of technology and its capacities and now technical requirements are based on precise practical needs.

This raises discussions about the interests of the employed officials and involves the question about the design of workplaces and work processes compared to the past when neither the employed - above all low-level-officials - nor their representatives had a chance to express their own ideas, knowledge, and interests.

Whereas in the past the use of technology in public administration was of virtually no interest for the political and administrative management - apart from very few individual initiatives - presently administrations are faced with political pressure for the use of IT and CT and comprehensive conceptions and federal development plans are being worked out.

The results of this irregular process are

- that almost all direct and indirect public administrations use IT (EDP including remote data processing). Routine mass work and quantitative work is mostly carried out with technical su ort, IT is also used for text production,

- that application schemes for the back-up of qualitative decision processes have been worked out (f.i. in employment administrations), and sporadic developments for mastering multi-com-
plex duties (as known in district governments) can be observed,

- that IT is also used as a means of communication (employment
administration, information systems of the pension fund); due to
the way it is used a separation of IT and CT is difficult in
public administration,

- that means of telecommunication are scarcely used in public
administrations except telephone and telex, disregarding some
specific administrative networks (f.i. police, tax administration, and others),

- that Btx as a means of communication is very rarely used;
there are single institutions (communities) using Btx for the
information (as a means of self-portrayal) of their citizens,

- that boards for economic promotion on federal and municipal
level take action to investigate the innovative potentials of
telecommunication offers (so-called "teleparks").

Today the topics in DP-administrations and special administration departments comprise

- the ratio of central and decentralised technology use,

- the systematic-organisational integration of PCs and text-
processing,

- the internal distribution of IT- and CT- competences,

- the further development of IT and its application.

2. Development Determinants

The design influencing factors are altogether not uniform. But
as I still intend to try to filter out certain development
determining factors in order to apply them prognostically I
refer to the research work of the "Forschungsgruppe Verwaltungsautomation" at the Gesamthochschule Kassel dealing with technology use in various administrations.

I would like to distinguish between

- the structure of administration work,

- the participants and their interests, insofar as they are
important for the further development of technology in administration, and

- problems deriving from the function of public administrations
in political systems.

2.1 Administration Work in View to Communication and Information Processing

As to its formal structure administration work seems to be especially suitable for information and communication technology back-up. The main administrative duties are the collection, processing and distribution of information. Facts are being stated, standardised and decisions are being made. The information will be forwarded to the client or to other departments of the administration. Corresponding to the different administrative duties the flow of information (i. e. the collection, processing and distribution of information) can be limited to a simple circle client-administration-client or between various administrative organisations. It can, however, also result in a ramified system between administration and client and various administrative organisations. The formal structure of the information and communication relations is as much ruled by organisation and competence regulations as informational requirements result from the communication contents of the duty in question.

The information is distributed by telephone, mail or messenger (above all within and between administrations), and - as already mentioned - by information technology.

Such a formal interpretation, however, is insufficient. In everyday work administrative duties turn out to be very complex, disregarding certain mass and routine work. The formal network of communication with its defined informational contents is overlied by an informal communication network and a great number of additional "soft" information, delivering orientation, understanding and evaluation, and which decisively determine the character of administrative actions and the quality of administrative work. This informational in-depth structure is the source of resistence of a great number of administrative duties against an IT and/or CT-linked - not: -supported - processing.

2.2 Participants and their Interests

The introduction of technology in public administrations depends on technology-political as much as economic and social policy influence. Although administrations are aware of their independent significance they sensitively adapt to political movements at the same time.

As the field of politics provides the budget it determines facts. The ministerial level can initiate programmes, representative corporations can give impetus to demands and plans in the way of parlamentary inquieries or at the occasion of debates concerning budget, organisation and employment, they can generate a pressure of expectation in administrations.

The "leadership" for provision and employment of new technologies is shifted to a great deal from technology-orientated data-centers to organisation departments of special administrations which adopted further competence. Another reason is that text processing and communication technology is mostly out of the influence of DP-organisations.

The management and officials' level (respectively their representatives) actively participate in planning and decision
processes for the employment of IT and CT - partly for various
reasons and different interests. Work-related and ergonomic
aspects increasingly form influencing criteria.

2.3 Lasting Structural Limitations?

Administration work is characterised by a structural continuity.
Its execution is related to specific administrative procedures
and ideas of correctness. This is both expressed by the stability of production processes and work regulations (where also
the written and documentary form belongs to). Only few administration duties are "time-critical". An obstacle for innovation
is the necessity to secure the regularity of normatively fixed
work compliance - which is also expressed by the status and competence of officials - in order to simultaneously grant the
interchangeability of personnel for the execution of administration work, as this is a special feature of bureaucracies. Therefore individual, workplace-related innovations are only feasible
to a small extent.

The organisational structures of administrations are multi-
dimensional and multi-functional and contribute to political
stability, services which are in line with legal prescriptions
and the clients' needs, securing of controllable work processes,
humane working conditions, and openness for innovations. The
creation of new administrative structures by the implementation
of information technology could invalidate this multi-functiona-
lity of single organisational structures and thus impede the
efficiency of the organisational system.

Well-tried solutions and working methods will only be abolished
when improvements are obviously possible. In doubt the
established working procedures - which also implies the
introduced technology use - will be maintained. If the political
trend urges an enlargement of the use of technology, it is more
likely that established systems will be improved by capacity
extension or attached systems than the trial of new technology
concepts. This attitude also results from scarce resources in
EDP-centers, DP-administrations and special administrations.

The problems of data protection represent another retarding
factor for the interconnection of existing IT-equipment, and
therewith for the use of CT in public administrations. Considering the possibilities and consequences of the application of new
technologies no reliable attitude has developed so far.

The way of budget- and investment planning in public administrations on one hand, organisational and legal requirements towards
administrative procedures on the other hand finally entail that
the planning and execution of innovative concepts in public
administrations result in medium- to longterm affairs.

In general the period between the development of a project or
innovative ideas and the start of its realisation is three to
five years, up to the "successful" end of the execution of a
plan certainly another two years. Conceptual modifications,
which means the abandon of familiar ways of technology require
even longer periods for their recognition and realisation.

These structural conditions hint at the integration of public
administrations into the political system, the functionalisation
of administrations for the stabilisation of the system and the
respective temporarily restricted - politically determined -
development lines. These lines develop in a sort of dialectic
process of external impulses (f.i. economic development, interest manifestations within parties and associations, legitimation
and acceptance requirements) and internal transformation into
practical strategies. This does not mean that political preconditions directly and immmediately result in technical-organisational solutions, but they determine the direction of development.

2.4 Further requirements?

It is difficult to forecast prospective developments, because
not only the structural elements themselves have different
weight, but the mentioned designing forces act on different
levels and partly follow different interests. While in the field
of politics a technical orientation related to efficiency
expectations prevails, plannings of organisation departments aim
at general weak points of the administration and the controllability of administrative processes. The officials' level on the
other hand stronger orientates at the requirements of single
duties and traditional working methods.

A practice-orientated approach limited to the evaluation of the
different participants is obviously insufficient. Such an
approach only seems fruitful in addition to a structural evaluation.

As far as the field of politics is concerned a fundamental
decidedness in favour of the use of IT and CT can be stated,
there is a tendency to functionalise administrations for a
certain kind of technology policy. We assume that this target
aims at the maintenance of the controllability in administrations when the quantity and complexity of their duties increase
and thus contribute to the rationality of the system.

My opinion is that despite this fundamental decidedness certain
conditions for technical innovations have to be provided, f.i.
their safe applicability, mainly for reasons of justification
but also with respect to experienced problems as to their realisation.

For new technologies and their application also a positive
public (private economy) evaluation is requested. Finally at
least potential rationalisation effects and service improvements
may have to be connected with the application of a new technology.

For the (middle) management level and the level of officials -
as well as their representatives - has to be obvious that a
definite relief of work, improvement of the work organisation
and service quality can be achieved by the application of new
technologies.

When evaluating the stated design determinants in their context I start with a continuous, inner-organisationally guided development where the following possible requirements and preparedness for innovations can be registered:

The precise technical possibility and necessity of support in the execution of certain duties is basical. Flexible technology offers have priority. The intention of the development is the overall technically supported official. Therefore in public administrations for knowledge-based, expert systems acceptancy can be expected as such systems limit the problems of providing information and the risks of decision-making and insofar stabilise bureaucratic behaviour.

The interest in the provision of management information increases in the administrative management. Especially for complex administration duties knowledge is understood as an independent resource which is technically disposable.

The requirements for central and decentralised system solutions complement each other. Improved communication possibilities are above all desirable for new administration duties such as environment protection, health, nuclear energy, as they are "time-critical" and due to the competence of various administrations demand inter-organisational coordination and reconciled action against the – frequently critical – public opinion.

The extension of the – especially communication-technical – infrastructure such as IT and CT application for intra-organisational duties and compound solutions is realised in long terms only – disregarding the already mentioned duties – unless it is ordered by political, system-planning and budget-based decisions. The reasons do not only lie in a certain scepticism of the employed officials against radical technology employment but also in the scarcity of the disposable budget, most of all, however, in the necessary analysis and organisation requirements. In contrary to data processing, above all the offer and application of workplace-related systems, the employment of communication technology requires coordination and integration, furthermore the comprehension of related workplaces in organisational and execution planning in advance and requires a strategically advanced diffusion.

3. Application Research

The recording of conditions and influencing elements in IT- and CT-application in public administrations is a necessary component of future-orientated application research but not sufficient to justify it as a scientific-political focal point.

The following duties of application research can be nominated

- investigation of possible further "requirements" of IT and CT (in public administrations),

- investigation of "application"-potentials of (prospective) IT and CT,

- analysis of the political-structural conditions of handling in public administrations,

- development of "adapted" technical-organisational concepts,

- transfer of application-orientated requirements to the development of technology,

- communication of legal requirements to the political area, and

- development of sufficient methodical instruments.

3.1 Starting Points: Structure of Administrative Duties, Market Development, Decision Behaviour, Political-Structural Frame

For the methodical question of how to assess further requirements and their conditions of realisation seven accumulating starting points result from the stipulated duties and the mentioned factors of influence for the field of public administrations:

The investigation of possible prospective "requirements" of IT and CT has to be based on an analysis of the administrative duties (1) concerning their suitability for IT- and/or CT-supported execution. It has to determine the structure of the duties and of its competent/involved organisations as much as their respective overlapping function (2) in their informational and communicational relations.

It also has to include present qualification profiles of the employed officials on different levels (3) and their possible further development as they co-determine the application possibilities of new technologies.

In my opinion it is important to include the history of technisation - the grown administrative strategies - into the analysis of duties, organisations and qualification profiles. Other than in private economy where an understanding for the replacement of a product by a new - better one - or the enlargement of the range of products exists, administrations are - as already explained - bound to continuity.

In this context it is necessary to elaborate fundamental knowledge about the real decision processes - influencing factors (5) - in public administrations related to the introduction and extension of technical systems; published statements mostly serve as a legitimation and say nothing about the accomplished processes, the relevant participant and the criteria which dominated.

The analysis of the efficiency of IT and CT also has to include their market development (6) and application in private economy, especially in the related service sector (insurance, banks). It does not only serve to recognise "applicable" potentials of IT and CT but characterises the surrounding of administrations and its influences.

Finally an analysis of the political-structural conditions of
activity (7) in public administrations is required. The political domain does not only decide about administrative duties and
legally regulated procedures but also about the provision of
resources and determines the administrative function within the
political-social system.

As to application research two different complementary methods
can be distinguished. They are

the investigation of the future requirements of the administration itself deriving from its duties and structure, from the
present administrative organisation, the organisational flow of
procedures, and the presently relevant designing influences
regarding the administrative behaviour,

and the investigation of "externally" uttered requirements
resulting from the attribution / or adoption of new duties or
new procedures (especially concerning interaction and communication relations) between administrations and their clients.

Better service for the client is a frequently used slogan in
administration. But this service is only development relevant
insofar as it is in line with the administration's own production interests (e.g. pension fund, employment administration).
There are, however, transfer effects from the private economy
production or service field, if the employment of certain information and/or communication systems provides facilitated conditions of action between the administration and its clients,
which in turn facilitates the conditions of production in
administrations.

Choosing an approach based on a view from outside of the administration a nearly infinite number of new administration services
or newly designed administrative procedures - feasible by means
of IT and/or CT - can be invented. If such an analysis is sin-
cerely worked out it has to explain if and to what extent the
clients are prepared to use such new services and procedures -
especially when they result in efforts for them -, and in which
way and what kind of (financial) means the administrative realisation of new services and procedures can be expected. Insofar
both the internal and external approach show common features.

3.2 Method-Mix

Application research depends on sufficient methodical instruments not only for the necessary analysis of the present state,
but also for the development of design concepts and the examination of the preparedness to accept such concepts. Especially for
the analysis of administrative duties, organisational structures, workplace relations, and the investigation of the historical process of technisation in single administrations a refined
methodical strategy is required.

Up to now the organisation research does not dispose of a sufficient basis - not only with respect to public administrations;
there is a lack of both systematic research results and organi-
sation-analysing empiricism and organisation-theoretical material. Further difficulties also derive from the provision of
communication analyses as a precondition of an appropriate and

efficient application of new technologies. Especially within less standardised administration procedures the administrative acts will be determined by a great number of differently structured interaction and communication relations.

The problem to deliver methodically secured forecasts is well-known. Helpful is the trend investigation on the basis of comparative case studies. I am not going to follow up the problems of a necessary abstraction and the representativeness of the results.

The use of the so-called "Delphi-method" seems to be less productive with respect to public administrations. Such methods can offer supplementary assistance when applied on the level of the so-called trend-amplification, as f.i. in associations or administrative "opinion and research institutions".

The "scenario-method" is of additional help for the discussion of future-orientated, alternative design models. Their function would be the presentation of newly designed administrative procedures and to check the practical realisation of analytically developed models including the necessary assistant measures.

Field tests and "pilot projects" are finally suitable to find out potential risks, to check acceptancy and the possibility of a transfer of design concepts.

3.3 The Importance of Application Research

Application research has to make sure which criteria its application and design recommendations have to correspond to. Refering to public administrations I consider the following general criteria as important:

- design has to be in line with duties, i.e. the complete and appropriate execution of administrative work has to be guaranteed which simultaneously implies the obedience of political regulations;

- the design has to meet the client's needs, which means that the he does not have to be burdened with administrative expenditure, the accessibility has to be adjusted to his specific situation;

- the design has to be in line with the officials' demands, they have to provide "humane working conditions";

- designs have to be economic, which means that among all possible designs allowing an optimal realisation of the other criteria, the most economic has to be chosen, evaluating the consequences for the employment situation;

- altogether the selected designs have to be taken into consideration regarding their social impact in the future.

Fundamental evaluation criteria are the administrative duties and their structural features as conditions for their execution by administrative organisations. Public administrations have been created to deliver definite services in a regulated procedure for a constitutional society. The application of IT and CT

has to enable the maintenance of the contents of service
requirements and the regulations for procedures, as they are not
only destined to secure the legality of administrative acts, but
also the clients' chance of participation and control. It is not
a matter of the technicians or some officials to introduce a
change in the duties or in the offically granted positions by
means of certain technology. Such changes are only subject to
political decisions. This represents a considerable difference
to technology use in private economy: the product and the way of
production are disposable for the company, the market decides
about the usefulness of the company's decision.

Usually technical-organisational design recommendations will not
be final in order to provide the chance of adaptation to the
situation of the administrations, their officials, and their
clients. Due to the methodical and practical problems for
example to develop complete communication analyses and communication-technical systems based thereon, design recommendations
will consequently adhere to the selection of duties, the presentation of the relevant communication context (skeletonised communication models) within the execution of work, the nomination
of suitable technology and thus to the stipulation of minimum
requirements for the employment of technology, after all it will
leave room for the free adaptation in practical work.

Application research is necessarily connected to the research of
design-related consequences. Only if the possible effects of
certain applications inside and outside of administrations will
be included they can be decided.

Application research also has to feed back its results regarding
a technology application that is in line with duties, clients,
officials, and economy to the producers of technology in order
to initiate application-orientated technology development. The
communication problems between producers and users have not been
clarified yet, corresponding instruments will have to be developed which can be regarded as another duty of application
research.

Finally application research has to make available its results
for politics, for example by the early nomination of legal
requirements or regulation demands with reference to their contents in order to avoid failures respecting the basic criteria
of the research, political conditions or constitutional demands.
After all it has to hint at possible alterations within the
political-social structures by the application of new information and communication technology, otherwise the prospective
development of IT- and CT-supported administrations would be
exposed to the "standardising power of facts".

Governmental and Municipal Information Systems
P. Kovács and E. Straub (Editors)
Elsevier Science Publishers B.V. (North-Holland)
© IFIP, 1988

STRUCTURED SYSTEMS ANALYSIS AND DESIGN METHOD
- A U.K. GOVERNMENT STANDARD

Michael C. GOODLAND

School of Information Systems, Kingston Polytechnic, Penrhyn Road, Kingston on Thames, KT1 2EE, United Kingdom.

The Structured Systems Analysis and Design Method (SSADM) has been used as a standard approach for the development of computerized information systems by the United Kingdom government since 1981. This paper presents a brief overview of SSADM and reviews its use by the UK government.

1. INTRODUCTION

In 1980 the Central Computer and Telecommunications Agency (CCTA), a unit which has responsibility for promoting good practice in government computing, were investigating the productivity of systems analysts and designers. As a result of this work a method for systems analysis and design was chosen to become the standard throughout government departments. Since its introduction in two pilot projects in 1981 its use has grown to the extent that in 1987 more that 350 government projects are estimated to have used or are using SSADM. In addition to central government use, it has been widely accepted by public utilities, local government, health authorities and commercial organizations who use SSADM or one of the commercial variations offered by private consultancies. It is now also promoted by the National Computer Centre (NCC) of the United Kingdom who publish a reference manual for SSADM [1].

SSADM has been used on a great variety of different projects. These range in size from the one person / six month project to the 40 person / 4 year project. The types of project have varied widely: manual systems being computerized, already computerized systems being enhanced or rewritten, maintenance of existing systems, the development of distributed and replicated systems, systems which will use application packages, systems which will be implemented using fourth generation languages, and systems for which there is no existing system. The range of information system application areas that SSADM has been used on is also great: welfare benefits, company and import taxation, legal administration, personnel, pay-roll, accounting, dental health care, immigration control, production of government statistics and many more.

The starting points for SSADM could range from a vague description of the project area to a full feasibility study report and the end products of a full study are a complete set of data, program, and system specifications. Feasibility studies are also carried out with SSADM. Thus the phases of the traditional systems life cycle addressed by SSADM are feasibility study, systems investigation, logical and physical systems design. By itself SSADM does not address: project selection and information systems planning, project management and control, the programming and implementation phases. However SSADM has been designed to integrate with these activities and specific guide-lines have been produced for integration with the PROMPT project management and control methodology [2] and Structure Design Method (SDM), the UK government version of Jackson Structured Programming [3].

2.   OVERVIEW OF SSADM

2.1.   Structural, Procedural and Documentation Standards

SSADM can be thought of as being composed of Structural, Procedural, and Documentation standards.

Structural standards divide the project up into six *stages*, each stage is subdivided into a number of *steps* and each step consists of *tasks*. Figure 1 shows the stages of an SSADM project. Similar diagrams show the inter-dependency of steps for each stage of a project. The products of each step and the interfaces between steps are clearly defined in the SSADM documentation[1].

Procedural standards define how each step and task is to be performed by providing development staff with a set of proven, usable, techniques and tools, and with guide-lines on how these should be applied.

Documentation standards define how the products of this development activity should be presented. Currently these are manifested as notational standards for diagrams and as paper forms. However many projects are now using computer support tools for developing these products.

2.2.   Underlying Principles

Certain basic principles underlie SSADM. These principles are not unique to SSADM - they are shared to a varying degree by many modern methods of systems analysis and design

Data-driven
All application systems have an underlying, generic, data structure which changes very little over time, although processing requirements may change. SSADM is a 'data-driven' approach in that great emphasis is put on determining this data structure, building it into the system architecture and ensuring that the processing structure is built around it.

Logical physical split
SSADM separates logical design from physical design. A hardware / software independent logical design is produced which can easily be translated into an initial physical design. Thus the developer is not concerned with file layouts, programming language or operating system constraints when engaged in the conceptual stages of analysis and design.

Different views of the system
Three different views of the system are developed in analysis. A view of the underlying structure of the system's data (the Logical Data Structure), a view of how data is used by the system and is transmitted into and out of the system (Data Flow Diagrams), and a view of how the system data is changed by events over time (Entity Life Histories). These views are regularly cross-checked to ensure that a consistent, complete picture of the system is maintained.

Top-down and bottom-up
SSADM is both a top-down and a bottom-up methodology. In the early stages of a project top-down techniques such as data flow diagramming and logical data structuring are used whereas in the design stages bottom-up techniques such as

relational data analysis and detailed process design are used to provide the detail and then reconciled with the top-down views to produce a validated logical design.

Iterative development
The previous two paragraphs have emphasized the consistency checking inherent in SSADM. It follows then that the development must be iterative with discoveries or decisions made in one view being reflected as changes in other, previously, constructed views.

User involvement
SSADM seeks to actively involve the user in the development of the system. This is encouraged by the use of easily understood, non technical diagrammatic techniques supported by short simple narrative descriptions. Users participate in formal quality assurance reviews and informal walkthroughs to ensure that the system being developed meets their requirements. At separate points during the development process users are offered a range of business options and a range of technical options. In some projects users have been trained in SSADM and have joined the development team.

Quality assurance
Formal quality assurance reviews are held at the end of each SSADM stage. The end products for the stage are scrutinized for quality, completeness, consistency, and applicability by users, developers and by experienced systems staff external to the project.

Self documenting
The products of each SSADM step form the project documentation and are used in subsequent steps. There is no possiblity of documentation becoming an 'after the event' activity.

2.3.   Techniques of SSADM

Logical Data Structure (LDS)
This is a method for describing what information should be held by the system. The approach used in SSADM is very similar to entity modelling in other methods. A diagram is produced showing the entities and their relationships, this is further documented by a set of entity description forms detailing their data contents. They are used in stages 1, 2, 4, 5 and 6 of SSADM.

Data Flow Diagrams (DFDs)
A widely-used method for representing flows of information through a system and between the system and the outside world. The approach used in SSADM is similar to that described by DeMarco [4] although the notation is like Gane and Sarson's [5]. They are used in stages 1, 2, 4 and 6.

Entity Life Histories (ELHs)
These are models of how the system's data is changed over time by events acting on entities. For each entity the sequence, selection and iteration of events affecting it are shown using a notation derived from Jackson [3]. They are used in stages 2, 5 and 6.

Logical Dialogue Design
A diagram, similar to a flowchart, is developed in Stage 2 for each update or enquiry that will be handled on-line. The Logical Dialogue Outlines show the data content of the user's inputs and the system's outputs.

Process outlines
These are descriptions of how events must be processed by the system. Each event may affect several entities; for each the operations performed and the data navigation are described. They are developed from Entity Life Histories in Stage 5 and and used for program specification in Stage 6.

Relational data analysis
A well-known technique for grouping data items into non-redundant, data independent, relations. The normalization rules are applied to the inputs and outputs to and from the required system It is used to fully define the logical data design in Stage 4.

First cut Data Design and first cut Program Design
The logical data and process designs are converted mechanically by application of a set of rules particular to the hardware/ software environment into first cut program and data specifications. These techniques are used in stage 6.

Physical Design Control
A technique, used in Stage 6, for predicting and optimizing the performance of the system. The system is tuned on paper before the programming phase begins.

2.4.   Steps and Stages of SSADM

The Stages of the project are shown below in Figure 1.

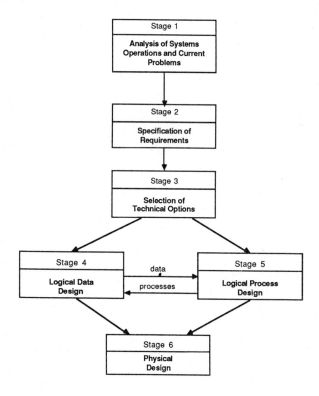

Figure 1   Stages of SSADM

2.4.1. Stage 1: Analysis of System Operations and Current Problems

This stage is concerned with the setting up the project, and performing a full analysis of the current system in terms of its operations, data, and problems. Data Flow Diagrams are used to describe the current operations and a Logical Data Structure describes the data held. A problem/requirement list describes in narrative the problems identified in the current system and the requirements for the new system. Severity/importance ratings are given to the problems/requirements; these act as a check-list which can be applied to the new system specification. Finally a formal quality assurance review is carried out with the users to ensure that the current system has been fully understood.

2.4.2. Stage 2: Specification of Requirements

A number of activities are involved in this stage:-

Firstly the Data Flow Diagrams which represent the current physical system are converted into a logical view. Thus the constraints implemented in the current system are not further considered.

The problem/requirement list is extended by including audit, security,control and any other new requirements. Each entry is expanded to give a full description and any duplications are removed.

By referring to the problem/requirement list and to the logical Data Flow Diagrams a number of Business System Options are developed and offered to the user. The selected option is then further described by a full set of required system Data Flow Diagrams and a required system Logical Data Structure. Supporting documentation is produced for both sets of diagrams.

Events are identified by inspection of the Data Flow Diagrams. A matrix is drawn up of events and the entities they affect, this is used to help develop the Entity Life Histories. These provide a third view of the system, linking the Logical Data Structure and the Data Flow Diagrams and revealing any inconsistencies in the different views.

Logical Dialogue Outlines are developed for the events that will be handled on-line. These provide the user with a clear view of the content of any on-line, man-machine dialogues.

Finally the products of this stage are formally reviewed to ensure that the Requirement Specification satisfies the users.

2.4.3. Stage 3: Selection of Technical Options

There will be a number of ways of implementing the Requirement Specification. Each will provide different levels of service, and will have different cost and benefits. A number, usually no more than three, of implementation options are offered to the user. After the users have made their selection, possibly assisted by the design team, the Requirement Specification may need to be modified.

2.4.4. Stage 4: Data Design

Stages 4 and 5 interact and to some extent are done in parallel. In Stage 4 a detailed logical data design is produced called the Composite Logical Data Design. Relational data analysis is performed on the inputs and outputs of the required system. All the results of individual analyses are combined to produce an optimized set of relations in Boyce-Codd normal form. These relations are converted to Logical Data Structure type diagram. This diagram, derived from relational data analysis, is the compared with the required Logical Data Structure, developed in Stage 2 by business analysis. Any differences are resolved with the user to produce the Composite Logical Data Design.

2.4.5. Stage 5: Process Design

Each event shown on an Entity Life History is developed into a Logical Update Process Outline. This details: volumes and frequency of the event, the entities affected, the operation performed on each entity as a result of the event, and the navigation through the Composite Logical Data Design required to process the event. A similar Logical Enquiry Process Outline is developed for each enquiry defined in Stage 2. The detailed logical data and process design are then reviewed together to ensure that they support each other.

2.4.6. Stage 6: Physical Design

The logical data and process designs are converted mechanically by application of a set of rules particular to the hardware/ software environment into first cut program and data specifications. These are rules, existing or easily developed, for converting logical designs into physical designs. A different set of rules is used for each proprietary file or database management system.

The first cut design is then subjected to Physical Design Control. The design is sized in terms of the amount of storage, the time taken for batch programs and on-line transactions, and the time taken to recover from hardware and software faults. The results of this sizing are compared with the performance objectives set by the users in Stage 3. If the objectives are not met the the physical design is modified and re-sized. This cycle of re-design and re-sizing is continued until the performance objectives are met or until no more improvement is possible. If the performance objectives cannot be met then the users are consulted and a change to either objectives, system software or to hardware agreed.

When the tuned design is satisfactory the full specification of the physical design is completed. Full program specification are developed, database or file definitions are loaded into the data dictionary, clerical procedures are specified, the user manual is prepared, operatin instructions and schedules are prepared, and plans are drawn up for programming, testing, data conversion, and change-over.

3.   REVIEW OF THE USE OF SSADM IN GOVERNMENT

3.1.   History

3.1.1. Selection of a methodology

In 1974 the CCTA, concerned about the escalating cost of government software developments, had introduced the Jackson method of program design (known in government as SDM) into government departments. Having achieved some improvements in programmer productivity and reduced program maintenance costs attention was focussed on systems analysis and design. At that time there was no systematic or standard approach to designing information systems in government and systems were often poorly specified and documented. Several different methodologies were commercially available and it was decided that CCTA should select one for trial use in government. Companies were invited to submit their method in the hope of winning the large training and consultancy contracts that would follow selection of their method. To be eligible for selection a method had to be:

proven in practice and immediately available,
concerned with the major activities of analysis and design,
teachable to and useable by government officers in a typical installation,
well supported in the UK by supplier,
compatible with SDM and with the government project control method.

In November 1980 five companies were shortlisted and in January 1981 the method put forward by Learmonth and Burchett Management Systems (LBMS) was chosen.

3.1.2. Method of introduction into government

A gradual approach was taken to the introduction of SSADM with two lead-in projects being initially selected to use the method. These projects were closely monitored by CCTA from several viewpoints. The amount and kind of training, the level of support and the documentation required for the method were assessed. The impact of using SSADM on the organization, on project management and its staffing implications were studied. The costs and benefits associated with using the method were also evaluated. CCTA staff gained practical experience with SSADM by working as team members on these lead-in projects. This early work enabled CCTA to develop a low risk strategy for the introduction of the method into other projects and eventually throughout government.

As it became apparent that the use of SSADM in the lead-in projects was proving successful CCTA began to promote SSADM more heavily. Seminars were held for senior managers in government departments, new projects were encouraged to use SSADM, and the frequency of training courses was increased. By the end of 1982, 18 months after its introduction, 35 projects were using SSADM. In January 1983, convinced of the benefits of SSADM, CCTA made the method mandatory for all new administrative information systems being developed for government. Since then its use has grown extensively, with a CCTA internal report estimating the number of projects at 250 in January 1986, these projects had an estimated total expenditure of £6 billion (ca. $10 billion). Although SSADM is no longer mandatory it is now used in all government departments with the exception of two: the Inland Revenue who use a version of the Yourdon Method and the Department of Health and Social Security who have integrated SSADM into a life cycle methodology that includes strategic planning, project control and management, and the programming and implementation phases. The number of government projects currently using or who have used SSADM is estimated at 350, with an estimated staff of 1500 having experience.

3.1.3. Development of SSADM

SSADM has been subject to constant review since its introduction. Version 2 of SSADM was released in December 1984 and Version 3 released in March 1986. Responsibility for development of SSADM has remained with CCTA although they consulted with private sector consultancies and SSADM users about each version.

Section 2 described SSADM Version 3. The main changes that were introduced with Version 3 were the introduction of the Logical Dialogue Design technique, some extensions to the Logical Data Structure notation, and some re-allocation of tasks to different steps. There was also the introduction of guide-lines to the use of SSADM in different ways: for maintenance projects, for microcomputer projects, for projects using computer support tools, and to estimating the resources required for SSADM projects.

The main changes that were brought about when Version 2 was introduced were modifications to the way in which Entity Life Histories were developed and the introduction of the Business System Options which sought to introduce a creative element into SSADM projects.

3.2. Central support for SSADM

The control and promotion of SSADM throughout government was provided by a section, within CCTA. This comprises on average 15 staff, both civil servants and external consultants. The work of this section and the central training requirements for SSADM are discussed below.

3.2.1. Training requirements

The UK government has a training college, the Civil Service College, who give, among many others, ADP courses. Initially the SSADM training was given by LBMS consultants at the Civil Service College but after a few months civil service trainers took over the courses. Over the last two or three years demand for training has been so high that many civil servants have been trained by commercial consultancies and training organizations.

Experienced systems analysts attend two SSADM courses, SSADM Part 1 and SSADM Part 2. The Part 1 course covers Stages 1 to 5 and the Part 2 course covers Stage 6. They are normally run as 5 day residential courses although some organizations offer slightly longer courses. Staff with no systems analysis training or experience normally go on a 4 week residential 'Basic Systems' course that includes SSADM Part 1 and 2 and some basic systems analysis skills. Other SSADM courses that have proved successful are: 'SSADM for Users' (a 2 or 3 day course for users who will be checking SSADM documentation), 'SSADM for project managers' (a 3 day course covering estimating, planning, and general project management issues), and ' SSADM for programmers' (5 days). CCTA appraises any new SSADM courses offered by commercial organizations and maintains a list of approved courses.

3.2.2. Consultancy

Since the introduction of SSADM the CCTA has provided free consultancy support to projects using the method for the first time. This support has taken several forms: advice on the application of SSADM techniques, estimation and planning of projects, tailoring SSADM to particular project environments, attendance at quality assurance reviews, training of users to understand SSADM documentation and advice on the use of computer support tools. Good consultancy support to SSADM has been a major factor in ensuring its success in government departments.

Initially projects were receiving about 2 man days of consultancy per month but with increasing adoption of SSADM this level of support could not be maintained. Another problem is that it has been difficult for CCTA to keep its support staff as they have become very marketable to the higher paying private sector. Some government departments have set up their own centres of SSADM expertise and some projects have made extensive use of consultants from the private sector. Now only the most critical projects are regularly supported by CCTA.

3.2.3. Documentation

A three volume reference manual to SSADM is produced and distributed by CCTA to government departments. Volume 1 describes the structural standards of SSADM giving detailed task lists for feasibility and full studies. Volume 2 addresses the procedural standards and gives guidance on all the SSADM techniques. Volume 3 includes the documentation standards (with all the standard SSADM forms), and sections on software support to SSADM, project management aspects, and the use of SSADM in specific project circumstances (with prototyping, with 4th generation languages, with application packages, in microcomputer projects and for maintenance of existing systems). Also included in Volume 3 are a worked case study, based on a government project, and a glossary of SSADM terminology. A condensed version of this manual is published by the National Computer Centre [1]. All training courses provide manuals.

3.2.4. User Groups and Promotion of SSADM

The first government SSADM user group meeting was held in December 1982 and they have been held twice yearly since. CCTA has retained responsibility for organizing the meetings and publishing the minutes. At each meeting there have been main sessions, parallel sessions and meetings for various working parties on computer support, training, project management, SSADM techniques and others. Speakers have been from CCTA, from government projects and from the private sector. In the early days of SSADM everyone who had been trained in SSADM was invited to the user group but numbers later became so large that, even after changing venue, invitations had to be restricted to one person per project. A user group is organized by LBMS for users of their commercial version of SSADM, LBMS Structured Development Method (LSDM).

CCTA has promoted SSADM outside government also. As many government computer contracts are awarded to software houses, for either a full systems development or for just the software, seminars have been arranged for the UK software industry. Interest was also stimulated in academic circles by a seminar for them and many polytechnics now teach SSADM.

3.3.   Current trends

Throughout the development of SSADM interest has been maintained in other fields of academic and commercial interest that could have an impact on the method. Thus CCTA have funded major studies into how expert systems technology can be employed to support SSADM, and into how the rigour of formal design methods, particularly the Vienna Design Method, can be applied to SSADM. However the main areas of interest have been the development of automated computer support tools to SSADM and the development of an interface between the later stages of SSADM and fourth generation environments (this term is used here to describe the environment in which a fourth generation language or is used, this could embrace the language, code generation, data dictionary, database management system, screen painter, and transaction processing software).

3.3.1. Automated support for SSADM

The area of computer assistance to systems analysis and design has been of great commercial and academic interest recently. Several 'analyst workbenches' are now marketed and used extensively. They provide varying support to such techniques as data flow diagramming, entity modelling, functional decomposition, relational data analysis, action diagramming, and database design. Most tools provide a graphics interface to the diagrammatic techniques, some provide consistency and completeness checks for techniques and across techniques, some provide support to specific methodologies, and some provide generation of database definitions and program code. These tools are generally single user, running on IBM PC/AT or compatible hardware, although some multi-user tools are becoming available. Another class of tools are the data dictionary products that have incorporated documentation of analysis and design.

Although many of the tools support techniques that are used in SSADM only two specifically support SSADM: MUST from CCTA and Automate/Datamate from LBMS Ltd. They are both used in government projects. The following features are shared by both tools: graphics support to data flow diagrams, logical data structures and entity life histories, consistency and completeness checking, reporting and query facilities. The main differences are that the LBMS tool provides support for relational data analysis, is single-user whereas the CCTA tool is multi-user product.

The general aim of CCTA's work on computer support for SSADM has been to help government departments to make optimum use of computers as a tool for managers, analysts, designers, and programmers. This work has involved the development of MUST, the appraisal of commercially available products, liaison with companies and research programmes, and support to departments on the selection and use of these tools.

A further component of CCTA's work has been the development of a meta-model of SSADM itself. This model, expressed as a Logical Data Structure, depicts and defines all the concepts used in SSADM and their inter-relationships. The use of the meta-model has been fundamental in the development of computer tools and in the definition of the interface to fourth generation environments described below.

3.3.2. Use with fourth generation environments

When SSADM was designed and first used most systems developed in government used Jackson program design techniques and were programmed in COBOL. Now many systems under development in government will use either solely fourth generation environments or will use a combination of these and COBOL.

It is clear that SSADM is a flexible approach and can be easily adapted to accommodate fourth generation environments. With a well specified interface between SSADM and the fourth generation environment ther may be an opportunity to directly generate code from the SSADM specifications. This opportunity led to a detailed study of this interface.

The approach taken was to build a meta-model of SSADM and data models of the fourth generation environments. Eight fourth generation environments were studied and a generic data model produced. This model included features from all eight and depicted an ideal environment in that it represented a super-set of features. The SSADM meta-model and the generic fourth generation environment data model were then compared to see if a smooth transition was possible. In general SSADM provided sufficient information to give direct translation into the 'ideal' fourth generation environment. However it was found that slight modifications were required to the SSADM approach to process specification to enable a complete translation. This work is currently under way. Further work has concentrated on three specific commercial fourth generation environments and adapted versions of SSADM have been produced for them.

3.4.   Problems and Benefits

Several internal reviews of SSADM have been carried out, the last of these was held in January 1986. The comments in this section are based on that review and on the authors own observations.

3.4.1. Benefits

Project Planning
The structural standards of SSADM have enabled managers to plan and allocate resources more easily. The approach taken in Stage 1 of drawing high level data flow diagrams has better defined the scope of many projects. This approach can be used for estimation of resources although this has caused problems (see below).

Project management and control
It was felt that SSADM enabled better use to be made of inexperienced staff and reduced the effects of transferring staff within or into projects. SSADM splits the project into tasks of limited scope with visible results which has improved staff morale and motivation. This structured approach has also facilitated monitoring of project progress and aided the the early identification of any necessary control measures.

User involvement
Communication with users is very important in ensuring that the required system meets their requirements. Data flow diagrams have proved particularly successful, being well accepted and understood by users. Recently the technique of logical dialogue outlines has proved valuable in giving users an idea of how they will interact with the on-line components of the system.

Quality of analysis and design
There was a broad consensus among the project managers that SSADM provided a better approach than those used previously. The different views of the system employed by SSADM and the cross-checking and quality assurance of results ensured a high quality design. However improvements in quality gained by the use of SSADM could not be quantified.

3.4.2. Problems

Several of the problems identified by the review were addressed by version 3 of SSADM and are not discussed below.

Estimating
Projects have had great difficulty in estimating how long it will take to carry out particular tasks in SSADM. Estimates have often been wildly inaccurate. CCTA are collecting data and have issued some estimating guide-lines to projects.

Over analysis of the current system
Some projects have spent an unnecessarily long time over analysing the current system using data flow diagrams. This has happened particularly in the early SSADM projects and the ones which did not receive consultancy support.

Documentation
Although it was recognized that the extensive documentation provided by the use of SSADM ensured a high quality product it was felt that the production and maintenance of this documentation is very costly. It is hoped that increased use of computer based tools will lessen this burden.

4.   CONCLUSION

The use of SSADM by the UK government has improved the quality of systems analysis and design. User involvement in projects has increased and project management has been aided by the use of SSADM. The role of a central group in introducing, promoting, controlling and supporting SSADM has been a major contributor in ensuring its success. Further work is necessary to ensure that SSADM is best adapted to any new technical developments.

ACKNOWLEDGEMENT

The author thanks CCTA for making various internal reports available to him.

REFERENCES

[1]   Longworth, G. and Nicholls, D., The SSADM Manual, National Computer
       Centre, Manchester, 1987.
[2]   Yeates, D., Systems Project Management, Pitman Publishing Ltd.,
       London, 1986
[3]   Jackson, M.A., Principles of Program Design, Academic Press, London, 1975
[4]   DeMarco, T., Structured Analysis and System Specification, Prentice-Hall
       Englewood Cliffs, New Jersey, 1979.
[5]   C.Gane and T. Sarson, Structured Systems Analysis: Tools and Techniques,
       Prentice-Hall, Englewood Cliffs, New Jersey, 1979.

Governmental and Municipal Information Systems
P. Kovács and E. Straub (Editors)
Elsevier Science Publishers B.V. (North-Holland)
© IFIP, 1988

POLICY PLANNING INFORMATION SYSTEM (PPIS) at MITI

Itsuko FUJIMORI

Office Director, Policy Planning Information System Office,
Ministers Secretariat, Ministry of International Trade and Industry
1-3-1, Kasumigaseki, Chiyoda-ku, Tokyo, Japan

The Policy Planning Information System (PPIS) is used to provide
information necessary for policy planning and to support the
sophistication of administrative planning functions.
It can be used via terminals located in almost all sections of the
ministry. Required information is produced through routine transactions and collected not only from NITI but from other ministries,
the private sector and other sources through the use of on-line
networks.
We are considering further altitude of user interface by using the
Artificial Intelligence technique.

1. Outline of information processing at the Ministry of International Trade
   and Industry (MITI)

The Ministry of International Trade and Industry (MITI) introduced the
Japanese MARK-A computer in 1961, and since then the Ministry has been
utilizing electronic computers in various administrative fields. Today, MITI
has installed five large capacity computers to enable more efficient and
sophisticated administration.
Initially, computers were introduced by MITI mainly to cope automatically
with work of a routine nature such as statistical processing and office
transactions. As, computer processing became more familiar and improvements
were made in information processing technology such as TSS (Time Sharing
System) and Data Base, computers were used more widely to permit more
effective and diversified application of information.
MITI is promoting an information processing system under the following
policies:
(1) More sophisticated planning and drafting of policies
    The Ministry is developing, the Policy Planning Information System in an
    effort to devise more appropriate and accurate policies more
    expeditiously.
(2) Improvement of such complex functions as information accumulation,
    retrieval and processing
    The MITI Data Bank has been established to enable the more effective use
    of various information. The Bank is furnished with information which is
    processed and later retrieved for use.
(3) Systematization of various routine transactions
    The Ministry is computerizing the processing of various statistics and
    office transactions in order to ensure more efficient, swift and labor-
    saving administration and to provide better service to the public.

(4) Promotion of computerization by means of computer utilities
     TSS (Time Sharing System) terminals have been installed at placed in the
     Ministry, making computers readily available to anyone, thus promoting
     the information processing mentioned above.

As shown in Fig. 1, MITI's information processing system is roughly divided
into two operations: the data yielding process and application of data.

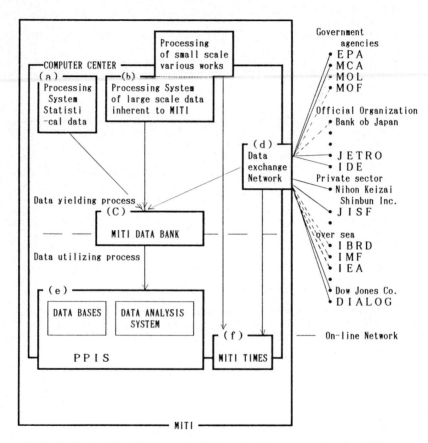

Fig.1 Outline of the Administrative Information Processing System at MITI

a) Statistical data Processing System
   Processing of statistical data such as census of manufactures, indicators of industrial production, etc.
b) Processing System for office transactions
   Large-scale routine transactions inherent to MITI such as patents, trade insurance and so on, have been processed by computers.
   By the introduction of multi-function computer terminals in '84, small-scale various transactions at each office such as Japanese word processing, Tabulation, Map, Graph are computerized.
c) MITI Data Bank
   Furthermore, the useful information produced through above work is accumulated at the MITI Data Bank for various application.
d) Data Exchange Network
   It is also used to support the information exchange network (on-line or magnetic tapes are used for media) with other governmental agencies such as the Economic Planning Agency (EPA), Management and Coordination Agency (MCA), Ministry Of Labor (MOL), Ministry Of Finance (MOF), Bank of Japan, Japan External Trade Organization (JETRO) etc., private sectors such as The Nihon Keizai Shimbun (Japan Economic Journal) Inc., The Japan Iron and Steel Federation (TJISF), Dow Jones Co., DIALOG, and international organs such as the UN and OECD etc.

Sophisticated use of computer has been achieved since the introduction of TSS in 1971.

e) PPIS (Policy Planning Information System)
   It became possible for anyone, anywhere to readily retrieve the information stored in the MITI DATA BANK using the TSS terminal. At the same time, Data Analysis system were developed, which enhanced value of the data and enabled more sophisticated use of it. In this respect, the Policy Planning Information System supports the planning function in specific fields such as trade, energy, industrial sectors, by providing data and analysis function.
f) MITI TIMES (MITI TSS Information Express Service)
   Since All of division of MITI has TSS terminals, it became possible to use as communication tools such as electronic mail, electronic board. MITI TIMES is such communication tool, and it is used to provide the latest information related to movement of In and Out of MITI.

Expansion of Information in the data yielding process bring the expansion of computer utilization or new method in the data utilizing process.

2. Policy Planning Information System

2.1. Basic concept

MITI has been developing a series of systems called "Policy Planning Information System," which enable users to utilize the sophisticated data processing capability of a computer at times of administrative decision making.
The objectives of this Policy Planning Information Systems are to support daily policy-planning and decision-making (administrative planning). The policy planning information systems which have already been developed and also which are now under development can be categorized into roughly three groups: Data Base System, Data Retrieval System and Economic Analysis System.
The Data Base System is divided into two groups by there subject.

The first is a group of some high-density sub-systems representing as many policy items such as trade, technology.

The latter is a group of sub-systems classified by industrial sector to serve the purpose of aiding the industrial information system currently being consolidated by the private industrial and financial community.

We contribute informatization in industry not only in MITI.

These two system groups complement each other in the administrative decision-making process, and can perform each administrative decision-making function by establishing close relationships between the groups. Each group systematically collects and consolidates related data for each policy field and each industry sector and permits appropriate retrieval, processing and analysis, by combining various data bases retrieval techniques and simulation models.

The Data Base System, however, is neither an 'integrated system' nor a 'comprehensive system'. The system group of important policy fields and the group of industry sectors have the mission of searching for local optimization, from their own standpoints, on the basis of the policy problems peculiar to the individual policy and industrial sectors.

And needless to mention, these are many Data bases in Japan which have been developed in private firms for their own purpose.

The Policy Planning Information System, on the other hand, constitutes a comprehensive network system engaging in the search for total optimization through aiding the development of information circulation and the technique for its utilization for mutually complementary purposes. It is said that an information-oriented society must depend on a poly-centric system for its source of intellectual creativity. The basic concept supporting the policy planning information system is, then, one realistic approach to the realization of just such a poly-centric system.

2.2. Data Bases

Data bases available in MITI are as follows:
1) Data Bases internal in MITI-Table 1
2) Data Bases external to MITI-Table 2

Table 1. List of Data Bases

FIELD	' DATA BASE '	CONTENTS	PERIOD
Enterprise	KIMS	Financial reports (about 400 items) of 2,700 major enterprises in Japan	1970 -
	MEIS	Financial reports (about 70 items) of 10,000 medium-sized enterprises in Japan	1975 -
Technology	TEC	Number of patents registered with Japanese Patent Office classified by item (IPC 7-digits)	1969 -
Trade	TRADE	Customs Clearance Statistics of Japan, classified by CCCN 7-digits (12,000 items) & 220 countries	Annual 7 years Monthly 36 months
	DOT	Direction of Trade Statistics, issued by IMF	1948 -
	EXTEN	Trade statistics of about 120 countries, classified by SITC 5-digits	1974 -
	WEIAS	Trade statistics of USA, UK, Germany (FRG), France and Canada	USA 1974 - others 1976 -
Resources & Energy	MRS	1 Production, consumption and international trade of 38 major mineral resources 2 Energy resources of the world	1 1968 - 2 1972 -
	IEA	Oil and Gas Statistics, Energy Balance and Basic Energy Statistics, issued by IEA	Depends on statistics
International Economy	IFS	International Financial Statistics, issued by IMF	1960 -
Domestic Economy	SDB	23,000 series of economic statistics (national accounts, production, prices, labor, etc.) in Japan	Depends on series
	IODB	Input-output tables & related tables of Japan	1970, 1975 - 81
Local Districts	AREA	Data on population, industry, finance, etc. for each city and town in Japan	Depends on items
	EVIS	Air pollution levels of about 4,500 points in Japan	1970 -
Industries	PAPS	Statistical data on paper & pulp industry	1967 -
Others	MARKET	Market prices of commodities	20 years
	LAWS	1 Full text of about 300 laws and ordinances related to MITI 2 Statutes and prefectural regulations concerning air pollution control	Latest editions of MITI statutes

Table 2. List of External Data Bases

PROVIDER	DATA BASE	CONTENTS
Economic Planning Agency	Economic Statistics Processing System for TSS (G. IRENE)	17,000 Series of National Economic Calculation and Mechanical Orders Statistics, etc.
	Economic Analysis Library	Least squares method Time differential correlation Seasonal adjustment method Equality test of coefficients Growth rate Estimating method for Almon lag Estimating method for limited information etc.
Management and Coordination Agency	Japanese Laws	Full texts of the Constitution, laws and orinances of Japan
	Diet Records	Records of proceedings in plenary sessions and committees of each House
	Cabinet Council Records	Records of Cabinet Councils and vice-ministers meetings, etc.
JETRO	Trade Statistics	Trade statistics of Japan, USA, EC, Great Britain, France and Italy collected by JETRO
	IFS	IFS statistics, issued by IMF
	BOP	BOP statistics, issued by IMF
	JETRO information Index	Titles of overseas information publicized or collected by JETRO
	EC National Economic Calculations	National Economic Calculations of EC member nations and their attachments, issued by the EC Statistics Bureau
	EC Business Office Statistics	Business Office Statistics of EC member nations, issued by the EC Statistics Bureau
	EC Production Statistics	Production Statistics of EC member nations, issued by the EC Statistics Bureau
	Retrieval of Periodical Materials	Titles of periodical materials (statistics, yearbooks, magazines directories, tables on tariff rates and Japanese statistics) collected by JETRO
	Information on the Economy and Trade by Country	Information on the economy and trade of various countries

Table 2. List of External Data Bases (Continued)

PROVIDER	' DATA BASE '	CONTENTS (examples)
Private Sector	NEEDS-1R	Headlines and summaries contained in the Nihon Keizai Shimbun (the Japan Economic Journal)
	NEEDS-TS	Statistical data on industries, economics, etc., and econometric models and other software for analysis
	NIKKEI TELECOM	New flashes, major economic indicators
	DOW JONES	Articles contained in the Wall Street Journal, outline and financial analysis of companies in the U.S.
	DIALOG	Diblio-data concerning science, economics and other fields
	NIPS	Biblio-data on 380,000 newly-published books
	SIS	Statistical data on iron & steel industry

2.3. Economic Analysis System

The Economic Analysis System of MITI allows everybody within the ministry to conduct various types of economic analysis merely by a simple operation from a TSS terminal.
Its major economic analysis systems are as follows:
    EAST (Economic Analysis System for TSS)
    MATE (Matrix Expression System)
    EMS (Econometric Model Building System)

  (i) East
    EAST mainly allows the following analysis and processing of economic time series data:
    * Term Conversion (month, quarter, half year, year)
    * Calculation of Basic Statistics (average, standard deviation, etc.)
    * Correlation Matrix
    * Distance Matrix
    * Seasonal Adjustment (MITI II Method, EPA Method, Link Ratio Method)
    * Growth Curve Fitting (Logistic Curve, Gompelz Curve)
    * Spectrum Analysis
    * Various Least Square Methods (Ordinary Least Square Method, Generalized Least Square Method, Stepwise Least Square Method)

 (ii) MATE
    * Calculation of Matrix
    * INPUT OUTPUT Analysis

(iii) EMS
    The functions of EMS partly overlap with those of EAST, but include additionally the following analysis.
    * Single estimation of simultaneous equation system model
    * Councurrent estimation of simultaneous equation system model
    * Model check and simulation
    * Seasonal Adjustment (Census Bureau Method II-X, II)

Table 3 is a list of softwares which exist in MITI.

Table 3. List of Software

SYSTEM	' SOFTWARE '	FUNCTION
Retrieval & Editing	MEU	Language for MITI end users: Retrieval, editing & display of the common data bases
	EDIS	Language for editing: Editing of data bases into time series and/or matrix form and storing of items in the users file
	TRADE	Language for TRADE data base: Retrieval processing & printing of Japanese trade statistics
Tabulation	CROSS	Tabulation of cross-section data in the common data bases
	TAB TAB2	Fixed-form tabulation of time series data in the users file
Graphics	GRAPHIC	Graphic display of data in the common data bases or in the user's file
Analysis	ARAN	Calculation and analysis of AREA data base
	MATE	Input, calculation and display of matrix data
	EAST	Input, calculation, analysis (seasonal adjustment, etc.) and tabulation of time series data
	MAP	Plotting of new technology coefficients on graphs
Economic Model	EMS	Language for economic model building: Estimation of a simultaneous econometric model and its simulation

2.4. Structure

The Data Bases include externally produced data as well as internally produced data through MITI activities.
Anyone can make use of the PPIS software to retrieve, tabulate, process, analyze and graphically output data primarily through the operation of terminals.

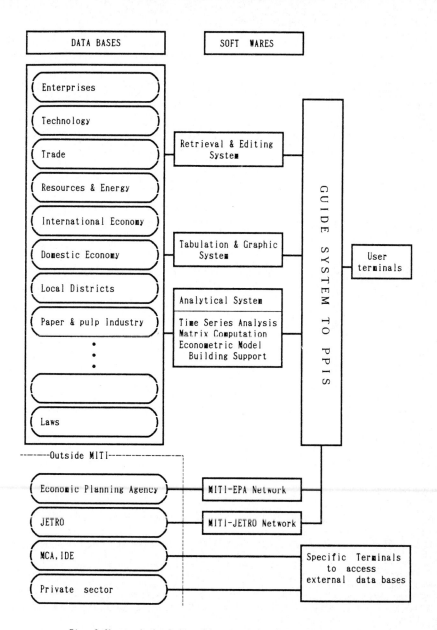

Fig. 2 Chart of the Policy Planning Information System

3. Technical Aspects of PPIS

Noteworthy progress has been made in the areas of both computer hardware and
utilization technique, significantly contributing to the upgrading of the
information system.
Some of the landmark achievements made within the contex of the history of
the Ministry's information system development program include:

(1) Introduction of TSS
     The introduction of the on-line real-time system has made a closer
     between office business and the computer possible and has facilitated
     computer utilization from remote locations. In this sense, this event
     had an epoch-making significance. The introduction of the time-sharing
     system was of particular significance not only in the sense that it
     served to drastically broaden terminal computer utilization, but also
     for the qualitative improvement it has realized in speed, convenience
     and thinking capacity.

(2) Utilization of General-purpose Data Base Management System
     At the time when we embarked on the development of the data base system,
     the practical application of system was not applicable because of the
     lack of suitable software, though its concept was familiar.
     At first we developed the Data management system for each Data Base by
     sequential filing, or random access filing through specific sub-routine.
     Now we use General-purpose DBMS named INQ which is relational type
     replaced from general-purpose DBMS of CODASYL type.
     We selected INQ from following standpoint.

     1) Facility corresponding complicated data structure;
     2) Easy contents retrieval and other retrieval operation;
     3) Flexibility to cope with various data structure, quantity of data and
        retrieval method;
     4) Well-designed end user interface;
     5) Easy maintenance;
     6) Easy linkage of different information systems.

The results obtained did not sufficiently satisfy all of the above enumerated
conditions. But the overall performance of the systems, especially shorten-
ing of a period of development and unification of user interface etc. showed
a significant improvement.
But computer users increased by using local software as word-processor are
not satisfied with the same interface as old.
It is needed to improve the new end user interface function.

(3) Establishment on-line Net Work
     Recently both in the government and private sector in Japan many organiza-
     tions have been developing data bases.
     MITI has established utilization system of such data bases by various
     methods according to the each partners condition.
     The one is the on-line computer network to enable the mutual utilization
     with EPA and with JETRO.
     The another is the on-line network to obtain and to maintain data file
     with a private Data service company.
     And others are data utilization by on-line through specific terminals by
     some data service organizations.
     These Technology of on-line computer network, with different computer
     systems have brought various merits to our PPIS.

(4) Altitude of terminals

Utilization of personal computers as multi-function terminals has brought drastic change to PPIS. For example conversational type interface are added to command type by using screen control function, paper manual are replaced by guiding system with Japanese character etc.

IV Subject for future.

As I said in the section I "basic concept of PPIS is network system", here after we must concentrate on the development of dispersed local Data Base and their network.

Namely we develop the network system that we can use any data linked local data bases containing minute secret information for each division, common data bases in MITI and public data bases out of MITI. (See figure 3.)

Following items are scheduled as actives for future.

1. Technology of development, maintenance, management of software

We expect availability of the technology needed to support an automation based software development. Because the significant portion of our efforts is occupied by maintenance of software for requirements from users or changes of conditions.

And increasing use of local softwares make impossible to manage them, under the circumstance that various kinds of terminals more than 300 are distributed all divisions in MITI.

So we need the technology which can manage and maintain them at center machine and apply them to various kinds of local terminals.

2. Linkage of Date Base

We expect the installation of OSI. And we must settle the code system for various data linkage; code of enterprise, country, manufacture etc.

3. Further altitude of user interface and Analysis of document

We are considering to make conversation with terminals by natural language, to get translated output from English to Japanese, and to analyze the contents from large volume of documents like news paper.

It will be realized by using the Artificial Intelligence technique etc.

Above all our most important subject is How to catch up Information needs of next age, How to develop new data, and How to let members of MITI use PPIS.

I think it is possible only through close communication and cooperation with staff of each fields.

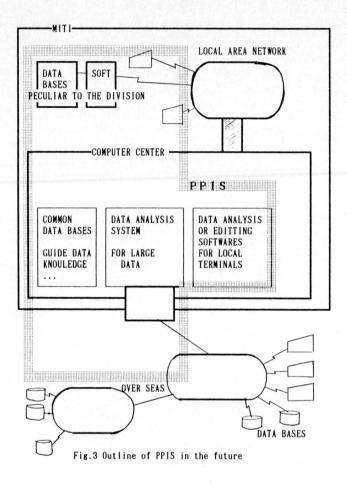

I. Fujimori

Fig.3 Outline of PPIS in the future

Governmental and Municipal Information Systems
P. Kovács and E. Straub (Editors)
Elsevier Science Publishers B.V. (North-Holland)
© IFIP, 1988

MIS OF THE CZECHOSLOVAK FEDERAL MINISTRY OF METALLURGY
AND HEAVY ENGINEERING

Jaroslav KEŠNER

INORGA, Institute for Industrial Management Automation, Praha, ČSSR

Three stages of MIS of Czechoslovak Federal Ministry of Metallurgy
and Heavy Engineering (MIS of FMMHE) development are being described
in this paper. Some problems of interactive user work, system
adaptability, project management and user - designer relations are
discused and some recommendations in this respect are given.

1. CONCEPTUAL INTENTIONS TO APPLY AUTOMATION IN MANAGEMENT OF THE SECTOR

The application of automation to management at the level of the mechanical
engineering sectors has a multiple years tradition. Today it proofs a number
of successes, though the experience from the earliest applications was not the
most stimulating. During the second half of the sixties some design teams from
research institutes tried to find a suitable subject for experimental purposes
and to verify the approaches of economic modelling being developed at that
time. The problems were in the nonexistence of linkups to wider automation
background in data and algorithms areas, in the unpreparedness of the user
audience, as well as in the inadequate approach from the conceptual viewpoint.
The designers were more prone to show off their cleverness and exclusivity in
tools they were working with than to solve management problems and user
interests. These factors even deepened the problems which designers usually
encounter at the commencement of work to develop an MIS i.e. in the field the
activities of which our team took on itself.

From the INORGA Research Institute's initiative in late 1969 a material was
prepared to propose an entire automated (i.e., computer-aided) solution of
management problems on sectoral level as a research contract. This material
was accepted at the Minister's Advisory Body meeting as a fundamental
rationalization measure in the management area. Approval was given to prepare
a feasibility study of the MIS and the Long-Term Conception of Automation
Development for the period till 1985. This "Conception" of 1971 anticipated
the accomplishment, during three five-year stages and in a stepwise manner, of
the following fundamental objectives:
- to support all the management areas on the sectoral level, both in batch
  processing mode and also enabling the communication mode for higher levels
  of management;
- to provide these services for all management levels including the top
  management level, i.e. Minister's Advisory Body;
- to cover entirely all management horizons from low level line management
  (i.e. operational management) to conceptual management upon which stress was
  laid;

- with an intention to achieve higher efficiency of management as well as higher effectiveness of system operation, to solve the interconnection with the systems of general directories (trusts);
- to solve both the content and model aspects of management, as well as to enable the verification, implementation and operation of the resolved (i.e., designed) MIS including its adaptability and its ability to be modified in accordance with changing economic environment;
- to implement the third stage of the automated system in a manner enabling further development with application of new hardware elements and management methods, which were not known during the preparation of the "Conception".

With respect to the large extent and complexity of MIS on the one hand and to the considerable variability of both economic and organizational conditions on the other hand the content orientation of the system was always formulated for five years (in accordance with the Plan of State Economic Research whose funds are used to finance the development of the system). Annually, precise lay-out into the so-called Operational Plan takes place, which is the fundamental tool of control and coordination of all research and implementation activities. Simultaneously these five-year and annual plans fulfil, from the economy and design viewpoints, the accepted long-term "Conception", in dependence also on the hardware items with which the respective stage is provided.

From the design viewpoint, the bulk of work during the 1st stage of MIS implementation on sectoral level was oriented towards the constitution of a data base and to providing its utilization in batch processing mode. For a number of reasons the actual development was limited only to solving problems of selected areas of management. The 2nd stage of implementation showed much higher qualitative characteristics. The intention of this 2nd stage (implemented during 1976 - 1980) was not only to cover, from actual content viewpoint, all the areas of management in the Ministry's departments with substantial upgradings of the algorithmic support of managerial activities, but also to create conditions enabling the transition to an entirely New Concept of MIS, which was planned for the 3rd stage for the 1981 - 1985 period.

The 3rd stage of implementation could have therefore been conceptually devised as the Hierarchical MIS of FMMHE. The formulation of the new qualitative characteristics was influenced especially by the following factors:
- the scope of the already implemented functions, and therefore the mastering of certain new management methods and work procedures under conditions of automation by the users, as well as the functional qualities of the new hardware made it possible to contrive the entire system in a new structure and with an innovated material orientation, where the automation tasks moved more explicitly to management;
- the external system linkups with subordinated general directories were viewed during the 1st stage of implementation as the unchangeable substantial environment of the system. During the 2nd stage these linkups were partially influenced in design primarily in the sense of data collection rationalization and of methodological guidance of MIS implementation on lower managerial levels in the scope of the resort. During the 3rd stage of development they became the subject of design solution;
- the success of the initial approach of the user to the computer on the level of acquiring information for the needs of management, accomplished already during the 2nd stage of implementation, enabled to elaborate the automated system further towards active cooperation between the user and the computer

when solving decision-making and management problems in real time, even to a larger extent than anticipated by the "Conception". When concluding the 3rd stage of implementation the system included more than 1000 automated functions (tasks) of which some 35 per cent were implemented in interactive end user mode supported by a dialogue;
- the structure of the system, the data base conception and the preparedness of users and designers became the basis of further development of the system towards the application of new automated technologies and to the control of the distribution of system functions enabled by hardware not known in time of designing of the Conception. This is the principal orientation of the current 4th stage of MIS of FMMHE implementation.

The content implementation in the individual stages was influenced to a large extent by the functional qualities of the available hardware, as shown in Table 1 below.

Table 1

STAGE	1	2	3	4	
1971	1975	1980	1985	1990	

```
1  IBM 1410
         2 EC 1030
                    3 IBM 370/138
                    + terminal network    4 IBM 4361, S/36
                                           +computer and
                                           terminal network
```

HARDWARE

1971-1973	1	IBM 1410 (80 KChar internal memory), 10 MChar disk capacity
1973-1978	2	EC 1030 (512 KB internal memory), 56 MB disk capacity
1978-1990	3	IBM 370/138 (1 MB internal memory), 800 MB disk Capacity, 39 local display terminals, 6 remote terminals, 15 handy printers; WANG 2200 MVP (two units), WORDPROCESOR (one unit), IBM 5110 (one unit)
1987	4	IBM 4361/4 (2 MB internal memory), 840 MB disk capacity; IBM S/36 (1 MB internal memory), 120 MP disk capacity; 14 color display terminals (of this 12 full-fledged PC XTs)

As follows from the indicated progress and operation of the MIS of FMMHE, it was possible during some eighteen years of development of this relatively large management system, implemented in changing economic environment and operated successively on hardware of several generations, to collect experience whose generalization can bring suggestions for future work of those who implement similar systems. In this paper we will concentrate especially upon such topics which have, according to our opinion, contributed expressively in the two last stages of implementation to the increase of fuctional capabilities of the developed MIS by way of maximal support of management activities by automation technologies. The experience of the earlier stages will be mentioned merely in the chapter treating project management during transition of the system to the higher hardware generation.

2 THE PROBLEM OF COMPUTER USER-FRIENDLINESS

Batch jobs which constituted the majority of computer work during the 1st stage underlined an obvious and not very effective characteristics. The periodicity of batch jobs corresponds to the needs of current, and mostly precisely defined and regularly repeated, administrative activities and of simple (routine) decision-making more or less of regular character. However, management on higher levels is limited rather by more broadly formulated authorities and responsibilities than by particular activities and fixed criteria. In addition it has further typical characteristics which cannot be ignored, since it is a sphere which would yield considerable effects in case of rationalization. Intervals between management acts are not always regular and mostly there is a very short period between fact-finding and the necessity to issue a management act. From this it is possible to draw the following requirements on MIS services and on the hardware which is to allow them:
- on time, i.e. as soon as possible, after ascertaining an event to yield information, or to make possible to assess the last states of affairs;
- to yield other necessary basic information for assessment of the situation;
- to give the possibility of analyzing and evaluating this information and of modeling a decision.

To cope successfully - from the point of view of subject-matter, hardware and also psychologically - with these requirements which were not realizable until by communication systems, we have elaborated what we called the "Conception of user-friendliness development", which was implemented in the following steps:

1st Step (implemented since 1979)

Display Information System (DIS)

Functionally:
- merely the level of keeping management personnel informed by way of pre-processed ready output formats;
- controlled communication, the computer yields a menu;
- light pen selection without possibility of user updating of screens;
- function of branched retrieval; returns, print, help, statistics, security via passwords.

Requirements on the User:
- none, except the knowledge of how to initiate and how to terminate communication and how to enter his personal password.

Goal:
- to break psychological barriers, to gain confidence;
- initial user approach to the computer, informing;
- to gain general minimum knowledge of the field of automation and of the entire MIS by the user;
- upon the evaluation of DIS statistics to control further utilization and elaboration of data base contents;
- to gain initial user experience.

2nd Step (since 1981)

Communication Planning and Analytic System (COMPAS)

Functionally:
- besides the DIS level to ensure also the possibility of access to these data base and the possibility of application of standard (ready) algorithms;
- user work controlled by dialogue (scenario).

Requirements on the User:
- experience with DIS is prerequisite, further knowledge gained by training, but not programming knowledge.

Goal:
- further user approach to the computer;
- to enable management personnel to prepare independently the necessary basic information for decision-making, namely that information which was not precisely defined and can be obtained by way of application of standard algorithms, i.e. of general dialogues;
- to provide management personnel with a tool for modeling and simulating the impacts of management acts by preparing specific dialogues;
- to obtain user experience with the implementation of a communication system of the given qualities, with linkups to a data base and an algorithms base, and with controlled work utilizing the metainformation system. Basically, this is a more broadly conceived concept of decision-making support system.

3rd Step (since 1984)

"Friendliness" of the users (or rather selected users) and designers with the computer on terms of work which utilizes interactive programming tools (languages) together with the support of the dialogue system, tending to indenpendent but monitored work of the users. At present this is the first step towards work in a distributed network of personal computers:

Existing good experience with interactive user work, especially the high degree of utilization of the existing communication modes, has confirmed that our approach was reasonable, in particular in an environment where there is a minimum of instruments to motivate more exacting (and of course more effective) approaches, which are now being implemented.

User interactive work in the environment of centralized intelligence made it possible to introduce a further new and efficient concept under which the MIS assumes an active role to the user. For this the method of control by exception and the method of addressed informing were utilized. Dialogue control is devised in such a manner that on the basis of defined bounds of certain indicator terms of reference, of convergence of critical conditions (which are "known" to the system from current processing), the system can advise the responsible personnel as to what should be done.This advice is displayed immediately upon the users' sign on, before they proceed with communication. Dialogue control can simultaneously (also without any request) notify the senior manager about the advices which his subordinates have received. For top level management dialogue control can aggregate statistics on progress task fulfilment including evaluation for purposes of stimulation and material interest.

3. THE PROBLEM OF DATA BASE CONTENTS AND UTILIZATION

The usual drawback of MISs that are being implemented at all management levels is the almost exclusive output derivation for decision-making and management based solely upon the processing of planning and statistical data. The algorithmic and model transformation of these two types of numerical data for the needs of management is the simplest procedure which may certainly increase the efficiency of the management of a respective economic system, but merely in its existing boundaries. This means, for instance, that the cost and profit parameters of a controlled system can be improved. However this approach does not ensure the system's efficient adaptation to changing conditions of a dynamical environment, especially to innovative trends. For the MIS to be able to aid management in this complex and solely correct manner, it must also have at its disposal information of scientific and technological nature, primarily of fact-describing type. Moreover, there must be the tools and algorithms for evaluating such information and joining it with planning and socioeconomic information into synthetical input information for decision-making. Incorrect concentration merely to easily algorithmizable transformations of only quantitative data by way of modeling approaches is, moreover, frequently preserved as unchangeable mode in the computer implementation.

The esteem of some managers for modern idols, as for them are mathematical models and computers, and the as yet rather partial successes of these appplications, make managers as well as designers blind in such a way that they are not able to realize any more that already at the phase of design they did not take into account the fundamental requirement of providing for the dynamical development of the economic system. An inadequate MIS conception could eventually lead even to the exploitation of the substantial internal sources of the organization for which the MIS is being developed, and to a loss of vitality with respect to the environment instead of using computers in the direction for which this technology· possesses such prerequisites as no other. For instance, for the introduction of efficient dynamics into the management system. Practically from the 1st stage of our MIS implementation we have strived to prevent the occurrence of this infavourable phenomenon. Today, the constitution of fact-describing data sets and their computer-aided evaluation for the purposes of conceptual management, technological progress management, investments, international cooperation, and further functions, is common. Tasks of this type oriented to these solutions of broader managerial connecions exhibit, in comparison with other functions, much higher effectiveness.

One more aspect of design is related to the work with data, where the still highly appreciated progressive methods and approaches can soon turn against those who established them as far as these mechanisms are not contained on time and with a new quality. Data base systems with their severe orientation to data and data structures are becoming dogmas to which even management mechanisms begin to adapt. This fetishism of data and data structures leads to extremes when management, particularly on higher levels, is limited by the extent and structure of a certain planning or statistical form. Economic thinking and considerations are degraded to formal manipulation with numbers and to playing with the data base as the target purpose of management. The manager becomes absorbed more and more into the structures and functions of data bank systems, particularly in case of communication work and work with the metainformation system and mainly with its DATA DICTIONARY part. There relations are mostly derived from the data and its structures and not from managerial activities as basic elements to which data elements together with higher structures relate.

We have consistently endeavored to adhere to the process approach, already when newly analysing the management system upon passing to the communication work mode as well as in the COMPAS concept (particularly in the conception of specific dialogues). There the economic process (managerial activities and their descriptions), to which the necessary data are assigned only later, is the basis of the entire design and implementation and the raison d'etre of automation. Despite our effort the approach has not been implemented fully in the design draft yet.

These activities should be completely concluded before installing new hardware, personal computers in particular. In addition to the already mentioned reasons for the choice of this approach, this solution is one of the prerequisites for preserving the integrity of the system under the conditions of distributed processing.

4. THE PROBLEM OF SYSTEM ADAPTABILITY

The solution of the system adaptability problem in a context as broad as possible was forced particularly by the fact that before the installation of computer hardware which enables interactive work the mere maintenance of more than 1000 batch jobs consumed more than 80% of programming capacity.

For this reason we have endeavoured to arrange conditions such that, making use of the interactive work of both users and designers, would provide for the necessary adaptability of the system at the level of:
- algorithms which increase the efficiency of system utilization due to the fact that this enable the user (with dialogue support of the COMPAS system) to adapt output (or an algorithm) to a new need or to change. At the same time this strengthens user identification with the new decision-making instrument in unpredictable situations;
- system structure and contents by way of the development of some methods and techniques supporting automation of design and thus enabling speeded implementation of new tasks which stem from the dynamics of the environment in which the MIS is functioning. This is resolved to a considerable extent with the support of the COMPAS system and its metainformation system;

- system design in such a way that new special data bases will be consecutively created and evaluated, oriented particularly to the areas of conceptual management and management of technological progress. It will enable the recognition in time of all changes in the substantial environment of the system which manifest themselves by new requirements on the system, and to become ready for such changes. In this field several functions were already implemented but the main part of the solution to this problem is facing us. We assume (and we have gained experience to this effect) that the possible way here could be work with bases of knowledge and the application of expert systems. These will enable to exploit better the new hardware whose installation lies just before us.

5. PROJECT MANAGEMENT AND COORDINATION DURING TRANSITION TO HIGHER
    GENERATIONS OF BOTH HARDWARE AND MIS DEVELOPMENT

From the approximately eighteen years of development and operation of our system we have acquired some interesting experience to this point.

The Structure of the MIS

It is interesting to note how does the former classical system structure (task, function, subsystem), which was fully justified with many arguments in time of implementation of batch mode tasks, start to change gradually with the transition to higher generations of hardware, particularly in the following directions:

a) The Separation of Cross-Sectional tasks (i.e. Functional Conjunction).
    First, tasks leading to unified implementation and to the separation of responsibility for data. This independent element of the management information system is generally accepted and fully supported both by methodological procedures and organizational methods (data administration). Later, as a separate cross-sectional element of communication systems which requires unified implementation in all application areas as well as central control of operation, the separation commences with the implementation of the communication system. Also, in our conditions a single implementation team proved true which cooperates with the individual application teams and is also responsible for communication control and administration.
    Of late it is necessary to solve anew, and as a cross-sectional problem, the questions of system reliability and security.

b) Increasing Internal System Integration.
    The level of cognition and mastering of new methods of work by users as well as designers leads gradually to the constitution of larger structural entities enabling to solve problems in a broader context, and thus on a level more efficiently supporting management. In our conditions, for instance, the following subsystems were gradually integrated into larger modules (i.e. blocks) : long-term planning, aggregated plan, economic analyses, and branch development, into a comprehensive decision-making block; the subsystems of material and technological procurement, production control and sales control into the block of reproduction process management; and, possibly, the subsystems of international cooperation, investments, scientific and technological progress management, and finance, costs and prices into the block of dynamical development factors.

c) Increasing External System Integration.
   Gradually we have more profound instruments for the unification of the
   data base contents on the individual levels of MISs, from the unification
   of algorithms through to the design of solving certain problems along the
   "management axis".
d) The Application of New Concepts With the Advent of New Technologies.
   For instance, this relates to Decision Support Systems (DSSs) or Expert
   Systems (ESs), the incorporation of a new system level (Office Automation)
   into implementation, and the development of new design and operation tasks
   (distributed systems).

The Structure of the Design Team

During years it was possible to trace the following tendencies in our
conditions :
- the team of designers, who were originally represented by application
  programmers in decisive majority, is required more and more to become
  familiar with particular subject-matter areas and to switch to management
  problems and exhibit the knowledge of management;
- new specializations are being separated which require a change in the
  implementation environment (data supervisor, communication supervisor,
  security officer, consultant to work with a specific program product, etc.);
- the work content of individual professions (operators, designers and users)
  is changing.

Organization of Work During the Transition to New Hardware

This is a very exacting problem, expecially where a large scope of automation
tasks exists and its positive acceptance by users has created a large
dependence of the users upon this system. This dependence could be disturbed
by new hardware installation, by adaptations in the computer centre premises
or by the transfer of tasks to the new computer.

The adaptation of the MIS itself to new hardware generations is also a serious
problem. The new functional properties of the hardware and thus also the
possibilities of applications, represent a qualitative break through, which is
usually beyond our full apprehension in the stage of preparations for
installation.

Therefore, whenever transition to new hardware occurred we have always strived
to ensure thorough preparation and organizational support. Moreover , we have
also kept to a certain policy, which fully proved correct in all cases:
- the installation of new hardware was never interlinked with the initiation
  of a new stage of the MIS where the design, programming and operational team
  (110 staff members in total) must cope with maximum volume of work;
- this allowed, during a relatively calmer period, to accomplish the complete
  preparation of the environment as well as the training and preparation of
  designers, operators and users for the new hardware;
- minimize the volume of conversion work under the condition of guaranteeing
  the fulfillment of all of the already implemented tasks, the transfer was
  performed with minimum modifications only partially utilizing the properties
  of the new hardware;
- this allowed better accomodation to the new functional properties of the
  installed hardware in order that the new quality of implementation could be
  fully exploited from the beginning of the next five-year design stage.

Applying this procedure such smooth transfer conditions were created during the already twice repeated transition to new hardware that our users never observed any degradation of computer centre services even though the number of tasks was immense.

Similarly we have started preparations for the next transition to new hardware in the middle of this year. However, the installation of distributed processing hardware forms far more complex conditions, where the project manager does not have in his hands all the tools that would enable the success of previous actions. Nevertheless, even now we search for ways to apply the principles mentioned above, particularly the minimization of conversion work, preserving system integrity through the support of only selected applications of personal computers at remote work stations in the first phase, etc.

The Development of Computer Centre Services

The following unambiguous trend in the development of Computer Centre services can be traced:
- from the former mode of in-house operation, when the Computer Centre was responsible for flawless performance of certain jobs, the Centre has been accepting gradually the responsibility for data, service parameters (job turnover time, response time), provision of various services for remote work stations including consultations and assistance to the solution of particular problems;
- the internal style of management in the DP Centre, with austere separation of specializations in assignments and with work organization oriented exclusively to the efficiency of the processing itself, is being changed to management by user needs.
  The monitoring of parallel runs of batch tasks and interactive work represents decision-making activity which has to be accomplished with knowledge of the particular applications and implemented by new instruments which monitor even the on-line work of users;
- the user audience and mainly the management personnel are beginning to grasp that it is not suitable to evaluate the work of the Centre by the amount of machine time, the multiprogramming coefficient etc. as the sole criteria, but first of all by the level and quality of services provided in complicated conditions.

6.   USER-DESIGNER AND OPERATOR OF THE SYSTEM RELATIONS

From the earliest stages of the development of MIS at FMMHE we were aware of the fact that the rate of success of our work does not depend only on the progressiveness of implementation and applied hardware but that it is given above all by the efficiency of the implemented MIS and the effectiveness with which this was accomplished. The best instrument if not used correctly or if it is incorrectly operated does not fulfill its purpose. Therefore, on the background of the prerequisites which qualify this final effect there is the human factor represented by all the three involved parties:
      the user - the designer - the operator of system.

The mechanisms which are recommended for the formalization of the relations between these parties, as e. g. the Steering Committee, work planning, team work, the formal heading of teams by a user etc., are well-known. In our opinion, to provoke an atmosphere of mutual understanding and responsibility for the fulfilment of a task it is necessary to concentrate above all on the following factors:

6.1 The Level of Knowledge as a Factor Qualifying Mutual Understanding

This concerns the level of knowledge of all partners which must be ensured as additional to the professional specialization of each of the parties to this process. Under our conditions and in particular at present this means:

Users:
- have at their disposal a system of periodical (annual) training courses, which are differentiated by level of management and are compulsory as part of qualification rating;
- have at their disposal and with an on-request basis consultants from the designer team for specific problem areas;
- a generator of teaching programs has been prepared for differentiated learning on personal computers and the first lessons will be ready soon;
- selected personnel joining the staff after graduating from universities have scheduled study stays in the designer team and at the Computer Centre totalling 2 to 3 months.

Designers and Selected Personnel of the operator
- besides a system of special training courses they have to become familiar (by additional study) with management in the application area for which they work;
- they take part in work consultation and coordination sessions held at their partner departments (i.e. they are 'to live' with the problems of users).

6.2 The Level of Design and Development as a Factor Qualifying the Mastering of Automation Tools

The notions of user comfort and differentiated user tools are commonly known approaches which improve the efficiency of user work. However, our opinion is that it is possible to do more in this area on the part of designers:
- to differentiate, in an expressive manner, the outputs of batch jobs by the purpose of application;
- to generate commentaries and guidelines for the particular management or control action as part of the required output;
- the outputs of model type should be completed with interpretation algorithms etc.;
- in a comprehensive way and to maximum extent to increase the readiness of outputs for use.

6.3 The Level and Quality of Services as a Factor of Trust Accrued by the User to the Computer Centre

This seemingly obvious fact , which presumes the organization and optimization of work at the Centre in accordance with users requirements and not with the internal interests of the Centre, was enforced with difficulties. Expecially the convergence of batch jobs and interactive work created difficult situations on a computer with limited resources. For instance, the process of ensuring reasonable response time lead to suppression of batch jobs, which frequently meant their transfer to night shifts. The monitoring of such jobs meant to ensure necessary subject-matter knowledge down to chief operator level so that he understands the necessity of interventions which otherwise mean exta work for him.

6.4   Integration of Responsibility as a Factor Qualifying System Efficiency

Long-term cooperation and adherence to the principles mentioned above allowed to set gradually higher and higher target objectives for both users and designers and to assign tasks on a higher qualitative level:
- the operations schedules according to which work on the development and operation of MIS is organized specify also the personal responsibilities integrated during the individual phases of the process as compulsory cooperation. The user participates in processing activities (he himself performs some of them) and the designer joins in the application phase;
- this has gradually created a new mode of cooperation upon which even the wage and incentive system is based. For instance, the premiums of the designers are dependent upon the confirmation of the due fulfilment of specified tasks by the user.

7   CONCLUSIONS

It is very difficult to present information about such an extensive system within the time allotted, in particular when it was also necessary, with regard to one of the specified topics, to outline the history of development as well.

Our main aim in this paper was to show the way in which we have gradually implemented our notions on the deepening of the effect of the implemented MIS and through this to show the actual effectiveness of the system, which components are the source of this effectiveness and who can influence them.

The evident truth that the computer and other hardware elements do not represent a goal and should represent a tool is currently recognized. However, not always do we reflect this principle into all mechanisms. Only after succeeding in the realization of the plans discussed above in all directions by way of both program and design, will we be ready to view for the computer, in particular under the conditions of distributed systems and new automation technologies, as an instrument of thinking and creative work, as an integral part to a higher system.

8.   LITERATURE

/1/   Kešner, J., Communication Systems and MIS of New Generation. Information Systems, Bratislava, 1983, pp. 103-104 (in Czech).
/2/   Kešner, J., The Integration of Text and Numerical Information in a MIS of an Industrial Resort. In Proceedings of FID 658 Conference, Prague, 1985, pp. 95-124.
/3/   Kešner, J., System Analysis and Design. A UNDP/UNIDO NTCTC Tutorial Material, 39 pages, Prague, 1986.

Governmental and Municipal Information Systems
P. Kovács and E. Straub (Editors)
Elsevier Science Publishers B.V. (North-Holland)
© IFIP, 1988

FORMAT AND CONTENT OF DESIGN SPECIFICATIONS

Dr. T. William Olle

T. William Olle Associates Ltd.,
2 Ashley Park Road,
Walton on Thames
Surrey KT12 1JU, England

1. INTRODUCTION

Much of the consideration of information systems analysis and design has focussed on the methodologies which should be used to perform these steps. The series of conferences organized by IFIP Working Group 8.1 [1,2,3] have made it possible to compare both the design process and the resulting design product for a single case study. The work by Madison et al [4] compared several widely used methodologies and it is clear that there is considerable similarity in the underlying techniques used although this similarity may be masked by terminology differences and the way the techniques are used.

Some information systems methodologies do prescribe a format for representing the resulting design, but many merely propose a technique or set of techniques to be used either for analysis or for design.

The aim of this paper is to illustrate as compactly as possible the major components resulting from the design of a non-trivial information system. Again, all too many case studies are based on trivial examples. When a user attempts to tackle a real life example of a non-trivial nature, the volume of documentation called for seems excessive.

2. DESCRIPTION OF CASE STUDY

The case study used in this paper concerns a health centre at which several doctors see patients. Unfortunately, the health centre is short of office space for the doctors but since some of the doctors do not spend a full five day week at the health centre, it is possible for an office to be used by different doctors on different days or half-days.

There are a number of time patterns established by the doctors which they use when setting up the times at which they are willing to take appointments. For example, a doctor may be present from 2 pm until 5.30 pm and be willing to see a patient every fifteen minutes during that period except for a rest break between 4 pm and 4.30 pm. This means that he can see twelve patients - eight prior to the break and four afterwards. For more time consuming appointments, possibly necessitating an examination, 30 minute appointments are necessary and this would mean that only six patients could be scheduled during a half day session.

It is necessary to keep track of appointments and of whether each patient has checked in for his or her appointment. During the course of an appointment a patient may be given a prescription for a kind of medication which needs a doctor's prescription. There is an approved list of such medications and only items on the list may be prescribed by a doctor.

3. COMPONENTS TO BE ILLUSTRATED

This paper illustrates several components which make up the system design. These are shown in Figure 1.

```
+--------------------------------------------------------------+



                    COMPONENTS OF SYSTEM DESIGN


             1.  Entity relationship diagram showing tables and

                 constraints

             2.  Overview of tables and columns

             3.  Invokable tasks and their categorization

             4.  Cross reference of tables and tasks

             5.  List of access control classes

             6.  Assignment of tasks to access control classes

             7.  Definition of tables, columns and constraints


+--------------------------------------------------------------+
```

Figure 1. Major components of a system design

3.1 Design philosophy

The design philosophy underlying the choice and preparation of these components is as follows. Firstly, the cornerstone of the design is the data oriented components, specifically the first two and last in the above list. A highly normalized approach is used in which the data is normalized not only with respect to the static dependencies but also with respect to the dynamic dependencies. This aspect will be explained in the design.

The design is construction tool independent. While it is clearly predicated on making use of a data base management system which can represent the normalized data base design, no specific DBMS need be identified.

Thirdly, the semantics of the data are represented as far as possible in the definition of constraints on the data. This approach is based on the 100% principle advocated in a recent ISO technical report [5]. The advantage of this is that the construction work, which may use a conventional programming language or alternatively a fourth generation language, is considerably simplified.

Fourthly, the all updating tasks and some retrieval tasks, any of which may be initiated by a non-technical user from a terminal, are specified in terms of the data tables in the highly normalized structure which each task must access.

Finally, full consideration is given to access control as an integral part of the design. Access control requirements influence the granularity of the user tasks and access control should not be added as an after-thought.

3.2 **Business activities**

Each of the seven parts listed in Figure 1 will be presented in turn.   Before
doing so, however,   Figure 2 shows a list of the eight business activities
which the system is intended to support.   This is not output from the system
design phase, but input to it from the Business Analysis phase. The system is
supposed to support each of these business activities.

The first business activity is called "system set up".   An activity such as
this is needed for every system design.   It covers the specification of the
various fairly static parameters which would vary,in this case for each health
centre using the system.   Once the system has been installed for a health
centre, any change would be very infrequent - such as adding new rooms or a
change of doctors assigned to the health centre.

```
+-------------------------------------------------------+



              BUSINESS ACTIVITIES SUPPORTED BY SYSTEM


                  1.   System set up

                  2.   Room assignment

                  3.   Define time patterns

                  4.   Time pattern selection

                  5.   Plan appointment slots

                  6.   Record appointments

                  7.   Patient check-in

                  8.   Issue prescription


+-------------------------------------------------------+
```

Figure 2. List of business activities supported

4. **ENTITY RELATIONSHIP DIAGRAM**

Figure 3 is an example of what is often referred to as an entity relationship
diagram, because of its widespread use in data analysis.   In the case of system
design, each rectangle represents a table (in the relational sense).   Each
arrow between two tables represents a constraint on the table pointed to,   or
more specifically on one or more of the columns which make up the table pointed
to.

In addition to the rectangles and arrows, it will be seen that each rectangle
contains a number.   This is an estimate of the number of rows in that table
which is expected to be present in the data base at any point in time.

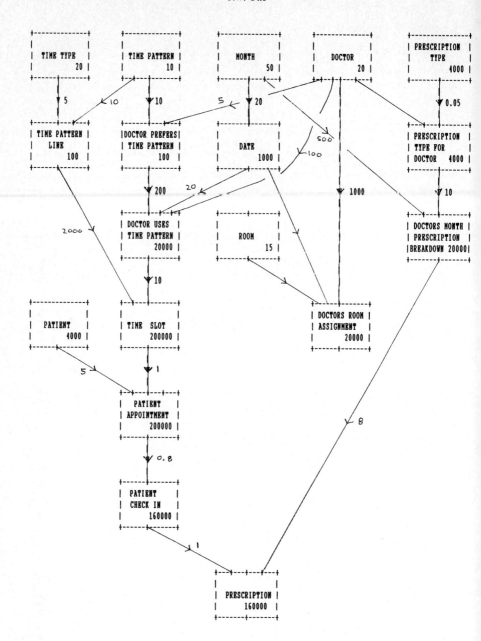

Figure 3. Entity relationship diagram for Doctors' Appoinments

Furthermore, there is a number alongside each arrow. This represents the estimated average cardinality of the relationship or constraint represented by the arrow. For example, since there will be 10 TIME PATTERNS and 10 TIME PATTERN LINES, then each TIME PATTERN will consist of an average of 100/10 TIME PATTERN LINES.

It should be noted that the diagram contains 18 tables, which is sufficient to be "non-trivial".

```
+---------------------------------------------------------------------+

    MONTH (YEAR, MONTH)

    DATE (CAL-DATE, YEAR, MONTH)

    DOCTOR (DOCTOR-CODE, DOCTOR-NAME)

    ROOM (ROOM-CODE)

    DOCTORS ROOM ASSIGNMENT (DOCTOR-CODE, CAL-DATE, ROOM-CODE)

    TIME TYPE (TIME-TYPE-CODE)

    TIME PATTERN (TIME-PATTERN-NUMBER)

    TIME PATTERN LINE (TIME-PATTERN-NUMBER, LINE-NUMBER, TIME-TYPE-CODE)

    DOCTOR PREFERS TIME PATTERN (DOCTOR-CODE, TIME-PATTERN-NUMBER)

    DOCTOR USES TIME PATTERN (DOCTOR-CODE, TIME-PATTERN-NUMBER, CAL-DATE)

    TIME SLOT (CAL-DATE, TIME-TYPE-CODE, TIME-PATTERN-NUMBER, LINE-NUMBER)

    PATIENT (PATIENT-ID, PATIENT-NAME)

    PATIENT APPOINTMENT (DOCTOR-CODE, CAL-DATE, TIME-TYPE-CODE, PATIENT-ID)

    PATIENT CHECK-IN (PATIENT-ID, CAL-DATE, TIME)

    PRESCRIPTION TYPE (PRESCRIPTION-TYPE-CODE, PRESCRIPTION TEXT)

    PRESCRIPTION TYPE FOR DOCTOR (PRESCRIPTION-TYPE-CODE, DOCTOR-CODE)

    DOCTORS MONTH PRESCRIPTION BREAKDOWN (PRESCRIPTION-TYPE-CODE,
                DOCTOR-CODE, YEAR, MONTH, NUMBER-ISSUED)


    PRESCRIPTION (PATIENT-ID, CAL-DATE, PRESCRIPTION-TYPE-CODE)

+---------------------------------------------------------------------+
```

Figure 4. Overview of tables and columns for Doctors Appointment

5. OVERVIEW OF TABLES AND COLUMNS

Figure 4 is an optional component.   For each of the 18 tables shown by a
rectangle in Figure 3, there is a row in Figure 4 which identifies the columns
in the table.   For example, the table DOCTOR contains two columns which are
referred to as DOCTOR-CODE and DOCTOR NAME.

Each of these tables has one unique identifier.   The identifier may consist of
one column or of more.   The column or columns which serve as the unique
identifier for a table are indicated in Figure 4 by being underlined.

It should be noted that some of the column names in Figure 4 are in italics.
This means that the column has been "propagated" from another table.   For
example, DOCTOR-CODE in the table DOCTORS ROOM ASSIGNMENT is in italics.   It
has in fact been propagated from the table DOCTOR.   Reference to the entity
relationship diagram in Figure 3 will show that there is a relationship between
the two tables DOCTOR and DOCTORS ROOM ASSIGNMENT.   This relationship simply
means that each DOCTORS ROOM ASSIGNMENT must be relatable to a doctor whose
DOCTOR-CODE is in the DOCTOR table.

Another way of saying this is to say that there is a constraint on the values
of DOCTOR-CODE in the DOCTOR table such that each value must already be found
in the column called DOCTOR-CODE in the doctor table. This kind of constraint
is called a referential constraint because it refers to another table.

6. INVOKABLE TASKS AND THEIR CATEGORIZATION

In simple terms, an invokable task is a task which a user can initiate (that is
to say invoke) from a terminal.   Whether the initiation is performed by means
of a touch screen, typing in an identification or by moving a mouse is not
relevant at this point.

There are several ways in which a task can be invoked. Figure 5 identifies the
tasks which may be invoked for each table.   Each task is firstly categorized as
one of the following

               Add
               Delete
               Modify
               Select

A task in the add category adds one or more rows to the table mentioned.   A
delete task deletes one or more rows from a table.   A modify task modifies the
content of columns other than those which comprise the unique identifier.
Finally, a select task retrieves one or more rows from a table but does not
change any of the rows.

The integer in the left hand side of each column indicates the Business
Activity in Figure 2 with which the task is associated.   For example, all the
tasks with a "3" in the left hand side of the column are in suport of the
business activity of defining time patterns.

The three letter code in the middle of each column categorizes each task in
more technical terms.   The first letter says whether it is an on-line task (0)
or a batch task (B). In this case, all tasks are on-line.

The second letter indicates whether it is a homing-in task (H) or an out-of-the-blue task (B). It will be observed that in this particular example almost all tasks are "homing-in". This means that the system is so designed that a user can perform the task by a process of homing in on the data he wishes to add, modify, delete or select. The tasks concerned with PRESCRIPTION TYPE are out of the blue. This means that the user at the terminal has to be able to enter the code for a PRESCRIPTION TYPE during the course of performing one of those tasks. Since there are 4000 PRESCRIPTION TYPES, this will require either a list at the terminal or a prodigious memory on the part of the user.

Table \ Task Type	Add	Delete	Modify	Select
MONTH	1 OHM			1 OHM
DATE	1 OHM			2 OHM
DOCTOR	1 OHM	1 OHM	1 OHM	2 OHM
ROOM	2 OHM	2 OHM	2 OHM	2 OHM
DOCTORS ROOM ASSIGMENT	2 OHM	2 OHM	2 OHM	2 OHM
TIME TYPE	3 OHM	3 OHM		3 OHM
TIME PATTERN	3 OHM	3 OHM		4 OHM
TIME PATTERN LINE	3 OHM	3 OHM		4 OHM
DOCTOR PREFERS TIME PATTERN	3 OHM	3 OHM		4 OHM
DOCTOR USES TIME PATTERN	4 OHM	4 OHM		5 OHM
TIME SLOT				6 OHM
PATIENT	6 OHM	6 OBM	6 OBM	7 OBM
PATIENT APPOINTMENT	6 OHF	6 OHF		7 OHF 2
PATIENT CHECK-IN	7 OHF	7 OHF		7 OHF 2
PRESCRIPTION TYPE	8 OHM	8 OBM	8 OBM	8 OBM
PRESCRIPTION TYPE FOR DOCTOR	*****			8 OHM 2
DOCTORS MONTH PRES. BREAKDOWN	*****			8 OHM 2
PRESCRIPTION	8 OBF	8 OBF		8 OHM 2

Codes used in this Figure:

1.	On-line	O		Batch	B
2.	Homing-in	H		Out of the Blue	B
3.	Menu driven	M		Fast track	F

***** Refer to discussion

Figure 5. Task specification and categorization for Doctors Appointments

The third letter indicates whether the task is menu-driven (M) or fast track (F). There are fast track tasks for PATIENT APPOINTMENT and PATIENT CHECK-IN. This is because these tasks will be performed with such enormous frequency that one cannot expect a user to work through a hierarchy of menus each time he wishes to invoke the task.

On some of the rows under "select" a "2" will be seen. This is to indicate that there is more than one select task associated with those tables. The design principle adhered to here is that only one task should be able to update any table (in any way). There can of course be several ways of retrieving data from a table.

The row of asterisks in the add column for the two tables PRESCRIPTION TYPE FOR DOCTOR and DOCTORS MONTH PRESCRIPTION BREAKDOWN are intended to indicate that rows are added to these two tables as a result of a calculation performed when some other table, namely PRESCRIPTION, is updated. In fact, these two tables are examples of stepping stones. These are tables introduced for performance reasons to enable an acceptable response to queries which would otherwise have to be derived from data in the PRESCRIPTION table.

7. CROSS REFERENCE OF TABLES AND TASKS

In order to perform some of the tasks, it is necessary to access tables other than that to which the table is related. In the course of performing a task, reference can be made to several tables and a table can be referred to by several tasks.

In order to give a complete specification of the relationship between tables and tasks, a complete cross reference table is needed. This is shown in Figure 6. Figure 6 contains a number of notes in the left hand column. This means that some word of explanation is needed for that particular Task. This is essentially a clarification from the designer to the constructor. In the following sub-sections, the rightmost number corresponds to the number of the note.

Table	Task Type	MONTH	DATE	DOCTOR	ROOM	DOCTORS ROOM ASSIGN	TIME TYPE	TIME PATTERN	TIME PATTERN LINE	DOCTOR PREFERS TIME PAT	DOCTOR USES TIME PAT	TIME SLOT	PATIENT	PATIENT APPOINTMENT	PATIENT CHECK-IN	PRESCRIPTION TYPE	PRESCRIPTION TYPE FOR DOCTOR	DOCTORS MONTH PRESCRIPTION BREAKDOWN	PRESCRIPTION
MONTH	A	S																	
	S	S																	
DATE	A	S	T																
	S	S	T																
DOCTOR	4			S															
ROOM	3				S														
DOCTORS ROOM ASSIGMENT	A		S	S	V	T													
	S		S	S		T													
TIME TYPE	3						S												
TIME PATTERN	3							S											
TIME PATTERN LINE	3							S	T										
DOCTOR PREF TIME PAT.	S			S						T									
	U			S				V		T									
DOCTOR USES TIME PATTERN	S		S	S			R	R	R	I	T								
	U		S	S						I	T	T							
TIME SLOT	S		S	S			R	R	R	I	I	T							
Note 1	A																		
PATIENT Note 2	4												S						
PATIENT APPOINTMENT	A		S	S			R	R	R	I	I	I	V	T					
Note 3	S1		S	S			R	R	R	I	I	I	R	T					
Note 4	S2	S	I	R			R	R	R	I	I	I	S	T					
PATIENT CHECK-IN	A		S	S										I	T				
Note 5	S1		S	S						I	I	I	R	I	T				
Note 6	S2		S										S	I	T				
PRESCRIPTION TYPE Note 2	4															S			
PRESCRIPTION TYPE Note 7	S1			S												R	T		
FOR DOCTOR Note 8	A															V	T		
Note 9	S2			R												S	T		
DOCTORS MONTH PRESCRIPTION	S1	S		S												R	I	T	
BREAKDOWN Note 10	A																		
Note 11	S2	S		R												S	I	T	
PRESCRIPTION	A		S	S										I	I	V	T	T	T
Note 12	S1		S	S									R			R	I	I	T
Note 13	S2												S	I		R			T

Codes used in above Figure for Task Types A Add; S Select; D Delete; M Modify; 4 A,S,D,M; 3 A,S,D; U A,D,M
Codes used in above figure for Roles S Starting point; I Intermediate point; F Infelction point; R Retrieval reference; V Validation reference; T Target

Figure 6. Cross reference table showing path for each task

7.1 Add TIME SLOT

This Task is not indicated in Figure 5 as a user invocable task, but new TIME
SLOTS are created automatically as part of the task

Add DOCTOR USES TIME PATTERN.

The indication for this task that TIME SLOT is a target table is consistent
with this.

7.2 Add, Modify, Delete, Select PATIENT

This is noted as a Task using a single table path. However, with an estimated
4000 PATIENTS in the table, some kind of artificial access path will be needed
for the Modify, Delete and Select Tasks.

This same note applies to the 4000 row PRESCRIPTION TYPE table. One solution
to this would be to introduce a new table called PRESCRIPTION CATEGORY to
categorize each PRESCRIPTION TYPE.

7.3 Select PATIENT APPOINTMENT, first option

This selection option lists, for a given DOCTOR on a given DATE, all his TIME
SLOTS and any PATIENT APPOINTMENTS assigned to these TIME SLOTS.

7.4 Select PATIENT APPOINTMENT, second option

This selection option lists, for a given PATIENT in a given MONTH, any PATIENT
APPOINTMENTS recorded in the system and indicates the TIME SLOT and the
DOCTOR.

7.5 Select PATIENT CHECK-IN, first option

This selection option lists, for a given DOCTOR on a given DATE, which PATIENTS
have checked in for their PATIENT APPOINTMENT.

7.6 Select PATIENT CHECK-IN, second option

This selection option lists, for a given PATIENT on a given DATE, the PATIENT
APPOINTMENT he has had, and whether or not he has checked in.

7.7 Select PRESCRIPTION TYPE FOR DOCTOR, first option

This selection option lists, for a given DOCTOR, the PRESCRIPTION TYPES
he is recorded as having used at any time since records were first
made.

7.8 Add PRESCRIPTION TYPE FOR DOCTOR, first option

This is not a user option, but is performed automatically by the system when
the task

Add PRESCRIPTION

performed successfully. The PRESCRIPTION TYPE referenced in the PRESCRIPTION does not have to be one already recorded in PRESCRIPTION TYPE FOR DOCTOR. If it is not, then a new row is added to PRESCRIPTION TYPE FOR DOCTOR.

7.9 Select PRESCRIPTION TYPE FOR DOCTOR, second option

This selection option lists, for a given PRESCRIPTION TYPE, all the DOCTORS that are recorded as ever having used it.

7.10 Add DOCTORS MONTH PRESCRIPTION BREAKDOWN

This is not a user option, but is performed automatically by the system when the task

Add PRESCRIPTION

is performed successfully. The PRESCRIPTION TYPE referenced in the PRESCRIPTION does not have to be one already recorded in DOCTORS MONTH PRESCRIPTION BREAKDOWN. If it is, then the value in the column number issued is incremented by one. If it is not, then a new row is added to the table DOCTORS MONTH PRESCRIPTION BREAKDOWN in which the value in the column Number issued is set to one.

7.11 Select DOCTORS MONTH PRESCRIPTION BREAKDOWN

There are two select options for this table. The first gives a breakdown of PRESCRIPTIONS issued by PRESCRIPTION TYPE for a given MONTH for a given DOCTOR.

The second gives, for a given MONTH and for a given PRESCRIPTION TYPE, the DOCTORS who have used the PRESCRIPTION TYPE and how many times.

7.12 Select PRESCRIPTION, first option

This selection option lists, for a given DOCTOR and a given DATE, which PRESCRIPTIONS he has issued and to whom.

7.13 Select PRESCRIPTION, second option

This selection option lists, for a given PATIENT, which PRESCRIPTIONS have ever been issued to him.

8. VALUE OF CROSS REFERENCE TABLES

The kind of cross reference table display in Figure 6 is not intended to be user friendly. Together with the preceding cross reference of the kind shown in Figure 5, it is intended to enable the designer to communicate his design to the constructor as compactly as possible.

It should be clear that a cross reference table of this kind is to some extent limited by the number of tables involved. Figure 6 is based on only 18 which is a fairly modest number, given the approach to data design which is being used.

If the data design produces a list of about 200 tables, the kind of cross reference table shown in Figure 6 is going to be rather difficult to prepare. The solution to this problem is to prepare a set of cross reference tables such that each of them relates to one top level Business Activity. Figure 5 identifies, for each task, the Business Activity with which the task is associated.

9. LIST OF ACCESS CONTROL CLASSES

Having established the tables and tasks, attention can be turned to the topic of access control. In practice, this is a very important aspect of system design. In an on-line system, it is undesirable and unreasonable to assume that every task can be invoked by every user. It is also unreasonable to define a separate password for each task although with some systems it is necessary for each user to have his own individual password.

The approach illustrated here is to define a set of access control classes. These are shown in Figure 7. It will be seen that there are six access control classes each representing either a class of people or an individual with a specific responsibility, such as the System Administrator or the Health Centre Administrator. One of the classes is for the general public. Each access control class is given a one letter code which will be used when assigning each task to an access control class.

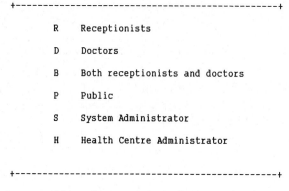

```
+--------------------------------------------------+

        R      Receptionists

        D      Doctors

        B      Both receptionists and doctors

        P      Public

        S      System Administrator

        H      Health Centre Administrator

+--------------------------------------------------+
```

Figure 7   Access control classes

10. ASSIGNMENT OF TASKS TO ACCESS CONTROL CLASSES

The assignment of each task to an access control class is shown in Figure 7. The access class to which each task is assigned is indicated by the inclusion of the code for the access class (see Figure 7) being included alongside the task.

The integer which is included in this table for each task indicates the business activity (see Figure 3) which each task supports. This shows that the tasks belonging to a given business activity are often assigned to different access control classes.

Figure 8 illustrates the kind of tasks, which would be assigned to a System Administrator - including many of the "delete" tasks which should be regarded as archiving.

The assignment refers only to tasks which can be invoked from a terminal. The tasks which are initiated as part of another task such as those for adding to the tables PRESCRIPTION TYPE FOR DOCTOR and DOCTORS MONTH PRESCRIPTION BREAKDOWN are not assigned to an access control class.

Table \ Task Type	Add		Delete		Modify		Select	
MONTH	1	S					1	P
DATE	1	S					2	P
DOCTOR	1	H	1	H	1	H	2	P
ROOM	2	H	2	H			2	P
DOCTORS ROOM ASSIGMENT	2	H	2	H			2	P
TIME TYPE	3	S	3	S			3	P
TIME PATTERN	3	S	3	S			4	P
TIME PATTERN LINE	3	S	3	S			4	A
DOCTOR PREFERS TIME PATTERN	3	B	3	S			4	P
DOCTOR USES TIME PATTERN	4	B	4	S			5	P
TIME SLOT							6	-
PATIENT	6	B	6	S	6	B	7	P
PATIENT APPOINTMENT	6	B	6	S			7	1 P
								2 P
PATIENT CHECK-IN	7	B	7	S			7	1 P
								2 P
PRESCRIPTION TYPE	8	H	8	S	8	H	8	P
PRESCRIPTION TYPE FOR DOCTOR	-						8	1 D
								2 H
DOCTORS MONTH PRES. BREAKDOWN	-						8	1 D
								2 H
PRESCRIPTION	8	D	8	S			8	1 D
								2 D

Figure 8. Assignment of Tasks to Access Control Classes

11.   CONCLUDING REMARKS

This paper has attempted to illustrate a compact but comprehensible format   for
the   presentation of design specifications.   There are many different views on
what   constitutes a suitable format for a design specification.   Even among
those who might agree on the format, there would be debate about what
constitutes a good design and what constitutes a poor design.

A design specification has to be complete.   In theory, a constructor should be
able to build the system, using the construction tool of his choice, on the
basis of a design specification prepared by a design team with whom he may be
able to have only limited contact.   In practice, there is no accepted yardstick
of "completeness" for the design specifications of computerized systems.

The   design   specification illustrated in the paper uses a data design as its
cornerstone.   The semantics of the data are defined in Figures 3 and 4.   The
relationships depicted in Figure 3 can also be thought   of as indicating
constraints on the columns in the corresponding tables as defined in Figure 4.
This approach is felt to be according to the spirit the "100% principle" as
expressed in the ISO report on conceptual schema concepts [5].   The essence of
thisd principle is that the semantics of the data should not be buried in
updating programs.

Other   aspects of the design are expressed in terms of the data.   It should be
noted that the data design is highly normalized.   This is a pre-requisite for
being able to define the user invokable tasks in terms of the four fundamental
relational operations add, modify, delete and select.

It is hoped that this paper will motivate further thinking on the questions of
what constitutes a satisfactory design specification and of what constitutes a
good design.

REFERENCES:

[1] Olle, T.W., Sol, H.G., & Verrijn-Stuart, A.A. (editors). "Information
Systems Design Methodologies: A Comparative Review".   Published by North
Holland, Amsterdam. 1982.

[2] Olle, T.W., Sol, H.G. & Tully C.J. (editors). "Information Systems Design
Methodologies: A Feature Analysis". Published by North Holland, Amsterdam. 1983.

[3] Olle, T.W., Sol, H.G. & Verrijn Stuart, A.A. (editors). Information
Systems Design Methodologies: Improving the Practice." Published by North
Holland, Amsterdam. 1986.

[4] Maddison, R.N. et al. "Information System Methodologies". Published by
Wiley Heydon Ltd. London on behalf of British Computer Society. 1983.

[5] van Griethuysen, J.J. (editor). "Concepts and terminology for the
Conceptual Schema and Information Base." Prepared by ISO TC97/SC5/WG3 in 1982
and available from ISO Headquarters in Geneva.

Governmental and Municipal Information Systems
P. Kovács and E. Straub (Editors)
Elsevier Science Publishers B.V. (North-Holland)
© IFIP, 1988

A DESIGN OF VIEWPOINTS-DIRECTED KNOWLEDGE SYSTEM FOR DECISION SUPPORT

Yoshinobu KUMATA
Masayasu ATSUMI
Department of Social Engineering,
Faculty of Engineering, Tokyo Institute of Technology,
2-12-1 Ookayama, Meguro-ku, Tokyo, Japan

As a framework of planning support by knowledge systems, four planning support forms are defined and design criteria of planning support knowledge systems are given. And viewpoints-directed knowledge
system which carries out viewpoints-directed support, which is one of
the planning support forms, is designed under these criteria.
Viewpoints-directed knowledge system consists of viewpoints base,
viewpoints control mechanism, knowledge base, and viewed-worlds area,
and has an object-oriented architecture which integrates object-
oriented representation of entities, rule representation, and logical
representation of methods in viewed-worlds using viewpoints. As a
formal model of viewpoints-directed knowledge system, viewpoints system is defined. Viewing conditions for building viewed-worlds and
two viewing algorisms are obtained from this model. Finally as an
example of planning support by viewpoints-directed knowledge processing, a qualitative prediction problem of air pollution diffusion is
considered. And possibility of planning support by viewpoints-
directed knowledge processing is examined.

1. INTRODUCTION

Recently local governments have been developing planning support information
systems and increasingly relying on these systems in planning. Planning process can be conceived as a cyclic and on-going process consisted of plan-
evaluation process, plan-formulation process, and plan-implementation process.
And a decision-maker group and a planner group organize a planning organization. Decision-makers request thier planners to evaluate effect of previous
plans, formulate new plans, and implement these plans. A planner group
analyzes the existing condition of town to be planned and what has caused problems, makes alternative plans to solve them, and monitors how plans are getting
along. A decision-maker group makes decisions on plans based on information
from a planner group. In planning of local governments, a decision-maker group
consists of a mayor, an assembly, various kind of councils, various kind of
resident organizations, and citizen. A planner group consists of a staff of the
planning department and planning experts of private office and university.
Planning support information systems are integrated computer systems to support
planner group activity. We call a composite of decision-maker group, planner
group and planning support information systems a planning information system.

Planning support information systems as an integrated computer system consist
of large data base, socio-economic models, a package of various statistical and
system analysis tools, and image processing functions for maps and diagrams.
These information systems present various data for planning support to
planners. Knowledge base systems and expert systems can store expertise systematically and carry out various expert tasks, partly replacing human experts.
They facilitate human experts to work more productively and make expertise
available for non-experts.

In this study, we present design criteria of knowledge systems for planning support. And we formalize and design viewpoints-directed knowledge system and consider its applicability for planning support.

2. A FRAMEWORK OF DECISION SUPPORT BY KNOWLEDGE SYSTEM

2.1. Planner Support Forms by Knowledge System

We will consider a planning system which consists of a decision-maker group, a planner group, and a planning support information system. We call this system planning information system. Figure 2-1 shows an organization of this system.

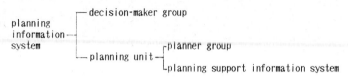

```
                      ┌─ decision-maker group
   planning           │
   information ──────┤
   system             │                    ┌─ planner group
                      └─ planning unit ────┤
                                           └─ planning support information system
```

FIGURE 2-1
Organization of planning information system

A planning information system consists of a decision-maker group and a planning unit. A planning unit consists of a planner group and a planning support information system. In municipal planning information system, a decision-maker group consists of a mayor, an assembly, various kind of councils, various kind of resident organizations, and citizen. And a planner group consists of the staff of municipal planning department and planning experts of university and so on. Municipal planning information system evaluates, formulates, and implement plans of a planning information system management and a city management.

A decision-maker group decides on plans. A decision-maker group requests a planning unit to evaluate effect of previous plans, formulate new plans, and implement these plans. A planning unit presents evaluation of previous plans, alternative plans, and degree of plans progress to decision-makers. We call tasks of a planner group in plan evaluation, plan formulation, and plan implementation "planning task" and divide it into three subtasks and four processing levels. Three subtasks are as follows; diagnosis task, prediction task, and plan-making task. Four processing levels are as follows; data production level, goal seeking level, understanding level, and learning level. Figure 2-2 shows the structure of planning task.

planning task

	diagnosis task	prediction task	plan-making task
	learning level		
processing level	understanding level		
	goal seeking level		
	data production level		

FIGURE 2-2
Structure of planning task

Diagnosis is the task of determination of disease states in a system to be planned based on interpretation of observed data. Prediction is the task of forecast of the future course of a system to be planned from a system model of the past and present. Plan-making is the task of creation of plans from a system model. A plan is goal states of a system or a program of actions that can be carried out to achieve goals. In these tasks, it is necessary to create a model of system to be planned. A model determines the meaning of observed data, actions, and goals. Goal seeking is the processing activity of solution search which satisfies goals based on a given model. Understanding is the processing activity of model construction based on planner's knowledge. And learning is the processing activity of knowledge acquisition for model improvement. Planning support information system is a computer system to support planners' planning task. Planning support is the task of data production for planners' planning task or of partial substitution of planners' planning task.

We discuss new planning support forms based on introduction of knowledge processing technique. We classify planning support forms of knowledge system by what part of processing level of planning task a knowledge system substitutes. We define four forms; a conventional support form, a goal-oriented support form, a viewpoints-directed support form, and a multiviewpoints-learning support form.

1)conventional support form
  a)definition
    For given instructions, a knowledge system executes conventional procedures and returns their results.
  b)substitution part
    Mainly data production for planners' planning task is a processing of knowledge systems.
  c)knowledge processing method
    Data analysis models, diagnosis models, prediction models and plan-making models are stored as procedural programs. Knowledge processing is carried out by these procedural programs.
  d)division of planning task between planners and knowledge systems
    Planners use procedural programs of expert knowledge for diagnosis, prediction, and plan-making.
2)goal-oriented support form
  a)definition
    For given queries, a knowledge system expands goal-search tree and returns answers and their reasons.
  b)substitution part
    A part of goal seeking for diagnosis, prediction, and plan-making tasks is substituted by knowledge systems.
  c)knowledge processing method
    A knowledge system consists of a knowledge base and an inference engine. For a given query, an inference engine expands a goal-search tree using knowledge in a knowledge base. A forward search method or a backward search method and so on are adopted for expanding goal-search trees by an inference engine.
  d)division of planning task between planners and knowledge systems
    Planners' expert knowledge or know-how for diagnosis, prediction, and plan-making are stored in a knowledge base. Planners use this knowledge system to solve their partial problems of a planning task.
3)viewpoints-directed support form
  a)definition
    For given queries, a knowledge system selects or creates world models for interpretation of queries. These world models are selected or created by viewpoints of planners or knowledge systems. Goal-oriented support is carried out in world models.
  b)substitution part
    A part of understanding level is substituted by knowledge systems.
  c)knowledge processing method
    A knowledge system consists of a knowledge base, an inference engine, and a mechanism for creating and modifying world models by viewpoints. Understanding is carried out by interpreting queries in world models. Course

of reasoning is determined by viewpoints.
d)division of planning task between planners and knowledge systems
   Planners and knowledge systems collaboratively create world models in
   working area of knowledge systems by operation of viewpoints. Solutions
   and their reasons by reasoning on these world models are returned to the
   planners.
4)multiviewpoints-learning support form
   a)definition
      In addition to viewpoints-directed support form, it is possible for
      planners to reason new results by learning facts or rules which construct
      new world models.
   b)substitution part
      A part of learning level is substituted by knowledge systems.
   c)knowledge processing method
      In addition to mechanisms of viewpoints directed support form, a knowledge
      system has mechanisms for generating new hypotheses and organizing them
      into its knowledge base.
   d)division of planning task between planners and knowledge systems
      Planners learn much from decision-makers or knowledge systems in planning
      process. At the same time, knowledge systems learn expert knowledge or
      knowhow from planners in planning process. In this support form, mutual
      learinig based on different viewpoints of planners and knowledge systems
      can be carried out.

2.2. Design Criteria of Planning Support Knowledge System

Planning task is formulated as a composite task of three subtasks; a diagnosis,
a prediction, and a plan-making task. In this section, we characterize these
tasks, and arrange design criteria of knowledge system for planning support.

Diagnosis, prediction, and plan-making tasks have following two common charac-
terictics.
1)Model of system to be planned is needed.
   In diagnosis, to understand the system organization and the relationships and
   interactions between subsystems is needed to identify causes of system
   diseases. In prediction and plan-making, it is necessary to understand how
   the system change over time by various actions.
2)Task execution under incomplete information is needed.
   In large complex problems, a planner has only partial information. The reasons are that the anatomy of systems is not fully understood, and that requirements or data are not fully known or change with time, and that task is
   divided into several subtasks and they are carried out by multiple planners,
   and so forth. To cope with these situation, planners must tentatively and
   contingently carry out tasks by hypothetical reasoning, information gathering, and so on.
These two properties characterize understanding and learning levels of planning
task. Each of diagnosis, prediction, and plan-making tasks has additional
characteristics. These characterize goal seeking level of each task.
Characteristics of diagnosis task are as follows.
3)Diagnosis depends on what status is considered to be correct.
4)There is causal relationship between diseases. A disease can sometimes be
masked by the symptoms of other diseases.
Characteristics of prediction task are as follows.
5)Explanetion of multiple possible futures is required for various actions and
assumptions.
6)It is necessary to indicate sensitivity to variations in input actions or initial state.
Characteristics of plan-making task is as follows.
7)In large complex problems, it is necessary to cope with complexities of system by dividing it into subsystems and interactions between subproblems.
8)To cope with plan modification, it is necessary to record justifications for

plan-making.

Corresponding to these characteristics of a planning task, we present six design criteria which should be considered to design planning support knowledge system.

[CRITERION-1]Planning support knowledge systems must equip data or knowledge needed for diagnosis/prediction/plan-making tasks and goal-oriented interpreters for carrying out these tasks.

[CRITERION-2]Planning support knowledge systems must be able to construct and modify system models to be planned in working area by collaborating with planners.

[CRITERION-3]Planning support knowledge systems must be able to execute hypothetical reasoning when information is not fully known.

[CRITERION-4]Planning support knowledge systems must equip mechanisms of accumulating and rearranging related knowledge in their knowledge base.

[CRITERION-5]Planning support knowledge systems must be able to explain their knowledge processing results by recording justifications.

[CRITERION-6]Planning support knowledge systems must equip man-machine interfaces which are intelligent and can display various diagrams.

2.3. A Framework of Planning Support by Viewpoints-directed Knowledge System

In this paper, a planner is characterized as an actor who execute data production, goal seeking, understanding, and learning for diagnosis, prediction, and plan-making tasks. In this characterization, a planner is an actor who executes goal-oriented, viewpoints-directed, multiviewpoints-learning knowledge processing. When a knowledge system has an ability of understanding, that is, a knowledge system carries out viewpoints-directed support, we name a planning model of planners and viewpoints-directed knowledge system "collaborative planning model". We show the collaborative planning model of planners and viewpoints-directed knowledge system in figure 2-3.

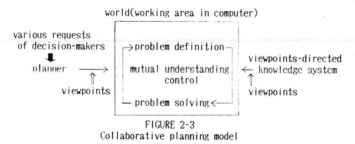

FIGURE 2-3
Collaborative planning model

This collaborative planning model is characterized by a mutual understanding control based on viewpoints control of planners and viewpoints-directed knowledge system. In collaborative planning, planners and viewpoints-directed knowledge system collaboratively define and solve diagnosis problem, prediction problem, and plan-making problem in worlds of computer's working area. This problem definition and problem solving process is controlled by viewpoints of planners and viewpoints-directed knowledge system, and forms a mutual understanding control cycle.
We aim at designing "viewpoints-directed knowledge system" which supports

planners in viewpoints-directed support form, realizes collaborative planning
process, and satisfies design criteria 1.2, and 3. Figure 2-4 shows elements
of viewpoints-directed knowledge system.

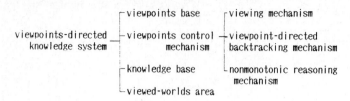

FIGURE 2-4
Elements of viewpoints-directed knowledge system

Viewpoints-directed knowledge system consists of a viewpoints base, a
viewpoints control mechanism, a knowledge base, and a viewed-worlds area. The
viewpoints control mechanism consists of a viewing mechanism, a viewpoints-
directed backtracking mechanism, and a non-monotonic reasoning mechanism.
These elements of viewpoints-directed knowledge system works as follows to
realize a collaborative planning process with planners.

1)Problem definition process is supported by a viewing mechanism.
A viewing mechanism is a mechanism which creates viewed-worlds using
viewpoints. As previously stated, it is necessary to build a system model to
be planned in diagnosis, prediction, and plan-making problem. Often information
for building a system model is only approximately known. Problem definition is
refered to as describing a system model and its belief which is necessary to
answer questions. Belief is described as premises or assumptions. Viewpoint
is a knowledge representation form which gives a framework to describe a system
model and its belief. Typical viewpoints for planning are implemented in a
viewpoint base by experts. A viewed-world is a space in which a problem is defined as a system model to be planned and its belief.
2)Problem solving process is supported by a nonmonotonic reasoning mechanism.
A nonmonotonic reasoning mechanism is an interpreter on viewed-worlds area
which reason consequences nonmonotonically from premises and assumptions in a
viewed-world. This mechanism resolves a diagnosis, prediction, or plan-making
problem which is defined in a viewed-world for a planner's query.
3)Problem modification process is supported by a viewpoints-directed backtracking mechanism.
A viewpoints-directed backtracking mechanism finds an assumption which causes
inconsistencies in a viewed-world by backtracking justifications and rejects
the assumption. Inconsistencies are indicated by planners or expert knowledge
in knowledge base. Rejection is carries out by selection of another assumption
from a set of possible assumptions, which are implemented in a knowledge base,
or justification of another possible assumption by another viewpoint, and so
forth. Selection of another assumption and selection of another viewpoint are
executed by planners or automatically by this mechanism. This rejection modifies viewpoints and viewed-worlds, which represent a problem to be planned.
4)Mutual understanding process is realized by viewpoints control mechanism.
A viewed-world under a viewpoint gives an interpretation for a query. A cycle
of problem definition, problem solving, and problem modification forms a mutual
understanding process between planners and viewpoints-directed knowledge system
and is supported by viewing mechanism, nonmonotonic reasoning mechanism, and
viewpoints-directed backtracking mechanism.

3. FORMAL DESCRIPTION AND TENTATIVE DESIGN OF VIEWPOINTS-DIRECTED KNOWLEDGE SYSTEM

3.1. Role of viewpoints in knowledge processing

We discussed that it is important to build a system model to be planned and reason hypothetically under incomplete information and knowledge in a planning task. For example, in prediction, future states depend on what kind of system model is assumed and what event is assumed to happen among possible events. Prediction is carried out by means of the integration of each future state based on each assumption. And in counter plan-making, one's actions depend on what kind of behavioral models are assumed for other actors and what actions are assumed to chosen among possible actions by other actors. Counter plan-making is carried out by means of the integration of each selected action based on each assumption. We call model building under incomplete knowledge understanding. To allow knowledge system to execute knowledge processing called understanding, in section 2-3 we gave a framework of viewpoints-directed knowledge system which consists of a viewpoints base, a viewed-worlds area, a knowledge base, and a viewpoints control mechanism to operate them.

Some systems which build worlds and manage assumptions have been proposed. Blackboard model[1] defines multiple worlds on a blackboard which correspond to multiple knowledge sources. Truth maintenance system[2] gives a modification algorism of assumptions and justified knowledge based on them. Script and plan in script applier mechanism and plan applier mechanism[3] are knowledge representation scheme which define worlds for understanding stories. MULTI-LOG[4] is a logic programming language which is able to define multiple worlds and inference mechanisms on them.

We define viewpoint as a knowledge representation scheme which is used for building world as a premises and assumptions system and managing inference on it. That is, viewpoint is a knowledge representation scheme which provides information needed for a world construction and assumptions management in the world. Knowledge processing based on viewpoints is different from knowledge processing of some knowledge system mentioned above and expansion of them, since viewpoint provides information needed for both world construction and assumptions management and viewpoint is used for reasoning control by viewpoints control mechanism.

3.2. A model of viewpoints system

We name a formal model of viewpoints-directed knowledge system a viewpoints system. Viewpoints system consists of a viewpoints space, a viewed-worlds space, a knowledge space, and a viewpoints control algorism. The viewpoints control algorisms consists of a viewing algorism, a nonmonotonic reasoning algorism, and a viewpoints-directed backtracking algorism. In this section, we formally define the viewpoints system and describe its behavior in knowledge processing especially focusing on viewing mechanism. And we obtain necessary conditions for building viewed-world by viewing, and present viewing algorisms which satisfy this conditions.

First of all, we define knowledge space formally.

[DEF 3-1] knowledge space
Let RO be a set of n-ary relations($n>=0$), let O be a set of objects, let O* be a set of n-ary elements of O, and let $P \subset RO \times O*$ be a set of knowledge primitives. Then knowledge space KB is defined by following three construction rules.
  1) $p \in P \rightarrow p \in KB$
  2) $p \in KB \rightarrow \hat{\ }p \in KB$
  3) $p1, p2 \in KB \rightarrow p1 \vee p2 \in KB$
The symbol $\hat{\ }$ describes negation and $\vee$ describes logical sum. //

A viewed-world is a premises and assumptions system which is created using knowledge in a knowledge base by a viewpoint. Next we define viewed-worlds space.

Let $W \subseteq KB$, let W^* be a family of finite subset of W, let WO be $W^* \setminus \{\phi\}$, and let W^+ be $W^* \cup \{\#\}$. Then nonmonotonic reasoning rule on W is defined as

$$Iw \subseteq W \times W^+ \times W^*$$

such that each element of Iw is one of following forms;

   $wp = (w, \{\#\}, \phi) \in Iw, \ w \in W.$
   $wa = (w, w^+, w^-) \in Iw, \ w \in W, \ w^+ \in W^*, \ w^- \in WO.$
   $ws = (w, \phi, \phi) \in Iw, \ w \in W.$
   or $wc = (w, w^+, \phi) \in Iw, \ w \in W, \ w^+ \in WO.$

We call w, w^+, and w^- of $(w, w^+, w^-) \in Iw$ justified antecedent, unjustified antecedent, and succedent respectively. And we call (w^+, w^-) justification of w under Iw. Nonmonotonic reasoning rule Iw means that if $w^+ \cup w^-$ is not ϕ and w^+ is justified and w^- is unjustified, then justify w. In this formalization, we assume that $\#$ is always justified. We call wp, wa, and wc premise, assumption, and consequence respectively. And ws represents possible but unaccepted assumption. We call it unaccepted assumption. A set of premises, assumptions and unaccepted assumptions is called base under Iw. Premises are regarded justified without regard to its ground. Assumptions and unaccepted assumptions are possible hypotheses in a viewed-world. Assumption is justified when unaccepted assumptions are not justified. Consequenses are regarded justified when they are derived from base under Iw. On above preparation, we define viewed-worlds.

[DEF 3-2] viewed-world
Let $W \subseteq KB$, and let Iw be nonmonotonic reasoning rule on W. Then viewed-world is defined as $M = (W, Iw)$ //

The value of any knowledge of viewed-world is 1 when it is justified and 0 when it is unjustified. We call a set of justified knowledge in a viewed-world a justified set. And we call a set of unjustified knowledge in a viewed-world a unjustified set.

[DEF 3-3] immediate conclusion
Let $M = (W, Iw)$ be a viewed-world. And let $W1$ and $W0$ be justified set and unjustified set on viewed-world respectively. Then w is a immediate conclusion from $(W1 \cup W0) \subseteq W$ iff $w \in W1$ or there exists some $w^+ \subseteq W1$ and some $w^- \subseteq W0$ such that $(w, w^+, w^-) \in Iw$ //

[DEF 3-4] Iw-derivation
Let $M = (W, Iw)$ be a viewed-world. And let $W1$ and $W0$ be justified set and unjustified set on viewed-world respectively. Then finite sequence $w1, w2, \ldots, wn (wi \in W)$ is a Iw-derivation from $(W1 \cup W0) \subseteq W$ iff $wi \in W1$ for any i or there exists some $w^+ \subseteq \{w1, w2, \ldots, wi-1\}$ and some $w^- \subseteq W0$ such that $(w, w^+, w^-) \in Iw$ //

[DEF 3-5] Iw-derivable
Let $M = (W, Iw)$ be a viewed-world. And let $W1$ and $W0$ be justified set and unjustified set on viewed-world respectively. Then w is a Iw-derivable from $(W1 \cup W0) \subseteq W$ [(W1 W0) I- w] iff there exists some Iw-derivation which includes w.
//

Let $M = (W, Iw)$ be a viewed-world and let Wp Wa Ws and Wc be premises set, assumptions set, unaccepted assumptions set and consequences set respectively. Then evaluation of knowledge in a viewed-world M is given by following evaluation function

   $Ew[Iw] : W \rightarrow \{1, 0\}$

      where if $w \in Wp$, then $Ew[Iw](w) = 1$,
            if $w \in Ws$, then $Ew[Iw](w) = 0$,
            if $w \in Wa \cup Wc$, then
                     if $(Wp \cup Ws)$ I- w, then $Ew[Iw](w) = 1$,
                     if $(Wp \cup Ws)$ I$\not$ w, then $Ew[Iw](w) = 0$.

Nonmonotonic reasoning algorisn on viewed-worlds generate lw-derivation from $(W1* \cup W0*)$ where $W1*$ and $W0*$ are premises set and unaccepted assumptions set respectively.

Next we define viewpoint. Let $R0$ be a set of n-ary relation($n>=0$). And we define R from $R0$ by following construction rules.
1)$r \in R0 \rightarrow r \in R$, 2)$r \in R \rightarrow \bar{r} \in R$, 3)$r1, r2 \in R \rightarrow r1 \lor r2 \in R$.
The symbol $\bar{}$ describes negation and $\lor$ describes logical sum.

Let $Rj \subset R$ and let $Rj*$ be a family of finite subset of Rj and let $Rj0$ be $Rj* \backslash \{\phi\}$ and let $Rj+$ be $Rj* \cup \{\#\}$. Then justification structure on Rj is defined as
$$J \subset Rj \times Rj+ \times Rj*$$
such that each element of J is one of following forms;
$$jp = (r, \{\#\}, \phi), \quad r \in Rj,$$
$$ja = (r, r+, r-), \quad r \in Rj, \quad r+ \in Rj*, \quad r- \in Rj0,$$
$$js = (r, \phi, \phi), \quad r \in Rj,$$
$$\text{or} \quad jc = (r, r+, \phi), \quad r \in Rj, \quad r+ \in Rj0.$$

We call jp, ja, js and jc premise justification structure, assumption justification structure, unaccepted assumption justification structure, and consequence justification structure respectively.

[DEF 3-6] viewpoint
Let $Rj \subset R$ and let $z=\{u1/x1, u2/x2, ..., un/xm\}$ be substitution of identification variables ui for arguments xi of Rj and let J be justification structure on Rj. Then viewpoints is defined as
$$v = (vi, z) \quad \text{s.t.} \quad vi = (Rj, J).$$
Identification variables gives identification of arguments in Rj. //

[DEF 3-7] chain
Let $v = ((Rj, J), z)$ be a viewpoint and let Rp be a subset of Rj element of which has a premise justification structure and let Rc be a subset of Rj element of which has a consequence justification structure. Then chain $C(v)$ on v is a subset of Rj constructed by following rules 1), 2).
1)If $r \in Rp$, then $r \in C(v)$,
2)For any $j = (r, r+, r-) \in J$, if $r+ \cup r- \neq \phi$ and $r' \in C(v)$ for any $r' \in r+$ and $r" \in Rc$ for any $r" \in r-$, then $r \in C(v)$. //

Now we formally defined viewpoint, viewed-world, and knowledge space. Next we discuss viewing algorism formally.

Four types of viewings are discussed. They are standard viewing, reverse viewing, strongly inclusive viewing, and connective viewing.

Standard viewing is a mapping which maps viewpoint to viewed-world. Let $M = (W, lw)$ be a viewed-world and let $v = ((Rj, J), z)$ be a viewpoint. Standard viewing is defined as
$$VG : (((Rj, J), z), d) \mid \rightarrow (W, lw)$$
$$\text{s.t.}$$
$$Rj (z \circ d) = W, \quad J (z \circ d) = lw,$$
and d is a substitution of objects for identification variables.
The symbol $\circ$ describes composition of substitution. We call d a viewing substitution. A viewing substitution prescribes knowledge base search and viewed-world construction by a viewpoint.

Reverse viewing is a mapping which maps viewed-world to viewpoint and viewing substitution.

We define following two relations between viewpoints.

[DEF 3-8] strongly inclusive relation between viewpoints : $\supset_v$
Let $v = ((R_j, (J_v \cup J_c)), z)$ and $v' = ((R_j', (J_v' \cup J_c'))$, $z')$ be viewpoints, where J_v and J_v' are sets of premises and assumptions and unaccepted assumptions justification structure of v and v' respectively, and J_c and J_c' are sets of consequences justification structure of v and v' respectively.
Then we say that "v strongly include v' " [$v \supset_v v'$]
iff $R_j \supset R_j'$ and $J_v \supset J_v'$ and $J_c \supset J_c'$ and
     there exists some substitution s such that $z \circ s \supset z'$. //

[DEF 3-9] connective relation between viewpoints : $<<_v$
Let $v = ((R_j, (J_v \cup J_c)), z)$ and $v' = ((R_j', (J_v' \cup J_c'))$, $z')$ be viewpoints, where J_v and J_v' are sets of premises and assumptions and unaccepted assumptions justification structure of v and v' respectively, and J_c and J_c' are sets of consequences justification structure of v and v' respectively. Let R_v and R_v' be sets of relations which have premises and assumptions and unaccepted assumptions justification structure of R_j and R_j' respectively. Let R_c be a set of relations which has consequence justification structure. And let $C(v)$ be chain on v.
Then we say that "v is connected with v' " [$v <<_v v'$]
iff $R_v' \supset (C(v) \cap R_j') \neq \emptyset$ and
     $R_v \cap R_v' = \emptyset$ and
     there exists some substitution s such that
            $R_c (z \circ s) \supset (R_c \cap R_j') z'$. //

We define two operators which generate new viewpoints using these two viewpoints relations. First of all, we define the strongly inclusion oprator SINCLUDEv using strongly inclusive relation between viewpoints.

[DEF 3-10] strongly inclusion operator: SINCLUDEv
Let v and v' be viewpoints.
Then SINCLUDEv is defined as follows.
   SINCLUDEv(v, v') = v if $v \supset_v v'$
                = v' if $\sim(v \supset_v v')$. //

Next we define the connection operator CONNECTv using connective relation between viewpoints.

[DEF 3-11] connection operator: CONNECTv
Let $v = ((R_j, (J_v \cup J_c)), z)$ and $v' = ((R_j', (J_v' \cup J_c'))$, $z')$ be viewpoints, where J_v and J_v' are sets of premises and assumptions and unaccepted assumptions justification structure of v and v' respectively, and J_c and J_c' are sets of consequences justification structure of v and v' respectively. Let R_v' be a set of relations which have premises and assumptions and unaccepted assumptions justification structure of R_j'. And let $C(v)$ be chain on v.
Then CONNECTv is defined as follows.
CONNECTv(v, v')=
   $((R_j \cup R_j', ((J_v \cup (J_v' | C(v))) \cup (J_c \cup J_c'))), ((z \circ s) \backslash s) \cup z')$ if $v <<_v v'$,
   undefined   if $\sim(v <<_v v')$.
where s is a substitution which defines connective relation and
$(J_v' | C(v)) = \{ j = (r, r+, r-) \in J_v' | r \; R_v' \backslash C(v) \}$. //

Connection operator construct a new viewpoint from two viewpoints that are in connective relation.
Next we define two relations between viewed-worlds.

[DEF 3-12] strongly inclusive relation between viewed-worlds : $\supset_w$
Let $M = (W, I_w)$ and $M' = (W', I_w')$ be viewed-worlds.
Then we say that "M strongly includes M' " [M w M']
iff $W \supset W'$ and $I_w \supset I_w'$. //

[DEF 3-13] inclusive relation between viewed-world : $\supset c$
Let $M = (W, Iw)$ and $M' = (W', Iw')$ be viewed-worlds.
And let $W1=\{w \in W | Ew[Iw](w)=1\}$ and let $W1'=\{w \in W' | Ew[Iw'](w)=1\}$.
Then we say that "M includes M' " [M c M'] iff $W1 \supset W1'$. //

Next lemma holds.

[LEMMA 3-1]
Let $M = (W, Iw)$ and $M' = (W', Iw')$ be viewed-worlds.
Then if "M strongly includes M' ", then "M includes M' ". //

Proof is given in APPENDIX 1.

On above preparation, we present the strongly inclusive viewing algorism and the connective viewing algorism. Next theorem holds.

[THEOREM 3-1] strongly inclusion theorem
Let $v = ((Rj, J), z)$ and $v' = ((Rj', J'), z')$ be viewpoints such that $v \supset v$ v'.
Let $M = (W, Iw)$ and $M' = (W', Iw')$ be viewed-worlds. And let s be viewing substitution for v and M and let s' be viewing substitution for v' and M'.
Then if $z \circ s \supset z' \circ s'$, then $M \supset w$ M'. //

Proof is given in APPENDIX 2.

This theorem gives a condition of viewing substitution for building another viewed-world which strongly includes one viewed-world. The strongly inclusive viewing algorism is constructed from standard viewing, reverse viewing, and strongly inclusion operator, and builds a new viewed-world strongly including a old viewed-world. The strongly inclusive viewing algorism SINCLUDEw is given as follows.

[ALGORISM 3-1] strongly inclusive viewing algorism
    INPUT: MO = (WO,IwO)
    OUTPUT: M = (W, Iw)
  step1: Obtain a viewpoint v0=(vi0, z0) and a viewing substitution d0 such that VG(v0, d0) = MO by means of reverse viewing RVG.
  step2: Obtain a viewpoint v=(vi, z) such that SINCLUDEv(v, v0)=v. The v strongly includes v0.
  step3 :Obtain a viewed-world M = VG(v,d) by a viewing substitution d such that $z \circ d \supset z0 \circ d0$ and a viewing substitution. //

The connective viewing algorism is constructed from standard viewing, reverse viewing, and connection operator. The connective viewing algorism CONNECTw is given as follows.

[ALGORISM 3-2] connective viewing algorism
    INPUT: MO = (WO, IwO)
    OUTPUT: M1 = (W1, Iw1)
  step1: Obtain a viewpoint v0=(vi0, z0) and a viewing substitution d0 such that VG(v0, d0) = MO by means of reverse viewing RVG.
  step2: Obtain viewpoints v and v1=(vi1, z1) such that v0 <<v v and CONNECTv(v0,v)=v1.
  Or obtain viewpoints v and v1=(vi1, z1) such that v <<v v0 and CONNECTv(v,v0)=v1.
  step3 :Obtain a viewed-world M1 = VG(v1,d1) by a viewing substitution d1 such that $z1 \circ d1 \supset z0 \circ d0$ and a viewing substitution. //

We obtain a next theorem as for connective viewing.

[THEOREM 3-2] inclusion theorem
Let $v=((Rj, J), z)$ and $v0=((Rj0, J0), z0)$ be viewpoints such that v <<v v0, and let CONNECTv(v, v0)=v1. Let d0 and d1 be viewing substitutions such that

$M0=VG(v0, d0)$ and $M1=VG(v1, d1)$. Let $C(v)$ be a chain on v, and let $W10$ be a justified set of $M0$.
Then if $z1 \circ d1 \supset z0 \circ d0$ and $\Phi*(C(v) \cap Rj0) \subset R*$, then $M1 \supset c\ M0$.
$R*$ is a set such that for any $r \in R*$, $r\ (z0 \circ d0) \subset W10$.

Proof is given in APPENDIX 3.

This theorem gives a condition for building another viewed-world which includes one viewed-world.

3.3. Tentative design of viewpoints-directed knowledge system

We design viewpoints-directed knowledge system as a system which has an object-oriented architecture. Viewpoints-directed knowledge system mainly con sists of a viewpoints base, a knowledge base, a viewed-worlds area, a viewpoints control mechanism and an interpreter. The interpreter processes message expressions, and executes knowledge processing. In this section, we outline design of viewpoints-directed knowledge system focusing on design of viewpoint and knowledge representation forms.

Knowledge in knowledge base is classified into three groups. These are entities, relations, and rules. Entities are divided into classes and instances, and forms a hierarchical knowledge organization. Figure 3-1 shows syntax of class and instance.

    <class>::=<class name><superclass part>
               <property_definition part><method_part>

    <instance>::=<instance name><instance_of part>
               <property_value part>

FIGURE 3-1
Syntax of class and instance

Methods of <method_part> are given as follows.

      <method>::=<message pattern>(<logical expression>)

Method is a procedure description for a received message and is described by logical expressions. Logical expression is given as follows.

      <logical expression>::=[<head sequence>]{<clause>}

      <clause>::=<head>:-<body>;|<head>;|<clause><clause>

Head sequences determine a control structure. Clause takes a form of a horn clause and its body is described by message expressions.

Figure 3-2 shows syntax of relation.

    <relation>::=<relation name>(<element number>)
               {<relation elements>;}

FIGURE 3-2
Syntax of relation

Relation describes the relationship between classes, instances and viewpoints. The is-a relation and the insrance-of relation are also described by this form.

Rules are described as a nonmonotonic rule form. Figure 3-3 shows an outline of rule syntax.

```
<rule>::=<rule name>              <rule body>::=
         <rule group>                  <succcedent definition>
              :                        <m_antecedent definition>
         <rule state>                  <n_antecedent definition>
              :                        <message expression>|
         <relative entity>            <succedent value>
         <rule body>                   <m_antecedent value>
                                       <n_antecedent value>
```

FIGURE 3-3
Syntax of rule

Rule body means that "if m_antecedent part is justified and n_antecedent part is unjustified, then succedent part is justified". The <m_antecedent defini-tion> part and the <n_antecedent definition> part define antecedent terms of rule and the <succedent definition> part defines succedent term of rule. And procedure for obtaining succedent from antecedents is described in the <message expression> of rule syntax. Rule group is a set of rules which has same an-tecedent terms and same succedent term. The <rule group> is a name of this rule group. Certainty factor can be described in <rule state>.

We define viewpoint as a knowledge structure for constructing viewed-world and managing knowledge processing in viewed-world. Viewpoints-directed knowledge system assigns viewed-worlds to any processings, and it assigns viewpoint to each viewed-world. Viewpoints are given by users or generated by system. Fig-ure 3-4 shows an outline of syntax of viewpoint which is given by users.

```
<viewpoint>::=<viewpoint name>
              <viewpoint owner>
                   :
              <viewpoint key>
              <viewpoint method>

<viewpoint key>::=<relative_entity key><base key><target key>
```

FIGURE 3-4
Syntax of viewpoint

Viewpoint keys consist of base keys which give a justification structure for bases, target keys which give a justification structure for queries, and rela-tive entity keys which are variables to be bound by classes or instances. Viewpoint methods are methods for various viewings. Viewing method creates viewed-world by searching knowledge in knowledge base and binding these keys of viewpoint. And viewing method generates a structure for representing a se-quence of justifications given or derived in viewed-world. This structure is used for managing knowledge processing in a viewed-world.

Viewed-world is described by rules, relations, and instances. Nonmonotonic reasoning mechanism carries out knowledge processing by applying rules to rela-tions and instances in a viewed-world. Application of rules is carries out by methods of logical expressions.

Thus viewpoints-directed knowledge system design aims at integrating object-oriented representation of entities, rule representation, and logical represen-tation of methods in viewed-world using viewpoint.

4. EXAMPLES OF VIEWPOINTS-DIRECTED KNOWLEDGE PROCESSING FOR PLANNING SUPPORT

As an example of planning support by viewpoints-directed knowledge processing, diffusion prediction of air pollution is considered. In this chapter, a simple qualitative model of air pollution diffusion is considered and viewpoints-directed knowledge processing in a qualitative model building and a qualitative reasoning[5][6] is discussed.

Figure 4-1 shows a framework of a qualitative model building and a qualitative reasoning by viewpoints-directed knowledge processing.

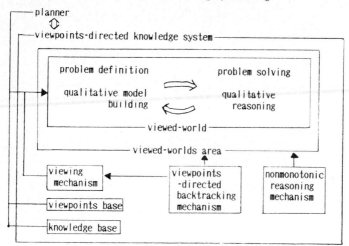

FIGURE 4-1
Qualitative model building and qualitative reasoning
by viewpoints-directed knowledge system

Qualitative model building is carried out by viewing mechanism. Given planner's query and premises information, strongly inclusive viewing searches a viewpoint which views system qualitatively, and builds a viewed-world which strongly includes the query and premises information. This viewed-world represents a qualitative model. Connective viewing searches another viewpoint which is connected with one viewpoint of a qualitative model in a viewed-world and modifies and expands the qualitative model. Viewpoint gives information for prescribing constituents and attributes of a qualitative model and managing possible assumptions. A qualitative reasoning is carried out by nonmonotonic reasoning mechanism. Nonmonotonic reasoning mechanism adds or deletes consequences derived from a qualitative model when the model is builds or modified. That is, it justifies or unjustifies consequences derived from a qualitative model. Viewpoints-directed backtracking mechanism finds causes of inconsistent behavior of a qualitative model and searches a viewpoint to resolve the causes.

An atmospheric diffusion model in which a space in which density is regarded as fixed is partitioned into one box and smoke outflow from the box and inflow to the box are considered is called a box model. Figure 4-2 shows a box model of atmospheric diffusion.

In figure 4-2, capital letters represent variable names which are used in this chapter. This box model is described by following three relational expressions.

E1: PROD-POLL + INFLOW - OUTFLOW - VERT-DIFF = POLL-ACCU
                           (equilibrium condition)
E2: OUTFLOW = f1(VEL-W, R-TEMPD-B, R-TEMPD-U, R-DAD,PROD-POLL)

E3: VERT-DIFF = f2(VEL-W, R-TEMPD-B, R-TEMPD-U, R-DAD, PROD-POLL)

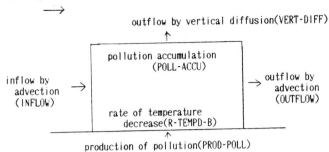

rate of dry adiabatic decrease(R-DAD)
rate of temperature decrease(R-TEMPD-U)

velocity of the wind(VEL-W)

outflow by vertical diffusion(VERT-DIFF)

pollution accumulation
(POLL-ACCU)

inflow by
advection
(INFLOW)

outflow by
advection
(OUTFLOW)

rate of temperature
decrease(R-TEMPD-B)

production of pollution(PROD-POLL)

FIGURE 4-2
Box model of atmospheric diffusion

Expression E1 is a equilibrium relational expression which gives equilibrium condition of the box. Expression E2 and E3 are causal relational expressions which give outflow by advection and outflow by vertical diffusion respectively. Atmospheric stability obtained from R-TEMPD-B, R-TEMPD-U, and R-DAD decides the box state. Atmospheric stability takes three states; stable, unstable and neutral states. This state decides a diffusion flow. This model explains causal relationship between pollution production and pollution accumulation by three relational expressions E1, E2 and E3.

A qualitative model is described by quantity space[7], qualitative relations, qualitative operators, and qualitative reasoning rules. Quantity space is a three-valued set {+, -, 0}. Figure 4-3 shows an example of qualitative description of atmospheric diffusion box model.

```
[PROD-POLL] = +
(== POLL-ACCU
   (+ (+ (+ PROD-POLL INFLOW)(- OUTFLOW)) (- VERT-DIFF)))
(<< VERT-DIFF PROD-POLL)
([(++ [(++ [(++ [PROD-POLL][INFLOW])]
          [(- OUTFLOW)])]) [(- VERT-DIFF)])] = x
   -> [PROD-ACCU] = x )
(<< A B) -> (== (+ A B) B)
```

FIGURE 4-3
Qualitative description of atmospheric diffusion

The [] is a qualitative value operator which defines a mapping from properties to quantity space. The ++ is a qualitative sum operator which is defined as figure 4-4. The == is a qualitative relation which represents "neally equal". The << and < are qualitative relations which represent "has far small order" and "has small absolute value" respectively. Qualitative reasoning rules are rules on qualitative operations and qualitative relations.

++	+	0	-
+	+	+	?
0	+	0	-
-	?	-	-

FIGURE 4-4
Qualitative sum

Let "atmosphere-box1" be viewpoint which provides a qualitative model for the purpose of reasoning qualitatively from pollution production and advection to pollution accumulation. That is, this viewpoint provides a qualitative model of equilibrium relational expression E1. This viewpoint is used to obtain a qualitative value of POLL-ACCU and qualitative relation between POLL-ACCU and PROD-POLL on the premises or assumptions of qualitative values of PROD-POLL, INFLOW, OUTFLOW, and VERT-DIFF and qualitative relations among them. Let "atmosphere-box2" be viewpoint which provides a qualitative model for the purpose of reasoning qualitatively from atmospheric phenomena to advection. This viewpoint is used to obtain atmospheric stability and qualitative values of OUTFLOW and VERT-DIFF and qualitative relation between PROD-POLL and them on the premises or assumptions of qualitative values of PROD-POLL, INFLOW, VEL-W, R-TEMPD-B, R-TEMPD-U, R-DAD and qualitative relations among them. By connecting this viewpoint "atmosphere-box2" with "atmosphere-box1", a viewpoint "atmosphere-box3" which provides a qualitative model for the purpose of reasoning qualitatively from pollution production and atmospheric phenomena to pollution accumulation is constructed. This viewpoint provides a qualitative model of relational expressions E1, E2 and E3.

For given queries or behavioral information of system, qualitative model construction is carried out by strongly inclusive viewing. In viewpoints-directed knowledge system, a viewed-world INPUTW which describes given premises is created in viewed-worlds area, and a viewed-world which strongly includes INPUTW is built by strongly inclusive viewing using queries as a target keys. This viewed-world describes a qualitative model. For example, when equilibrium relational expression of air pollution and qualitative values of pollution production and inflow by advection are given by user, following input viewed-world is created.

```
(VW inputw (I1 F (== POLL-ACCU
                  (+ (+ (+ PROD-POLL INFLOW)(- OUTFLOW))
                  (- VERT-DIFF)))))
(JW inputw (I1 j (#)()))
(VW inputw (I2 F ([PROD-POLL]=+)))
(JW inputw (I2 j (#)()))
(VW inputw (I3 F ([INFLOW]=+)))
(JW inputw (I3 j (#)()))
```

And viewpoint "atmosphere-box1" is selected as a viewpoint which provide a viewed-world which strongly includes this input viewed-world.

Let "atmosphere-world1" and "atmosphere-world2" be viewed-worlds built by viewing of "atmosphere-box1" and "atmosphere-box2" respectively. Assumptions in a viewed-world "atmosphere-world1" are for example described as follows.

```
(VW atmosphere-world1 (I1 F (<< VERT-DIFF PROD-POLL)))
(JW atmosphere-world1 (I1 j () (I2)))
(VW atmosphere-world1 (I2 F (< VERT-DIFF PROD-POLL)))
(JW atmosphere-world1 (I2 u ()()))
                      :
```

These mean the assumption that "if VERT-DIFF is not compared with PROD-POLL then VERT-DIFF is negligible in comparison with PROD-POLL". In "atmosphere-world1", we suppose that an assumption (<< VERT-DIFF PROD-POLL) concludes a consequence (== POLL-ACCU (+ PROD-POLL INFLOW)). At this time, if possible but unaccepted assumption (< VERT-DIFF PROD-POLL) is justified as an assumption or a consequence, then (<< VERT-DIFF PROD-POLL) and its consequence (== POLL-ACCU (+ PROD-POLL INFLOW)) loses their justifications and another consequences are concluded. In a viewed-world, nonmonotonic reasoning mechanism modifies justified consequences by managing justifications when justified assumptions are modified.

In "atmosphere-world1", it is possible to explain the relationship between VERT-DIFF and POLL-ACCU based on various assumptions about magnitude of VERT-DIFF, but it is impossible to explain magnitude of VERT-DIFF based on other causes. Connective viewing builds a viewed-world "atmosphere-world3" by searching a viewpoint "atmosphere-box2" when causal relationship between atmospheric stability and VERT-DIFF is for instance asked. In this viewed-world, it is possible to explain magnitude of VERT-DIFF from atmospheric stability. A qualitative relation (<< VERT-DIFF PROD-POLL) can be concluded for some atmospheric stability. For example, qualitative reasoning rules

```
([ATM-SmB]=-) & ([ATM-S-U]=+) -> ([VERT-DIFF]=0),
[A]=0 & not[B]=0 -> (<< A B)
```

concludes above qualitative relation in "atmosphere-world3".
The ([ATM-S-B]=-) means that atmospheric stability in box is unstable, and the ([ATM-S-U]=+) means that atmospheric stability above box is stable. This rule means that there isn't exist outflow by vertical diffusion when there exists a inverse layer. Atmospheric stability ATM-S-B and ATM-S-U are derived from following qualitative rules in "atmosphere-world3".

```
([R-TEMPD-B]=-) & (< R-DAD R-TEMPD-B) -> ([ATM-S-B]=-)
([R-TEMPD-B]=-) & (< R-TEMPD-B R-DAD) -> ([ATM-S-B]=+)
([R-TEMPD-B]=0) -> ([ATM-S-B]=+)
([R-TEMPD-B]=+) -> ([ATM-S-B]=+)
(== R-TEMPD-B R-DAD) -> ([ATM-S-B]=0)
```

Nonmonotonic reasoning on viewed-worlds area is carried out by means of justifying assumptions in one viewed-world as consequences in another viewed-world by connective viewing.

5. CONCLUSIONS

Consequences of this paper are summarized in five points as follows.

1)We classified planning support forms by knowledge system into four forms as follows; a conventional support form, a goal-oriented support form, a viewpoints-directed support form, and a multiviewpoints-learning support form. And we presented six design criteria of knowledge system for planning support.
2)As a framework of knowledge system for viewpoints-directed planning support form, we presented a design framework of viewpoints-directed knowledge system which consists of a viewpoints base, a viewpoints control mechanism, a knowledge base and a viewed-worlds area.
3)As a formal model of viewpoints-directed knowledge system, we defined a viewpoints system formally and obtained viewing conditions for building viewed-worlds and viewing algorisms of two viewing - strongly inclusive viewing and connective viewing.
4)We designed viewpoint and knowledge representation forms and outlined design of viewpoints-directed knowledge system as a system which integrates object-oriented representation of entities, rule representation, and logical representation of methods in viewed-world using viewpoints.
5)By an example of qualitative prediction of air pollution diffusion, we discussed qualitative model building and qualitative reasoning by viewpoints-directed knowledge processing and examined possibility of viewpoints-directed support form in problem definition and problem solving.

REFERENCES

[1] Hayes-Roth,B.:A Blackboard Architecture for Control, Artif. Intell.,pp251-321, 26(1985)

[2] Doyle,J.:A Truth Maintenance System, Artif. Intell.,pp231-272, 12(1979)

[3] Schank,R.C. and Riesbeck,C.K.:Inside Computer Understanding:Five Programs Plus Miniatures, Lawrence Erlbaum Associatess, Hillsdale,N.J. (1981)

[4] Kauffmann,H. and Grumbach,A.:Representing and Manipulating Knowledge within WORLDS, Proc. of 1st Int. Conf. on Expert Data Base Systems, pp61-73,(1986)

[5] de Kleer,J. and Brown,J.S.:A Qualitative Physics Based on Confluences, Artif. Intell.,pp7-83, 24(1984)

[6] Bourgine,P. and Raiman,O.:Economics as Reasoning on a Qualitative Model,Economics and Artificial Intelligence International Conference, AIX-EN-PROVENCE FRANCE, pp185-189,(1986)

[7] Bobrow,D.G.:Qualitative Reasoning about Physical Systems:An Introduction, Artif. Intell., pp1-8, 24(1984)

APPENDIX 1   Proof of Lemma 3-1

If $M \supset w M'$ then $Iw \supset Iw'$. Let $WI=\{w \in WI \mid Ew[Iw](w)=1\}$ and let $WI'=\{w \in W'I \mid Ew[Iw'](w)=1\}$. And let Wp and Wp' be set of premises of M and M' respectively and let Ws and Ws' be set of unaccepted assumptions of M and M' respectively. Since $Ew[Iw'](w)=1$ for any $w \in WI'$, $w \in Wp'$ or $(Wp' \cup Ws')$ I- w hold. And since $Iw \supset Iw'$, $Wp \supset Wp'$ and $Ws \supset Ws'$ hold. Hence $w \in Wp$ or $(Wp \cup Ws)$ I- w hold. And $Ew[Iw](w)=1$, that is $w \in WI$, holds. Therefore $WI \supset WI'$, that is $M \supset c M'$.

Q.E.D.

APPENDIX 2   Proof of Theorem 3-1

$W = Rj(z \circ s)$ and $W' = Rj'(z' \circ s')$ hold. Since $v \supset v v'$, $Rj \supset Rj'$ holds. And $z \circ s \supset z' \circ s'$ holds. Therefore $W \supset W'$. Next let Jv and Jv' be sets of premises and assumptions and unaccepted assumptions justification structure of v and v' respectively. And let Jc and Jc' be sets of consequences justification structure of v and v' respectively. $Iw = (Jv \cup Jc)(z \circ s)$ and $Iw' = (Jv' \cup Jc')(z' \circ s')$ hold. Since $v \supset v v'$, $Jv \supset Jv'$ and $Jc \supset Jc'$ hold. And $z \circ s \supset z' \circ s'$ holds. Therefore $Iw \supset Iw'$. Hence $M \supset w M'$.   Q.E.D.

APPENDIX 3   Proof of Theorem 3-2

Let WII be a justified set of MI. And let $Wp0$ and $Wp1$ be set of premises of $M0$ and $M1$ respectively and let $Ws0$ and $Ws1$ be set of unaccepted assumptions of $M0$ and $M1$ respectively. And let $Rp0$ be a subset of $Rj0$ element of which has a premise justification structure, and let $Rp1$ be a subset of $Rj1$ of $v1$ element of which has a premise justification structure. And let $Rc1$ be a subset of $Rj1$ of $v1$ element of which has a consequence justification structure. Since $M1 \supset c M0$ is equivalent to $WII \supset W10$, we show that "for any w, if $w \in W10$ then $w \in WII$". When w W10 hold, w Wp0 or $(Wp0$ Ws0) I- w hold.

1)When $w \in Wp0$ holds, there exists some $r \in Rp0$ such that $\{r\}(z0 \circ d0)=\{w\}$.

(a)When $r \in Rp0 \backslash C(v)$ holds, $r \in Rp1$ holds by the operation CONNECTv. Since $z1 \circ d1 \supset z0 \circ d0$ holds, $\{w\}=\{r\}(z1 \circ d1) \subset Wp1 \subset WII$ holds.

(b)When $r \in Rp0 \cap C(v)$, $r \in Rc1$ and $r \in C(v1)$ hold by the operation CONNECTv. Since $z1 \circ d1 \supset z0 \circ d0$ holds, $\{w\}=\{r\}(z1 \circ d1) \subset (Wc1 \cap WII) \subset WII$ holds.

2)When $(Wp0 \cup Ws0)$ I- w holds, $w' \in Wp0 \rightarrow w' \in WII$ holds by 1). Therefore $w' \in Wp1$ or $(Wp1 \cup Ws1)$ I- w' hold, i.e. $(Wp1 \cup Ws1)$ I- w' holds for any $w' \in Wp0$. And since $C(v) \cap Rj0 \subset R \ddagger$ holds, $C(v) \cap R$ d0 $= \phi$ holds. Therefore R d0 $\subset R$ d1. Since $z1 \circ d1 \supset z0 \circ d0$ holds, W d0 $\subset W$ d1 holds. Hence $(Wp1 \cup Ws1)$ I- w hold. That is $w \in WII$ holds.   Q.E.D.

Governmental and Municipal Information Systems
P. Kovács and E. Straub (Editors)
Elsevier Science Publishers B.V. (North-Holland)
© IFIP, 1988

SIGMA: SOFTWARE INDUSTRIALIZED GENERATOR AND MAINTENANCE AIDS

Noboru Akima, Fusatake Ooi

SIGMA Project, INFORMATION-TECHNOLOGY PROMOTION AGENCY,JAPAN
5F Akihabara-Sanwa-Toyo Bldg.
3-16-8 Soto-Kanda, Chiyoda-ku, Tokyo, Japan

Information-technology Promotion Agency, Japan (IPA) is a government (MITI) related quasi-governmental organization promoting computerization of Japan, particularly from a standpoint of software. IPA started a new project in mid-1985, which is to improve software development environment for better productivity and quality. The name of the project is SIGMA. The gist of the project is to industrialize software production process, by promoting distributed software development environment.
This paper covers the objectives and the basic features of the project, the functions and the structures of the software development environment proposed by the project, and ongoing and planned activities.

1. INTRODUCTION

As society continues to rapidly transform itself into an information society, the role of computer systems in economic and social life becomes more vital. As this transformation continues, there will be an increasing demand for computer software. It is already evident, however, that the gap between software demand and supply capacity is widening. Furthermore, the requirements for software quality are increasing. These have given rise to the advent of what is now called "software crisis". Born to cope with this problem is SIGMA Project, which is a Japanese nation-wide project.
The gist of the project is to industrialize software production process, by means of computerized development facilities and nation-wide network. SIGMA Project is expected to make a great contribution to the development of Japanese software industry as an independent entity, the improvement of the working software development environment, and the solution to satisfy the demand for software. In other words, the ultimate goals of the project are to produce software as a manufactured product instead of a manually produced product, and to transform the software industry from the labor intensive to the knowledge intensive industry.
In October 1985, SIGMA System Development Office was officially organized in IPA, as a nucleus for constructing SIGMA System. And the efforts of one and a half years have made the image of SIGMA System rather clear than ever. This paper covers the objectives and the basic features of the project, the functions and the structures of the software development environments proposed by the project, and ongoing and planned activities.

2. SOFTWARE CRISIS AND SIGMA PROJECT

2.1 SOFTWARE CRISIS IN JAPAN

We recognize the following items are the contents of the software crisis in Japan, which brought us SIGMA Project.

(1) Widening gap between software demand and supply capacity
As Japanese society becomes computerized one rapidly, the demand for the number of software engineers becomes larger at the rate of 26% a year. On the other hand, the software productivity is supposed to be improved at the rate of only 4% a year. We estimate the rate of increase in number of software engineers as 13% a year, which can not fill the gap.

(2) Rising software development cost
In last decade, computer hardware got higher performance with lower cost. On the other hand, computer software got larger in its scale and more complex. As a result, software development cost occupies relatively far more in a total cost of a system.

(3) The need for high quality software
With the changing social situations and the progress of the information revolution, Japanese society is increasingly depending on the good operation of computer systems. Nevertheless the quality of software is often worse than what it should be, and sometimes much worse.

2.2. THE PROJECT OBJECTIVES

The main purpose of SIGMA Project is to construct a working system that fulfills the following objectives;

(1) to improve software quality and software productivity
(2) to prevent duplicate investments in software development
(3) to consolidate software development facilities, accumulate technical know-how, and raise technical capabilities
(4) to promote efficient training of software engineers

In order to achieve these objectives, SIGMA System is now in the course of its development. And we have taken the following approaches to put the system into operation;

(1) To establish a common software development environment independent of the hardware that will execute the programs developed(i.e. *target computer*)
(2) To construct a network system for retrieving and transmitting programs and technical information

2.3 THE MAIN FUNCTIONS OF SIGMA SYSTEM

SIGMA System provides its users with broad functions which support every activity in their software development processes. The functions provided by SIGMA System mainly comprise the following three;

(1) Software Development Support Functions (tools)
Software development support functions, also described as software development tools, are functions that directly support the software development process. These functions will be used on SIGMA Workstation discussed later to computerize the various processes and activities involved in software development. Using these functions will make a great contribution toward realizing beneficial development techniques, and improving software productivity as well as the quality of the developed software. These tools (*named SIGMA Tools*) can be categorized into two major types by function: *basic tools and application tools*. The basic tools are those which can be used in common in the development of software, and are independent of the variety of application fields and the phases in development processes. The application tools fulfill different requirements for different activities, phases, applications, etc.

(2) Database Services Functions
SIGMA System allows its users to make access to the database of SIGMA related

information; namely tools and services available for SIGMA Users, references to other databases and technical information, etc. This service is further planned to enable the users to make access to the other databases outside SIGMA via the gateway provided by SIGMA System. As an example of the effectiveness of these database services, there is a growing recognition of the roll of the database information on various software products already on the market. Because it will serve to promote re-use of application programs, and consequently to prevent duplicated investments in software development.

(3) Network Services Functions
Network services functions are those functions required to enable SIGMA System users to exchange information, and to make use of resources of target computers such as mainframe computers linked up to SIGMA Network.

3. THE FEATURES OF SIGMA PROJECT

Software crisis should be recognized as a common problem for Japanese industries. SIGMA Project which is planned to solve it, therefore, has the following unique features.

(1) The project is a 5-year project (FY1985-FY1989). Then full service will be furnished from FY1990. A total budget for 5 years is scheduled to be 25 billion yen. Most of the funds are either invested or donated by supporters of the project in both the private and public sectors. At present, over 160 private companies are financially supporting the project.

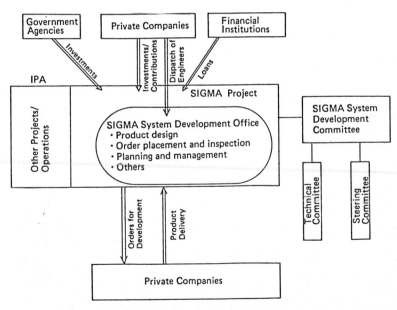

Figure 1. Conceptual Diagram of SIGMA Project Organization

(2) In October 1985, SIGMA System Development Office was organized in *IPA*, as a nucleus for constructing SIGMA System, considering the public aspects of SIGMA Project. It is staffed by approximately 50 engineers loaned from private

companies. They do primarily making the overall plan of the system and overall management and design of the project. On the other hand, most of the actual development works due to the specifications put forth by SIGMA staffs are contracted to various private companies.

A special committee -SIGMA System Development Committee- has also been organized to study and discuss the contents and direction of the plans and specifications formulated by the office from a general standpoint of view. This committee comprises over 50 members, all of whom are leading figures in the worlds of academia and industry. The committee is supported by two expert committees. Technical Committee is in charge of technical matters, and Steering Committee is in charge of matters related to employing SIGMA System. These expert committees are comprised of approximately 15 members each (See Figure 1).

(3) In spite of numerous software engineering tools existing, few of them are truly applicable to real software development. Therefore, SIGMA Project aims at attaining its objectives by a two-stage approach, instead of embarking on overall development efforts to develop a full-fledged operation at a stroke. The first stage (Oct. 1985 - Sept. 1987) is for a prototype SIGMA System to evaluate the market's reaction. And the second stage (Oct. 1987 - Mar. 1990) will focus on enhancing and improving the prototype system. More specifically, the types of work to be carried out during the second stage will include the addition of functions not originally incorporated into the prototype system; incorporation of other new functions become available during the course of the project by advances in technology; refinement of performance and usability in response to discoveries made during the test operation of the prototype system; and the conversion of the prototype system into a practical system.

(4) Once SIGMA System is complete, a user will generally be able to use the system without any restriction if he or she signs a contract for the use of the system. The contract requires the user to pay the required charges. And it will be made available to as many users as possible to help improve their software development environments in the broadest sense of the term. The income earned from SIGMA System utilization fees will be used to operate the system, as well as to maintain and improve it. The schedule calls for the system to be put into widespread commercial use beginning in April, 1990.

4. SIGMA SYSTEM OVERVIEW

4.1 SIGMA SYSTEM CONFIGURATION

The configuration of SIGMA System is shown in Figure 2. The system consists of SIGMA Center, SIGMA Network and SIGMA User Sites.

4.2 SIGMA CENTER

The role of SIGMA Center is to support SIGMA System users in their construction of software development environments and in the subsequent development of programs using those environments. To carry out this role, SIGMA Center manages and controls the whole system, and provides the database services, a part of the network services and the demonstration services. The readers of this paper should be aware the fact that we don't put such roles on SIGMA Center as TSS (Time Sharing System) and RJE (Remote Job Entry) services.

(1) Database Services
The database services of SIGMA Center are planned to provide the following six types of data.

(a) *Software Information* consists of catalog data concerning software products

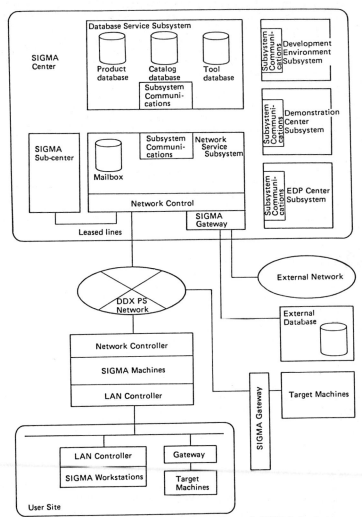

Figure 2. Overall Configuration of SIGMA System

on the markets, such as software development tools, application packages, database management software and system software.

(b) *Services And Companies Information* includes data describing various outside database and network services; introductory information on software houses; and other information on software-related education and events.

(c) *SIGMA System Information* consists of those information necessary and useful for the users to use SIGMA System, and includes data on utilization guidance and the fixed bugs of SIGMA System.

(d) *Hardware Information* are also catalog-type data about hardware equipments, computers, peripherals and others.

(e) *Reference Information* consists of technological articles in newspapers and magazines, plus other data related to the software standardization, Japanese

Industrial Standards (JIS), ISO and so forth.

(f) *Precedent Information* is a vehicle of having common property in the software industry. It includes examples of previously constructed software development environments; software and system development examples; and fact data which can serve as the basis for cost estimation.

(2) Network Services
The followings are the types of network services provided by SIGMA.

(a) *Message Communication Functions* will be used among SIGMA System users. The messages should allow Japanese language representation. These functions include electronic mail, electronic newsletter, electronic bulletin board and electronic conversation.

(b) *File Transmission Functions* enable users to have rapid and easy transmission and distribution of data, programs and documents.

(c) *Target Machine Access Functions* enable the users of SIGMA Workstation to access and use the resources of target systems. For example users will be able to test their programs in the equivalent environment of a target computer by using remote login to the computers connected to SIGMA Network. Target Machine Access Functions also include virtual terminal and remote job entry functions.

(3) Demonstration Services
Generally speaking, when one considers to purchase a certain software product, it would be necessary for him to see, feel, compare and evaluate the candidates. This is also true for SIGMA System, especially for SIGMA Tools. Taking these into consideration, we will construct a typical SIGMA User Site which will give opportunity to the users to feel and touch the effectiveness of SIGMA Tools (see Figure 2; Demonstration Center Subsystem). Furthermore, the consulting service will be available at Demonstration Center.

4.3 SIGMA NETWORK

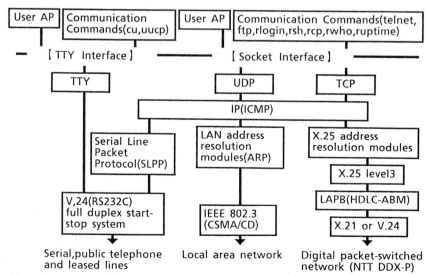

Figure 3. Communication Functions and Configuration

SIGMA Network refers to the UNIX-based inter-network and logical network which will be used to connect SIGMA Center and SIGMA User Sites, the individual User Sites themselves and SIGMA Center and external networks. Thus SIGMA Network will play a roll of infrastructure in SIGMA System. The electronic community of the software engineers realized by SIGMA Network will make a great contribution to the industrialization of software development processes.

SIGMA Network will make use of the DDX(PS) network, leased lines and the public telephone network provided by Nippon Telephone and Telepgraph Corporation (NTT). Figure 3 shows communication functions and configuration of SIGMA Network. Due to the transmission cost, speed and reliability, DDX(PS) is selected as a main network between SIGMA Center and SIGMA User Sites.

4.4 SIGMA USER SITES

(i) Single SIGMA-Machine System

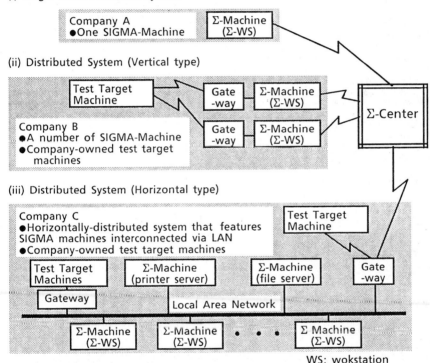

(ii) Distributed System (Vertical type)

(iii) Distributed System (Horizontal type)

WS: wokstation

Figure 4. Examples of SIGMA User Site Configurations

User Sites are users' locations where users can utilize SIGMA System services and functions, and develop their programs. A typical SIGMA User Site comprises SIGMA Workstations with SIGMA-OS(Operating System), LAN(Local Area Network), SIGMA Gateway and so forth.

The elementary hardware facilities to be installed at User Sites are SIGMA Workstations. These SIGMA Workstations will be of a variety of different makes and brands, but they will all operate alike, i.e. they will all run software with the same functions and use the same communication protocols. This will enable the SIGMA System users to freely install and hook up their own choice of

SIGMA Workstations, and to construct these sites in a range of sizes, from simple single-machine sites, to much more complex, multiple workstation sites, all in accordance with their particular requirements. Figure 4 shows examples of some of the various types of User Sites possible. The software development environment advocated by SIGMA Project calls for each software engineer to be provided his or her own SIGMA Workstation on which many useful tools will run.

It is almost impossible to discuss software development environments without mentioning hardware aspects. Although this is not the prime emphasis of this paper, we will briefly describe the hardware features of SIGMA Workstation. Also the operating system should not be separated from the hardware; both constitute the virtual machine interface that users actually access. The actual development of the SIGMA Workstations and their provision to SIGMA System users will be entrusted to a number of computer manufacturers. Table 1 lists the proposed specifications for a SIGMA Workstation. These specifications constitute what is called an "image guideline" for hardware manufacturers. This guideline is made of the following requirements.

(1) Basically for personal use(dedicated workstation) so that each user can enjoy the powerful computing power
(2) Powerful network functions providing efficient system-to-system transfer
(3) Resource-sharing functions in a distributed environment(i.e. LAN)
(4) Advanced user interface: high-resolution display, mouse, graphics
(5) Minimum affection for designing tools to run on them

Table 1. Proposed Specifications for the Prototype Σ Workstation(Extract)

Item		Requirements for ΣOS-V0
Price		3 million yen
Control	CPU	32 bit (Internal Registers)
	Floating Point Processor	Built into CPU board (IEEE format)
	Main Memory	4 MB min.
	Addressing-Space(Logical)	8 MB min.
File	Hard Disk	20 MB min. for user's area
	Floppy Disk	5"(2HD) or 8"(2D) for data exchange
	Backup Device	Necessary for a system
Display	Display Unit	Bit mapped (1000 × 768 dot min.)
	Key Board	Revised JIS model,10 Function Keys min.
	Pointing Device	Mouse (2 buttons min.)
	Printer	Not specified
External Interface	Serial Interface	RS232C(V.24) 2 or more
	Parallel Interface	CENTRONICS interface (option)
	LAN Interface	IEEE 802.3 interface
	DDX-P Interface	V.28(X.21 bis) or V.11(X.21)
	GP-IB Interface	For ΣICE interface (option)

The specifications put forth in this guideline are for use with the prototype SIGMA System. The workstation envisioned for use with the commercial SIGMA System is expected to be greatly improved with respect to its functions, performance and price. Hardware similar to the guideline is currently being developed by several Japanese leading workstation manufacturers. And SIGMA System Development Office has already purchased a number of such machines for use in developing and testing software for SIGMA System.

One of the important activities of SIGMA Project is to set a de facto standard OS to assure the portability of tools. SIGMA OS is the operating system for the

SIGMA Workstations. SIGMA System Development Office is not planning to develop SIGMA OS itself but defines the external specification of the OS, and let the manufacturers develop the OS following the specification and put them on the market. When they install SIGMA OS in their workstations, they can make changes to the hardware-dependent part of SIGMA OS and upgrade its performance. They should not, however, make changes that affect any external specifications of SIGMA OS. Thus the software such as tools which are supposed to run on SIGMA Workstations will be portable, and run on a number of different makes of workstations. SIGMA OS will function as a means of consolidating and standardizing software development environments, independent of target computers.

Our intensive work including various examinations and discussions on what the requirements of SIGMA OS should be and how to implement it, has brought us to the conclusion that SIGMA OS should not be developed from scratch, but rather should be a revised version of UNIX operating system developed and licensed by AT&T. UNIX OS was selected because it already fulfills a number of requirements for SIGMA OS. The features of the requirements for SIGMA OS are summrized as follows and also Figure 5 shows the conceptual configuration of SIGMA OS.

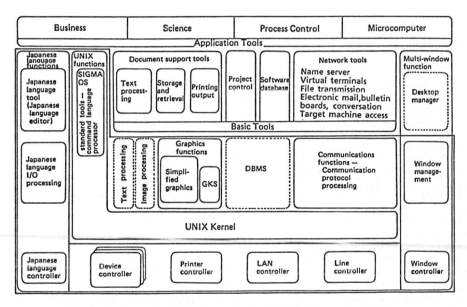

Figure 5. Conceptual Configuration of SIGMA Operating System

(1) The functions of SIGMA OS are derived from both AT&T System V and 4.2 BSD versions of UNIX (i.e. AT&T and Berkeley versions). All of the functions provided in AT&T version should be incorporated into SIGMA OS, whereas only those functions considered beneficial to software development should be selected from 4.2 BSD for incorporation into SIGMA OS.
(2) However, as UNIX does not satisfy all of the requirements for SIGMA OS, some functions must be added and/or strengthened. The functions concerned are Japanese language processing, graphics, multi-window, database and communication functions.

The development of SIGMA OS Version 0 for the prototype SIGMA Workstation has almost completed. SIGMA OS Version 0 is based on AT&T System V Rel. 2.0 and 4.2 BSD versions of UNIX. Those functions available in System V Rel. 2.1 and 3.0, as well as those in 4.3 BSD will be considered for incorporation in later versions of SIGMA OS.

5. SIGMA TOOLS

With the exception of the software developed in relation to SIGMA OS and SIGMA Center, most of the software being prepared for use with SIGMA System is being developed and will be provided in the form of tools.

5.1 DESIGN CONSIDERATIONS OF SIGMA TOOLS

SIGMA Project furnishes many tools for software development and they run on a number of various SIGMA Workstations. These tools are named SIGMA Tools. There will be two categories of SIGMA Tools;

(1) Those newly developed or adapted from existing tools for use in SIGMA System and provided by SIGMA System Development Office.
(2) Those tools developed and commercially provided by the parties other than the Development Office.

In terms of functions, these various tools can also be categorized into two major types; basic tools and application tools (see §2.3 (1)). The major design considerations of SIGMA Tools provided by the Development Office are as follows.

(1) Optimal Integrated Software Development Environment
The software development environment supports all of software development phases, and reduces the degree to which the development efficiency is dependent on the skills and experiences of each individual engineer. However, different software projects require different development environments. Futhermore, the software development environment should keep grow and be improved, by having various advanced tools introduced into the market by various sectors. SIGMA System allows the development environment designers to customize the nominal to create an optimal development environment of their own. With the aboves in minds, the following considerations are made.

●SIGMA System Development Office will develop and provide many useful tool-sets that will be applicable to wider range of software development processes: from requirement analysis phase to installation and maintenance phase. Furthermore, the tools directly applicable to a specific phase of the software lifecycle are able to effectively be integrated so that the user could make re-use of information created in former phase at later phases (e.g. implementaion etc.) and so on.

●The idea of *fully integrated software development environment* has been in fashion for sometime. Many experts, however, have now claimed that too much integration is not good. By forcing a single paradigm over a whole environment, it may result in constraining developers too much prohibiting a better, flexible environment. Therefore in the SIGMA Software Development Environment, the emphasis should be more on *multi-paradigm* environments that allow communication between difference of users, tools, methods, languages, and target computers. To achieve this, the functions for accommodating the SIGMA Environment to the practical world of a specific user should be designed especially. The functions used to define a development process in scenario form, to define the contents of a dialect of a specific pogramming language specification, to define the hardware information of a specific target computer, are the good examples.

●As there would be a case where the functions for accommodation could not satisfy the user's requirements, the venders of SIGMA Tools would be provided with source codes of those tools.

(2) Promoting Technology Transfer
Existing tools and technologies whose effectiveness and applicability to the practical world of software development have already been evident at leading companies are taken as the base of SIGMA Tools. In this sense, SIGMA Software Development Environment would function as a vehicle of making technology transfer in the industries. Furthermore, using the existing tools, as described above, would greatly help us to not only develop effective and practical tools, but also save the project's cost and time.

(3) Recognition of the Roll of the Future Tool-products on the Market
The resources (budget, man-power, time etc.) of SIGMA Project is limited. In this sense, we expect that various useful tools will be *kept* introduced into the market by many companies as their businesses. Especially as for the tools which support exclusively a specific methodology, target computer and target OS, we expect those to be put on the market in the near future as many as possible. The following considerations will greatly promote the advent of the above tool market.

●Tool-kit approach should be adopted in SIGMA Tools to enable their users to select, combine and compose the optimal development environment. Also Tool-kit approach will prevent duplicated development efforts among SIGMA Tools.

●A communication protocol such as the pipe mechanism of UNIX can be said to be the unifying element for integrating software development environment. But the pipe mechanism of UNIX, although remarkably powerful on paper and for simple uses, turns out to be insufficient for more serious applications. In addition to the pipe mechanism, therefore, we define more sophisticated communication protocol (i.e. interface among SIGMA Tools). This communication protocol have been named "*SIGMA Data Architecture*", and defines the various information such as design information, program-chart information and so on. The defined Data Architecture will be opened to the public to enable the software product vendors to develop and distribute more advanced tools than the existing SIGMA Tools at that time.

5.2 SIGMA TOOLS

We suppose that most of the users would follow the steps of those in Table 2 in the courses of their software developments, although the details of the model might vary. And Figure 6 shows the eventual image of the software development environment designed and provided by SIGMA System according to the design considerations of §5.1, when SIGMA System will be put into widespread commercial use.

(1) Basic Tools
The basic tools scheduled to be provided with the prototype SIGMA System are: documentation tools, network tools, and project management tools.

●The documentation tools enable the user to write and update documents by simple operation. The types of documents possible include Japanese language texts comprised of KANJI, KANA, alphanumerics and symbols, plus diagrams that consist of combinations of straight and curved lines and circles, tables, graphs and formulas.

●The network tools enable the user to utilize message communications functions (electronic mail, bulletin boards and newsletters), plus file transmission, RJE and interactive virtual terminal functions required for use of remote systems.

Table 2. Phases in the Software Lifecycle

Phase	Activity
Planning	●Exploration ●Requirement analysis ●Conceptual design ●Overall project planning (budget,schedule,constraint definition)
Design	●System design(Functions,Performance etc.) ●Detailed plan for the rest of the project ●Define the main data-flows and processing-flows ●Software design(Decompose the system into subsystems and define the main data structures) ●Program design(Decompose each subsystem into programs) ●Detailed design(Decompose each program into modules)
Implementation	●Program writing ●Desk checking ●Compile and linkage edit
Checkout	●Design test cases,programs and operation-procedures ●Implement test programs, data, drivers and stubs ●Unit testing ●System testing ●Validation
Maintenance	●Distribute the system and its documentation ●System in operation ●Maintenance

●The project management tools are designed with the philosophy that project management activities should be done according to the cycle of P(lan)-D(o)-C(heck)-A(ction). These tools support the user to plan, measure and analyze the objects which are schedule, cost and quality. However, different companies require different project managements. Therefore, the project management tools provide enough functions for user's accommodations.

(2) Application Tools
Application tools scheduled to be provided with the prototype SIGMA System include:
    -Languages: Cobol, Fortran, C and a few microprocessor assemblers;
    -Applications: Business, scientific, process control and microcomputers;
    -Phases: Downstream of design, implementation and checkout.
The Development Office is constructing these tools for use in the prototype SIGMA System. Some tools from scratch, but others are by adapting existing tools for use with the prototype SIGMA System. Basic design work is completed, and some of the required tools are in the implementation phase now.

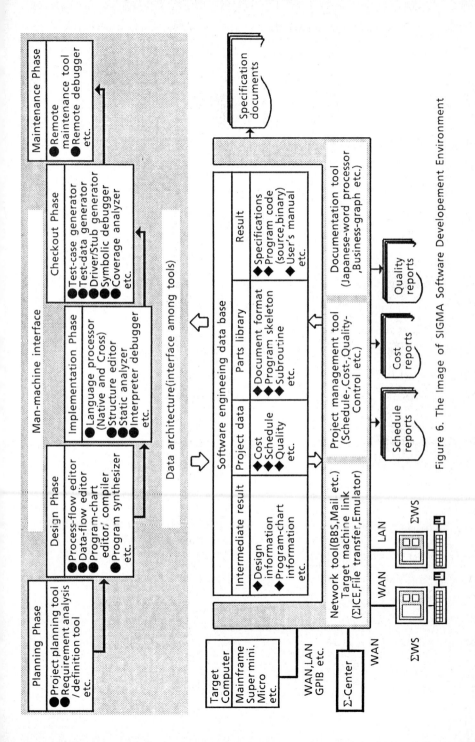

Figure 6. The Image of SIGMA Software Developement Environment

6. FUTURE OUTLOOK

The Development Office has already finished design work of the prototype SIGMA System, and is now working full-time on implementing it. This construction work, including integration and testing, is expected to take roughly half more year.

When the prototype system is completed, it will be test operated. This test operation, called monitor testing will employ outside parties, i.e. those parties that did not participate directly in the design and implementation of the prototype system. The results of this monitor-type test operation phase will serve as feedback for the improvement of the prototype system.

The Development Office plans to continuously upgrade the SIGMA OS in response to
● revisions of specifications used in the AT&T and/or Berkeley versions of the UNIX OS;
● trends in international standardization;
● demands from SIGMA System users.
It will also update as needed the communications capabilities built into the SIGMA System to keep up with developments in OSI protocols and other communications techniques.

As for SIGMA Center, the Development Office will continue to improve the center's overall functions; to enhance its database capabilities; to improve the level of its security; and to test its user registration and management functions. This will ensure the expansion of the prototype SIGMA Center functions and facilities in preparation for its commercial operation.

The Development Office will constantly enhance the functions incorporated into the software development environment of the prototype SIGMA System. For example, it plans to develop an integrated software development tools that encompass the requirement analysis phase, and to introduce new engineering technologies into SIGMA System. In line with this, the Development Office will also work to increase the number of firms that develop software tools for SIGMA System.

These endeavors, combined with increased utilization of SIGMA Workstations, should enable the realization of even better environments for software developers. And the better the software development environment, the greater will be the contribution of SIGMA System toward software productivity and the sound progress of the information processing world.

Governmental and Municipal Information Systems
P. Kovács and E. Straub (Editors)
Elsevier Science Publishers B.V. (North-Holland)
  IFIP, 1988

COMPUTERS IN SWEDISH GOVERNMENT AGENCIES

Lars Hellberg

STATSKONTORET
THE SWEDISH AGENCY FOR ADMINISTRATIVE DEVELOPMENT (SAFAD)
Box 34 107, S - 100 26 STOCKHOLM, Sweden
(Telephone +46 8-738 40 00)

The Swedish government has decided on a number of standards, among others for operating systems, for decentralized multi-user computer systems (departmental computers). It has also negotiated call-off contracts regarding such standardized systems in order to get a uniform development and run-time environment. This is the result of a long-range plan for computer support in the administrative routines in the government agencies.

SAFAD, the Swedish Agency for Administrative Development, is a government agency under the Ministry of Public Administration. This agency is among other things responsible for the acquisition of all computer equipment for the Swedish government agencies.

SAFAD buys approximately $ 100 M of computer equipment each year. Historically, large central computer systems were acquired in the 1960's, and these computer assisted routines are still running. Nowadays, the trend is towards more decentralized data processing, and terminals, personal computers, "briefcase computers", word processors and standardized computer systems are procured under call-off contracts.

SAFAD consequently has a big interest in the efficient use of the computers. This can be achieved by including carefully developed standards to the requirements when buying the computer systems.

Accordingly, SAFAD has put emphasis on standards and has several persons assigned to committees of Swedish and international standards organizations. SAFAD also issues its own standards or recommendations, often in cooperation with corresponding bodies of the other Nordic countries.

The goals of this effort on standards are extendability, exchangeability, integration and a standardized work station, which in turn can be interpreted as

- common software development
- more effective systems development
- access to common support efforts and education
- exchange of experience
- extended exchange of information within a government
  agency and between agencies.

Thus, in order to gain a standardized development, training and technical environment, as well as lower costs, SAFAD has developed a policy for the acquisition of departmental computer systems, including a package of standards aimed at the above goals.

The software for such a computer system includes

- Unix operating system
  (Unix is a trade mark of Bell Laboratories)
- data base management systems
- system development tools
- local and global data exchange
- office support
  - document handling
  - text processing
  - electronic mail
  - personal computing facilities
  - office information systems
- general administrative applications
- applications for the specific agency

The supporting hardware is based on standard components. It consists of modern Unix systems for ADP on the local level and work stations with good ergonomy.

So far, some 350 systems have been procured under these and related contracts. The experience of these systems is that they work reasonably well both in applications specific to the agency and as general office support.

SAFAD is now in the process of negotiating new call-off contracts regarding the second generation of standard computer systems. These "departmental" systems should be more powerful and be able to support up to more than a hundred directly connected work stations. The operating system should be Unix system/V and much emphasis is put on data communication and development tools. Wherever possible, international, national or governmental standards have been used. Personal computers should be natural components in the systems. Contracts are due to be signed before July 1st, 1987.

One of the standards that SAFAD has adopted is on the development and run time environment, among other things the operating system Unix system/V. The Unix operating system is created by A T & T Bell Laboratories in the USA. It is a building-block system from which higher levels can be created.

People commenting on Unix often forward the opinion that Unix might be difficult to learn and not very friendly to the user. This is both true and false. The specific installation should be adapted for its intended use (which is easy - Unix has all the tools) and the end user then eventually will not see it at all. I think it must be admitted that Unix has a lot of functions and facilities which can make life somewhat complicated for the amateur but on the other hand makes it a programmers dream.

Unix is also said to lack in security. Because Unix is such a wide-spread operating system, many reports have been dealing with this issue. Unix is an open system and you add the security that you need and are willing to pay for. So this is rather a matter of implementation.

Unix is wide-spread. Today there are some 250 000 Unix systems in the USA and about 40 000 systems in Europe. You can have it on a PC or on an Amdahl or Cray or on practically any computer system in production today, either from the computer vendor or from elsewhere.

SAFAD standardized on Unix five years ago, not primarily because of its technical superiority but because of its vendor independence and market penetration. No other multi-user operating system from an "independent" supplier has such a market penetration.

But there are many Unixes. Apart from the main-stream AT&T Unix there are 2 widely spread ones. The Berkeley 4.2 bsd from the University of Berkeley, California is regarded to be more efficient, especially on data handling. Xenix from Microsoft is said to have a better user interface.

AT&T has published a document "UNIX System V Interface Definition", which specifies Unix. On this document now most implementors rely.

In order to strengthen their position on the market, a number of computer vendors have got together and formed the X/OPEN group. It was founded by a number of European computer manufacturers. Now vendors like DEC, BULL, UNISYS and Ericsson are members. Even A T & T has joined. They specify interface definitions and not specific products. The basic subject of specification by X/OPEN is that of Unix.

MS-DOS is an operating system originally developed by Microsoft for the IBM PC. It has become the de facto standard for personal computers. Although there are other interesting possibilities, it has been adopted by SAFAD as the standard operating system besides Unix for single user work stations. There is now much activity in this area and the standard may soon be revised.

A number of SAFAD activities have resulted in program packages, suitable for the government environment. Existing and evolving packages are:

- personnel administration
- financial administration
- purchasing
- library
- registry
- administration of premises
- internal education

These packages are written for an Unix environment and are therefore relatively easy to transport to different computers in different agencies. So development costs can be divided between several agencies, agencies may communicate in standard formats and education can be carried out more effectively. Many of today's centrally managed internal administrative functions can be carried out directly by the individual employee having access to computer support.

Behind these activities is a long-range plan that promotes decentralized data processing. The technical development carries many attractive opportunities. The starting point for a long-range plan must still be the information needs, the administrative culture and the decision pattern of the organization. The desired changes, for instance regarding decentralization or committing of authorithy, will be supported by the proper selection of technique.

Among the factors demanding attention are the proliferation of small computers, the direction of office automation, the alternative ways to communicate data, the more or less common data bases, and the distribution of tasks between users and EDP personnel. Add to this the questions regarding the already installed computer-assisted routines. Existing large central systems have to be renewed and coordinated with numerous new systems of different size and character.

The advantages of using small computers in different applications are growing as the included electronics gets cheaper and more powerful the software gets better. Faster systems development, less investment in equipment and a decentralized organization are among the benefits. The common need for information interchange between different applications are demanding some sort of coordinated planning, though. Depending on the rest of the data processing of the organization the local small computers might also be used as terminals to larger systems. This, then, also calls for technical coordination.

The use of small computers develops both as an alternative to and as a complement to the traditional data processing and puts the decision makers at a cross-road. Office automation exemplifies this. Word processing equipment is often used today mainly for one single basic function and is used separately. It can also be performed on more general small computers or terminals connected to larger computers. Other functions can then be performed as well, as mentioned here earlier. A development towards such an office information system, at the same time avoiding incompatibility, demands a well kept-together longrange plan.

The total effectiveness in information processing grows more and more dependent on the integration between data processing and data communication. The selection of data communication method may be an act of strategic nature which calls for attention by the management.

Data administration is particularly important. If the organization works with cammon information to a great extent, then this should be reflected in the structure of the data bases and the data structures. The efforts to reach this goal may be very large and may affect large parts of the organization.

The introduction of computer assistance in the offices often affects the distribution of assignments. It will also mean new ways to perform functions, it will affect the quality of work, and it will influence the way people think. A new administrative culture will emerge.

This new culture may be better or worse in different ways and depending on how you look at it. The contents of the new administrative culture will be influenced by a series of decisions made within and outside the specific organization. A long-range plan will help filling this culture with a desirable content.

Conclusions

The Swedish government has regarded it necessary to form a conception of how a future administrative system should be designed. This conception has been taken as a starting point in the computerization of the government agency office. It was then possible to obtain a suitable model for a future office information system. Thus, a computerized office information system with the ability of concurrence between places of work, data, and programs is being successively aquired.

- 0 -

Governmental and Municipal Information Systems
P. Kovács and E. Straub (Editors)
Elsevier Science Publishers B.V. (North-Holland)
© IFIP, 1988

IMPLEMENTATION OF COMMUNICATION SYSTEM IN MIS FMMHE /ČSSR/

Bedřich ČÁMSKÝ

INORGA, Institute for Industrial Management Automation, Praha, ČSSR

The Management Information System at the Czechoslovak Federal
Ministry of Metallurgy and Heavy Engineerig /MIS FMMHE/ has attained
a rather advanced level. The dialogue mode of work has reached the
stage of practical realization and it became an integral part of the
managerial activities of the ministry personnel. The results which
have been reached together with the new technical means of computer
equipment are the basis for further development of the informational
support to the decision process and for the overall improvement of
conditions for the work of management personnel at ministerial level.

1. INTRODUCTION

The automation of management at the Czechoslovak Federal Ministry of
Metallurgy and Heavy Engineering /FMMHE/ has attained a rather advanced level.
The processing presentation of information for management purposes is
materialized in MIS FMMHE in the form of printouts and graphical and text
outputs. The users have the possibility of everyday communication in dialogue
with the computer. The realization of interactive nonprogrammer-user work with
the computer system has expressly supported the propagation of conditions for
more rapid reaction to changing requirements of information support - that is,
the adaptivity of the system. Later in 1987, significant innovation and
advancement of the technical base of MIS FMMHE is to take place. This will
enable a broader exploitation of computing technique for increasing and
improving the support of management activities of the specialized departments
at FMMHE. The following systems are to be installed and gradually used:
a) the present main-frame IBM 370/138 with an extensive terminal network,
b) the new main-frame IBM 4361,
c) IBM PC/XT personal computers, IBM compatible personal computers,
d) IBM S/36 system.

The rational use of this computer equipment, in agreement with the character
of the management functions of the FMMHE departments, will guarantee maximum
fulfillment of the requirements of these departments.

The present paper discusses two basic approaches to computer utilization in
MIS FMMHE:
- the direct use of computing equipment by management personnel, i.e. use of
  terminals of the main-frame system and personal computers,
- complex office automation and text processing.

2.   DIRECT COMMUNICATION OF MANAGEMENT PERSONNEL WITH THE CENTRAL COMPUTER
     SYSTEM

The development of the technical base has considerable influence on the
possibility of the further development of interactive systems and their use by
management personnel in MIS FMMHE. FMMHE offices are already equipped with 45
displays and 15 printers linked to the main-frame IBM 370/138. The users may
use the following interactive systems:

KOMPAS   - is a system of general and one-purpose dialogues for interactive
            work, oriented primarily to the retrieval and presentation of data.
            However it has limited possibilities of algorithmic data processing.
PODAGRA   - works with a data-base which also includes, besides data, the
            context and character of the representation. It possesses extensive
            possibilities for algorithmic processing, the output for the users
            is arranged into publishable form. It ensures linkage to personal
            computers which can wors in the mode of a main-frame display.
DDB   - simulates the functions of a personal computer on the terminal of a
            large-scale computer. It worke with a specifically organized
            data-base, it possesses very flexible algorithmic means which the
            user himself may modify and control.

A survey of user interest and requirements has shown that it is possible to
classify the applications of interactive work with the computer into the
following groups of tasks:
- Isolated tasks which the users can approach at the moment when there is the
   possibility of their active direct involvement using their "own" equipment
   (personal computers) and when they are ready to cope with these tasks
   independently themselves. As a rule, these tasks are not included in the
   conception of MIS FMMHE development. However, they might introduce positive
   changes in the technology of management.
- Tasks using a dedicated data-base designed to serve their specific
   requirements. The processing of these problems is carried out in batch as
   well as in interactive modes. For this type of task it is normal that
   changes take place rather frequently. For this reason, from the user
   standpoint, interactive approaches are a very suitable and particularly
   flexible tool.
- Tasks using centrally administered data whose maintenance and updating the
   users leave to the problem-solvers. To this group we rank problems for the
   processing of large amounts of input data, with relatively simple
   algorithmical background but a broad variety of output requirements. Here,
   interactive work is a supplement to batch processing, it may even serve for
   the initiation of batch processing.
- Algorithmically complicated tasks working in a data-base environment, where
   the elaboration of interactive applications is left entirely to
   professional programmers while the user's role is limited only to the
   passive utilization of prepared dialogues.

At the centre of user interest in the use of interactive forms of work with
the computer we find at present the processing of individual partial tasks,
and not work with extensive data-bases which would be used for the complex
soluing of the problems and to ensure interlinkage. This is also confirmed by
the structure of tasks needed to be prepared for user work on personal
computers. This trend, which also shows itself in the contemporary experience
of other organizations, is temporary and typical particularly for the initial
period of the use of a decentralized computer environment. Thus it cannot
serve as the conclusive criterion for conceptual decision-making on a

long-term scale. The reason is, first of all, that this orientation is of a disintegrative character and violates the developed system links in the managerial activities of FMMHE.

In the further development of user interactive work it is therefore necessary to start with the demands of user departments, the considered managerial spheres and problems, according to the character of the logical structure of management functions, of the respective data-base, and the links to the environment of the system. From this position it is possible to distinguish:
a) managerial spheres with considerable internal and external information links and an extensive data-base. From the technical and design point of view, the approach is oriented to an interactive system realized on the central computer and, according to the character of the tasks, to the parallel utilization of the PODAGRA and DDB communication systems,
b) managerial spheres with orientation to autonomous data processing which is realized on independent personal computers, with the possibility of link-up to the central computer.

For the use of the decentralized computer equipment, methodical instructions have been prepared which specify the process of implementation of relatively isolated tasks on personal computers with the use of available programming instruments, with the purpose to increase the effectiveness of these activities under the condition of substantially changed environment as compared with central computer applications. At the same time, this material specifies assistance offered to users with the aim of maintaining the integrity of the system under the conditions of decentralized processing:
- accessibility of standard program products,
- development of an integrated data-base and data transfers,
- preparation of individual scenarios for specific tasks of the different users,
- consulting assistence,
- training on specific non-standard functions.

3. OFFICE AUTOMATION AT FMMHE

The aim of office automation at FMMHE is not only text processing but also the execution of further administrative functions, information processing and information transfer via the computer system in the management ranks of the ministry.

The technical equipment which is available at FMMHE from this year makes it possible to proceed with the complex approach to office automation. The equipment of the work-stations enables superior processing of text outputs as well as the complex execution of further functions of office automation. In particular, we mention the transfer of messages to other work-stations of this system, electronic mail, text conferences between the different departments, the formation of catalogues, archive records and messages on magnetic media, their common utilization; furthermore, additional use can be made of the capacity of the personal computer at the work-station, etc.

The IBM S/36 system, designed for the management of office automation tasks,enables verification of the approach in horizontal as well as vertical interlinkage of FMMHE departments. The basic functions of office automation

are realized by using adapted software of the supplier. Therefore the work is
concentrated on mastering the conditions of work and the tasks of the
respective departments and of the methodical, organizational and other
prerequisites for successful implementation, including user training. Personal
computers with which the individual work-stations are equipped serve as
terminals for text-processing and for the realization of further office
automation tasks, including linkage of the IBM S/36 system with the central
computer. Besides this, these personal computers are, in part of their
capacity, used for data processing.

The central aspect of the approach to office automation consists in the
analytical mastering of the problems and specific conditions of the activities
of top management secretariat and their demands, in the effective design, in
the realization of the corresponding set of tasks, and in creating the
necessary methodical, organizational and realizational conditions. For this
reason, in designing and realizing the task of office automation at FMMHE we
start from elementary text-processing tasks in the range corresponding to the
routine of text processors. These are directly followed by the development of
further functions from the range which office automation systems make
possible. The realization itself is divided into the following steps:
- automatized text-processing,
- functions such as archive, catalogue, task tracing, calendar, etc.,
- data processing,
- massage transfer,
- electronic mail,
- internal information system.

4. CONCLUSION

Direct user communication with the computer system and the approach to office
automation are elements of automation technologies which are realized in
relation to material problems in the individual domains of management, with
concentration on achieving new qualities in the level of information backup of
the decision-making process by FMMHE personnel. This progressive trend
represents a further expressive user shift in direction to user development of
management instruments not only at the level of partial solutions but also in
deepening the approach to the entire system. At the same time, this leads to a
principal change in user responsibility for the realization and thus
costitutes a real basis for the further increase of MIS FMMHE effectiveness.

<u>Literature</u>

(1) Kešner, J. etal; Feasibility study of the MIS FMMHE project (INORGA,
     Praha, 1985) /in Czech/
(2) Čámský, B.; Results and Aims of the MIS FMMHE project (ASŘ Bulletin
     INORGA, 1987) /in Czech/
(3) Planning your System 36 office (IBM, 1986, SC 21-9481-1)

Governmental and Municipal Information Systems
P. Kovács and E. Straub (Editors)
Elsevier Science Publishers B.V. (North-Holland)
© IFIP, 1988

ADAPTIVE INFORMATION SYSTEMS TO CONTROL ORGANIZATIONS
ACTIVITY

V.N. BURKOV, V.V. TSYGANOV

Institute of Control Sciences, 65 Profsoyuznaya,
Moscow, 117342, USSR

The paper presents the analysis of the problem dealing
with designing the information subsystems for adaptive
mechanizms of functioning (AMF) of the socio-economic
systems. The AMF also include the subsystems of decision
making in planning control and stimulation of organizations. The designing of adaptive information systems
(AIS) caused the development of an approach, based on
the obtained problem solutions of progressive AMF synthesis. The paper contains detail consideration of two AIS
main types. The first one is intended for maintaining
the processes of forecasting, planning and control. Under consideration are the adaptive econometrical procedures of time series forecasting and designing of regressive models. The second type i.e. rank AIS, is designed
to provide information for decision-making (classification and pattern recognition). They are used mainly for
estimation of the state, control and organizations stimulation.

1. INTRODUCTION

Systemic investigations of the problems dealing with the design
of the information systems to control organizations, include, as
the main component, analysis and account of a human factor effect
which should be understood as an activity manifestation of the
people or collectives (elements of control system) which is caused by the availability of their own aims, not necessarily coin-
ciding with the goal of the system in its entirely [1]. Such
elements may utilize available information channels connected
with the system control (the centre) in order to improve a current or future state. On the other hand, provision of ability to
control complex socio-economic organizations in their dynamics
with incomplete information is, as a rule, based on application
of adaptive information systems (AIS) which provide identification of a controlled object structure and parameters of external
environment and finally, generating of controlling actions making use of current information, obtained from an object element
in order to achieve the optimal state of the system. For example,
reconstruction of economy control, together with the structure
change, includes as well an adaptive adjustment of procedures
and parameters in a new control mechanism with the view to its
optimization. Hence, in developing and designing the AIS' it is
necessary to consider the activity of its component elements.
For example, in manufacturing organizations the most significant
manifestation of this activity is a various degree of their production potential utilization. Their production potential is to

be determined with account of internal resources, appeared as a result of the scientific-technical progress [2,3]. To avoid undesirable distortion of information, sent by the elements to the centre, the problem of designing an optimal AIS should be considered in complex, together with the problems of synthesis of planning, control and stimulation procedures adopted in the given mechanism of organization control.

2. PROGRESSIVE ADAPTIVE MECHANISMS

In recent years quickly develop the newly appeared direction in the theory and practice of control for hierarchic organizations with a stochastic structure. It has been connected with the designing of AMF'. In these mechanisms, information received from organizations in the process of functioning is used by the centre for decision-making with the view to achieving the optimal state of the system.

A way to avoid undersirable distortion of information is in designing the so-called progressive AFM's wherein the values of the elements goal functions corresponding to the solution of the game increase with the increase of the efficiency of functioning of their elements. Formal statements and solutions of synthesizing the progressive AMF (I,P,Q,F) are presented in [2, 3]. These AMF together with AIS I include decision-making procedures: planning P, control Q and stimulation F (see fig. 1).

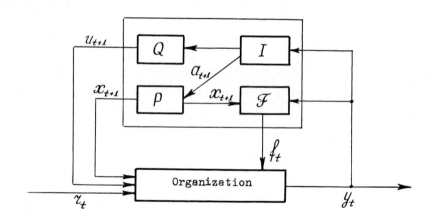

FIGURE 1

AMF structure. Here y_t - output, a_t - parameter estimate, x_{t+1} - plane, u_{t+1} - control, z_t - input, f_t - stimuli, t - time period.

Such AMF ensure possibility to identify an internal structure of organizations and environment parameters as well as the utilization of internal resources by the organizations in accordance with the goal of the system in its entirely.

The methods for designing progressive AMF have been studied and developed (see fig. 2).

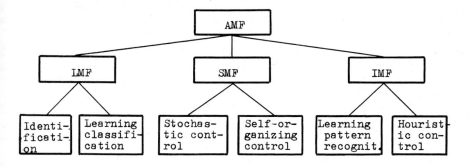

FIGURE 2
AMF classification

Learning mechanisms of functioning (LMF) should provide for an estimate of the state and parameters of organization potential in its dynamics, supplying more information for planning the organization output indices at the account of learning processes [2]. Information provision in LMF' is realized by means of corresponding identification procedures: analysis and econometrical forecasting of time series, designing of factor (regressive) models, etc. Besides, LMF' with detection (recognition) of deviations from the normal functioning mode and their classification are being developed for control and well motivated decision-making.

Stochastic (self-organizing, dual) mechanisms (SMF) should provide for combination of learning and planning for an output organization (the way it is done in LMF') with the control of its inputs (i.e. direct influence on the potential of an organization) [3].

Intellectual mechanisms (IMF) combine learning with indistinct and qualitative commands from the centre and control on the basis of these commands [2]. Designing of such mechanisms requires hierarchical man-machine systems with such intellectual abilities as multi-level learning. The example of LMF is a mechanism with the learning of pattern recognition [2].

3. ADAPTIVE INFORMATION SYSTEMS

With application to the synthesis of AIS for planning, control of resources distribution and stimulation, the sense of obtaining the theoretical results consist in the idea that progressiveness of AMF' can be ensured by "sufficiently flexible" application of information with the view to redistributing the scheduled tasks, resources and stimuli among organization. Hence, it results in their persistent interest to discover their own resources and to find the abilities of identifying the states on the basis of information obtained from them as well as the possibility to realize their gradual outcome on a assigned trajectory of development. Simultaneously the validity of forecasting

computations and future plannings can be sufficiently high by
virtue of the high-level reliability in determining the charges
coefficients (norms) based on identification of organization
structure. The developed approach is aimed at designing of the
adaptive system of methods, algorithms, and programs for information analysis and forecasting the state (potential) of production elements with high degree of approximation and decision-making procedures based on this information with due account of
organization activity. Such a system is, firstly, a component
part of the complex control of the economic system in its entirely. Secondly, it is adaptive, i.e. it is learning and self-
learning in the varying conditions of functioning. Thirdly, it
should be based on a problem-oriented information language which,
on the one hand, ensures the system effective utilization by
decision-makers and, on the other hand, it provides the possibility to apply mathematical methods and computers, i.e. a dialogue in the man-machine system, including formal, expert and combined methods for designing the identifiers and forecastings.

The direct result of AIS is information provision for decision-
making procedures (planning, control, stimulation). Another indirect result of AIS functioning is a specially built and periodically updating database for decision making. Norms and regulation documents included in this database are bring generated
by means of processing the statistical and expert information of
organizations functioning in previous and forthcoming planning
periods. With this aim in view we use such methods of economic
cybernetics as adaptive identification of economic systems, econometric forecasting, regressive models and others. Thus, we
ensure introduction in the control practice the system of progressive economical norms and utilization of norming methods on
all levels of planning and control.

The AIS structure is illustrated in fig. 3.

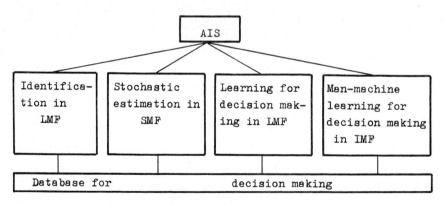

FIGURE 3
AIS structure

The main components in identification of parameters for the LMF
are adaptive and statistical methods and procedures of econometrical analysis, forecasting of time series and designing the fac-
tor-regressive models of organizations.

Let us, at first, consider the case, where the LMF is based on factor (regressive) model of organization.

4. FACTOR MODELS

Let the model of organization constraints with any **external** action ($\overline{z}_t$) be assigned by stationary random process and we shall estimate the organization output indices in the period t by means of the following expression:

$$\hat{y}_t = \sum_{k=1}^{n} C_k \, z_{kt} \; . \tag{1}$$

There z_{kt} are factors (resources) of a plant of k -kind, C_k are adjustable coefficients, $k = \overline{1,n}$. The value C_k has the sense of an output increment norm with the increase of k - factor of production by one, $k = \overline{1,n}$. The linear procedure for adjusting the parameters of model (1) (or a procedure of learning) has the form [2]:

$$\overline{C}_t = \overline{C}_{t-1} + \beta_t (y_t - \hat{y}_t) \; , \quad \overline{C}_0 = \overline{C}^o \; . \tag{2}$$

Here $\overline{C}_t$ is an estimate of a parameter $\overline{C}$ which is optimal from the view point of minimizing some estimate quality criterion. In LMF the procedures of planning and stimulation are based on these estimates. Usually the optimal plan (x_t^o) is equal to the optimal estimate of an output (i.e. $x_t^o = \hat{y}_t$). However, in a general case the plan in the period t (x_t) may differ from the estimate $\hat{y}_t$. Then, in order to improve the production effectiveness, the stimulation procedures are traditionally used depending on the degree of plan fulfilment (i.e. depending on the difference $y_t - x_t$). On the other hand, stimulation for attainment of increased main indices, obtained by means of forecasting model (1) with adjustable coefficients (2) is sufficiently natural for maintaining the interest in improving the production effectiveness and intensive planning at the account of internal resources utilization. Intensity of a plan is characterized by the difference between the value of the given plan x_t and forecast value of the index $\hat{y}_t$, obtained on the basis of a considered forecast model:

$$\delta_t = (x_t - \hat{y}_t)/x_t \; . \tag{3}$$

The denominator x_t is entered for showing the plans intensity index which is to be comparable for various conditions of functioning (for example, in the case of comparing estimate of plan intensity in different enterprises at the same moment of time or in one enterprise at different moments of time and so on). Production effectiveness estimate is characterized by the difference of a real value of a given index (y_t) and its forecast value ($\hat{y}_t$):

$$\varepsilon_t = (y_t - \hat{y}_t)/\hat{y}_t \; . \tag{4}$$

The denominator $\hat{y}_t$ is introduced to compare the indices of control effectiveness in various conditions. The dynamics of organization output indices depends on the dynamics of the main production factors - material and labour resources as well on

the level of their utilization. Therefore index (4) corresponds
to a quantitative amount of the share belonging to the informative-
managerial factor (with the accuracy determined by a chosen forecast model accuracy) in the final results of enterprise production activity. At the same time the mechanism of isolating
the informative-managerial factor is designed on the priciple of
commensurability of the main production factors dynamics (production resources) and final result dynamics. Note, if a plan
task for a plant x_t is equal to its optimal forecast estimate
$\hat{y}_t$, determined according to (1), (2), then estimate (4) is
reduced to the known estimate of a plan fulfilment degree. Since
the above indices (3), (4) increase with the increase of a plant
functioning effectiveness then stimulation can be closely connected with these indices. For example, giving a bonus and an-
nouncing the results of socialistic competition are realized taking into account the plans intensity and commitments for some
degree of resources utilization (i.e. depending on the norms $\bar{C}_k$,
$k = \overline{1, n}$). However, in determining corresponding procedures of
stimulation it is necessary to make allowance for the circumstance that a prescient element can forecast to a certain extent
the consequences of decision-makings. In this case we deal with
the influence of current indices, chosen by the elements at the
moment of times on the estimates of intensity coefficients showing the realization of resources in future $C_\tau, \tau > t$. Thus, according to (1), (2) current indices influence the forecastings
$\hat{y}_\tau$, $\tau > t$, as well as the estimates of the plant utilization
of internal resources - estimates of plans intensity (3) and
control effectiveness (4). Therefore the bonus value for prescient element in future, with $\tau > t$, depends on the chosen
current indices. It may occur that indices constraints (not revealing all the potentials) will be beneficial for a plant in a
current moment in order to ensure preferable estimates of the
plan fulfilment degree, plan intensity and control effectiveness
in future.

It has been already described that the requirement of progressiveness is the important one in designing such systems. It means
that the growing production effectiveness should be followed by
the element stimulation increase (with account of its prescience).
Formal problem statements for synthesizing the progressive LMF
are considered in [2] with formulations of theorems, containing
the constructive necessary and sufficient conditions for their
existence. In the course of their fulfilment the parameter vector $\bar{C}_t$ meets the plant maximal capacities. In this case C_{kt}
has the sense of a progressive norm for a production output increment with the increase of k -factor by 1.

On the basis of the developed approach we can develop the
method for estimating the effectiveness of a plant control. The
control effect is characterized by variations of the level de-
monstrating the realization of the main production factors -
material and labour factors. This method has been applied to the
estimate of economical effectiveness of control systems in enterprises and production complexes engaged in instrument engineering. This method includes the techniques of output estimates, estimate of the three main production factors ($k = 3$),
cost of a control system. Control effectiveness estimate is performed by means of model (1) with adjustable coefficients (2).
Heuristic procedures to determine the initial values of these

coefficients ($\overline{C}^o$) have been designed. Another factor (regressive) model served the basis for the method for determining the dependencies of total expences causes by introduction of new technique on such main factors as production output, productivity, specific weight of high-quality products and others.

It is of great significance that AIS design does not require the complex databases. In fact, the learning procedures of type (2) require only on-line information (y_t) and a current estimate of the parameter (C_{t-1}).

5. ADAPTIVE ECONOMETRIC FORECASTING

Adaptive econometric forecasting is a component of the LMF and it includes the analysis of an achieved level of indices and already formed tendencies. The adaptive methods are used to improve the accuracy of economic development forecastings under the varying conditions, incomplete information and uncertainty. Real economical processes occur in the varying environmental conditions to which they are adapting. The model in its turn adapts to a time series, representing this process. Adaptive methods are especially valuable in forecasting the time series with "short history". In the practice of organization branch control we have to work either with "new" series or with "old" ones but undergone such essential changes that the use of all series points is practically impossible. Adaptive forecastings of instrument engineering organizations and subbranches have been formed on the basis of the following models groups:
1) adaptive polinomial Brown's models (zero; first and second-orders; 2) Theil-Wage model; 3) Trigg-Lich-Shown-model; 4) models of adaptive filtration. Each of them served the base for designing the algorithms and a program for computing the forecasting indices, realized on computers EC and CM type (FORTRAN). Validity of forecast time series was for the term of 5-15 years. The number of indices characterizing the control plants reached 30. This information has been processed by a computer. As a result of extrapolation we obtained short-term forecastings for development of organizations and their subbranch complexes. The obtained analytical and forecast information has been successfully applied to operative and short-term planning of the above organizations and subbranches activity. Besides, it became the basis of the database in planning and financing of organizations and subbranches.

6. STATISTICAL FORECASTING

Statistical forecasting methods are also based on the analysis of time series of the forecast object characteristics. Under conditions of short strongly fluctuating time series a characteristic approach is applied. On the first stage feasible types of functional dependencies are heuristically selected. In the second stage they are parametrically adjusted to minimize some criterion of forecasting quality. It is the collected initial information that represents the short time series (10-15 observations). The chosen model was checked for adequacy as real process parameters. The check involved the analysis of the index design value deviations from the real values.

The checking results allowed us to draw a conclusion on the

adequacy of the model. The forecast values for indices have been
obtained, confidential intervals have been determined. All this
resulted in the development of a procedure, algorithms and programs a statistical forecasting of subbranch organizations development.

7. STOCHASTIC ESTIMATION

Stochastic estimation of the states is necessary for designing
the stochastic selforganizing (or dual) mechanisms [3], in which
learning and organization outputs planning as well as the control
of organization inputs are realized. Consider, for example, the
problem of controlling the technological power of the branch.
This power is decomposed into separate relatively independent
hierarchically ordered blocks to be refered to as technological
power modules. The centre knows each module's cost values (norms),
corresponding to the attainment of the assigned power level of
a branch with respect to the module in the several periods of
system functioning (for example, months, quarters, years). On the
other hand a factual level of the module power is a random function not fully known to the centre. Therefore the controlled organizations can be viewed as objects with a nondeterminated
structure, defined by a random noise.

The problem consists in constructing such controlling actions on
the part of the centre which are in the form of centralized resources destributions and other managerial decisions under which
the extremum of some control quality criterion is attained. The
theoretical solution of this problem was obtained by the optimal
synthesis of SMF organizations with nondeterminated structure,
defined by a random noise [3]. At the same time typical algorithms
of stochastic states estimation (Kalman-Busy's filter) are applied.

8. RANK AIS

Many control problems in organizations are reduced to classification of observed situations and events, connected with the
functioning of the lower level elements. The examples to be
shown, are identification of "both necks" in production and measures taken to eliminate them, determination of reasons due to
which the real indices deviate from the planned indices, winners
of competions and etc. Classification of the observed situations
is performed by some identification system on the basis of some
decision rule. Any decision is made depending on the result of
the classification. Such control mechanisms are called ranking
mechanisms.

With the lack of information for decision-making the necessity
of learning arises.

In [2, 4] designing of the rank LMF' is considered. Simultaneously the classification and identification is realized on the basis of in-coming information and accepted decision rules. Planning and stimulation is implemented depending on the result of
the classification. The problems of learning the classification
("without a teacher) and learning the pattern recognition
("with a teacher) have been considered. Conditions of optimality
for corresponding rank mechanisms have been obtained. The inves-

tigation results were used in designing and introduction of the
rank systems for estimating the state and stimulation as well as
in summing-up the results of socialist competition in organizations of the branch. For example, the following emulation rank
system of stimulation[4] is used in the mechanism of socialistic
competition among the national economy branches organizations.
At first, the activity of each organization is estimated, depending on a degree of the assigned conditions attainment and with
due account of its functioning conditions. This estimate computation involves the technique which is known as computer-aided
quantative complex Estimate of Activity Results (AKKORD-Russian
abbreviation) [1]. Further, the ordering of all organizations is
realized with the scalar estimates of AKKORD diminishing. With
the increase of a rank, the bonus (material, moral) becomes
higher. Note that an organization state is characterized by some
set of indices. Therefore, the procedure of clustering the state
indices, which ensures the realization of ordering, is of great
significance in designing of the rank AIS.

9. AKKORD OF ORGANIZATIONS

The AKKORD system is an important element of science and technology progress control. The system purpose is to determine the
correspondence of the activity results to the given tasks. The
AKKORD is performed on the basis of objective quantitative data
from the existing statistical, accounting and operative records
as well as from the quantitative expert estimates. The main principles of AKKORD formation are adaptiveness and progressiveness.

Adaptiveness is provided by flexible adjustment of the system to
the goals of the centre (a branch in its entirety) accomplished
by adjusting the norms of estimation, indices revealing the significance of various directions of work and special matrices of
meaning clustering, which formally express the strategy in the
field of science-and-technical progress. Particularly, the
AKKORD adjusting procedure scheme, utilizing the learning techniques of pattern recognition, is shown in fig. 4.

A decision maker (DM) plays the role of an expert-teacher. A
system developer becomes an interpreter of teacher's commands
in the AKKORD language. Upon completion of the learning process
the AKKORD functions in automatic mode, thus the centre is not
performing routine operations.

Progressiveness is achieved by such combination of adaptive adjustment procedures and stimulation in the LMF which makes an
assigned rank LMF a progressive one. This maintains the interest
of organizations in the improvement of production effectiveness
and quality of work at the cost of utilized internal resources
(reserves) generated due to utilization of science-and-technolo-
gy progress achievements.

Activity estimation is carried out by using current results (total data by the end of a planned period) and by prospects (forecast and prospect plans data). Estimate is formed by combining
the current and prospect estimates. The current (prospect) estimate totalizes current (prospect) estimates of effectiveness and
quality. Effectiveness estimate characterizes economical or some
other effectiveness (for example, profit, etc.). Quality estimate
characterizes a scientific-and-technical level, significance,

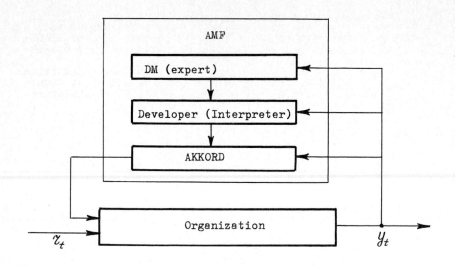

FIGURE 4.   Learning of pattern recognition
in the AKKORD system

orientation, rhythm of operations as well as fulfilment of current plans. The AKKORD draft estimate is to be considered and
corrected by the branch management.

10. CONCLUSIONS

The paper presents the principles and methods for designing the
AIS as a component of the AMF in the organizing-and-economical
system. Two types of the AIS are considered in detail. One of
them is connected with creation of the analysis, planning and
forecasting system in a branch complex system of hierarchic me-
chanisns with adaptation and problem-oriented information language (APPROXIMATSIA). The second type of adaptive information
systems, described in this paper, are flexible systems for
analysis and estimation of activity, in particular AKKORD. At
present the above principles and methods are being successfully
introduced into the control practice of instrumentation, automatization means and control systems in conditions of selffinan-
cing and self-repayment [4].

REFERENCES

[1] Burkov V.N. and others, On Some Principles of Planned Econo-
    my Management, in: Proceedings of the 9th Congress of IFAC
    (Pergamon Press, Oxford, 1984) vol.3.
[2] Tsyganov V.V., Adaptive Control of Hierarchical Socio-Econo-
    mic Systems, in: Preprints of the 4th IFAC/IFORS Symposium
    "Large Scale Systems. Theory and Applications" (Pergamon

Press, Zurich, 1986) pp.694-698.

[3] Burkov V.N., Tsyganov V.V., Stochastic Mechanisms of the Active Systems Functioning, in: Preprints of the 2nd IFAC Symposium on Stochastic Control (ICS, Moscow, 1986) pp.259-263.

[4] Tsyganov V.V., How to Urge up the Professional Competition in the Field of Large-Scale Systems in the Socialist Countries, in: Optimizarea Structuru si Proceselor de Conducere (ICSIT-ICS, Bucuresti, 1985) pp.170-184.

Governmental and Municipal Information Systems
P. Kovács and E. Straub (Editors)
Elsevier Science Publishers B.V. (North-Holland)
© IFIP, 1988

TRENDS IN MUNICIPAL INFORMATION SYSTEMS, 1975 - 1985

Kenneth L. KRAEMER, John L. KING, Debora E. DUNKLE,
and Joseph P. LANE

Public Policy Research Organization*
University of California
Irvine, CA 92717   U.S.A.

1. INTRODUCTION

The role of computers in city management has continually evolved since their introduction during the 1950s. Though initially used primarily to replace clerical operations, computers have come to be viewed as an essential tool of city management because of their capabilities for improving productivity, information use, and communication.

In the earliest days of their use, computers were viewed as replacements for the "clerical armies" engaged in municipal record-keeping operations such as accounting, payroll processing, and utility billing. Their chief advantage was that they could perform such tasks faster and more accurately, and sometimes cheaper, than people. By the 1960s, the "management information crisis" was perceived to be a major part of the "urban crisis," and computerized databanks were viewed as vehicles for providing information badly needed by the city's managers to deal with urban problems. These databanks about a city's people, housing, transportation, and real estate would assist city officials to identify community problems, evaluate alternative solutions, and monitor the programs set up to solve these problems.

With the onset of "fiscal crises" in cities in the 1970s, computers were viewed as a means of increasing productivity in government operations. The expectation was that productivity gains from computerization would help offset budgetary pressures while enabling cities to meet expanding service demands. The introduction of microcomputers in city hall in the 1980s further enhanced both the productivity and the information that could be provided by computer workstations, and added a whole new dimension of communications. The introduction of microcomputers has distributed familiarity with the technology and information-based tasks more broadly within city hall. By so doing, it has simultaneously expanded the means of com-municating via mainframe or other networks throughout the growing community of computer users in city hall. And such communication has extended beyond city hall to networks of city officials, managers and staff throughout the nation.

It is this ever-expanding role of computers in city management that accounts for the continued and dramatic growth of computer-based information systems in the nation's cities.[1] Today, more cities are using computers than ever before. Moreover, in absolute terms these cities are spending more money to perform more tasks with computers than ever before.

This report examines trends in the growth, organization, resources, usage and change of computers in cities from the 1950s to 1985. It is based on information from two surveys, conducted in 1975 and in 1985. Both surveys focused on the data processing installations in a city, whether single or multiple installations, and involved a survey of "computer equipment and applications" and of "computing management and policy" in municipalities 10,000 and over in population.

*This paper is based on a survey funded through a research agreement with the IBM Corporation.

Response rates for the 1985 surveys were 71% for cities over 50,000 population and 45% for cities between 10,000 and 50,000 population. The response for cities over 50,000 was equal to that of our 1975 survey (Kenneth L. Kraemer, William H. Dutton and Joseph Matthews, "Municipal Computers: Growth Usage and Management," Urban Data Science Report, 7(11), November), the highest response rate ever achieved for any nation-wide survey of cities. Thus, the survey data should accurately depict computing in U.S. cities. In addition, we believe these data are also generalizable to city/county and county governments. Our 1975 survey of cities *and* counties indicated surprising similarities in computing use, and our 1985 pre-survey case studies in five cities and two counties showed they remain similar. Further, both units of local government have been subject to the same changes in environmental factors at the community, state and federal levels.

In summary, the 1985 surveys replicated the 1975 surveys and covered new topics as well. Both surveys examined five general areas of computing in cities:

1. The extent of computer adoption and growth in cities.
2. The arrangements for provision of computing services.
3. The extent and character of computing resources.
4. The uses of computers in municipal operations.
5. The areas and rates of change in computing.

The remainder of this report reviews changes in municipal computing between 1975 and 1985, discussed in order of the five general areas listed above.

1.1.   Changes in Municipal Computing Use

Our previous surveys of computing have shown a seemingly inexorable trend towards increasing use of computers among cities.[2] The introduction of microcomputers in the early 1980s was expected to fuel that trend.

Consequently, there are a number of interesting questions that can be asked about the trends in computing use in cities between 1975 and 1985. What is the change in computer use among cities? What changes have occurred in the types of computing arrangements that cities follow? Do cities still primarily use their own in-house computers? What is the pattern of computing adoption over time? Have some cities been earlier adopters while others lagged behind? What changes have occurred in the local government functions which are served by computing? And, how has the depth and breadth of automation changed in these functional areas?

Comparison of data from the 1975 and 1985 surveys provides some surprising answers to these questions.

Extent of computing use. Table 1 shows the extent of computing use in municipal governments.[3] As of 1985, 97% of the cities surveyed report computing use in some form. All medium and large cities (> 50,000 population) appear to use computing, as do over 90% of small cities (< 50,000 population).

As Table 1 shows, computing was already widely used in municipal governments by 1975. Just over half the cities surveyed, including virtually all large cities, reported computing use. Across all cities in 1985, 97% used computing in some form, an increase of over 90% during the past decade. Computing use remains a function of size with larger cities more likely to have adopted automation. Presently all cities over 50,000 population use some type of computing.[4]

Table 1: Municipal Computing Use, By Population, Comparison Between 1975-1985

	Response (N)		Computing Users		Computing Users as % Response (N)	
	1975	1985	1975	1985	1975	1985
Cohort:						
Total	2,294	754	1,177	732	51	97
> 100	157	170	154	170	98	100
50 - 100	246	273	227	273	92	100
10 - 50	1,891	311	796	289	42	93

Rates of adoption. Although the overall percentage of cities reporting some type of computing use is quite high, the patterns and rates of computing adoption over the past 30 years differ according to city size. Figure 1 contains individual adoption curves for small, medium, and large cities, as well as a composite curve for all cities.

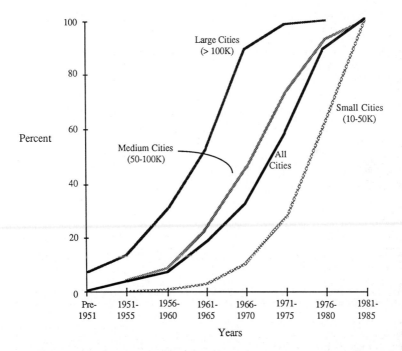

Figure 1: Rates of Computing Adoption Over Time, as Cumulative Percentages of All Municipalities Reporting Year of Adoption[a]

[a] Curves based only on cities reporting computing use and providing year of initial adoption (N = 355). Each curve represents cumulative percentage of cities using computing, as a percentage of the total number of cities presently using computing in that cohort, at each specified time frame.

Large cities (> 100,000) were the first to initiate computing use. Their collective pattern of adoption is an elongated s-curve. The rate of adoption in medium cities (50,000 - 100,000) follows a very similar pattern, although their cumulative percentages lagged behind those of large cities by about five years, and their s-curve is steeper. These two features imply that medium-sized cities were later adopters, but the rate of adoption was faster than for large cities, once adoption commenced. The rate of adoption curve for small cities (10,000 - 50,000) exaggerates both features because their adoption lagged behind medium cities by about ten years, but their s-curve is even steeper. Although last to adopt computing, the rate of adoption is fastest in small cities. The s-curve representing all reporting cities clearly corresponds to the standard logistic curve for the diffusion of a technical innovation.

1.2.   Changes in Municipal Computing Organization

Types of computing arrangements. More cities now operate in-house computing installations, as shown in Table 2. Ninety percent of all cities reported in-house computing arrangements in 1985, as compared to about 70% in 1975. Nearly all large cities have in-house installations, as do over two-thirds of the smaller cities.[5]

The changes in use of external arrangements are more mixed. The use of FMO arrangements have increased across all cities. The use of both public regional and service bureau arrangements has decreased overall, although large cities show increased use of both arrangements. While the use of service bureaus has increased in large cities, it has decreased by more than half in the small cities. The dichotomy in service bureau usage might be explained by the dynamics of computing adoption, especially surrounding in-house usage. For example, ten years ago computing capabilities were more expensive to obtain and the breadth of services was more limited. Large cities purchased their own systems to service this limited use, while small cities relied on service bureaus to fulfill their needs.

Table 2:   Percentage Distribution of Computing Arrangements, By Population, Comparison Between 1975 and 1985[a]

	In-House				External Arrangements					
	(N)		Installation Computing (%)		FMO Contract (%)		Public Regional (%)		Service Bureau (%)	
	1975	1985	1975	1985	1975	1985	1975	1985	1975	1985
Cohort:										
Total	1089	415	72	90	1	4	14	11	41	15
> 100	126	131	91	98	3	5	11	13	12	16
50 - 100	180	163	75	92	0	4	12	10	24	12
10 - 50	783	121	58	79	0	3	15	9	49	17

[a] Total row percentages may add to over 100% due to the use of multiple arrangements by individual governments.

By 1985 the relative cost of hardware had declined substantially, while the range of available applications had expanded greatly. Departments in larger cities are now using service bureaus primarily because they want "specialized" (versus generalized) computing services. That is, they have specialized applications (e.g., modeling and simulation packages for urban development, transportation, engineering and planning), databases (e.g., municipal bond and securities prices for municipal cash management and investment), or other automated capabilities (e.g., timesharing, electronic mail, computer conferencing) that the city doesn't have and cannot develop for economic or political reasons. In other words, service bureaus provide an efficient means to provide particular capabilities to departmental users.

Smaller cities are rapidly developing in-house capabilities in response to cost reductions in computing technologies, and so are becoming less reliant on service bureaus, at least until they move into the "specialized" domains described above for large cities.

The movement away from service bureaus for "general" data processing services has been occurring over the past 30 years as the cities in each population cohort reached the point of economic feasibility for their own computing installations. The continuous decline in the entry cost of computing has probably now put computing within reach of even the smallest cities (< 10,000 population).

Multiple installations. In addition to the expansion in computing use to new cities, use has also expanded within cities over the past decade. Increases in the number of cities with multiple installations is one measure of this expansion. Table 3 reveals that the percentage of medium and large cities with multiple installations has doubled (1975 data not available for small cities). While the percentages remain related to city size, the growth rate over the past decade exceeds 100% for all reporting cohorts. Thus, the observed growth in multiple installations is occurring at about the same rate regardless of city size.

Table 3: Multiple Computing Installations, By Population (Populations > 50,000), Comparison Between 1975 and 1985

	(N) With Computing		(N) With Multiple Installations		% With Multiple Installations	
	1975	1985	1975	1985	1975	1985
Cohort:						
Total	307	374	39	98	13	26
> 100	127	128	26	58	20	45
50 - 100	180	151	13	29	7	19

This is a very significant change. Although there were some multiple installation sites in 1975, the general trend in cities was towards the consolidation of computing into a single, central installation. Although only one-fourth of all cities reported multiple installations in 1985, the increase shows the trend of the mid-seventies has clearly been altered.

However, it is important to note that these multiple installations are not all "general purpose" sites serving city-wide functions. That is a task usually assigned to one "central" installation. Many are "special purpose" departmental installations serving the specific needs of a limited group of users. The new trend of "special purpose" installations should accelerate over the next decade as the cost of computing continues to decline, and as the expertise of users continues to grow, thereby creating additional demand for decentralized computing resources.

1.3. Changes in Municipal Computing Resources

Monetary resources. In terms of budgeted expenditures for computing installations, Table 4 shows the obvious increase in dollar amounts across all cohorts.[6] Overall, the large cities (> 250,000) and small cities experienced the greatest growth in expenditures between 1975 and 1985.

Table 4:   Municipal Computing Budgets, By Population,
Comparison Between 1975 and 1985

Cohort:	(N) 1975	(N) 1985	Mean Computing Budgeted Expenditure [Thousands] 1975	Mean Computing Budgeted Expenditure [Thousands] 1985	Computing Budget as % of City Operating Budget 1975	Computing Budget as % of City Operating Budget 1985	Mean Hardware Expenditure as % Computing Budget 1975	Mean Hardware Expenditure as % Computing Budget 1985
Total	997	348	$193	$1,506	0.9	1.5	43	27
> 100	118	126	297	3,491	1.1	1.8	36	26
50 - 100	190	140	137	507	1.0	1.4	47	27
10 - 50	689	82	43	163	0.5	1.4	--	29[a]

[a] For comparative purposes, number omitted from calculation of totals.

When computing budgets are expressed as a percentage of city operating budgets, they reveal the proportional growth of expenditures over time irrespective of monetary inflation. The results show that computing budgets now account for nearly 50% more of an average city budget than they did in 1975 (1.5% as compared to 0.9%) Of course, the actual figures only represent direct computing funds spent by the central installations, so the total amount spent on computing within cities at both times is probably much higher. However, it is even more likely, given the increased distribution of computing to multiple departments, that the relative increase in computing expenditures over the past decade is significantly greater than 50%.

The distribution of expenditures has also clearly shifted over time. The percentage of budgets expended on hardware declined from nearly one-half in 1975 to about one-quarter in 1985. The declines appear negatively correlated with city size, with smaller cities experiencing greater declines in budget portions spent on hardware. Perhaps as more recent adopters, the smaller cities are building on a more modern and thus less costly technological base. However, in absolute terms, cities which now dedicate the highest percentage of expenditures to hardware are the small cities. This could be attributed to changing budget distributions for computing. For example, larger cities have developed multiple installations and have more dispersed computing, which would lessen the hardware expenditures reported by the central computing installation. In comparison, small cities are still building their basic in-house installations, so more of their expenditures are probably concentrated in the central installation, which was reported here.

Hardware resources. Hardware resource comparisons are summarized in Table 5. Overall, during the past ten years the number of central processing units doubled, average core memory increased by 5,000%, and the average number of terminals increased tenfold. Improvements in the price/performance ratio for hardware explain the first two forms of growth, while the increased distribution of computing use--horizontally across functional areas and vertically through the organizational hierarchy--summarizes the third. Combining the increased access to mainframes through terminals with the multiplicity of departmental systems provides some estimate of the true growth and impact of computing in local governments.

Table 5: Computing Hardware Characteristics, By Population, Comparison Between 1975 and 1985

	(N) 1975	(N) 1985	Mean Number CPUs 1975	Mean Number CPUs 1985	Mean Core Memory[a] 1975	Mean Core Memory[a] 1985	Mean Number Terminals 1975	Mean Number Terminals 1985
Cohort:								
Total	647	363	1	2	.16	8	9	111
> 100	127	126	2	4	.57	17	19	251
50 - 100	178	150	1	2	.09	5	2	46
10 - 50	358	87	1	1	.04	1	--	18[b]

[a] Average core memory expressed in megabytes.
[b] For comparative purposes, number omitted from computation of totals.

Computing staff. According to Table 6, the number of computing staff employed by user departments has grown at a faster rate than has the number of staff employed in computing installations. Overall, the number of staff in computing installations has remained about the same, while computing staff in user departments have nearly tripled. This trend is most evident in the medium-sized cities, where the computing staff employed by user departments has increased eight-fold, and now equals the number of staff employed by computing installations. Although 1975 data are unavailable for small cities, in 1985 these small cities reported several times as many staff employed by user departments as compared to computing installations.

Table 6: Municipal Computing Staff, By Population, Comparison Between 1975 and 1985

	(N) 1975	(N) 1985	Mean Staff Employed By Computing Installations 1975	Mean Staff Employed By Computing Installations 1985	Mean Staff Employed By User Departments 1975	Mean Staff Employed By User Departments 1985
Cohort:						
Total	308	366	20	22	5	13
> 100	118	127	40	51	11	24
50 - 100	190	148	8	8	1	8
10 - 50	--	91[a]	--	3[a]	--	7[a]

[a] For comparative purposes, number omitted from computation of totals.

These dramatic changes in computing staff in user departments are coincident with the increasing decentralization of equipment to user departments, and these two trends have probably reinforced one another in two ways. First, most of the user department growth was probably caused by the decentralization and expansion of data-entry tasks. Second, as the computing expertise in user departments has increased, users have demanded and received their own computing capabilities, which in turn has increased their expertise and numbers, thereby generating additional demand for equipment and staff.

1.4.   Changes in Municipal Computing Applications[7]

Total operational applications. In terms of total operational applications, the average
number of applications has nearly tripled in ten years (see Table 7). Of course, the number of
applications within application categories has shown similar growth. Thus, changes in total
numbers is as much a function of expanded options as increased use of existing applications.

**Table 7:   Mean Number of Operational Applications, By Population,
(Populations > 50,000), Comparison Between 1975 and 1985**

	(N)		Mean # Operational		
	1975	1985	1975	1985	% Change
Cohort:					
Total	305	286	31	84	271
> 100	127	129	43	101	235
50 - 100	178	157	23	70	304

Applications in functional areas. The 1985 survey organized applications within five
functional areas: (1) public safety; (2) finance and administration; (3) general government;
(4) community development, public works and utilities; and (5) human resources. When
application inventories for the two time periods are aggregated at the level of these functional
areas, they reveal two types of information. First, when quantified as percentages of total
applications they reveal the relative distribution of applications across the functional areas.

Figure 2 shows that in terms of both commonality and intensity of use, all five functional areas
essentially maintained the same relative rankings in 1985 as they held in 1975.[8] Finance and
administration remains the most commonly automated area, followed by public safety, general
government, and community development, with human resources in a distant last place.
However, both the general government and community development areas have increased their
relative share of applications, primarily at the expense of finance and administration. Certain
categories of applications concerned with revenue generation, expenditure control, and the
provision of basic services account for most of this shift, as will be detailed in the following
section which reviews changes in these application categories.

The relative intensity of applications development contains slight variation but is also essentially
the same as in 1975. Public safety remains the most intensively automated area, followed by
finance and administration. Public Safety was the only area to increase its share of applications.
The remaining three areas have maintained their order of intensity.

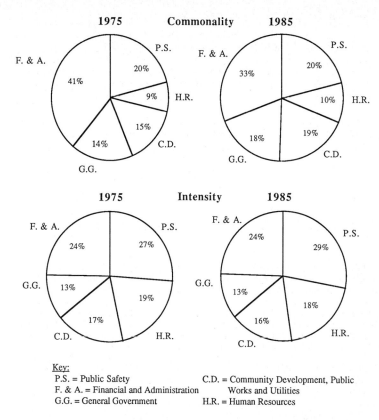

Figure 2: Applications Distribution (Cities > 50,000 Population) By Functional Area, Comparison Between 1975 and 1985

Second, when quantified as percentile and numeric values for commonality and intensity respectively, application inventories provide some indication of absolute growth for each functional area. As shown in Table 8, four of five areas are now common to about half of all cities, as compared to the area in 1975, and the mean intensity of application development across the five functional areas has increased over 50%.[9]

**Table 8: Commonality and Intensity of Operational Applications
(Cities > 50,000 Population) by Functional Area,
Comparison Between 1975 and 1985**

	Application Commonality (%)		Application Intensity	
	1975	1985	1975	1985
Functional Area:				
Public Safety	32	51	3.7	6.7
Finance & Administration	66	84	3.3	5.5
General Government	23	45	1.7	3.1
Community Development,				
Public Works & Utilities	24	47	2.3	3.6
Human Resources	15	24	2.6	4.2

Application commonality is highest for finance and administration, with over 80% of cities now running applications in this area, compared to 66% in 1975. While about half of all cities have applications in public safety, general government and community development, automation intensity does not correspond directly.

The intensity measures for both general government and public safety are somewhat overstated because each contains one functional category which is heavily automated. General government contains the application category for computing departments (i.e., data processing), in addition to other general function categories (e.g., clerk/recorder public information, central garage). Likewise, the public safety data on application intensity is skewed by the tremendous growth in police applications over the past decade. Thus, public safety and financial administration have about equal automation intensity. Human resources is not commonly automated, but where certain functions occur (public health and public welfare), the intensity of automation is quite high.

The data in Table 8 is plotted on a graph to better convey the comparative growth in commonality and intensity for each functional area (see Figure 3).

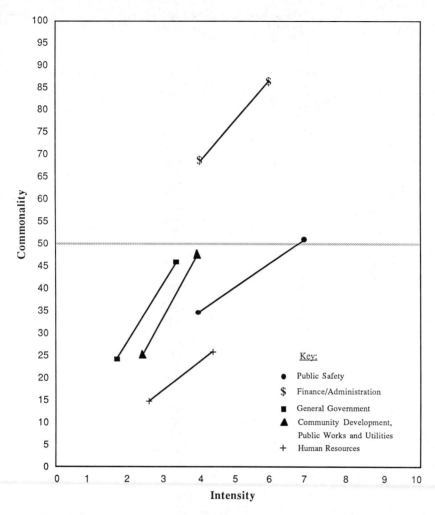

Figure 3: Mean Change in Applications Distribution (Cities > 50,000 Population) By Functional Area, Comparison Between 1975 and 1985

Note in Table 9 and Figure 4 that only three application categories (accounting, treasury and collections, and police protection) were common to more than 75% of the cities in 1975. In comparison, all applications common to at least 50% of the cities in 1975 are now present in over 75%. In fact, all but one application category grew in commonality during the past decade.

Application categories. The commonality and intensity data at the level of application categories, for both 1975 and 1985, are listed in Table 9 for reference.[10] The application distribution data for the two time periods is also plotted on graphs for comparative purposes (see Figure 4).

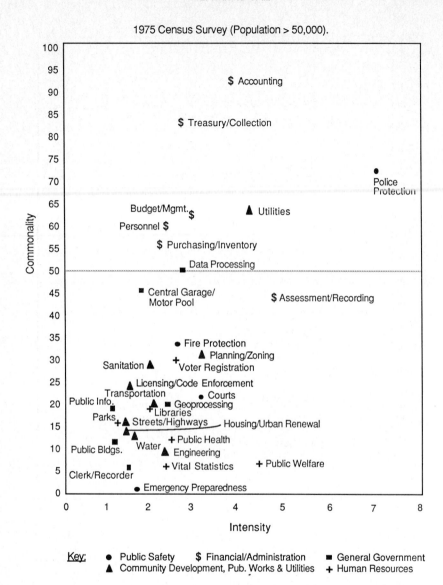

Figure 4: Applications Distribution (Cities > 50,000 Population), By Application Category, Comparison Between 1975 and 1985

1985 Census Survey (Population > 50,000).

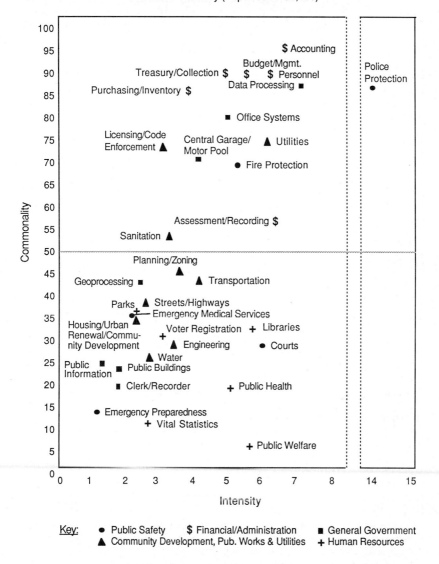

Key:
- ● Public Safety
- $ Financial/Administration
- ■ General Government
- ▲ Community Development, Pub. Works & Utilities
- + Human Resources

Figure 4 (continued): Applications Distribution (Cities > 50,000 Population), By Application Category, Comparison Between 1975 and 1985

Table 9: Application Distribution (Cities > 50,000 Population) By
Application Category, Comparison Between 1975 and 1985

Application Category	(N) With Application		Application Commonality (%)		Application Intensity	
	1975	1985	1975	1985	1975	1985
Total	**305**	**288**				
Public Safety						
Police Protection	221	258	72	90	7.2	14.2
Fire Protection	104	198	34	69	2.7	5.2
Courts	65	85	21	30	3.2	5.9
Emergency Preparedness	3	40	1	14	1.7	1.4
Emergency Medical Services	--	103	--	36	---	2.3
Finance & Administration						
Accounting	281	271	92	95	4.0	6.6
Treasury/Collection	253	255	83	89	2.9	4.5
Assessment	135	160	44	56	4.8	6.6
Budget/Management	188	251	62	88	3.2	5.2
Purchasing/Inventory	170	244	56	85	2.3	3.9
Personnel	182	257	60	90	2.5	6.2
General Government						
Data Processing	153	251	50	88	2.9	7.1
Office Systems	--	232	--	81	---	5.0
Geoprocessing	57	121	19	42	2.6	2.4
Public Information	55	73	18	26	1.1	1.4
Public Buildings	33	69	11	24	1.2	2.0
Clerk/Recorder	17	55	6	19	1.4	1.8
Central Garage/Motor Pool	139	204	46	71	1.8	4.4
Community Development, Public Works & Utilities						
Planning/Zoning	94	128	31	45	3.3	3.6
Housing/Urban Renewal	44	99	14	35	1.5	2.3
Licensing/Code Enforcement	70	212	23	74	1.6	3.2
Engineering	26	87	9	30	2.5	3.6
Transportation	58	128	19	45	2.2	4.1
Streets/Highways	49	110	16	39	1.5	2.6
Sanitation	87	154	29	54	2.1	3.4
Water Supply	35	76	12	27	1.7	3.0
Utilities	191	214	63	75	4.4	6.3
Human Resources						
Public Health	37	62	12	22	2.6	5.3
Public Welfare	24	29	8	10	4.5	5.9
Parks/Recreation	49	107	16	37	1.3	2.5
Vital Statistics	21	35	7	12	2.5	2.7
Libraries	54	90	18	32	2.1	5.7
Voter Registration	90	95	30	33	2.6	3.1

The licensing and code enforcement category made the largest surge in commonality from less than 25% to about 75%. The office systems category posted growth of a different sort because it was non-existent in 1975 but is now used in over 80% of all cities. The observed growth in these application categories, along with less spectacular but equally significant growth in utilities, sanitation and all the financial/administrative categories, reflects the recent declines in local government coffers, and corresponding needs to increase revenues, accelerate their collection and enhance internal productivity. In addition, these factors all exert pressure on governments to narrow their scope and scale of operations by concentrating on provision of basic services.

Growth in application intensity is common to all but two categories, with both emergency preparedness and geoprocessing showing slight declines. Overall, intensity growth has been marked. For example, while half of all application categories had less than 2.5 applications in 1975, half the categories now contain at least four applications. Intensity growth follows the same general pattern as commonality, with revenue-based and basic service application categories showing the highest growth.

1.5.   Changes in Municipal Computing Change Rates

Comparing actual and estimated change rates for 1975 and 1985 gives some idea of the relative stability of computing installations during the two time periods. Computing manager responses regarding changes to their installation's organization, hardware, and software are compiled in Table 10. Overall, the percentages reported for actual recent changes decreased between 1975 and 1985, while the percentages reported for estimated changes in the near future have increased. According to computing managers the aspects of installations that traditionally caused change are actually a little more stable now than ten years ago. Hardware changes are the only type exhibiting an increase, although hardware is surprisingly stable considering present rates of technological innovations. Some managers commented that new demands and capabilities (i.e., end-user computing, more multiple installations, office automation, and communications) are increasing the complexity of the computing environment, and thereby expanding the range of issues with potential for change. Thus, although fewer changes are reported for specific issues, the overall environment is perceived as less stable than ever.

Table 10:   Recent and Expected Changes in Municipal Computing Installations (Cities > 50,000 Population), Comparison Between 1975-1985

	Percent Indicating Change Occurred in Past Two Years		Percent Indicating Change Planned During Next Year	
	1975	1985	1975	1985
Change:				
Organization:				
Top Computing Management	31	33	6	7
Mainframe Vendors	17	13	8	7
Physical Location	21	17	14	14
Departmental Location/Status	22	17	11	13
Installation Relationships	12	15	7	13
Hardware:				
Machine Generation	40	47	17	30
Number of CPUs	10	33	8	27
Significant CPU Upgrade	57	58	--	52
Software:				
New System Development Priorities	42	38	24	34

Past rates of change seem to be influencing the perceptions of computing managers regarding future change because their estimated rates of change for the near future have increased from 1975 to 1985. However, managers continue to estimate change rates in the near future as lower than their most recent experience would suggest is realistic. This might be attributed to rather optimistic perceptions that past changes reduce the likelihood of future changes, although some change must be expected anyway.

2. SUMMARY

Nearly all local governments (with populations greater than 10,000) used computing services of some type in 1985; the culmination of about thirty years of adoption. Computing adoption began in earnest in large cities (over 100,000 population) during the early 1950s, and reached full adoption by the mid-1970s. Adoption in mid-size cities (50,000 to 100,000 population) followed a pattern similar to large cities about five years behind; beginning in the late 1950s and reaching 100% use in the early 1980s. Small city (10,000 to 50,000 population) adoption lagged by an additional ten years, with marked growth in the adoption rate occurring between the late sixties and the present. Although the last to initiate computing use, small cities have shown the most rapid adoption rate.

Virtually all the quantifiable attributes of municipal computing (e.g., number of installations, scope of operations, scale of resources invested, and extensiveness of application inventories), can be summarized in two ways. First, they are positively related to city size (with population acting as a surrogate for all measures of relative magnitude)--which is itself positively related to length of involvement with computing. Larger cities tend to have more of each attribute than smaller cities. Second, the mean measure of each of these attributes across all cities is about equal to the mean value for cities at the 100,000 population level. That is, cities with populations greater than 100,000 have more of each computing attribute than the mean, and cities with smaller populations have less. Descriptions of each attribute are as follows.

At present, most cities operate in-house computing installations rather than obtaining services through contracts with external entities (e.g, service bureaus, facilities management organizations, regional centers, state agencies). In fact, over 90% of cities have at least one in-house computing installation, located in either a departmental sub-unit or an independent computing department. Departmental sub-units are twice as common as independent departments across all cities, although larger cities are more likely to have both.

In a pattern characteristic of all cities early in their adoption of computing, most small cities operate their computing installations as departmental sub-units (usually in the finance department), although these sub-units function as independent departments by providing general computing services throughout the city. Medium and large cities have moved beyond this arrangement by establishing independent computing departments to provide a broad range of general services. However, these larger cities are also implementing additional sub-unit installations in order to provide special purpose capabilities to particular departments (i.e., police dispatching, library circulation, public works simulations).

The growth in such special purpose installations, presently comprising about one third of all departmental sub-units, is increasing the number of cities with multiple installations. The general trend in cities during the mid-seventies was towards consolidating computing into a single, central installation. This trend has now reversed with the number of cities of all sizes operating multiple installations doubling in the past ten years. The "all purpose" independent installation is itself becoming specialized as a general services provider, while the sub-units carve out task-specific niches. These special purpose installations are surfacing in all the major functional areas (e.g., public safety, finance and administration, public works and utilities, and even human resources), although police and finance operate the majority.

Tremendous reductions in the price/performance ratio of hardware over the past ten years, using 1975 as a baseline, have generated major changes in all three components (i.e., dollars, equipment and staff) of the computing resource mix in cities. First, the amount of real dollars expended on computing has effectively doubled, although the percentage devoted to hardware has been nearly halved. The largest and smallest cities now dedicate the greatest percentage to hardware; large cities are expanding the number of installations while small cities are still investing in their main installations.

Second, the sheer amount of equipment has increased along with the equipment's capacities. The number of CPU's has doubled, average core memory increased by over 400%, and the number of terminals increased tenfold. The exponential growth in number of terminals attached to mainframe or minicomputers indicates the increased distribution of computing access. As further evidence of computing expansion most cities now have microcomputers (on average about 20 per city), with about one-third of them linked to mainframes or minicomputers.

Third, computing use and expertise has become more distributed organizationally. The number of staff employed by central installations has remained stable, while the number employed by user departments has doubled. The ratio of central computing staff to user department staff has declined from 4:1 to 2:1 since 1975. Since this shift is coincident with the increasing decentralization of equipment, it is likely the two trends have reinforced one another.

Technological advances have increased the quantity and distribution of computing resources, and the average number of operational applications in cities has shown a corresponding increase of nearly three-fold over the past decade. However, declines in the fiscal health of cities have largely determined the functional application areas to which computing resources are applied. Reductions in federal and state revenue assistance, and tax reduction initiatives by the citizenry, have generated an orientation toward the provision of basic services and greater internal control in municipalities.

Finance and administration, and public safety show the greatest increases in both commonality and intensity of application development. Over 90% of cities currently run accounting applications, and 75% have automated some aspects of police operations. Applications in other functional areas also emphasize financial concerns such as revenue generation and collection, cost control, and productivity improvements (e.g., utility billing, fleet management, office systems, and computer-aided emergency dispatching).

Finally, based on instances of change reported by computing managers, the computing environment within cities has itself been altered over time. Computing installations have become more stable in terms of internal structures and operations, but have maintained the rate of technological change necessitated by the pace of external advances. However, new demands and capabilities (e.g., end-user computing, office automation, and communications) are increasing the computing environment's complexity, and thereby expanding the range of issues with potential for instigating change in the future.

---

1 Throughout this report the words "cities" and "municipalities" are used interchangeably and are meant to reflect cities, towns, townships, villages, and boroughs.

2 Three types of computing use are included. Cities that own and operate one or more computing installations, defined as a set of hardware (mainframe or minicomputer) and staff operating essentially independent of any other set of hardware and staff, are the primary type of computing users. Cities that contract with outside sources (e.g., service bureau, facilities management organizations, regional installations, state agencies), for hardware or staff constitute a second type of computing user. Cities with only microcomputers, in either stand-alone or networked configurations, are a relatively new but legitimate third type of computing user. In this broad definition, only cities with fully manual operations are considered "non-users."

3 Since this survey studied all municipal governments with populations greater than 10,000 population, categories were established to differentiate between large (> 100,000), medium (50,000 - 100,000), and small (< 50,000) cities. As a convention for this report, unless otherwise noted, tabular data are presented in four rows. The top row of each column contains sum or mean values across all population cohorts, and the three subsequent rows report values for the three cohorts in descending order of population size.

4 A portion of the tremendous increase in computing use between 1975 and 1985 is attributable to the growth in external service agencies and the appearance of microcomputers. Whereas in 1975 the difference between a user and non-user represented substantial capital and personnel investments, in 1985 "user" status accompanied a

microcomputer purchase. Data on in-house computing installations in Table 1 provide a better comparison of computer use as it existed in 1975.

5 In-house computing installations are the main interest of this study because they comprise the majority of municipal computing activity. In fact, the survey instruments were specifically designed to gather data about computing installations. Virtually all the data presented in the remainder of this report is drawn from, and so best represents, cities that operate at least one in-house installation.

6 These budget figures should be used with caution for comparative purposes, because reported budgets of computer installations are generally conservative estimates of total municipal expenditures on computing. They may or may not include computing expenditures in user departments, overhead and support costs, or management and administrative costs related to computing. An additional complication is that comparisons of computer resources across a full decade are made difficult by price/performance changes in the technology, structural and budgetary changes in installations, and monetary inflation. We did not normalize the data because their values are instructive for specific comparisons, and because comparing percentages and means across cohorts clearly indicates the observed growth in resources.

7 The 1975 data on computing applications in small cities (<50,000) was not collected through the same instrument used for the medium and large cities (>50,000) in 1975, and used for all cities in 1985. Thus, comparisons and generalizations are limited to applications in medium and large cities.

8 Commonality and intensity are two measures of application use within the distribution of operational applications. Commonality is defined as the percentage of cities with one or more operational application(s) in each application category, for all cities reporting the use of computing. Intensity equals the average number of operational applications in each application category, for all cities with one or more operational applications in that category. Combining the commonality and intensity measures provides a clear indication of where municipalities are directing computing resources and for what purpose.

9 In the course of updating our 1975 survey instrument we nearly doubled the number of specific applications listed in the applications inventory (total applications listed: 1975 = 261; 1985 = 468). The intensity figures cited above reflect this absolute growth in the total number of available applications over the past decade. Thus, caution is advised when using the above numbers to measure changes in intensity over time, and any such comparisons must be mindful of this growth in the baseline inventory.

10 A caveat is required for utilizing the intensity measure at low levels of aggregation. The actual number of files and records reported for each application category may understate the full intensity of development, because some integrated systems and turnkey packages were reported as one application although they encompassed several. Therefore, the intensity numbers are most valuable for relative, rather than absolute, comparisons.

Governmental and Municipal Information Systems
P. Kovács and E. Straub (Editors)
Elsevier Science Publishers B.V. (North-Holland)
© IFIP, 1988

INFORMATION SYSTEM USED AS A PLANNING TOOL IN THE DANISH
SCHOOL SECTOR

Gunhild Marie Andersen

Kommunedata
P.O. Box 720
DK-9100 Aalborg, Denmark

This paper describes the construction and use of an information system used in school planning in Denmark. The
system which is called **the School Planning Model** has been
developed by the Danish municipalities' data center
- Kommunedata -

1.   INTRODUCTION

1.1. The School Sector in Denmark

Denmark consists of 275 municipalities. There is a long tradition for municipal autonomy. State influence is ensured by
legislation.

A municipality can be considered as an independent economic unit,
where expenditure must balance with income. Income is mainly
procured by levying taxes.

The municipality is divided into a number of sectors each of
which manages its own area. Each sector is run by a committee
made up of politicians from various parties. Control of the
school area thus lies within the school sector.

The school structure in a municipality covers a number of municipal schools with appurtenant school districts and private
schools. Most children normally go to a school appertaining to
the district in which they live. However, they are also allowed
to go to other schools.

In Denmark all children must normally go to school for at least 9
years (1st-9th form). However, it is possible to start one year
earlier in a nursery school class and continue to the 10th class.
Thus, the Danish state school offers children 11 years of schooling. The compulsory school age stretches from 5 to 17 years of
age.

By level of service in a municipality is meant the service which
a municipality offers its citizens in the field of education.
Fewer pupils in classes or more lessons for the individual pupil
may, for example, be ways of extending a higher level of
service.

1.2. Problems in the school sector

The school sector is today facing many problems.

The general economic cuts in municipal incomes have meant that it is necessary to save money - also within the school sector.

Furthermore, population estimates show future decreases in the number of children and increases in the number of elderly.

This means an increased economic pressure on the school sector as resources must be moved over from it to other sectors.

The general decrease in the number of children affects the various areas in a municipality with varying degrees of force. In some areas the elderly remain, whilst families with children move away. The falling birthrate tendency is thus felt more intensely in these areas.

In other areas new housing estates are built and younger families move in. The number of children increases and extra pressure is put on the existing schools.

It is, therefore, necessary for many municipalities to make a more thorough analysis of the school structure and the service offered to their citizens.

Some questions which it might be relevant to analyse are:

- how can resources be utilized better?
- must the school structure be changed?
- what level of service should the municipality offer in the future?
- is it possible to pursue a policy so an undesired development can be avoided?
- what are the consequences?

In order to make such an analysis it is necessary to know something about the following:

- how will the number of children develop in the future within the individual districts?
- how are demand patterns, i.e. how are children distributed between the schools?
- what level of service does the municipality offer? How do the principles for forming classes, distribution of teaching hours, etc. work?

The Danish municipal data center - Kommunedata - has developed a school planning model which is a tool for analysing the questions raised.

It is this model and its use potentials which will be discussed in this paper.

2. THE PRINCIPLES FOR KOMMUNEDATA'S SCHOOL PLANNING MODEL

Kommunedata has developed several types of planning models for use in municipal planning. The school planning model is one of them.

The model is built up in 5 stages of calculation, each with its own prerequisites, calculations and results.

The stages of calculation are illustrated in fig. 1.

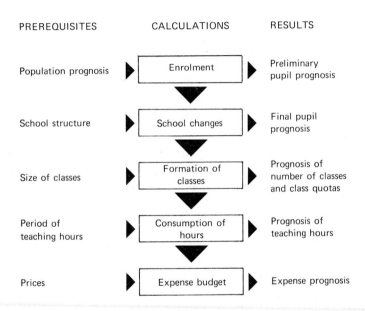

PREREQUISITES	CALCULATIONS	RESULTS
Population prognosis	Enrolment	Preliminary pupil prognosis
School structure	School changes	Final pupil prognosis
Size of classes	Formation of classes	Prognosis of number of classes and class quotas
Period of teaching hours	Consumption of hours	Prognosis of teaching hours
Prices	Expense budget	Expense prognosis

FIGURE 1

Stage of calculation

Results are available after each stage of calculation.

The basis for calculation is a classification of the schools as regards the type of school (municipal or private school) together with a statement as to whether the schools are with or without an appertaining district.

The calculation is made for each school individually and can be summarized for a random number of schools of own choice.

3.   ENROLMENT

The basis for being able to calculate the development of the
number of pupils is:

> - determination of the division of districts.
> - a prognosis for the development of the number of
>   children within the districts.
> - determination of demand patterns.

Prior to a child being able to start school the parents must have
enrolled the child in the school in question. The concept of
enrolment is thus connected with the official act which has to
take place in connection with the commencement of the child's
schooling.

Information at commencement as to how many children are enrolled
at a school can be transferred automatically from Kommunedata's
pupil administration system to the school planning model. This
enrolment information states whether a child goes to the district
school, to a private school, to a school in another school
district or maybe does not go to school at all. Furthermore, the
child's age and stage of schooling is stated. Children who are
already enrolled are followed throughout the whole course of
their schooling by means of the school planning model's calculations.

Kommunedata's population prognosis is the basis for calculation
of future demands and usage. Among other things, the result of
this is an estimate of the municipal population in number of
people, divided into age groups and districts. Prerequisites for
the population prognosis are among other things housing development, patterns of moving, and fertility.

Data for the 5-17 year olds can automatically be transferred from
the population prognosis. By means of this transfer the school
planning model creates school districts based on the division of
districts in the population prognosis.

The population prognosis results are coupled together with
prerequisites as to future **enrolment** patterns - i.e. information
as to which school and stage of schooling together with at what
age the children in the prognosis period start their schooling.
Children from the population prognosis are thus allocated to
schools according to some allocation figures.

The municipalities must themselves evaluate and state how
expectations are for the pupil's future enrolment patterns i.e.
state from which class the pupils leave school.

The result of the enrolment calculation is a prognosis of the
present number of pupils at the district's schools, distributed
in age groups and classes.

4. CHANGE OF SCHOOL

Some children will go to school at a different school than that which they started at. This may be due to the fact that not all schools have the last three forms (8th-10th form) or cannot offer special lessons. It may also be a case of a school being shut down or a new school being built.

At this level of calculation pupils can thus move **from one school to another**. The result is a final pupil prognosis for all schools

This stage of calculation makes it possible to make consequential calculations as regards the effects changes in the school structure, changes in districts, closing down of schools, etc. will have on the number of pupils at the various schools.

5. FORMATION OF CLASSES

The principles for formation of classes and period division can have great importance for resource consumption in the future.

This stage of calculation deals with formation of classes. Some principles for how classes should be formed must, therefore, be given.

The principles partly cover future class quotas and partly the question of whether the classes may be divided or amalgamated during the course of schooling. The class quotas are stated as a required maximum and minimum number of pupils in the classes.

The use of the division or amalgamation principle make it possible to form classes as close to the desired class quota as possible. In class stage intervals where it is not possible for division/amalgamation of classes the number of classes remains constant.

The calculated number of classes can be replaced by a reported number if this is desired. It is in this way possible to join several classes together to form one class.

When the calculation has been carried out the municipality has a prognosis of the number of pupils and classes at each stage of schooling. The result shows the first actual consequences of the fixed school structure. Is there, for example, a risk that there will in future be too many "small classes" at some schools?

If the municipality wishes to evaluate the consequences of the changes in prerequisites, for example, another goal as regards size of classes the calculation can be repeated as often as wished.

Furthermore, the prognosis forms a basis for calculating derivative consequences as regards resources. This takes place in the next stage of calculation.

Fig. 2 shows an example of a pupil and class prognosis:

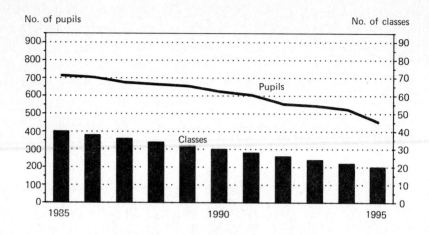

FIGURE 2

Development in number of pupils and classes

Municipal total

6.   CONSUMPTION OF HOURS

At this stage of calculation the consumption of weekly teacher wage hours together with the need for teachers and nursery school class leaders is calculated.

There are two types of teacher wage hours. **Timetable hours** are spent directly with teaching and are divided into normal teaching and special lessons. **Reduction hours** are assigned to teachers who take care of other functions as, for example, student guidance, library, etc.

It is the municipality themselves who fix the number of timetable hours, whilst a considerable number of the reductions hours are fixed in accordance with duty hour regulations.

There are several possibilities and degrees of detail for the setting up of prerequisites:

- hours stated per pupil
- hours stated per pupil, but dependent on class and number of pupils in the class
- hours dependent only on class level.
- a fixed pool

together with a combination of these. The information of consumption of time is assigned to types of consumption hours, which can be freely defined.

The need for teachers is calculated on the basis of teacher's working hours (full-time jobs).

The result of the calculation shows among other things the development of hour consumption per pupil in accordance with fig.3.

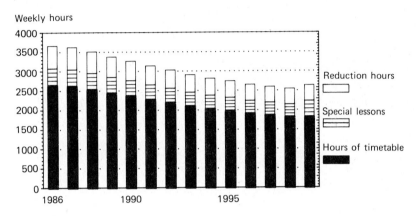

FIGURE 3

Development in number of teaching hours

Municipal total

Expenditure to teachers' wages forms the greatest part of the running expenses of the schools. Knowledge of how development in usage of teaching hours can be affected is, therefore, of particular interest. A correlation of this kind can be determined by means of the school planning model's possibilities for setting up and calculating new alternatives with other prerequisites in accordance with para. 3, 4 and 5. The municipality thus procures a better basis for controlling developments and pursuing a better policy in this sector.

The consumption of teaching hours is also in focus in evaluating the degree of service the municipality wishes to offer its citizens within the school area (level of service).

If there is a great divergence between the individual schools in the municipality or in relation to the country's average the municipality should consider starting an investigation as to the causes of this. The school planning model can also be of assistance in making such an analysis.

7.   EXPENSES

The economic consequences of a given pupil-, class number and consumption of hours can be calculated at this stage of calculation.

This takes place by means of a coupling of the expenditure entries and corresponding amounts. Teacher wage hours are an example of an expense entry, where the amount is the number of teaching wage hours and the unit is the expense per teacher wage hour. A budget amount can also be specified. The result is an expense budget, divided into accounts with the corresponding expenses.

The municipality has thus a basis for making an evaluation of resources in relation to the consequences budget-wise.

8.   USE OF THE MODEL

It may often be fitting to start by determining a reference prognosis. The purpose of this is to obtain a basis for setting up the relevant alternatives and at the same time establishing a basis for comparison.

The reference prognosis will typically be an estimate of the present structure and level of service.

The result can, for example, be a surprisingly large increase in consumption of teacher wage hours per pupil. This is a sign that a more thorough analysis should be made.

The cause will typically be found in the general fall in the number of pupils. If the distribution of hours is not fully dependent on the number of pupils, schools with "small classes" will have relatively more teacher hours per pupil.

It can also be a case of a greater part of the school's pupils moving up to the higher class levels, a fact which normally means more hours per pupil.

Finally, it can be because of a greater pressure on special lessons. This can, for example, be the case in a municipality with a considerable influx of foreign-language children.

Often both the actual problem and the cause will appear in the results from the school planning model.

The question is then how can the problem be solved. Is it necessary to make structural changes? Must the principles for formation of classes or distribution of hours be changed?

> - must slight changes in districts be made, so the class quotas for all the schools are retained at a more suitable level?

- must a school be closed down? Which other schools should the children then be moved to?

- must the principles for division of hours be changed, so the distribution of hours for the individual class is directly dependent on the number of pupils?

- is the municipality's level of service generally too high in comparison with other municipalities?

The alternatives in the school planning model are set up in such a manner that the consequences of the various solutions can be illuminated.

It is then up to the politicians to make decisions as to which solution should be chosen.

Governmental and Municipal Information Systems
P. Kovács and E. Straub (Editors)
Elsevier Science Publishers B.V. (North-Holland)
IFIP, 1988

AUTOMATED LAND ADMINISTRATION - DETAILED

By: J. Kochav, Architect.

1.   PROBLEM AND PURPOSE

The dynamic development, which is characteristic of Israeli towns, is being
delayed, since the authorities do not always have at their disposal
sophisitcated information systems for collecting, storage, extraction and
processing of data according to immediate requirements. A great need exists to
obtain reliable and up-to-date information on land plots: their designations,
use, location, layout, value, ownership, and the rights in connection
therewith. This information is important for the citizen, town, local authority
and for the Ministry of Interior.

The amount of information relating to the subject is tremendous and divided
among the local authorities. In most cases, it is recorded manually.

There are situations where money is spent on:

* Manual collection of information at the Municipality, causing a waste of
  personnel time.

* Field surveys relating to the use of the land for planning purposes.

* Infrastructure surveys, since it is impossible to establish in a multilayer
  superposition manner under or above ground infrastructure systems.

* Circulation system (transportation, garbage collection); inefficient and
  wasteful with respect to manpower, equipment and in service to the citizen.

Needless to say that, in the present situation, the likelihood of making
incorrect decisions is great, in view of incomplete, unreliable or inaccurate
information. Such decisions will undoubtedly lead to wasteful funds in the
wrong direction and to unnecessary expenditures, and sometimes to erroneous,
irreversible decisions after a "point of no return" caused by facts created on
the spot.

Complot (83) Ltd. naturally offers its services mainly to Authorities (cities,
towns, municipalities, local councils, district councils, etc.), to the
Ministry of Interior (district master plan, country-wide master plan, etc.) of
whom updated and quick land information is important for the purpose of current
work and for receiving quick and reliable information presented in the form of
tables and drawings, and identical to the original. Additional bodies could be:
National Lands Authority, Ministry of Defence, Housing Ministry
(neighborhoods), Transport Ministry (roads, junctions, the Council for
Prevention of Road Accidents), the Ministry of Communications (country-wide
communications network), the Ministry of Agriculture (agriculture lots, nature
reserves), the National Water Authority (spreading pipelines throughout the
country), etc.

2.   METHOD

The basis fundamental and leading principal is:

* Organization of information on a unique geographical basis (according to
  coordinates).

Feeding all the data at once into a computerized, alphanumeric and graphic
(maps) pool, enabling:

A. The data input of each parcel in town (including all designations) and its
    location on a map drawn with country-wide coordinates.

B. The compilation of approved plans and the data input of instructions and
    regulations still valid for each parcel in town.

C. The data input of building rights of detailed plans that were previously
    approved, and warnings about irregular issues such as: betterment,
    expropriation, corner plots, and unification/separation of parcels.

D. Keeping a follow-up of plans in process.

E. The display of graphic and alphanumeric information on each individual
    parcel in a block, at any required scale.

F. Reaching a common denominator and creating a unifying factor of land
    designations in all the detailed plans spread over the whole town.

G. Making a rapid extraction of building rights over each parcel: always
    reliable and standard.

H. Rapid processing of data avilable in the file for the preparation of
    programs relating to planning, surveys and research.

I. Principlal or detailed urban planning and updating the TBP thereafter.

The method to be explained hereinafter is designed to meet the requirements of
the town engineers assignments, namely:

* Planning new areas.

* Re-planning existing/old areas.

* Approval of town building plans.

* Approval of building licences and building supervision.

* Responsibility over the execution of expropriations.

* Regular maintenance of the Authority's property.

* Planing maintenance of infrastructure and piping systems in towns.

* Supervision, inspection and approval of plans by outside planners.

The principal and important layer for all this information is that layer which
deals with land designations, which is the "leading" layer in all the
information.

There are two main files in the process that builds the method for feeding land
designations (Town Building Plan):

A. A graphic file (drawings) – containing the coordinates of each parcel, unified in each block and enabling a colored and complete drawing of the city in the T.B.P.

B. An alphanumeric file (details file) – containing the basic data on each parcel (alphanumeric) and all T.B.P. regulations applying thereto.

Another system, which is very important to the city:

System for handling building licence: The system is composed of 3 files:

* Main master file.

* History file.

* Tables file.

3. A FILE CREATING PROCESS

The computerized file for land designations is composed of graphic information that includes maps of land designations, and an analytical information including administrative data, building rights, instructions and limitations, and statutory data.

The information is organized, as mentioned, on a defined geographical basis – a parcel in a block of the Department of Survey (belonging to the Ministry of Construction & Housing) is received on a country-wide network of coordinates. In accordance with this, the process is implemented as follows:

1. Drawing foundation maps by means of a Plotter, including a table of areas for all of the parcels in the block (after a series of auxiliary programes for correcting errors).

2. Data input and drawing of alterations made in existing plots and the creation of temporary parcels (not yet recorded in the Survey Department's block maps).

   i.e. updating of block's maps and creation of land designation maps by means of division and unification of the existing parcels, in accordance with instructions of the detailed plan, indicating at the same time that the new lot has not been officially arranged and has a temporary number, and emphasising its connection with the original parcel.

3. Data input of the land designation for each and ever single parcel, and drawing (with a Plotter) a map of land designations, in color, with each of the designations being indentified by a color dotter.

4. A table of areas for each parcel in the block, and calculation of areas.

5. Data input of block maps by means of digital signs – by entering the coordinates.

6. Input of administrative data for each parcel, including:

   * Block and parcel numbers.

   * One address, or two addresses (in corner plots).

   * Width of road in front of parcels.

* The statistical zone and number of Parcel area: if the block has been
arranged, the area is indicated in the block map and checked by computer.
If the block has not been arranged, the area is graphically calculated by
computer, adjusting the total of the temporary parcel with the original
parcel.

7. Data input of plans applying to parcel and building rights detailed in each
plan, including:

   * building percentages.

   * number of floors.

   * total amount of built-up area.

   * density

   * building lines.

8. Data input of plans in process applying to each parcel and the stage at
which they are pending approval.

9. Data input of plans approved in the past for each parcel, including plans
in archives (if necessary).

10. Creation of a file that includes a list of plans according to their
statutory position, and the last position data.

11. Creation of an alphanumeric, special remarks file for each parcel.

12. A remarks file for all town building plans – detailed/regulationary.

13. A remarks file for each street – according to street signs and details of
sections.

14. Location details of objects in street.

Governmental and Municipal Information Systems
P. Kovács and E. Straub (Editors)
Elsevier Science Publishers B.V. (North-Holland)
IFIP, 1988

THE SWEDISH LAND DATA BANK SYSTEM

Mr Olof Wastesson
Head of Division, Master of Urban and Regional Planning

Central Board for Real Estate Data, P.O. Box 1363,
S-801 38 Gävle, Sweden

ABSTRACT

The need for information on land and on land-related
activities and conditions is recognized among decision-
makers within governmental, municipal and private bodies
all over the world. The need for appropriate systems for
land administration and urban and rural planning is growing. Simultaneously the rapid technological development
offers new and advanced tools.

In many countries existing information systems are under
reorganization. New systems are being built up and implemented in order to facilitate and make more efficient the
handling of information.

Systems designed for the purpose of handling land-related
information are generally known as Land Information
Systems (LIS). A LIS is a tool for legal, administrative
and economic decision-making and an aid for planning and
development.

The Swedish Land Data Bank System (LDBS) is the largest
project in the field of LIS in Sweden. It is an EDP-system
for collecting, storing, processing and presenting land-
related data. The decision to start the project was made
in the early seventies, the purpose being the reformation
of the registration of land and real properties and to
make land-related data more available and useful for
urban and regional planning and other utilization in
society.

The LDBS has been the subject of a large number of studies and evaluations during the seventies and eighties.
This means extensive data and a very good and thorough
knowledge is available in the field of LIS - development,
data capture/data conversion, implementation, maintenance,
training, etc.

This paper discribes the system and some of the experience gained from the development, implementation and operation of the LDBS.

1. INTRODUCTION

Sweden has been at the international forefront within the field
of computerized information systems since the early seventies.
Consequently the country has long experience in development,
implementation and maintenance of public information systems. The
greatest concentration of work within the field of Land Information Systems (LIS) is the Land Data Bank System (LDBS).

2. THE LIS CONCEPT

Land Information Systems (LIS) can be described and discussed
from varying viewpoints.

Firstly there are the **functional aspects** and the pure positive
role land information systems can play in today's society as a
means of registration, for obtaining information on land, for
facilitating administrative procedures concerning land, for
land-taxation purposes, for planning purposes, etc.

The connection of data to points or areas on the surface of the
earth has made different **aspects of geographical reference** of
special interest in land information systems, e.g. the definition
and identification of spatial units, the use of co-ordinates and
co-ordinate methods, and the graphic presentation of data.

Thirdly there are **the technical aspects** such as system design,
register and database organization, database management systems,
data security, technical equipment, methods for data capture,
updating, etc.

In addition to this there are the more **general aspects of data
policy** concerning among other things questions of decentralization, privacy, integrity and influences on other matters in
society.

Some of the questions mentioned above will be dealt with in this
paper.

3. LAND-RELATED DATA IN SWEDEN

For a long time the real property has been the least common geographical unit in the division of land and water in Sweden. To
this unit land-related data - such as population, land-use and
building regulations - are assigned.

Sweden is divided into about 3,5 million real properties. Most
properties are owned by private land owners, but also companies,
municipalities, the church and the state own land. Registration
of the division of land into real properties and of the owners
has a long tradition in Sweden. It has been performed in a systematic way, covering all kind of properties and every spot on the
ground, since the beginning of this century.

There are several registers and systems in Sweden containing
land-related data.

The **Property Register** (cadastre) is the basic register with data on the division of land into real properties (real estates). The register gives each real property an identity of its own and gives information on it's basic **legal-material** status regarding area, boundaries, approved land-use plans etc. The registration is performed by local property registration agencies within the land survey organization (National Land Survey of Sweden).

The Land Register provides, in a corresponding way, information on the basic **legal-economic** status of the real properties. The purpose of the register is to give publicity and legal protection of acquisition of rights concerning real properties - ownership, mortgages, etc. The registration is performed by local land register agencies at the district courts. These agencies are attached to the courts organization (National Courts Administration of Sweden).

These two manually kept registers are now replaced by the Land Data Bank System (see below!).

The Land-Taxation Register contains data on land-use, buildings and other matters of interest in valuation and planning concerning real properties. The register was computerized many years ago and is in operation with a central-regional system design. The assessment is carried out by authorities within the Swedish Tax Administration.

In **the Population Register** each individual is assigned to the real property in which he lives. This computerized register has been in operation for many years.

Other registers with land-related data are **population and housing censuses, the national farm register** and the **register of firms**. All of them are computerized and run by Statistics Sweden (the National Board of Statistics).

Within the National Road Administration a **Road Data Bank,** with data on public road networks and traffic, has been developed. This computerized system has also been in operation for many years.

How this land-related information in different registers can be used through integration will be commented upon later in this paper.

An **Environmental Information System** serving authorities and organizations that require data on environment, pollution, etc, has also been developed.

4. THE LAND DATA BANK SYSTEM

4.1. General

No change in the division of land in Sweden can be made without having it registered at the local property registration agency. There are in all 55 such agencies. In the same way transfer of ownership has to be registered at the local land register agency. The number of land register agencies are 95. The local property registration agencies handle 50 000 registration cases every

year. The number of land register cases, including applications
for mortgages and similar, are 2 million per year.

The registration of real property and land in Sweden is in the
process of being automated. This is currently the most important
single development in the field of LIS in Sweden. An EDP-system -
the Land Data Bank System (LDBS) - is replacing the manual register books which were used earlier. The system is being implemented in order to make the registration of real property and land
more efficient, and also to make information more readily available for purposes other than registration like urban and regional planning, taxation, etc.

A government agency - the Central Board for Real Estate Data
(CFD) - has the main responsibility for the development, implementation and technical operation of the new system. CFD was
established in 1971 for the purpose of performing these tasks.
CFD is a very specialized organization with people from different
fields working together: surveyors, lawyers, computer specialists,
urban and regional planners, economists and others, giving CFD a
unique competence in the field of LIS.

The reform work is carried out in close co-operation with the
National Land Survey of Sweden and the National Courts Administration. They are in turn responsible for the contents and up-to-
dateness of the implemented system. Also, the cities and municipalities are deeply involved in the reform work.

The Land Data Bank System is funded by the Government and has
legal status. By September 1987 some 2.0 million of 3.5 million
real-property units will be registered in the LDBS. The system is
scheduled to cover the whole country by the beginning of the
nineties.

The LDBS is divided into two main registers - the Real Property
Register and the Land Register. The Real Property Register
contains facts on area, centroid co-ordinates, plans and regulations affecting the unit, etc. The Land Register stores information on legal and economic matters concerning the real-property
units, ownership, mortgages, etc. LDBS also contains information
on assessed values derived from the Land Taxation Register produced by the National Tax Board. The registers are kept up-to-
date by real-property register agencies and by the land register
agencies respectively.

LDBS is based on the old manual systems for real-property and
land registration. The process of converting the old system into
the new Land Data Bank System is complicated and involves many
different stages.

4.2. Data Capture/Conversion

The major part of the information in the Land Data Bank System is
derived from the manual property and land registers. On an average
900 characters are captured per real property, 400 coming from
the property register and 500 from the land register.

Experience shows that the data capture preferably should be performed by specialists, exclusively concentrating on the task.
Preparation and "cleaning up" of the manual property register

takes on average 3 minutes per real property. Corresponding work for the manual land register takes 5 minutes. Also the transfer to an EDP-readable medium takes 3 and 5 minutes respectively. A minicomputer system (key-to-disc system) is used for this purpose. Registration is performed by two independent operators. The system checks that the registered data is identical and plausible. There is no need for manual checking.

The total cost for the data conversion from the manual registers amounts to about 60 SEK per property. The figure includes costs for the development and maintenance of the data conversion system, and loading of the data bases.

Another 40 SEK per property is used in order to collect certain information which can not be found in the old registers. Examples are: co-ordinates and map references, street address of the property, assessed value of the property, land use, approved plans and regulations affecting the property, and address of the owner.

The figure just mentioned also includes reformation of the identifiers of the properties. SEK 100 correspond in relation to the value of a property in Sweden to less than 0.05%.

4.3. Identifiers

Questions of identifiers have been considered very thoroughly in Sweden. With these considerations as a base it was decided to implement a civic registration number and a uniform real property designation system over the whole country.

For population registration there exists for every individual a unique civic registration number comprised of digits for the year, month and day of their birth, plus digits for their sex (an example: 301206-2335). This system has been widely used for more than 20 years.

The identifiers of the properties consist of the name of the municipality as a first part, the name of the district within the municipality or the name of the block as a second part and property number (lot number). Examples are: Stockholm Bromma 4:3 and Stockholm Mercurius 5.

This designation is considered to be convenient for the public and other users as well. It is easy to remember and gives easily understandable indication as to the position of the property and therefore is thought to be widely-used. It offers possibilities of preserving valuable and tradition-bound names of villages and farms. A change over to co-ordinates or similar as an official designation of properties would be impossible in Sweden. There is no such requirement for computer-technological reasons either.

The real property designation is the primary identifier in the Land Data Bank System. The co-ordinates for the central points of the real properties are registered in the system. These are not primarily identifiers but a means of localization, of selection and of automatic mapping. In the same way addresses are not primary identifiers but search arguments and a means of finding the official designation. Regarding physical plans and other approved plans the LDBS has been designed to provide the designations of all real properties affected by a certain plan as well as designations of all plans concerning a certain property.

4.4. Data transfer

There are regular transfers of data appertaining to the property division from the Land Data Bank System to the Land-Taxation Register and of data relating to assessed values and land-use from the Land-Taxation Register to the Land Data Bank System. The real property designation is used as an integration key.

From the Population Register there is a regular transfer of addresses of owners of properties. The civic registration number is used in this context.

4.5. Information Retrieval

The handling of real-property and land registration does not change in any major respect after LDBS has been introduced. The registration is performed by the same authorities and by the same staff but with the use of new and more effective instruments. To ensure equal treatment, it is important that the same procedures be used in the old and the new systems since they will be in operation side by side for several years.

LDBS is run on a central computer installed at CFD in Gävle. The authorities are linked to the system by means of terminals. Registration is made on-line, checks are performed and stamp duty and fees are calculated automatically. Changes in the registers brought about by the process of registration are substantiated in so-called journals that are printed out locally at the agencies. Official documents like certificates of registration are ordered on-line, printed out at the Gävle facility and distributed to applicants.

Traditionally the information contained in the Real Property and Land Registers is open and available to the public. Banks, local authorities, brokers, insurance companies, regional and local planning authorities and other organizations that deal with land information can get direct access to LDBS by renting equipment form CFD or by connecting their own terminal or office computer equipment. In January 1987 some 1 500 terminals and printers were serviced by the system.

The main search key in LDBS is the official designation. The user obtains access to the unit by stating the designation or the address. This access method is satisfactory in most cases but not in urban and regional planning situations where data on several real-property units must be selected and compiled. However, LDBS does have the ability to meet these demands. Information can be aggregated in many different ways, for example by area (an entire local administrative area or a part of local authority), by type of ownership (private or local government), by use of land (farming, industry, recreation). The availability of co-ordinates makes it possible to compile information about real property within arbitrarily delimited areas and to display the information on maps. Information is selected and compiled off-line (batch-processing). The information is produced on special order from the user.

4.6. Use in Local Administration and Planning

Sweden has 284 local authorities. The number of inhabitants ranges from 650.000 in Stockholm to some 5.000 inhabitants in the smallest local authority areas. The land area also varies considerably from 19 000 square kilometers in the far north to some 20 square kilometers in densely populated areas. Local authorities administer social services, public utilities like roads, water, electricity, etc. and play a key role in the provision of urban and regional planning and housing. The activities are financed mainly by taxes/ rates paid by the inhabitants but to some extent also by subsidies from the national government.

Swedish legislation grants broad powers to local authorities. They alone are entitled to plan land-use, they have pre-emptive rights. Local authorities are governed by directly-elected councils on land of interest to the community and they have the right to expropriate land for housing and roads.

The government also provides local authorities with wideranging controls over housing construction through the regulations which apply to financing.

Local authorities are organized in a variety of ways depending on size, tradition, etc. Generally, however, activities with a bearing on real estate are handled by offices within one of four basic groups.

The **Real Estate Department** administers housing production according to plans approved by the local council, and manages local authority owned buildings and land. This department also buys and sells publicly-owned real estates.

The **Town Engineer's Office** deals with surveying and the production of large-scale maps needed by the local authority.

The **Town and Country Planning Department** is responsible for physical planning - planning for housing provision and the preparation of master plans. The department makes inspections in connection with building permits, and houses the offices of the Building Committee which issues building permits.

The fourth group consists of **public utilities** like the Department of Water and Sanitation and the Department of Streets and Traffic.

Local authorities can obtain data from LDBS in several ways

- by direct access on terminals
- by ordering extracts or maps
- by subscribing to LDBS change notification

Direct access by terminal is the most common way of obtaining information from LDBS regardless of organization. Besides, there are several types of standard extracts with different sets of information that are tailored to suit several different demands. In addition, the local authorities can order special analyses according to individual specifications. Thematic maps containing information on population or housing are also produced.

For some time now, Swedish local authorities have been planning to set up internal information centres containing data on real estate. Several local authorities are proceeding gradually to create local land information systems, and incorporating oppressive and administrative tasks like handling building permits or managing waste disposal operations or local land management.

The success of a system for local users is dependent on the information being up-to-date and complete. Recognizing the need for real-estate data in local systems, CFD has created a method of transferring data on changes in LDBS to local registers. As the planned local government information systems come into service, it is expected that the product will become one of CFDs most important services.

All these different possibilities have meant that LDBS is an important tool in local planning and land management. The system has resulted in significant improvments for these users since they can carry out work for which they previously lacked the technical and staff resources.

4.7. Use in Urban and Regional Planning

Information of value to urban and regional planners and other users can be found in many different public computerized registers. In Sweden there are (besides the Land Data Bank System) registers for population, for land-taxation purposes, for public roads, for farms, for firms, for vehicles, for censuses (population and housing) to mention some. It is obvious that different users can be facilitated if data in these different registers can be integrated. If, also, data in the registers mentioned can be linked to the co-ordinate register it can be related to geographical positions on a detailed level. Finally, modern techniques make it possible to handle large amounts of data and to integrate information from different registers.

For such an integration you need one or several identification keys. Four circumstances are of special interest in the work with integration in Sweden.

Firstly, the real property designation is unique and widely used in registers. Secondly, every individual has a civic registration number of its own. Thirdly, the inhabitants are registered on the real properties where they live. And fourthly, Sweden has decided to register also the co-ordinates for every real property unit.

Using these four circumstances, different registers can be linked together. The civic registration numbers and the real property designations are used as identifiers.

The connection with the co-ordinate register gives, above all, three advantages. The co-ordinates are a means of providing a more accurate localization of real properties. Another is the possibility to produce statistics for functional as well as geographical areas. The third is the possibility to use the co-ordinates for analyses of geographical data (distance analyses) and for presentation of statistical data (thematic maps).

Some examples how the integration of registers has been used will be given. The examples are based upon an integration by means of the real property designation and the civic registration number. The co-ordinates have been used for selection, processing and presentation.

One very important use of co-ordinate-based data is to delimit freely chosen polygons on a map, digitize the co-ordinate values of the polygon corners and let the computer collect all co-ordinate-registered objects and data within the polygons. Data for the polygons can then be presented in tables and list forms, or be represented by different hatchings, colours or diagrams on a map. If data is already given for polygons such as cities and municipalities (administrative areas), co-ordinates are necessary only for the graphical presentation.

This method can be used in the production of real property lists, for example, giving designation, owner's name and address for each real property within the desired areas. It is also possible to produce tables and statistics about e.g. area and type of real property (one-family houses, weekend houses, etc).

The co-operation between the Statistics Sweden (National Bureau of Statistics), the National Land Survey of Sweden and the Central Board for Real Estate Data has resulted in a regular production of thematic maps. Some of these maps are demographic, others describe geographically unique census variables such as type and degree of employment, housing conditions, households and commuting patterns.

Through integration between the Land Data Bank System and the Land-Taxation Register data about buildings is automatically obtained. The variables of special interest are class of standard of buildings, class of age of the buildings and owner category.

Selection can be made on many different variables. The selected items are then tabled or mapped in the form of dot, square grid net or isarithmic maps.

The method for calculation of a certain isarithm also gives the possibility to an automated delimitation of densely built-up areas. The mapped items and items within delimited areas are also presented in tables with more aggregated figures.

The nuclear power plants need special evacuations plans. The principle for the use of co-ordinate-based data in this case has been as follows: a circle with the plant in the centre is divided into several sectors. Each sector is divided into smaller areas by concentric circles. For each of these small areas, the number of inhabitants, the size of arable land and so on are calculated.

Another application dealt with the information needs in comprehensive municipal planning, comprising:

- survey of building stock, housing development, land ownership conditions and population distribution. The presentation was made in the form of square grid net, dot and isarithmic maps

- automatic delimitations of densely built-up and densely populated areas and description of building stock, proprietorship conditions, land values, etc. within certain areas.

Other applications are: presentation of yearly changes of population per grid net square, background data for location of service facilities (e.g. schools, post offices, shops, bus stops) and for civil defence planning.

These applications are just a few examples. Through combination of unique real property designations, unique civic registration numbers and co-ordinates, the Land Data Bank System offers plenty of possibilities for compilation of land information and of land-related information.

4.8. Effects

LDBS has now been in production for more than 10 years. It has legal status and has been proven an effective and economic system. It has had the following effects

- the quality of data is higher than in the manual system and has resulted in significant quality improvements for individuals, for the staff affected and for interested parties in the public and private sectors

- the information is always up-to-date and accurate

- increased efficiency at the Property and Land Register Agencies, that is faster job performance, less people involved, etc., and also for all other activities that involve the handling of land and real property information (banks, brokers, local authorities, etc)

- changes of addresses, assessed tax values and land-use are automatically entered into the LDBS which means a very important rationalization of data flows between Government agencies

- the information has been made more available and accessible, since it is stored in one place, can be presented in different ways and is easy to read by linking the computer to the user's own terminal

- the system is available to users in urban and regional planning and in other fields of activity; new possibilities to compile, analyze and present the contents of the Real Property and Land Registers and to integrate these registers with other registers with data important for urban and regional planning and development; the products of the system have resulted in significant improvments for these users since they can carry out work for which they previously lacked the technical and staff resources.

4.9. Economy

The investments being made as regards development, building the system and so on, have been considerable. In spite of these investments, the Land Data Bank System is profitable within a relatively short period. Savings are made through reduction of staff and reduced costs for premises at the register agencies. Investments will be paid back within 10-15 years by rationalizing the work at the authorities. The costs of implementation and of running the system are covered by charges. The charges, also, cover the maintenance and the further development of LDBS.

In a wider sense LDBS is economically beneficial for society as a whole be giving a higher degree of service as regards accessibility to data, increased amount of data, shorter turn-around time and so on.

5. CONCLUSION

The Swedish Land Data Bank System has now been run with legal power for ten years in some areas, and is very much appreciated by all users, such as land and property register agencies, cities and municipalities, banks, credit organizations, companies, etc. The experience gained is extremely positive.

The work with the system has resulted in a very good and thorough knowledge about costs, benefits, and administrative, technical, and legal aspects of EDP-based information systems for central, regional and local authorities, particularly in the field of Land Information Systems. There are lots of experiences on, for instance, data capture/conversion, different ways of using the data throughout the society and how to make systems economically favourable by creating many sources from which income may be obtained. The experience gained from the implementation of these systems has proved to be very interesting from an international point of view.

THE SWEDISH LAND DATA BANK SYSTEM

SYSTEM OVERVIEW

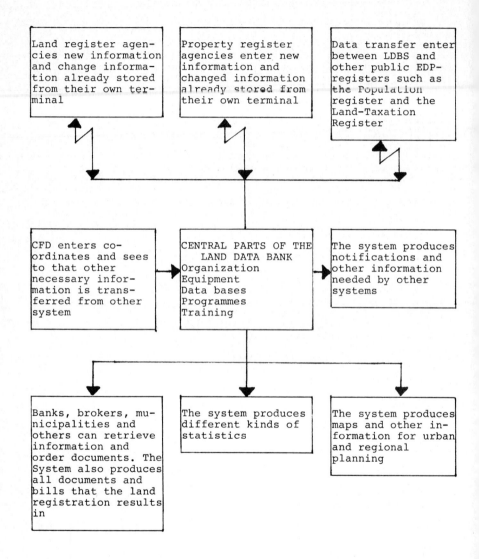

FACTS ABOUT LDBS

1.1 Information contents

The most important particulars of the system are
the following:
the identity of the property (identifier),
its origin,
its location (municipality, parish, etc.),
coordinates (centroids) and map references,
street address,
acreage of the property,
survey measures and other proceedings concerning the
property,
servitues, easements and other rights bound to the
property,
plans and other land regulating stipulations affecting
the property,
property classification and land use,
assessment values for land and buildings,
legal owner of the property (including address),
owners of objects on the property e.g. a house, and
mortgages and other restrictions encumbering the property.

1.2 Technical equipment (January 1987)

```
  1 IBM 4381-PO2    Computer with memory size of 16 MB
  7 IMB 3380        Disk storage à 2.4 GB ⎫
  4 IBM 3350        Disk storage à 300 MB ⎬ Total 18.0 GB
  7 IBM 3420        Magnetic tape units   ⎭
  2 IBM 3203-5      Printer
  1 IBM 2501        Card reader
  1 IBM 3725        Communications controller
240 Alfaskop        Display terminals
    (Ericsson IS)
115 Alfaskop        Terminal printers
    (Ericsson IS)
200 Nokia MPS2      Display terminals
 75 Siemens PT89    Terminal printers
    or OKI
250 Customer owned terminals connected via switched lines
700 Videotex terminals
```

DB/DC-system: AROS/ROSAM

1.3 Some figures for 1986

700,000 register extracts, certificates and other documents are
produced by the computer and distributed from CFD.

900,000 questions are "asked" from leased/owned/Videotex-terminal.

12,000 real property register cases are handled by means of the
Land Data Bank System (some 55,000 cases are handled in Sweden
every year).

1,345,000 land register cases are handled (in Sweden there are
about 2 million land register cases per year).

Governmental and Municipal Information Systems
P. Kovács and E. Straub (Editors)
Elsevier Science Publishers B.V. (North-Holland)
© IFIP, 1988

CITIZEN IMPACTS OF A MUNICIPAL INFORMATION SYSTEM
SOME EMPIRICAL EVIDENCE

Bernd H. LIEDTKE

Gesellschaft fuer Mathematik und Datenverarbeitung
Postfach 1240
D – 5205 Sankt Augustin 1
Federal Republic of Germany

The paper reports on a project which has led to the introduction of information technology into the administration of a West – German municipality with 60,000 inhabitants. The project was conducted under very favorable circumstances. The paper centers on the project's explicit objective to make the task – handling and service – delivery of this administration more effective – from the citizen's point of view – and how this objective fared.

1. LOGIC à la CARROLL, or ... "WHAT ARE WE TALKING ABOUT"?

This paper is concerned with citizen impacts of information systems development and use in a municipal administration. Do positive effects outweigh negative effects (or vice versa) when information technology is introduced into public administration and more specifically into local administration? In fact, are there any effects at all worth mentioning? The usual answer is "it depends ...".

The answer depends not only on how well a development project is endowed with time and skills, how well these resources are used, restrictions observed and opportunities exploited to make the information system meet the specifications, but also on the point of view of the different actors in the implementation game on how well the system's specifications meet their perceived needs, their expectations, or their interests. The metaphor can be stretched. Hirschheim [1] recently reminded us with respect to office automation that the answer also depends on the beliefs, values, and tastes of the spectators and commentators of the implementation game. Beliefs, values, and tastes of researchers affect their preferences of research methodologies as well as the kind of research questions asked and thus the research results produced.

This situation, of course, is special neither to office automation nor to information systems in general. It is typical for all human activity, be this policy or study. However, in studying social impacts of information systems, this situation is aggravated by a number of problems of which once again Hirschheim [1] has made us aware, and which I would like to summarize as follows: We have not yet succeeded in naming, isolating, and measuring firstly the causes and, secondly, the effects with any validity for theory and with any relevancy to practice.

The first point is not surprising because it characterizes much of normal science. When, for example, my colleagues Lange and Sippel cite research by Brinkmann [2] and Blannerhasset [3] which contradicts their own findings, they merely conform to scientific convention. They discovered, by the way, a marked (although spurious) correlation between the use of computers in the offices of a particular segment of public administration and the quality of services delivered to the citizens as "customers" of these offices (cf. Lange [4]; [5]). *Figure 1* shows their findings which on first sight are indeed impressive.

The second point is more alarming as it usually characterizes the birth of a new scientific discipline or a paradigm change within an established discipline: terminology is ambiguous (is "citizen outcomes" the same as "citizen impacts", what is the difference between "effects" and "implications") and concepts are fuzzy. What sort of social or citizen impacts are or should be our "real" concern? Are they long – term and not short – term effects, latent (covert) against manifest (overt) effects, unintended versus intended effects, more the creeping than the swooping effects, indirect or direct effects? Perhaps those long – term, subtle, latent, indirect, and unintended effects are the most important which we cannot yet name (or research) because of lack of imagination. Be it as it may, the findings by Lange and Sippel may be doubted just by calling in question the relevance of their conceptualization and operationalization of the effect variable "quality of service". So – like Alice behind the looking glass – we find ourselves in a situation where different researches on one and the same information system *may and may not* discern any effects, or outcomes, or impacts or whatever, and may assess similar effects as *good and* as *bad*, and thereby declare this information system to be a *success and a failure*.

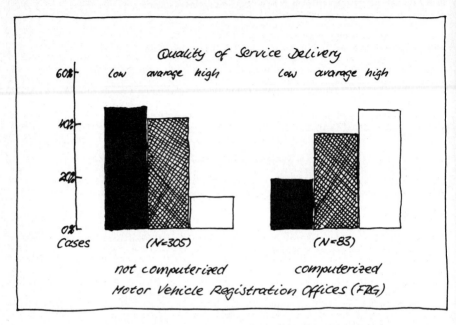

Figure 1
Use of information systems and quality of service (adapted from Lange [4])

This situation of Carrollian logic has not changed much during the past few years. In this situation of relative ignorance another case study on the impacts of public information systems on the citizen has been conducted. The "case" is a research and development project which was primarily and expressly targeted at improvements for the citizen in task – handling and service – delivery of a municipal administration and in which information technology played a major part. I dare tell the story despite the opinion of acknowledged researchers "case – study, so what?" (Lange [4]).

My story loosely follows the outline of a classic research report. In the Section 2 I shall describe the "problem", i.e. the features of the Citizens Office as a new administrative unit in a municipal administration and the rationale behind it. In Section 3 (method) it is argued that researching citizen impacts, in the context of the project citizens office, could imply nothing but try to contribute to the project's main objective. Section 4 (results) is concerned with the findings that people believe that the citizens office has made it easier for them to settle their affairs with the city administration. I shall argue that, for all we know, this subjective impression is only partly due to objective changes in administrative "output" accompanying the implementation of the citizens office. It seems more due to the credit the citizen gives the city (council and administration) to have *visibly tried* to change something within the administration for his or her sake. In Section 5 (discussion) I shall present my view of why there can be no guarantee of positive citizen outcomes even when they should be the main concern of a development project. There are weaknesses inherent to any such concern which become virulent in all projects regardless of whether they are conducted under favorable conditions (like the citizens office) or under less favorable conditions (like the majority of re – organization projects in public administration). There are similarities between the policy problem and the research problem.

2. THE CITIZENS OFFICE (CO)

2.1. The "case"

Not knowing whether "citizens' office" or "citizen's office" is the literal translation of "Buergeramt" I have already spoken and shall continue to speak of the "citizens office". The citizens office is not part of the classic division of a municipal administration into departments, offices, and bureaux. On the contrary it is to date a singular experiment in administrative reform in the Federal Republic of Germany.

The experiment has been conducted by the administration of the municipality of Unna. Unna is a town with a population of about 60,000 and is situated at the eastern edge of the Ruhr District conurbation. The idea for this experiment dates back to 1978 when it was first discussed in connection with plans for a new city hall. Since 1980 there has been a contract of cooperation between the town of Unna and the Gesellschaft fuer Mathematik und Datenverarbeitung (GMD) which, as its name suggests, supplied the expertise on information systems (development). Until 1983 the joint project had been generously funded by the Federal Ministry of Research and Technology; in fact, this project has been amply endowed with resources throughout all its stages. In 1984 the Citizens Office opened its first stage of completion. Since then its range of tasks has grown continuously. By the middle of 1987 the joint project will come to its formal end.

The project is documented in detail (Dunker [6]); there are also shorter reports in German (KGSt [7]) and in English (Dunker [8]). My description is restricted to those aspects of the outcome which have direct bearing on the assessment of citizen impacts. The name "citizens office" itself hints already at the delicate relationship between "citizen – orientedness" on the one hand and "bureaucracy" on the other.

2.2. Rationale

The idea behind the citizens office is straightforward. Under the conditions of competitive markets the motive to make profits induces a striving not only for better quality products but also for higher quality services. In contrast, in public administration, the pursuit of the common well – being is not a sufficient driving force to guarantee a continuous monitoring of the adequateness of task – handling and service – delivery and its adaptation in case of malfunctioning from the point of view of the citizen. This holds not only in the citizen's role as tax – payer but also, and especially, in his role as client and customer of public offices. But for citizens the comparison between the quality of private and public services is becoming more obvious. And public administration must be cautious not to suffer a loss of legitimation because of unfavorable comparisons.

Unna's city director has again and again argued that many of the difficulties of the citizens stem from their confusion regarding which bureau does what in public administration, which in turn can be traced back to an intra – organizational rationality by which the division of labor in public administration has evolved historically. So why not try by using all organisational and technical means available today to restructure this division of labor wherever possible and, where this is not possible, to provide qualified council and advice to reduce the remaining difficulties. It was up to the joint research & development project not only to model this idea into a solid systems concept but also to implant the concept into a living organization.

2.3. Features

Figure 2 shows how the original vision has become manifest in the range of tasks and services of the citizens office today. It is not necessary to discuss all the details of this figure which show many local and at best national idiosyncracies and are thus only of restricted interest for an international audience. Nevertheless, I do want to point to the fact that around the basic tasks of the former residents registration department a number of other tasks have been integrated into the citizens office which up to then had been attached to several different divisions of this particular municipal administration. These tasks have a common feature in that people usually come personally to the office, that the tasks are of a relatively simple structure and therefore in most cases can be settled on the spot. A diversified offer of information and advice/counseling services supplements the task profile of the citizens office.

"Functional concentration of tasks" and "upgraded information and advice/counseling services" are but two features of the citizen office. Together with two other features these give the citizens office its unique *Gestalt*. "All – round task handling" paraphrases the principle that all officials working in the citizens

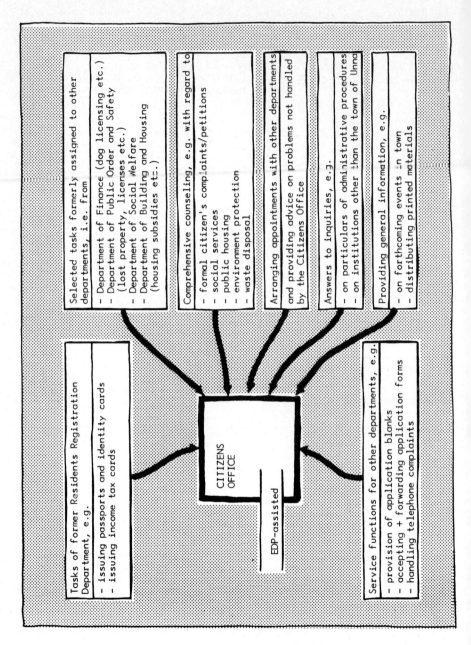

Figure 2
Tasks and services of the citizens office today (adapted from Dunker [8])

office shall be qualified and responsible, with respect to all tasks performed in the office (including advice and counseling), which is advantagous for the organization (e.g. cover for absenteeism) as well as for the clients (free choice of official). Lastly the citizens office consists of a head office downtown, which will be situated in the foyer of the new city hall some day, and two branch offices in the suburbs. A third branch office will be opened as soon as suitable accomodation is found. The realization of such a feature which we call "locational decentralization" is dependent on the functional concentration of tasks and their all—round handling. It makes possible not only shorter distances to the office for suburban dwellers but opens the possibility for the citizens to get their business done in whichever office is most convenient to them — regardless of where they dwell, shop or work.

Changes in	Main features of the citizens office			
	Functional concentration of tasks	Upgraded information and advice services	All-round task-handling	Locational decentralization (branch offices)
Organisational structure	X			
Qualification of personnel		X	X	
Use of information technology		X	X	X

Figure 3
Major prerequisites (X) for implementing the CO

2.4. Major development tasks

In *Figure 3* the different features of the citizens office are related to changes in the different strata (personnel, structures/procedures, technology) of an administrative department which have been necessary in order to get the citizens office in shape and on its way.

- **Changes in organization:** changes with respect to organizational structures and procedures were necessary to work towards the objective (= feature) of functional concentration of tasks; criteria for CO suitability had to be developed, tasks fullfilling these criteria had to be detected and the feasability to transpose the task into the CO had to be checked, not only from the perspective of the future CO but also from the perspective of the administrative unit in which the task traditionally resided.

- **Changes in the qualification of personnel:** higher qualified and well motivated personnel was a prerequisite to reach the objectives of upgraded information and advice services and the individual competence to perform all CO tasks. Qualification measures had to be developed with respect to professional knowledge as well as with respect to communicative knowhow.

- **Changes in the use of information technology:** with the exception of the functional concentration of tasks, all other CO features need some infrastructure of information technology; up – to – date and comprehensive information is needed for many advice and counseling tasks which are best kept in some form of computer based system on which all officials can draw. All – round task handling needs other qualifications than just knowledge on procedural details though this knowledge must be present if needed. And locational decentralization with respect to tasks which rely on registers of some sort or the other (lost property, or a voters' register, for example) has become feasible with the advent of on – line data processing.

I have elaborated on *Figure 3* because I felt it necessary to stress that the information system "citizens office" encompasses not only information technology (without which the CO surely would have not been possible) but also (organizational) procedures/structures and personnel, all of which have to be "programmed" and mutually adapted and fine – tuned in order to effect optimal performance. Kraemer [9] has taught us this lesson. I might add that in the case of the citizens office the potential "customers" of public services should also be regarded as an operational field in which systems development must be done. The citizens have to be made aware of the changes in structures and procedures, for example, in order not to evoke new difficulties in their interactions with public bureaux.

3. RESEARCHING CITIZENS IMPACTS

3.1. Involvement of citizens and employees

Change ellicits resistance and inertia has to be overcome. The above description has hopefully induced the notion that the scope of the project "citizens office" was such that many members of the administration saw personal interests (or the interests of a particular bureau) to be affected in one way or another. In fact it seemed that in the end there could be many loosers but few winners.

For example, a change in the task structure is always a change in the power structure of an organization. The possibility that a task may be transfered from a particular bureau to the citizens office is a menace for the image, power, and careers of those working in this particular bureau (or heading it). It will be the more so the more the task in question is considered to be a basic task of the bureau with which the members identify themselves strongly. Or, to take another example: Up to the beginning of the project the town of Unna had its data processing done in the local Common Computer Centre (CCC) of which Unna is a member (together with other municipalities). It was clear to all concerned that the town of Unna would use the project as a means to reduce its (financial) engagement in the CCC as far as possible and to build up computing resources of its own. More than a negligible amount of time and effort were spent because of the conflict of diverging interests which arrose out of this situation. Similarly, conflict of hopes and fears with respect to individual careers, pay, job security, demands on qualification, job enrichment etc. were virulent within the personnel.

In this situation, the major task was to convince people of the merits of the project, to recruit allies, to canalize fears and make hopes fertile in order to prevent an untimely end of the project and for the sake of a "good product". Moreover provisions had to be made which would allow the vague idea of "to change something in the interest of the citizen" to become operationable in the sense of how what should be changed to which extent – without denaturing the idea of its very essence.

In order to achieve the above ends, a strategy of participative systems development was followed. I need not explain the details of this strategy here as aims, form, and success have been described elsewhere (Mambrey [10]; Ehrenberg [11]). A short exposition of its main rationale exists in English (Oppermann [12]). I just want to mention that, on the local level, employees as well as the management of the administration, ordinary citizens and politicians, the local union as well as an advocate who voiced the interests of the elderly, the handicapped, and the poor, were brought into the development process via working groups and committees. These groups met regularly. The citizens working group, for example, met 42 times during a three year span with practically no turnover in membership. All groups and committees, as well as Unna's formal councils (i.e., town and staff councils), had the right to hear and the right to be heard. Looking back there was no major decision which was pushed through against the will of any one interested group participating in the project.

3.2. Matching process and method

In the same way in which the involvement of citizens and employees in the development process is part of the "case" citizens office, its description could be part of the case story of Section 2. But the original considerations which led to a participative systems development strategy as well as the actual involvement of citizens and employees in the development process had peculiar implications for the design and conduct of impact research within the project. And the design and conduct of research determines, of course, the kind of results.

A strategy of participative systems development implies that the product does not have any features which touch the interests of those participating more than they are willing to bear. If taken seriously, the idea of participative systems development also implies that no development (or research) activity is performed against the interests of anybody participating if he does not consent to it. In short, in participative systems development one never knows what one gets (or whether one gets anything at all) or how one gets it. If everything happens as originally envisaged then something goes wrong. In a situation like this it is rather futile to try to follow a design of rigorous scientific research with any rigor. Questions may not be asked because they may impinge on the perceived interests of somebody and questions must be asked which do not make much sense in any theoretical framework. Scientific rigor may even be detrimental for the development tasks if it should prevent flexible action, or a change in plans, where this is called for.

Nonetheless there were information needs, perhaps more so than in conventional development projects. These were partly due to the indeterminacy of the goals as well as of the design features and enhanced further by the characteristics of the design strategy. In this situation it seemed necessary to give as much support as possible to the very general aim "foster positive citizens outcomes" in accordance with the participating bodies who should articulate the interests of the citizens. We chose to do the research on citizen impacts in the fashion of "utilization – focused evaluation" (Patton [13]) which during the course of the constructive phases of the project was thought to be "formative" and during the assessment phase to be "summative" (Weiss [14]). The formative part of the research question thus was "how can positive outcomes for the citizens be enhanced and negative outcomes be prevented" and the summative part was how far (and for what reasons) have positive outcomes been effected and negative outcomes not been prevented".

With our activities we did not remain passive observers but defined ourselves as active participants in the development process. Every activity we wanted to perform for research reasons had to be checked for its contribution to solve the development task. We became aware that any research activity could serve purposes beyond the satisfaction of some particular information need.

3.3. Summary of research activities

We followed the logic of an *ex – ante* → *in – actu* → *ex – post* research design. In particular we performed, at the very beginning of the project, a series of expert interviews in and outside the town administration of Unna to get a first impression of the field. During the analysis phase a survey among the clients at most of the town offices was done with the purpose to contribute to the goal function; a mailed survey among the general public was performed to coroborate the concept (Liedtke [15]; [16]). During the constructive phases of the project we participated in systems specification, program testing, and documentation. In autumn 1986 we began the duplication of the original research steps but this time in reverse order. We started with the survey of the general public. A survey among the clients of the citizens office and its branch offices will get under way at the beginning of May 1987. With another series of expert interviews data collection will be finished. Wherever it makes sense results of one research step are followed up in the next step.

It looks like a very conventional collection of research activities. It could be so because these activities were supplemented by the information gathered by the advocate planner and because preparations and results were scrutinized by the citizens' working group, for example. These activities also had to be conventional, because not all research steps could be performed as planned. We could not convince the employees, for example, that it would be as much in their interest as in the interest of the clients to know more about the peculiarities of the situations of face – to – face contact between official and client with respect to possible requirements for the man – machine interface. A systematic observation of such situations was blocked vehemently and, from the employees' point of view, successfully.

3.4. Formative evaluation: an example

While the next section of this presentation provides a glance at the summative part of our research I want to illustrate here the formative part. I use the survey among the clients at the offices of the town administration as an example.

- **Functions:** the survey was conducted near the very beginning of the project. It served three functions which were derived from the main needs at that stage of the project's progress.

  - **Information (and motivation) function:** the survey was intended as a means to make public the existence and purpose of the project Citizens Office. Interest of the citizens should be roused and, as far as possible, motivation created to participate in the project.

  - **Exploratory function:** it was intended to get to know as specifically as possible positive as well as negative experiences of the clients of public administration with regard to visits to public offices. The study was not intended to be an opinion poll or an image study.

  - **Sensibility function:** the survey was intended to serve as a means for making professional systems analysts aware of and give them a feeling for the problems of customers of different town offices in face – to – face contacts (also to provide them with a background of personal experience for assessing the summarised results of this survey).

- **Design and conduct:** the three functions led to several contradicting specifications with regard to questionaire – design and conduct which resulted in compromises.

  The central theme of the interview was the current visit to the office and its circumstances. The interview was divided into a section which was conducted when a client entered the office and a section which was completed when he left. This made it not only possible to ask further questions but also to contrast the expectations of the client with regard, for example, to duration and success of this visit with his actual experiences. To get the full flavor of the answers and to have an instrument which could be used in all parts of the administration, most of the questions were open – ended.

  The interviews were performed by all the full – time project members including the project manager. Over a span of two months 851 clients of 11 different town offices (a cross – section of the administration) were approached, out of which 564 agreed to be interviewed.

  An intensive press campaign before and during the survey was intended to heighten the attention for it as well as for the project. This is quite against the rules of rigorous social research (thou shall catch your interviewees unawares).

- **Results:** the results of this survey were put in the form of recommendations under four headings of near equal weight.

  - The project must be aware of the fact that many clients consider a personal visit to an office as the most convenient and "safest" way to get business settled with the office.

  - Spatial decentralization of the administration accompanied by functional concentration of tasks should be extended.

  - The citizens office should also bring improvements for the clients of very specialized departments, e.g. social welfare.

  - "Information and advice/counseling" should get the status of an independent administrative task.

  These recommendations reflected the advantages and disadvantages associated with the citizen's visit to a municipal office. All of these recommendations have to some degree been taken into account in the development of the citizens office. There was no recommendation with regard to the use of information technology because in none of the offices were computers used during a client – official contact at that time. Such a recommendation had to be formulated by drawing on other sources of information.

4. EVALUATING THE CITIZENS OFFICE

4.1. The evaluation scheme

Several models for a citizens office which differed in some major aspects had been developed and put forth for discussion. Both public employees and citizens, both the city council and the management of the town administration, selected the most ambitious model for realization. It best incorporated the requirements from the citizens' point of view which had evolved during the course of the project. Of course, this model also was the most frail with regard to the possibility that the final implementation would not quite meet the expectations. A comprehensive evaluation of success and failure of the project and its outcome should thus give answers to the three following questions:

- How successfully does the citizens office operate?

- How successfully does the town administration as a whole operate after the establishment of the citizens office?

- How weighty are the changes in the municipal administration of Unna with respect to encounters of the citizens with other parts of the public administration?

One might perhaps miss an evaluation question with respect to the success of the information technology put to use in the citizens office. When any information technology is used by people whithin an organisational context I see analytical difficulties in neatly separating the effects of one from the other. I also see no need for such an evaluation question because, from the citizens' point of view, technology, organization, and staff factually constitute the "bureau", in which deficiencies of technology may be compensated for by a proficient staff, and advantages of technology may be counter-acted by poorly trained and unmotivated personnel.

Success in the context of the above questions is a multi-dimensional measure covering performance aspects as well as output and impact aspects. I summarize these dimensions under 5 headings:

- Reduction of mental stress of the clients in their encounters with public bureaux. This stress is often caused by lack of knowledge on possible and/or necessary routes of action, and by feelings of uncertainty with respect to circumstances and success of these routes.

- Reduction of the citizen's efforts involved in settling his business, as a result of obtaining immediate information, thus saving time spent waiting, time and money spent travelling from one office to the other, or time lost due to inquiries and check-backs.

- Higher quality of service with respect to professionalism and communicative competence of the officials, speed of task delivery, accuracy in decision-making, reliability and comprehensibility of information.

- Transparency of public administration because of lucidity of organisational structure, accountability of acts to officials, control of the citizen on personal data kept in the administration.

- Effectiveness of public administration, e.g. presence where needed, responsiveness and adaptability with regard to (changing) requests.

This list is similar to those proposed by others (Sterling [17]; Kraemer [9]; Kling [18]; Lange [5]). In its elaboration it is enumerative and may be expanded almost at will. It must be differentiated still further when we recognize that "the citizen" is a phantom. There are many citizens and they differ not only in sex and age but also in their experiences, knowledge, expectations, attitudes, and needs in relation with public administration. Success of the citizens office may be assessed differently by an occasional visitor to a public bureau than by a long-standing client of a social agency.

We have neither enough data nor are the data we have always conclusive to fill the assessment scheme. This is due not only to the "soft" research design described in the preceding section but also due to measurement problems irrespective of the actual design. I use this scheme to get some order into the data I have – to make them coherent and somehow meaningful – to discern a picture even as one can still see the motive of a jig – saw puzzle when a few pieces are missing. I present no proofs but hints and conjectures and hope they are suggestive.

At the time of writing, the ex – post data collection has not yet been completed. Only the results of the mail survey are available.

4.2. The search for effects

In autumn 1986 questionaires were sent to approx. 4200 persons in Unna aged between 16 and 75 years. Questions on different topics relating to the citizens office were raised. In design the survey was a near to exact replica of the one we used in 1982. The random sample was stratified with respect to age and address of the potential respondents. Both older persons, because of their known reluctance to answer questionaires, and suburban dwellers, because of their relatively small number, were over – represented. The two surveys were embedded in a press – campaign related to the (planned) citizens office.

There was a difference in the thematic range of the questions asked in the two surveys. The 1982 survey contained questions relating to the citizens office as well as questions on the satisfaction with the local infrastructure and local politics. This mix of themes was considered inducement enough for participation in the survey. No personal "reminder to participate" seemed necessary. We expected a response rate somewhere between 20% and 25%. The actual response rate was near to 27% which was considered satisfactory remembering the stratification effects. The 1986 survey contained a reduced set of questions relating to the assessment of the citizens office (and some background information on the respondents). This time, to compensate for the missing motivation induced by the questions on local politics and infrastructure, we included a personal "reminder to participate". The actual response rate was more than 39% which we consider to be excellent. After all, in the eyes of the public both surveys were activities of the town administration. The questions were on topics of which either a bureaucrat should know more about than an ordinary citizen (organisational reform) or of which large parts of the population had not yet experienced (information technology as a tool and as an organizational means).

The second survey was performed at a time when more than half of the population ought to have experienced business with the new citizens office, thus enabling a comparison to be made of the answers of those who had been to the citizens office (n = 865) with those who had had no personal contact with it (n = 733).

At this point of my presentation I am in a fix. On the one hand the project was expressly targeted at changes in the municipal administration which would be perceived as improvements by the citizens. Ideally, these perceived improvements would foster the willingness of the citizens to actively look after their interests against public administration. And I myself tried to contribute toward this objective. On the other hand common sense reasoning suggested that the hope that changes within the administration would be consciously perceived by the clients would turn out to be futile. Apart from an admittedly significant minority of citizens most citizens have few encounters with a public bureau. Every five years personal identity cards and/or passports have to be renewed. There may be encounters with the police because of minor traffic offences, etc. At times there may be a limited period of extensive and frequent encounters with public bureaux – say if somebody plans to build a dwelling or if somebody becomes unemployed for a short period. Usually these encounters involve little or no business with the citizens office.

Often, the encounters with public bureaux are not only rare but also do not imprint themselves on the minds of the clients. After a short while you can hardly remember that you have been to an office, causing difficulties when being asked what you have seen, or whether there have been any changes since your previous visit. There need to be a lot of changes before they become imprinted on the customers' minds. This common sense reasoning seems to be corroborated by scientific research (cf. Sharp [19]).

Whatever the findings on the impacts of the citizens office are, they may be doubted. Should there be few adverse effects or only positive impacts then these are biased results because of the active engagement of the researcher in the development process. Should there be no effects at all then the researcher has not tried hard enough to disprove his preconceptions (by using a soft research design as described above). Perhaps the researcher is prejudiced *and* incompetent?

Well, I shall turn first to the question of the role of information technology in the citizens office as perceived by the public. Then I shall try to shed some light on the question how the citizens office, as it presents itself today, is assessed by the public.

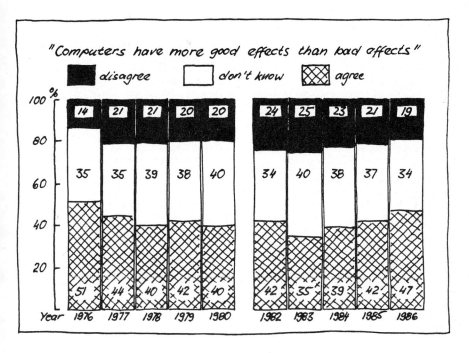

Figure 4
Change of attitudes towards IT in the FRG (adapted from IBM [20])

4.3. The role of information technology

Until the citizens office opened the citizens of Unna in their encounters with the municipal administration were confronted solely with printed computer output. There are, for example, decrees on local fees and taxes for homeowners, decisions on rent and housing subsidies, or calculation sheets for social welfare benefits, part of which was done at the Common Computer Center and part of which is still done at one of the computer centers operated by the state. The citizens office has changed the situation drastically. Terminals and key – boards are placed on all desks, and several local print – stations are visible for all to see. Many but by no means all tasks are performed utilizing on – line data processing. This change in appearance of the city administration was considered to be risky and problematic for several reasons.

One of which had to do with the general discussion of the pros and cons of information technology in the Federal Republic where a tendency to become more critical and more sceptical has been effective since the mid – seventies. In this period a major national theme has been the "citizen of glass" or what the state should or should not know on any one individual. This discussion climaxed in 1984 when the supreme court decided that the legal basis of the decennial population census in the FRG was at fault. Since then, it is said that the tide has turned (cf. *Figure 4*). Our snapshots in Unna also show a more optimistic assessment in 1986 than in 1982 (cf. *Table 1*). Time must show how stable this new tendency really is.

A second reason had to do with the specific economic situation of the Ruhr District. For years already this old industrial center of coal – mining, foundries, and steel – works has suffered an economic slump.

"On the job, at home, and in school more and more computers are used. It is said that this is just the beginning. How do you feel about this development all in all?

	1982	1986
I am enthusiastic about this development - or - I see more good effects than bad effects	31%	41%
I don't know	37%	41%
I see more bad effects than good effects - or - this development will be disastrous	27%	15%
no response	4%	3%
	(n=1190)	(n=1638)

Table 1
People in Unna assess information technology more optimistically in 1986 than in 1982

"Have you gained already any experience with computer technology in school or at your job?"

Rank order of respondents grouped for age/sex according to proportion answering:

Yes, but not many - or - yes, have worked with it for a longer time already

1982		1986	
16-30/male	50% (210)	16-30/male	58% (247)
31-60/male	50% (228)	31-60/male	52% (242)
16-30/female	36% (207)	16-30/female	43% (227)
61-75/male	23% (91)	31-60/female	25% (329)
31-60/female	18% (204)	61-75/male	18% (251)
61-75/female	7% (133)	61-75/female	6% (308)

base of percentage

Table 2
Older women have the least experience with computer technology

The rate of unemployment is significantly and constantly above that of the FRG as a whole. The Daily Papers abound with news of works' closures and workers' lay – offs. A considerable portion of the population of Unna has been or still is commuting to neighboring Dortmund or to other cities of the Ruhr District to earn a living. So it comes to no surprise that in the 1982 survey as well as in the 1986 survey the most frequent comment (about 3 in every 10) spontaniously added to the question cited in *Table 1* was "more computers = more unemployed".

A third reason had to do with the fact that a large proportion of the general public had not yet had any personal experience with computers. Not much has changed in this situation between 1982 and 1986. While in 1982 33% of all respondents answered that they had had some experience with computer technology, in 1986 it was 37% of all respondents. In *Table 2* the figures of our surveys are broken down with respect to age and sex of the respondents. Older persons are – as is to be expected – the least experienced and more than 90% of the older women have no experience with computer technology at all. If you are unfamiliar with something when the person opposite you seemingly is not and if you believe you are dependent on this person for whatever reason then this "something" advances to an object of power and magic. If you see the official in front of you manipulate information technology it does not necessarily arouse your curiosity but, on the contrary, may arouse feelings of insecurity and anxiety, depending on the circumstances of your encounter. The feelings of inferiority may even be re – enforced by the image of speed, impartiality, and efficiency of the computer, especially in the eyes of those who are unexperienced in this technology. Now, lack of compassion is said to be an outstanding feature of bureaucratic procedure (Thompson [21]).

The computer as job – killer, as big brother, and as the symbol of matter – of – factness ..., these notions in the minds of the clients in the citizens office could well be detrimental to the objective to make it easier and more relaxing especially for less experienced clients to get their business settled in the citizens office. While the performance aspect of information technology will be subsumed under the general assessment of the citizens office, the question here is directed to the mere existence of computers, i.e. whether or not the *visible use* elicits adverse reactions.

But how visible is information technology in the citizens office? By chance the implementation process in Unna – it resembled a field – experiment in this respect – offers some answer to this question. Since the opening of the citizens office in February 1984 information technology was used in the head office as well as in the branch offices. The head office was rebuilt and newly furnished for this occasion. In the branch offices business was done as usual for quite a while; one branch office was re – modeled shortly before the survey started, the other after the survey was finished.

Despite any possible bias due to differential return rates *Table 3* shows astonishing percentages of respondents having noticed changes in the bureaux between the time of their last visit and the time before 1984, thus contradicting much common sense reasoning. Apart from this, the figures induce the conjecture that they are a direct reflection not of the visible use of information technology but of the different points in time at which the appearance of the offices was brought up – to – date. Supporting evidence is provided by the comments of the respondents that they had noticed some change in the office in comparison to former times. With respect to the head office only one out of five commented on "computers", "displays" etc., whereas with respect to the branch offices, one out of four mentioned information technology. It comes as no surprise that the computer is mentioned so infrequently by clients of the branch offices. The question on noticed changes was often used as an opportunity to express deep satisfaction with these offices and with the officials working there ("I have *always* had friendly counsel").

In the citizens office, clients seem to be more impressed with the atmosphere of the bureau and the personality of the officials and less impressed by information technology (in other words, the computer), although displays and keyboards are placed on the desk – top between them and the officials. It is also true to say that the majority of respondents evidently is not disturbed when officials use a terminal in their presence. This aparently is the general feeling, independent of whether they have or have not visited the citizens office.

In *Table 4* the overall results are broken down for respondents with various bureaucratic experiences and whether or not they have visited the citizens office. Of course there are widely differing percentages of "don't knows" whereby the rank order can be predicted. The more the respondents know about bureaux in general, or the citizens office in particular, the smaller is the percentage of "don't knows". Let us discard the "don't knows" for the moment and look at the proportion of respondents who feel irritated by

"If you know the citizens office already: Have you noticed any remarkable changes compared to the times before 1984?"

(Respondents only who know the offices from former times)

	Visitors to		
	headquarter office (n=432)	branch office A (n=157)	branch office B (n=73)
Yes, I have noticed some remarkable changes compared to former times	77%	46%	22%

CO headquarters opened in 1984 in rebuilt and newly furnished rooms.
Branch office A opened also in 1984 but was re-furnished shortly before the survey.
Branch office B opened in 1984 and was re-furnished after the survey.

Headquarter and branch offices are equipped with information technology since 1984.

Table 3
There are changes due to the citizens office which are more remarkable than the introduction of information technology

"When you go to an office and data-displays are used there – do you in any way feel irritated in your conversation with the official?"

Respondents who ...	don't know	feel not irritated	feel irritated	base of percentage
... do not yet know the CO and ...				
... have little or no experience with bureaucratic procedures	35%	58% / 90%	7% / 10%	492 / 318
... have moderate or great experience with bureaucratic procedures	16%	74% / 88%	10% / 12%	233 / 197
... know the CO already and ...				
... have little or no experience with bureaucratic procedures	21%	71% / 90%	8% / 10%	414 / 327
... have moderate or great experience with bureaucratic procedures	9%	77% / 85%	14% / 15%	445 / 404

Table 4
Clients feel little irritated when officials use IT in their presence

the visible use of IT in relation to the proportion of respondents who do not. Astonishingly constant proportions (about 1 to 9) become visible over all groups of respondents (hand – written figures). Should an analyst attempt to give another interpretation of these differing ratios, it is impossible to base an explanation on the influence of information technology. Do these respondents see something that less bureaucratically experienced respondents are unable to see? Perhaps it is their notion how IT is *actually* used by bureaucrats?

10% of the respondents answered that they indeed felt irritated by the visible use of information technology. Most of them have commented why. As can be expected the majority of these comments had to do with different facets of the role of information technology in inter – personal communication. But there is a remarkable difference in the quality of the answers of those who have been to the citizens office and of those who have not. While the latter very generally criticise the situation as "impersonal", respondents who have been to the citizens office remark very concretely "the official pays more attention to the machine than to my problem". Nearly half the comments of visitors to the citizens office have this quality. If there is a grain of truth in these answers there could be different reasons: the official uses the monitor to hide from the client (as he has used stacks of paper in former times), the official does not know how to structure the conversation with the client and when to use the monitor (cf. Cruickshank [22] for similar problems arising in medical consultations); or the official has difficulties in mastering the terminal. In any case the remedy lies in better training and qualification of the official and not in a change or abolishment of information technology (with the exception perhaps that the best training is not sufficient to cope with bad software and hardware).

Another cluster of comments was concerned with the fact that the visual display screen cannot be observed by the client in the citizens office. There are arguments for and against such an arrangement. The administration in Unna preferred this arrangement (while other administrations prefer other solutions) as it gives better protection to personal data displayed on the screen. The arrangement can be altered to please the curiosity of the clients – that is not a problem of information technology as such. These results will be followed up in the survey of clients of the citizens office. If there seems to be little impact of information technology as such on the citizen let us ask whether the use of this technology is more impressive. As argued above this question is equivalent to the question how the citizens office as a whole is assessed by the citizens.

4.4.   The citizens office in the eyes of the public

Very bluntly we asked the citizens "After all you know by now – do you believe that for you personally the citizens office has made it easier or more difficult to get your official business done?" Respondents who had not yet been to the citizens office also had a chance to answer other than "don't know". A leaflet in which the citizens office was described was enclosed with the questionaire. While practically none of the respondents answered "more difficult than before", a noticable proportion answered "as easy or as difficult as before". Of course the respondents projected many of their hopes and fears, and also their attitudes and prejudices towards public administration into their answers. *Figure 5* shows the main result.

The information in *Figure 5* is reduced to the bare minimum necessary to assess this result visually. The figure is purposely hand – drawn in order not to fake exactness when the data might contain error margins. The two squares represent the two categories of respondents, those who had not yet visited and those who had visited the citizens office. The rectangular areas within each square represent the number of respondents who answered (as explained in the legend), and are arranged within each square for the following two comparison. Firstly, you can assess the proportion of don't know answers (cannot say) to the proportion of "know" answers by orienting your eyes on the horizontal lines of the square. (Naturally, the proportion of "don't knows" in the group of respondents who have not yet been to the CO is much greater than in the group who had not been.) Secondly, you can assess the differentiation among the "know" answers by orienting your eyes on the vertical lines of the squares. (One must make the comment that the proportion of respondents who think the CO has made official business easier relative to the proportion of respondents who believe it is as easy or as difficult as before *seems* to be among those who have already been to the CO somewhat greater than in the other group.) You can use a ruler and elementary arithmetics to roughly reconstruct the original frequencies. Actually this graphic representation is equivalent to the numeric representation used in *Table 4*.

Obviously, at least part of the increase in the proportion of respondents who believe the CO has made their official business easier is simply due to increased knowledge of those who have been to the CO.

This is not a very thrilling result. But also, part of the increase (visible as the difference in the ratio between "same as before" answers and "easier than before" answers in the two groups) must be due to something else, e.g. chance errors, attributes in which the respondents themselves differ, or characteristics of the CO.

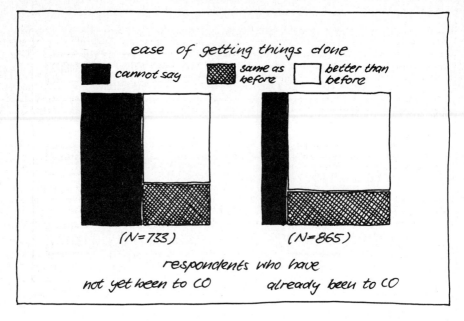

Figure 5
Assessment of the "utility" of the citizens office by both those who have and have not been there

Chance errors: Any difference between proportions is significant if the sample becomes just large enough. It is highly probable that the direction and the magnitude of the difference in the ratios shown in *Figure 5* are not due to chance. From the policy point of view, is the observed difference in proportion in any way remarkable? The results shown certainly are not as spectacular as the results of Lange and Sippel (cf. *Figure 1* above). And why should the differences shown in *Figure 5* be given more weight than those shown in *Table 4*? If it should be possible to show that these differences can be explained with characteristics of the citizens office, then it is indeed a remarkable result. After all, it must be remembered that there are citizens who are so proficient in getting their affairs settled in public bureaux that the CO does not offer any improvements. Then there are citizens who are perhaps not so proficient but have business mainly with other bureaux than the CO; for them also the opening of the the CO has brought little or no change for the better.

Personal attributes: People who know the citizens office may differ in many personal attributes from those who do not yet know the citizens office. We know, for example that more married women visit public bureaux than married men, simply, because fewer married women are the principal bread – winners. The most important personal attributes I can think of which influence the individual assessment of the citizens office are differential experiences with bureaucratic procedures (especially whether or not oneself is engaged in such procedures in private or public bureaucracies) and one's attitudes towards (public) bureaucracy in general and the town administration in particular. One of the hypotheses would be: respondents who know the CO assess the CO more positively than respondents who do not know the CO because more of them are generally more positively inclined towards public administration. The way we measured it, this hypothesis has to be refuted, together with any similar hypothesis on differing degrees of "bureaucratic experience".

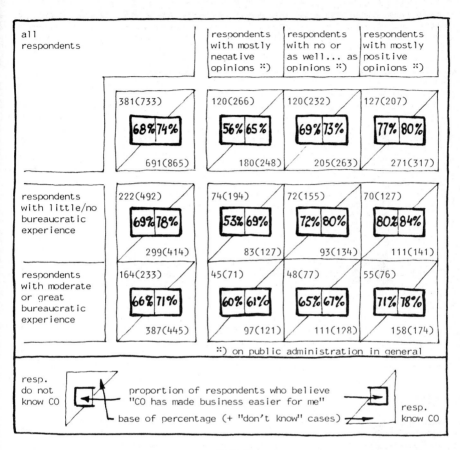

all respondents	respondents with mostly negative opinions *)	respondents with no or as well... as opinions *)	respondents with mostly positive opinions *)
381(733) **68% 74%** 691(865)	120(266) **56% 65%** 180(248)	120(232) **69% 73%** 205(263)	127(207) **77% 80%** 271(317)
respondents with little/no bureaucratic experience 222(492) **69% 78%** 299(414)	74(194) **53% 69%** 83(127)	72(155) **72% 80%** 93(134)	70(127) **80% 84%** 111(141)
respondents with moderate or great bureaucratic experience 164(233) **66% 71%** 387(445)	45(71) **60% 61%** 97(121)	48(77) **65% 67%** 111(128)	55(76) **71% 78%** 158(174)

*) on public administration in general

resp. do not know CO — proportion of respondents who believe "CO has made business easier for me" — resp. know CO — base of percentage (+ "don't know" cases)

Table 5
Regardless of experiences with/in bureaucracies and regardless of opinion on public administration in general, more respondents who know the CO than those who do not believe that the CO makes their official business easier

In a mail survey we cannot measure all variables as accurately as methodological purists wish. We did not actually measure attitudes towards public administration but gathered responses on a sample of opinion statements on public administration which we used in turn to differentiate between three groups of respondents: those with distinct positive opinions; those with distinct negative opinions; and those with no opinions or with very balanced opinions. Respondents with either excessively favorable or unfavorable opinions were excluded from the analysis. Similarly we did not measure the degree of "objective" exposure to bureaucratic procedures but asked whether the respondents considered themselves experienced with work and procedures in offices and bureaux. We know that this self – assessment is correlated with the extensity and intensity of "exposure" to bureaucracies as well as with the inclination to voice one's interest against public administration. We have grouped together the respondents who considered themselves basically inexperienced with bureaucratic procedure and those who considered themselves moderately or well experienced.

In *Table 5* a three – dimensional topic is represented whereby the prime information is the percentage of respondents who believe that with the opening of the CO the handling of official business has become easier for them. This percentage is hand – written. It is based on the number of respondents who have *not* answered "don't know".

It is this table on which my argument rests, that *Figure 5* presents the basic result with regard to the assessment of the citizens office by the citizens themselves. Compare all the percentages between those who do not know the CO and those who do know the CO. Whatever combination of the personal attributes (experience and opinion) you look at, more respondents in the group who have been to the CO assess it positively than those in the corresponding group who have not been to the citizens office. This holds despite the small size of the bases which makes the calculation of percentages look rather awkward. Furthermore, most of the additional information which is contained in the marginal distributions is mirrored in the lowest level of aggregation. For example, the marginal distribution with respect to differences in opinion suggests that the more favorable the opinion the higher the proportion of positive assessments regardless of whether or not the respondents know the CO. This relation holds without exception when the data are disaggregated. For some of the relations there are of course exceptions which make more or less sense. All in all, the data displayed in *Table 5* are very consistent. I am confident that people who have been to the citizens office indeed tend to assess it more positively than people who have not been there yet – regardless what they think of public administration and what they know of the bureaucratic way of life. *Figure 5* expresses all this.

I may add that, with respect to the question *how* impressive the CO is, *Table 5* is also suggestive. While those citizens who do not think well about public administration and know much about bureaucracy are little impressed by the citizens office, citizens who also do not think well of public administration but admit they have little or no experience are likelier to be positively impressed by the citizens office once they get to know it. This is just but a hypothesis.

Characteristics of the CO: It is time to ask, what is it that makes the CO to be so positively assessed by its clients. As yet, there are no figures to give a detailed answer. After having studied series of cross – tabulations and reading all the comments by the respondents, I suspect that it is not so much what the citizens office has to offer to its clients (i.e. the effects of the design features of the CO mentioned above) but what it stands for in the eyes of the citizens. The citizens office is a *visible sign* of an earnest attempt to change something within the administration in the interest of the citizen. The citizens office, as a symbol and not so much the actual "performance" of the citizens office, is honored by the clients. Of course, the performance must be without major faults and flaws so that the citizens office can satisfy its symbolic function successfully. This is my personal assessment which is not shared by all project members. I shall present some corroborating evidence, not so much to prove my point of view but to illustrate it. After the survey among the clients of the citizens office we hope to know.

It goes without saying that there have been changes in procedures with the opening of the citizens office and some tasks are either done quicker or with less effort on the citizen's side, e.g. blanks for passports and identity cards have no longer to be filled out by the applicant. He just signs an application form which has been prepared and printed by the system in his presence. The use of information technology in the citizens office has not made all task – handling faster. The astonishingly frequent remark of the respondents "things go faster (and officials have become friendlier)" only partly describes objective reality. It may simply be an expression of satisfaction. But there are also several possibilities for a distortion of perception. Computers are synonyms for speed, the use of computers ought to make task – handling faster. Or, sitting in front of the official and watching her do this and that makes time pass faster than waiting at a counter while the official does her task unseen in the back of the bureau.

It fits into the picture that there is no difference in the assessment of the citizens office when the respondents are grouped according to the business they had settled in the citizens office, whether it was a task formerly done in the citizens registration department, whether it was one of the tasks formerly residing in one of the other departments, or whether respondents had asked for information and advice. The ratio between the respondents believing official business has become easier and those who see no difference remains the same. It also fits into the picture that more of the respondents who usually visit one of the branch offices felt that things have become easier for them then in the average ... although in the branch offices there have been the least changes. Time and again during the course of the project, people in the suburbs had been confronted with the threat that the branch offices could be closed for cost reasons. The citizens office has resolved this to the satisfaction of the people in the suburbs.

SURVEY 1982	SURVEY 1986
"Do you believe that a citizens office as it is described in the leaflet will be rather useful or rather superfluous for the citizens here in Unna?"	"After all you know by now – do you believe that for you personally the citizens office has made it easier or more difficult to get your official business done?"
(1190 respondents)	(1638 respondents)

rather superfluous	**6%**	same as before	**18%**	
rather useful	**63%**	easier than before	**50%**	
don't know	**28%**	don't know	**28%**	
no response	**3%**	no response	**3%**	

Table 6
Citizens have given advance credit to the municipal administration with regard
to the usefulness of the citizens office (authors'data)

I would like to add my final impression. Is it not surprising how many of the respondents believe the CO has made official business easier for them although they have not yet been there? *Table 6* shows the original percentages (adjusted for stratification effects of the sample) and compares them with the answers to a similar question in our first survey. I cannot but interpret these figures as an expression of advance laurels with which the original plans of the municipal administration have been credited by the citizens. These figures have more to do with trust and mistrust of the citizen than with the actual output of the citizens office. And the municipal administration seems to have not disappointed the hopes and expectations of the citizens. While in 1982 quite a few respondents critically remarked on costs and effects of the project, hardly such a remark was made in 1986 ... and the citizens of Unna are very critical with respect to other public enterprises, where they have not changed their opinions during the past four years.

5. IS THERE A LESSON TO BE LEARNED?

I am sorry that I cannot present findings which are sensational, in the sense that something awfully bad resulted for the citizen despite the good intentions of all concerned with the development and implementation of the citizens office. Quite to the contrary facts and impressions suggest that the citizens office operates successfully (in the citizens' judgement) – at least for the moment – and that irritations which do exist can be cured with reasonable effort... if, so might be added, these cures (longer opening hours, more staff – training in client – official communication etc.) are really wanted. It should also be mentioned that there still are some discrepancies between concept and reality particularly with respect to the integration of tasks of a somewhat more complex nature into the citizens office (e.g. rent and housing subsidies which are now attached to the department of social welfare). These amendments also seem possible if they are to be pursued hard enough.

Of course, there are circumstances which make the product of (near to) all non – trivial systems development projects sub – optimal in one aspect or the other. We all have experienced them at times: missed opportunities, lack of skills, phantasy, or patience, slacking morale, ups and downs in motivation, uneasy compromises. These and many other circumstances are so common that they are regarded to constitute "normal" systems development. In fact, in order to compensate for their effects it is not unusual to set goals higher than can be achieved realisitically and to be quite satisfied if a reasonable part of these goals is realized at all. (It is intriguing but out of place here to follow the thought of what this understanding of normal systems development means in the context of a participative development strategy where goals reflect hopes and expectations of those affected by the system in the future as well as promises of those who actually build the system.)

The citizens office project, which lasted 7 years and in which up to 15 specialists have been engaged at times, also suffered under such circumstances. I do not want to stress the fact that the project has fallen somewhat short of its original aims. Instead I want to tell you of an observation which seems to have significance beyond this particular project. The project was conducted under very favorable conditions. It was richly endowed with personnel, expertise, time and money. "Positive citizen outcomes" was the paramount objective. There was strong partisanship for this objective as well as a political climate in the municipality which was conducive for the project. Nonetheless resources were limited and the support for citizen – oriented objectives not unbounded.

Because of these limited resources, choices had to be made as for what or for what not to use them. Because the support for citizen – oriented objectives is limited there exists a possibility that choices are made in favor of other objectives. Actually in situations of choice there seems to be a bias "away" from citizen – oriented objectives which is due to their very nature. Let us consider once more the objective to reduce the citizens' costs and effort in settling their affairs with public offices. I have already shown that any such concept must be multi – dimensional. I have also mentioned that the logical and empirical relations between the dimensions of such a concept are not at all clear and that there are measurement problems. Apart from these problems there are problems of identifying relationships of cause – and – effect. There is no simple and straightforward relationship between any one measure of administrative reform or any one systems development activity and this objective. (A comfortable astmosphere in a bureau does not necessarily induce comfortable feelings in a client visiting this bureau.) There are many competing causes and intervening variables which make it uncertain to which effect a single activity or a package of administrative reform will really lead. Some of the policy problems and some of the research problems with respect to (positive) citizen impacts have the same roots.

If choices are made between alternative actions the one will be selected which promises the higher pay – offs. With regard to an action which supposedly contributes to a citizen – oriented objective you cannot calculate the pay – offs let alone calculate differences in pay – offs between this and another action contributing, say, to the efficiency of administrative procedures. Even when there is strong partisanship for a citizen – oriented objective, this objective has a difficult stand. The more so, if the efficacy of the rule "a bird in the hand is worth two in the bush" for decision – making should remain unnoticed and thus uncontested. There are risky but nonetheless worthy goals of information systems development projects. Citizen – oriented objectives are among them. We can never be absolutely sure whether we will be right or wrong in what we do in information systems development. All we can strive for is a solution which is considered to be appropriate by those who are affected by this system. As long as no complaints are voiced we shall feel free to believe that our task is well done. And when dissatisfaction is voiced because afterwards "one always knows better" then, by all means, we should be sure to have thought of this possibility and to have made provisions in order to remedy the defects.

REFERENCES

[1]   Hirschheim, R.A.: The Effect of A Priori Views on the Social Implications of Computing, ACM Computing Surveys 18 (1986) 165 – 195.

[2]   Brinckmann, H. et al., Automatisierte Verwaltung (Campus, Frankfurt, 1981)

[3]   Blennerhasset, E., Information Technology and the Public Service, paper presented at the EIPA Seminar "Information Technologies and their Utilisation by Sub – Central Government" at Maastricht – NL – May 6/8 1985 (Institute of Public Administration, Dublin, April 1985, xerographed)

[4]   Lange, K. and Sippel, F., Citizen – Benefits from Information Systems, paper presented at the IFIP WG 8.2 Working Conference on "Information Systems Assessment" at Noordwijkerhout – NL – 27/29 August 1986, procedings in print.

[5]   Lange, K. and Sippel, F., Verwaltungsautomation und Buergerservice. (Westdeutscher Verlag, Opladen, 1986)

[6]   Dunker, K. and Noltemeier, A., (eds.), Organisationsmodelle fuer ein Buergeramt und deren Realisierung in der Stadt Unna (Gesellschaft fuer Mathematik und Datenverarbeitung, Sankt Augustin – D – , 1985, GMD studies No.95)

[7] Kommunale Gemeinschaftsstelle fuer Verwaltungsvereinfachung (KGSt), Das Buergeramt Unna (KGSt, Cologne, 1986, report No.16/1986)

[8] Dunker, K., Introducing IT in Local Government, paper presented at the EIPA Seminar on "Information Technologies and Their Utilization by Sub – Central Government" at Maastricht – NL – May 6/8, 1985 (Gesellschaft fuer Mathematik und Datenverarbeitung, Sankt Augustin – D – , October 1985, xerographed)

[9] Kraemer, K. L., Proposals for Research on Citizen Outcomes from Information Technology in Public Administrations (Public Policy Research Organization, Irvine CA, November 1980, xerographed)

[10] Mambrey, P. et al., Computer und Partizipation, (Westdeutscher Verlag, Opladen, 1986)

[11] Ehrenberg, U., Anwaltsplanung im Rahmen partizipativer Systementwicklung. (Gesellschaft fuer Mathematik und Datenverarbeitung, Sankt Augustin – D – , September 1986, GMD working papers No.218)

[12] Oppermann, R., User Participation – Some Experiences and Recommendations, Systems, Objectives, Solutions 4 (1984) 157 – 168.

[13] Patton, M. Q., Utilization – Focused Evaluation, 2nd ed. (Sage, Beverly Hills, 1986)

[14] Weiss, C. H., Evaluation Research (Prentice – Hall, Englewood Cliffs NJ, 1972)

[15] Liedtke, B. H., Buergerumfrage Unna 1982 – Konzept und Durchfuehrung (Gesellschaft fuer Mathematik und Datenverarbeitung, Sankt Augustin – D – , 1984, GMD studies No.83)

[16] Liedtke, B. H., Ergebnisse der Publikumsbefragung 1981 und der Buergerumfrage 1982 in Unna (Gesellschaft fuer Mathematik und Datenverarbeitung, Sankt Augustin – D – , 1984, GMD studies No.92)

[17] Sterling, Th. D., Guidelines for Humanizing Computerized Information Systems – A Report from Stanley House, Communications of the ACM 17 (1974) 609 – 613.

[18] Kling, R., Citizen orientation of automated information systems, Information Age 4 (1982) 215 – 223.

[19] Sharp, E. B., Responsiveness in Urban Service Delivery – The Case of Policing, Administration and Society 13 (1981) 33 – 58.

[20] International Business Machines Corporation (IBM) Germany, (ed.), Computer Image Studie 1986 (Sindelfingen – D – , November 1986, xerographed)

[21] Thompson, V. A., Without Sympathy or Enthusiasm – The Problem of Administrative Compassion, 3rd print. (University of Alabama Press, University AL, 1975)

[22] Cruickshank, P.J. et al., The computer in the consultation and the reaction of the patient (MRC/ESRC Social and Applied Psychology Unit, University of Sheffield, Sheffield – UK – , undated [1984], memo No.653)

Governmental and Municipal Information Systems
P. Kovács and E. Straub (Editors)
Elsevier Science Publishers B.V. (North-Holland)
© IFIP, 1988

INFORMATION SERVICES TO REGIONAL AND LOCAL AUTHORITIES — NEW DIMENSIONS

Gunnar Karlström, Director, Kommun-Data AB
S-125 86 Älvsjö, Sweden

ABSTRACT

Parallell to the technical orientation of information technology (IT), in recent years some questions concerning different kinds of the consequences of IT have been focused e. g. consequences on privacy, vulnerability, organization, work environment, efficiency. This paper will briefly highlight various tendencies from the point of view of technical, economic and human aspects concerning the use of IT in local governments in Sweden.

1. INTRODUCTION

Kommundata was founded in 1965 by the Swedish Union of Local Authorities. In 1976 the Federation of County Councils became a part owner to 1/3 of the stock. Kommundata operates in competition with other alternatives to provide information services to local governments e. g. own services, other service bureaus. Kommundata, however, holds a strong position on the market. 275 out of 284 communes and 13 out of 24 county councils are mainly served by Kommundata and its subsidiaries. Sales in 1986 was about 850 Million SEK equal to 130 Million US $.

The original role of the company was that of a traditional service bureau — systems development combined with computer services on central computers. In recent years the company has analysed and developed its activities to meet the future demands from its customers. The result is a concrete plan covering a wide variety of aspects. The realization of this plan started a couple of years ago and will continue the following years.

A long range plan covering the next three years has been worked out. Some main elements in this plan from the point of view of the customer are
- policies and development concerning hardware, software and applications
- a widened set of IT services
- IT in new organizanal structures in local governments aiming at deepened democracy and improved services
- questions concerning security and vulnerability
- cost-benefit aspects on the use of IT

From the point of the company some elements are
- reformulation of business idea
- definition of new business areas
- economic goals
- policies for marketing, systems development, methods etc

2. BUSINESS IDEA

A fundamental basis when establishing Kommundata was to develop standard applications for local government administration and planning, applications to be utilized by a great number of customers and easily modified to meet special requirements from certain customers. From this basis combined with the possibilities and demands of today and in the future the following business idea has been outlined:

> — Kommundata provides on a business oriented basis services that benefit local government activities.
> — The deep experience in IT and customer activities profile Kommundata as the natural partner for local and regional governments.
> — Kommundata provides a spectrum of services: computer services, software, hardware consultancy and training.

The business idea will stress business orientation, benefit to the customer, skill and a wide range of services.

3. BUSINESS AREAS

The computer services, on a service bureau-basis, are estimated to decrease in relation to other areas, although this has not yet occurred. The business areas of the company have been analysed in order to meet future demands. The different business areas, their relative proportion of the total business in 1986 and a forecast for 1990 is shown below.

Business area	Share of total revenue	
	1986	1990
Service bureau and computer services	72	68
Software	8	10
Consultancy	8	10
Training	2	5
Hardware	10	7

4. MARKET ORIENTATION

Like other companies in most branches the earliest phase of Kommundata was production-orientation, when technique was dominating. The next phase was product-oriented and since the early 80's the company is organized on a market-oriented basis. This has meant a sector-oriented organization based on divisions serving the different customer sectors — local authorities, county councils and companies owned by those bodies.

The market-orientation also has meant a decentralization of the company to regional and local offices. During the first ten years the company only had its main office, in Stockholm. Today there are 25 offices throughout the country, some of them with comprehensive computer installations.

The decentralization have had a great impact on the deversification of knowledge and use of IT.

5. HARDWARE AND SOFTWARE

In the early 80's Kommundata outlined a hardware concept including central and regional mainframes cooperating with minis, micros and PC:s according to customer demands and applications design. Due to size, organization etc customer demands are very varied.

Principal features of the hardware concept are

Level	Use	Manufacture
central	batch, interactive	IBM, Unisys
region	interactive	IBM
local	interactive	Datapoint, Ericsson, IBM, Unisys

The above concept shows the actual situation of an ongoing process.

For details as to hardware and systems software see appendix 1.

Tendencies for the future in the above concept are
- the applications will in many cases be available alternatively on mainframes, minis or PC:s
- extended coordinated use of computers of different size and from different manufactures

Guidelines for recent development are
- use of high-level languages
- portability as to hardware and software
- user involvment in systems design by means of data modelling

Applications designed on these bases are e. g. for environmental control, for fire prevention and a comprehensive system for health care based on dedicated computers for each clinic. This system includes inpatient and outpatient care, care records etc.

These applications are developed on basic computers (super minis) according to the specifications of the National Office for Administrative Rationalization and Economy. UNIX operating system and 4th generation languages, mainly MIMER and PROGRESS, have been used.

6. COMMUNICATIONS

Communication will play an important role in future IT in order to use equipment from different manufacturers in a net. On the local level there are nets from the different manufacturers, SNA from IBM, DCA from Unisys, ARC from Datapoint. Apart from these nets Kommundata has chosen NOVELL for local communication between PC:s. Nationwide communication between Kommundata's centers and its customers are at present provided by the PTT. For net services in the future, designed to meet the various demands of the customers, Kommundata is analysing the possibilities to establish a nationwide net based on leased lines with net services provided by Kommundata.

7. VALUE-ADDED APPLICATIONS

A project group of local government board members and managers is engaged in specifying an IT tool for decision support, planning and access to internal and external databases. In this way the comprehensive databases built up during a long period for local government administration may be given a substantially widened use for decision support and planning by commissioners and management.

Examples of databases for these purposes are those for staff, economy, population, care for children and elderly, external databases from banks, central government offices, information databases etc. Easy-to-learn, easy-to-use, presentation in graphics characterize the design.

The example below shows the presence of staff and children in day nurseries which might be of value to a decision-maker.

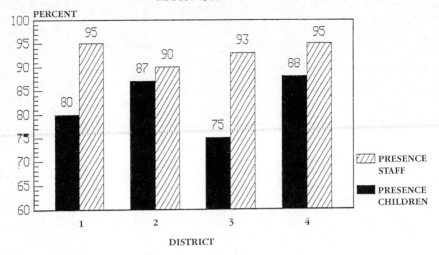

PRESENCE CHILDREN AND STAFF
DISTRICT 1—4
AUGUST 1987

8. IT IN NEW ORGANIZATIONAL STRUCTURES

An ongoing development is the decentralization of political decision functions in order to increase the involvement of the citizens. Besides to deepen democracy and stimulate involvement the goal is to improve services for better correspondence to the demands of the citizens. Means of doing this is decentralization and integration of services to the basic level. The former strictly sector oriented organization will be replaced by decentralized bodies serving various functions. New organizational structures under evaluation are local boards responsible for a number of sectors and cost/revenue responsible work-teams.

New organizational structures also mean new demands on IT. The applications are often developed in total for a local government, staff administration, general ledger etc. The needs of the local office serving various functions will mean easy access to information of various kinds — staff, economy, population etc. Realizing this requires
       — a communication structure
       — standardized terminal procedures
       — activity oriented applications instead of sector oriented

Jointly Kommundata and some communes work in project aiming at illustrating the IT requirements in a long-range process of change satisfying the need from the following viewpoints:
       — new control functions
       — decentralized local government activities
       — deepened democracy and involvement from the citizens

The IT-needs are analysed from the aspects of the following groups:
       — citizen
         - access to information on local governments services
       — staff
         - liability and authority will be delegated to basic units with cost/revenue
           responsibilities
       — commisioners board and management
         - efficient tools for target formulation and control

9. STRATEGIES AND PLANS FOR IT

Politicians and trade unions have more and more started to pay attention to use and development of IT. As a result of this several municipalities have adopted policies and plans for their use of IT. An IT policy adopted by the municipal council might have the following main components:

— scope
  - the policy shall include data processing word and image handling
— basic view
  - IT development shall be activity-driven
  - by means of the benefits of IT resources shall be allocated from adminsitration to service
  - special attention shall be paid to staff conditions, job security, work environment, professional skill, education and training
  - free access to public documents may not be affected by new technique
  - high standard of security shall be kept up to avoid interruptions and unauthorized use
— organization
  - IT policy questions shall be handled by the executive board
  - the current planning and coordination shall be performed by a steering committee, chief officials and staff representatives

Some concrete projects in connection with these policies will be mentioned in the following, those concerning security and vulnerability, job environment and cost/benefit analyses.

10. INTEGRITY, SECURITY AND VULNERABILITY

The increasing use of IT focuses questions on the integrity of the individual, security and vulnerability. The balance between the needs of the authorities to provide efficient services and the individuals' needs for their sphere of integrity is continuously beeing discussed. A means of satisfying these interests is a high degree of security in IT-use.

Two aspects on this theme will be discussed in the following. The first concerns authority to access information. Kommundata recently has published its specification to an access control system to be used internally in systems development and externally when formulating demands on suppliers of hardware and software. The access control system also has to satisfy The Legislation on Privacy and Security.

The specifications of the access control system includes the following main components:

— identification
  - design of identity, duration, uniqueness
— verification with password
— verification with question - answer
— verification with magnetic card
— design of access and access control
  - individual and group access
  - various possible limitations as to access
— access control administration
  - registration, logging
— security functions

Another operational instrument for methodical analysis of security and vulnerability is the SBA-method, jointly developed by the Vulnerability Board and the Swedish Federation of Data Processing Users in cooperation with industry and authorities. The method will in a few hours enable a company or a government agency to analyse whether security weakness exists in their data processing systems (DP systems).

The method is based on the following requirements:
- The company/government agency should itself be able to assess the vulnerability of its DP systems.
- The company/government agency should be able to test its own vulnerability and dependence on external systems.
- The testing method should be well-defined and easy to understand, and little time should be needed to train people to use the method.
- The method should be applicable both to a total assessment of the company/government agency's DP systems, as well as to assessments of individual DP systems.

11. WORK ENVIRONMENT

The increasing use of IT will mean changes in work environment for certain groups. This circumstance has since long been observed by the trade unions. In IT-policies they have defined their attitudes to a number of questions concerning IT. They all express a fundamental positive view on IT, provided that the consequences will be better services, efficiency and a good working climate.

Below some of the demands are quoted.
- job security and meaningful jobs shall be warrented to everyone
- an IT policy and a long-range development plan shall be worked out in local and regional governments
- operations at a terminal may not be the dominating part of the job
- participation in systems development
- ongoing education and training in new techniques
- fundamental job experience may not be lost

Some groups are estimated to be more concerned when IT-use increases e. g. doctor's secretaires, office employees, map-drawers. To make preparations for the new work environment Kommundata and the trade unions jointly have developed a training programme for doctor's secretaires. The present work of the secretaires has been analysed, possible changes have been considered and on these bases a training programme has been developed including the following parts.
- to use a PC
- word-processing
- calculations
- database handling

12. COST-BENEFIT ANALYSES

The demands for services provided by regional and local governments are continually increasing, demands for a higher aspiration level, demands for better services. As well the demographic structure of the population will claim increased services. The costs for public services are even today so considerable that rationalization by means of IT is desirable. Today the total costs for EDP in local and regional governments still are very low, 0.5—1.0 percent of the total expenditure.

Competing with other necessary investments it will be more and more important that investments in IT will give an added value, higher than the costs for this investment. Cost-benefit analyses of IT-projects has often been neglected due to lack of methods.

The costs of an investment in hardware or software may be calculated, although above all the investments in software have been underestimated.

Due to difficulties to quantify certain variables the return of the investment is still harder to estimate. There is some experience in certain areas. Two of these will be briefly described below.

Some fundamental variables of benefit are
- increased production
- increased quality
- savings

Further we can talk about direct and indirect effects.

The implementation of an information system in the health care sector can illustrate the different effects.

	Examples of	
	Direct effects	**Indirect effects**
Staff costs	Less case record handling	Shorter average caretime
Other costs	Less need for paper	Less costs for drugs

The medical staff, in general, spend about 35 percent of their time to keep case records. The direct effects on revenue when using an information system is 5—15 percent depending on the kind of care. In addition to that there will be indirect effects e. g. shortened average care time which gives substantial cost reductions.

Another example from day nurseries. Here the costs for administration are very low whereas the costs for running the day nursery are very high. When implementing an information system the cost reductions for administration are of less interest. On the other hand an effective information system for treating supply and demand for day nurseries will increase the capacity of the day nurseries by about 10 percent.

13. REFERENCES

1. Gustafsson A: Local Government in Sweden. The Swedish Institute, Lund, (1983).
2. I.T. in Municipalities and County Councils, SOU 1983:35. Stockholm (1983).
3. Coordinated Public Information, SOU 1984:68. Stockholm (1984).
4. Swedish Information Technology, A Basis For A National I.T.-program. Stockholm (1984).
5. Freese Jan: The Swedish Data Act. The Swedish Institute, Stockholm (1982).
6. DASIS. Informationsystem for the healthcare sector. Effect-study. STU info 610-1987. Stockholm (1987).

KOMMUNDATA HARDWARE AND SYSTEMS SOFTWARE **Appendix 1**

Device	Manufacturer	Model/version	Number
Processors	IBM	3090-150	3
		4361	1
		4381	8
		3083	1
	Sperry	1100/92	1
		1100/81	1
		1100/74	1
		1100/72	1
Disk systems	IBM	3380	44
		3370	10
	Sperry	8480	15
		8470	36
		8433	8
Tape systems	IBM	3420/8	32
	Sperry	U 36	38
Impact printers	IBM	3283	8
		4245	3
	BASF	6603	2
Laser printers	Sperry	0777	7
	Siemens		2
Communications processors	IBM	3725	11
		3705	3
	Sperry	DCP/40	7
		DCP/10	2
Operating systems	IBM	MVS/XA	
		DOS/VSE	
		VM	
	Sperry	05-1100	
Database systems	IBM	IMS/DB	
	Sperry	DMS-1100	
Networking systems	IBM	ACF/VTAM	
		NCP NCCF	
		NPDA	
	Sperry	DCP/TELCOM	
		CMS 1100	
Access methods		VTAM	
Programming languages		COBOL	
Programming aids		Oliver	
		Simon	

Governmental and Municipal Information Systems
P. Kovács and E. Straub (Editors)
Elsevier Science Publishers B.V. (North-Holland)
IFIP, 1988

COORDINATE REFERENCE /GEOCODE/ FOR SPATIAL ORIENTED DATA

Gyula   DEME

Geodetic and Cartographic Department, National Office of Lands and
Mapping, Ministry of Agriculture and Food, Hungary
P.O. Box 1, Budapest 55. H-1860

Due to the rapid spreading of microcomputers, the computer resources
and data bases are gradually decentralized. This flow which may
better benefit the potential users lays an emphasis on exact spatial
or areal entity definitions, structuring concepts and, not least, the
problem complexity of geocoding. In order to create a common basis
on which the decentralized systems may act and develop together, the
fundamental requirements have been recently regulated by the Law of
Geocoding in Hungary.

1.   INTRODUCTION

A spatial data base should be a multifaceted model of geographic reality.
This statement whose veracity timelessly stands its ground has its certain
meaning in the world of integrated data systems. Its explanation, however,
should be newly considered in the era of microcomputers, when the creation and
access of data bases mostly because of distribution possibilites both for computer resources and data should be reconceived. Being bound toward a new situation in data storage, which seems to be a more user friendly solution than
large central data banks, one may regard in Hungary as a milestone the creation of a unique identifier, since it provides a nationally accepted reference
scheme which is based on unique geodetic coordinates.

1.1. Historical precedents

Recently a provision of law regulating the application of the coordinate reference based schemes, simply stated, Law of Geocoding has been enacted in
Hungary. The research founding this legislation dates back to a roughly ten
year period. Of course, such activity cannot be immune to external effects.
Some Hungarian researchers as early as in the mid-70s had a faint picture
about the Swedish Land Data System, where centroid coordinates were used for
both the cadastral units and the buildings, too, in addition to the cadastral
code. Geographic information systems were implemented in several municipalities in the United States, e.g. in St.Louis, in Des Moines etc., where the
geographic data were identified and retrieved also by centoid coordinates.
The census blocks in the Dual Independent Map Encoding (DIME) system were also
provided with coordinate identifiers. In the land parcel registers of Ottawa
(Ontario, Canada) calculated centroids replace the parcel enumeration numbers.
Certainly, other historical precedents could have been listed up, too, which
exerted some effect when the concept was formed on the basis of which the
aforementioned Law of Geocoding was conceived, worded and tabled.

1.2. Aspects of classification

The different types of geocoding are treated in the Manual of Remote Sensing
(1976, Vol. I. p. 620; source: Tomlinson, 1972). There are four fundamental
types of geocoding as:

- external index: this includes all the list-type identifiers, such as: serial
numbers, parcel enumeration numbers, postal codes etc.

- arbitrary grid (raster or implicit) encoding: each square grid is identified
by its starting coordinate, and of course, the grid properties should be also
given. This is the standard format to which the remotely sensed and scanned
images are encoded.

- explicit boundary: vector polygons of loose-type lines, or lines circumscribing an area are used for encoding.

- point coordinate reference: centroids (central location points, centers etc.)
are used for area encoding. In this encoding system, points and lines can be .
considered as special cases of areas and can be treated in the same way.

1.3. Why point coordinate reference has been preferred

Conversely with the possible opinions which think a geodetic coordinate very
hard for many categories of users, the choice fell on the type of the point
coordinate reference, because it was preconceived, that

a/ the coordinate identification system can be easily added to the contents
of the existing maps of various scales. Thus the majority of users meets only
the graphic presentation of geocoding: a marked point on a screen or on a map.
One can select an interested area by positioning a floating index or a sensor.
A potential user may have little business to the numerical value of a centroid.

b/ In special cases of application, the other types of geocoding could be of
assistance. As was mentioned, some types of information can be stored more
advantageously in an arbitrary grid system. Moreover, for circumscribing a
socio-economic entity, simply stated, an areal object, vector polyogons are
inevitably necessary. The system designer has to find an effective solution,
the sooner the better, to the sometimes penalizing raster/vector interface
problem. In our concept, by means of point coordinate reference, which super-
imposes both, and by its linking mechanism the various ways of geocoding can
be effectively amalgamated.

c/ Similarly, the point coordinate reference does not mean the exclusion of
any list-type identifier. All the old and new identifiers and codes referring
to the same object should be included in an attribute system, where each
attribute permits a converse access to the centroid concerned.

d/ Comparing a list-type key with a coordinate identifier, the latter turns
the balance, since
- it provides the spatial information for a direct geographic relation
- it provides the information for unique identification
- it strongly supports the so-called "geometric way of retrieval" where the
selection from the data files is made of an inquiry area, simply stated
"window", given by geodetic and/or geometric parameters.

The aforementioned considerations have led to the decision that point coordinate reference was envisioned as legal means for the identification of spatial oriented data, as well as effective tool for associating the map data with nonmap data. Since the name "geocode" for a coordinate identifier was generally accepted, moreover, became rapidly popular, this name is used throughout the legal text and also here in the following.

2.   A short digression to mathematics

It is supposed, that at the majority of geocode applications, the solution where a point with special location separates and simultaneously identifies the aggregations of spatial points, or sets of vectors, was conceived and applied upon empirical considerations. This solution, however, must have mathematical background, too. That may have its roots in dimension theory, possibly in the section, where the expansion number of dimensions and the separative aggregation is defined.

On the basis of some findings in the special literature it can be stated, that a Russian mathematician, P.S. Urison (1898-1924) defined firstly the aforementioned notions, and obtained, that an aggregation of dimension expansion n can be separated correctly by an other aggregation of dimension expansion n-1. Consequently, an aggregation of lines (number of expansion: 1) e.g. a linear map, presenting land parcels and other socio-economic entities circumsrcibed by vector polygons, can be separated into any portions by points with mathematical correctness (number of expansion: 0). Unfortunately, these mathematical considerations has been so far poorly explicated in the context of geocodes.

3.   The complexity of legislation and information management

Turning back again from the unperturbed ideas and models of mathematics to the daily practice, question can be arisen, why legislation can assist in a field where the problems can be solved mostly by information management and organization.

In general, the introduction of a unique identifier in the use of which a wide range of appliers and users are interested needs a major, to say the most, national consent. In the course of the preparation stage of the legislation, the experts interested have the opportunity to get acquainted with the draft and may have word in any detail. The preparation of a provision of law is in general a customary way how the opinions, for and against, and at last the official consent can be obtained. Moreover, in the blueprint stage it can be also cleared up, which institutions will provide for the basic tasks. E.g. the Law of Geocoding prescribes, that the Land Offices have the task to collect the geocodes in registers and they have to control their map presentation. Also they have the responsibility for the maintanance, and for passing the data to the users who pay fee for them. The determination of the geocodes can be carried out by entrepreneurs who possess the skill of surveying and mapping. The latter have the obligation to hand over the replicas of the geocodes with their map presentation to the competent Land Office, free of charge.

The Law of Geocoding deals not only with the licensed activities but it imposes the main features of data organization adherent to the application of geocodes. These regulations serve as basic principles for data organization, and provide for logical conditions for linking the various data structures and contents, by the special means of legislation. Nevertheless, the Law of Geocoding is far from replacing the data organization activity needed for concrete projects and tasks.

3.1. Objects of identification

An object to be identified by a geocode can be any spatial or areal socio-economic entity (a customary example: ownership unit) which can be distinguished by a criterion and can be circumscribed by physical or non-physical (e.g. legal, assumed, fictive) border. An object should have stable form in a certain time interval.

A spatial or areal object can be portrayed on a map at adequate scale. Conventionally any spatial or areal object can be represented by its mapped figure. Its border can be determined by coordinates which can form vectors. Consequently, any border encompassing an object can be represented by a set of vectors which go round clockwise or counter-clockwise. An object but point and line covers a certain map area. Point-like mapped figures and lines can be regarded as special kinds of objects. A point is an object with zero area covering and zero border. A line is an object with zero area and with coincident direct and reverse encompassing vectors. (The treatment of vector coincidences means minor difficulty with a modern computer software, since such cases occur many times at the processing of linear map in conjunction with adjacent land parcels.)

A linear map which in general contains a certain aggregation of the objects can be transformed into computable form by digitizing (accuracy problems and deeper questions of technology must be here disregarded). Following an adequate method at digitizing, the circumscribing vectors and simultaneously, the geocode values can be obtained. They should be loaded into a special data store, namely, surveying and mapping data base, where all sets of vectors are linked to the appropriate geocode i.e. which has an approximately central location within the mapped figure of the object. (Other location is also allowed for objects of peculiar shape but the connection between object and geocode should appear.) As a result from this arrangement, the subscribing vectors of an object can be keyed to a map or to a screen by the help of the geocodes.

3.2. Finiteness of the object sphere

It can be noticed, that the object concept is in fact a new approach to old notions. Objects has been presented long ago on cadastral maps as well as on maps of various scales and that of special contents. Regarding these finite map contents, there is a practical finiteness in the object sphere, too. New object generation can come into being in accordance with map presentation and digital transformation, moreover, the updating capacity should be kept always in the forefront. This step cannot be jumped over because the jungle of spatial information cannot be controlled otherwise, since the objects serve as logical units for the spatial information.

By means of map and graphic screen presentation, the objects and their aggregations can be always overlooked, controlled and manipulated under certain circumstances.

3.3. Relation between objects

The objects may have various spatial locations related to each other. They can be scattered (e.g. farm yards) or adjacent (e.g. land parcels). A larger object can overlap a group of smaller objects so that the latter fill out continuously the area of the larger object (e.g. land parcels fill out a block). In a lot of cases the relations among smaller and larger objects follow the so-called "mosaic principle". If a stable mosaic principle dominates over the object sphere, it is recommended, that vertical relationship, in other words, hierarchical structure would be fixed by linking the geocodes. The resulting geocode structure renders the hierarchy of the objects at any time and presents a basis for retrieval subroutes.

If several hierarchical structures exist, they can ben connected at certain nodal points by means of their common geocodes, if needed. For instable relations temporary geocode aggregations can be created where the retrieval subroutes are used only for a short time.

3.4. Ampleness in structures and reaggregations

Conversely with the practical finiteness of the objects, there is a theoretical infiniteness in structuring and reaggregating the geocodes. By connecting the existing hierarchies, new structures come into being in significant number where selection can be made among numerous retrieval subroutes.

Geocode aggregations can be created by selection, which can be carried out on the basis of the object attributes. It is recommended, that the attributes of an object, among them all the traditional identifiers: land parcel number, postal code etc. should be separately collected, listed up and stored under the geocode concerned. All these solutions multiply the possibilities how geocodes can be regrouped. Regarding, however, the not endless demands and rather, the finite budget of the users, practically these possibilities mean rather an ampleness than infiniteness for structuring and reaggregating the geocodes.

3.5. Raster objects

Lots of information cannot be connected with ease to the normal objects circumscribed by a vector polygon. In several modern data acquiring systems e.g. airborne scanners used in remote sensing surveys, the way of information acquirement has inherently a raster-type nature. A raster unit which contains the information is called raster object and can be identified by its starting coordinate. Of course, a grid system, or in other words, a system of raster objects distributes the sphere of normal objects into portions.

In order to recommend a software-oriented solution to the vector-raster interface problem, in other words, to make use of the raster-oriented information in an object-oriented system, a new solution of identification should be applied.

This solution needs a certain set of map grid intersections, where the coordinates of grid intersections of a certain density (e.g. 100 m) are listed up and stored under the geocode concerned. If the grid system of the raster objects and that stored under the geocodes belong to the same coordinate system, the normal and raster object areas can be rapidly and adequately adjusted to each other (otherwise the grid system of the raster objects should be transformed into the object-oriented system).

A set of map grid intersection values stored under the geocode is very useful for the so-called "geometric way of retrieval" (windowing). Windowing is a customary way of data selection and retrieval for automated map plottings and for graphic screen representations.

The way of retrieval based on map grid intersections especially useful for the retrieval of linear or polygon-shape objects where one dimension of an object is relatively great. The delineation of such an object should be approached and followed by a set of grid intersections whose coordinate is linked, directly and reversely, to the geocode, thus providing for several access subroutes.

4.   Basic principles of application

The Law of Geocoding explicates also the basic principles of the geocode application. A geocode has dual function: on one hand, it acts as common identifier, simultaneously in several data stores, where it identifies

a/ the vector polygon of the object, which imposes a logical unit for storing various thematic (map or nonmap) data;

b/ different thematic data sets. Obviously, a geocode should be repeated as many times as independent identification task it has. Therefore heed should be paid to geocode synchronizing, especially at updatings.

On the other hand, a geocode acts as "object representative" and in this capacity, it "leads a life" independent of the data set it identifies in its first function. In other words, the geocodes can act as means for creating various (stable or temporary) geocode sets or aggregations, at the users' best convenience. When the suitable set of geocodes has been compiled, the necessary data could be keyed to those from the thematic data bases. As was treated in the foregoing, some auxiliary data bases (e.g. hierarchical structure, grid intersections etc.) are needed, mostly, in order to support this second function. (In the use of these auxiliary data bases, the geocode acts again as identifier.)

4.1. Outlines of geocode application in distributed systems

Theoretically, the aforementioned basic principles could be applied to either integrated or distributed data systems. Regarding, however, the rapid conquest of microcomputers, it is more actual if one thinks rather of a distributed application. (The special details of interdependence between distributed system concept and microcomputer network as well as the related hardware and software problems though actual and of great importance are not treated here, because they are dispensable from our narrow subject.)

An information system can be distributed to two main subsystems: at least one central directory and, in theory, no matter how many thematic data bases. Of course, however, the number of individual thematic subsystems is in fact limited by hardware and software features.

4.2. Individual thematic subsystems

It may be supposed, that in a microcomputer network the central directory can be placed onto a microcomputer server or a large mainframe having been inserted in the network. The thematic data bases can be put up to several microcomputers having been installed at competent users who have also the responsibility for the maintanance of the data. Under certain conditions, the competent user may supply other users with data, if the data request can be satisfied by the subsystem of his own. If the data request can be satisfied by two or several individual subsystems, the data request should be raised to the central directory. Assuming, however, a more sophisticated subsystem network, the best way is to put up all request to the central directory. The directory can give a detailed picture at any time, what kind of information are at one's disposal in the distributed system.

It is important, that in the rank of the individual thematic subsystem the surveying and mapping data base should be also aligned, since it contains the circumscribing vector polygons, and further, it operates under the direction of the competent Land Office, which has the responsibility for issuing the geocodes, both at their primary determination and at later updatings. It is prescribed in the Law of Geocoding, that the geocodes should be updated together with the maps on which they appear.

4.3. Experience and further project

As for the question of the praxis, we have some experience only about the implementation and management of the surveying and mapping data base, since a project of an area of 30 square km has been finished recently, where the large scale maps of town Szeged has been put on computers. This can be regarded as an individual thematic data base, with geocodes and vector polygons, updated and suitable for providing digital data source for automated mapping and for some other special task. But that could be more effective as a subsystem of a distributed system where the utilization of data bases could come up to a higher level.

Therefore we make preparatory work in order, that several thematic data bases, together with a central directory could come into being, based on the rules of the Law of Geocoding. A decision is underway to implement a distributed micro computerized system for town Győr, with the following thematic data bases:

-surveying and mapping; operator: Land Office
- land registers; operator: Land Office
- gas pipelines; operator: Municipal Gas Works
- water supply; operator: Municipal Water Works
- electricity, sewage system and
  even two or three other utility
  networks; operators: local companies

- building and house register,
  regulations for constructions; operator:Local Council
- central directory; operator: Local Council

It is important, that the rank of the thematic bases need not be determined for good and all. It can be enlarged, between conventional limits.

5.   Closing remarks

According to technical predictions, the logic based on the philosophy of spatial objects will be much more general already in the 1980s, since the use of the spatial information will enlarge. That means, the spatial data should be effectively addressed and rapidly retrieved, in order to keep pace with the challenges to information use and extraction. We do hope that the Law of Geocoding even if it should be sometimes overlooked and when necessary corrected, will help the progressive flows in technology and will manifest itself in realized systems.

                              R E F E R E N C E S

Klinghammer, I. — Papp-Váry, Á.: Mapped grid at disposal of terrestrial data
    supply and planning. (in Hung.) Geodézia és Kartográfia, 1973/4.
Pittman R., Jr. — Samoska, E., G: Remote graphic display an economical aid for
    environmental considerations .(74-111). Proceedings, of the American Congress
    on Surveying and Mapping. Fall Convention, 1974.
Sweitzer, H.R., Jr.: Computer Mapping with the Census Bureau's Geographic Base
    (DIME) Files (74-112). Proc.of the Am. Congress on Surveying and Mapping.
    Fall Convention, 1974.
Labonté, M.: Memorandum about the method used to find the parcel limits from
    the automated map files of the N.C.C., July, 1976. Manuscript.
Reeves, G.R. (ed.): Manual of Remote Sensing I-II. American Society of
    Photogrammetry. Falls Church, 1976.
Mrs. Májay, P.: Report on study tour in Sweden. (in Hung.)
    1980. IX. 30. - X. 6. Manuscript.
Deme, Gy.: The theory and functions of the geocode. (in Hung.) Geodézia és
    Kartográfia, 1983/3.
Guptill, S.C. — Starr, L.E.: The future of cartography in the information age.
    ICA Commission report on Computer assisted cartography research and develop-
    ment, 1984, pp. 1-15.
Szentesi, A.: Remote sensing and spatial information systems. (in Hung.)
    Thesis of candidature, 1984.
Boda, I.: Distributed data bases. (in Hung.) SZÁMALK, Budapest, 1984.
D.R.F. Taylor: The educational challenges of a new cartography. CARTOGRAPHIA,
    vol. 22. No.4. 1985 pp. 19-37.
Deme, Gy.: A uniform aspect for spatial information. (in Hung.)
    Vezetéstudomány, 1986. augusztus /XVII. évf./, 27-34.o.

P.C. Kelly: A revolution in the provision of cadastral data in Australia: implications at federal level. Paper. FIG XVIII. International Congress, Toronto, Canada 1986.

N.R. Chrisman, D.F. Mezera, D.D. Moyer, B.J. Niemann jr., J.G. Sullivan, A.P. Vonderohe: Soil erosion planning in Winscosin: an application and evolution of a multipurpose land information system. Paper. FIG XVIII. International Congress, Toronto, Canada, 1986.

T. Kalms: Land registration within the concept of LIS. Paper. FIG XVIII. International Congress, Toronto, Canada, 1986.

Balogh, Gy. — Deme, Gy.: The geocode method as new approach in the methodology of the storing and utilization of Cadastral and Land Management Data. Paper. FIG XVIII. International Congress, Toronto, Canada, 1986.

Governmental and Municipal Information Systems
P. Kovács and E. Straub (Editors)
Elsevier Science Publishers B.V. (North-Holland)
© IFIP, 1988

INFORMATION SYSTEMS TO IMPROVE CITIZEN INTERACTION WITH PUBLIC
ADMINISTRATION

Klaus LENK

Universität Oldenburg
P.O.Box 2503
D-2900 Oldenburg

Based on research concerning information needs of citizens, a model
of a Citizen Information System (CIS) is sketched. Special attention is given to its structure, mode of operation, and information
contents. Prospects for implementing CIS are briefly discussed.

1. INTRODUCTION

Concluding from one of the first empirical investigations into the interaction
of public administration with the public, Janowitz et al. wrote in 1958 (3):
"Public Administrators ... must face the reality of a relatively uninfor-
med citizenry. The majority of the population finds it difficult to
translate its self-interest into an adequate level of understanding of
key social welfare programs." And they pursue: "Analyzing administrative
behavior from the point of view of public perspectives is almost certain
to result in policy considerations pointing to the need for public informational programs. (This) is not merely a task of disseminating more
information..."

Three decades later, the complexity of public administration is greater than
ever before, with the citizen being probably less informed about its operations. The information which he receives via the mass media is mostly incohe-
rent. Moreover, he receives it generally at the wrong time.

Yet within the time span considered here, and with the perspective of automated information retrieval, data banks, and remote information processing, a
"better informed citizenry" became an objective of information systems design.
The idea of "Information Utilities" providing information via a network much
like electricity or water, was born (9). In the seventies, national governments, e.g. in Canada, France and Japan, were seriously considering major
information policy choices. Broadband information systems based on bidirectio-
nal Cable TV networks were imagined. Later on, the development of videotex
systems took up the idea of providing administrative information and other
information of general interest.

And yet, only a handful of such systems are operational today. There are still
almost no information systems that would constitute some sort of encyclopaedia
for everyday use (including a store of "instant" information to permit a first
orientation in many practical questions of everyday life). In the more restricted field of information on public administration which is the focus of
this paper, the situation does not look much better. No technical information
systems exist that actually supply answers to the day-to-day problems of citizens applying for public benefits or simply being at loss in their dealings
with the large administrative machineries of the industrialized countries.

It might be worthwhile to investigate why the promise of information technology and an obviously existing demand did not yet meet. There was no lack of critical voices asking repeatedly why information technology was not brought to bear on everyday problems that plague many people in the industrialized countries (8). Whatever may be the reasons for the non-existence of CIS, one thing is obvious. Although some interesting experiences with information technology-based citizen information systems can be identified, there is a lack of adequate concepts that could guide the application and indeed the very development of information technology beyond what is technically feasible.

The present paper aims at filling this conceptual void. A model of a Citizen Information System (CIS) is presented which lends itself to further elaboration. It is expected that its presentation will lead to a more thorough discussion and trigger some new ideas (not necessarily conforming to what is imagined here).

In doing so it is hoped to contribute to identifying socially useful ways of making use of information technology, in accordance with a R&D program on "Man and Technology" launched by the Land of Northrhine-Westphalia, Federal Republic of Germany. The work reported here is carried out under a research grant from this program.

2.   INFORMATION NEEDS

    2.1. Experiences and methodological problems

After an evaluation of incremental videotex-based CIS, it is obvious that new approaches to their design are required. The country where experiments were most widespread and best evaluated is France. The experiences made here since 1980 are important in several respects. Among other results, they show that the importance of administrative information had been grossly overestimated, that the information was often not well presented, and that the difficulties in making use of the information were not only related to information technology.

The results of the evaluation studies cannot be reported here in detail. Special reference is made to (2), (6), (9). Summing up, one is again reminded of the fact that the appeal of a technology looking for a market is an invitation to designing systems that promise a good solution to the wrong problem.

Great care in identifying the problem correctly is therefore required. The first step in developing a CIS must be an assessment of the information needs to which it should respond. For several reasons, this is far more difficult than it seems at first glance.

(1) People rarely identify an "information need" as such. Rather they see it imbedded into a choice of possible courses of action. When making such choices they rarely behave conforming to the model of rational man. An "information system" will in most cases be quite distant from the assumptive world in which its "user" lives.

(2) While citizens and public administration can readily agree upon the statement that "more information is needed", they do not conceive of "information" in the same way. Public agencies will tend to provide raw information, concerning e.g. rights and duties, adresses and opening hours, whereas a citizen C may want an answer to his specific problem. In most cases, this answer cannot be inferred from the raw information provided without further efforts which C himself is not always able to make (7).

(3) "Better information" for the citizen can be an easy-at-hand formula for diverting pressures aimed at changing existing structures in a way that would benefit the public. It can be presumed that information technology was used more than once as a means of preserving a fragmentated scenery of specialized agencies, which brings inconvenients to C (as an "inter-organization client") (4).

(4) The political and legal issue of "freedom of Information", i.e. an administration open for inspection by the public may be an important goal in itself. Yet it is only weakly related to those information needs felt most intensely by the public. The information most people lack in their day-to-day life is of a kind that is already openly available in all major administrative systems in the industrialized world. It may even be feared that insisting too heavily on widening access to administrative records will detract attention from the more urgent information problems.

(5) Most important is the fact that available research findings are far from giving a complete picture of the information needs of citizens in their dealings with public administration. Research originally geared to other topics indicates that many such needs do exist. Few studies, however, give indications that are clear enough to permit the design of information systems. This is not astonishing, given that information problems of citizens with regard to public administration are difficult to identify by applying the classical instruments of social research.

Especially for the last mentioned reason, CIS design encounters an important methodological problem. Obviously, this problem is linked to traditional conceptions of systems design where all the information required has to be present before implementation starts.

Alternative ways of systems design consist in deliberately proposing prototype systems based on incomplete information, with a view to finding out, through their actual working, what the real problems are to which they should give a solution. This implies a well designed and constant feedback and an adaptation of CIS to expressed needs.

2.2. Towards an analysis of information needs

Due to the difficulties outlined so far, CIS development must be predominantly experimental. However, some analytical efforts will help us to systemize our reduced knowledge.

One possible approach to roughly assessing presumed information needs consistsin asking what types of relationships between a citizen C and public administration exist, and what are the typical questions which may arise in their context. The following taxonomy of relationships is proposed:
- applying for welfare benefits and services;
- seeking redress of grievances;
- participating in local planning processes, in shaping one s environment;
- understanding, scrutinizing, monitoring the administrative machinery.

Information needs may vary with these types of relationships. In all cases, particularly when applying for benefits and services, the information needs are most intensely felt prior to establishing contact with an agency. Once there is such contact, it can be assumed that clients learn rather quickly about the procedure to follow, especially about what is expected of them.

In the case of applying for welfare benefits or services, but also in most other practical circumstances, the following questions will occur quite frequently, and at an early stage:

I: Is there any program/legal provision from which I can benefit? Does
      it concern me? This entails further questions: How do "they" call
      it? Am I eligible? Roughly, what can I claim?

II: What have I got to do in order to get things started or influenced?
      How does it all work?

III: Where can I address myself? (Agencies, their location, opening hours
      or accessibility by phone, documents to present, forms to fill in
      before or while applying?)

IV: What can I ask for? How much am I entitled to get? Will I get it
      really? Will they believe me? How much time, effort and money will
      I have to spend in order to get what I am entitled to?

V: (If there is no immediate answer to the questions listed above:)
      Where can I get further information and advice?

Many citizens will not find exhaustive answers to questions I - IV quickly.
Information needs are especially high when C applies for a service for the
first time, when his cultural distance to the administrative world is high, or
when he has no good command of an official language.

Bad information, or the complete lack of information can have several effects.
First, it could cause important losses of time and waste of energy e.g. in
trying to find one's way.

Second, the restricted amount of information that C can glean constitutes a
factual base on which he will repeatedly assess the opportunity of taking further steps. More or less consciously, a personal cost-benefit analysis is performed at several stages before, during and after an administrative procedure.
In the early stages of orientation and of search for information its result is
crucial for deciding whether C will apply for a service at all. Later on, it
may perhaps induce C to desist before a perhaps lengthy procedure has come to
its end.

Third, information must not be seen as of instrumental use only. Information
needs are not limited to instrumental knowledge. C may want to learn details
about administrative action even beyond the strictly necessary, by curiosity,
by the desire of enhancing his general knowledge about the politico-admini-
strative system, or by a general distrust of this system and the desire to
monitor its functioning whenever possible. Answers to questions of this kind
will often have to go into depth: what happens behind the scene? And why?

3.   OBJECTIVES OF A CIS

With regard to presumed information needs, a CIS should:
      -    support the matching of felt needs with entitlement categories ex-
           pressed in administrative language,
      -    constitue a user's guide, contributing to surmounting practical
           barriers which otherwise might have a discouraging effect,
      -    supply an information base for the citizen's personal cost benefit
           analysis: information on rights and duties, e.g. for calculating the
           amount of benefits,

provide the means and ways for deeper scrutiny of administrative action.

It does not seem very realistic, in the immediate future, to aim at developing comprehensive systems fulfilling all these functions. It is proposed, therefore, to split up CIS design into three parts. First, a general CIS would provide better information on a large variety of questions which may not be confined to public administration in a narrow sense. Such an overall CIS would basically provide answers to questions I - III and V.

A second type of CIS would deliver in-depth information on rights and duties needed in support of the mentioned personal cost-benefit analysis. This amounts to individualized advice, or legal help. In other words, such a CIS would interfere with the world of professional experts. Experimental systems of this type have been developed in one special field, namely social aid (supplementary benefits) claims (1)(5).

A third type of CIS could provide direct access to administrative procedures in real time. This would benefit C when he wants to know how long he will have to wait before getting a result, or in inspecting the data held by public administration on his person or his case. Freedom of information regulations could be made more effective in the same way, opening the files for public scrutiny, wherever this is warranted by access regulations. Such CIS delivering case-by-case information will be effective only when office automation will have penetrated more deeply into public administration.

The following description deals with CIS of the first type only.

4.   A SHORT DESCRIPTION OF A MODEL CIS

   4.1. Functions and elements

A CIS as a generalized system providing better information on a large variety of subjects will have to fulfill two basic functions, namely:
   -   providing information (which implies the storage, retrieval and linkage of internally stored information as well as the ad hoc search of new information in its environment);
   -   presenting the information in a way that fits the demand, i.e. translating it into a language which the citizen understands and which corresponds to his assumptive world.

In order to fulfill these requirements CIS should consist of:
   M   a human person, called the mediator, and
   TS_i one or more technical systems supporting him.

It is assumed that the two functions mentioned are distributed in a way that a technical system TS_1 carries the bulk of information storage and retrieval, whereas the translation function is performed by M. It is thus a human mediator who is in charge of explaining the information to the client and tailoring it to his particular situation and presumed information need. In doing so, he may be partly supported by an "intelligent" TS. Besides, he may use one or several other TS, e.g. for storing supplementary information which for practical reasons cannot (yet) be entered into TS_1.

Furthermore, CIS should comprise the following information channels and communication links:
   -   from CIS to citizens asking for information;
   -   from CIS to instances in its environment providing information to be stored or for ad hoc use;

-    from CIS to other CIS or to similar advice institutions. Such a link
     is required for referral in cases where demands for information or
     for assistance, for monitoring or the like cannot be satisfied by
     the CIS addressed by C;
-    from CIS to administrative agencies, for initiating action on the
     subject on which information is asked for, especially for securing
     the "intake" of the client in an administrative process concerning
     welfare services delivery.

4.2. Mode of operation

The typical functioning of CIS can be described as follows: C adresses M,
possibly face-to-face, by phone, or via a mailbox service. A dialogue between
C an M is then started which may consist of several speech acts, their number
being rather small when the dialogue is disconnected in time. If M is not sure
he can answer the question exhaustively and in a way C unterstands, he opens
an intermittent "dialogue" with TS_1. This might take the form of a conventional information retrieval. Alternatively, a learning component could be built
into TS_1 which might help a less competent M in his translation effort or
improve his overall skill in dealing with C. The dialogue between C and M ends
when one or both deem the information demand satisfied. Alternatively, it
ends with the referral of C to another CIS or advice institution, or with M
initiating some kind of administrative action, in favor of C.

There is an alternative way of accessing CIS. A first link is established
between C and TS, with M entering the relation only when C asks him to do so.
It is assumed that there are classes of C who would prefer such a rather
impersonal procedure. However, from research available on the interaction of
citizens and public administration, it can be concluded that, for most groups
of C, few benefits will be derived from such an arrangement.

Regardless of the way C addresses the CIS, there is an important requirement
if CIS is to be of real help in situations of dearth of information. As many
information problems arise well before first contacts with an administrative
body are made, CIS must be perceived, by C, as a relevant and trustworthy
source of information. In other words, the visibility of CIS must be extremely
high if it is to compensate for the lack of information on the workings of the
administrative machinery. High visibility of CIS can be achieved e.g. by a
uniform phone number throughout a country, or by uniform denomination.

4.3. The institutional framework

The model sketched so far is fairly neutral as to its implementation within
the framework of either existing or newly created organizations. A CIS could
be attached, more or less closely, to local or central government, or to single major agencies. As CIS constitute a relais between C and public services,
there are also institutions outside the domain of public administration where
CIS could be easily integrated. These include consumer organizations, advice
bureaus, legal help institutions, social workers, and neighborhood centers

Furthermore, a CIS could be part of, or congruent with institutions serving as
mediators, ombudsmen, tutors, advisory bodies, intake bodies etc. As, with
more "intelligent" TS, the qualification and competence requirements of "M"
roles can be lowered, most public officials and most "go-betweens" eventually
could assume this role, including e.g. aldermen, lay people with an interest
in neighborhood welfare or even persons who are often addressed by their relatives and neighbors when a day-to-day problem arises.

Finally, the scope of CIS could be widened beyond administration-related
information in the sense defined above. They could provide day-to-day informa-

tion on things of immediate interest, e.g. cultural life of a community, opening hours of stores, etc.

4.4. Information contents of TS₁

The information to be provided by CIS is stored, to a large extent, in one
technical system TS_1. It is expected that experienced M will rely, for most
routine demands made by C, rather on their memory and a variety of simpler TS
like scratchpads, blackboards, etc. Still, most of the information of relevance for citizens, especially before they establish first contacts with an agency, should be contained in TS_1.

The following types of information have to be included in the knowledge base
of TS:

I   (General) information on programs, on rights and duties,

II   (General) information on administrative procedures, possibly in
     graphical representation,

III Information on competences (e.g. graphical organization charts), on
     office location, opening hours, documents required for applying or
     complaining, forms to be filled out,

V   Documentary information, referring to other information sources like
     CIS, advice bureaux, booklets.

Not included is information for answering questions of type IV, i.e. exhaustive (mainly legal) information on rights and obligations.

The amount of information thus to be stored appears impressive at first glance. Yet it has to be recalled that a CIS for general information is not designed to give specialized advice on all kinds of problems. After providing a
first orientation, the CIS would refer C to the appropriate sources for information and advice, especially for complete information on rights and duties.

As far as information type I is concerned, the example of the Service d'information et de diffusion of the French Prime Minister (SID) database demonstrates that less than 10 000 pages in standard videotex format could suffice. The
volume of information of type II depends to a large extent on the intelligent
structuring of such information. Information type III may show significant
local variations. A CIS installed in a small town hall need not show all details of access to e.g. a central body which is only rarely accessed. Information type V will probably fall into two parts. One is a handful of adresses
to which people are quite often referred. To give an example, the telephone
directory of the City of Hamburg lists about 200 of such institutions, in a
haphazard way. If, on the other hand, an exhaustive repertoire of institutions
and printed media offering help and advice in even the most particular situations is to be provided, one could take the example of two exhaustive French
referral manuals, the "Guide des guides" and the "Guide des services d'accueil
et de renseignement", both edited by the SID. As of 1985 and 1987, they total
212 and 113 pages. Both are primarily designed to serve local administrators
in referring citizens to written information on special problems, and to agencies and associations, respectively.

Still, the sheer size of the information which CIS would contain is not a problem by itself. The main problem stems from the fact that such information
will have to be drawn together from a large variety of sources. These include
virtually all tiers and branches of central and local government, quasi-governmental institutions, and voluntary associations. Several of these insti-

tutions may not be willing to provide all the information required in due
time, unless they are offered something in exchange.

Furthermore, the information provided must undergo a selection at a central
point in the system. It has to be edited. In order to ascertain its correctness, it will in many cases have to be approved by the body providing the
information. Moreover, clear provisions must exist as to how and at what time
the information is entered into TS_1.

All these requirements are crucial. Public expectancies as to accurate information are significantly higher with regard to information technology-based
CIS as to printed media. However, in CIS experiments carried out so far, these
requirements were most difficult to comply with. The continuous update of the
information requires elaborate organizational provisions. These may be seen as
part of an information management function. The importance of this function is
still underestimated. It follows from this that the tasks of information management related to CIS must be given at least the same importance as the design
and implementation of TS_1.

5.   PROSPECTS FOR CIS

The model developed here is open enough to permit its adaptation to various
settings. Its implementation could enhance the effectiveness of the services
of information and advice bureaus, receptionists, etc. Eventually CIS could
become so widely diffused that all categories of administrative staff dealing
with clients as well as voluntary organizations would make use of it.

CIS will have many resistances to overcome before they are built up to any
larger extent. The good will of bringing information systems design to benefit
ordinary man may be widespread. Still, it is competing with firmly established
beliefs on the proper functioning of public administration. The rather subcon-
scious existence of such an "administrative philosophy" as well as its
strength are revealed by a series of arguments that repeatedly come to the
surface when a CIS (information technology-based or not) is proposed. Among
these arguments are concerns over liability in case of giving wrong information, over protection of personal privacy, as well as over the willingness of
staff to effectively make use of CIS. Furthermore, lack of resources is often
alleged.

Although many of these arguments are not altogether unfounded, systems design
could take them into account so as to build CIS that avoid undesirable side-
effects. All too often, this opportunity is deliberately overlooked.

Moreover, much of the new opportunities for a better public administration
seems to be channeled towards improving existing structures instead of serving
as an instrument for responding to new challenges. Although there are new
technological instruments for bringing about a more responsive and open administration (without jeopardizing its overall effectiveness and efficiency),
traditional policy choices are preventing their implementation to any greater
extent. The literature on social impacts of information technology is replete
with indications that negative impacts of information technology use in public
administration were the effect not of information technology as such but of
policies guiding its design and introduction.

Yet it can be hoped that, in face of a turbulent world, the political and
administrative systems will not only innovate in an instrumental sense but
also with regard to policy choices. In that sense, a more citizen-oriented
public administration is a major issue for the future. Models like the one
presented here can show that such an administration is feasible.

REFERENCES

(1) Adler, M. and du Feu, D., Technical Solutions to Social Problems? Some
     Implications of a Computer-based Welfare Benefit Information System,
     Journal of Social Policy 6 (1977) 431-447.

(2) Enel, F., Télématique et relation administration-administrés, Rapport de
     synthèse, Institut Français des Sciences Administratives, Paris, 1983.

(3) Janowitz, M.; Wright, D.; Delaney, W., Public Administration and the
     Public, University of Michigan Press, Ann Arbor, 1958.

(4) Lenk, K., Computer Use in Public Administration: Implications for the
     Citizen, in: Mowshowitz, A. (ed.), Human Choice and Computers, 2, North-
     Holland, Amsterdam 1980, 193-211.

(5) Liedtke, B., WIBES Projektskizze, paper, Gesellschaft für Mathematik und
     Datenverarbeitung, St. Augustin, 1987.

(6) Marchand, M., and Ancelin, C. (eds.), Télématique. Promenade dans les
     usages, La Documentation Française, Paris, 1984.

(7) Noël, P., Le tambour de ville, ou comment l'Administration écoute, ren-
     seigne, informe, La Documentation Française, Paris, 1982.

(8) Reinermann, H., Bürger und Computer - Hat die EDV uns Privatleuten etwas
     zu bieten?, Die Verwaltung 11 (1978) 413-438.

(9) Sackman, H., and Boehm, B., Planning Community Information Utilities,
     AFIPS Press, Montvale N.J., 1972.

(10) Télématique et services publics. Clés pour une réussite, Centre d'études
     des systèmes d'information des administrations (CESIA), Marseille, 1986.

Governmental and Municipal Information Systems
P. Kovács and E. Straub (Editors)
Elsevier Science Publishers B.V. (North-Holland)
© IFIP, 1988

INFORMATION SYSTEM TO FORECAST MUNICIPAL TAX REVENUE AND
GOVERNMENTAL PAYMENT FOR MUNICIPAL SERVICES

Jens Kammer Laursen

Kommunedata, P.O. Box 720,
DK-9100 Aalborg, Denmark

This paper describes how the Danish municipalities can
forecast some of their main incomes by means of an EDP
model. The calculation involves both tax revenues as well
as income and expenditure in connection with the municipal
adjustment and subsidy schemes.

1. INTRODUCTION

When a municipality is making a budget it is naturally very important to have an overall view of future revenues. Kommunedata
can offer assistance in several ways in this connection. One
method of assistance is Kommunedata's income prognosis as described in this paper.

Kommunedata is one of Denmark's largest EDP service agencies
(approx. 1700 employees). It is owned by and serves the Danish
Municipalities and Counties.

2. BACKGROUND

There is a long tradition in Denmark for extensive municipal
autonomy. The municipalities and Counties have independent
responsibility for carrying out many tasks which they, in part,
finance by levying taxes. Furthermore, they carry out tasks on
behalf of the state which the state then refunds in part or
whole.

There is also a long tradition in Denmark for treating citizens
on equal terms and for making it possible for them to receive
approximately the same public benefits irrespective of where
they live in the country. This has resulted in the establishment of a number of adjustment and subsidy schemes which help
to counterbalance the differences between "poor" and "rich"
municipalities and between municipalities with different
requirements for public expenditure.

There is, therefore, a complicated system of financial transfers between municipalities, counties and the state. Figure 1
on the next page shows some of the most important transfers.

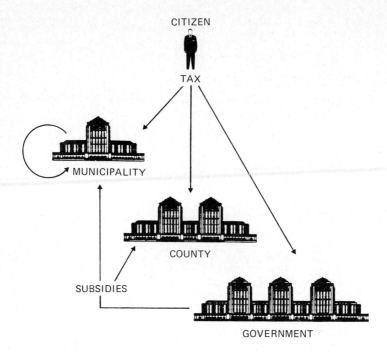

CITIZEN

TAX

MUNICIPALITY

COUNTY

SUBSIDIES

GOVERNMENT

FIGURE 1

Financial transfers

3. KOMMUNEDATA'S PLANNING MODELS

Kommunedata has gradually built up a number of EDP models for use in municipal planning. In order to achieve the greatest possible degree of flexibility, all models are written in the programming language APL, and they are run via terminal with direct updating and immediate calculation. The basic model is the population prognosis which exists in several versions, each based on its own theory. The population prognosis gives a picture of a municipality's population for several years, divided into sub-areas and 100 age groups from 0-100.

Many of the remaining models receive a great deal of their data from the population prognosis. Among these is the revenue prognosis, which is used by the municipalities to forecast the main part of their basis for income.

A new and improved version of the income prognosis has just
been drawn up. It is divided in three parts:-

- prognosis for income tax
- land tax prognosis
- adjustment and subsidy.

These three parts are examined in the following paragraph.

4.   PROGNOSIS FOR INCOME TAX

4.1. Standard calculation

This module calculates a municipality's present and future income
from personal income tax. Data is drawn automatically from three
sources in this calculation:

- final tax assessment statistics, which contain a
  synthesis of tax assessments for a municipality.
- population prognosis for the municipality, which among
  things gives an estimate of the number of future
  taxpayers.
- a common data bank, which, for example, contains the
  rates for personal deductions and price and wage
  estimates.

The module can in principle make the whole calculation from this
data. In practice though changes will often be made in this
standard calculation by varying one of the following four areas:

- grouping of taxpayers
- grouping of assessment entries.
- calculative entries.
- rate of taxation

4.2. Grouping of taxpayers

If the municipality so wishes the taxpayers can be divided into
groups. This grouping can be done according to sex, trade or
age. It is important that taxpayers are grouped, as far as is
possible, in groups with the same wage trends and deductions to
enable them to be forecast in the same manner.

4.3. Division of assessment entries

Assessment entries are the individual entries on income tax
return forms. The muncipality themselves can fix the group of
assessment entries to be forecast. For each assessment entry
the number of taxpayers with the relevant income or type of
deduction is forecast. Calculations are then made as regards
price and wage developments. Finally, special expectations can
be incorporated if, for example, it is estimated that one tax
group will in the future weigh heavier than others.

4.4. Calculative entries

Calculative entries pertain to personal deductions and the degree to which these are utilized. This data can be altered by the municipality. Furthermore, the calculative entries are forecast individually according to developments in the age group in question.

4.5. Rate of taxation

When the module has calculated a basis for assessement this is compared with the rate of taxation and the municipality's tax revenue is then calculated.

5.   PROGNOSIS OF LAND TAX

The module for the land tax prognosis is based on the taxable land value at the commencement of the year in question. This is then forecast on the basis of an estimate of the value of new land and increases in the value of land. Finally the land tax proceeds are calculated by means of some thousandths of this total land tax value.

It is also possible to calculate "backwards", i.e. one calculates the land tax percentage on the basis of the proceeds which are desired.

6.   ADJUSTMENT AND SUBSIDIES

6.1   Background

The module for adjustment and subsidies calculates a great deal of municipal revenue and expenditure. Without going into details, they can be grouped in the following main sectors:

- Adjustment of basis for taxation between municipalities. That is, "rich" municipalities pay an equalizing sum to the "poorer" municipalities.

- Adjustment of expense needs between municipalities. This means the municipality with a great need for expenditure (for example due to a rapid population growth) receives an adjustment sum from municipalities with a lesser need for expenditure. Of course, this is the source of many serious discussions as to how these expense needs should be measured and the rules are often changed. At the moment expense needs are defined by 12 so-called "objective" criteria.

  For example:
  . total number of inhabitants
  . number of 7-16 year olds.
  . number of inhabitants over 75 years old.
  . total length of roads
  . number of unemployed

The criteria have each their own carefully fixed rate of importance which, of course, is also the subject for many animated discussions.

- General state subsidy which is given to all municipalities as compensation for the municipalities having taken over certain tasks from the state.

- Special subsidy to municipalities with very special problems.

6.2   Calculation

When calculating subsidies and adjustments data from several sources is made use of:

- the municipality's population prognosis is transferred automatically.
- prognosis for income tax supplies a basis for taxation and rate of taxation.
- land tax prognosis supplies land values and rates of land taxation. a common data bank which contains much
- country-wide data used in the calculations.
- the municipalities' own reported data regarding for example the "objective" criteria.

The calculation is made on-line and the desired graphs are written immediately. The figure (fig.2) shown below shows some of the ways in which the above-mentioned facts are connected with one another.

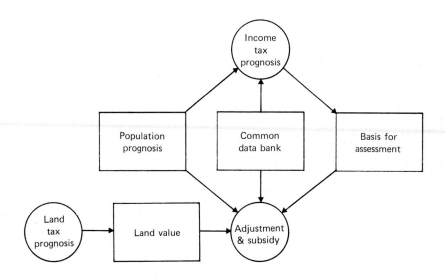

FIGURE 2

Data flow

7.   FLEXIBILITY

One of the main design criteria in the preparation of this model
has been taking as much consideration as possible to future
changes in legislation. This has, for example, been taken care of
by removing from the programme a large number of the constants
which are contained in the calculations and placing them in the
common data bank where they can be quickly altered.

Furthermore, the total model, consisting of all three modules,
offers ample possibilities for making fast consequential calculations when needed.

It is expedient if the municipal user of the model runs it at
least once a year so the results can be used in the municipal
budget.   In addition it is often necessary to make new calculations. There are a few examples of this in the following.

Final tax assessment statistics showing the total results for the
municipal tax assessment are calculated several times a year in
more accurate versions. It is relevant to make a new run of the
model when the municipality receives a new version of the final
tax assessment statistics.

When the municipality receives a population prognosis it may be
interesting to see what effect the new population figures have on
tax revenues, adjustments and subsidies.

There is a data bank containing much common data in the system.
A great deal of this data is based on estimates of developments
and these estimates are regularly revised.   When considerable
changes take place in the data bank it would be a good idea to
make a new run of the model in order to see what effect these
changes have had.

The government often changes legislation regarding adjustments
and susbsidies.   When such alterations in legislation take place,
or whilst they are being discussed the municipality can quickly
calculate the consequences for their economy.

By means of experimenting with the model the municipality can
maybe also procure arguments in favour of changes in the
regulations!

Governmental and Municipal Information Systems
P. Kovács and E. Straub (Editors)
Elsevier Science Publishers B.V. (North-Holland)
© IFIP, 1988

ON THE IMPLEMENTATION OF LAIOS

A LOCAL AUTHORITY INFORMATION & ORGANIZATION SYSTEM FOR GREECE

A. B. Sideridis1, G. I. Pangalos2

Abstract

A full range program for the automation of the greek local authority services gets well under way. The project is supervised by the greek Ministry of the Interior and has been included in the mediterranean integrated programs sponsored by the European Economic Community. The design philosophy of the corresponding MIS, the conclusions of an especially conducted study, the implementation recommendations and the problems encountered so far have been analysed and are reported for the successful integration of LAIOS and any other similar operation in other countries.

Key words: Information system, MIS planning, local authority automation.

Author's addresses

1. Informatics Laboratory, Agricultural University of Athens, Iera Odos 75, 118 55 Athens, Greece.
2. Information processing division, Greek Productivity Centre (ELKEPA), 28 Kapodistriou St., 106 82 Athens, Greece.

1. INTRODUCTION

The Greek Ministry of the Interior among its other duties is also responsible for the decentralization of the central government's activities and the coordination and harmonization of the local administration as a whole. Acting in this capacity has naturally concentrated, the last two years, in planning a Management Information System (MIS) that will meet the information needs of the local governments [1]. The system should also support automatic decision making procedures which should be developed in successive stages and attached to it. Thus, the information system should be gradually tranformed and integrated to a decision support Local Authorities Information and Organization System (LAIOS) [1, 2].

The overall structure of LAIOS consists of different applications for the various levels of the organization such as operations, management control and planning, as well as applications of service support to the public and to various management activities of the local authorities and mainly those requiring control and decision making.

Given the urgent need to utilise better information techonology in order to ease some of the problems currently encountered by the Greek local authorities, the Ministry of the Interior decided to proceed immediately to the implementation of LAIOS. For this purpose, a major nationwide study has been undertaken recently in order to examine the implementation problems and priorities and suggest alternating solutions. This study   proposed a methodology for the development of the appropriate computer applications both at national and local levels. Its recomendations have already been accepted by the government and will form the basis for the future development of the local government information systems in Greece.

In the present paper the structure of the Greek local government is considered in section 2 and since LAIOS has been fully described in [1] here is very briefly referred in section 3. In section 4 the study undertaken in implementing LAIOS strategy is analysed in detail. Finally, in section 5, recommendations made by the studying team are evaluated and conclusions drawn so far are discussed.

2. PRESENT STRUCTURE OF THE GREEK LOCAL GOVERNMENT

Greece is divided into municipalities (dimi) and communities (kinotites) which form the so-called first level of local government [3]. Municipalities are the capitals of the 52 prefectures, as well as all cities with population over 10,000. Municipalities with population over 15,000 can be divided into districts (diamerismata). Two or more municipalities or communities can be linked together to form a union (syndesmos) in order to undertake major projects, utilise better equipments e.t.c. In Greece there are today 276 municipalities and 5,760 communities. A classification according to their population appears in figures 1 and 2 [2, 4].

Local government in Greece is going to be strengthened further in the near future with the decentralisation of more responsibilities and funds. According to the new legislation [5], there will be three levels of local goverment: the central level which will have mainly planning and co-ordinating responsibilities, the peripheral level which will have mainly responsibilities on planning and technical support, and the prefectorial level where the remaining responsibilities will be decentralized. The principle objectives of the new structure are [5, 6]: to provide better services to the citizens, improve efficiency, minimize beaurocracy, utilise better the human resources, improve communications between local authorities and the government, make available more and more reliable data.

The well planned and co-ordinated introduction and subsequent utilisation of modern information processing technology has been accepted [1] that can play a decisive role for the acomplishment of these goals.

3. LAIOS 's DESIGN PHILOSOPHY

3.1. System's functioning and architecture

The functioning of LAIOS, at a typical local government environment, comes up from:
- strategic, managerial and planning needs,
- the need of participating organization of the citisens, administrators and operators involved in every procedure,
- the need of meeting the users and operators requirement and,
- the need of feeding back to the system all the necessary information so that new processes could be researched, explained, developed and adopted.

POPULATION SIZE	NO OF COMMUNITIES
1 - 500	3,377
501 - 1,000	1,442
1,001 - 3,000	842
3,001 - 5,000	75
5,001 - 10,000	24
	TOTAL : 5,760

figure 1:
Classification of the communities in Greece according to their population.

POPULATION SIZE	NO OF MUNICIPALITIES
1 - 5,000	105
5,001 - 10,000	48
10,001 - 50,000	98
50,001 - 100,000	17
100,001 - 500,000	7
500,001 - and over	1
	TOTAL : 276

figure 2:
Classification of the municipalities in Greece according to their population.

The functions above are covered by LAIOS's three stage MIS model [7, 8]. These three stages are:
- strategic information systems planning, including preplanning and formal systems planning,
- organizational restructure, information requirements analysis, systems development and implementation and,
- systems adiministration of the municipal activities and allocation of both MIS appliction and operational resources.

The system's architecture includes all the todays efficient information tools and facilities such as data bases and model bases linked by a powerful decision support mechanism in a local environment (see fig. 3). Telecommunication software could extend the domain of application of LAIOS at a regional level which should cover the minicipalities and administration of a prefecture. Common aotivitico between the local governments of a certain prefecture should necesitate linkage among themselves, the prefecture and other public or private organizations, industry, etc.). Finally, the local authorities, through the prefecture's common linkage to the central administration should have direct access to the national fully Integrated Management Information System (IMIS) of the public administration [2].

3.2. Factors in LAIOS success.

It is evident that a fully detailed plan of LAIOS should include specific targets and involve a long range time-table. The plan should not underestimate the various difficulties due to limited experience in the development of integrated management information systems, the organizational obstacles which may develop in the course of implementing those systems and the vulnerabillity in considering a straightforward implementation of a comprehensive LAIOS as having goals or objectives of its own. It should also emphasize the basic factors, among the various technical and nontechnical ones, upon which depend LAIOS's successful implementation. The most important of these factors are:
- continuous, throughout its implementation stage, political support,
- active municipal participation from the MIS planning phase,
- availability of DP expertise at a local level and
- purchaising of the most appropriate software and hardware [8].

3.3. LAIOS time - table

LAIOS provide an interrelation of computer applications and the way decisions are made and feed back with information the various systems which are in operation. These systems are classified in [1] into:
- Operational Support Systems (OSS) design for the automation of daily activities
- Management Control Systems (MCS) devoted to various data services and,
- Planning Systems (PS) design to assist management for an evaluation of future alternatives.

The OSS have been given the first priority in the LAIOS implementation time-table. In particular, since the first phase of the program started last year, OSS have been analysed and their application software is currently developed under UNIT and MS-DOS. It is estimated that the corresponding OSS packages should be available to the municipalities by the end of 1988. The development and disposal procedure of these packages to the data processing centres of the interested municipalities will be

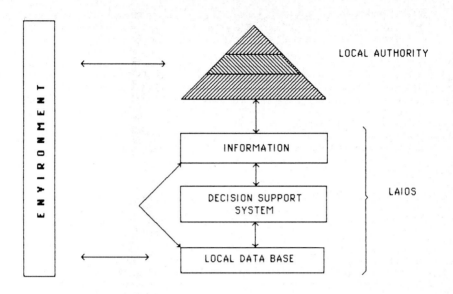

figure 3 :
LAIOS 's structure

controlled by an especially authorized public enterprise named "Hellenic Agency for Local Development and Local Government (EETAA)", whose the board of directors include members of the National Union of Local Authorities (KEDKE).

The time-table of the program for the full operation of the OSS, MCS and PS is subject to the availability of the necessary funds. It is estimated that, apart of the initiation stage (i.e. the completion of the preplanning phase which took a year's time), the second turning point, which remarks the integration of the formation, production and OSS, MCS and PC functioning, will require two more years. Finally, is expected that LAIOS will advance to maturity after the consolidation phase in five years since its initiation. This period could be further extended if the pre-estimated funds either will not be available in time or prematurely curtailed [1].

3.4. Personnel needed

Since the availability of skilled personnel is an important factor for LAIOS successful implementation, a specific program has been devised which encompasses the retraining of the existing management and administrative personnel and the encouragement of computer scientists, from the local universities, to participate in LAIOS project. This program is taking into account the different specialities needed to support the minicipal data processing centres and, in particular, those needed to deal with the more complex data base and tele-processing technologies.

4. THE STUDY

4.1. Objectives and methodology

The major objective of the study has been to make a global and in depth investigation of the present and future information processing requirements of the greek local authorities and to propose an implementation methodology on the following issues:
a. The technical characteristics of the local government
   information system at a national level.
b. The type, structure and technical characteristics of the computer systems
   required by each category of local authority.
c. The appropriate strategy and methodology for the development of the
   necessary application software.
d. The bodies which will provide the necessary technical support
e. The overall implementation plan and costs involved.

The implementation of the study has been accomblished in the following five stages:
   Stage 1 :   Collection and analysis of all available data, i.e. documentation
                available, existing legal framework and related legislation, expe-
                rience from similar implementations in other countries e.t.c.
   Stage 2 :   Study of the experience gained and of the problems encountered
                from the application of modern information processing technology
                so far by the greek local authorities.
   Stage 3 :   Collection of detailed information on the profile, structure,
                activities, work-flow and work-load characteristics, e.t.c. from
                all 6,000 local authorities in Greece.
   Stage 4 :   Classification, processing and analysis of all available data.
   Stage 5 :   Coclusions and compilation of the report.

Detailed information on the objectives and methodology of the study, particular data, or parts of the final report (four volumes) can be obtained from [6].

4.2. Identification of the information processing needs

The detailed identification of the profile and the information processing needs of the individual local authorities has been found to be necessary before any recommendation is made on the structure and the technical characteristics of the information processing systems required in each case. This identification has been carried out through a survey which covered practically all local authorities in Greece. This survey has been carried out:
a. By personall interviews on sight. These interviews covered all local authorities which already use computers (over 60), as well as a representative sample of the rest. The appropriate sample has been defined in co-operation with KEDKE.
b. By detailed questionnaires. The questionnaires have been compiled again with the co-operation of KEDKE and have been posted to all local authorities (except those in (a) above). Following instructions by the greek ministry of the Interior, the accuracy of the data filled in has been certified by the local councils. In this way practically all local authorities (more than 95% of the total) have completed and returned on time the questionnaires.

The data collected were subsequently fed into a computer data base and processed using appropriate statistical packages and application programs. This extensive survey, which has been performed for the first time in Greece, has produced a huge amount of valuable information about the greek local authorities. This information provided an accurate basis for the formulation of the overall strategy and the definition of the technical parameters proposed in this study.

4.3. Major conclusions on the present situation

From the analysis of the data collected through the nationwide survey and the on-sight study of the representative sample, it appears that:
a. Most municipalities and communities in Greece face a serious information flow problem today. This is mainly due to the heavy work-load, the unsatisfactory work procedures, the organizational problems, the shortages in personell e.t.c.
b. The operational costs in most cases are high. A major reason for this is the limited use of automation and the excessive use of human resources.
c. Management information is in most cases inadequate. This is regarded to be a major problem since it seriously affects the planning activities and the desigh and implementation of local strategies and policies.
d. The level of activitico and the work-load characteristics of a significant number of local authorities (and especialy the bigger ones) justifies the immediate introduction of modern computer technology.
e. The introduction of automated information processing methods although it does not necessarily affect directly the existing organizational sructure and mode of working, it is expected that will help the re-organization and simplification of a significant number of currently unsatisfactory procedures.
f. Most local authorities strongly favour the introduction of information processing technology, which is expected to help provide better services to the public, reduce operational costs, improve the currently time consuming procedures, produce the necessary management information, and improve working conditions.

Based on the above conclusions, it has been recommended by the study that the use of information processing technology can provide significant help to the local goverment and should therefore be used extensively. Given the present situation, however, this introduction must be accomplished in the a systematic and well-planned way proposed in [1].

Fourteen major activities which are common to the majority at the greek local authorities have been identified and analysed. For each one the objectives, limitations, detailed work flows and problems currently encountered have been studied. An analysis has also been made on the feasibility and the expected advantages from the use of computer technology in each case [6].

4.4. System's communication

An information system that will ootiofactorily cover the needs of the greek local government should not only satisfy the information processing requirements of the individual local authorities, but also cover their data communication needs. From the analysis of the data collected, it appears that there are three important data communication levels in the greek local government:

a. Communication between local authorities, especialy those which participate in the same union.
b. Communication with the prefecture (nomarchia).
c. Communication with the ministries and other govermental bodies.

The analysis of the data collected on the information flows, the communication needs, e.t.c. suggests that the general architecture presented in figure 4 is the most suitable for the greek local government [1, 6]. The implementation of such a network is however a difficult task. It has been found for example that no public data transmition network is available and that at least 10% of the local authorities face serious telephon communication problems. A small example of the technical difficulties that must be solved.

4.5. Definition of local needs

The big number of local authorities in Greece (approximately 6,000) made it very difficult to study each one individually. It has been therefore necessary to classify the total population in such a way that the results obtained for each category would provide adequate information to the individual local authorities to choose and develop the appropriate type and size of computer system. A number of criteria have been examined for this classification i.e. population, budget, geographical position e.t.c. It has been decided and tested (using the PEARSON corelation principle), that among those the population one gives best results. Using the above criterion the entire population of Greece has been classified into thirteen major categories.

For each category, the information processing requirements of the fourteen major common activities of the greek local authorities have been calculated. In order to do that, the various types of input, files and output have been identified for each application. The average values (based in the number of transactions, file sizes e.t.c.) for the specific category were then calculated for each one. The minimum configuration required for each category was finally defined on the basis of those calculations [6]. Detailed guidelines have been produced in this way for all categories, which enable the local authorities to choose the appropriate type and size of equipment.

LOCAL LEVEL

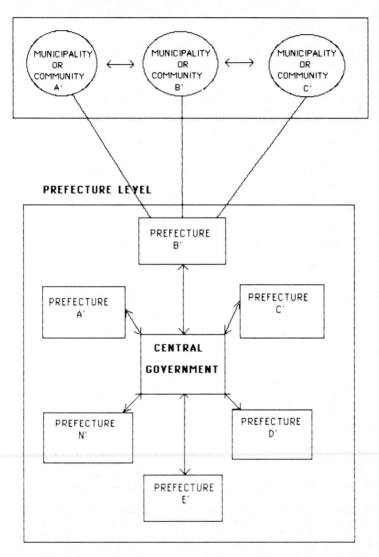

figure 4:
Suggested structure of the new computer based information
system for the greek local government.

5. CONCLUSIONS AND RECOMMENDATIONS

The presumptions made in section 3 and 4 cannot of course guarantee the successful development and application of a complex local authorities information system such as LAIOS. For example, the minicipal participation to the development of the system from the MIS planning phase cannot always ensure a complete information requirements analysis, since the continuous process of decentralization often necessitates a redetermination of the information volumes and flows. Thus, the managerial staff can not conceive their future information requirements, which continuously expand as the decentralization process is getting materialized. In addition, because of their insufficient retraining in subject areas as informatics, they can not perceive the qualitytive difference of the available information by the new automated procedures. As a result of this, there is a clear need in defining processes and determinig systematically information requirements of todays and future applications. For this reason it has been proposed the establishment of a committee of users and experts regulating LAIOS and its performance evaluation on an on-going basis [1].

In order to bypass some of the implementation problems, it has been also decided that the following two principles will be followed for the implementation of LAIOS:
a. The system will be implemented in stages. This is helped by its modular structure.
b. The local information systems will be implemented independently by the individual local authorities.

The implementation will follow, however, strict specifications and compatibility rules which will make possible the integration of the local systems into a national network at a later stage.

A major advantage of the above approach is that individual local authotities can quickly develop their information processing systems according to the local needs and resources available. The introduction of strict specifications and compatibility rules also ensures that it will be possible to interconnect the systems developed at a later stage in order to cover the communication needs of the local goverment.

As far as the compatibility problems is concerned, it has been decided that the philosophy of the Open Systems Interconnection architecture (OSI) should be followed for the implementation of the information system. An important advantage of this architecture is that it allows the subsequent addition to the network of an unlimited number of local systems (nodes), under the restriction that these systems will comply with a given set of compatibility rules. For this rurpose the relevant "guidelines" [6] suggested by the EEC have been adopted. A detailed description of the seven layers proposed by the OSI architecture , as well as the compatibility rules can be found in [6]. The "guidelines" specify, for axample that, as far as the operating systems are concerned, the systems chosen by the local goverment should use either "MS-DOS", in the case of single user systems, or "UNIX" in the case of multi-user systems, or a very limited selection of other operating systems in the case of big main-frames [6]. This recommendation has been also fully adopted.

5.1. Development of the necessary software

The comlexity of the problems, the limited resources usually available and the shortages in well-trained personell, make the development and support of the necessary software a major problem for most local authorities. The autonomous approach to the development of the necessary software, which has been followed by most greek local authorities so far, combined with the lack of co-ordination from the part of the state, has already led in a situation where many local authorities spend a lot of time and resources for the development of identical or very similar software, on computers which do not conform to any compatibility standards.

Another problem has been that, because of the shortages in well educated perconell, local authorities had usually to rely exclusively on external help for the selection, development and subsequent modifications of the required software. This can be expensive and dangerous, especially in the cases where there is no one in the local authority who can co-ordinate, supervise and control the whole operation.

The centralised development is an alternative to the above approach in which the required software is developed for a smaller or bigger number of local authorities. In this case the development is usually made according to agreed specifications. This method of development offers a number of significant advantages. It avoids the parallel development of identical or very similar software and makes easier the systematic and planned development according to the specifications. It also reduces the requirements for well educated personell. For these reasons, and taken into account the dissadvantages of the previous approach , it has been decided that the centralized mode of development is more appropriate for the greek local authorities.

In order to help further the development of the necessary information systems by the local authorities, a detailed implementation plan, guidelines on how to proceed for the call for tenders, a set of model conditions for the purchase of the necessary computer equipment and other related material has been compiled and distributed to the local authorities. Education programs have also been organized for the local authorities at a peripheral level.

REFERENCES

[1]. A. B. Sideridis, "Informatics and Municipalities: The Greek Approach", Report TRI/1986, Ministry of the Interior, Athens, Greece, 1986.
[2]. A. B. Sideridis, "Informatics in regional and Local administration", Proceedings of symposium "Informatics and Greek Economy", Athens, 1986.
[3]. ETE, Legislation on the organization and structure of the greek local government: N1065/80 - 1270/82, Ethnikon typographion, Athens, 1982 (in greek).
[4]. KEPE, Five year plan for economic and social development in Greece: 1983-1987, KEPE, Athens, 1983 (in greek).
[5]. Local government trainning board, Information technology for managers in local government, Local government trainning board, U.K., 1982.
[6]. "Study for the introduction of data processing in the greek local authorities", ELKEPA, Athens, 1986.
[7]. B. Bowman, G. Davis and J. Wetherbe, "Three stage model of MIS Planning", Information Management, V6/1, February, 1983, pp. 11-25.
[8]. K. L. Kraemer, W. H. Mitchel, M. E. Weiner and O.E. Dial, "IMIS Planning, Development, and Administration", in "Computers in Public Administration: An International Perspective", Pergamon Press, Oxford, 1976, pp. 4-34.

Governmental and Municipal Information Systems
P. Kovács and E. Straub (Editors)
Elsevier Science Publishers B.V. (North-Holland)
© IFIP, 1988

NEW METHODS FOR BASIC EDP TRAINING
M. Hentzel / Sweden

Background

In Sweden, basic EDP training has been provided for more than 15 years for
people who work in companies and other organizations. In one way or another
these people are in contact with computers in their daily work.

The training is carried out by the employer, who also bears the cost of the
training. The basic aim of this kind of training is, of course, to raise productivity and thereby the effectiveness of the company or organization.

The employees did not receive any computer training at school and thus have
very little or no knowledge of computers and EDP.

Today, EDP has been introduced as a subject at different levels in the Swedish
school and we hope in the future to have a situation where practically everyone has received basic EDP training at school. Training within our companies
and other organizations can then be focused on other topics.

Why basic EDP training ?

We in Sweden are quite convinced of the importance of computers as part of
almost every activity in our society. We believe that it is impossible to work
efficiently if we do not make use of the tools that are available. We consider
that the use of computers today is a necessary basis for a good, prosperous
and competitive society. We are aiming at a situation where everyone will find
the use of computers a natural element in creating even better conditions in
society.

We also believe that the effective use of new technology depends on the manner
in which the technology is introduced. An important factor in this connection
is the approach used to involve the end-users in the introduction process.

Accordingly we have to ensure that the people who work in our companies and
organizations have an elementary knowledge of computers, of the favourable and
unfavourable effects of computerization and of how computers can be used to
make all our activities more effective.

Basic EDP training during the '70s

During the '70s, basic EDP training was mostly carried out using classical
educational technigues, i.e., an EDP specialist tried to explain fundamental
EDP principles to a group of people. Typically, the group consisted of about
15-20 people. One course lasted for about 3-4 days.

The course of instruction was normally theoretical and technical. The teacher
tried to explain how a computer worked and how to program computers. Not much
was done to show how users could employ computers to improve their work in
their own sphere.

The outcome of these courses was quite poor in that the students seldom had
any opportunity to apply the theoretical knowledge acquired during the courses.

In addition, the courses were expensive for employers, especially if the costs representing the time that the students had to be away from their normal occupations were taken into account.

Basic EDP training during the '80s

During the '80s we discovered that it was necessary to look for new ways and methods for providing this kind of training. The reasons for this were

o   fast developments within the EDP field that made the use of computers increasingly valuable to the business sector and to public authorities

o   the increasing number of people who, in one way or another, came in contact with computers in the normal course of their work

o   the numbers of terminals and personal computers available.

The new methods employed were based upon the idea that any company or organization could itself carry out its own basic EDP training. At the same time, the training could be largely adapted to the applications and technology used within the employers' organization.

In the early '80s we discovered that about 1.1 million people in Sweden needed some kind of basic EDP training. In view of the large numbers it was not possible to manage this educational project through the ordinary training companies and organizations. Instead, the training companies focused on developing training materials in the form of packages that they could sell to the user companies. At the same time, the training companies offered training for trainers. This would enable the user companies to carry out their own training, using their own specially trained staff for this purpose.

The training materials that were developed are very comprehensive and include various kinds of tools and guide-lines for teachers. Examples of such materials are trainers' guides, educational student material, slides, transparencies, tapes, video tapes and a large number of training exercises. Sometimes the training material also included computer programs that enabled the students to carry out practical exercises if a terminal or a personal computer were available.

The training for trainers lasts about 2-3 days and is focused on how a trainer should use the training material and how he can conduct his own training sessions.

A normal in-house course based upon a training package of this kind lasts about 2-3 days and is normally held inside the employer organization. One basic aim of these courses is to give the students a wider view of the use of computers in practice and the way in which computers could be used within their own organization och within their own field. It is hoped, at the same time, that the course will raise the motivation of all students.

The results of these courses are quite good and the knowledge acquired is much more serviceable in the everyday reality of working life. By using a pedagogically designed training package and practical exercises, we have also attained an educational effect that is superior and longer-lasting than before.

By using trainers from the user organization we have increased the total number of trainers considerably. This, in turn, means that we have been able to increase the number of people that can be trained in a limited span of time. It has also been possible to reduce the cost of the training since we use staff members as trainers. We have managed to reduce direct costs by 50%,

compared with the situation during the '70s. Indirect costs are still almost
the same since students must be away from their normal work for almost the
same period. In some cases we have also managed to reduce indirect costs by
providing training in the evenings, during holidays, etc.

Basic EDP training during the '90s

Today we face a situation characterized by even more rapid developments in the
EDP field. Our children are learning about EDP and computers at school and a
growing number of places of work are using computers for an increasing part
of their throughput. In many cases, it is likely that new products and services
would not have been developed if we had not used computers.

Accordingly it is even more essential that all the people who work within our
companies and other organizations should have at least some basic knowledge
about EDP and computers, preferably about the way in which these tools should
be used effectively in their work.

In Sweden about 10% of the population still need this kind of training.

In some large organizations this situation has led to radically new training
methods where we try to train more people at the same time and to use less
time for this training. The reason is obvious since the indirect cost of the
training is the more expensive part. What we try to do is simply to train more
people at a lower cost than before. Our latest advance in this respect is
called PrataData (CompuTalk).

Within a PrataData activity we can train up to 200 people at a time. By
creative use of modern educational methods, we have managed to shorten the
training time to one day instead of 2-3 days. This means that we can attain
the same training effect in one day, with an obvious reduction in indirect
costs. Besides, since we can train up to 200 persons per day, we now have a
real chance, for the first time, of giving everyone the necessary basic EDP
training. Thus, the educational backlog can be reduced substantially.

PrataData training activity consists of three separate modules, as follows:

o A 4-hour lecture in a theatre, where the students are very much involved.
   In this lecture we use modern equipment and techniques, such as computers
   and video, and the possibilities the stage form gives us, such as light-
   and-sound effects, large screens, music, etc;

o An exhibition where the students can see how their own company or
   organization is using computers and what plans exist for the future;

o A practical exercise in which the students use peronal computers. Here
   we use specially designed and developed programs that ensure that nobody
   fails and that everyone can attain some result with a computer. This
   exercise is based on computer-assisted training.

Another essential feature is that every student receives high-quality
documentation from this training program. One purpose of this documentation
is to motivate the student to go through it in his spare time. In our assessments we have found that this is also the case.

Up to now we have trained about 40,000 people in PrataData programs and our
experiences have been quite satisfactory. We believe that we obtain the
same educational effect by using this technique as we obtain by using the
older techniques. We can also reduce the cost of this training dramatically.

Our estimated direct costs per student are about 15% of the costs that we had during the '70s.

Indirect costs have been cut dramatically. Since we only need to use one full day instead of three, we have managed to reduce this cost down to one-third.

The experience we have gained up to now is based upon training performed inside large companies and organizations, i.e., each PrataData training program is directed towards people who work within the same organization.

A company that intends to train its employees in basic EDP by the PrataData method needs to have at least 1,000 employees for the method to be cost-effective.

Conclusion

Based upon the experience we have gained in Sweden, we believe that the use of computers is essential in order to promote good business and to create efficient organizations. Moreover, we think that the efficient use of computers is necessary if we wish to create a competitive society.

We also believe, that efficient use of computers means that every person involved must have an elementary knowledge about computers, computer applications and the effects of computerization. This leads to the conclusion that every man och woman in our society needs basic EDP training.

Today, we have developed new methods and techniques enabling us to reach this goal in such a way that we can afford the cost involved, whether this cost is paid from public funds or by employers.

Governmental and Municipal Information Systems
P. Kovács and E. Straub (Editors)
Elsevier Science Publishers B.V. (North-Holland)
© IFIP, 1988

INFORMATION MODELLING OF MUNICIPAL ACTIVITIES

K.Krepler, L.Pősze, A.Zamahovszkij

Government Computer Service for State Administration (ÁSZSZ), Information Systems Division for State Administration (ÁFI), 1502 Budapest, P.O.Box 135, Hungary

Methods and forms of automatization of municipal informatics in Hungary are considered including information collection and estimation, information modelling for database design and structurization of information flow.

1.   Introduction

Information Systems Division for State Administration (ÁFI) was founded by KSH as part of ÁSZSZ in order to complete the tasks for interbranch development of government information systems according to the point I/22 of ATB directive 5022/1985 which other organizations do not deal with. Our division proved to be most effective in communications with regional and city councils providing coordination, information and development activites in collaboration with 15-20 municipal councils and special committees. Our division is involved in following tasks:
- research under the contract by KSH in both present and future states of government institutions;
- analyzing and working out suggestions for complex use of national registers (databanks);
- participating in efforts for decentralization of these registers, especially for integrating them with municipal information systems;
- modelling of municipal informatics.

2.   Computer support establishing the municipal information model

2.1. Formulation of objections for modelling

The development of municipal information systems in VII. five years plan has the aim at establishing an informatics which provides unification of municipal activity with preserving specifics of sectorial activities. One of the essential principles of implementation is that all this may be performed only after examination and putting in order the information enviroment. However this demands the improvement of affinity of municipals for national databanks and modern computer techniques as well. This approach includes inititatives of some municipals, expanding of sector specific systems, and developing of standard systems for municipals initiated centrally.

The key for further steps is recognition of such problems as:
- method and speed of request satisfaction for data on the regional or lower levels,
- work-place systems for administrators,
- integrative decisions for implementation of municipal functions.
It seems necessary and up-to-day constructing such a model that will:
- take into consideration various levels of municipal activities,
- provide connection between registers (databanks) and separate files, spheres of activities and elementary data,
- explore flow of elementary data, files and databanks,
- explore information flow between municipal and its surrounding.
Collected information would provide the possibility to:
- establish the list of registers (databanks) to be computerized,
- build shared central databases,
- define complete list and structure of data.
On the level of data it would be possible to provide:
- the index of data which may be accessed by municipal personal and methods for it,
- background information with list of possible sources for decision support,
- parallel dataservice.
In the spheres of activity it would be possible to perform:
- more effective classification of spheres and bringing more order into organization structure,
- balanced loading of administrators and sectors of municipals.

2.2. Organisation of model data base

At the start of modelling it became clear that the big volume of data demands computer support. Due to the claim of completeness measurement would be performed on the level of:
- small town,
- big town,
- region.
Such a broad measurement similiar in purposes to our modelling   was already   completed (e.g. in the town of Sárospatak),however it   was evaluated manually, and while providing valuable information   for specialists, limited the aims and obtained results.
Beyond the evaluation of big amounts of data computer support satisfies the claim for multiaccess and analyzing of collected data with the help of computer.
Establishing the purposes of modelling were followed by choosing appropriate software. Essential in this choice was that limitations of software might not bound the original aims. The consideration of various task-driven and general types of systems being on sale both in the country and abroad showed the absence of tool which would not bound the original aims.
Finally relational type DBASEIII was choosed which is considered to be already classical for various implementations.

2.3. Collection of information for modell

Broad collection of information provides basis for establishing computer model of municipal informatics. The pattern for data collecting was worked out in iterative process with extensive use of specialists, and on the ba-

se of early gained experience and results of previous information gathe-
ring efforts.
Data entering is provided by two data sheetes:
I . One for information about spheres of municipal activities,
II. Another for information in documents (files).
The first data sheet mainly reflects logical links between types of acti-
vites and documents used in them. This sheet consists of parts A and B.
"A" part contains names of specialized agencies of municipal and sphere of
activity, its code and several qualifying characteristics.
"B" part contains data about documents corresponding to the sphere such as
short name of document, its origin, number of requests for it, destinati-
ons if passed further, etc.
The second data sheet aims at profound description of data occuring in documents. Beyond the name of data item such information is provided as code
of data group, if item is used as key for repeated request, origin of data
item, etc.
Three things at least follow from this:
- no document or type activity and due to it no data item, which while
being useful will not be present in the collected information,
- links are established in some degree between various special agencies
of municipal and commonly used registers (and data in them),
- in order to provide such gathering personal involved in it must be
very careful and collaborative.
Program system provides possibilities for entering, modification, deleting
and querying according to described 2 data sheets. This system is implemented under DBASEIII and may be used on IBM PC compatible computers.

3. Information modelling of municipal activity

3.1. Modelling strategy

Municipal activity being the important part of modern society may be undo-
ubtely considered as complicated universe of discourse with not only complicated but often not well defined structure of knowledge and data. One of
the goals of information modelling of it must be clarifying the structure,
defining the concepts and relation between them. This goal being achieved
in some degree will provide the good basis for automatization and computerization of this acitvity.
Various formalisms were suggested for so called conceptual modelling and
there exist numerous data models including semantic features for performing this task /1, 4, 5 /. It must be noticed that out initial conditions
and information, and our finite goal play the determining role in the
choice of method for information modelling. At the start beyond the general knowledge of municipal activity due to the efforts in analyzing of it
a big amount of data about documents which take part in the information
flow in municipal services was collected and represented in the database
managed by DBASE3 on IBM PC, as described in section 2.
Being oriented to the usage of the same DBMS further on, it would be wise
to use when possible relational model methods provided DBASE3 is close
to relational data base model. Due to all this it seems adequate to
choose semantic network (SN) representational techniques and relational
data model (RDM) for higher and lower levels of information modelling
respectively. They are described briefly in following subsections.

3.2. Semantic Networks (SN)

In order to represent complicated universe of discourse one of   the broadly used devices are SN's. In this approach universe of   discource is
considered as a set of concepts connected by (or being in) relations. Concepts form two general classes:
- tokens, i.e. real beings,
- types, i.e. classes of tokens, or subclasses.
This approach presupposes that for the majority of domains following relations between concepts are sufficient:
- IS-A,
- PART-OF.
Often IS-A is the only one. These relations provide 4 organizational axes for structuring the set of concepts / 3 /:
- classification (IS-A),
- aggregation (IS-A, PART-OF),
- generalization (IS-A),
- partition (PART-OF).
It seems clear that much may be represented using this method,   nevertheless as an implementation device it lacks many of necessary features, such as well defined semantics, impossibility of   supporting big
amounts of data and so on, not mentioning that most of programming software supporting this model is experimental. But for high-level information
modelling it is quite appropriate.

3.3. Relational data base model (RDM)

RDM considers universe as set of relations, operations on them and integrity constraints (IC).   Relations (or predicates in logical notation)
are used for representing entities and relations between them in real
world, operations provide querying facilities of DB, IC's model the semantic features (constraints) between attributes.
Various types of constraints were suggested as IC's /5/, the most useful and used are functional dependencies (FD), which say that some group
of attributes uniquelly defines another group of attributes.
Interesting from practical point of view,is that if we have a set of atti-
butes R, and the set of functional dependencies $F=\{f\}$, where $f:A \rightarrow B$;
$A,B \subseteq R$ (say defined by designer) for every FD g we can decide if g is
a logical consequence of F, i.e. if every state of DB which satisfies F
must satisfy g . Moreover such finite relation on R may be constructed,
which satisfies these and only these FD's which are consequences of F.
This relation is called Armstrong relation / 2 /. Clearly precise definition of the set of FD's gives a relevant model. In practice due to the size of attribute set and numerous FD's designer generally can not define
completely the set of FD's on R, and some are not exposed. That is why
Armstrong relation was suggested for extracting FD's from it in / 2 / as
part of design process and called <u>dependence inference</u> , with further adding to or modifiyng the original set F of FD's. So the design process looks like this:
- defining set of FD's F,
- constructing Armstrong relation,
- dependence inference,
- modifying F
and may be of course iterative.
The connection between this design process and collected information desc-

ribed in section 2 is straightforward: we consider the latter as Armstrong relation on the universal schema or set of Armstrong relations on independent schemas, which possibly must be modified in order to satisfy FD's in F if they are not already satisfied by it.

4. Structural model of municipal activity

The structural model has its aim at such regulation of information processes which gives opportunity for unified administration of affairs in automatization of concrete municipal activites. So no traditional methods are revised, only rationalization of them is aimed. New in it is that basic registers (BR) are brought into consideration with decentralizing them at least on the region level. It is assumed that there exist corresponding local registers,e.g. hardcopy BR on settlements and local register in Territory Institution.
The structured model is presented on fig.1. New elements of existing now BR's are marked by 1.
Essential is establishing such registers of transactions of affairs (documents) where the latters may be searched repeatedly not only by the number of transaction (document) but also by:
- name (personal, or of institution),
- address,
- identifying number (personal number, or some kind of indentifier for institution).
This provides the possibility for establishing connections between transactions corresponding to the same client.
Those registers which have no equivalents on the national level are marked by 2. Actualization and processing of new types of registers (marked by 1) may be done with the help of basic registers by extending them with identification numbers and addresses.
This structural model doesn't change depending on whether partially or in full automatization is performed. That is:
- at the begining such registers as local, individual, sectorial, and those for concrete administrators will be computerized in order to improve the inner work of agencies,
- computerization of summary registrars and by way name-,address- and sectorial registers provides connection between individual registers, as well as their effective use,
- decentralization of national basic registers provides basic data for local institution.
Fig. 2. gives the structure of system for current implementation.
Fig. 3. gives the simplified schema of transactions of affairs in computer support.
Participation of municipals is indispensible for research- development in municipal informatics,so collaboration agreements set up with 10-15 regional and city councils provide benefits for both sides.
Collaboration takes place mainly on the levels of special committees providing mutual information and advice services for computerization.
These agreements are based on following general principles:
- those municipals wich collaborate are doubtlessly interested in modernization of municipal informatics,
- municipals are willing to make sacrificies, but do not want "surface" decisions,
- in consideration of main task unified point of view was obtained,
- readiness for distributing of tasks in interest of rapid progress

and effectivity.
At the present time special committees were estalished in the following fields:
- registration, file registers,client and information services,
complex registers for actual clients,
- rationalization of manual writing work, formulas and catalogs databanks on computer,
- system for private property,
- computer support for settlement registers.
For establishing and effectivness of municipal information systems implementation ÁSZSZ has set up information and advice service. In the frame
of this service ÁSZSZ accepts responsibility for:
- occasional information and advicing,
- reports on current state of development,
- organization of working meetings in the country and abroad in
the field of municipal informatics,
- defining short-, middle- and longterms strategies for establishing municipal information systems,
- maintaince of courses with inner and invited lecturers.

References
/1/ King, R. and Mcleod,D., Semantic data models, in: Jao, S.B.,(ed.),
    Database Design, (1985).
/2/ Mannila,H. and Räihä,K.-J., Design by example: an application of
    Armstrong relations, J.of Computer and Systems Sciences, 33, 126-141.
    (1986)
/3/ Mylopoulos,J. and Levesque, H.J., An overview of knowledge represen-
    tation, in /4/.
/4/ Brodie,M.L., Mylopoulos, J. and Schmidt, J.W., (eds.), On conceptual
    modelling. (Springer Verlag, 1984)
/5/ Ullman, J., Principles of database systems, (Pitman, 1982).

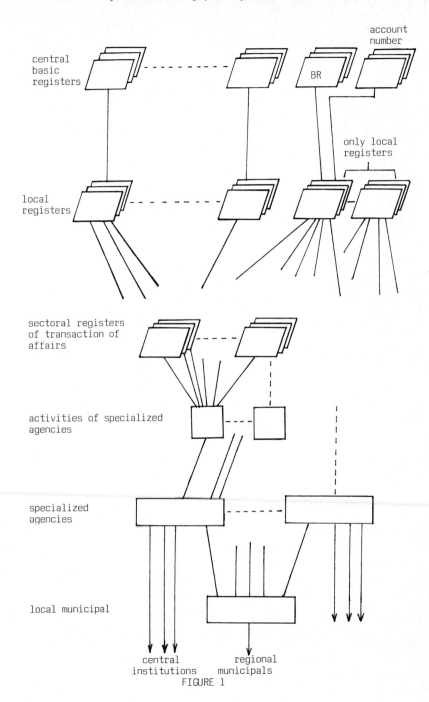

FIGURE 1

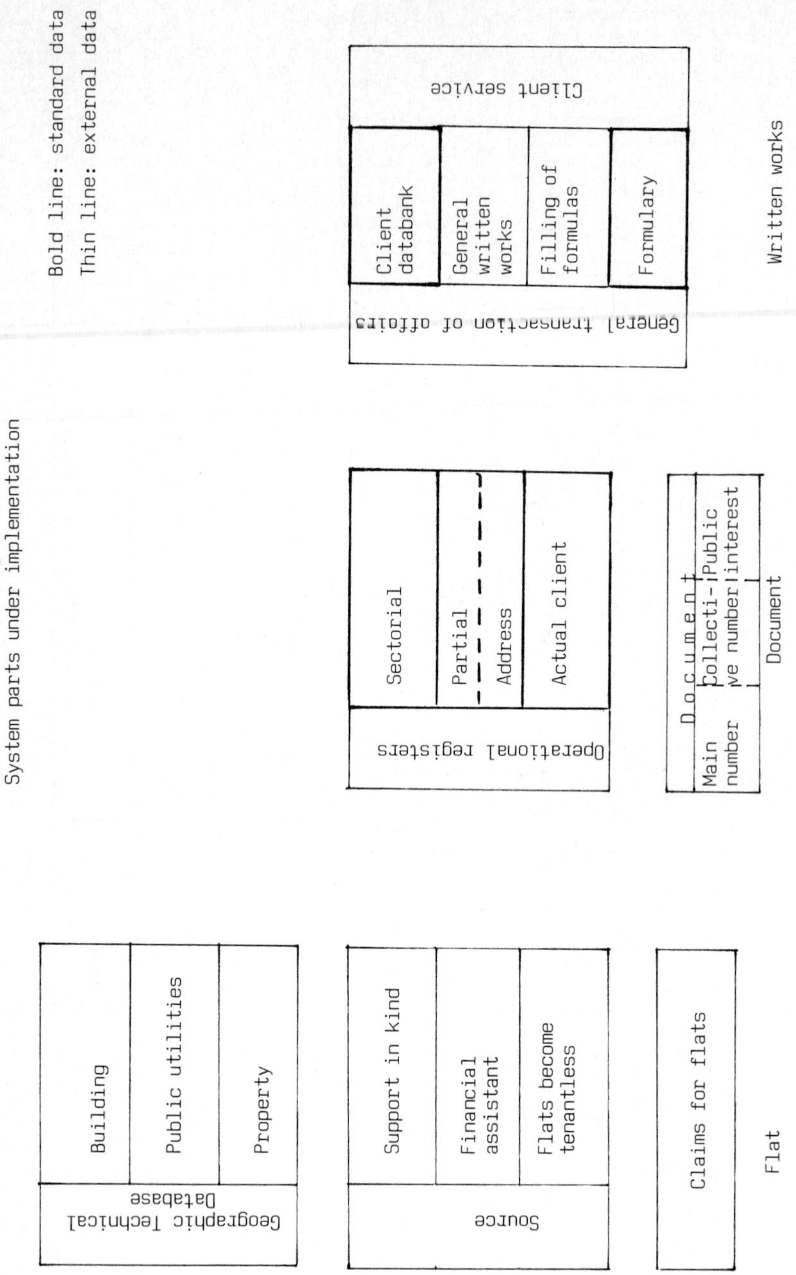
Bold line: standard data
Thin line: external data
System parts under implementation
Client service
Client databank
General written works
Filling of formulas
Formulary
General transaction of offairs
Written works
Operational registers
Sectorial
Partial
Address
Actual client
Document
Main number
Collecti-ve number
Public interest
Document
Geographic Technical Database
Building
Public utilities
Property
Source
Support in kind
Financial assistant
Flats become tenantless
Claims for flats
Flat

FIGURE 2

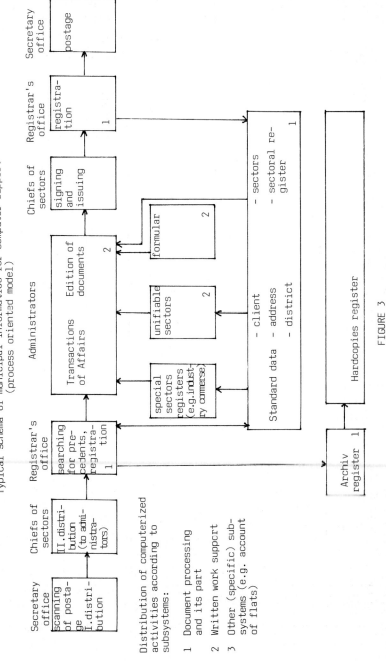

Typical schema of municipal informatics for computer support
(process oriented model)

FIGURE 3

Governmental and Municipal Information Systems
P. Kovács and E. Straub (Editors)
Elsevier Science Publishers B.V. (North-Holland)
© IFIP, 1988

SYSTEM OF FACTOGRAPHIC INFORMATION IN THE FIELD
OF THE AGRICULTURAL TECHNIQUE IN POLAND

Doc. dr inż. Adam Górski

Generally under the conception of factographic information
one should understand factual, converted information and preparing
for indirect utilization by the user.

Preparing relys on the proper selection and chosing from among
all sources of information, pertinent to the actual need, their
verification, through analysis and proper scientific description,
in the conclusions from the realization of analysis', studies,
researches and expert appraisement. In the connection factographic
information occurs not only in the tables, outlines and diagrams
- for what would indicate mentioned definition - but it is also
supported with appropriate explanations, opinions reviews and
analitic - syntetic analysis'.

Very often we meet the ordinary factographic information. It is
furnish in the information station, in the railiway, bus stations,
airport etc, when we receive concrete and complete answer for
questions. So far in the area of science and technology, factographic information has not been popularized and universalized,
although it can be occured in branches of economic activity.
However most information is unit for use in the technique field,
and in the classical use - for information in the range of manufactured products by the particular industries, where is used for the
users information about particular facts, concerned with these
products.

For a better illustration of the problems above can be used the
"International System of the factographic Information in the Field
Tractors and Agricultural Machines" so - called "MOSFI" utilized
in Poland and all countries participating in the International
System of Scientific and Techniqual Information" which belong to
"Council For Mutual Economic Aid".

Generally the "MOSFI" System can be defined as a system of
information in the range of manufactured products by the manufactures of tractors and agricultural machines all over the world
It is designated to collect and compile with the help of computer's
technique, international materials and to give users the run of
apropriate facts concerning those products.

Basic principles of the "MOSFI" action

On the "MOSFI" system all products the branch of tractors and
agricultural machines are well - ordered and form so - called
factographic groups. And for example tractors form factographic
group number 001, drills seeder - 016, combines and harvesting
devices - 083.

A profile of the factographic groups can include no more then
999 factographic groups. At present in the data base system are
gathered factographic data for about 200 (two hundred) factographic groups.

For each factographic group has been established certain factographic data, which is the best characterize of the certain product,
especially its technical - exploiatation paramteters. In the
subordination of the concrete discription of factographic groups
settled by the specified data. The maximum number of the data
amount - facts is 99.

These facts are devided into two parts: One part forms the first
of the 16^{-th} facts which is processing and then found in the
Electronic of the Numeric Machines (ENM), this according can be set
to the name of the facts and the trade marks (so - called direct
occess). This is the descriptive part. For example in the factographic group 011 includs tractors, for the first part facts
collected enter the following dates:

01 - products mark, 02 - country - producer, 03 - producer -
concern, 04 - product's name 05 - driving mechanism type,
06 - towing power class, 07 - workmanship, 08 - conditions use,
09 - type of engine, 10 - mark's engine, 11 - operator's cabin
type, 12 - PTO driving system, 13 - location of PTO, 14 - driving
mechanism system, 15 - hitch decive system, 16 - technological
equipment.

The second part is formed of such facts, which processing and
finding in the Electronik of Numeric Machines can take part only
with the onomastics facts, is so called nondescriptive part.
This type of factographic data are chosen from the particular
sources of information and put into the system of adata base.
Obviously not each source of information includs all settled data
for particular factographic group. Morever analysis of the series
of different sources of information allows to fully acquire factographic data, characterize technical - exploatation parameters
of certain product.

Factographic information which is put into "MOSFI" system are
chosen on a basis of present analisis from the following types
information sources: - monographs, - periodic publications,
- materials from conferences, congresses, - prospects and manufactures catalogues, - trade publication from centres of information,
- special collections/patent discription, exploitation instructions, technical conditions, norms, reports from research centers.

Gathered factographic data are entered into the system base
concerning particular products groups and then are open to users
in two versions of information services:

1) Preparing information for specific questions
   (finding information in the retrospective direction)

2) Preparing periodic of current information for given themes.
   (finding information in the direction, so - called Selective
   Destrebiution Information).

Generally questions, themes can be reduced by questions about
definitive parameters of particular types of tractors or agricultural machines, and can also hold a wide range of information,
including all data of factographic products in certain factographic group.

Answers in this system are realized in the print read - out
form - tabulations on which are specified by designation of specific

factographic group, product's name, product's trade names of
factographic data and well - ordered to them size or data qualifications, Besides, each position of printed read - out includes data
of certain product or products group given bibliographic data of
information source, from which is chosen data.

Apart from the discussed form of reciving answers from the
"MOSFI" system, exists also different tabulations forms. For
instance these tabulations' foresee printed read - out, where
certain chosen fatographic's data for different product types
(from the same factographic group) are realized in table from.

User can choose the form in which he wants to receive answers
for his questions. Program "AJTOS" - which has been used in this
system, makes possible realization of different sizes of printed
- read - out. If the answer for question on the magnetic disk or
magnetic tape and can create data bank for here own needs.

The Significance of factographic systems are increasing all
over the world, and the rate of developing documentary systems is
clearly decreasing. During the last years the number of the factographic data bases increased almost two times.
First of all it results from the increase of application for
factographic information. For example 70-80% notificationed
questions by the scientists of in restigations back up facilities
concerned factographic information.

Governmental and Municipal Information Systems
P. Kovács and E. Straub (Editors)
Elsevier Science Publishers B.V. (North-Holland)
IFIP, 1988

SOME PROJECTS OF WIDE AREA NETWORKS IN POLAND

Zbigniew HUZAR, Andrzej KALIŚ

Computation Centre, Technical University of Wrocław,
Wybrzeże Wyspiańskiego 27, 50-370 Wrocław, POLAND

The paper describes two projects of computer networks of
WAN type. The first one, called MSK had been accomplished
in the period from 1980 to 1985 within the research program sponsored by the Ministry of Science and Higher Education and coordinated by the Technical University of
Wrocław. Since 1986 the MSK computer network has been developed within the new research program also coordinated
by the Technical University of Wrocław. The aim of this
program is to gain a fully operating computer network,
called KASK, joining a majority of academic computer centres. The second project, called SKJS2 version 1 had been
realized in the period from 1984 to 1986 by the Technical
University of Wrocław. The SKJS2 version 1 computer network was examined in a laboratory installation and now is
offered as a commercial product.

1. INTRODUCTION

Problems connected with construction and exploitation of computer
networks in Poland, there are in the experimental phase. However,
some works are carried on, that create possibility to spread them
in the near future. Two elaborated projects of Polish computer
networks - MSK and SKJS2 version 1 - are strongly connected with
Polish computer manufacturers activities. The mainframes produced
by ELWRO such as ODRA1305 and EC1032, on which the Polish informatic and the main computer applications are based, became the basic
components of the above mentioned networks. The ODRA computers,
which were launched at the beginning of the seventies as a result
of co-operation with the ICL firm, are very popular due to very
fine properties of operating system GEORGE3+MOP. The EC1032 computers, generally accepted as a standard in socialist countries, are
fully compatible with IBM360 system and were launched in Poland in
the mid-1970's. The conceptions complete with realizations of the
MSK and SKJS2 computer networks were worked out by the Technical
University of Wrocław, full of vitality research center in training of computer applications. Among other things, at the Technical
University of Wrocław took place the first multiaccess system in
Poland. The program of construction an experimental computer network MSK for Polish academic environments was created in the latter part of the seventies. The first project works began in 1980
and the pilot version of the MSK network became operational in
1985 and has operated continuously since then. On duration of the
project phase and the resolution as a whole, the important influence had economical difficulties in Poland, especially, the lack
of the technical infrastructure at the universities. The second
project of the SKJS2 computer network began in 1984 and completely
finished in 1986. Created software had been confirmed and tested

during about one year. It means that this computer network has
been built during two years only.
As far as the MSK computer network is concerned, the activity was
oriented toward the development of the network techniques and its
starting point was the training of specialist staffs in computer
network area as well as in the methods for access to information
resources. On the other hand the SKJS2 computer network is fully
commercial product, ready for use, for example, in banking business. The MSK project was sponsored by the Ministry of Science and
Higher Education. The SKJS2 version 1 computer network was sponsored by Polish computer industry.

2. THE INTERUNIVERSITY COMPUTER NETWORK

2.1. Assumptions and requirements

As it was mentioned in the introduction, the idea of an experimental interuniversity network MSK /MSK - an abbreviation from Polish
Międzyuczelniana Sieć Komputerowa/ dates from the late 70th, but
the MSK project had started in 1980. The main aim of the project
was to built an experimental configuration of a heterogenous computer network and next, after a period of its examination, to
transform it into a permanently functioning academic network.
The basic assumptions, requirements and realization plans were
contained in the program of the project, elaborated by the Computer Centre, Technical University of Wrocław in 1980. The basic
assumptions were concerned with the logical architecture and standards of the computer networks. To meet the requirements of the o-
penness and heterogennity, the ISO reference model had been accepted. Because at that time as the reference model as well standards of the network services and protocols had not been matured
yet, therefore the MSK standards were elaborated in a considerable
extent on the base of the national standards utilized by countries
advanced in a network technology, particularly by Great Britain.
The second important question was related to the data transmission
subnetwork. Services rendered by the Polish post organization were
supported on a channel switching technique only. Despite of this
fact the decision choosing a packet switching technique had been
taken. The decision has appeared to be of strategic value and adequate for networking purposes.
The realization demands were the following:
- the hardware equipment of the network should be produced in
  Poland or in the others socialist countries,
- a special telecommunication equipment, like line adaptors,
  should be designed and manufactured within the project,
- the software of the network should be designed and implemented
  by self-dependent programming staffs.

2.2. Hardware and software configuration

Both host computers, i.e. the mainfraimes ODRA1305 and EC1032, are
coupled to the data transmission subnetwork via front-end-processors. For the ODRA1305 computer it is the minicomputer ODRA1325,
which are linked together via the intercomputer adapter ADM305.
For the EC1032 computer it is the communication controller EC8371
/the counterpart of the IBM3705/.
The standard operating systems, GEORGE3 with the multiaccess MOP
option and OS/JS 5.OP with the TSO option form the programming environment for networking software, of ODRA1305 and EC1032, respectively.

The main role of the front-end-processors is to concentrate terminals /mosaic printers with keyboard and monitors/ and to co-oper-
ate with data transmission subnetwork. Their software was designed
and implemented from scratch.
The data transmission subnetwork consists of the set of communication nodes linked together by means of duplex telephone lines. The
data transmission is carrying out in synchronous mode with the
rate 1200/2400 b/s. The communication nodes were realized in two
versions: on the base of SM3 and MERA60 minicomputers. Just as for
FEP´s the software of nodes was designed and implemented from
scratch. A typical fragmnet of the MSK configuration shows Fig. 1.

2.3. Services and protocols

The data transmission subnetwork supplies packet switching services founded on the X.25.3 standard recommended by CCITT[7]. The
implemented services contain SVC /Switched Virtual Calls/ and PVC
/Permanent Virtual Calls/ connections. The designers did not decide to implement a datagram service. This appeared to be in accordance with the further development of X.25.3[6] excludes this
service. The X.25.3 defines the interface between the communication subnetwork and its users, while the protocol between nodes
was also defined on the base of X.25.3 as its semidatagram modification. The other standards applicated in the communication subnetwork are: X.25.2 /LAP B/ [18] for the data layer and X.21 bis
[17] for the physical layer. The software of the communication
node performs also additional functions concerning with control,
diagnostic and measurement[1]. A description of performance measurements of the communication node is presented in [9].
The software of the front-end-processors supplies transport and
virtual terminal services. It enables a user of a network terminal
to establish connection with a given network application situated
in a given host computer and a connection with any other network
terminal /a substitute of an electronic mail service/. The above
services are based on the following recommendations. The transport
service and protocol was worked out by oneself and is founded on
the ISO document[14]. The transport entity implements the class 1
of the transport protocol as the primary protocol for a recovery
of services after communication failures. The virtual terminal was
elaborated on the working documents of the ISO and ECMA as a base
[20]. The implemented version realizes the simplest class for
teletype devices. The scope of the implemented virtual terminal
corresponds to services offered by the session and presentation
layers in the ISO reference model.
The network software of the host computers, except services of
their standard operating systems, offers the file transfer and manipulation service. The first pattern of this service was the
British standard[12,15] implemented in the JANET computer network
[19] and PAXNET network[11]. On the base of the file transfer the
job transfer and manipulation service was implemented /for ODRA
host computer only/. Additionally, also for ODRA host computer, t
the system of data base management and retrieval, called IDOL, was
implemented. By means of IDOL system its users have possibility to
access in conversational mode to bibliographical data bases.

2.4. Results and their appraisal

The final result of the MSK project was the pilot configuration
connecting the computer centres placed in the Technical University
of Wrocław, the Silesian Technical University in Gliwice and the
Institute of Computer Science at the Polish Academy of Science in

Warsaw. In recapitulation of services offered by it to the users
contains the following facilities:
- to run under control of the operating system of the choosen host
  computer,
- to transfer messages to any other network terminal,
- to transfer sequential files between any pair of host computers,
- to retrieve information in bibliographical data bases,
- to transfer jobs /ODRA computers only/.
How to evaluate these results? It is unambiguous matter bacause
the experimental phase of the MSK activity has not been exceeded.
There are several reasons for this situation, but the following
two are the most important:
- an underdevelopment of the technical infrastructure of the computer centres linked to the network,
- a lack of the essential results in the creation and development
  of programming network resources.
Independently of this insufficiency there are some valuable results:
- the experimental structure forms the technical and organizational nucleus for the future development,
- the achievement of the several original hardware and software
  solutions,
- the constitution of the experienced teams of designers and programmers familiar with modern network standards.

3. THE SKJS2 VERSION 1 COMPUTER NETWORK

3.1. Assumptions and requirements

Starting to construction of the SKJS2 version 1 computer network,
some requirements and limitations were assumed:
a/ users requirements
    - to ensure communication between any terminal and any choosen
      local or remote resources /terminal-to-host/,
    - to ensure connection between one terminal and any other one
      linked to the network /terminal-to-terminal/,
    - to ensure transfer of sequential files /by host-to-host in-
      teractive connection/,
b/ designers requirements
    - to ensure possibility of creation any network configuration,
    - to ensure possibility of the network extension by joining
      additional hosts, nodes and new resources /configuration
      flexibility/,
    - to ensure easy organization of the owners systems,
    - to ensure acceptance of various terminal devices.
c/ manufacturers requirements
    - equipment used to completion of the network have to be pro-
      duced by ELWRO,
    - software distributed by ELWRO among users, should be largely
      utilized in the network.
d/ exploitation requirements
    - possibility of the network diagnozing,
    - possibility of the network reporting and measuring.

3.2. The SKJS2 computer network configuration

A computer network is composed of transmission facilities and communication hardware in addition to terminals and computers. System
configuration of the SKJS2 version 1 is presented in Fig. 2. Dis-
tinctive feature of the SKJS2 computer network is that the commu-

nication controller EC8371.01 /IBM3705/ brings together functions of the network node and terminals concentrator /it acts both as interfaces between the host computers and the network and as packet-switching node/. Communication controller is located at each host site. Two or more communication controllers are interconnected by means of modems through leased telephone lines.

The following components are used in the network:

a/ host computers - the mainframes such as EC1032 /IBM360/,EC1055 EC1034 /IBM370/,

b/ Fep and node - communication controller EC8371.01 /IBM3705/,

c/ terminals - EC8577M /connected to the communication controller/ EC7910 family /EC7911,EC7914,EC7915,EC7917/ linked to host and communication controller,

d/ transmission equipment - any terminal is connected to communication controller by means of two wires through modem EC8006 /600,1200 b/s/. The communication controllers are linked each other by means of four wires through modems EC8013 /1200,2400 b/s/.

3.3. Software

The operating system OS/JS 5.0P /OS/MVT/, telecommunication access method /TCAM5/ and the network control program /NCP/ in conjunction with EC8371.01 communication controller are used. All the above mentioned software components are sold by ELWRO.

For realization of network processing mode and communication services, the following program modules were elaborated:

a/ HOST. The main module MLOT controls terminals and realizes virtual connections in the network. Generated program MCP /telecommunication access method/ serves the terminals directly linked to the host computer on the physical level only, and in addition it is "a medium" for messages that flow bidirectionally between MLOT and applications. Module MLOT has been coded in Pascal360 languages with elaborated access method between Pascal modules and program MCP. File transfer services are realized by the file transfer station /FTS/. It is originally new application that uses the host-to-host interactive connections to transfer a data file between hosts.

b/ FRONT-END and NODE PROCESSOR. Software that realizes functions connected with the front-end and node processor are located in communication controller EC8371.01. This software is divided into several program module as follow:

- network access method entity,
- transport entity,
- operator entity,
- network entity.

Software structure of the SKJS2 version 1 network is depicted in Fig. 3.

3.4. Services

The elaborated program modules give us possibility to manage the network configuration, effect changes, and monitor the use of network resources.

The main equipment base of the network is composed of devices produced in Poland, especially by ELWRO /of course, it not means that other compatible devices produced in the other countries would not be used. However, it means that all equipment and software are sold by one contributor only/.

The main resources are as follows:

- customer information control system /CICS/,

- time-sharing option /TSO/,
- file transfer station /FTS/,
- applications elaborated by the owners, for example, the electronic mail.

The access to the resources is possible from:
- local terminals directly connected to the host,
- remote terminals linked to the communication controller.

The way in which the virtual connection is made is independent of
the resources localization. The virtual connection sustaining and
the control of flow information in the network is invisible for
the users /communication services are transparent to the user/. In
addition, the software is able to report the main states of the
network, connect together of system operators and manage recovery.

3.5. Results

The all programe modules were fully confirmed and tested on the
configuration composed with three computers /two EC1032 and one
EC1055/.
Measuring and testing were made with respect to the early prepared
testing plans. The special measure-diagnostic device was constructed that was able to trace all bit streams flowing between two communication controllers and interpret them.
Obtained results demonstrates that the network SKJS2 version 1
complies with all assumed requirements, particularly, time-sharing
option has better facilities than this original one.
Each time a connection either enters or leaves serving host, data
about this connection are accumulated by the host computer. When
a connection finally terminates the connection's statistics are
logged by the host /module MLOT/.

4. FINAL REMARKS

The both described projects have essentially an explorative feature
but they can be treated as a turning-point in the development of
computer networks in Poland. The achieved experience proved that
the main problems in the network design and exploitation are these
of economical and organizational nature connected with the "network of people" responsible for the creation and maintanance of
network resources. A relative success of the MSK project formed
a basis for its further continuation. The new project of the National Academic Computer Network, called KASK had been started.
Its main aim is to build computer network, joining the majority of
Polish academic computer centres. This network is expected to operate in a fully usable mode. The undertaking works are concentrated, among others, on the following problems:
- the adaptation and attachment of new operating systems options
  to the network purposes,
- an adaptation of data base management and retrieval systems running on EC computers,
- an attachement of new types of host computers /EC1061/,
- an enrichment of the set of network terminals by an exploitation
  of IBM PC microcomputers.

The emaginable success of this enterprise and especially a dissemination of achieved solutions, will be depended in considerable
scale on the data transmission services developing by the Ministry
of Communication.
Also the project of the SKJS2 computer network is to be continued
but the main effords will be directed towards an application of
the already gained results in a practice.

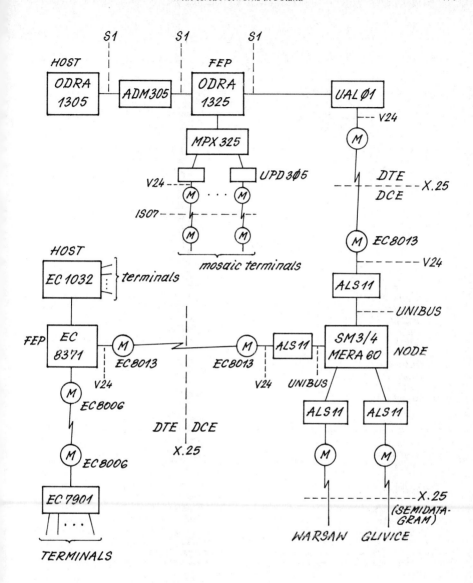

Fig. 1 The MSK computer network configuration

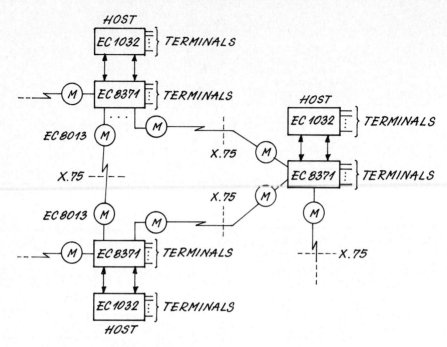

Fig. 2   The SKJS2 version 1 computer network
         configuration

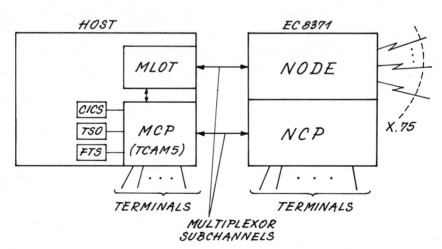

Fig. 3   The SKJS2 version 1 software configuration

REFERENCES

[1]   Bieleninik E. et al., MSK Communication Subnetwork, Informatyka, 1986,no.11-12,pp.15-38.
[2]   Bilski E., Open System Architecture, in[16],pp.13-23.
[3]   Bilski E., Fryźlewicz Z., Huzar Z., Kaliś A., Wide Area Computer Network, Informatyka, 1985,no. 9,pp.4-11.
[4]   Budzianowski L., MSK Computer Network Protocol Interaction, in[16],pp.233-250.
[5]   Budzianowski L. et al., ODRA1305 as a Host in MSK Computer Network, Informatyka, 1986,no.7-8,pp.16-19.
[6]   CCITT Recommendation, Red Book, Geneva 1985.
[7]   CCITT Recommendation, Yellow Book, Geneva 1981.
[8]   Dubielewicz I., Network Layer Protocol, in[16],pp.49-98.
[9]   Dubielewicz I. et al., Performance Measurements of the Communication Network Node, COMNET´85 Int. Symp., Working Papers, John von Neumann Society for Computing Sciences, Budapest, 1-4 Oct. 1985, pp.7.102-7.117.
[10] Hudyma E. et al., The Structure of the Reliable control and Measurement System in the Computer Network, ibid.,pp.8-29-39
[11] An Introduction to PAXNET, Rep. Class 1,no.2,July 1984, KTAS
[12] Kaszuba R., File Transfer Protocol, in[16], pp.152-215.
[13] Kaszuba R. et al., User Characteristics of File and Job Services, COMNET´85 Int. Symp., Working Papers, John von Neumann Society for Computing Sciences, Budapest, 1-4 Oct. 1985, pp.1.36-1.40.
[14] Muhleisen T., Transport Layer Protocol, in[16], pp.99-121.
[15] A Network Independent File Transfer Protocol. File Transfer Protocol Implementers Group. NIFTP-B/80/, Feb. 1981 /"Blue Book"/.
[16] Protocols of the Interuniversity Computer Network /MSK/, /ed./ E. Bilski, Wrocław Technical University Press, 1987, /in Polish/.
[17] Stanisz A., Physical Layer Protocol, in[16], pp.24-30.
[18] Stanisz A., Packet Level Protocol, in[16], pp.31-48
[19] Wells M., The JANET Project, University Computing, vol.6, 1984, pp.56-62.
[20] Wietrzych J., Virtual Terminal Protocol, in[16], pp.122-151.

Governmental and Municipal Information Systems
P. Kovács and E. Straub (Editors)
Elsevier Science Publishers B.V. (North-Holland)
© IFIP, 1988

OFFICE AUTOMATION IN THE GOVERNMENT
OF THE UNITED KINGDOM

Ewan Sutherland

Faculty of Social Sciences and Business Studies, Polytechnic of Central London,
32 Wells Street, London, W1P 3FG, United Kingdom
Telephone + 44 1 486 5811 ext 6464, Telecom Gold/Dialcom 87:WQQ223,
JANET sutherla@uk.ac.pcl.lynx

Abstract

The use of office automation in the UK Government is described and analysed.
The factors encouraging and discouraging the use of OA are considered. Certain
problems in the formulation of IT and OA strategies are identified. The results
of pilot projects and trials are discussed. Staffing issues are analysed. A conflict
between industrial policy and procurement of OA equipment is discussed.

1 INTRODUCTION

The development and use of office automation (OA) in Her Majesty's Government is considered includind the work of departments of different responsibilities, sizes and subject areas.
There is considerable diversity in the use of OA, even within one department.

Over the last thirty years HMG, the Government of the United Kingdom, has been slower
to develop its use of information technology (IT), and OA in particular, than the private
sector.

In most departments today, or a very few years ago, support for staff consists of a typing
service primarily relying on electronic typewriters and a data processing centre for transaction processing and statistics. There are a number of large data processing centres, e.g.
the Driver and Vehicle Licensing Centre. Major distributed data processing systems are
currently being developed for the Inland Revenue and the Department of Health and Social
Security.

Office automation in a number of departments has now reached a stage of "early contagion",
i.e. rapidly spreading use of some OA tools with pilots of multi-function systems. A
very few are at the stage of "advanced contagion", but none has yet reached the point of
"consolidation". [1]

2 IT STRATEGIES

The general movement in the commercial world has been towards the development of IT
"strategies" and this approach has been adopted by the Civil Service [2]. When used in
the private sector, it has proved relatively, but not completely, straightforward to identify
business objectives and critical success factors. In public sector industry, it has been more
difficult to determine and to rank goals. However, this has been extremely difficult in
Government departments. [3]

The reason for this difficulty has been the lack of recognisable objectives - indeed they are
almost totally absent. The main function of the Civil Service is to advise on ministers on
policy and then carry out that policy. Most senior Civil Servants focus on policy formulation
because that is what ministers are interested in. Consequently administration is put in
second place. [4,5]

IT is seen primarily as a way to save money, usually through staff savings [6,7,8]. HMG is
aiming to cut levels of staff back to what they were in the 1940's. OA is not easily shown
to achieve this, the costs are too high. It also presumes the ability to reallocate time saved
which requires some degree of organisational flexibility. However, efforts are now being
made to use IT to help in policy formulation.

There is little evidence of enthusiastic high ranking Civil Servants influencing the adoption of OA in the way that frequently occurs in commerce and industry. At lower levels there has been very little financial scope for do-it-yourself OA and a considerable tradition against such moves, though this is common outside.

Unlike the practice in commerce and industry, where it is increasingly common to find a director or other senior executive with sole responsibility for IT, in HMG it is left in the hands of middle ranking staff, under the supervision of IT committees.

OA is a much lower priority than in the private sector, there being a much less pressing demand for correspondence, information and reports.

Committees have been established to work on IT strategy in most departments. In better cases, these consist of the departmental Permanent Secretary and deputy, the Establishment Officer, the Head and Deputy Head of IT and a representative from the CCTA. In other cases it will be at a lower level, reporting to the management services committee.

The IT strategy committee identifies areas within the department where IT is to be developed and any necessary infrastructure. Once the strategy has been devised, the problem is often one of finding the necessary money to pay for it. A lack of funds has made development much more *ad hoc* and less strategic than departments wish.

There is an emphasis on cost benefit analysis within HMG which would otherwise characterise a less mature user of OA. Discounted cash flows based on time and staff saved are a common requirement for the purchase of an OA system.

Coincidentally, a new accounting procedure has been introduced which has had significant effects on departmental administration. The Financial Management Initiative (FMI) gives individual managers responsibility for their cost centres, in the same way as in the private sector. Any savings made in a cost centre can be spent within that cost centre, for example, on IT systems. [9] It therefore becomes necessary to persuade managers to accept procedures, standards and strategies for OA procurement and use since they will have to pay for them.

The combination of IT and FMI has caused considerable disruption to the way in which the Civil Service operates.

An important addition to the work on IT strategies has been the adoption of international standards, especially OSI and X.400. OSI is seen as the most effective way of ensuring the availability of a wide range of systems and suppliers and of achieving long term value for money. There is now a presumption in favour of OSI in all procurement. A subset of OSI has been defined as the Government OSI Profile (GOSIP). [10,11]

In OA it has been recognised that certain problems exist in regard of standards; multimedia documents, integration of a greater diversity of manufacturers and services and the sophistication of user expectation.

3 USE OF OFFICE AUTOMATION

The use of office automation in HMG has been severely restricted for many reasons; technical, financial and organisational.

Controls on departments come from the Treasury and its Central Computer and Telecommunications Agency (CCTA). The former's control is financial, while the latter offers "advice" on IT. Most departments are able to buy systems up to the value of £100,000 (approximately the GATT government procurement limit) without approval, although this varies from department to department, depending on its experience in IT.

Where a system costs more than the departmental limit, approval and advice must be sought. However, it is not possible for the Treasury and the CCTA to compel a department to buy a particular type of system or to prohibit them from buying one they want. The strength of individual departments in bargaining permits each to follow its own chosen path. As a last resort, the CCTA can insist on a post-installation evaluation.

The historically low level of spending on office equipment has meant that it has proved difficult to obtain the necessary money to implement large scale projects, since it appears to be a large jump from the previous budgets. The cost of installing the infrastucture is very high, especially during a period when HMG has sought to minimise capital expenditure.

Since 1977, HMG has imposed severe financial restraints on itself.

There is a shortage of experienced and qualified IT staff in the Civil Service and it is virtually impossible to recruit from outside. Attempts have been made to resolve this by training its own staff, especially young graduates. However, this has proved only partially successful. "Head-hunting" by private organisations has been a serious problem.

The previously very low level of use of IT amongst staff has meant that the Civil Service starts lower down the IT "learning curve" than equivalent commercial organisations.

Manpower restrictions and limits are imposed on units in order to achieve the required overall reductions. The effect is to force those units to look to OA to help them out.

The types of solution adopted have tended to be IBM PC's (or clones) and Unix mini-computers linked by LAN's. The Unix "boxes" either providing an integrated OA system or used for specific applications to supplement facilities on PC's. In one case where the software runs on Unix systems, the functional requirement specified response times rather than a size or number of processors, leaving the supplier with the unpleasant job of sizing.

3.1 Central Computer and Telecommunications Agency

The CCTA's roles are advice and help, identification of key issues and development, inter-departmental communications and procurement [12]. As part of it development programme, CCTA's current trials include linking PABX's using Digital Private Network Signalling System [13], voice mail [14] and text distribution [15].

It has rapidly and effectively changed its role from one of determining departmental requirements. Departments find the new arrangements much more helpful and flexible.

The CCTA has suffered considerable problems in maintaining adequate levels of qualified staff.

HMG has sought to develop methodologies in the CCTA, usually in collaboration with outside consultants, with a view to their wider use. Considerable success has been achieved with Structured Systems Analysis and Design Methodology (SSADM). A methodology for OA implementation has recently been produced [16,17].

4 OFFICE AUTOMATION PILOT PROJECTS

To encourage the use of information technology in HMG (and in the UK in general) a programme of Office Automation Pilot Projects was run by the Department of Trade and Industry (DTI), lasting from 1981 to 1985. The Pilot Projects were intended to help users, manufacturers and consultants located in the UK to develop there expertise in office automation.

The enthusiasm of the IT industry, and of potential users, was so great that the scheme was expanded from three to twenty projects. At each site approximately £250,000 worth of equipment was installed. The systems were used in proper working environments. Of the projects, six were in central government, eight in public sector industry and six in local government. Of the suppliers, twelve were UK-owned one was Dutch and six were based in the USA (including IBM). For each system, a member of a consortium of commercial management consultancies carried out an initial study. Later, another firm of consultants undertook an assessment of the use made of the system.

The effect of the Pilot Projects was to accelerate the use of office automation in HMG. This was achieved by offering a route towards office automation with low cost and reduced risk, or at least limited consequences, of failure. They also stimulated considerable interest in other departments, especially those which had been unsuccessful in requesting a Pilot Project.

The sites of the Pilot Projects were extensively visited by representatives of both private and public sector organisations. For example, fifteen hundred vistors saw the system at the Greater London Council's Scientific Branch.

Interim and Final Reports were produced by the consortium of consultants monitoring the Projects [18,19]. The Final Report was widely disseminated, with free copies being sent to the heads of all Government departments, chief executives of local authorities and managing directors of public sector industries.

In the reports, the applications of office automation were classified as

Text Production going beyond word processing to include electronic document distribution and storage, included the use of systems by end-users.

Case Handling the use of OA to support administrative transactions in organisations where work tasks are related to individuals, companies and projects and where staff need to store, retrieve, update and control information about them.

Management Support covering a range of acrtivities, including collective planning and decision making, executive communications and personal management support.

The greatest successes were achieved in word processing, with modest successes in the other areas.

Some systems failed completely, in a technical sense, and were removed. However, this was seen as inevitable in an experimental programme. In some cases manufacturers (including well-known firms) had overextended themselves.

The success in word processing, both in the Pilot Projects and elsewhere, has been developed into tests of considerable sophistication used in selecting new products. These use samples of departmental work to test potential office automation packages at suppliers' premises.

A further DTI pilot is planned to demonstrate Open Systems Interconnection (OSI) for office automation involving at least three different suppliers.

In addition to these DTI sponsored pilots, a significant number of departmental pilots have been run for their own purposes, these continue today [20,21]. Some of the early pilots lacked clear objectives which made them more difficult to build on. Pilots are recognised to present a danger in being open-ended, staff might not want to commit themselves, however it helped to persuade staff to accept systems. The results of pilots are made available to all departments through the CCTA.

5 STAFFING

Other than in specialist functions, the Civil Service is composed almost exclusively of "generalists", it possesses few engineers, scientists or MBA's - this is also true of the House of Commons. This makes more difficult the processes of decision-making, training and the implementation of OA and end-user computing.

The Civil Service has yet to adapt its career patterns to the use of information technology. Those selected for rapid promotion do not usually find themselves appointed to implement IT or to other "support" posts, e.g. in organisation and methods. Instead, the "high flyers", those destined for the top jobs, are usually assigned to deal with policy issues. Consequently, the top staff are usually not available to oversee the introduction of office automation systems. This will have longer term effects through the lack of experience of senior staff in day-to-day decision making regarding IT and office automation.

Civil Servants are generally enthusiastic about IT and have taken well to the systems they have been given. There are very rarely volunteers to lose their systems. However, they are relatively easily put off by complex or unpleasant systems or features of systems. Secretarial and clerical staff are well aware of the personal benefits from learning how to use IT systems, especially word processing. The usual age barrier has been observed with fewer senior secretaries or staff taking to office automation with enthusiasm, while some younger staff meddle and "hack".

A major reason for this enthusiasm is the poor level of typing service, which is frequently very slow. While ministers and top civil servants have a private office and relatively senior staff have personal secretaries, other staff must use a divisional secretary or typing pools. Frequently, secretaries to senior staff are asked to type work which should properly go to the typing pool. Work takes from two to four days to be returned from a typing pool and often longer, this is very much poorer than in equivalent commercial organisations. It is therefore worthwhile for staff to do their own word processing, especially if only simple changes are to be made.

The London market for secretarial staff is notoriously competitive and HMG offers relatively poor pay rates. It is therefore unable to increase the size of typing pools, even if it were inclined to do so. It has transferred work to some typing pools outside London where spare capacity exists.

Enthusiasm goes beyond word processing and electronic mail. Generalist staff seem happy to write their own applications in fourth generation languages. In the medium and long term the variety of systems, primarily between departments, must make more difficult the transfer of staff.

The trades unions have made many fewer objections to office automation than might have been predicted, which can be attributed to a number of factors. There has been considerable general Governmental pressure on trades unions. Pre-emptive and preparatory work by the departments (e.g. pilot studies, staff involvement in planning and evaluation, etc) has helped. A good liaison system has been established with the Council of Civil Service Trades Unions. The main focus of union bargaining has been on pay-related issues. While there is no national agreement, there are a number of new technology agreements in individual departments.

The low salaries, even with the special increment for data processing specialists, have made it difficult to recruit specialist OA staff. The bonus was only paid to office automation specialists after 1985, previously it had been restricted to data processing staff. Within the Civil Service, CCTA and departments are now in competition for such specialist OA staff as there are.

A wide range of skills is required of staff dealing with OA; organisation and methods, computing, networking, project management and personal skills. Technical staff, despite their valuable knowledge, are usually very poor at communicating with non-specialist staff. Instead, non-IT staff have to be specially trained.

Yet considerable human resources are needed to implement new OA systems, indeed they are the main constraint in their introduction. Relatively few staff are available to train and support new users, which forces the slow introduction of OA.

Support for users of OA systems takes the usual forms of courses (generally in-house) and help-lines. However, there are signs of a growth of two sophistications to these approaches. Firstly, support by wandering about (c.f. managing by wandering about [22]) and secondly of "seeding" the organisation with more knowledgeable users.

Staff shortages have forced HMG to rely on commercial consultancies which are amongst the best paid jobs and among the more aggressive head-hunters.

6 SECURITY

Security in OA systems has been a much greater problem for HMG than for private organisations. Each installation is vetted by the "security officers" to determine the classes of documents which can be put on it. Usually, this is only "confidential" although one system is cleared to "classified". Most of the papers in most departments are only confidential, rather than secret. Many of these, although not particularly important in terms of national security are either personally or commercially sensitive. Therefore departments are obliged to regard the information as requiring appropriate security.

Some "tempest-proofed" units exist but they are small and isolated. Some PC's have removeable hard discs which can be put in safes for added security. Typewriters and traditional paper files are used for more secure work in parallel with the OA systems.

Brightly coloured LAN cables are left visible even in the corridors of nineteenth century buildings in order that any illicit taps can be seen easily. In one case, PC's networked to minicomputers, have locks on the PC's, on the NIU's and a password is required to logon to the minicomputer. In others, ID cards are used for access to each terminal in addition to passwords.

Security considerations have limited the interconnection of systems with the presumption being against a system, until it is proven to be sufficiently secure. This has limited access from office systems to databases, both internal and external.

In order to comply with the Public Record Act, paper copies of most documents must be kept in addition to any electronic records.

In common with most commercial users of OA systems, there is little evidence that disaster planning has been undertaken.

7 ELECTRONIC MAIL

Most departments maintain an hourly messenger service to all offices delivering and collecting mail and photocopies. This service is expected to be maintained for many years, despite the growing use of electronic mail.

Electronic mail is used extensively within OA systems, even in relatively small systems. In addition to messaging it is used both to circulate draft documents and to return word processed material from pools. Users are keen to see electronic mail extended to more widely. In one small system electronic mail is so well accepted that it is used for gossip.

The Inter-Departmental Electronic Mail (IDEM) service indicates the beginnings of electronic interconnections between departments [23,24]. It is a message handling system conforming to CCITT X.400. IDEM provides two services, mailboxes for direct users and a gateway service for office systems with their own electronic mail facility. In addition to conventional X.400 services, IDEM contains a restricted mail service, accessible only from encoded telephone lines - non-restricted messages can be passed to the unclassified section.

Work is currently being planned on a Government Data Network (GDN) which will match the existing Government Telecommunications Network (GTN). However, this has met with public disquiet. For the future, an Integrated Services Government Network (ISGN) has been proposed, based on ISDN. [25]

8 THE LIBERATOR

A major study of "knee-top" micro-computers was undertaken by the CCTA to determine their suitability for use in the Civil Service [26]. The trial lasted nine months, cost £30,000 and included forty-four users. The results were very favourable, with considerable benefits identified: improved turnaround time for document production; use of "dead time", e.g. travelling; use at home and as a low cost electronic mail terminal. Payback periods varied, according to the user's grade, from fourteen to forty weeks.

Thorn-EMI, a UK manufacturer, produced a "knee-top" computer based on a specification drawn up after the trial. "The Liberator" is small, light (less than 2kg) and very easy to use. The aim was to provide a quick and effective way of converting ideas into text. [27]

They are used mainly for text production with some use of the telecommunications facilities. Staff issued with Liberators also use them in their offices to provide a faster typing service than their typing pool. Problems have been experienced when connecting The Liberator to word processors and micro-computers.

Success in the diffusion of The Liberator has been "patchy". Some departments have had good results where it has been pushed. However, where it has not been marketed, it has not been a success. In one department it was felt that portable dictation machines were more cost effective. This appears to be a misconception of the use of the Liberator by the department concerned.

The Liberator has not sold in significant quantities in the commercial market.

9 INDUSTRIAL POLICY

The use of OA by government has caused a clash between two policies, those of cheap and efficient administration and the sponsorship of the UK OA industry. The application of the rules of the GATT and the European Community [28,29] have meant that HMG uses a very open tendering process. Typically 50-150 enquiries are received to an invitation to tender with 10-20 proposals resulting from these, from which a much smaller short-list is drawn.

The Government has been severely criticised by UK OA suppliers for failing to use its procurement of IT for wider policy goals, i.e. to help them. The potential for UK firms in OA had been expected to be high. [30] However, there are few integrated office system available from UK suppliers.

Before open tendering was introduced, there was a very strong "Buy British" policy. As a result of this, HMG was using so many ICL systems that when that firm found itself in financial difficulties in 1981 it was obliged to help. Failure of ICL would have been disastrous for the public sector. [31]

10 CONCLUSION

In spite of many obstacles, the UK Government has made significant advances in its use of office automation and continues to do so. Nonetheless, it has been uneven and remains somewhat isolated, both electronically and organisationally.

The wider potential benefits of greater automation to support the Civil Service seem not to have been recognised. In France, the benefits of a more economic government bureaucracy are seen in terms of improving international competitiveness [32], this has not occurred in the United Kingdom. It is not clear that, even in France, the potential benefits of greater flexibility in Government are appreciated. There is no political force for the greater use of office automation and therefore progress is slow. Such pressure as there is, comes from dissatisfied users.

Government emphasis since 1977 has been to reduce expenditure, or at least to minimise the growth and to reduce manpower levels. Therefore, spending on running costs, even with potential long term benefits are not welcomed. The effect of this, in restricting growth in IT, has been considerable.

Until the use of basic OA tools of word processing and electronic mail are in much greater use, it will be difficult to assess the overall effects and real benefits.

Bureaucracy has considerable reserves of inertia and the UK Civil Service is no exception, so that it will be some years before a truly automated system supports the human Civil Servants and Ministers.

ACKNOWLEDGEMENTS

To the various Civil Servants and consultants who gave me their time. To the Polytechnic Wolverhampton which permitted me to undertake the initial part of this research and to Mr Philip Moore and Mrs Olive Ransom for their advice and support. To Professor Tom Carbery for his advice, support and comments on my prose. To Dr Yves Morieux and Mr Miles Atchison for their comments on earlier drafts of this paper.

REFERENCES

[1] Soane, Giorgina. The Organisational Issues of Office Automation *CCTA News*, No. 61 (1986) 2-4.

[2] CCTA. Guidelines for Strategic Planning for Information Technology (CCTA, London, 1986). Dd8933965 CCTA J0016

[3] McCosh, Andrew M. The Organisation, its Aims and Using Information Technology to Achieve Them *Information Technology and Public Policy*, 4 (1985) 23-35.

[4] Bruce-Gardyne, Jock (Lord). Ministers and Mandarins (Sidgwick and Jackson, London, 1986). ISBN 0283994150

[5] Lyn, Jonathan and Jay, Anthony. The Complete Yes Minister; the diaries of a Cabinet minister by James Hacker, MP (BBC, London, 1984). ISBN 0563203234

[6] House of Commons, Treasury and Civil Service Committee. Efficiency and Effectiveness in the Civil Service (HMSO, London, 1982) HC (1981-82) 236-I. ISBN 0102930821

[7] HM Government. Efficiency and Effectiveness in the Civil Service (HMSO, London, 1982) Cmnd 8616. ISBN 01018605

[8] House of Commons, Committee of Public Accounts. Management and Control of the Development of Administrative Computing in Government Departments (HMSO, London, 1984) HC (1983-84) 361. ISBN 0102361843

[9] HM Treasury. Financial Management in Government Departments (HMSO, London, 1983) Cmnd 9058. ISBN 0101905807

[10] CCTA. Standards for Open Systems Interconnection. (HMSO, London, 1986) *IT in the Civil Service* **12**. ISBN 0113300034

[11] CCTA. Open Systems Interconnection - CCTA's Expectations and Suppliers' Implementation (HMSO, London, 1986) *IT in the Civil Service* **15**. ISBN 0113300123

[12] CCTA. Central Computer and Telecommunications Agency: progress report (HMSO, London, 1985) *IT in the Civil Service* **11**. ISBN 0113300026

[13] *CCTA News*, No. 63 (1986), 12.

[14] Bayliss, Jon. CCTA Voice Messaging Project (VOMP) - an interim report, *CCTA News*, No. 63 (1986), 8.

[15] Hunter, Philip and Rowland, Peter. Text Distribution by IT - throwing words about in Government, *CCTA News*, No. 63 (1986) 5.

[16] CCTA/MPO. COMPACT; a management guide (MPO, London, 1986).

[17] Sangway, Diana. COMPACT - solving problems in the office. *CCTA News*, No. 69 (1987), 2-4.

[18] The Economist Informatics Unit. DTI Pilots; Interim Report (Department of Trade and Industry, London, 1985).

[19] KMG Thomson McLintock. Profiting from Office Automation (Department of Trade and Industry, London, 1986).

[20] CCTA. Early Experiences with Multi-User Office Systems (HMSO, London, 1984). *IT in the Civil Service* **7**. ISBN 0116307250

[21] Symons, Martin and O'Leary, Tim. The Revenue's Experience *Computer Bulletin* **3** (1987) 24-26.

[22] Peters, Tom and Austin, Nancy. A Passion for Excellence (Collins, Glasgow, 1985). ISBN 0006370624

[23] CCTA. Inter-Departmental Electronic Mail (HMSO, London, 1985) *IT in the Civil Service* **9**. ISBN 011330000X

[24] CCTA. Inter-departmental Electronic Mail: Stage 2 (HMSO, London, 1986) *IT in the Civil Service* **14**. ISBN 0113300115

[25] *Hansard* Sixth Series **113** Written Answers *107-108* (24 March 1987).

[26] CCTA. Who Needs Kneetops ? - a report on the trial of simple, easy-to-use, portable, text creation devices with communication capabilities (HMSO, London, 1985) *IT in the Civil Service* **10**. ISBN 0113300018

[27] McDonald, Sylvia. The Liberator Launched *CCTA News*, No. 56 (1985) 10-12.

[28] European Community. Council Directive 77/62 *Official Journal* L 13 (15.1.1977) 1-4.

[29] European Community. Council Directive AT/767 *Official Journal* L 215 (18.8.1980) 1-28.

[30] National Economic Development Office, Office Systems Sector Working Party.

[31] *Hansard* Sixth Series **1** (19 March 1981) 435-440.

[32] Salmona, Jean. Information Technologies in French Public Administration - towards major changes *Futures*, **18** (1986) 318-324.

Governmental and Municipal Information Systems
P. Kovács and E. Straub (Editors)
Elsevier Science Publishers B.V. (North-Holland)
© IFIP, 1988

OFFICE AUTOMATION IN JAPAN TODAY AND FUTURE CONSIDERATIONS
FOR THE PUBLIC SECTOR

Y. Yamadori / Japan

Thanks to technological innovations and lower prices for
business-related machines and equipment, the office automation (OA) movement in Japan has made very rapid progress
over the past few years. This movement has been especially
active at private enterprises where high-performance OA
equipment are being networked together to create comprehensive in-house systems and/or intelligent buildings.

This situation has increased the need for OA equipment
and systems in the public sector as well, and various
government agencies are already either carrying out feasibility studies or taking concrete steps to automate their
offices.

It is therefore a good time to review the extent to which
OA has penetrated the private sector, and based on these
findings, to give some serious thought as to just how
the public sector should approach OA.

1. INTRODUCTION

1.1. Everyone's talking about "OA"

Over the past 4 or 5 years, the term "OA" has become firmly established among Japanese as an abbreviation for office automation.
A number of stories have been reported of Japanese businessmen
in the office automation field asking their American counterparts
about the "OA" situation in the U.S. and getting a puzzled look
in response.

The fever over office automation that has swept Japan has been
generated mostly by the mass media, office automation equipment
salesmen and the managers of user companies. Most office automation specialists on the other hand are a bit perplexed by all
the fuss that has suddenly arisen over office automation and are
worried about a reactionary decline in interest.

Their anxiety stems in part from the nature of Japan's mass communication media (which incidentally, are referred to as MassCommi,
a rather odd abbreviation, as a more natural one would be MassComm).
These media know that the Japanese are quick to warm up to a subject but are even quicker to cool off. Therefore, since it is
easier to write for an enthusiastic audience, they come out with
article after article while their readers are still warmed up
to it. But once they sense that the fever has passed, they stop
completely.

First of all, I would like to elaborate the situation of installation and shipments of computers and OA related machines.

1.2. Computer Systems in Operation by Industry

Table 1 provides figures on general-purpose computer systems in operation by industry as of the end of March 1986.

Table 1.   General-purpose Computer Systems in Operation by Industry
(As of end of March, 1986)

(Values: in millions of yen)

Industry	No. of Systems	Value	Average Value Per System	% of Value
Agriculture	248	6,740	27.2	0.1
Forestry	163	1,451	8.9	0.0
Fisheries	317	4,863	15.3	0.1
Mining	273	6,215	22.8	0.1
Construction	6,017	106,906	17.8	1.4
Manufacturing	61,061	2,645,451	43.3	34.6
Electricity, Gas and Water	1,165	106,450	91.4	1.4
Transportation and Telecommunications	9,456	546,740	57.8	7.1
Wholesalers, Retailers and Restaurants	104,140	1,189,171	11.4	15.5
Finance and Insurance	10,130	1,324,116	130.7	17.4
Real Estate	819	9,730	11.9	0.1
Services	36,397	995,900	27.4	13.0
General Services	11,292	185,636	16.4	2.4
Information Services	17,923	510,326	28.5	6.7
Hospitals	3,212	56,867	17.7	0.7
Educational Institutions	3,970	243,071	61.2	3.2
Government	6,566	510,895	77.8	6.7
Local and Municipal	3,648	172,807	47.4	2.3
National	1,520	186,407	122.6	2.4
Government-related Agencies	1,398	151,681	108.5	2.0
Corporate Bodies and Farm Co-ops	7,174	174,494	24.3	2.3
Religious Organizations	104	2,431	23.4	0.0
Others	118	4,907	41.6	0.1
Total	244,148	7,636,461	31.3	100.0

Source: MITI's "Survey on Computer Deliveries & Trade-ins"

As shown in the figure, government is also one of the important industry sectors as for general-purpose computer systems in operation.

1.3. Small Business Computer Shipments

According to the fiscal 1985 survey, shipments of SBCs during that fiscal year amounted to 105,365 systems (up 35.7% over the previous year) worth a total of 390 billion yen (up 1.9% over the previous year).

1.4. Personal Computer Shipments

The market for personal computers (PCs) has passed from the phenomenal growth exhibited at the outset to a period of stable growth. The overall size of the

PC market is around 555 billion yen now, and is expected to reach the 1,000 billion yen level within a few years.

Factors contributing to OA and present status of OA are shown in figure 1 and 2.

Figure 1. Factors Contributing to Office Automation

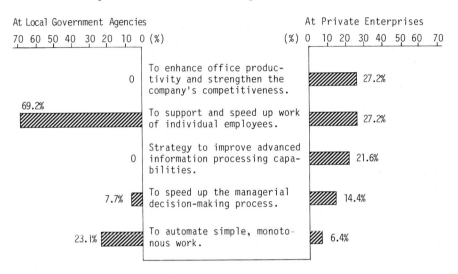

Figure 2. Present Status of Office Automation

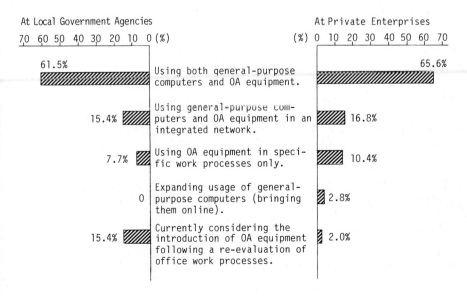

2. PUBLIC SECTOR APPROACH TO OFFICE AUTOMATION

Although there are any number of mutually-related steps involved in introducing
OA equipment into government offices, the following is considered the most basic
approach. And, proposed integrated OA network system is shown in figure 3.

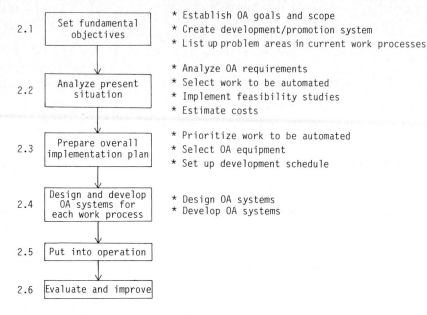

2.1 **Set fundamental objectives**
* Establish OA goals and scope
* Create development/promotion system
* List up problem areas in current work processes

2.2 **Analyze present situation**
* Analyze OA requirements
* Select work to be automated
* Implement feasibility studies
* Estimate costs

2.3 **Prepare overall implementation plan**
* Prioritize work to be automated
* Select OA equipment
* Set up development schedule

2.4 **Design and develop OA systems for each work process**
* Design OA systems
* Develop OA systems

2.5 **Put into operation**

2.6 **Evaluate and improve**

Figure 3.   Proposed Integrated OA Network System

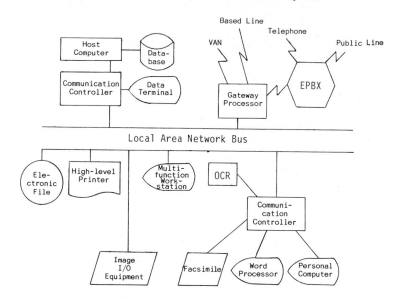

2.1. Establish Fundamental Objectives

For the efficient promotion of OA in Japan, we will have to come up with some fundamental ideas concerning the objectives and extent of that promotion. We will also have to set up appropriate organizations for the promotion and development of OA technologies. This is because the degree to which OA is promoted in Japan will depend in large measure on the comprehension and cooperation of the individuals involved in that promotion process.

(1) OA Objectives and Extent of Promotion

[1] Establish OA objectives
[2] Set the extent of OA promotion

(2) Promotion and Development Organization

Generally speaking, the following type of organizational structure will be necessary for the promotion of OA. We will also have to select and/or combine certain of these elements so as to meet with the objectives and extent of OA desired.

[1] Projects section
[2] Dedicated OA promotion section
[3] EDP section
[4] General affairs section
[5] Central coordinating section

2.2. Analyze Present Situation

(1) Sort Out Problems Inherent in Current Work Methods

a. Study work processes

Work flows (the flow of information and work processes), workloads and inter-sectional work relations, etc. should be clarified, and hearings should be conducted to gain a comprehensive understanding of the current work situation, i.e. are there any contradictions inherent in existing rules and regulations, and which vouchers are used the least.

Studies sould also be carried out on the kinds of problems faced by the people in charge of various types of work; on the aspects of their work they would like to improve; on the limitations they must work under; and on the degree to which they are counting on OA to improve their work situations.

b. Study existing computer system

Studies should be made on work currently being processed by the computer division, such as overviews of input and output processing and processing times, to determine user problems and areas that could be improved. Efforts should also be made to grasp the relationship between the existing computer system and OA, to include how these technologies might be configured in future.

c. Sort out problems

Based on the results of your work studies and study of the existing computer system, list up the problem areas discovered, the work aspects in need of improvement and the various limitations turned up, and then sort out and analyze the problems, research their causes and work out proposals for making improvements. This job should not be left entirely up to the people directly responsible for carrying out the work; management level opinions should also be solicited.

(2) Analyze OA Requirements

Next, analyze and prioritize OA requirements. A detailed, concrete understanding of user requirements is a must to ensure that no major changes are
wrought as a result of developing and implementing OA schemes.

(3) Select Work to be Automated

Based on the results of your work studies and analyses of OA requirements,
apply OA schemes to those jobs where it should prove the most effective.
At this point make sure you understand the entire process involved in the
work being automated, and clarify the relationship between the automated
jobs, the existing computer system and other jobs.

(4) Conduct Feasibility Study

A number of factors must be analyzed in relation to the various jobs
selected for automation. These include the functions of current OA equipment, their levels of utilization, the systems being used to promote their
use, the budgets required for their purchase and operation, legal restrictions on their usage and the relationships between the jobs to be automated
and other work processes. The results of this feasibility study will tell
you whether or not it is possible to carry out your automation scheme.

To determine the suitability of introducing OA schemes into certain selected
work processes, you will also have to carry out cost-performance analyses.

(5) Estimate Costs of OA

In calculating the estimated costs of your OA scheme, you should take the
following two points into consideration.

[1] Method of introduction

You will have to decide whether you want to purchase your OA technology
outright, or whether it would be more economical for you to lease or
rent the equipment you need.

[2] Required expenses

A variety of different types of expenses are involved in the introduction of OA equipment into your operations. Table 2 breaks these
expenses down by category.

2.3. Prepare Overall Implementation Plan

(1) Prioritize Work to be Automated

Attempting to introduce your OA scheme into all the work processes you
selected at once will probably put too much of a burden on you, both
economically and personnel-wise. It is better to prioritize the work to
be automated, and then to introduce your OA scheme into one work process
at a time in the order decided. The criteria used for prioritization are:

[1] Degree to which OA required
[2] Urgency of OA
[3] Cost-performance results
[4] Promise for future

Table 2. Expenses Related to OA

	One-time Expenses	Recurring Expenses
Facilities-related expenses	∘ Equipment room remodelling and expansion costs ∘ Facilities construction costs (power and communication equipment) ∘ Fixture expenses	∘ Floor space costs ∘ Utilities charges
Hardware-related expenses	∘ Hardware purchase costs ∘ Delivery and related costs	∘ Hardware rental costs ∘ Hardware maintenance charges ∘ Line leasing charges
Software-related expenses	∘ Software purchase costs ∘ Software development costs	∘ Software rental costs
Other expenses	∘ Data production costs ∘ Education and training costs	∘ Expendable supplies costs ∘ Data updating costs

(2) Select OA Equipment

When selecting your OA equipment, make sure you accurately understand the functions and features of each type of equipment, and clarify the effects that can be expected by introducing that equipment into the work processes selected for automation.

Some common points to keep in mind when selecting OA equipment are:

[1] Higher cost-performance
[2] Relationship to other work processes/sections
[3] Capabilities for mutually effective use
[4] Satisfaction of installation environment conditions
[5] Little worry of malfunctions; ease of operation
[6] Development trends for equipment in question

Points to keep in mind in the selection of OA equipment by equipment type are as follows:

A. Word Processors

    a. Effects of introducing into operations

        [1] Enhanced quality of texts and other printed materials
        [2] Reduced workload thanks to use of form letters and other general-purpose texts stored in memory, and abbreviated correction/revision work
        [3] Reduced printing costs and shortened printing times

    b. Points to keep in mind when selecting a word processor

You must make sure that the functions capable with the word processor you select satisfy the requirements of the work process involved.

- Input   : Input method, units and keyboard alignment
- Display : Size and color of screen, illumination control, character patterns and layout
- CPU   : Number of resident KANJI characters
- Storage : Vertical write display, format, standard floppy disk, floppy disk capacity and basic word storage

```
            - Output   : Printing method, character pattern, typeface, character
                         size, printing speed, noise and the type and size of
                         paper used
            - Password function
            - Communication functions
```

B. Personal Computers and Intelligent Terminals

    a. Effects of introducing into operations

        [1] Timely document preparation, accurate data management, fast data
        retrieval and effective utilization of data
        [2] Speedy work processing
        [3] Reduced amount of work
        [4] Reduced personnel costs
        [5] Enhanced government services

    b. Points to keep in mind when selecting a PC/intelligent terminal

        [1] You must make sure that the functions capable with the PC or
        intelligent terminal you select satisfy the requirements of
        the work process involved.

```
            - Display : Size and color of screen, illumination control,
                        character patterns and layout
            - Storage : Format, standard floppy disk, floppy disk capacity,
                        standard hard disk and hard disk capacity
            - Output  : Printing method, character pattern, typeface, char-
                        acter size, printing speed, noise and the type and
                        size of paper used
```

        [2] Software

```
            - Program language      : BASIC, COBOL, PASCAL or FORTRAN
            - Business programs     : Spreadsheets, data retrieval, integrated
                                      programs, graphics capabilities and
                                      simplified word processors
            - Application packages : Finance, payroll, accounting and word
                                      processing
            - Operating system      : CP/M, MS-DOS, UNIX
```

C. Facsimiles

    a. Effects of introducing into operations

        [1] Speedy document exchange
        [2] Reduced document exchange

    b. Points to keep in mind when selecting a facsimile machine

    You must make sure that the functions capable with the facsimile
    machine you select satisfy the requirements of the work process
    involved.

```
        - Continuous send function
        - Multi-point communication function
        - Auto-dial function
        - Automatic receive function
        - Polling function
        - Telephone reservation function
        - Book scanning function
```

D. Microfilm Equipment, and Electronic File Devices

    a. Effects of introducing into operations

[1] Space savings
[2] Speedy retrieval

b. Points to keep in mind when selecting microfilm equipment and/or electronic file devices

You must make sure that the functions capable with the microfilm equipment and/or electronic file device you select satisfy the requirements of the work process involved.

Microfilm Equipment

- Microfilm camera   : Type of film, photography method, subject width, reduction ratio and photography speed
- Microfilm reader   : Type of film used, expansion ratio, screen, feed speed, number of frames storable, focus adjustment, image revolution and retrieval functions
- Microfilm printer   : Reproduction speed, reproduction size, paper feed method and continuous prints

Electronic File Device

- Optical disk device : Revolution speed, data transmission speed and seek time
- Display   : Color, number of dots and image display function
- Keyboard   : Key alignment, numeric pad and function keys
- Scanner   : Maximum size of paper capable of being input
- Image processing function
                     : Partial movement, expansion, deletion, revolve, reverse and character insertion

E. Digital Private Branch Exchange and LAN

a. Effects of introducing into operations

[1] High-speed, high quality data communications
[2] Increased efficiency thanks to interconnectability of OA equipment

b. Points to keep in mind when selecting digital private branch exchanges and local area networks

You must make sure that the functions capable with the private branch exchange and local area network you select satisfy the requirements of the work processes involved.

Digital private Branch Exchange

- Relay functions: : Trunk line relay method, distributed relay method and direct online method
- Service functions : Extension line reset call, variable automatic transmission, extension line status display, extension line camp on, electronic mail and ACD functions
- Non-telephonic terminals

Local Area Network (LAN)

- Transmission medium
- Topology
- Access method
- Transmission method

- Transmission speed
- Terminal interface
- Maximum nodes per topology
- Maximum terminals per topology

(3) Development Schedule

You should put together a development schedule that calls for detailed planning based on long-term outlooks. Coordinate the individual plans put forth by each department, and then determine the overall development schedule based on these. Your final schedule should also include detailed schedules for implementing your OA scheme in each section of every department.

2.4. Design and Develop OA Systems for Each Work Process

(1) OA System Design

Design your OA system in the following manner:

[1] Divide the work processes to be automated into their smallest possible job denominations
[2] Clarify the function and objective of each job
[3] Estimate the amount of processing to be required for each job in the near future
[4] Ascertain the restrictions of each job
[5] Determine the approximate specifications for the OA system functions required to execute each job function
[6] Create the overall process for the OA system
[7] Estimate total costs

(2) OA System Development

Use the OA promotion and development organization you set up earlier to develop your OA system. You must decide whether you want to carry out this development entirely in-house, or farm a part or all of it out to outside developers.

2.5. Put into Operation

2.6. Evaluate and Improve

(1) Significance

The amount of OA equipment introduced into government offices has been increasing tremendously recently, but not enough has been done to analyze the effects of this automation on government work. The introduction is very costly and has a direct impact on the way government work is performed. Therefore, in the promotion of OA, not only must we be fully aware in advance of the effects that can be expected from introducing OA into government operations and of the suitability of those effects on the types of work involved, but we must also determine just how well the introduction of OA has met with our initial expectations.

This type of evaluation is related to the review and enhancement of the current state of OA utilization, and should form the basis and justification for promoting and expanding OA in future.

It will also be necessary to evaluate the profitability of promoting OA, especially under the austere economic conditions we now find ourselves in.

(2) Evaluation Methods

The methods for evaluating OA can be broadly divided into the following two categories:

[1] Relative evaluation methods (checklists and scoring models) which do not calculate the effects of OA in direct monetary terms; and
[2] Evaluation methods that compare the total costs of OA with its effects calculated in monetary terms (cost-performance analysis).

Relative evaluation methods, such as those cited in [1], allow for a far-reaching grasp of the effects of OA from both a quantitative and qualitative standpoint. However, because this approach does not use the absolute values associated with money, but rather relies on the judgements of the evaluators, it tends to lack conviction.

Relative evaluation methods are generally used in cases such as those outlined below (See Table 3).

Table 3. Factors Evaluated in the Analysis of OA Effectiveness

Main Factors	Secondary Factors
Qualitative improvements in work performance	° Accuracy of work performance ° Advancement of work performance ° Ease of work performance ° Improved readability of documents
Improvement of information management	° Speed of data transmission ° Accuracy of data transmission ° Ease of data utilization ° Centralization of data management ° Shared/mutual use of information ° Handling of increased amounts of data ° Data protection
Labor savings	° Reduction of personnel ° Curbs on personnel increases ° Reduction of operational expenses ° Shortening of work time ° Cut backs in overtime
Improvement of office environment	° Effective utilization of space ° Reduction of simple, repetitive tasks ° Improvements in communication ° Improvements in morale
Improvement of government services	° Simplification of procedures ° Accuracy of services ° Speed of services ° Enhancement of services
Qualitative improvements in government work	° Speed of administrative policy decisions ° Handling of diversification of administrative demands ° Assurance of reliability

a. To compare expected and actual effects (Degree of effectiveness achieved)
b. To establish priorities for the introduction of OA equipment and/or the development of applications
c. To evaluate and select various makes and models of equipment
d. To compare similar cases in a relative manner.

In contrast with this, the cost-performance-type evaluation methods described in [2] determine whether or not OA is profitable, and if so, to what degree, by arriving at the monetary balance between the costs involved in introducing OA and its effectiveness (in terms of increased productivity

and/or personnel savings, etc.). However, calculating the effectiveness
of OA in monetary terms is not easy, especially when you are dealing with
such qualitative factors as enhanced quality of administrative policies
and improved government service.

3. PROBLEMS RELATED TO THE PROMOTION OF OA

The advance of office automation (OA) into workplaces throughout the public and
private sectors in Japan, and the increased applications to which OA technologies are being put in line with this, could clash with traditional ways of doing
things, and the rules and regulations that have governed office routines to
date. The promotion of OA in Japan should therefore be carried out with the
following matters in mind.

3.1. Originality of Magnetic Files

The computerization of registration-type work has meant that registers and
ledgers are now created in the form of electronic files stored on magnetic
media. This has given rise to the problem of duplicate originals, i.e. the
hardcopy ledger used to date and the electronic ledger. As it stands now,
there are no provisions that enable us to treat electronic files as original
works. At present, the only thing we can do to deal with this problem is to
revise specific laws on a case-by-case basis. Some examples of the types of
electronic files for which pertinent laws have been revised to deal with the
problem of duplicate originals are as follows:

[1] Patent Registries (Patent Registry Ledgers)
[2] Automobile Registry Files
[3] Registration Files
[4] Resident Cards
[5] School Age Registries

3.2. Microfilm: Originality and Authenticity

The chief of the Criminal Bureau of the Ministry of Justice, in a statement
made on February 11, 1959, put forth the view that microfilm negatives of
official documents can be considered probative and can therefore be used as
authentic transcripts of original documents because (1) they prove the existence
of the original photographed document; (2) they serve as accurate copies of the
original document; and (3) they are properly maintained. There are those, however, who continue to maintain that the original document should be preserved
for a specified period of time even after it has been microfilmed.

3.3. Official Document Seals

Having to affix official seals by hand to large volumes of public documents output from computers runs counter to the merits achieved by computerizing the job
of preparing such documents in the first place. Therefore, when judged not to
be detrimental, the image of the official seal can be printed on the document
in question at the same time as it (the document) is being output, thus basicly
eliminating the problem of hand-affixed seals on official documents.

One area where this problem still exists, however, is facsimile reproductions.
Facsimile machines are coming into widespread use in the transmission of official documents between government ministries and agencies, and between central
and outlying government offices. But there is still no public interpretation
as to whether the seals reproduced on documents sent by facsimile are acceptable
as official seals, or whether they will have to be printed on these documents in
accordance with government instructions.

3.4. Printing Methods and Authenticity

Documents output from personal computer and/or word processor printing devices are acceptable as public documents on the conditions that they possess high resolution, are easy to read and are capable of being maintained for long periods of time.

Meeting these conditions depends on the printing method and character format (degree of resolution) used. The Ministry of Justice has stipulated the following specifications for Japanese-language public documents printed out using word processor printers:

Printing Method	Character Format
Wire-dot impact method	24 x 24 dots
Thermal transfer method	24 x 24 dots

3.5. Office Procedures and Regulations

The advance of OA into various facets of administrative (government) work has resulted in cases where the new OA technologies can not be readily applied to traditional or conventional work procedures and regulations, thus giving rise to duplication of effort, ledgers and other documents. This is very ineffici-ent. We must therefore, on a case-by-case basis, review and revise work regu-lations and improve and standardize work management and document control pro-cedures for existing work processing methods, the order and flow of that work, bookkeeping methods and document storage and control procedures to meet with the incorporation of OA technologies into government offices.

3.6. Ringi System

For some time now, there have been those in Japan who have pointed to the fact that the use of the "ringi" system (The process of obtaining the sanction of superiors to a plan by circulating the draft proposal of that plan to all con-cerned.) is too time consuming, and should therefore be simplified and rational-ized.

However, if we attempt to speed up the approval process by using electronic mail and other OA technologies, it will be necessary to review the various electronic processing methods to determine which are most suitable for the job, i.e. which fit in the best with the practice of affixing personal and official seals and with conventional revision methods.

3.7. Data Protection

With the progress of OA, huge amounts of diverse types of personal and corpo-rate data (information) are being stored in a variety of different types of OA equipment on various kinds of media. This data must be protected. Even so, it is still likely to "leak" outside the organization.

This problem is currently being dealt with by means of the "Working Rules for the Protection and Control of Computer Processed Data."

3.8. Office Environment

The progress of OA will bring with it the need to create suitable office environments capable of meeting new working conditions.

(1) Office Layout

Office furniture, desks and OA equipment will have to be arranged with safety and mobility uppermost in mind.

(2) Work Environment

The working environment for employees required to spend long hours in front of video display terminals, as well as their workloads and overall physical health, will have to be considered when designing offices in the future.

Governmental and Municipal Information Systems
P. Kovács and E. Straub (Editors)
Elsevier Science Publishers B.V. (North-Holland)
© IFIP, 1988

MULTIDATABASE MANAGEMENT SYSTEMS
SYSTEM ARCHITECTURE AND APPLICATION PRINCIPLES

Witold Staniszkis

CRAI
Contrada S. Stefano
87030 RENDE(CS)
Italy

ABSTRACT

The emerging multidatabase system technology is a response
to the growing need to integrate the preexisting databases
and to allow for uniform treatment of the heterogeneous
data resources. The need to integrate data stems from the
gradual development of information systems over many years
as well as from the availability of the technological
infrastructure in the area of data communications. We
present the architecture of Multidatabase Management
Systems (MDBMS) as well as the principal aspects of the
application development methodology. The future trends in
the area of multidatabase systems are presented.

1. INTRODUCTION

The present information processing systems have grown gradually over many
years. Such situation is typical for all large organizations, in particular
government agencies, industrial organizations, banks and many others, where
the gradual development of information systems, and consequently of data
resources, has followed the evolution of the data processing technology.

The result of the above process is the existence of many distinct information
systems, representing the various functional aspects, within a single
organization. The heterogeneity of data processing tools and techniques used
to develop applications over years makes it practically impossible to
integrate the existing data resources.

The need of integration has been recognized many years ago and consequently
the Information Center concept has been introduced in the late 70ties.
Although the required hardware infrastructure has been available (computer
networking equipment, teleprocessing networks etc.), the principal problems in
providing satisfactory solutions have resulted from the lack of software tools
and techniques to integrate the heterogeneous, preexisting data resources.

Intensive research and development activities have led to development of a
number of the MDBMS prototypes. The relative novelty of such systems and the
class of information processing systems (command and control systems) that
stimulated most of the development work result in very little published

information regarding the multidatabase application experience.

The possible alternative approach would be to attempt to convert the existing applications and data repositories into a single integrated information processing system. The already mature centralized database management systems would be the best candidates to provide the technological support for such a venture. Unfortunately, the software effort involved, in view of the already extensive capital expenditures and the growing required application backlogs, precludes this straightforward solution.

The integration problems seem to be discussed mainly in the context of the formatted databases due to their principal role in the classical information processing systems. Although the importance the formatted database integration is not questioned, there exists an important family of databases, namely the information retrieval databases, that seems to gain increasing importance in the modern information processing systems.

The availability of the public information utilities, accessible through the generally available telecommunication networks, is an important factor in development of the new generation, intelligent information processing systems. The legal, economic, or geographical information available through the public information utilities will most certainly be the important data resource for the modern governmental information processing systems.

The integration problem in the case of the public information retrieval systems is oriented towards providing standard, user friendly, intelligent interfaces to such systems. The major problems confronting the present users of the public information utilities is the variety of query languages and access conventions. Additional burden placed on the user, who may have the need to access many information bases of varying domains, is the need to be familiar with the object domain to be able to pose the topical queries.

Due to the growing importance of the public information utilities in the area of governmental systems, we discuss the preliminary architectures of the intelligent information retrieval support systems regardless of their disparity with the generally accepted concept of a multidatabase management system.

The paper is organized in the following way; first of all we present the state of the art and the general architecture of multidatabase management systems, then we present an outline of the multidatabase application development methodology. Finally we present the preliminary architecture of the knowledge-based, intelligent information retrieval support systems.

2. MULTIDATABASE MANAGEMENT SYSTEMS

A multidatabase management system may be defined in terms of the following characteristics:

1. Integration of heterogeneous databases - this implies that the underlying databases, accessible through the system, are managed by different DBMSes and may represent diverse logical data models.

2. Distribution - the fact that data are not resident at the same site (processor) and that all sites are linked via a geographical or local network.

3. Logical correlation - the fact that data have some properties that tie them together, so that they may be represented by a meaningful,

common data model.

The first characteristic distinguishes the multidatabase management systems from distributed database management systems, although both types of systems belong to a wider class, namely the distributed data sharing systems. The above two types of systems have many common characteristics, yet they are sufficiently diverse, in terms of their objectives and potential utilization, to merit separate treatment.

Distribution may not always be a necessary condition to justify an application of a multidatabase management system. Clearly, there exist cases, where different centralized database management systems are present at a single site, and a multidatabase system may be used to provide for the required integration of data. However, the lack of distribution capabilities would be a serious limitation with respect to most applications.

Logical correlation implies existence of a common logical data model with its corresponding data language. Since many different data models already exist, corresponding to the various centralized databases accessible in the realm of a multidatabase system, the necessary mappings between those data models and the common data model of a multidatabase management system must be provided. This is the major distinguishing factor between the multidatabase and the distributed database management systems. In the case of the latter class, a common logical data model is applied and the data are physically distributed.

Presently, there exists little user experience in the area of the multidatabase systems, and the existing applications may be considered, at best, to be experimental prototypes. However, the limited experience suggests a number of principal user requirements.

The following requirements have already been reported as desirable in [STA83,DAY82a,DAY83]:

1. The data model that supports a non-procedural, end-user friendly data language.

2. The complete distribution transparency providing for the manipulation of data, as if the user were accessing a unique centralized database.

3. The local data model transparency relieving the user of the complexity of dealing at the same time with many, diverse logical data models.

4. The explicit support for definition of data abstractions providing means for correct representation of the multidatabase system semantics.

5. Minimal interference with the local processing of the centralized databases included in a multidatabase system.

Current objectives of multidatabase systems, exemplified by the above user requirements, show that interrogation functions take precedence over the distributed update capabilities. In many cases, allowing the multidatabase system users to update the underlying centralized databases would be considered too much of an interference in the local applications. However, transaction processing based update capabilities may be useful, and they are comprised in some of the current multidatabase management system prototypes. This creates serious technical problems, particularly in the area of concurrency control. We shall later discuss problems associated with multidatabase transaction processing in more detail.

Most of the currently implemented systems have adopted the relational data
model as the global data model. In some cases, mappings from network and
hierarchical data models are supported. Extensions of the relational data
structure definition facilities have also been proposed to provide explicit
support for data abstraction.

Since multidatabase systems utilize already existing databases, the possible
interference of the global and local functions may be considered from two
perspectives; the need to modify existing database design to support the
multidatabase system needs, and degradation of the local application
performance resulting from additional workload generated by a multidatabase
system.

Modification of existing database systems to meet the specific requirements of
the multidatabase systems users would seldom be permitted. This fact has
determining influence on the multidatabase system design methodology.

The need to minimize the multidatabase system workload causes the processing
cost, rather than response time, to be the principal goal of query
optimization. Apart from the query optimization strategy, this fact has an
important influence on implementation of the multidatabase management system
user interfaces.

For example the asynchronous query processing approach, based on queueing
queries rather than holding up user terminals, seems to be more appropriate in
the multidatabase system environment.

Typically, a multidatabase management system would support the following data
abstraction architecture:

1. **The Global Schema**
    The Global Schema constitutes the principal integration level. It
    comprises all logical data structure objects resulting from data
    abstraction and integration processes performed on the data objects
    defined in the local database schemata. This level provides an
    integrated view of the underlying databases, supporting, in most
    cases, distribution and data model transparency.

2. **The User Schema**
    The User Schemata correspond to the concept of the External Schema of
    the ANSI/SPARC DBMS architecture. They comprise all of the user view
    and snapshot definitions.

3. **The Local Schema**
    The Local Schemata, defined in the host DBMS data description
    language, represent the logical data structure of the underlying,
    local databases to be integrated into a multidatabase system.

4. **The Auxiliary Schema**
    The Auxiliary Schema is stored, in some cases fragmented, in all
    sites of a computer network. It comprises data model mapping and
    other information related to the local resources, as well as
    information used to resolve incompatibilities of the local databases
    and the respective host DBMSes.

In the majority of multidatabase systems the Global Schema is replicated in
all sites of the computer network. This fact and the need to access data
residing in distinct, geographically distributed databases creates new
problems in the area of database administration and design.

In the following section we present a number of multidatabase management systems, mostly developed as research prototypes. Subsequently, the principal features of a generalized multidatabase management system architecture and implementation principles are discussed. Finally, problems related to multidatabase system design and the future trends in multidatabase management technology are presented.

2.1. The Current Research and Development Work

The state-of-the-art survey of the distributed database management technology has been given in [CER84,MOH84,STA85]. Both types of systems, namely the distributed database and the multidatabase systems, have been presented. We shall briefly summarize information regarding the most important developments in the area of multidatabase management systems.

A representative sample of the current research and development work includes such systems as ADDS [BRE84,BRE86], MERMAID [BRI84,TEM83,TEM86a], MULTIBASE [SMI81,LAN82], NDMS [STA84a], SIRIUS-DELTA [LIT82], DQS [DQS85], AIDA [TEM86b], and MULTI* [MUL87].
A survey of the current multidatabase management systems is presented in [STA86].

Most of the above multidatabase management systems do not match the principal user requirements. This is the result of the evolving multidatabase system technology and the varying objectives of the organizations sponsoring the research and development work. Although the relational data model prevails as the global schema representation, many systems do not support heterogeneous data models of the underlying databases. They are still considered multidatabase management systems, because integrated access to databases managed by diverse DBMSes is supported.

In most cases, distributed transaction processing is not supported. This is due to unresolved problems of concurrency control in the multi-DBMS environment. The difficulty results from the fact that multidatabase management systems utilize the host DBMSes on the level of user interfaces, that is on the query language or the data manipulation language level. Hence, it is impossible to apply most of the concurrency control algorithms developed for the distributed database management systems.

The lack of cooperation between local and global locking mechanisms may, for example, lead to undetectable global deadlocks. A detailed presentation of concurrency control problems in multi-DBMS environment may be found in [GLI84a,GLI84b].

We present NDMS and its commercial derivatives DQS and MULTI* developed at CRAI as examples representative of our approach to the MDBMS architecture.

NDMS (Network Data Management System)

NDMS has been developed to provide a facility for retrieval and distributed processing of data residing in distinct, preexisting databases and data files installed in a heterogeneous computer network.
The current version of the system operates on a network of IBM and VAX computers integrating local databases supported by ADABAS, IMS/VS, IDMS DB/DC, RODAN and INGRES database management systems.
The global schema, replicated in all sites of the computer network, is relational with SQL supported as the data language.
User schemata are supported by the view definition mechanism of SQL and, both

permanent as well as temporary, snapshots may be defined.
The auxiliary schema comprises mapping definitions controlling materialization of global schema relations.
Query processing is based on an intermediate data manipulation language designed to exploit the inherent parallel execution capabilities. A centralized query planner generates a query plan, defined as a sequence of the intermediate language operations, resulting from the query optimization algorithm. The goal function of the query optimization algorithm is minimization of the overall query processing cost, including the communication cost as well as the CPU and I/O operation costs. Query postprocessing is not necessary, since all local database accesses are performed via the host DBMS data access modules developed in the respective data manipulation languages.
Distributed transaction processing is supported and the concurrency control approach is based on the two-phase commit protocol and the corresponding host DBMS facilities.

DQS (Distributed Query System)

DQS has been developed as a commercial system based on the research and development experience stemming from NDMS development work.
It provides facilities for distributed query processing on an integrated collection of heterogeneous databases residing in a SNA network of IBM mainframes.
The system is integrated with the CICS TP environment and it currently supports integration of databases controlled by IMS/VS, IDMS DB/DC and ADABAS database management systems. Integration of operating system access method files (ie. VSAM) is also supported.
The global schema is relational and SQL has been implemented as the distributed query language. Distributed transaction processing is not supported.

MULTI* (Multistar)

Multi* has also been based on the NDMS experience. The prototype and the ensuing commercial versions of the system have been developed in the UNIX System 5 environment. The system is functionally integrated with the DQS distributed query processing environment in order to provide for integration of the departmental level databases into the multidatabase information processing system.
The query language is SQL, standardized according to the X Open System architecture proposed by ECMA.
The limited update capability, via the SQL queries, is also provided.

2.2. Logical System Architecture

A multidatabase management system installed in a computer network consists of two principal components; the MDBMS software and the System Dictionary. The control software provides all necessary data management and data communication services and the System Dictionary comprises all necessary data and environment definitions. The multidatabase system users are accessing the system at their respective nodes. A schematic representation of a multidatabase system architecture is shown in figure 1.

Mirror images of the MDBMS software must be installed at all sites of a computer network containing databases to be integrated into a multidatabase system. If heterogeneous computer system hardware environments are supported by the multidatabase management system, as in the case of NDMS [STA84a], functionally equivalent versions of the control software must be developed for each computer system environment.

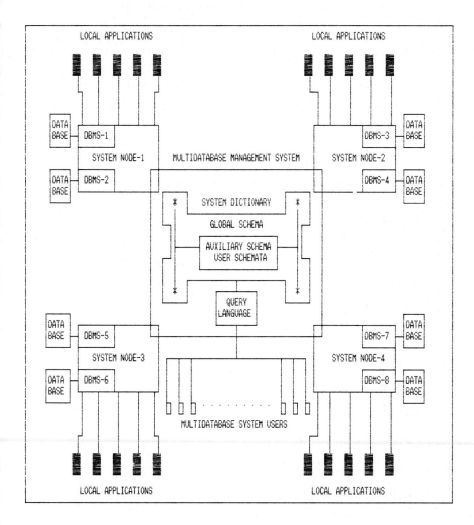

Figure 1. Logical architecture of a multidatabase system.

The System Dictionary may be seen as a distributed database, managed by the MDBMS, comprising data descriptions pertaining to the respective schema levels as well as the multidatabase system user descriptions and the data administration information.

The Global Schema is replicated in all system nodes, due to the requirement to access the base relation schemes during the query translation and optimization phases. Partitioning of the Global Schema would result in significant delays during the query acceptance phase of the query processing cycle.

The User Schemata are partitioned according to the user location within the computer network. This imposes a slight restriction on the multidatabase system use by allowing system users to pose queries only at their native nodes. A feature to accept foreign users at other system sites, while processing their queries in the native sites, may be introduced as a possible solution to the above problem.

The Auxiliary Schema is partially replicated and partially partitioned among the system nodes. The replicated information characterizes distribution of the Global Schema relations and provides the corresponding statistical information. The partitioned information pertains to the mapping information required for materialization of the base relations.

Databases, managed by the respective database management systems, are concurrently used by the local applications and accessed by the MDBMS data manipulation functions. The respective MDBMS functions, extracting data to materialize the base relations, are seen by a local DBMS as an additional application task.

User definitions comprise authorization information as well as the possible restrictions, such as the expected query size, the working storage size etc., that may be imposed on the users by the system node data administrator.

Distribution of data administration functions resulting from the above multidatabase system environment calls for an additional level of coordination. Such level may be created by a body, comprising all individuals responsible for the local databases and the multidatabase system node administratioegulations.

3. MULTIDATABASE APPLICATION DEVELOPMENT METHODOLOGY

The nature of the multidatabase information processing systems, particularly the fact that the principal objective is to integrate the preexisting databases, creates a host of new design problems that do not appear in the classical distributed database system design methodologies.

On the other hand, the system designer is given much less freedom with respect to the design decisions that may be implemented in the multidatabase system environment. For example, the fragmentation design as well as the fragment distribution design, typical phases in the case of the classical distributed database technology, do not apply to our design task since we are dealing with already existing databases. For the same reason the physical database will not typically be undertaken. Only rarely the preexisting databases would be physically reorganized to suit the query requirements of the multidatabase system.
As a result of the above requirements a specific design methodology, pertaining to the multidatabase system design requirements, must be developed. A proposal of such a methodology has been presented in [MOS87].

The multidatabase system design methodology comprises the following design phases:

1. Requirements Analysis.
   The principal objective of a multidatabase system is to allow distinct user communities to share data resources distributed over a set of heterogeneous databases residing in a computer network. The system is not to substitute the local database applications providing the respective users with the required application support. It is rather to create an image of a "superdatabase" representing the required level of abstraction with respect to the local databases and thus substantially enlarge the information space available to the multidatabase system users.
   Hence, the requirements analysis must define the boundaries of the Global Schema, as well as the specific, application dependent, view requirements of distinct user groups. Such requirements must subsequently be reconciled with the availability of data in the source databases.

2. Global Schema Design.
   The Global Schema must represent semantics of the "superdatabase" data to be abstracted from the underlying, local databases and to reconcile all semantic conflicts that may exist on the required abstraction level.
   The principal steps are the analysis of the local database semantics, construction of the intermediate conceptual data models based on a unique formal representation, integration of the partial conceptual data models, and decomposition of the integrated conceptual data model into a set of Global Schema relation schemes.

3. Application Schemata Design.
   Application Schemata represent the higher abstraction level with respect to the Global Schema. Each user community is to share an Application Schema supported by the Node Administrator acting as their representative versus other user communities as well as providing all necessary local support. All necessary transformations are expressed as relational views.
   The enhanced performance requirements are also considered at this stage and they may be resolved by introducing the data storage redundancy. The redundant storage requirements are defined in terms of permanent views (snapshots).

4. Auxiliary Schema Design.
   The Auxiliary Schema comprises the local database schemata/Global Schema mapping rules controlling base relation materialization at the query execution time, the query optimization criteria and the quantitative description of base relations.
   The mapping rules are distributed over the computer network sites and their definition is the responsibility of the local Database Administrators. The principal criteria for mapping rule definitions are the expected performance characteristics of the host DBMS base relation mappers executed during processing of distributed queries.
   The query optimization criteria reflect the relative cost of the various processing resources, namely the relative CPU, I/O, and data transmission costs, as well as the main memory constraints at each site. The query optimization criteria are replicated at all sites of the computer network.
   The quantitative descriptions of base relations are to be automatically derived from the source databases with the use of a statistical data analysis function. The quantitative information are replicated at all sites.

The above preliminary multidatabase system design methodology is currently
being verified by the first DQS users. It seems that the major problem
encountered at most DQS sites is the problem of the global schema semantics
and the related problem of extracting semantic information from the underlying
source databases.

Automatic design tools, similar to those presented in [ALB85], are being
studied to extend the existing MDBMS architectures with the required
conceptual and logical design tools.

4. INFORMATION RETRIEVAL SUPPORT SYSTEMS

The increasing complexity of our civilization places an excessive burden on
the governing bureaucracies. Implications of everyday decisions made by the
governing bodies have a profound effect on the well-being of not only the
single citizens, but whole nations, or even a vast international community. It
seems that no enlightened government may exist today without having access to
an extensive body of information dealing practically with every aspect of the
modern society.

The need for such information-oriented government has long been recognized and
the growth of the technological infrastructure as well as the availability of
the public information services, both national and international, being placed
practically at the user fingertips by the modern hardware/software technology,
leads one to believe that such an ideal, informed government is indeed
possible.

However, attempts to construct information systems based on access to
heterogeneous sources of information, both formatted and unformatted
databases, have encountered serious difficulties stemming from the following
principal factors:

    1)   A considerable domain knowledge is required to pose intelligent
         queries against a professional (e.g. legal, medical, economic,..)
         information utility. Difficulties arise in selection of the
         appropriate keywords as well as in interpretation of system
         responses.

    2)   It is difficult to make further use of the selected information by
         means of automatic tools. Problems are aggravated, if more than one
         information source is utilized to meet a particular information
         requirement.

    3)   Sufficient command of a specific query language (or a number of query
         languages, in the case of cross-referencing different information
         bases) is required in order to interact with the information
         retrieval system. In most cases the languages available in the
         present systems may not be considered user-friendly.

One of the approaches taken today, if such difficulties are encountered, is to
introduce an intermediary human role, acting as an agent between the
information user and the information retrieval system, dubbed sometimes
"information specialist".

An information specialist is to shield the end user from the complexities, or
unfriendliness, of the information system and to provide for the required
level of information presentation. Clearly considerable data processing skills

may be required, coupled with the sufficient domain knowledge pertaining to the required realms of information, in order to provide the satisfactory Information Center services.

We have listed the problem areas according to their relative importance, but we shall deal with possible solutions starting from the most, given the state of the multidatabase technology, immediately achievable.

The solution to the syntactic problem, namely the disparity of the query languages available in different information utilities, may be based on introduction of a standard, user-friendly interface. It also would be desirable to have the same linguistic tool to access both the formatted and the unformatted databases.

One of the possible solutions has been born in the area of office automation, more precisely in the area of multimedia databases utilized in the office systems. Straightforward extensions of SQL have been proposed in [DEM84,CHR84] to handle queries posed against textual databases.

This approach may immediately be applied to a multidatabase management system serving as a front-end to the multiple information retrieval systems available via a telecommunication network.

The first two problem areas may be considered as representatives of the semantic problem class. In such cases, an "intelligent" solution is required. This implies either the human intervention, possibly aided by more sophisticated information presentation and interpretation tools, or the "expert" system approach to provide the user with the required domain-oriented support.

The second direction seems more attractive and it already draws interest of the database and AI research community. The preliminary proposals of systems that comprise intelligent user interfaces have been presented in [SAC85,BRO85].

The KIWI system [SAC85] utilizes a knowledge base coupled with an inference mechanism to provide the required domain expertise. Any number of domain experts may be constructed within KIWI, some making use of information retrieved from the information bases, others aiding query formulation and result interpretation tasks.

The use of knowledge representation techniques and logic programming in the user query processing or application development interfaces has been proposed in [FUR86,JAR86,SIB86].

The above proposals, although indicative of the general development trend, are at best preliminary. Much research and development work is required before the end users of public information bases are provided with the required support.

One of the major problem is the performance of proposed intelligent interfaces, that, being based on the knowledge processing techniques, inherit all the performance problems of the knowledge based systems.

A possible solution is to design hardware/software systems implementing the required functionality and exploiting the potential of massive parallelism available in the fifth generation computer system architectures. The goal is to develop a dedicated information gateway system that would provide the user with all required facilities abstracting in the same time from complexities of the underlying technology.

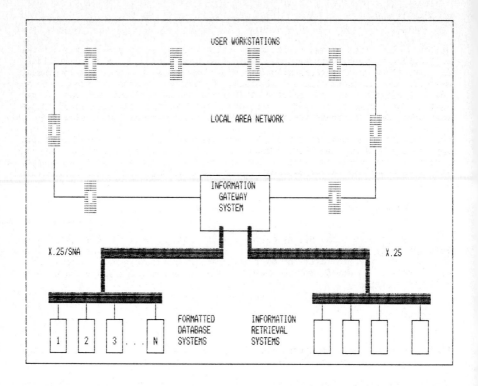

Figure 2. Application context of the information gateway system.

The application context of an information gateway system is shown in figure 2.
The system aids the user, utilizing a workstation connected to the system
within the local area network, in accessing all available information
resources, both formatted and unformatted, is if they were available locally.

The uniform, user friendly interface, coupled with the domain expertise of the
knowledge based system, should provide for the complete information type,
distribution, as well as data model transparency.

The processing and storage capabilities of the information gateway system will
provide the necessary support for the information presentation and correlation
tools.

The information gateway system may easily be interfaced with the multidatabase
management system environment, such as DQS or MULTI*, to make use with their
heterogeneous database integration capabilities.

In the case of the information retrieval systems, the information gateway
system will translate the standard user interface queries, formulated with the
aid of the appropriate domain expert system, into the target query language. A
particular user request may generate one or more information retrieval queries
requesting information from more than one information base.

5. CONCLUSIONS

Although the last five years have witnessed an increased interest in the multidatabase management systems, their real potential will only be exploited, if significant applications stimulate their commercial success. The government systems, due to their size and diversity of information sources, seem to be an ideal candidate for the pilot multidatabase system applications. Indeed, the initial development of NDMS undertaken by CRAI has been stimulated by the government need to create the transportation control information system.

Our research and development efforts are currently directed towards automatic application design and development tools (e.g. a fifth generation language interface) as well as towards the knowledge based systems for interrogation and management of heterogeneous information available within a multidatabase system.

ACKNOWLEDGMENTS

I am grateful to all my colleagues, in particular to M. Kowalewski, A. Dutkowski, S. Mezyk, W. Kaminski, G. Turco, and T. Mostardi, who worked with me at CRAI in the area of multidatabase management systems. Without their collaboration I would not be able to gain the experience that allowed me to write this paper.

REFERENCES

ALB85   Albano, A., De Antonellis, V., Di Leva, A., (Editors), Computer-Aided Database Design, The DATAID Project, North Holland, 1985.

BRE84   Breitbart, Y.J., Tieman, L.R., ADDS – Heterogeneous Distributed Database System, Proc. of the 3rd Int. Seminar on Distributed Data Sharing Systems, F.A. Schreiber and W. Litwin (Eds), Parma, Italy, March, 1984, North Holland, 1985.

BRE86   Breitbart, Y., Olson, P.L., Thompson, G.R., Database Integration in a Distributed Heterogeneous Database System, Proc. of the Int. Conference on Data Engineering, February 5-7, 1986, Los Angeles, USA, IEEE Computer Society, 1986.

BRI84   Brill, D., Tempelton, M., Yu, C., Distributed Query Optimization in MERMAID: a Frontend to Data Management Systems, Proc. of the Int. Conference on Data Engineering, Los Angeles, April 1984.

BRO85   Broverman, C.A., Croft, W.B., A Knowledge-Based Approach to Data Management for Intelligent User Interfaces, Proc. of the 11th VLDB Conference, Stockholm, 1985, VLDB Endowment, USA, 1985.

CER84   Ceri, S., Pelagatti, G., Distributed Databases – Principles and Systems, McGraw-Hill, 1984

CER84a   Ceri, S., Pernici, B., Wiederhold, G., An Overview of Research in the Design of Distributed Databases, Database Engineering, Volume 7, Number 4, December 1984.

COD71   Codd, E.F., A Data Base Sublanguage Founded on the Relational Calculus, Proc. of the 1971 SIGFIDET Workshop, San Diego, USA, November 11-12, 1971, ACM, 1971.

COD79   Codd, E.F., Extending the Database Relational Model to Capture More
          Meaning, ACM TODS, Vol. 4, No. 4, December 1979.

DAV81   Davenport, R.A., Design of Distributed Data Base Systems, The
          Computer Journal, Volume 24, Number 1, 1981.

DAY82a   Dayal, U., Hwang, H.Y., View Definition and Generalization for
          Database Integration in Multibase: A System for Heterogeneous
          Distributed Databases, Proc. of the 6th Berkeley Workshop on
          Distributed Data Management and Computer Networks, May 1982.

DAY82b   Dayal, U., Goodman, N., Query Optimization for CODASYL Database
          Systems, Proc. of the ACM/SIGMOD 82 Int. Conference on Management of
          Data, 1982.

DAY03   Dayal, U., Processing Queries over Generalization Hierarchies in a
          Multidatabase System, Proc. of the 9th Int. Conference on Very Large
          Data Bases, Florence, Italy, October-November 1983.
DQS85   Distributed Query System, User Documentation, CRAI, Rende(CS), Italy,
          1985.

FUR86   Furtado, A.L., Moura, C.M.O., Expert Helpers to Data-Based
          Information Systems, Proc. of the 1st Int. Workshop on Expert
          Database Systems, L.Kerscheberg (Ed.), The Benjamin/Cummings
          Publishing Company Inc., USA, 1986.

GLI84a   Gligor, V.D., Luckenbaugh, G.L., Interconnecting Heterogeneous
          Database Management Systems, IEEE Computer, Volume 17, Number 1,
          1984.

GLI84b   Gligor, V.D., Popescu-Zeletin, R., Concurrency Control Issues in
          Distributed Heterogeneous Database Management Systems, Proc. of the
          3rd Int. Seminar on Distributed Data Sharing Systems, F.A.,
          Schreiber, W. Litwin (Eds.), Parma, Italy, March 1984, North-Holland
          1985.

JAR86   Jarke, M., External Semantic Query Simplification: A Graph-Theoretic
          Approach and its Implementation in PROLOG, Proc. of the 1st Int.
          Workshop on Expert Database Systems, L. Kerschberg (Ed.), The
          Benjamin/Cummings Publishing Company Inc., USA, 1986.

LAN82   Landers, T., Rosenberg, R.L., An Overview of Multibase, Proc. of the
          2nd Int. Symposium on Distributed Data Bases, H.-J. Schreiber (Ed.),
          Berlin, September 1982, North-Holland, 1982.

LIT82   Litwin, W., Boudenant, J., Esculier, C.,Ferrier, A., Glorieux, A.M.,
          La Chimia, J., Kabbaj, K., Molinoux, C., Rolin, P., Stangret, C.,
          SIRIUS Systems for Distributed Data Management, Proc. of the 2nd Int.
          Symposium on Distributed Data Bases, H.-J. Schreiber (Ed.) Berlin,
          September 1982, North-Holland, 1982.

MOS87   Mostardi, T., Staniszkis, W., Multidatabase System Design
          Methodology, Proc. of the 10th Int. Seminar on Database Management
          Systems, October 19 - 24, 1987, Cedzyna, Poland, CPIZI, 1987.

MUL87   MULTI* Functional Specification, CRAI, Rende(CS), Italy, 1987.

SAC85   Sacca', D., Vermeir, D., D'Atri, A., Liso, A., Pedersen, G.S.,
          Snijders, J.J., Spyratos, N., Description of the Overall Architecture
          of the KIWI System, ESPRIT '85: Status Report of Continuing Work, The
          Commission of the European Communities, North-Holland, 1986.

SIB86   Sibley, E.H., An Expert Database System Architecture Based on an Active and Extensible Dictionary System, Proc. of the 1st Int. Workshop on Expert Database Systems, L. Kerschberg (Ed.), The Benjamin/Cummings Publishing Company Inc., USA, 1986.

SMI81   Smith, J.M., Bernstein, P.A., Dayal, U.,Goodman, N., Landers, T.A., Lin, W.-T.K.,Wong, E., MULTIBASE -- Integrating Heterogeneous Distributed Database Systems, Proc. AFIPS NCC, Volume 50, 1981.

STA83   Staniszkis, W., Kowalewski, M., Turco, G., Krajewski, K., Saccone, M., Network Data Management System - General Architecture and Implementation Principles, Proc. of the Third International Conference on Engineering Software, Imperial College of Science and Technology, London, England, April, 1983.

STA84a   Staniszkis, W., Kaminski, W., Kowalewski,M., Krajewski, K., Mezyk, S., and Turco,G., Architecture of the Network Data Management System, Proc. of the 3rd Int. Seminar on Distributed Data Sharing Systems, F.A. Schreiber and W. Litwin (Eds.), Parma, Italy, March, 1984, North-Holland, 1985.

STA84b   Staniszkis, W., Grano, A., Kaminski, W., Kowalewski, M., Mezyk, S., Orlando, S., Turco, G., NDMS Query Planner, in NDMS Working Papers, W. Staniszkis (Ed.), CRAI Research Report 84-24, Rende, Italy, October 1984.

STA85   Staniszkis, W., Distributed Database Management, State-of-the-Art and Future Trends, Proc. of the 8th Int. Seminar on Database Management Systems, October, 1985, Piestany, Cechoslovakia.

STA86   Staniszkis, W., Integrating Heterogeneous Databases, in Relational Databases, State of the Art Report, D. Bell (Ed.), Pergamon Infotech Limited, 1986.

TEM83   Tempelton, M., Brill, D., Hwang, A., Kameny, I., Lund, E., An Overview of the MERMAID System -- A Frontend to Heterogeneous Databases, Proc. of the 16th Annual Electronics and Aerospace Conference, Washington D.C., September, 1983.

TEM86a   Tempelton, M., Brill, D., Chen, A., Lund,E., MERMAID - Experiences with Network Operation, Proc. of the Int. Conference on Data Engineering, February 5-7, 1986, Los Angeles, USA, IEEE Computer Society, 1986.

TEM86b   Tempelton, M., Brill, D., Chen, A., Dao, S., Lund, E., MacGregor, R., Ward, B., Introduction to AIDA - A Front-end to Heterogeneous Databases, to appear in a IEEE publication.

ZAN79   Zaniolo, C., Design of Relational Views over Network Schemas, Proc. of the ACM/SIGMOD 79 Int. Conference on Management of Data, 1979.

Governmental and Municipal Information Systems
P. Kovács and E. Straub (Editors)
Elsevier Science Publishers B.V. (North-Holland)
   IFIP, 1988

THE TIME BOMB

Knud Lysgaard

Kommunedata I/S, P.O. Box 720,
DK-9100 Aalborg.

It is a common practice to omit the century in dates.
This article deals with the problems this causes in EDP
systems as we approach the year 2000.   In particular
problems in large EDP installations are dealt with and
there is a description of how Kommunedata I-S, Denmark,
tackles this matter.

ADJUSTMENT OF TIME: YEAR 2000

In the early days of computer programming data storage was expensive and in many situations limited. Therefore, no superfluous
information was stored. As almost all dates could be assumed to
be in the 20th century there was no need to store the century. It
became a habit to store dates with 2 digits for the year - just
as it is a habit in many everyday situations only to note 2
digits, for example, 15/06-87.

The programmes to process the dates were, therefore, designed
on the assumption, that the first two digits in all years are 19.
At some point as we draw closer to year 2000 this assumption
will, however, no longer qualify and programmes will either give
wrong results - or simply refuse to produce results.

As almost all EDP systems store and process dates and as the
majority of these dates are still stored and processed on the
assumption that we are in the 20th century what we actually have
here is a delayed-action time bomb ticking under our information
society. If we do not act it will explode on 1st January 2000,
at the latest - in many cases considerably earlier as systems are
assumed to be able to handle dates forward in time.

NO HELP FROM SUPPLIERS

We have to do something. We cannot blame the problem on others
than ourselves. Unfortunately, we cannot reckon on others
solving it for us either.

It's true it is not only we users of EDP technology who have a
problem. The EDP vendors have in many cases built up their operating systems on exactly the same weakness and for exactly the
same reason: the high price and limited storage space. The EDP
suppliers who wish to be on the market in 2000 will, of course,

K. Lysgaard

contrive to solve their own problems. They will probably offer
some tools which can assist the rest of us a little in solving
our problems but there is no indication that the suppliers are
able to contribute markedly to a solution of our problem.

CONVERSION OF FORMAT

If we had worked out all date formats with all 4 digits in the
year it would not have been necessary to incorporate assumptions
in our programmes and the turn of the century would neither have
given us headaches nor sleepless nights.

What is more obvious than changing all 2 digit years to 4 digits?

From a technical point of view such a conversion is just routine,
but the disadvantage is that many elements in a EDP system are
affected:

                    - structures, for example:
                      - forms
                      - data screens
                      - temporary files
                      - registers
                      - reports, etc.
                    - programmes
                    - stored data
                    - documentation, among other things:
                      - system descriptions
                      - user manuals
the task rapidly becomes very extensive.

ALMOST IMPOSSIBLE TO CONTROL

Furthermore, it is such that changes in many elements are dependent on one another inasmuch as they actually must commence at
the same time (on the same run). For example, alterations of one
single date field in a register will lead, at the least, to the
following changes in activities:

                    - changes of record structure
                    - conversion of actual register data together with
                      possible back-up versions
                    - adjustment of all programmes using the field
                    - recompiling all programmes using the record
                    - adjustment of the system description

Conversion in 1 field at a time will mean that each register and
every programme must be changed many times. Conversion of a
record or a register at one time makes it difficult to maintain a
comprehensive view. The risk that not all the necessary corrections have been done right is ever present and one should be
prepared to be able to return to an earlier version.
In the case of large installations with hundreds of on-line data
sets and thousands of programmes a conversion from 2 digit to
4 digit years will demand a very large control effort and the
risk of errors, with following interruptions in operation, will
still be considerable.

At Kommunedata each system is developed and maintained in one of
five development centres, whilst operation is done at three
regional central stations. Thus, there is an increased need for
control and as far as Kommunedata is concerned the method of
changing all date formats to 4 digit years will be almost
impossible to control.

SELDOM A TRUE DOUBT AS TO THE CENTURY

Before starting with conversion of date formats, let's see if it
is really necessary.

If at all times a date has a relevant range of less than (or
equal to) 100 years, then a 2 digit year is theoretically
adequate to identify the year within the relevant interval of
time.

Example on conversion table with relevant interval = 1975 - 2015

2 digit year	75	87	00	15
Actual year	1975	1987	2000	2015

As end users know the relevant interval they will never be in
doubt as to the meaning of the 2 digit year.

If the relevant interval can be greater than 100 years it is
maybe not possible to make do with 2 digits in the year, but in
99% of such situations 4 digits will already be used in the year.
Otherwise it may be necessary to convert such date fields - but
the task will in any case be reduced to a fraction.

CHANGES IN PROGRAMMES ARE ADEQUATE

If information as to the valid time interval is added to the
programme - maybe just the start year for the 100 year interval -
the programmes will be able to handle all time calculations
correctly. Information that the relevant interval starts in
1955 will for example, mean that 55 - 99 is interpreted as 1955 -
1999, whilst 00 -54 is interpreted as 2000 - 2054. The relevant
time interval will often be definable relatively in relation to
a run parameter or, the day's date field on a data screen. In
this way a maintenance load is avoided in definition of the time
intervals.

MINIMUM CONTROL

The advantages of only changing the programmes is that the number
of elements in the conversion is drastically reduced and - maybe
even more important - there is no need to coordinate the conver-
sions. All programme changes are independent of one another.
They just have to be effected before it is too late. This means
the programmes can be corrected at a rate which fits in with
other activities, that is it can be done at the same time as
normal maintenance.

With this method of procedure control is minimal as one must just
ensure that all programmes are made "bomb proof".

STANDARD ROUTINES ARE IMPORTANT

It is obvious the programme logics are made more complicated in
relation to the present situation. Date manipulations are, however, already rather complicated so this added minor complexity
is not so important.

The use of standard routines is a great help, it reduces both
the manual effort as well as the risk of errrors. Already today,
most date manipulations take place via standard routines and as
more operations, which were previously very simple, become more
complicated as we approach year 2000, the standard routine
library should probably be extended in connection with demounting
of the date bombs.

PROBLEM ANALYSIS IS NECESSARY

When one chooses to change only the programmes it is necessary to
discover which operations in the programmes will go wrong in year
2000. Such an analysis is also a fine basis for judging which
standard routines that should be offered to minimize the resource
effort.

In the following we attempt to make a fairly comprehensive
problem list.

DATE CALCULATION

By this we mean:
- number of days between two dates (or year, month
  and day)
- estimating from one date to a new date by stating
  the number of days between (or year, month and
  days)
- week day for stated date
- type of day (week or Sunday, Bank Holiday,etc.)
- conversion from one date format to another (for
  example on presentation of data screen, report
  or the like).

The above can easily be solved with 2 digit years and statement
of relevant interval.

SORTING

Sorting of 2 digit years with usual utility programmes will
result in erroneous chronological number order. Correct number
order is achieved as follows:

- definition of sorting sequence for first digit
  in year (decade), for example 6789012345 for
  time interval 1960-2059. This method can only be
  used if the interval is at the start of a decade.
- temporary addition of auxiliary fields stating the
  century and included in the sorting criteria.
- a sorting routine which can sort with transposed
  zero point. If the transposition for a 2 digit
  number area is set at '60', the order of the
  sorting should be 60-99, 00-59.

A special problem presents itself if one has a 6 digit date included in the primary key of a file organised index sequentially. In many cases it will probably be advisable to convert to a 8 digit date - with the problems this involves.

'00' AND '99'

Many people know that '00 and '99' in a year have been attributed a special meaning as for example 'not filled in', 'first' or 'last'. If one had 4 digits in a year one would probaly have used '0000' and '9999' and thus been able to continue with this for a very long time. When 1999 and 2000 no longer are improbable or illegal years, can '99' and '00' on the other hand no longer be used and a new solution must be found.

In the case of date fields this problem probably does not exist except for clean year fields. '00' and '99' are still illegal values for months and days.

COMPARISON OF DATES

This problem is named separately, as many programmes test according to which of two dates is the latest. This is done apart from the standard routines as opposed to the more complicated date calculations.

Around year 2000 this test will become more complicated and must be re-programmed with consideration to the relevant time intervals or be done via new standard routines.

There may be other simple (at present) date manipulations which can be done apart from standard routines where the same considerations can be made. Please note though that the simple test of whether two dates are the same, will continue to work, as long as the relevant time interval is less than 100 years.

CALCULATION OF YEAR

Calculation with years is at the moment so simple that it is not done via standard routines.

With 2 digit years on both sides of year 2000 these calculations will become more complicated and it may be necessary to carry them out via new standard routines.

PRESENTATION OF DATES

That which gives problems with presentation of dates for the end user is that there usually is no doubt as to what extent 05 should be interpreted as 1905 or 2005. The problem is that there is more than one commonly used number order of year, month and day (at least in Denmark). Year - month - day (87-06-30) and day month year (30-06-87). After year 2001 doubt can, therefore, easily arise as to the meaning of 01-02-03. Is it 1st February 2003, or 3rd February, 2001?

Therefore, at some future point it may be necessary always to
present dates with 4 digit years or, to state the format
(yy-mm-dd).

Transcribing 4 digit years does **not** require storing or keying in
4 digits.

KOMMUNEDATA'S PLAN

After an analysis of the problem at Kommunedata a method or procedure has been chosen which is briefly as follows:

4-DIGIT YEARS WHEN DEVELOPING NEW SYSTEMS

Full information as regards the year is the most simple to handle
and is set as a requirement in future developments. A complete
set of standard routines is first constructed and made available
for all non-trivial date manipulations.

Dating in forms and data screens can still use shortened years,
if it is thought expedient, but stored years **must** contain 4
digits.

RUNNING ADJUSTMENT OF EXISTING PROGRAMMES

Gradually as programmes are changed as a link in the maintenance
plan, adjustments and tests are likewise made to manage year
2000. Only if it is probable that they survive year 2000 though.
Programmes which are tested and found (time) bomb safe, are
specially marked and noted on a special list.

Also in this case a set of standard routines will first be made
available to make it possible for statement of the valid time
intervals. If this is not used, a standard interval which is
made up-to-date every year or, every other year is used.

Standard routines also include conversion between various date
formats - for example dates which are exported from an old
system (shortened year) to a new system (full year).

SYSTEMATIC DEMOUNTING OF TIME BOMBS

In plenty of time prior to 2000 (1995-1997) a systematic inspection of the programmes not yet registered as "bomb free" is to
be started.   Maybe mechanical tools will be used to disclose
which programmes use date fields.

The programmes which must survive year 2000, are adjusted by use
of the new standard routines.

DECISIVE ADVANTAGE

When choosing the procedure outlined, Kommunedata stresses the
fact that there is thereby achieved a number of really decisive
advantages in relation to a slavish conversion of the date formats.

MINIMUM MANUAL RESOURCE EFFORT

The extent of the task is simply considerably reduced as it is
only programmes which have to be altered. The extra logical
complexity is unimportant.

MINIMUM RISK OF ERROR

As the individual programme correction can stand alone, the risk
of error due to lack in coordination is avoided. Fewer operation
stops again mean greater productivity. Return to an earlier version is easier with this procedure.

INDEPENDENCE

The lesser need for coordination is a great relief for a firm
such as Kommunedata. This, together with the fact that programme
changes can be fitted optimally in the remaining work, again
means greater productivity.

ALSO ADVANTAGEOUS FOR OTHERS THAN KOMMUNEDATA

The problems are not unique for Kommunedata

If these problems sound rather similar to the ones in your EDP
installation, then I am certain there must be an advantageous
solution close to the one chosen by Kommunedata for you.

Anyway, here is the suggestion at your free disposal.

Governmental and Municipal Information Systems
P. Kovács and E. Straub (Editors)
Elsevier Science Publishers B.V. (North-Holland)
IFIP, 1988

ATTEMPTS TO MASTER LARGE SCALE NEGATIVE EFFECTS
OF EDP

Per Svenonius, Ministry of Public Administration,
S-103 33 Stockholm, SWEDEN

A single EDP system is vulnerable due to numerous
reasons. Very likely the system owner is aware of
this. He can blame nobody else, if his system fails
due to system errors, incompetent operations, old
documentation, poor premises, deficient access
controls, etc, etc. We regard it a system owner responsibility to keep the security at a proper level.
By risk analysis he should regularly check that the
security level matches his responsibilities towards
the direct users, the outside world and his own
interests of having the system running.

The Swedish government agencies operate to a large
degree independently from the State Cabinet.
Within given instructions they are on their own
designing their working methods. While more than 400
000 civil servants are employed at the agencies the
overall Cabinet staff is under 4000, distributed
among 20 Cabinet ministers and 14 Ministries.

Within given resources the agencies are expected
to use EDP provided that it enhances their
effectiveness. The driving forces behind the
administrative development are normally found inside
the agency. Some large reforms involving heavy
computerization have been initiated by the

politicians, but once the system is implemented,
the continuation efforts to cut costs and improve
services fall within the regular responsibilities
of the pertinent agency.

The basic principle is simple. Each agency is fully
responsible for its work with regard to working
methods as well as results.

This does not mean, however, that the impacts of
EDP have been disregarded politically. The first
Royal Commission minding EDP matters was appointed
in 1955, and through the years a large number of
commissions have been studying various aspects of
the development. Suffices it here to remind of the
pioneering work we have done in Privacy Protection
through our Data Act, adopted in 1974. I do not
intend to expand on this, but we still regard it
necessary to mind and protect the citizen's right
to a private sphere and thus to limit the
collection, exchange and sale of personal
information by government or private enterprises.

Special commissions will be needed also in the
coming years to take a closer look at arising new
issues. But as a result of the continuous growth
of EDP-related topics, a special Cabinet group -
consisting of five Cabinet ministers - has been
appointed with the special assignment to mind long
term and inter-ministerial EDP strategies. Its
major function is to facilitate the best possible
use of the technology, both in government and by
society as a whole. By action it may amplify some
trends and discourage the evolvement of others.

To the Cabinet group are linked two advisory
bodies - a Reference Group concerned with EDP
policies and an Expert Group concerned with EDP
and security at large.

The Reference Group covers a broad spectrum of
representatives of political parties, unions,
commerce, industry, administration, research, etc,
etc. The composition is such, that large fractions
of the society have an open link for communication
with the Cabinet. Over this link they can exchange
views on EDP and its impacts on society. The
purpose is of course to facilitate mutual exchange
of views on EDP matters and thus to reach the best
possible understanding and acceptance of the long
term EDP strategies.

The Expert Group is much smaller. Representatives
are coming from different parts of public
administration and from industry. The group shall
analyze negative effects - "vulnerabilities" -
that are related to the EDP development. The group
shall not only advocate vulnerabilities
(manifested of feasible) but also propose actions
to reduce or eliminate these negative effects. The
nature of such suggestions may be anything between
mild advice to the EDP users and firm legislation.

We have studied a number of potential hazards that
might cause nation-wide concerns. I am not going
to cover these studies comprehensively but shall
comment on some of them.

Disturbances to vital and unique EDP systems -
like many of the governmental ones, e.g.
population, taxation or land registers - could of
course create serious societal concerns. Similar
examples can be found in the private sector. We
have as an example noted that a very large part of
all payments in Sweden are cleared daily through
two giro systems. This gives room for fears that
very bad incidents might occur. Just imagine that
both systems run into trouble at the same time.

From such observations we have concluded that the
basic awareness of EDP hazards need to be raised
both among EDP professionals and - still more so -
among those (general or managing) directors, who
will be held legally responsible if "their"
systems go wrong. We think that the weaknesses of
to-day's EDP very much is related to the fact,
that directors do not realize to which degree
their whole business depends on EDP. We have
developed a special model for risk analysis of EDP
just to give the top manager the means to easily
estimate the potential hazards in this respect.

We have asked ourselves how it comes that serious
EDP hazards tend to be overlooked. Broadly
speaking, the creation of a new system goes
through four phases: specification (basic design
and functional specification), final design,
implementation and operation. We have found that
security concerns sometimes are regarded only
marginally important in the first phase. In the
final design security considerations merely get
established as the final touch to the design.

Another possible explanation , and a more alarming
one, has to do with the technological
development. Even if security constraints are
defined in the original specifications, technical
innovations may get introduced at a later stage in
a way that offsets the original specifications. In
the end, very likely, the system gives more and
better service than originally anticipated, but
equally likely the system security is no longer
fully adequate.

We have concluded, as a firm recommendation, that
the specification - the functional specification
originally adopted by top management as the system
to be developed - among many other things also
shall specify rather precisely the security
requirements. Properly treated this should work
two ways. Top management should become better
aware of security costs and hazards and system
designers should become more careful in analyzing
security consequences of design changes.

To operate sensitive information (e.g. business,
personnel, medical or police records) in a
telecommunication environment calls for special
care. Only a very limited number of users should
have the right to access very sensitive
information, otherwise the data base can not be
regarded as reliably protected. But, to be honest,
we do not know of any such software in the market
that meets the need for individualized access
rights to a sensitive data base with numerous TP
users. This is an example that demonstrates how

innovated use of technology may take place faster
than security can follow. The market is in strong
need for a very advanced access authorization and
control scheme.

A different large scale effect would result from
threats that at the same time affect a number of
otherwise unrelated EDP systems. This could e.g.
happen through breakdowns in the electric power or
the telecommunication networks. It might also be
the outcome of restrictions in international
trade. At present we are e.g. partially subject to
US trade limitations in our field. We feel
confident that the current conditions are mutually
satisfactory - but things may change. Swedish
government stimulates research and encourages
industry both to maintain high technological
competence and to minimize their ties to foreign
restrictions.

In the early history of EDP it was often
understood that EDP would reduce the need for
written documents. The information would be
available on terminal screens linked to
databases. Not yet has this forecast come true.
Printed outputs are produced in very large
quantities. But time is ripe now to seriously look
into the technological and legal aspects of
paperless applications, primarily related to
business agreements and money transfer. This will
therefore be one of the major areas for continued
investigations in our group.

Governmental and Municipal Information Systems
P. Kovács and E. Straub (Editors)
Elsevier Science Publishers B.V. (North-Holland)
IFIP, 1988

AN INFORMATION MANAGEMENT APPROACH TO THE MICRO EXPLOSION

Ilmari PIETARINEN

Senior Adviser for Information Technology
Ministry of Finance, Finland*

1. INTRODUCTION

The past decade or so has seen remarkable changes in Government
data processing and in the environment in which Government data
processing has to operate. The near total revolution in technology
and price-performance is well known and documented, and I need not
dwell on it. Yet it needs to emphasised that the consequences of
these developments as regards an administration's ability to meet
the demands placed on it, have hardly begun to be drawn. This environmental change will continue strong upon us for the remainder of
this century.

Irrespective of this environmental change, an inner change has
been slowly taking place in the thinking of those who are responsible for information processing and its development, both at the
individual agency level and in coordinating organizations that
exist in many, perhaps in most countries participating at this conference. This change, I submit, has to do with the way employers
view those who are working at the different echelons of public administration: decreasingly as standardized performers of predefi-
ned routine tasks but increasingly as individual human beings endowed in varying measure with intelligence, initiative, and problem
solving capabilities.

This change in thinking is not coming about as a result of sudden
change of heart on the part of employers and supervisers but it
is, rather, a consequence of rising salary levels. Man is already
well on the way to pricing himself out of jobs in the industrial
sector. The rising cost of manpower is sorely felt in the public
sector as well. However, public administration cannot operate without people. Yet people can be used either wastefully, by being forced to follow standard routines that insult the intelligence, and
thus eliciting a minimal performance, or economically, making the
most of their capabilities and motivation. In the economical mode
of human utilization, attention focuses on man as an information
processing subsystem, and on the management of such subsystems.

Thus the concept of information management could have developed as
an outgrowth of organizational management without the intervention
of computers and office automation. As it happens, we have the in-
credible progress of information technology at the same time. It
is providing us with the tools for getting the most out of people
as information processors. These tools can take over many routine
aspects of white-collar work but, mor important, they can support
the qualitative improvement of administrative work.

---

* Currently on leave of absence as Director of Information Technology Development Institute, a research organization.

2. THE MICRO EXPLOSION: SOLUTIONS IN SEARCH OF USES

It is a general observation that the explosion of microcomputers
and small systems on the market has caught administrators and poli-
cymakers everywhere unprepared. This does not apply only to the
public sector. Many a tale of woe has been heard about how private
firms have been caught in the micro revolution. The early text processors were intended to replace typewriters and thus bought by managers traditionally responsible for office equipment procurement.
Then followed a wave of enhanced text processors that could be
used for other jobs as well but were sure to be incompatible with
the first generation text processors. And with the personal computers being bought by other people in the same organization. It is
a familiar story to many, as is the not unusual situation where
data has to be copied manually off the screen of one microcomputer
and then typed into another.

One should not, perhaps, be too harsh on those who made the decisions that led to acquiring incompatible or perhaps useless micros
and text processors. It is easy to be wise after the fact. How is
one to see several years into the future in a frantically evolving
field? There is no way. But I think we have by now acquired enough
hindsight to project it modestly into the future, and with the
help of concepts such as information management, hoping to avoid
the obvious mistakes.

3. THE INFORMATION MANAGEMENT CONCEPT AND ITS APPLICATION

3.1. The Concept

The concept of information management has been recently gaining
ground as a general expression of an approach that assigns systematic information processes an important role in the activities of
an organization. In general terms, one might say that the aim of
information management is that all those who need information,
whether inside the information generating organization or as members of a legitimate interest group outside of it, get the information that they need or want, and that they get it fast enough,
accurate enough, and in a usable form.

The content of information management would then be to see to it
that this aim is fulfilled. Obvious questions at this point arise:
what information is exactly required? how can we make sure the
need is justified? what part of the required information is available? if some is missing, how can it best be obtained? how can the
aim be reached in the most economical way?

My guess is that the rest of this century and a good part of the
next will be spent in answering this and similar questions, consequences of considering information as a resource in its own right.
In developing information management policies for the Finnish
Government, information management has been analyzed into the following types of activities within an organization:

1) to acquire, maintain and develop the personnel and material resources needed for information activities

2) to organize these information resources into information systems that effectively serve the activities and aims of the organization

3) to ensure that the information systems, separately considered, are efficient, and together make up a consistent network

4) to maintain the quality and integrity of information

5) to assign rights and duties relating to the access and use of information, and see to it that they are observed

6) to ensure necessary compatibility and communication with information systems outside the organization.

There are, of course, other ways of cutting the cake. It seems that Anglo-Saxon usage prefers the term "information resource management", which can be read in two ways: management of information resources (corresponding to 1 and 2 above), or as management of information as an organizational resource (perhaps close to items 3, 4 and 5 above). For example, a U.S. Government circular defines information resources management as

— the planning, budgeting, organizing, directing, training, promoting, controlling and management activities associated with

— the burden, collection, creation, use and dissemination of government information and the related resources, such as personnel, equipment, funds and technology.

3.2. The Coverage of Information Management

In practical application, the essential point about information management is that it should cover all the systematic information activities of an organization. These include not only ADP operations and development and office systems of the "new" or "traditional" type, but also records management and archives, libraries and information research (if any), and telecommunications including telephone service. The organization may also maintain an information service to put out press releases, answer citizens' requests for information or to provide for data access under privacy laws, or it may be in the business of disseminating information. These activities belong under information management as well.

The above is not only a list of the main systematic information activities of a typical organization, it also maps out the hunting grounds of the microcomputer salesman. The minimum need is to restrain uncoordinated purchases on the impulse, but much more is at stake. To say that one should consider all these functions as being subject to a coordinated information management is not to say that they should be placed under the iron-clad control of an information czar and forced to follow uniform practices. Some of the services, such as a library, may have requirements that are in many ways different from those of the others.

Technology has by now irrevocably married text production with personal computing, and no organizational boundaries should be allowed to impede the coordinated management of these activities. The integration of computing and office systems with communications is well on the way. It is inevitable. This should be taken into account in any decision with consequences for the 1990's.

It seems fairly natural that, as the next step, the organization's records and archives should be brought under integrated information management. The case of the librarians and information retrieval people may be a thorny one, used as they are to to their own established and "scientific" modes of operation.

4. INFORMATION MANAGEMENT AND THE MICRO

4.1 Resources Management

Systematic information activities represent no small proportion of
an organization's personnel and its resources. Thus one cannot expect that the coordinated management of all information resources
can be implemented quickly. In a large organization, it may take
years even if top management is fully committed. What is involved
is a change in thinking from the top down. The new thinking and
the new attitudes have to be, to a large extent, home grown from
the goals and the culture of the organization. There is today no
generally accepted overall theory of information management; there
are checklists of factors to consider.

It seems clear that a CIO, chief information officer, is needed in
every organization. This may be a function in its own right, or it
may be integrated into the functions of the CEO, chief executive
officer. The latter is probably the better course, for what is a
top manager's job if not to manage the most important assets in
the organization. Whatever the choice, an educational effort is
needed to train the CIO-office holder, as well as lower level information managers. But to get a reliable quality of education for
the CIO, we may have to wait until the universities have developed
the proper theory-backed courses to teach information management.

The educational and training task does not end here, of course.
All those involved in information activities that are systematic
or are to be systematized must be inculcated with the appropriate
concepts and procedures, and be given the mental tools to participate in the building of information systems that will be important
in their work. The information center approach, where assistance
and training is provided by a group set aside from the organization's own staff shows promise in this regard, although it might
serve to sidetrack the career paths of the people concerned. These
questions could be the topic of another conference.

Besides human resources, information management involves acquiring
and maintaining material resources needed for information activities. The list of activities to be brought under the umbrella of
the information management concept, as given in the beginning of
the preceding section, also yields a map of the hunting grounds of
the microcomputer salesman.

The minimum need, then, is to restrict uncoordinated purchases on
the impulse. Controlling procurement does not necessarily mean
that every purchase decision has to be centrally made or that only
items - whether hardware or software - appearing on the approved
shopping list can be acquired. But some degree of organization
wide coordination seems to be definitely needed. How rigid and how
detailed coordination should be depends on the type and size of
the organization and on how it has responded to the other requirements of information management: efficiency, uniformity, compatibility, integrity, etc.

As a general rule, coordination should be rigorous enough to pre-
clude procurement decisions that underlyingly run counter to the organization's information management policies. On the other hand,
such contradictory decisions could be made consciously to allow
for special cases.

4.2 Effective Information Systems

Organizing information resources into information systems that effectively serve the activities and aims of the organization is daily bread for ADP departments. But it may not be equally familiar
to the records keeper, archivist, librarian, press officer, telephone system planner, or the manager who is toying with his new
PC. And even though the problem be familiar, solutions do not come
easy or cheap.

Most if not all administrative information systems being developed
today incorporate microcomputers in one way or another: as terminals to a mainframe or mini, as servers, as partners in a micro
network, or as standalone PC's. It seems to be accepted that when
an established ADP department designs and implements a new system,
it does its homework properly: feasibility studies, cost-benefit
analyses, training programs, checking and rechecking. There is a
measure of confidence that the system will be useful and economical – even when it includes micros.

But there is far less confidence in the outcome if a user department installs a micro network or buys a set of PC's. Judged in
purely economic terms, the overwhelming evidence seems to be that
such purchases have been outright disasters. Money is spent in
buying the micros, time is spent in various activities around
them, but positive impacts on organizational effectiveness, such
as staff savings or increased output can rarely, if ever be observed. Negative impacts have been observed more frequently. This situation is said to exist particularly in the private sector, and
often in those countries that took part in the first wave of microcomputers.

What should be the approach from the viewpoint of information management? There is no unique answer. I have noted two opposing
schools of thought: the hard dollar approach and a "soft", perhaps
a broader, longer view that I will call the evolutionary approach.

The hard dollar approach follows naturally from the fact that public administration is increasingly pressed by budget limitations
that give little leeway to developmental experiments. New items in
the budget are being viewed as investments that have to pay for
themselves fairly quickly. Viewed as an investment, the purchase
of a single PC or micro can never be cost-justified, because its
impacts are too varied and minor to be measured. An economic evaluation can make sense when a number of PCs, or text processors,
or a network of micros, are acquired to perform a set of specified
tasks. One can then compare inputs and outputs before and after
the change. The hard dollar school teaches us that installing micros or PCs is legitimate only if it brings net benefits that can
be expressed in money terms.

From the "evolutionary" viewpoint the hard dollar approach is too
narrow. Information processing organizations, such as public administrations, are undergoing profound changes in their way of working. They are slowly evolving, if not to the paperless office, towards a paper-cum-telematics type of operation. The first reasonably stable realizations will be reached in the early part of the
next decade, but we do not yet see clearly what they will be like.
What will take place in the meantime is not only feverish technological development by the vendors, but a fundamental learning process by the users, involving the whole personnel, from the tradi-

tional "office" workers to managers, who have to learn to become
information managers. The transformation of organizational cultures is so broad and complex that we cannot properly plan it, let
alone cost-benefit it. Yet we know that the change must take place.

In concrete terms, the evolutionary approach would encourage intelligent experimentation and tolerate, for the time being, less than
full resource utilization in order to speed up the necessary learning process. This is not to say that waste should be tolerated,
nor that micro-based systems should be installed planlessly.

4.3 Efficiency and Consistency

Some of the considerations presented above also concern efficiency. One cannot expect anywhere near 100 per cent utilization from
a micro. In that respect, a personal micro is more like a personal
telephone than a traditional computer. The main efficiency characteristics concern the compatibility of equipment, data media and
software.

The information manager should be able to exert a measure of control over purchases so as to prevent the introduction of incompatible equipment into an environment where data sharing is necessary,
or likely to become necessary. The latter is extremely hard to judge, however. A prospective PC user may be convinced that all he
will ever need is a purely personal operation. Yet experience
shows that, sooner or later, he will want to share data or text
with other people in his office, or with people in another office,
or with the central computer. The lack of compatibility among diskettes, for example, is well known, and has effectively ruled out
passing data between micros of different makes, except in a few
cases. The recent emergence of what are called industry standards
for micros and diskettes is now beginning to change this exasperat-
ing situation, however.

Another source of incompatibility and inefficiency is the fact
that small desktop devices are not only offered by the micro salesman but also exist as intelligent terminals to mainframe computers, to information retrieval services, or to videotex systems.
They will soon be provided by your telephone company as well, in
the form of "glorified" telephone sets. The latter are basically
for voice and data transmission but can handle computation and
text processing on the side. And incompatibility with everything
else is practically guaranteed. This "nightmare" prospect of end-
ing up with three or four boxes and screens on each desk points
out the importance of considering all the major information activities: DP, office systems, telecommunications, information retrieval, etc, under the same concept - and practice - of information management.

4.4 Quality, Integrity and Security of Information

The traditional yardsticks of information quality, as it relates
to automated systems, are timeliness, speed of response and accuracy. The introduction of personal computing is likely to improve
the values of most of these parameters. Reports generated from material kept up to date in the personal micro are likely to be timely. The speed of response of the system is nearly instantaneous.
There are no intervening processing steps that would introduce errors beyond those introduced by the user himself.

The early MIS-type systems have tended to confuse output quantity with quality. By producing reams of paper, they have often served to hide the relevant facts. To that extent, one might almost say that there exists a reverse relationship between reporting quantity and quality. The innovative reporting systems, particularly the graphic output facilities that are available on modern micros, by themselves bring about an improvement in the quality of management information.

However, a more fundamental question concerns the extent to which data and information reliably relate to the organization's needs and aims. If there are many independent points in an organization that enter and maintain data about an organization, there will inevitably coexist many meanings and definitions — explicit or implicit — as well as formats for the representation of each item of information. Clearly it will be difficult or impossible to agree on action on the basis of a conflicting and inconsistent body of information. This touches on an aspect of quality that is sometimes called the integrity of information.

Ideally, there should exist one and only one "master copy" of each item of information in an organization. Other instances of the same information would then be exact replicas of the master. This can only be achieved if a centralized and authorized data dictionary is maintained. This task is a natural part of the information management function.

In general terms, integrity could be defined as "all the relevant facts and nothing else". An essential omission or an irrelevant redundancy are likely to lead to misleading information, a loss of integrity. At the same time, the definitions and formats of the various items of information should be consistent among themselves.

It is easy to see that the ideal conditions are unlikely to be realized in a fully distributed computing environment with a large number of independent-minded users. It will be next to impossible to have them submit to an authorization of the data files they might create. Nevertheless, some overall standards are essential. Information management will have to devise a palatable recipe of rules, standards and recommended practices, and see to it that it is used. The "recipe" should be one that strikes a balance between the organizational need for information integrity and users' need for flexibility while taking into account, when necessary, the data subjects' need for data protection and confidentiality.

ADP center managers have, by now, come to grips with the requirements for the security of their installations and the data stored in them. In personal computing and fully distributed networks, the state of security today is deplorable. This is a universal condition and one for which no general solution seems to be in sight. It is possible to get protection for one's programs and data against equipment or network malfunctions by taking frequent backup copies, as some users do. But the vast majority do not, and I think it unlikely that they can be made to mend their ways. Perhaps the long term solution here is to connect all micros into networks and make backup security a built-in network function.

However, programs and data on diskettes, whether originals or backup copies, are highly vulnerable to unauthorized access, accidents, vandalism or fire. Particularly if they are left lying around on desks and in unlocked drawers. Is it reasonable to expect that, some day, at the end of the day, micro users will lock

up their floppies in fireproof safes and cart backup copies of
them off to a secure site? I think not. Some other solution will
have to be found. In the meantime, information management has to
deal with the security issue, identifying potential losses and de-
vising procedures to minimize them.

4.5 Rights and Duties Relating to Information

As information is not fully perceived as an "object", it is not
surprising that rights and duties relating to it are not adequately defined in an organization such as a government agency. Even
though the agency has, in essence, always worked with information.
But, until now, it has knowingly dealt only with documents, concrete objects made of paper. A document exists in one or a few originals and a variable number of copies. Precise rules are usually
laid down as to what is done with the original(s) and less precise
rules may cover the fate of copies. But the the thing that really
matters, the information content of the document, has received
scant attention.

To be sure, many of the rules that govern documents can be tran-
scribed in terms of information. One who has access to a document
should also have access to the information contained therein. However, the computer age has introduced new and complicating factors.
Which is "original" information and what is a copy? Who "owns" a
particular record that floats about in a network? Is access to one
record different in kind from access to a thousand?

Some of the main categories of information rights are

— the citizen's right of information, as defined in recent legislation in several countries and, incidentally, practiced in Finland and Sweden since 1776

— the utilization, in the national interest, of the "Government
Warehouse" of information.

— the universal interest of scientific exchange

— particular rights to information that follow from a person's organizational function.

Some of the duties typically encumbent upon the information hand-
ler are to maintain confidentiality, to keep up security, to ensure information integrity, to preserve a historical or an auditing
record of the organization, and to safeguard privacy of the data
subject whether or not there is a privacy protection law in place.

The assignation of rights and duties relating to information, and
ensuring their observance, is part of information management regardless of the kind of information processing technology in use.
However, a highly distributed computing environment is likely to
make the task, particularly enforcing the observance of the duties, much more difficult.

4.6 Communication with the Outside

It is, to me, a curious phenomenon that users and managers consistently seem to take a very narrow view of the communication requirements of their information systems. A personal computer tends to
be viewed as Personal indeed, and the need to share data with near-
by PC users comes then as a surprise. An office system or network

tends to be seen as self-sufficient, with little thought expended
on the eventual need to link it up with the rest of the department. At the limit, a government department or agency is considered a mini-universe, separated by light years from other bureaucratic galaxies.

Eventually, linkages among the various systems will become necessary. It is usually impossible to see today what interactions will
become necessary in a few years' time. Therefore, systems should
be built to be open for eventual linkage. As we know, this is done
by observing standards. The purpose of this paper is not to extol
OSI, but I would urge that a network planner who is proposing an
OSI-incompatible solution be made to justify his ideas very carefully. Insisting on compatibility throughout does not mean that
every system will eventually be connected with every other. The
criminal records system is unlikely to be linked with fishing licence information. But the best defense of a system lies not in incompatibility but in proper security procedures.

Linkages and data sharing should be foreseen not only vis-a-vis
other government entities, but with the enterprise sector as well.
Part of the job of information management is to facilitate the dissemination of government information to the outside and to make it
possible, where legitimate, for firms and citizens to make use of
the government information warehouse. Each of the thousands of micro installations in government is a potential point of contact.

The reverse side of the coin, so far largely unexplored, concerns
easing the reporting requirements that government agencies place
on the enterprise sector. Such reporting should be made as automatic as possible. Private sector computers conversing with government computers, as it were.

OSI does not today, and will not in the foreseeable future provide
all the interfaces and protocols needed for government-wide or nationwide networking on the scale implied here. Information management needs to devote increasing attention to standards work to define protocols and formats for high-level interfaces in the different application areas where inter-system interaction is necessary.

5. CONCLUDING REMARKS

Where does this all leave us as responsible or prospective government information managers? With a very extensive bill of goods,
indeed. I shall only pick up two items from it.

The brief history of administrative data processing has demonstrated the unwillingness of managers to deal with the hard question:
what precisely am I doing, where exactly do I want to go. When the
second computer generation came into administrative use many managers expected the machines to do company planning for them, and
were, in fact, relieved to abdicate some of their most important
decisions to the ADP people. I can see it happening again, microcomputers being too often regarded as the panacea to problems that
management is unwilling to tackle head-on.

Information management must resist such escapism. There is absolutely no alternative to knowing what you are doing. However fast or
intelligent your machine, only the driver can tell it where to go.

My second concluding point is that the introduction of machine
intelligence into the working lives of millions of people consti-

tutes a tremendous social change from within. There has never been
anything of the kind. To deal with it, and with its consequences,
we should know more about people, and we should know more than we
know today, about people in relation to their work.

AUTHOR INDEX